ASPECTS OF SAXO-NORMAN LONDON : 2

FINDS AND ENVIRONMENTAL EVIDENCE

DATE DUE FOR RETURN

ASPECTS OF SAXO-NORMAN LONDON : 2

FINDS AND ENVIRONMENTAL EVIDENCE

edited by Alan Vince

with contributions by Patrick Allen, Marion Archibald, Justine Bayley,
Tony Clark, Anne Davis, Jennifer Hillam, Ian Freestone, Frances Pritchard,
Anne Jenner, Glynis Jones, Clare de Rouffignac, Peter Stott, Vanessa Straker
and Alan Vince

London & Middlesex Archaeological Society
Special Paper 12

Published by the London & Middlesex
Archaeological Society

Typeset and printed by BAS Printers Limited,
Over Wallop, Hampshire

Design and production: Melissa Denny of Diptych

The cover illustration by John Pearson shows a
reconstruction of the interior of an 11th-century
building excavated at Pudding Lane.

ISBN 0 903290 37 5

**The Society is grateful to English Heritage for
a grant towards the publication of this Special
Paper**

CONTENTS

ABSTRACT

Alan Vince

In the late 9th century the centre of settlement in London was moved, almost certainly by royal instigation, from the undefended *wic* along the Strand into the walls of the Roman city. The growth of London in the 10th and 11th centuries was phenomenal and by the middle of the 11th century the town was a thriving port with contacts in Scandinavia, the Rhineland, and Northern France.

In this volume various studies of finds and environmental evidence from sites within the walled city and dating between the late 9th and mid 12th centuries are presented. The first of the eight unequal parts is a brief essay on the nature of the deposits from which the evidence was derived.

A corpus of Saxon pottery from the City of London is presented in Part 2, together with the reasoning behind the chronological framework which underlies most of the other papers. Furthermore, by combining petrological analysis with a study of pottery from contemporary sites in the surrounding countryside it has been possible to establish the source, or source area, of much of the City's pottery.

Small finds composed of antler, bone, copper alloy, fired clay, glass, iron, ivory, lead, leather, stone and wood are considered in Part 3. All stratified 10th and 11th centuries small finds are included here, except those from sites where no stratigraphic data was available. The leatherwork is of particular interest since there is sufficient of it to extend the sequence of styles and techniques previously established for the 12th to 15th centuries back to the 10th century.

Recent excavations have yielded relatively few Saxon or Norman coins, but the study of earlier finds and the comparison of coins from within the walled area with coins from the surrounding area is crucial to the interpretation of the pottery and other finds. An essay and illustrated catalogue of these coin finds is therefore included here as Part 4, while a companion paper on associated lead pieces postulates that these objects were used in some way as receipts for toll.

The problems of residuality and contamination which affect the studies of pottery and small finds also affect botanical remains and are considered in Part 5. Despite these problems the value of the study of botanical remains from London can be demonstrated. In Part 5.ii a study of the absolute frequency of parasite eggs within a deposit has shown that it is possible to differentiate between deposits which are composed almost entirely from decomposed human cess, those which contain an appreciable cess content and those with other, incidental, constituents.

In Part 6 the preliminary results of a study of late Saxon crucibles is presented. It demonstrates that Stamford ware crucibles were preferred to those from other sources, especially for the melting of silver.

In Part 7 two short reports on scientific dating of late Saxon deposits, using dendrochronology and archaeomagnetism respectively, are published.

Finally, in Part 8, the topographic and functional development of London from the late Roman period to the Norman Conquest is summarised, using information from both Volumes One and Two of the series. The main concern of this paper is to establish the archaeological context of Saxon finds from within the walls of the City, although in order to do this it is also necessary to look outside the walls.

Following the printed report are microfiche on which will be found site by site reports enabling the user to relate stratigraphy, pottery, small finds and environmental data from a deposit.

INTRODUCTION

Alan Vince

This volume grew out of several separate and independent post-excavation projects started in the late 1970s and early 1980s. That it has taken so long to complete and will be seen even now to be a far from perfect presentation of the evidence requires some explanation and apology. Until the early 1980s it was the policy of the DUA to publish sites and their associated finds sequentially and separately. The first sites to be excavated became the first sites to be studied and prepared for publication. This approach is as good as any other for dealing with the stratigraphic evidence from the City of London. So long as parts of the city remain to be excavated there cannot really be a final statement of the city's development, nor can one avoid making conclusions which later excavations show to have been in error. For the publication of finds, however, the policy was demonstrably a failure. In the main the problem was that a multi-period site would reveal small quantities of a whole range of artefacts, each of which required classification and study before the particular finds from the site could be adequately interpreted. The need for original research across a wide range of material, from the early Roman to the post-medieval periods, stretched the resources of the DUA finds section too far and in 1981 work was still underway on sites excavated in 1974 and 1975, including the New Fresh Wharf site.

In 1981 it was decided to instigate a new policy. Those sites where publication work was nearly complete were to be published as site reports while finds from other sites were to be published thematically. The order of publication was to be decided by the logic of the finds themselves, so that the sites and assemblages which would provide the dating evidence would be dealt with before those where the finds would be needed to provide the dating framework for the site analysis. Thus, the dated assemblages of medieval pottery and other finds from the Thames waterfront were selected for study first since they could be independently dated through their stratigraphic position and by the use of dendrochronology and other dating methods (Pearce *et al* 1982; Pearce *et al* 1985; Cowgill *et al* 1987; Grew & de Neergaard 1988; Pearce & Vince 1988). A similar scheme was proposed for the publication of the Roman pottery using the material from the extensive area excavation at Newgate Street to provide a framework, although that from New Fresh Wharf was published as a separate assemblage with the site report (Richardson 1986; Davies & Richardson forthcoming). Following this change of policy the preparation of a Saxon pottery corpus began, using the New Fresh Wharf sequence and a draft report by Clive Orton and Louise Miller to provide an admittedly incomplete chronological framework. A project to study the seeds and other botanical remains from pits at Milk Street was also in progress at this time and it was therefore necessary to widen the pottery project to provide some dating evidence for the pits whose contents were under examination. At about the same time a project was proposed to catalogue and discuss the remains of timber buildings found on sites around Cheapside, such as Milk Street, Watling Court, Well Court and Ironmonger Lane. This project too was widened and altered subsequently by the addition of sites around the bridgehead: Peninsular House, Pudding Lane and Fish Street Hill. The report on this project now forms Volume One of *Aspects of Saxo-Norman London* (Horsman *et al* 1988). At that time it was intended to include Miles Lane within the bridgehead sites, to mirror its treatment in *The Port of Roman London* (Milne 1985) but the basic site post-excavation work for the post-Roman parts of the excavation was not completed in time.

A further complication was provided in 1984 when the newly-created English Heritage made it clear that they intended to provide funds only for a limited period of post-excavation work on sites for which they had funded the excavation and therefore felt responsible for the publication of the results. The change of policy was subtle, since the character of the proposed publications was the same but there was no longer any possibility of returning to earlier sites at a later date to use the results of initial research. Material from further waterfront sites (Swan Lane, Billingsgate Lorry Park and Seal House) was added and a seven year programme was imposed so that, as before, work was progressing on a broad front instead of in a logical progression. A cursory scanning of material from sites not included in the companion volume was made, where possible, and similarly some material from pre-DUA sites directed by Peter Marsden has been examined and incorporated where it was thought that it would add significantly to the evidence presented.

The reader will therefore find that certain parts of this volume deal with certain groups of sites whilst some, such as that on the coins, cast an even wider net and include material from outside the City altogether. It was felt that there was little point in trying to impose a neat but restrictive framework when what was important about the papers was the research whose results they present. Most of the work included here was completed by 1987/8.

The volume is divided into eight unequal parts. The first is a brief essay on the nature of the deposits from which the finds and environmental evidence was derived. It is in many ways another apology, not for the method of publication or analysis but rather the scrappy nature of the raw data. There is little point in elaborate discussion of the significance of the finds and environmental data for the reconstruction of past activities on the site when most of the features are truncated, unrelated to each other and can be demonstrated to contain large quantites of redeposited material. In many cases it is as much as can be done to determine a date after which the feature must have been filled.

A corpus of Saxon pottery from the City of London is presented in Part 2, together with the reasoning behind the chronological framework which lies behind most of the other papers. By combining petrological analysis with a study of pottery from contemporary sites in the surrounding countryside it has been possible to establish the source, or source area, of much of the pottery. There are three principal conclusions. Firstly, that the pottery used in the earliest late Saxon city is quite different from that used in the preceding *wic* along the Strand. Secondly, that there are few imports associated with this earliest late Saxon

pottery while, thirdly, there are major changes in the source and character of the pottery which can be dated through dendrochronology to the period between *c.*1040 and *c.*1055. Another valuable result is that where an area was supplying London with pottery in the Saxon period it is possible to use the dating framework established in London to date local pottery.

The study of the Saxon small finds from excavations in the city, published here as Part 3 of the volume, has been a mammoth task, principally because of the difficulties of distinguishing residual Roman finds from those of late Saxon date. Many of the finds described are from the Saxon waterfront excavations at Billingsgate but this study was undertaken at the same time as the dendrochronological analysis of the timbers and only material stratified in contexts of the excavator's archive Period V or earlier has been studied in detail. There is, therefore, a grey area between the finds covered here and those being published as part of the *Medieval Finds from Excavations in London* series and for the 12th century the reader is advised to use both sources. For the 10th and 11th centuries, however, the coverage should be full, except for sites where no stratigraphic data was available. Objects of iron, copper alloy, wood, bone, stone and glass are amongst the finds while the leather footwear is of particular interest since there are sufficient finds to extend the sequence of styles and techniques established for the 12th to 15th centuries back to the 10th century (cf Grew & de Neergaard, 1988). Other items of interest include the fittings for a wooden door, a wood-working axe found with its wooden shaft intact, knives decorated with inlay and one knife found within its scabbard.

Relatively few Saxon or Norman coins have been found in DUA excavations and yet the evidence to be gained from a study of earlier discoveries and by a comparison of coins found within the walls of the city with those from the surrounding area is crucial to the interpretation of the pottery and other finds. An essay and illustrated catalogue of these coin finds is therefore included here as Part 4, with a companion paper on associated lead pieces which postulates that these objects were used in some way as receipts for toll. The paper demonstrates the value of treating unstratified coins as archaeological finds and shows that, although there is a concentration of pre-Viking coin finds in the Strand area, the walled city has also produced a reasonable quantity. The presence of these finds, when contrasted with the evidence from a study of the pottery, is another factor to be considered when discussing the function of the walled city in the 7th to 9th centuries. In other ways, however, the pattern recognised archaeologically – an extensive extra-mural settlement in the 7th to 9th centuries, the rapid decline of that settlement and the growth of the intra-mural town from the late 9th century, gradual at first but then spectacular in the later 10th and 11th centuries – is to be seen just as clearly in the coin finds.

The problems of residuality and contamination which affect the studies of pottery and small finds also affect botanical remains. Only where concentrations of seeds are found can one be reasonably sure that they were actually deposited within a short time of their disposal. Even when concentrations of seeds have been recovered it is necessary to establish how they came to be preserved before one can offer an interpretation. These and other points are considered in Part 5.i and show that despite these problems the study of botanical remains from London has been worthwhile. The absence of cereal rachis fragments suggests that grain was entering London after winnowing while the purity of a bread wheat deposit from Well Court suggests that grain was sieved before use. They suggest, further, that the Well Court deposit was accidentally charred while being parched prior to grinding, and that this was a secondary function of the oven in which the deposit was found. A similar oven from Botolph Lane, however, seems to have been fired with the remnants of animal fodder. Samples from occupation layers within buildings have produced quantities of sedge and rush seeds, probably brought into London with flooring. By studying the absolute frequency of parasite eggs within a deposit, it has been possible to differentiate between deposits which are composed almost entirely from decomposed human cess, and those which contain an appreciable cess content and 'background noise' (Part 5.ii). It is worth noting that even samples from occupation deposits contained small quantities of parasite eggs and, therefore, had once contained human excrement.

In Part 6 the preliminary results of a study of late Saxon crucibles is presented. It demonstrates that Stamford ware crucibles were preferred to those from other sources, especially for the melting of silver. The distribution of crucible fragments suggests that metalworking was practised on a small scale over most of the occupied area of the city whilst the stratigraphic context of the finds shows that there was little if any non-ferrous metalworking before the early 11th century.

In Part 7 two small reports on scientific dating of late Saxon deposits, using dendrochronology and archaeomagnetism respectively, are published. They are included for completeness, as part of the publication of the sites included in Volume One, while the most valuable dendrochronological report, that on New Fresh Wharf and Billingsgate (Hillam forthcoming), will be published in the volume on the waterfront in the Saxon period.

Finally, in Part 8, the topographic and functional development of London from the late Roman period to the Norman Conquest is summarised, using information from both Volumes One and Two of this series. The first version of this paper was prepared in 1983-4, at a time when the idea of a substantial extra-mural settlement in London in the mid-Saxon period was unorthodox. Since that time, the archaeological confirmation of this thesis has been overwhelming and no attempt has been made to incorporate recent discoveries by the Department of Greater London Archaeology. The main concern of this paper is to establish the archaeological context of Saxon finds from within the walls of the City, although in order to do this it is necessary to look outside the walls, both to the Strand and to Southwark, whose development is inextricably linked with that of the walled area.

Since many of these reports refer to the same publications a combined bibliography has been included. Like the papers, it is only complete up to 1988. Following the printed report are microfiche on which will be found site by site reports enabling the user to relate stratigraphy, pottery, small finds and environmental data from a deposit. Fuller details are available on request from the Museum of London Records Department but for most purposes the information supplied on microfiche should be sufficient.

I. THE ARCHAEOLOGICAL CONTEXT

Patrick Allen and Alan Vince

The finds and environmental data described in the following papers come mainly from excavations carried out by the DUA since 1974. A substantial unpublished archive exists frror each site and is available for study in the Museum of London, accessible by the site code and year of excavation (Fig. 1.1).

For all these sites a level III archive report exists in which the Saxon and early medieval features and their stratigraphic relationships are described and their interpretation discussed. To facilitate reference to these reports, the text section in which a feature is described is given in the catalogue (Appendix 1). Generally, however, the reader will find ample information in the published data in *Aspects of Saxo-Norman London*: Volumes One and Two.

Two other sites included here (Public Cleansing Depot and St Nicholas Acon) were excavated before the formation of the DUA but have been retrospectively given the site codes PCD and SNA for ease of reference and consistency. Level III reports comparable to those for more recent sites do not exist.

Date and interpretation

Typically, a London site of this period contains isolated late Saxon and early medieval features cutting through much earlier deposits. Individual features can only be stratigraphically related where they intercut, and it is therefore usually impossible to show from the stratigraphy alone which features were in contemporaneous use. The pottery found in the fills of these features (Part 2) has been used to give the layers in which it occurs a *terminus post quem*. If more than one layer occurs in a feature, the possibility that the feature took a long time to fill, or was recut, or had a compensatory fill in the top is considered. If the feature is related to other Saxon or medieval features, the implications of this for the dating of the

sequence are then examined. Finally, a relative date for the features is arrived at, the date of the pottery and any other dating evidence (such as dendrochronology, coins, or archaeomagnetic dating). The usefulness of these other methods of dating is variable. Dendrochronology has proved invaluable on the waterfront, where large structures containing numerous datable timbers have been excavated. The timbers from inland sites have been less useful but could have been crucial if sunken-featured buildings, or plank-lined pits or wells with well-preserved timbers had been found (Part 6). Coins have provided corroborative evidence for the dating of the ceramic sequence, but have not been found in sufficient quantity to provide a close date for any feature (Part 4). Archaeomagnetic dating has been attempted on three Saxon sites; two of these have also been dated by pottery and stratigraphy, where it can be shown that the archaeomagnetic dates are not as accurate as they should be (due to the movement of the burnt features after firing). However, the usefulness of the technique was shown at 29–31 Knightrider Street (TAV81), where an isolated hearth, cutting through natural brickearth and thought to have been used in mortar preparation, was dated to the late Saxon period, although it had previously been thought to be Roman (Part 7).

With the exception of a few sites where circumstances have led to the preservation of substantial horizontal deposits, the features could be of any date after that of the pottery found within them. Nevertheless, several long sequences, involving four or more separate deposits, have produced pottery assemblages with progressively later *termini post quos* (Figs 1.2-1.3). Thus, the stratigraphic sequence confirms an independently determined sequence based on pottery. As a reminder that these dates are relative, and only tenuously tied to an absolute chronology, the term 'Ceramic Phase' is used instead of an absolute date. Fig 2.1 shows the phases and their

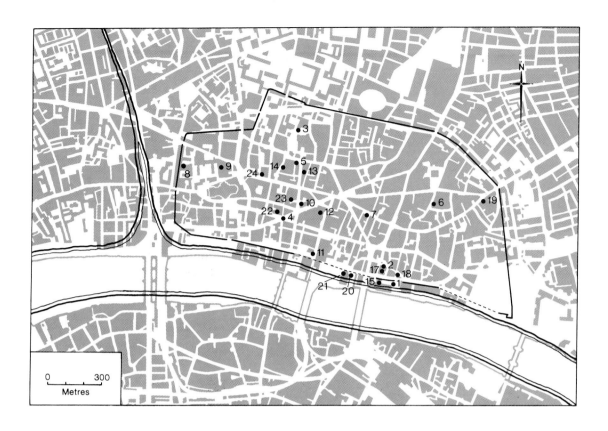

Code	Site name	Site report	No
BIG82	Billingsgate Lorry Park	in prep	1
FMO85	Fish Street Hill – Monument Hill	Horsman *et al* 1988	2
IRO80	24–5 Ironmonger Lane	Horsman *et al* 1988	13
MLK76	1–6 Milk Street	Horsman *et al* 1988	14
NFW74	New Fresh Wharf	in prep	15
PCD59	Public Cleansing Depot (Dowgate)	Dunning 1959	11
PDN81	Pudding Lane	Horsman *et al* 1988	17
PEN79	Botolph Lane (Peninsular House)	Horsman *et al* 1988	18
PUB80	The George PH, 86 Fenchurch St	unpub archive report A Upson	19
SH74	Seal House	in prep	20
SM75	St Magnus House (New Fresh Wharf)	in prep	15
SNA59	St Nicholas Acon, Nicholas Lane	Marsden 1959	7
SWA81	Swan Lane	in prep	21
WAT78	Watling Court, 11–14 Bow Lane, 41–53 Cannon St	Horsman *et al* 1988	22
WEL79	Well Court, 44–48 Bow Lane	Horsman *et al* 1988	10
WOW79	Woolworth's, 130–1 Cheapside	unpub archive report J Milner	5

1.1. Sites and Site Codes

currently suggested absolute dating (argued in full in Part 2).

Interpretation of the finds is even more difficult than their dating. As already mentioned, the sites mainly consist of the bottoms of features cutting through earlier stratigraphy. Streets were examined at two sites but neither produced contemporary finds. The types of Saxon and Norman

Pit	Dating	CP	Total	Wt	LSS	EMS	EMFL	EMS	EMSH	ESUR	BLGR	LCOAR
Pit 44	Roman pottery only											
Dark earth												
Pit 45 (initial use)	914+	1	1252 gm	100								
Pit 45 (later backfill)		3	1343 gm	64	20	16	0					
Dark earth	pottery not quantified											
Pit 55	1017+	4	584 gm			11			31	20	31	6
Pit 56		5	21 gm							57		42

1.2 Pottery from a representative stratigraphic sequence at Milk Street (percentage by weight excluding Roman pottery).

CP	CNAME	Ed	B1co	B1us	B2us	B2du	B3	B4co	B4p1us	B4p2co	B4p2us	B4p2du	B4p3co	B5co	B5us	B5usear	B5usfi	B5du	Total
	RPOT	2645	2	487	340	1109	474.2	130	9.5	140.5	324.7	.	.	223	16	7	.	739.5	6646.9
CP1																			
	LSS	155	7	2	83	121	290.5	38	3	11	41	4	.	111.4	.	16	.	759	1641.9
	MISC	43	.	10	18	44	8.5	34	.	.	.	.	.	28	.	.	2	.	187
CP2																			
	EMS	.	4	47	67	144	108.5	12	.	.	19.7	.	.	8	.	.	6	124	540.2
CP3																			
	REDP	.	.	3	.	.	.	.	.	.	.	.	.	.	8	.	5	6	22
	STAM	.	.	.	5	6	3.5	.	.	.	.	.	.	.	.	.	.	.	14.5
	EMFL	.	.	.	.	12	.	.	.	.	.	.	.	.	.	.	.	.	12
	EMSS	.	.	.	.	4	2	.	.	109.5	.	.	.	.	.	5	.	.	120.5
	EMSH	.	.	.	.	54	23.5	.	3	.	12	.	.	19	.	5	.	238	354.5
CP4																			
	ESUR	.	.	.	.	.	.	13	.	32.2	11.2	.	.	63.7	.	2	.	58	180.1
	EMCH	.	.	.	.	.	.	.	.	5.5	6	.	.	6	.	.	.	.	17.5
	LOGR	.	.	.	.	.	.	.	.	.	108	.	12	9	.	39	.	16	184
MISC	GREY	.	.	.	.	.	.	.	.	.	19	.	.	.	.	.	.	.	19
	EMSH	.	.	.	.	.	.	.	.	.	608.5	.	.	47.3	.	87	4	46.5	793.3
	THET	.	.	.	.	.	.	.	.	.	.	.	.	.	.	.	1	.	1
CP5																			
	LCALC	.	.	.	.	.	.	.	.	.	.	.	.	.	.	.	10	149.5	159.5
	LCOAR	.	.	.	.	.	.	.	.	.	.	.	.	.	.	.	.	19	19
	ANDE	.	.	.	.	.	.	.	.	.	.	.	.	.	.	.	.	8	8
	SHER	.	.	.	.	.	.	.	.	.	.	.	.	.	.	.	.	45	45
	Total	2843	13	549	513	1494	910.7	226	15.5	189.2	1259.6	4	12	515.4	24	161	28	2208.5	10965.9

1.3. Table showing quantities of pottery (in grams) from a stratigraphic sequence at Pudding Lane. Starting with a 'Dark Earth' deposit (Ed) followed by the construction, use, modification and disuse of buildings PDN1, PDN2, PDN3, PDN4 and PDN5. The area subsequently was used as a yard or external surface. The small size of most assemblages should be noted, together with the consistently high quantity of residual Roman pottery (see Fig. 1.5).

deposit which produced finds can therefore be discussed in three groups: building levels, pits and wells, and exterior strata.

BUILDINGS

Fragments of several timber buildings, mainly of 11th- and 12th-century date, have been excavated. Finds were recovered from the construction, occupation and disuse deposits within them. Floors and hearths were also sampled for plant remains. With few exceptions, the finds assemblages from these buildings are meagre and throw little light upon the activities carried out within them. Rarely, it is possible to identify pottery vessels which were smashed on a floor surface and left there. Two such examples were found at Pudding Lane, both 11th-century storage jars or spouted pitchers (Fig 1.4; Nos 125 & 136). In general, however, floors in actual use seem to have been kept clean and the most common pottery

finds are sherds of Roman pottery (Fig 1.5). The seeds recovered from soil samples taken from building floors suggest that rushes were often used to cover the floor. When rotten, this flooring would normally be taken out of the building for burning or burial, also taking with it any artefacts which had been lost or discarded in the building. It is possible that fragments of lava quernstone are more frequent in building deposits than in other features (Part 2), partly due to the reuse of the querns for levelling, as at Pudding Lane, where fragments were found acting as supports for a timber sill beam, or, as at Well Court, as post-packing.

There is a difference between the type of deposits found in some sunken-floored buildings and those found in ground-level buildings. It seems that some of the former were recut, removing earlier occupation deposits. This is thought to have happened at Milk Street (MLK2) and at Ironmonger Lane (IRO2). The earliest assem-

1.4. A brickearth floor of Building PDN11 *with fragments of an* EMCH *spouted pitcher lying on its surface.* CP4 – *late 11th to early 12th century.*

blages found within such a building may therefore be smaller and less well dated than those from the later phases or from ground-level buildings. Similarly, most of the finds from these buildings come from disuse, or backfill, deposits and post-date the actual use of the building.

PITS AND WELLS

By far the most frequent late Saxon and Norman features on the sites included here are pits. They vary considerably in size and shape, as in the nature of their fills. Although some may have been dug for industrial purposes or as quarries there is no evidence for this from the finds or environmental data examined. Almost all pits

%AGE	CP1	CP2	CP3	CP4	CP5	TOTAL BLG	TOTAL EXT	TOTAL PITS	TOTAL
0–9	1	1	1	2	0	2		3	5
10–19	1	0	0	2	2	3		2	5
20–29	2	1	1	2	3	2		7	9
30–39	0	0	2	1	3	3		3	6
40–49	1	1	1	2	3	3	1	4	8
50–59	1	0	1	0	1	1	1	1	3
60–69	2	4	2	0	0	2		6	8
70–79	0	0	1	1	0	2			2
80–89	0	0	1	0	0	1			1
90–100	1	0	0	4	0	2	3		5
TOTAL	9	7	10	14	12	21	5	26	52 ASSEMBLAGES
MEAN	42%	32%	43%	52%	43%	44%	65%	28%	44%
N = (Kg)	12	4	9	12	14	16	16	19	51

1.5. Percentage of Roman pottery in assemblages containing more than 100 gm pottery from Pudding Lane. Note that external deposits contain a high percentage of residual Roman pottery, pits contain a smaller percentage but that deposits associated with buildings are variable.

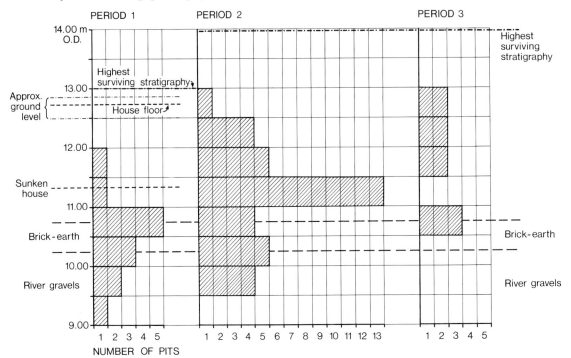

1.6. A schematic section through the 1976 Milk Street site (MLK76). The height from which pits must have been cut is shown by the floors of the surviving ground-level buildings, MLK4 *and* MLK5. *The upper levels of almost every pit have been removed by later disturbance. The height of natural gravel and the probable Saxo-Norman water table are indicated.*

seem to have ended their life acting as cesspits and general refuse pits, usually a mixture of the two (Part 5). Many pit fills were excavated as a single deposit but at Milk Street, where particular attention was given to the stratigraphic excavation of pit fills, analysis of the finds has shown that joining potsherds often occur throughout fills and that there is likely to be little difference in date between successive layers. Horizontal strata which have slumped into the tops of pits, and levelling thrown into the resulting depressions to compensate for the consolidation of the fill can be of any date after the date of backfilling but few examples of such deposits were excavated, due to the truncation of most pits by post-medieval and modern cellar floors (Fig 1.6). Finds from slumped deposits in the top of a pit which could be interpreted as part of a later stratigraphic unit have been included as part of that unit in this report. If, on the other hand, the only surviving part of a later deposit is to be found in the top of a pit it has been interpreted as a later pit fill. For example, at Ironmonger Lane it is thought that there was a significant break between the initial and compensatory fills of Pit 7 and these are consequently treated separately.

Many pits produced evidence that they were lined, with wattle, clay, planks or barrels (Figs 1.7-1.9). This suggests that they could have been emptied. Evidence for such reuse is not uncommon in late and post-medieval stone-lined pits, in the form of thin skims of previous fills, containing demonstrably earlier pottery. These late pits were sometimes used from the 13th to the 16th centuries. No such reuse could be demonstrated for any Saxon or Norman pit, although several were re-dug on the same spot. This may partly reflect the greater ease with which pottery of the later medieval period can be dated.

A few Saxon and Norman wells were excavated. They are normally distinguishable from rubbish or cess pits by their greater depth and by their lining (Fig 1.9). There are, however, a few borderline cases, features which would have cut down to the Saxon watertable and whose final use was as cess or rubbish pits, for example MLK P7. Difficulties of excavation meant that most could not be fully emptied.

The preservation of artefacts and organic remains varies considerably between pits, and from layer to layer within their fills. This can be seen in the condition of metal artefacts (Fig 1.11), in the degree of preservation of organic finds such as wood, leather and textiles (Fig 1.10), and in the presence of 'waterlogged' seeds. As shown in Fig 1.6, few pits actually reached the contempor-

1.7. A wattle-lined pit, P65, from Watling Court. CP4 – late 11th to early 12th century. Building WAT3 is in the background. (0.5m scale).

ary water table, although most were dug down to the natural gravel, to allow their liquid contents to flush away. The main reason for differential preservation appears to be variation in the amount of oxygen present in the soil. Oxygen is removed from the soil by bacteria, feeding on organic refuse, while a soil with a clayey texture will inhibit the circulation of groundwater and the replenishment of the oxygen supply. So many factors affect preservation – for example, depth of burial, organic content and texture of the deposit – that it is difficult to compare assemblages. For example, the absence of leather from a pit may mean that it was never present, or that conditions for its preservation were poor. These factors have made the interpretation of the environmental evidence very difficult (Part 5).

Only pottery and worked stone are likely to be both well-preserved and rigorously collected and these materials alone can be usefully compared, not only between features on a site but also between sites.

1.8. A ?plank-lined pit, P55, from Milk Street. CP4 – late 11th to early 12th century. The curious shape of the walls of the pit suggests that the plank lining rotted in place after the pit had been filled and that pressure from the surrounding earth caused the sides to bow in. The feature had been cut down to the top of the natural terrace gravels. (1.0m scale in pit).

1.9. A barrel-lined pit, P46, from Watling Court. CP4 – late 11th to early 12th century.

1.10. Wooden vessels and other artefacts in Pit 15 at Milk Street. (0.1 m scale).

1.11. An axe with wooden shaft and iron head both well-preserved in the fill of Pit 55 at Milk Street (see 1.8). This pit also produced a coin of Cnut, dating the backfill to 1017 or later.

Exterior deposits

On a few sites, notably Watling Court and Pudding Lane, areas of horizontal, external stratigraphy of Saxon or Norman date survived. These can be roughly grouped into those probably formed by horticulture, involving little importation of material, and levelling deposits which substantially raised the ground level on the site. The former were recognised at Milk Street, sealing some pits and cut by others. The latter were found at Watling Court, Periods xii and xiii, although only small areas survived. An earlier dump, of Period xi, may have been local and insubstantial, intended to level areas previously occupied by sunken-floored buildings and pits. The implications of these deposits for the study of finds and environmental evidence is slight for the earlier phases, since there is no evidence for large-scale make-ups until Ceramic Phase 5 (early to middle 12th century). For later periods it is quite possible that large quantities of finds were imported onto a site with spoil and do not reflect any activities taking place on the site itself. Dumps of late medieval bronze-casting moulds have been observed at Fenchurch Street, reused as road metalling, and a deposit of mid-17th-century glass manufactur-

ing waste from Aldgate is also thought to have been tipped onto the site (Charleston *et al* forthcoming). External surfaces, composed of gravel or brickearth, survived and were excavated in small patches at Watling Court, Botolph Lane and Pudding Lane. They produced no finds of any type and so must have been clean, freshly imported material.

Finally, no discussion of external deposits in Saxon London would be complete without a mention of 'Dark Earth'. This is found immediately overlying 2nd and 3rd century levels on many sites where the appropriate levels survive, especially in the west of the city. Since there is usually no sign of tumbled or other building debris lying *in situ* within it, the deposit cannot be a natural soil formed over mouldering remains of Roman buildings. Mosaic floor fragments at Milk Street which immediately underlay the dark earth appear to have been covered before weathering and showed no sign of plough or horticultural disturbance. This indicates that dark earth was on occasion deliberately dumped make-up. Once dumped on the sites the dark earth may have been cultivated, although no definite evidence, such as plough or spade marks, has been found (or would be recognisable if the ploughing took place solely within the dark earth). Neither is there any evidence for the formation of a soil profile. Such a development would seem to have been inevitable if the deposit was left undisturbed for up to seven centuries. The finds evidence also suggests that the upper part of this sequence is missing. 'Dark earth' deposits either contain solely mid to late Roman finds, perhaps with a few intrusive Saxon

and medieval artefacts, or they contain sufficient late Saxon finds (as at Botolph Lane, area E) to suggest that the deposit is actually a dump of Late Saxon date (see for example the Billingsgate Triangle report, where the problem was unresolved. In places in that work a particular deposit is interpreted as a 3rd-century dump and in others as one of the late Saxon period, Jones *et al* 1980). The dark earth certainly does not contain finds of early- or mid-Saxon date and cannot be used as evidence for or against the agricultural use of the City during the Dark Ages. The presence of redeposited Roman dark earth in Saxon and Norman features is indicated by 3rd and 4th century coins and pottery and can be noted during excavation by the quantities of Roman tile, especially in the upper fills of pits (Fig 1.12).

Conclusion

The main factors influencing the distribution of finds on sites appear to be the methods used to dispose of, or to reuse, artefacts and domestic waste, and the different types of preservation found. This should not deter others from searching for intra-site variability, since London has suffered more than most sites from later disturbance of its Saxon and Norman stratigraphy.

1.12. A cross-section through a typical pit, Milk Street Pit 12. CP2 – late 10th or early 11th century. At the base is a thin deposit formed by slumping of the Roman stratigraphy through which the pit was dug. Overlying this is a thick layer of organic refuse. In the upper levels much more residual Roman material can be seen. The upper fill includes a high proportion of redeposited earth. (1.0m scale).

2. THE SAXON AND EARLY MEDIEVAL POTTERY OF LONDON

Alan Vince and Anne Jenner

ABSTRACT

The Saxon pottery found within the walls of the City is described here as a type series and the evidence presented for its date. Five ceramic phases spanning the 10th to the 12th centuries can be recognised and these can be used both to relate the stratigraphic sequences found on sites in different parts of the City and to reconstruct the development of the ceramic industry supplying London. A programme of petrological analysis and a comparative study of Saxon and early medieval pottery in the Thames Basin has shown that the source areas of several distinctive fabrics can be localised.

The range of forms found in London is briefly described and illustrated as a type series, arranged by fabric and supposed source. Each identified fabric is described, and the implications of its petrological composition for characterisation explored. Short codes, developed initially to aid the computerisation of the data, have been used to identify fabrics throughout this report and the DUA archive (Fig 2.1). Evidence is presented for the existence of clearly defined ceramic phases, identifiable throughout the City, together with a discussion of the dating of the sequence (Fig 2.2). Finally, the economic implications of the ceramic evidence are discussed.

Introduction

Opinions about the date and sequence of Saxon and early medieval pottery types in the London region have varied widely over the last half-century. A knowledge of how these opinions were formed and how they have developed is useful when reading reports of early excavations and syntheses. This section will therefore try and chart this development and put the present study in its historical context.

Pottery of Saxon and early medieval date from London has been collected from building sites and dredging in the City and the surrounding region from the mid-19th century onwards. Gradually

Code	Common name	First occurrence in London (CP)
ANDE	Andenne ware	4
BADO	Badorf ware	1 ?
BLGR	Blue-grey ware	3
CROW	Crowland Abbey-type bowls	4
DEVS	Developed Stamford ware	6
EMCH	Early med chalky	4
EMCW	Early med coarse white ware	4
EMFL	Early med flinty	2
EMGR	Early med grog-tempered ware	5
EMIS	Early med iron-rich sandy wares	4
EMS	Early med sandy	2
EMSH	Early med shelly	3
EMSS	Early med sand and shell	3
ESUR	Early Surrey ware	4
IPS	Ipswich-type ware	0
LCALC	Calcareous London-type ware	5
LCOAR	Coarse London-type ware	5
LOCO	Local Coarseware	5
LOND	London-type ware	5
LSS	Late Saxon shelly	1
M40	M40 ware	6
NEOT	St.Neots ware	1 ?
NFRE	Misc North French wares	1
NMDX	North Middlesex Ware	4
NORG	Normandy glazed ware	4
NORM	Normandy gritty ware	4
REDP	Pingsdorf-type ware	3
SATH	Sandy Thetford-type Ware	1 ?
SEMS	South Essex Medieval Shelly ware	5
STAM	Stamford ware	3
THET	Ipswich Thetford-type ware	3
THWH	White Thetford-type ware	4
WINC	Winchester ware	3 ?

2.1. A list of mnemonic codes used in this volume (and in the DUA archive) to denote Saxon pottery fabrics.

these collections have coalesced so that by the 1930s there were only two large collections, those of the Guildhall and London Museums (now amalgamated as the Museum of London collection), although important pieces were, and still are, to be found in other collections, for example

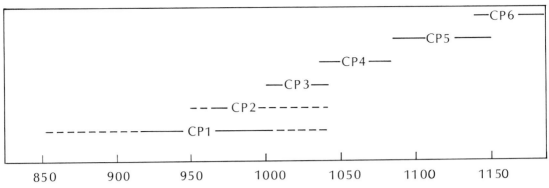

2.2. Absolute dating of Ceramic Phases 1 to 6.

the British Museum, the Cuming Museum and Maidstone Museum.

In 1935 Mortimer Wheeler produced a catalogue of the Saxon pottery in the London Museum with a briefer list of similar vessels in the Guildhall Museum (Wheeler 1935, 156-9, 187-8, 192-3). This catalogue contains much of value although most of the identifications and attributions must today be revised. Early Saxon pottery from cemeteries at Mitcham, Ewell and Hanwell was described, together with Early Saxon pottery from an occupation site at Hanwell. Three unstratified vessels were recognised as being of mid-Saxon date. Two, a complete globular pot in a local sand-tempered fabric and a rim sherd of Ipswich-type ware, were found at the Savoy together with annular loom weights while the third, a chaff-tempered vessel, was recovered from the Thames at Mortlake. From within the City walls three early Saxon vessels were recognised: a complete wheelthrown Merovingian jar from Gresham Street (Wheeler 1935, 156 Fig 32 No 1); a small stamped bowl from Aldermanbury, paralleled with 6th-century Frankish vessels (Wheeler 1935, Fig 44 no 2); and a small dish from Christ's Hospital also identified as a Frankish vessel of 6th-century date. The Aldermanbury bowl is probably not Frankish, although the remaining two vessels are (Nos 306, 308).

Several pottery types were attributed by Wheeler to the mid-Saxon period. A spouted pitcher of LSS (cf Nos 26-30) was dated by the absence of the type from both Early Saxon graves and accredited post-Conquest groups, by parallels in Merovingian and Carolingian contexts in the Rhineland and France, and by a 'partially analogous vessel' from Richborough, found in the vicinity of coins of Offa. A probably 12th-century spouted pitcher from Lime Street was compared with the LSS vessel. A few Rhenish red-painted spouted pitchers were dated to the late 9th century or earlier because of the suggested destruction of the Pingsdorf kilns in a Norse raid in 881, although a 9th- to 10th-century date was attributed to the remainder (although those imported to London are now thought to date to the 11th and 12th centuries, cf No 253). Finally, wheelthrown greyware jugs, of late 12th and 13th-century South Hertfordshire type (Hooson forthcoming), were identified as being of mid-Saxon date, on the basis of parallels in Frankish cemeteries. None of these attributions would be accepted today, although most of the pottery is of late Saxon date.

In 1937 an early Saxon pot was found at Drury Lane and studied by Myres (Myres 1937, 432-6). Parallels between the fluted decoration of this vessel and those from the middle Thames and Surrey were noted but no date suggested. Subsequently Myres has attributed a 7th-century date to this vessel in his *Corpus* (Myres 1977, no 713).

In 1964 the discovery of the first dated Saxon pottery assemblages from London was recorded. They were found during excavations at St Nicholas Acon, Nicholas Lane, and dated to the mid-11th century, c.1020-80. However, although the fact of their discovery was published and the results of a preliminary analysis of the pottery used to date other pottery (such as that from Aldgate, Clark 1973, 40-41, Fig 19), there are no details in print of the range of forms or fabrics found (See Appendix 1).

In 1959 Gerald Dunning published the first survey of London's Saxon and early medieval pottery since that of Wheeler, as part of a general survey of late Saxon pottery in England (Dunning 1959). Several wares were identified, in particular the Rhenish red-painted and blue-grey wares (REDP and BLGR) and a distinctive greyware decorated with bosses (THWH). The high proportion of Rhenish imports in early medieval London was noted in Dunning's paper and just as his work was approaching publication a remarkable assemblage of pottery was discovered at the Public Cleansing Depot, Dowgate. A note on this group was included as an appendix to Dunning's report.

Some Saxon pottery from London has been included in *corpora* of Saxon pottery, in particular those by Hurst on Thetford-type ware (Hurst 1956) and St Neots-type ware (Hurst 1955) and by Hurst and Kilmurry on Stamford ware (Hurst 1957; Kilmurry 1980). However, London is on the extreme edge of the distributions of all three of these wares, and little can therefore be learnt about the dating or composition of London's late Saxon to early medieval pottery sequence from their identification amongst unstratified collections.

For a long time the only stratified pottery sequence covering the Saxon and early medieval periods in the London area was that obtained by John Hurst at Northolt Manor, Middlesex (Hurst 1961, 254-67). Many of the types present at Northolt are also known from the City of London although the sequence for this early material is dated only by parallels with the pottery forms and fabrics rather than by the site stratigraphy. The Northolt sequence remained the only complete Saxon to medieval pottery succession to be published from the area for over a decade and the need to supersede this work was noted by Hurst as one of the most urgent priorities in the Saxon and medieval archaeology of the region (Hurst 1976a, 65-6).

In 1973 the newly-founded Department of Urban Archaeology (Guildhall Museum) excavated several sites producing late Saxon and early medieval pottery, and the results of these excavations were published over the next few years in *Transactions of the London and Middlesex Archaeological Society* (Rhodes 1975; 1980). As at Northolt, however, the pottery could only be dated by comparison with material from other areas where it was hoped that the dating of pottery was based on sound principles.

In 1974 a breakthrough was made following the discovery of the New Fresh Wharf Saxon waterfront. Pottery was found in apparent association with the earliest post-Roman occupation of the site which was initially dated by a Carbon14 determination to the late 9th century. This was a historically attractive date, since it is just at this period that one would expect to find evidence for Alfred's reconstruction of the town. Accordingly, the New Fresh Wharf assemblage was used as a datum to divide pottery assemblages into three groups; those which could be argued to be earlier than New Fresh Wharf; those containing the same range of types; and those containing types not found in the New Fresh Wharf assemblage and therefore probably later than it (Rhodes 1980a, 139).

Subsequent work has shown that the late 9th-century date for the New Fresh Wharf material must be abandoned. Dendrochronological analysis of the New Fresh Wharf timbers has taken place parallel with the development of the master tree-ring curves for Saxon and medieval London, so that initially there was no means of checking the validity of the late 9th-century Carbon14 date. Subsequently, analysis managed to show that the first New Fresh Wharf structure could be dated c.60 years earlier than the second, which produced timbers with felling dates clustering at the end of the 10th century. Further revision has now shown that the latest timbers in the second bank were probably felled c.1020, to which date an unknown period must be added for the reuse of the timbers. Finally, detailed analysis of the stratigraphic contexts of the sherds said to be associated with the first bank showed that not one was in a sealed context while statistical comparison of the assemblage with that from the second bank showed that the two were indistinguishable. Thus, although it is still thought that there was late 10th-century activity on the waterfront there is no pottery which can be associated with it. Pottery types which were previously being dated by this excavation to the mid-9th century can now be seen to be in all probability 200 years younger.

Excavation at the neighbouring site of Billingsgate Lorry Park in 1982 produced a small group of pottery from the first Saxon waterfront, coin-dated to the late 10th century or later (a date used in a recent survey of London's Saxon and Medieval pottery, Vince 1985d, 31). The dendrochronological evidence from this structure has since dated its construction to c.1039-1040. Since further excavation along the waterfront has shown that there is little activity east of the mouth of the Walbrook before the late 10th century, the only possibility of obtaining earlier assemblages dated by dendrochronology lies in the examination of sites close to Queenhithe, known from documentary evidence to have been in existence in the late 9th century (Dyson 1978), the chance survival of waterlogged wood on a non-waterfront site or the discovery of stratified assemblages of pottery associated with coins.

A late 9th-century *terminus post quem* for the Saxon ceramic sequence in the City can be inferred through the demonstration that a substantial mid-Saxon settlement using different pottery types existed immediately to the west of the City (Vince 1984; see p.38). The date-range of chaff-tempered ware in the London area is clearer following the publication of assemblages from Clapham (Densem and Seeley 1982, 181-4, Fig 5) and Tottenham Court (Blackmore 1983). Nevertheless, the precise starting point for the City sequence is still uncertain, within a bracket of *c*.850 to *c*.950.

The chronological sequence presented here is based on the analysis of pottery from building sequences excavated by the DUA at Pudding Lane in 1981, Botolph Lane in 1979, Watling Court in 1978 and other sites within the City walls. Study of pottery from other DUA sites has mainly revealed a series of pit groups with few interrelationships. Some of these sites, such as the 1976 excavations at Milk Street, have produced the best preserved fragments of pottery and provide much of the material used in the present type-series.

Many aspects of the Saxon and early medieval pottery of London have yet to be determined; for example, closer dating of the sequence and the precise provenance of much of the pottery. It is to be hoped, however, that the present study, and in particular the archive which was prepared as part of the study, will prove to be a useful starting point for future research.

DATING

Introduction

For the high medieval period, from about the middle of the 12th century until the middle of the 15th century, it is possible to construct a pottery sequence for London based on the analysis of large quantities of data obtained from well stratified and independently datable sequences. For the early medieval and late Saxon periods this cannot be done. As shown above, the excavated sites hardly ever produce large quantities of pottery of this period and there seems almost to be an inverse relationship between the size of the assemblage and the quality of the stratigraphic relationships. The quantity of pottery within the building sequences at Pudding and Botolph Lanes is much smaller in total than that to be found in a sample from a single medieval waterfront deposit. However, although some of the pottery types found in London are identical to those known elsewhere, and for which date ranges have been suggested, it has been decided to try and demonstrate the London sequence and its date using stratigraphic principles and material from London itself. The main reason for this is that at almost every other site where one might wish to use the pottery dating, the sequence is either less well dated than that in London or appears to be based on equally uncertain foundations.

There are two independent stages in the establishment of a dated sequence. Firstly, the relative date of the wares and types must be established, and then evidence for the absolute date of the sequence inserted.

Relative dating

There are many lines of reasoning which can be used to establish the relative date of pottery types. Typological arguments, which have been successfully used to date much medieval pottery, are of less use for this period because of the similarity of forms used throughout the period. Nor does the examination of intercutting rubbish pits produce clear-cut evidence for the relative date of pottery types because of the high quantity of residual material in most pits, and because the relationships are quite often not clearly defined on the ground, due to the similarity of fills and the slumping of overlying deposits into the top of pits. Even when the two assemblages are clearly differentiated, there is often little useful data regarding the relative date of the types because the interval between the deposition of the groups is too great.

The best evidence for the relative sequence of types comes from the excavation of long stratigraphic sequences, examination of trends within the pottery data and then the comparison of these trends with other sequences and assemblages. The building sequence at Pudding Lane Area A (Fig 1.3) is the longest single sequence covering the late Saxon period. That at Botolph Lane Area E suffers from the lack of stratigraphic correlation between separate excavation trenches (C, S and SS) and from the very small quantities of pottery from each makeup/floor sequence. It is possible to relate most large assemblages to one of the phases of occupation at Pudding Lane, and there is little disagreement in the basic sequence of pottery types.

Another extended sequence is found at Milk Street, where P44 was sealed by a deposit of dark earth, then cut by P45 (which has a primary and secondary fill), which was in turn sealed by more dark earth, then cut by P55, which was finally cut by P56 (Fig 1.2).

The best sequence, however, is that from the Billingsgate Lorry Park site. This sequence starts later than the two mentioned above but is continuous from its starting date through to the end of the medieval period. For the earlier medieval period the site is divided into two stratigraphic sequences, divided by an inlet. That to the west of the inlet is the more complete sequence and can be closely dated by dendrochronology. The first post-Roman activity was the construction of a revetted bank (App 1, BIG Period IV.1). This bank had a period of use (App 1, BIG Period 4.1US, Period IV.7) followed by a refacing (App 1, BIG Period IV.4). After a further period of use (App 1, BIG Period 4.6FS), the new face fell forwards and was replaced by a new bank and revetment (App 1, BIG Period V.1). Subsequently, a completely new waterfront was erected to the south of the previous line (App 1, BIG Period VI) and the inlet was filled in (App 1, BIG Period VII).

The earliest groups in these City sequences contain mainly sherds of LSS (CP1). These are succeeded by assemblages containing mainly LSS, with EMS and EMFL (CP2) and then by those containing EMSS in addition to the previous wares (CP3). These in turn are replaced by assemblages containing ESUR, SHEL, EMCH and ANDE in addition to the previous wares (CP4). Some closed groups of this phase show that LSS had by this time ceased to be used, although it is found throughout the Pudding Lane sequence. In the next phase, sherds of LOND and LCOAR glazed wares and various handmade sandy wares (such as LOGR and EMGR) are found, although again alongside wares introduced earlier (CP5). The final phases at Pudding Lane contain sherds of wheelthrown cooking pots, mainly SSW, and can be correlated with the earliest material from the medieval waterfront reclamation sequence (CP6), dated to the second half of the 12th century.

Alongside these fairly common wares there are rarer types whose date range might be useful for sub-division of the sequence, but the majority of these types are imports which might vary in frequency for reasons other than date (as, for example, at the Dowgate foreshore which on the basis of local wares would be dated to CP5).

Absolute dating

There seems little doubt that the five ceramic phases outlined above are valid, given large enough contemporary assemblages and that it is possible to assign any large group to a 'ceramic period'. It should then be possible to calibrate the sequence by inserting the termini post quem obtained from absolute dating methods. However, there are so few of these absolute dates, and so much doubt about their correct interpretation, that this absolute dating is much less secure than the relative sequence. Scientific dating methods - for example thermoluminescence or radiocarbon dating - have been used to date late Saxon pottery, for example at St Aldates in Oxford (Durham 1977). While such methods can be of use where the date of a ware is unknown to within a couple of centuries, they are of little use where the whole sequence must fit into a period of three hundred years, c.850-1150. The conditions under which these methods will work are also limited. Thermoluminescent dating is most accurate where the natural background radiation is known, by means of samples of the soil in which the sherds were buried; and radiocarbon dating of pottery itself, rather than of the context in which it was found, depends on the isolation of contemporary organic material within the pottery fabric. The method should work on chaff-tempered pottery, but the quantity of pottery recovered from the city is so far too small for sherds to be spared for destructive analysis. Horizontal stratification - by which material is dated through the shift of activity across a site is of some use, since the balance of probability is that most sherds found within the City walls post-date the abandonment of the extra-mural mid Saxon settlement. Similarly, finds from sites to the south of Thames Street are unlikely to have arrived there before the 11th century (when that area was part of the river), although they could, of course, have been redeposited in the 11th century or later. Such arguments, however, cannot be used where the theories upon which they are based are themselves unproven.

Dendrochronology has supplied nine usefully dated contexts from the City and one, Hibernia Wharf, from Southwark. Of these groups one is stratified within a building sequence, at Botolph Lane, and can therefore give a *tpq* to the remainder of the sequence. Another, from Milk Street P45, gives a *terminus post quem* to some wood fragments thrown into a pit and thus gives a *tpq* to the remaining pits in this sequence (see above), while the remaining dates come from waterfront revetment structures (Fig 2.3).

Site	Group	CP	Dendro *tpq*
Peninsular House	PEN E16	1	912 +
Milk Street	MLK P45	1	914 +
New Fresh Wharf	NFW 2.4	3	1014 +
Billingsgate	BIG 4.1	3	1039-40
Billingsgate	BIG 4.4	4	1055
New Fresh Wharf	NFW 3.2	4	1055 + (prob 1084 +)
Billingsgate	BIG V.1	5	1080 +
Seal House	SH water front I	5	1133-49
Billingsgate	BIG VII	5	1144-83

2.3. Table showing assemblages dated by dendrochronology. The quantity of pottery (by fabric) in each group can be found in Appendix I.

Eight 10th- to 12th-century coins have been found stratified in later Saxon or Norman deposits in London but of these only one is of 10th-century date, and that now appears to be within a deposit of mid 11th-century date, at Billingsgate Lorry Park (although originally thought to date the construction of the first bank and inlet to the 10th century, Vince 1985b). Examination of each assemblage shows that although the date of loss of each coin is securely known, it provides no proof that the associated pottery was deposited within similar limits. A comparison of the pottery phases and coin dates is shown in Fig 2.4.

Site	Group	CP	Coin tpq	Coin date of loss
Milk Street	MLK P55	4	1017	before 1050
St Nich Acon	SNA	4	1025??	before 1050??
Pudding Lane	PDN ESB5	4	1062	before 1066
Milk St	MLK P41	4	1074	before 1077?
Peters Hill	PET	5	1083	before 1086?
Billingsgate	BIG IV.6FS	5	1080	before 1083?
Seal House	SH pre-wI	5	1056	before 1100

2.4. Table showing assemblages dated by coins. The quantity of pottery (by fabric) in each group can be found in Appendix I.

Other artefacts are too imprecisely dated themselves to be used to date the context in which they were found. They consist of decorated artefacts, such as the 'motif pieces' from Milk Street and Seal House. Since most of these objects are likely to have had a longer period of use than their associated pottery there is little to be gained from a study of their intrinsic dating. Another potential means of calibrating the pottery sequence is to examine the likely duration, or relative duration, of the different pottery phases. At Botolph Lane area E, for example, the number of re-floorings per pottery phase can be calculated. Similarly, at Milk Street, it is possible to work out the average number of intercutting pits per pottery phase. However, this method assumes that the occupation of a site was uniform throughout the late Saxon and early medieval periods, which is unlikely.

The combined evidence for the absolute date of the pottery sequence (summarised in Fig 2.2) is therefore as follows:

Late 9th century: transfer of domestic settlement to within the City walls. Use of LSS in the London area is later than this movement and can therefore be given a tpq of post-840 but is probably substantially later than this.

Late 9th to 10th century: Use of LSS alone (CP1). Dendrochronological date of 912 + from Botolph Lane and 914 + from Milk Street P45.

Mid-10th to early 11th century: Use of LSS with EMS and EMFL (CP2). No absolute dating evidence but the beginning of this phase must lie between the mid-10th and early 11th centuries. It must end before 1040.

Early to mid-11th century: Use of LSS with EMS and EMSS (CP3). Dendrochronological dates from New Fresh Wharf (c.1014 +) and Billingsgate Lorry Park (c.1039-40).

Mid- to late 11th century: Absence of LSS, presence of ESUR and EMCH (CP4). Coin dates from St. Nicholas Acon, Milk Street pits 41 and 55 and Billingsgate Lorry Park. Dendrochronological dates from New Fresh Wharf period 3.2 (1055 +, probably 1084 +) and Billingsgate Lorry Park period 4.4 (c.1055).

Late 11th to mid-12th century: Use of London-type and Coarse London-type ware alongside miscellaneous unglazed greywares (LOGR) and types found in previous phase (CP5). Dendrochronological dates from Seal House Waterfront I (1133-49) and Billingsgate Lorry Park (periods V.1, 1080+ and VII, 1144-83).

Manufacture

The main division in manufacturing techniques is into vessels thrown on a wheel and those formed by hand. In many cases the use of the wheel is unequivocal. Such vessels include non-local English wares, such as NEOT and STAM, and continental imports such as REDP, ANDE and NFRE. In a few instances, however, it is unclear whether the vessels were thrown on a wheel or merely rotated as a finishing process. In particular, the method used for LSS is uncertain. Some of these vessels are undoubtedly handmade (cf. No 6) and exhibit regular thumbing on the underside of the shoulder, as well as near-vertical undulations on the inside of the body. Some, however, have parallel striations from the rim to just above the base on both the inside and outside of the vessel. However, there is not one example with pronounced ribbing on the inside and only one vessel, the sprinkler (No 35), on which the characteristic 'stretch marks' caused by the twisting of the clay on the wheel can be seen. The sprinkler is good evidence that the wheel was used to throw, as opposed to finish, some LSS vessels, but since hand-forming techniques were also definitely used in the same industry there will always be an element of doubt over the method used for individual vessels. There is no evidence from London to support a chronological progression from handmade to wheelthrown vessels within this industry.

There is no doubt, however, that the wheel was not used in the production of most of the early medieval coarsewares used in London. These vessels were made by coiling, although the coils were usually competently smoothed into each other so that construction evidence is only rarely seen. Several other hand-forming methods are known, or have been postulated, but, with the exception of a possible use of a former (to make the rounded bases of LCOAR vessels), such methods have not been identified on Saxon or Norman pots from London.

The bases of almost all LSS and early medieval coarseware vessels are convex even when the vessels were wheelthrown. Experiments by Natalie Tobert suggest that it would be difficult to produce these bases by pushing out a flat base

without also producing cracks. Some of the less extreme examples may have been produced by 'rocking' the pot on a hard surface to smooth off the base angle. This is more likely to have been a finishing process than the method of manufacture. Natalie Tobert has suggested that the bases could have been produced by press-moulding and that the base, still within the mould, might have been used as a base for the construction of the walls. It must be admitted that the precise method of production is still unclear, with no obvious means of choosing between alternative hypotheses. There is no doubt, though, that the sagging bases were produced deliberately.

Finishing

Few late Saxon and early medieval pots from London seem to have been fired without their surfaces being finished off, to remove blemishes caused by the manufacturing process. Detailed examination of the surfaces can often identify a sequence of finishing processes, varying both with the type of tool used and with the wetness of the clay.

A few vessels show signs of a fine slip covering all or parts of the surface. This is probably due to what is known to modern craft potters as 'self-slipping' and is caused by rubbing a wet hand

2.5. A Late Saxon Shelly Ware cooking pot (No 2) showing the 'self slipped' surface on the body.

2.6. The inside of an Ipswich - Thetford type storage jar showing throwing lines obscured by extensive knife trimming.

over the pot soon after manufacture, causing the coarser particles to sink below the finer ones. The method has been consistently noted on LSS, possibly because a wetter clay was needed to produce a wheelthrown vessel (Fig 2.5).

Most handmade vessels show signs of rough smoothing. Detailed examination can distinguish differences which depend on the hardness of the smoothing agent. At one extreme the palm of the hand itself 'rides' over large inclusions in the pot, while at the other the knife either cuts through the inclusion or forces it out of the way. The effect of any smoothing also depends on the consistency of the clay. A knife can produce quite different surface textures if used immediately after the pot has been made from those produced on a leather-hard vessel. Early medieval coarseware vessels typically have surface textures which show that the outside of the pot was first given an irregular finish with the hand, followed by horizontal smoothing produced by running the hand around

the rim. These horizontal striations usually extend only a finger's depth on the inside and outside of the pot. There is no proof, nor apparently any need, for a tournette or turntable to be used to produce this effect, nor is there any evidence for the use of a cloth or other material than the human hand to produce the smoothing. A leather pad, however, would probably give rise to an effect identical to that of using the palm. There is also evidence to show that vessels were often given a final palm smoothing after the use of a knife or similar tool.

On a few vessels a sharp-edged tool was used to pare off clay from the vessel. This gives a faceted appearance to the surface and usually numerous parallel striations, plucked grains and shallow furrows with an inclusion at one end. This method is known as 'knife-trimming', although there is no proof that the implement was an iron knife. There are two main ways by which the method was applied. On some vessels clay was removed from both the inside and outside of the pot while on others the clay was removed only from around the outside of the base. The first method was used extensively on the mid-Saxon pottery used in the London area, for example IPS, and it is interesting that it appears most frequently on later Saxon pottery with a continental or east coast origin (Fig 2.6). It was used extensively on THET, REDP and on ANDE while it has not been noted on LSS or the locally-made early medieval coarsewares (Fig 2.7). The more limited use of knife-trimming, around the outside of the base, was also a relatively rare technique at this

2.7. Andenne type ware costrel (No 275) knife trimmed where it was taken off the wheel and on the 'side' to provide a flat base.

a

d

b

e

c

2.8. a-e. Miscellaneous early medieval coarsewares with individual stamp decoration.

time, although it became standard on mid-12th-century and later LCOAR and LOND. The only examples noted are on 12th-century LOGR and EMGR and on STAM pitchers. The former vessels usually show signs of hand smoothing both before and after knife-trimming.

Decoration

The majority of vessels examined are undecorated, but examples with individually applied stamps, roller-stamps, freehand decoration applied with various tools, applied strips and finger-impressions are also found.

Individual stamps, presumably cut from wood, bone or antler, are common on 6th and 7th century pottery in the London area. Examples are known from Clapham and Tottenham Court. By the mid-Saxon period, however, the use of stamps was restricted to a few Ipswich-type ware vessels. Stamping remained a rare technique in the late Saxon and early medieval periods but examples have been noted on LSS (Nos 30, 34), a NFRE glazed ware pitcher (No 277) and various early medieval coarseware vessels (Fig 2.8). The stamps are without exception circles divided either into squares (grid stamps) or into triangular segments (wheel stamps). There is no

possibility, given the small number of examples and the simplicity of designs, of identifying individual dies.

The use of roller-stamps, small wheels on which a design was cut and then rolled over the pot, is also rare on late Saxon and early medieval pottery in London. A single roller-stamped LSS vessel has been noted (No 10) while the method is more common on 12th-century LOGR spouted pitchers (No 177; Fig 2.9). The latter designs are extremely simple and consist mainly of lines of squares. The most common use of roller-stamping was on ANDE and NFRE vessels, many of which have horizontal bands of diamond pattern roller-stamping (Nos 271, 276, 287, 293-4; Figs 2.10, 2.11).

Freehand decoration was applied using a variety of techniques. Firstly, there is a single vessel, thought to be a Low Countries import, on which a round-ended tool has been used to produce burnished lines, applied in a lattice pattern (No 309 Fig 2.12). Burnishing appears to be a common decorative method on 7th to 9th century

2.9. Detail of roller-stamping on a Local Greyware spouted pitcher (No 177). The poor impression appears to be made with a diamond lattice roller stamp and has been obscured by subsequent smoothing.

2.10. Sherd of an Andenne pitcher with diamond lattice roller stamp.

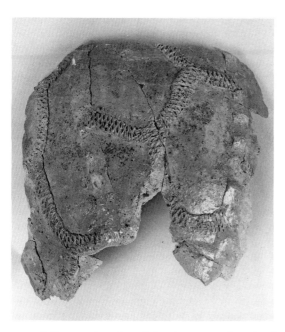

2.11. Roller-stamping of applied strips on a yellow-glazed North French pitcher (No 276). Note also applied strips with thumbing.

2.12. Burnished decoration forming a lattice pattern on a Low Countries import (No 309).

continental imports and is found on Ipswich-type ware of the same date. There is no other example known from London of the use of the technique in the late Saxon period. Secondly, a round-ended tool could be used to produce deeper grooves. Crude designs, usually of wavy lines, were used to decorate the shoulders of early medieval coarseware spouted pitchers (eg Nos 63, 136, 154-5). Finally, a 'comb' could be used to produce similar patterns. From inspection of the type of impressions left by these tools it appears that in some cases a snapped twig or any other piece of wood with a jagged edge could be used to produce such 'combed' lines on a pot (Fig 2.13). On ESUR cooking pots such simple combs were mainly used to produce a zone of rilling around the girth and shoulder (Nos 140), although more complex patterns were used on spouted pitchers (Nos 154-5).

Applied strips of clay were added to some late Saxon and early medieval vessels, probably both to strengthen the vessel and to provide decoration. The technique was used extensively on THET, on which wide, usually vertical, strips were secured and decorated by thumbing while the pot was on its side. This technique produces a distinctive result on which the thumb impressions are

2.13. Detail of the shoulder of an early Surrey cooking pot showing rough grooves, probably made with a jagged piece of wood.

asymmetrically placed on the strip (No 205; Fig 2.14). Other examples of applied, thumbed strips have been noted on NFRE (No 276), ANDE (Nos 270, 272), STAM (not illustrated) and EMCH (No 138).

Finger-impressions on the rim of a vessel are frequently the only decoration present on early medieval coarseware pots, especially EMSS. There is some variety in the distance between impressions and in the way in which they were made. For example, there is a difference between rims which have been decorated by pressing straight down onto the rim and those where the decoration is around the outer or inner edge. There are a few examples where only part of the rim of the vessel has been decorated in this manner. This characteristic was noted on a late 11th- or early 12th-century vessel from Gloucester but was thought then to be an aberration on the part of the potter (Vince 1979, No 107).

Bossing, or the pushing-out of the walls of a pot as a form of decoration, is a rare technique on late Saxon and early medieval pottery in London.

The main example of its use is on THWH pitchers on which bosses were formed by the simultaneous pinching of the outside and pushing of the inside of the pot. Dunning defined the area in which the technique was current, predominantly in the Low Countries (Dunning 1959, 67). A similar technique, on which the walls of the vessel have been indented in long vertical grooves, has been noted on STAM pitchers from Gloucester.

Glaze

Glaze was used on only a small number of vessels, mostly of known non-local origin, such as ANDE. The next most frequent Saxo-Norman glazed ware in London is STAM (Kilmurry 1980, 155-170). A few sherds of WINC, NFRE yellow-glazed wares and the LCOAR complete the picture. Three methods of application can easily be distinguished. The first, in which the vessel is either dipped into a liquid containing the glaze (for an external covering) or the glaze is poured into the vessel (for an internal glaze) cannot be demonstrated on any Saxo-Norman vessel from London and may well have been too wasteful of glaze. It is nevertheless the most likely method to have

been used on the earliest, 10th to 11th-century, glazed wares such as the NFRE pitcher from Pudding Lane (No 276) and a few sherds of STAM. The second method, in which the glaze is sprinkled onto the pot, either as a powder or a liquid, gives rise to irregular spots and dribbles of glaze. This method was definitely used on LCOAR and LOND (Pearce et al 1985, 4-5) and appears to be the method used on some of the STAM and WINC vessels. The third method is the application of glaze with a brush, which would have given the potter good control over the areas glazed but unless a very thin application is used it is not possible to see individual brush strokes. This method was almost certainly used on ANDE, as can be seen from the way in which glaze is absent on that part of the body shielded by the handle (Fig 2.15).

It is furthermore possible to distinguish variations in the texture of the original glaze mixture, although probably not its precise composition. Many early glazes are characterised by minute pits, often in the centre of a circular spot of glaze.

2.14. A sherd of Ipswich Thetford-type ware spouted pitcher, showing the way in which the applied strip has been thumbed from one side.

2.15. A sherd of Andenne-type ware pitcher (No 272) showing that the glossy, crazed glaze was not applied underneath the handle.

These are caused by the reaction of the glaze with the fabric of the vessel, and show that the glaze contained a coarse element, such as metallic lead shavings, a lump of frit or small lumps of ore. On some LOND and LCOAR vessels the centre of the pit is filled with a globule of metallic lead. This could as easily have been produced by reduction of an ore fragment as by melting of a lump of metal. Such pits are virtually never found on the other Saxo-Norman glazed wares, and suggest that the glaze was either crushed and sieved before use or applied as an oxide.

All the glazes used were lead-based, as demonstrated by XRF analysis at the Ancient Monuments Laboratory (carried out by Justine Bayley), and no examples of green glaze coloured by copper are present. However, some of the colour range found on ANDE glaze is due to the addition of iron. This sometimes occurs as spots or streaks, demonstrating that the glaze was not fritted before use (which would have homogenised the constituents). Most of the glazes have a yellow colour, caused by small amounts of iron and an oxidized firing. The iron could be present as an impurity in the glaze but is more likely to have been taken up from the clay fabric. A light green glaze, found on a small number of vessels of all wares, was produced by reduction of this iron. Isotope analysis of the lead in the glaze would probably enable the sources to be determined but, due to inaccessibility of the equipment, analysis has not been undertaken.

Firing

Although it is possible to determine, within limits, the conditions under which a pot was fired, only a limited amount of work has yet been undertaken on the Saxon and Norman pottery from London. Various techniques could be employed, including refiring test sherds, examination of polished sections under the scanning electron microscope and differential thermal analysis - comparing the physical characteristics of the test sample and a control at different temperatures, but the following analysis is based solely on observation. Almost all the wares from London were fired at relatively low temperatures. This is shown by the hardness of the fabrics, most of which can be scratched with a steel blade, and by the optical properties of the clay matrix in thin-section. At high temperatures (the actual temperature depends on the clay composition and firing conditions), the clay minerals

in a pot fabric are completely altered to form a ceramic which does not transmit crossed polarised light (XPL). Such a ceramic is termed isotropic, while those that show interference colours in XPL are termed anisotropic. High temperature firing is sometimes accompanied by the formation of new minerals, such as mullite. The only ware not usually fired at low temperatures is REDP, much of which must have been fired at stoneware temperatures. High fired sherds of other wares are sometimes found but these are accidental, and are sometimes accompanied by the vitrification of the sherd. A further limit on firing temperature can be seen where vessels contain unaltered shell or other carbonate inclusions. In oxidizing conditions, the survival of these inclusions would suggest a firing temperature below 850°C, but a reducing atmosphere would allow higher temperatures to be reached while the presence of finely divided sodium chloride leads to the formation of a stable, protective halo around the carbonate inclusion. Few vessels seem to have suffered through the alteration by heat of their carbonate inclusions, even where the vessel has an oxidized surface and is unlikely to have contained salt in its fabric. It is therefore likely that a temperature of 850°C was seldom reached. Firing below 600°C leads to the formation of very soft pottery, which on burial can revert to its unfired clay state. It is therefore likely that the majority of Saxon and Norman pots were fired between 600° and 850°C. Such temperatures can easily be reached in a bonfire firing and, with the exception of REDP, there is no ware which could not have been fired in a simple bonfire.

Although a wide range of clay colours is found in the Saxon and Norman pottery from London, there are only a small number of firing patterns, suggesting that firing conditions, like the temperatures achieved, were similar for most of the pottery. Most clays contain organic matter, either as distinct inclusions, such as roots or decayed leaves, or as microscopic fragments, perhaps even chemically bonded to the clay minerals. Upon firing, this material is first converted to carbon and then burnt out of the fabric. In a short duration firing, or a very thick pot, the carbon is not completely removed and this leads to the formation of a black fabric. Few of the wares found in London show this feature, which is, however, typical of much early to mid-Saxon pottery. The fabrics of most of the pottery have colours which depend on the iron content and firing conditions alone. Oxidizing conditions lead to the formation of pink, brown or red clays, while reducing conditions lead to the formation of blue-grey clays. It is normally straightforward to distinguish one from the other, but can be difficult when vessels have a very low iron content. Few vessels have a homogeneous colour throughout their fabric. LSS vessels usually have a thin, reduced, grey core with oxidized margins, while early medieval coarseware vessels have a thicker core and oxidized margins. A few types, notably THET, THWH, LOGR and EMGR, have deliberately reduced surfaces, sometimes over the top of oxidized margins, and can be grouped together as 'greywares' or 'reduced wares'. A distinctive feature of many vessels is that the surface colouration is patchy. They have eliptical marks with concentric zones of varying colour. Normally, the centres of these zones are less oxidized than the rest, giving the impression that they were formed by jets of reducing gas during the firing (Fig 2.16). Such jets might be found where green timber was used as a fuel, causing steam to play over the vessels. It is clear that these conditions were transient, as there is sometimes evidence for overlapping jets and the mottling is rarely more than a surface phenomenon. This mottling is most common on early medieval coarsewares with oxidized surfaces, but can occur on LSS and the greywares as well.

2.16. An early medieval gritty ware spouted pitcher (No 189) showing elyptical reduced areas.

Vessel forms

There are only a handful of common pottery forms used in late Saxon and early medieval London, and these can be simplified further into cooking vessels, serving vessels and others. Quantitative analysis of selected groups confirms the impression gained from surviving complete vessels that cooking vessels greatly outnumber all others, and serving vessels form a minor element, although becoming more common through the period. Other forms are very rare and are each represented in London by a handful of examples. Within each form, however, there is considerable variety. Much of this is due to the differences in pottery source, and there is a strong correlation between the form and typology of vessels and their fabric.

Cooking vessels

Jars, termed here cooking pots, and bowls were used for cooking. The cooking pots greatly outnumber bowls and occur in a wide range of sizes and forms. They are the major product of the LSS and early medieval coarseware industries and rarely, if ever, occur in those industries concentrating on the production of serving vessels.

Leaving aside the few non-local and imported vessels, there are four main forms. These approximate to fabric groups, so that the earliest form is that produced in LSS which was roughly globular with an everted rim. This type was superseded by a form produced in several early medieval coarseware fabrics (mainly EMS, EMSS, and EMSH). All these types have a roughly cylindrical body with a well-defined shoulder and vertical or everted rim. Similar forms occur over much of southern England, all apparently starting in the 11th century, perhaps as early as c.1000. A slightly later introduction is the form typified by the ESUR cooking pots. These vessels have straight sides which narrow slightly towards the rim, which is usually everted and infolded. Very similar forms occur in the Welsh borderland, from south Wales to south Worcestershire, starting in the later 11th or early 12th centuries, perhaps a generation or so after the conquest. There is no doubt, therefore, that the ESUR vessels are earlier than those found further west. Finally, the last basic form was introduced. This type has a squared rim and a globular body and is typical of the wheelthrown cooking pots produced in the London area from the mid-12th century (Pearce *et al.* 1985, 42, Nos 341-7). The early to mid-12th-century examples discussed here are in greyware fabrics and were produced without the use of the wheel.

Straight-sided bowls, many of which may have had socketed handles or spouts, are found in a number of fabrics throughout the period. They are particularly common in LSS, EMS and EMSS but have not been noted in ESUR. Many examples have heavily sooted sides, showing that they were used for cooking, but it is uncertain whether they were used for exactly the same purposes as cooking pots or whether they had a more specialised function.

Serving vessels

A small number of vessels are distinguished by the presence of a spout and sometimes a handle and glaze. Such vessels also have a higher incidence of decoration, little or no sooting and, when made in a calcareous fabric, often have heavy leaching on the inside of the vessel. These vessels are grouped together as serving vessels, although it is clear that there may well be an overlap in many characteristics with liquid storage vessels, such as that from Winchester (Cunliffe 1964, Fig. 34, No 1), which also have handles, spouts, decoration and leaching of the interior. The distinction between the vessels must be made on grounds of size. The Winchester vessel and those like it could not have been moved when full, whereas the majority of examples from London were little different in size from contemporary cooking pots.

When recording the London material, tall spouted, handled vessels have been distinguished from squatter, spouted handled vessels. The former, which occur mainly in glazed wares, are termed pitchers, and the latter spouted pitchers. The two forms look quite different but this is probably due to the fact that they were produced in separate regions, using different techniques. Two further forms are recognisable. Firstly there is a type with a relatively narrow rim, a spout but no handle. This type is found in REDP (No 253), LCOAR (No 194 and Pearce *et al* 1985, 39, Nos 40-42), EMGR (Nos 186-9) and LOGR (Nos 171-8) and first appears in the early to mid-12th century. Secondly, there is a type found in one fabric only, THWH, which appears to be of cooking pot form,

although no sooted examples are known. The form is handled but an almost complete vessel has no spout (No 222).

Tripod pitchers are usually glazed, handmade vessels, with spouts, handles and three feet. They are known from Winchester and south-east Wiltshire from the end of the 11th century but few appear to have been imported into London until the mid-12th century (and those not from Wiltshire but from east Berkshire). The majority of tripod pitchers appear to be in locally-produced LCOAR (eg No 193).

Other forms

The remaining forms account for a small fraction of the pottery. Excavations at 10th to 11th century kiln sites show that occasional oddities, such as ring vases and costrels, were produced at many centres (Hurst 1976b, 314-48, Figs 7.15, 7.20). The present list from London is therefore likely to be extended, slowly, by further excavation.

Beakers have been found in REDP. They can be distinguished from the spouted pitchers in sherd collections only by their much smaller size. Storage jars have been found, and are mainly distinguished from cooking pots in the same fabrics by their much larger size and the absence of sooting. However, some vessels which were definitely used for cooking were of considerable size (eg No 119 which is sooted). There is a danger, alluded to above, of confusing these storage jars and fragments of spouted pitcher, but storage jar fragments have been positively identified in LSS and some early medieval coarsewares. Several varieties of lamp have been noted. The earliest examples, of LSS, usually have a pedestal base (Nos 36-41) while the later ones were made for suspension (Nos 92-3, 182-4). The latter type continued into the later 12th century in London-type ware (Pearce *et al* 1985, 46, No 428). A few cups have been found, some decorated all over with stamping (Nos 301-5). There are a few examples of costrels, in STAM (No 245) and ANDE (No 275; Fig 2.17), glazed STAM, NFRE and NORG pitcher lids (Nos 244, 290, 296), sprinklers in LSS (No 35), STAM (No 246) and NFRE (Fig 2.18; Fig 2.116) and a few vessels whose complete form and function are unknown (for example a NFRE glazed ware vessel from Watling Court, No 291; Fig 2.19).

Crucibles were used from the late 10th or early 11th century and a number of forms and fabrics have been recognised. Only one ware, STAM, was used for both domestic vessels and crucibles. The

2.17. A complete Andenne-type ware costrel (No 275).

a

2.18 a. *The side view of a North French sprinkler (No 291a)*
showing applied roller stamped strips and b, the base which
has been pierced with 5 holes before firing.

reasons for this appear to be that the pottery clay available at Stamford, was, by chance, suitable for use as a refractory clay (Part 6, p.403).

2.19. Unidentified North French object (No 291) decorated with roller stamping, free hand incised lines and stamped circles.

b

The study of late Saxon pottery is still hampered, over a quarter of a century after the first late Saxon pottery symposium (Dunning *et al* 1959), by the lack of primary data. The comparison of the London sequence with that from other sites is therefore often hindered by the fluid dating of the comparative material and the lack of data from much of the surrounding region. Indeed, until 1985 there was little mid-Saxon pottery from central London and thus no body of data with which to contrast the City finds. It might be argued, therefore, that this is not the time to draw conclusions from the study, and that it would be better to wait for further comparative material, but the most likely stimuli for further work on the subject are hypotheses which 'explain' all the currently available facts, since they focus attention upon crucial areas of research, such as the need to produce a more detailed chronology for late 9th- to 10th-century pottery from London, or the lack of knowledge of late Saxon pottery distribution in the southern Chilterns. In the following discussion many of the statements are based on inadequate samples, usually from unstratified collections, and there is no doubt that much will be erroneous. Consequently, the function of this section is to stimulate further work as much as to summarise present research.

The transition from mid-Saxon to late Saxon pottery

In eastern England the ceramic division between 'mid-Saxon' and 'late Saxon' is clear-cut. It is represented by the introduction of the potter's wheel and by a range of pottery forms exemplified by the products of the Thetford-type ware industries (Hurst 1976b). In East Anglia this division can be seen to apply at numerous sites, due to the proximity of the Ipswich and Thetford-type ware kilns. Further afield there is circumstantial evidence pointing to the continuity of 'early Saxon' handmade black-fired wares throughout the Saxon period. Some of the pottery produced in the centre of Gloucester in the late 10th and early 11th centuries would not have been out of place in mid-Saxon Southampton (Vince 1979, Fig 8). It would have been quite feasible for London to belong ceramically to this more backward zone. Nevertheless, it is now clear that London belongs to eastern England in this respect, since the latest pottery assemblages from the mid-Saxon settlement are dominated by Ipswich ware with few handmade, black-fired wares still in use (see, for example, the Treasury site assemblage, Huggins forthcoming). By contrast, the earliest vessels from occupation within the City walls are of LSS, many of which were wheelthrown vessels. The contrast between the pottery used in the two settlements is striking.

Shell-tempered wares have been found at two mid-Saxon sites, the Treasury and Jubilee Hall, but they do not contain the same type of shell temper as that found in LSS (and were probably produced closer to London, possibly from outcrops of the Woolwich Beds clay). There is therefore a clear division in London between mid-Saxon and late Saxon pottery. The separation is in fact too clear cut to sustain the hypothesis that the intra-mural occupation sequence follows directly on from that in the Strand. At no other point in the pottery sequence is such a sharp break noted. The variable life of the vessels themselves normally causes apparent blurring of ceramic changes, however abrupt they might be for the industries concerned. Prized vessels, amongst which we might class the Ipswich ware spouted pitchers and certain mid-Saxon imported vessels, would probably have been retained in households long after the source of supply had changed. We have, therefore, strong grounds for believing that we have either not yet discovered any occupation debris belonging to the initial inhabitants of the walled City, or not yet found pottery from the latest settlement along the Strand.

The possible reasons for this have implications for the interpretation of events. Perhaps the scale of settlement was initially quite small, although the Queenhithe charters (Dyson 1978) show that at least parts of the infrastructure of the town (the street grid, trading within properties, trading on the shore) were in being soon after Alfred's re-occupation of the City. Perhaps, then, the Strand settlement itself was shrinking during the 9th century and the reoccupation of the town took place in the 880s but with a different population? The small quantity of data available for the Strand settlement does not indicate any contraction in the settlement area during the 9th century. The three excavated sites have produced evidence consistent with 9th-century occupation (although they could have been abandoned within the century, rather than towards its end). Similarly, two 9th-century stray coins have been found, at Northumberland Street and Fleet Street (see p.285).

The Waterloo Bridge hoard dates to c.870 and is almost certainly associated with the Viking occupation of London in 872 (see p.286). At present there are no means of determining which, if either, of these alternative explanations is correct. The most likely seems to be a compromise: that the Strand settlement was declining in size during the 9th century, and that the remnants of its inhabitants moved inside the walls in the 880s, but that initially the extent of this intra-mural settlement was limited and its intensity low.

The late 9th or early 10th century change in pottery supply was itself a remarkable event. London in the mid-Saxon period and later in the 11th century was supplied with pottery from sites within the Thames Basin, supplemented by a small amount of imported pottery from the east coast of England and from the continent. Between these dates, the complex links were severed and a single, non-local, pottery industry came to supply almost all of the pottery in use in London (and, as will be suggested below, the surrounding region). It also appears that this phase was not a short disruption of normal trade patterns since it persisted throughout the 10th and into the 11th century. Nevertheless, comparison with other parts of England shows that the London evidence fits well with other known pottery distributions of this date.

Before moving on to examine this comparative data we must look at the evidence for the introduction of wheelthrown pottery, which is taken here to mark the beginning of the late Saxon period. The earliest documented production of wheelthrown pottery in Midland England was in late 9th-century Stamford. Here, a case has been made by Dr Kilmurry for the importation of the technique by the Vikings some time in the late 860s or later (Kilmurry 1977, 183-4). Sherds from what may well be this phase of production were found at Repton in disturbed deposits above the remains of late 9th-century burials, perhaps associated with the Viking occupation of 874 which resulted in the takeover of eastern Mercia (Garmonsway 1972, 72-3). The same ware is found in the earliest occupation levels at Flaxengate, Lincoln, which are coin-dated to the late 9th century (Adams Gilmour 1988, 123-33). Several sherds from one red-painted Stamford ware vessel of this early type have been found at Victoria Street, Hereford, stratified above sherds of Chester-type ware (now thought to have been produced at Stafford) and late Saxon Gloucester products (Vince 1985c, 79). There are, however,

several reasons, none conclusive, for believing that the Stamford ware vessel found in Hereford must have been deposited in the mid-10th century. Firstly, there is an aceramic occupation phase at Hereford, from which a single coin of Alfred was recovered giving a *terminus post quem* of c.887. Secondly, the Victoria Street sherds were recovered from an erosion deposit post-dating stage 3 of the Hereford defences, for which an early 10th-century date is postulated. Thirdly, the Stafford kilns themselves are likely to post-date the documented construction of the *burh* in 917. Chester-type ware has been found on many sites along the Welsh border but at none of these is there any dating evidence, except at Chester itself. The term 'Chester-type ware' derives from the discovery of a hoard within a roller-stamped jar dated c.972-3 at Castle Esplanade (Webster *et al* 1953; Carrington 1977). Chester-type ware has been found in Chester in contexts post-dating the construction of the Aethelflaedan defences of c.907, but the considerable sequence excavated at Lower Bridge Street only produced pottery in the latest pre-Conquest phase, V, and the end of the preceding phase, IV (Mason 1985, 33-4). The starting date for Chester-type ware could therefore be as late as c.970 but could be as early as the 920s.

The Chester-type ware industry, like that producing London's LSS, was operating on the fringe of the area in which wheelthrown pottery was the norm. Further south the starting date for the isolated wheelthrown pottery industries may be even later. At Cheddar, fabric B can be shown petrologically to have been locally produced, and Rahtz's excavations at the Palace demonstrate that it came into use after c.1000, accompanied by handmade wares. Similarly, the evidence from Exeter suggests that the Bedford Garage kiln may be of early 11th rather than 10th century date (Allan 1984, 9), while, in southern Hampshire, Michelmersh ware was definitely in production in the early 11th century, as was Porchester ware. In both cases a late 10th century origin has been suggested but has still to be proved (Addyman *et al* 1972; Cunliffe 1976). Earlier wheelthrown pottery has been recognised at Winchester, though petrological analysis has failed to suggest a source, nor are the reported finds of this ware sufficient in quantity to prove a local origin (Biddle and Collis 1978, 133-5).

On the fringes of the wheelthrown pottery heartland we can therefore see a slow diffusion of the technique, which arrived later and was rarer as it spread south. Turning back to the East Midlands and East Anglia we find little dating evidence for the use of wheelthrown pottery with the exception of the Morley St Peter hoard pot, a Thetford-type vessel dated c.925 (Clarke and Dolley 1958) although it is a reasonable assumption that there was continuous production at Stamford from the end of the 9th century onwards.

On the basis of the data described above, it is suggested here that there were four ceramic zones in late 9th to early 11th-century England. In the central zone, which includes Stamford and Ipswich and the source(s) of St Neots-type ware, wheelthrown pottery completely replaced handmade wares c.900 and continued to be used throughout the 10th and 11th centuries. In the second zone, which includes Stafford and quite probably Northampton, Leicester and the other Midland kilns, Gloucester and the source of LSS, wheelthrown wares replaced handmade wares later in the 10th century and in two cases, Gloucester and the LSS industry, wheelthrowing was used side by side with handforming techniques. In this zone the potter's wheel fell out of use during the 11th century. London would fit into this zone. In a further zone, south of the Thames, wheelthrowing started in the late 10th or early 11th century, never completely replacing handmade production, and lasted at most for a generation or two. Further afield, the wheel appears to have not been used at all in this period. Politically, zone (a) corresponds to the Danelaw, zone (b) to English Mercia, where the Danes were only ever in control for a matter of years, if ever, and zone (c) to Wessex. This correspondence is sharp enough to suggest that the military reorganisation of society in the Danelaw and Mercia was in some way responsible for these changes in pottery production.

Tenth-century pottery

Although, as noted above, the starting date of many late Saxon wheelthrown wares is unknown, there is little doubt that most were in use during the later 10th century and were broadly contemporary with those from London. This enables three types of comparison to be drawn. These are (i) the range of forms used, (ii) the presence or absence of contemporary wares in London, and (iii) an analysis of the distribution pattern of LSS

to see how much of the marketing process can be reconstructed.

The main form used in London, as everywhere, was the 'cooking pot'. There is abundant evidence, in the form of sooting and food deposits, that the majority were actually used for cooking. Their shape follows a broad regional pattern. Those from the Midlands and East Anglia are taller than they are wide and have narrow bases, while those from the south are as wide as they are tall. Insufficient complete profiles have been recovered to tell whether these differences are reflected in the capacities of the vessels. This trend did not have its origin in the mid-Saxon period since the few complete profiles of handmade vessels from mid-Saxon Southampton are tall, whereas Ipswich ware vessels are more similar in overall shape to those found further south in the late Saxon period. The next most common forms in LSS are straight-sided bowls or dishes, probably always spouted. These forms have been noted in the Thetford-type ware industries but not in contemporary industries to the west or south. They are found, however, in later 11th-century industries in Oxfordshire (fabric AC), Berkshire, the London area (for example, EMS and EMSS) and in Somerset (Rahtz 1974, Fig 6). If the form represents a distinctive style of cooking then this diffusion is of some interest, since it implies a spread of this habit from the Thames valley to the south and south-west.

The remaining forms found in LSS, such as large storage jars and spouted pitchers, lamps and the sprinkler, are so rare that knowledge of their distribution in other industries is limited to those from which large kiln waste deposits are known. All are paralleled in Thetford-type wares, but are unknown in the southern wheelthrown industries. A single lamp has been found in the Gloucester late Saxon ware (Vince forthcoming) from the Bell Hotel site, Southgate Street.

Many of the wares contemporary with LSS also continued in use later and it is not possible, except in sealed deposits, to be certain that an association of LSS and, for example, NEOT is real rather than a fortuitous association of residual 10th-century pottery and later 11th century wheelthrown wares. Sites where sealed 10th-century deposits exist, such as Botolph Lane and Pudding Lane, indicate that LSS had a monopoly in the London pottery market. The most noticeable absentee is Ipswich Thetford-type ware (THET), since pottery from this source was present in the 9th century and again in the 11th century. There are no known differences in typology between 10th and 11th century THET, and it is therefore possible that there are some pieces of 10th- century date from London. A few sherds of a coarser-textured Thetford-type ware (SATH) have been found in London. These too have been found in later, 11th-century contexts. NEOT is found in small quantities in London, but no sherds have yet been found in conclusively 10th-century contexts. A couple of sherds of Chester-type (Stafford) ware have been tentatively identified, but no examples of Gloucester late Saxon ware. Several distinctive hand-made wares of late Saxon date are known from England south of the Thames, for example small groups of pottery stylistically late Saxon rather than early medieval have been found at Bisham Abbey (Reading Museum) and Wraysbury (Wessex Archaeological Unit) in Berkshire and at Reigate (Jones forthcoming) in Surrey. All three wares have distinctive fabrics but have not been recognised in London. None of the handful of chaff-tempered sherds from intra-mural sites in London were found in 10th-century contexts, although that from New Fresh Wharf came from an 11th-century deposit which may contain a high proportion of late 10th-century material. A single glazed northern French pitcher and lid were found in a 10th-century group although other sherds have been found in definite 11th-century contexts. Finally, no examples of Rhenish imports of this date have been noted. A small number of sherds of Badorf-type relief-band amphorae have been found in London, but all in later deposits and not, apparently, associated with other residual mid-or late Saxon pottery. Sherds of several other wares have been found in CPI contexts but are interpreted as intrusive (this interpretation has been checked against the relevant site records).

Although late Saxon pottery industries and their products are known in all the areas surrounding London, there is as yet no proof that their wares, or those from abroad, were being traded to London. Even if they were, there is sufficient evidence to show that any trade was on an extremely small scale, as in the case of the northern French glazed ware. This tendency for late Saxon pottery industries to distribute to exclusive markets has also been noted in the Severn valley and the West Country (Cheddar E ware). Particularly interesting are the presence, apparently, of three industries supplying settlements on the Thames between Oxford and London whose wares were not sent to London. This suggests either that LSS was being transported to London overland or that the traders transporting pottery downstream from the Oxford area did not pick up further goods on their journey. This is quite different from the sort of distribution pattern found along the coast in the later medieval period, the best example being the Bristol-Dublin trade in the 13th century, where goods were bought and sold all along the coast between the ports. It is also different from the pattern of river trade in pottery found in the Thames valley in the 12th century.

The distribution of LSS is at present not fully known. Three attempts have been made to plot it. The first (Mellor 1980, Fig 1) indicated a south Oxfordshire origin for the ware with trading contacts to the north (Northampton), north-west (Worcester) and west (Swindon and Gloucester). The second showed that the distribution extended into the Thames Basin but suggested that London was at the extreme eastern end of the market region (Vince 1985, Fig 6). Since then, five more findspots have been recognised. Those at Hendon, Waltham, Springfield and Orsett show that the ware must have been traded to the north and east of London (Vince 1990, Fig 52), while that at Winchcombe is to be expected, given the previous discoveries at Worcester and Gloucester. Colchester, however, has produced sherds of NEOT but not LSS, suggesting that north Essex was outside the market area. Similar 'negative evidence' is present at Walton, near Aylesbury, and at St Alban's Abbey. These three sites seem to show the northern limit of the distribution; in each case the late Saxon ware present was NEOT. To the south the limit at present is the Thames, although there are no known late Saxon sites in Surrey between Battersea and Reigate, nor in Berkshire except on the Hampshire border (Silchester and Netherton), so it may be that the present map, like the previous two, underestimates the market area of LSS.

It seems at present that the marketing areas covered by Stafford ware and London's LSS were much larger than those to be found in the Danelaw, where the density of known kiln-sites is higher. The explanation for this is unlikely to be that transport and marketing were more highly developed along the Thames and in western Mercia. It more probably indicates a smaller demand for pottery in these areas, either because of lower population density or because pottery was in less frequent use in English Mercia than further north.

Eleventh to early 12th centuries

A major change took place in the supply of pottery to London during CP2 and CP3. At the beginning of this period, LSS comprised virtually all of the pottery used, whereas by the end it had been replaced by other wares. The wares which replaced it were different in a number of ways. Firstly, the majority of them were from sources much closer to London. Secondly, there was no single major source; instead, the market was divided among three or four major suppliers and several minor ones. Thirdly, and most interestingly, these new wares were in general technically inferior to LSS. In particular they were produced without the potter's wheel and without the use of a kiln.

What circumstances might lead to such changes? One of the first points to establish is whether the observed facts were the result of a single event, such as the devastation of an area by warfare, or whether they were more diverse. It is clear that this sequence is not found in London alone. Exactly the same change is noted in the Severn valley, for example. However, it is clear that this technical decline was not nationwide. The Stamford industry continued, and even grew in scale, during the 11th century, although handmade pottery was produced nearby, at Blackborough End. In York too there is no trace of any decline at this period. The second point to establish is whether the replacement of wheelthrown pottery by handmade wares took place at the same time in the affected areas. This is difficult to establish and should perhaps be considered in two ways. Firstly, when did wheelthrown wares cease, and, secondly, when did handmade wares start? For London neither point is satisfactorily resolved. Two coin-dated contexts suggest that CP4 (the first from which LSS is completely absent) may have started by the reign of Cnut (see Fig 2.4). However, it has also been suggested that the coins of Cnut could have been circulated up to c.1050 and there is always the possibility that neither association is valid, because of the high proportion of residual finds. The dendrochronological date of the largest assemblage of CP3 (when LSS was still present), from New Fresh Wharf, now suggests a deposition date of c.1030 (Hillam, forthcoming), while the smaller group from Billingsgate Lorry Park would suggest that LSS was still current in 1039-40. It is therefore fairly certain that LSS disappeared from use in London between c.1030 and c.1050.

At Oxford, Mellor has suggested, the production of the ware ceased abruptly in the early 11th century, as a result of the Danish sacking of the borough in 1014. This presupposes that the pottery kilns were located in Oxford or its environs, for which there is no positive evidence (although it would not be surprising and would probably be consistent with the petrological evidence). It also provides a single historical context for the cessation of one pottery production centre, but not a reason for the cessation of other wheelthrown pottery production, nor for the replacement of well-produced wares by inferior ones in the area once served by LSS. Thus, before accepting this explanation it must be considered whether it is consistent with the dating evidence from London which would imply that a high proportion of the pottery used in the City was over 15 years old when broken. We have no comparable figures for the medieval period, but for the 17th and 18th centuries this would not seem an unreasonable estimate. For contemporary peasant pottery (low-fired earthenwares, comparable to late Saxon wares) it would be an extremely long 'life', since the average life of a utilitarian pot is closer to one year (Vince 1977). Reluctantly, therefore, the 1014 end-date for the production of LSS must be rejected until more precisely dated groups are available. If the evidence for the cessation of production of Gloucester late Saxon ware and Stafford ware is examined, it must again be concluded that an early 11th-century demise for these industries is too early. At Hereford the defensive circuit was refurbished in 1056 by Earl Harold and the soil levels which accumulated beforehand contain predominantly sherds of Gloucester and Stafford wares. There is then an almost complete break in occupation, and the earliest succeeding contexts on most sites must date to the early 12th century (Vince 1985c). If the Stafford and Gloucester wares fell out of use in the early 11th-century, then 11th century occupation in Hereford has yet to be discovered. The few sherds of glazed Stamford ware (STAM) from Hereford (from Berrington Street site 4) confirm that the latest Stafford and Gloucester wares are of mid 11th-century date. A similar conclusion has been reached at Gloucester, again on the basis of the few Stamford ware imports and the fact that Gloucester late Saxon ware had gone out of use before the construction of the timber castle in the 1060s. From these three regions it can be suggested that the wheelthrown wares had ceased production before the Conquest, perhaps a decade or two beforehand, but almost certainly not as early as the Danish wars of the first quarter of the 11th century.

It is now necessary to examine the evidence for the starting date of the inferior wares. Dunning defined these wares as 'early medieval' since both typologically and technically they are the ancestors of the coarsewares used in the post-conquest period. Fabric analysis shows that many were produced from the same clay sources as their successors and that there was therefore probably a continuity of production from the 11th into the 12th centuries. In London the earliest of these wares is EMS. The first use of this ware marks the beginning of CP2, although there is no doubt that LSS was still the major ware. A number of similar wares followed on from this, still apparently forming a minority of the wares in use. The fact that two stages in the introduction of these wares can be recognised suggests that the changeover took an appreciable time. The dating evidence for these phases is discussed above (p.24), where it is suggested that CP2 is late 10th or early 11th century and CP3 is early- to mid-11th century. There is, however, no absolute date for CP2, and two dates, of *c.*1030 and *c.*1039-40, for CP3. Elsewhere, the best dated evidence for the start of early medieval wares comes from the Severn Valley and the West Country. At Cheddar such wares are found with coins of *c.*1000, which provide a *terminus post quem* only, and were absent from deposits later than *c.*930. At Silbury Hill an occupation of the hilltop was associated with a coin of Cnut and early medieval pottery from several sources. At Gloucester and Hereford it has been suggested above that early medieval wares started *c.*1050 or later, although at Winchcombe two sites have produced evidence for an early medieval ware associated with Gloucester late Saxon ware and a radiocarbon date of 1020±80 (Saville, Haddon-Reece and Clark 1985, 135). At none of these sites, therefore, can early medieval wares be shown to have come into use before the mid-11th century, while at Hereford they were probably absent in *c.*1050. Such evidence suggests that the changeover to handmade pottery took place over large areas of southern England at the very end of the Saxon period. It is therefore more likely that CP2 and CP3 span the early to mid-11th century than that CP2 starts in the 10th century.

The explanation for this change in ceramic production must allow for the likelihood that there was a substantial chronological overlap between the wheelthrown industries and their early medieval successors, and for the fact that the changeover took place at different times between *c.*1000 and *c.*1050. There is little doubt that early medieval wares were in more frequent use (or at least were more frequently thrown away) than their predecessors. This can be seen by comparing the average size of pit assemblages of different Ceramic Phases from London, although this figure is of course influenced by the size of the pit itself, which also increased during this period. It is also certain that early medieval pottery was produced at many more places than its predecessors. Some, if not all, of this production was rural, and in some centres large-scale industries developed during the late 12th and 13th centuries (see below, pp.46-7). In the 11th century, however, production seems to have been almost always on a small scale. Distribution evidence shows that the centres supplying London, for example, were operating over distances of 20-30 miles at most. This in turn suggests that their products were marketed by the potters in areas within a day's journey of their settlements, probably with some redistribution through markets and fairs. Although it cannot yet be demonstrated, it is likely that early medieval wares in southern England were being produced and marketed in a similar manner to wheelthrown wares in East Anglia and the East Midlands, where rural kiln sites are known and where the spacing of production sites suggests that the wares were distributed over smaller areas than Stafford ware and London's LSS.

It can be suggested that between the 9th and 11th centuries pottery production in southern England changed from a situation in which pottery was not common, but where it was in use might well be traded, to a situation in which pottery was in common use, to the extent that a network of production centres could be supported. In between these two states there was a time when demand was growing, but was not yet great enough to support a local industry, and it is to this transitional stage that the widespread distribution of Stafford and LSS wares belongs. The contrast between the distribution areas of these 10th-century wares and those of their 11th-century successors cannot therefore be used to indicate a dramatic decline in overland transport but may merely indicate that pottery had changed from being a rare novelty to become an item of everyday use. We are still left with the problem of why the early medieval potters did not use the wheel. Possibilities include a lack of personal capital (for a workshop, kiln, firewood or transport for the finished pots) or a demand for pottery which outstripped the supply of trained potters. It may be significant that the potter's wheel disappeared from use in the part of the country where the manorial system was already well-established before the Conquest, perhaps inhibiting individual enterprise.

The sources of London's early medieval pottery are only vaguely known, since there is no archaeological evidence for production, nor perhaps is there likely to be any since early medieval potters may not have used permanent kilns for firing their pottery. Petrological evidence shows that there were four main groups of fabrics. The earliest and most frequent ware contains fossil shell temper, sometimes combined with a rounded quartz sand. The sand could be derived either from a drift deposit or an earlier geological deposit, such as the Bagshot Beds, and is therefore of little use in providing a provenance for the pottery. The shell is of Tertiary origin and therefore, in the London area, almost certainly from the marine facies of the Woolwich Beds. This deposit outcrops as a narrow strip along the south bank of the Thames from Charlton eastwards. The difference in fabric, and slight differences in typology, suggest that there were at least two separate sources: EMS and EMSS together form the larger one while EMSH is the smaller. Although both would have been in contemporary production for much of the later 11th and early 12th centuries, in CP3 and CP4, EMSH becomes more frequent during the early to mid-12th century, in CP5.

The next largest source of early medieval coarseware in London is in Surrey, producing wares (ESUR) whose white-firing clay was tempered with a sand composed mainly of weathered iron-rich sandstone. The closest source of such a sandstone is the Lower Greensand, while the Reading Beds apparently contain lenses of white-firing clay, used, for example, in Wiltshire for the 13th-century Laverstock pottery and from the mid-13th century at Kingston-upon-Thames. Although petrology shows that this ware must have been carried some distance to London, insufficient fieldwork has been done to map the location of the potential resources. Not all of the Reading Bed clays are white-firing and not all of the Lower Greensand is iron-rich sandstone. Even less certain is the extent to which alluvial sands in Surrey are derived solely from iron-rich sandstone. The sand used in Kingston-type ware is

more varied in composition but that used for Coarse Border ware in the later medieval period is very similar. A source in western Surrey, northeast Hampshire, or even eastern Berkshire, is therefore more likely. The only settlement site at which sherds of ESUR form the majority of those seen is Aldershot, close to the borders of all three counties.

A fourth source area of early medieval coarsewares lies to the north-west of London and, like EMSH, its products become more frequent through the period. EMCH is a distinctive ware whose source may be localised using petrology. Thin-section analysis has shown that this ware was probably made from a river clay to one side of a chalk outcrop, since its clay matrix is similar to both the Gault clay and some of the basal deposits of the London Clay. Petrology cannot yet pinpoint the source but the distribution of the ware may help to define the source area. At present only one site, apart from London, is known where this ware has been found in quantity, St Albans Abbey. The nearest area to St Alban's where the right deposits may be present is to the north-west, in the direction of Berkhamstead.

Another ware, EMFL, is sufficiently distinct in its petrology to show that it was not locally produced, but the range of potential sources is too great to hazard a guess as to its source. Although never more than an infrequent ware in London, the sherds found do suggest that it was present during CP2, as early as EMS. Finally, there is LOGR and other, miscellaneous, quartz- tempered wares, some of which are similar in petrology to wares known to have been produced in the London area but which on petrological grounds could come from anywhere within the Thames Basin. These wares increased in frequency during the period and in some deposits of CP5 they form the majority of coarsewares present. Insufficient work has yet been done on the distribution patterns of these handmade coarsewares for them to be analysed in detail, although they were obviously distributed over much smaller areas than LSS.

Wheelthrown non-local wares

Small quantities of wheelthrown English wares are found in 11th- to 12th-century London assemblages. A few of these have a known source, such as STAM and THET. Others, such as WINC and NEOT have a generally recognised source area, although no kilns or production sites are known. There are also two wares whose sources are unknown, although they are distinctive in appearance. The first is a sandy Thetford-type ware, SATH, of whose source all that can be said is that Essex and Hertfordshire appear to have been outside the production area of this style of pottery, while known kilns at Ipswich, Thetford, Norwich and Grimston, and indeed throughout the East Midlands, produced similar but not identical products. A source in East Anglia or the East Midlands is likely. The other ware, THWH, has a distinctive fabric in thin-section and is decorated by the unusual technique of bossing, yet no examples have been reported outside London. In 1959 Dunning suggested a Low Countries origin but despite much work in this area since that time no clear parallels have come to light.

In form these non-local wheelthrown wares differ from the early medieval coarsewares since they include mainly spouted pitchers with few cooking pots. Other forms are also more common in these wares than in local wares, for example the STAM sprinklers and costrels, although few of these types occur in archaeological contexts. There are no examples of non-local wheelthrown wares in CP1 and they are most frequent in CP3 to CP5.

Continental imports

Imports from the Middle Rhine, the Meuse valley and northern France are found during this period. Of these, the latter are scarce but include both glazed pitchers and unglazed whiteware cooking pots. Coarse gritted sherds from Normandy (NORM and NORG) are found, from both cooking pots and pitchers, but others, of unknown origin, are more common (NFRE and NFRY). A few of these sherds are decorated with red paint. There is some evidence to suggest that the importation of northern French pottery increased after the Conquest, since it is absent from New Fresh Wharf in CP3 but present in the CP4 deposits which follow, and in similar deposits from Billingsgate Lorry Park, dated c.1055. The Meuse valley products, ANDE, occur in the same CP4 deposits but not in CP3. They too must have been introduced well before the Norman Conquest.

Wares from the Middle Rhine valley are by far the most common imports, from CP2 or CP3 onwards. Red-painted Pingsdorf-type ware (REDP) vessels are the most common and few groups - whether from the waterfront or inland

- fail to produce sherds of such vessels. A few examples of Pafrath-type (BLGR) cooking pots and ladles have been found, in late 11th to mid-12th-century deposits, and a sherd which may be of this ware was recovered from the CP3 bank at Billingsgate. This ware may therefore first appear in London in the early to mid-11th century.

A few imports from unknown sources have been found, of which the most distinctive are the rare sherds of glazed hemispherical cups, with stamped decoration, known from their first recorded discovery as Crowland Abbey-type bowls. Excavations in London have produced fragments of two of these vessels, while the British Museum has a third example from London. The distribution of these vessels - London, Crowland Abbey, Oxford and Dublin - is too diffuse to indicate their source, or sources. The sherds are either unavailable for petrological analysis (the Crowland vessel was lost during the war) or are too scarce to be spared for destructive analysis.

By and large the continental imports found in London in the 11th and 12th centuries do not give the impression of being deliberately traded goods, since they are rare and from disparate sources, with the possible exception of the Red-painted and ANDE vessels. A deposit found on the foreshore at Dowgate in 1959 contained a very large collection of REDP, as well as a number of BLGR ladles. Analysis has shown that most vessels showed signs of use and the high concentration must therefore be either due to their use on board German ships or to the proximity of Dowgate to the Steelyard, the German quarter of London in the later medieval period.

Comparison with other areas

The evidence from London demonstrates the growth of a network of small potteries in the Thames Basin during the 11th and 12th centuries. A similar growth is recognisable over much of southern England, at much the same time. Too little is known of the pottery used in Middlesex, Surrey and Essex at this time for the routes by which this pottery entered the City to be demonstrated, although it is tempting to see ESUR being carried by boat downriver and EMCH being carried overland, along Watling Street. It is interesting, in this regard, that an 11th-century abbot of St Albans is said to have had a strip of woodland to either side of Watling Street cleared, to make the road safer for travellers.

The relative quantities of non-local English wheelthrown wares suggest that the majority were carried to London by ship. STAM, NEOT and WINC are remarkably scarce in comparison to wares from land-locked sites such as Oxford, which is as distant as London from the source areas, whereas THET is rarely found in the Thames Valley outside London, nor is it apparently found in central Essex, which is closer than London to Ipswich. The continental imports undoubtedly entered London by ship, either as the personal belongings of the crew or passengers or as a make-weight used to fill the hold on the return journey of a ship which carried a more valuable cargo on its outward voyage. As excavation fills in the present gaps in our knowledge of the pottery used in the areas surrounding London, so it will be possible to determine which wares were traded in London, and therefore found at surrounding sites, and which were incidentally imported, and therefore confined to the port itself.

In conclusion, the 11th to 12th-century pottery sequence in London demonstrates a wide range of contacts between London and its immediate hinterland, with other regions in southern and Midland England, and with continental Europe. In this respect the pottery is little different in character from that used in the mid-Saxon settlement, or in the later medieval City. What is surprising is that this mature trading pattern seems to have arisen early in the 11th century. The present study suggests that the pottery trade in the late 10th and early 11th centuries was atypical, and that work should be undertaken to see to what extent this is a reflection of changes in the economy of London, general economic trends or merely a phenomenon of the pottery industry.

The transition to high medieval pottery

Three features differentiate the pottery of the mid-12th century from that of the later 12th century. The first is that there are far fewer sources for late 12th century pottery than for the mid-12th century. Few, if any, of the pottery fabrics are the same in each period. It is possible that some groups of potters worked throughout the century but changed the composition of the clay they used. Petrology shows, however, that some areas supplying London in the mid-12th century ceased to supply the City in the later part of the century. The second difference is a change in the technology used to produce the pottery. The most obvious features are the use of the potter's wheel and the increasing use of glaze, but it is also clear from examining the regularity of colour of complete vessels that the later pots were fired in a kiln whereas the earlier ones need not have been. A quantitative analysis of mid- and late 12th-century pottery assemblages from London shows that glazed, wheelthrown, kiln-fired pottery was present in the mid-12th century, in the form of LOND and LCOAR. The quantities present, however, are minimal. In the later 12th century these glazed wares were much more common and new wheelthrown cooking vessels were introduced. The latter may have been produced in the same areas as some of their handmade predecessors. SSW, for example, contains a similar shell temper to EMSH, although less was used in the fabric and the larger fragments were excluded. It is just as likely, however, that unconnected groups of potters used the same basic clay sources in both periods. With the exception of the London-type wares the amount of overlap between the periods was minimal. Since well-dated mid-12th-century groups may be as early as c.1140 and the later 12th-century groups as late as c.1190 this leaves half a century for the changeover to have taken place. However, the ease with which groups can be placed into CP5 or CP6 on all sites suggests that the change was actually much quicker than that, perhaps lasting a decade or two.

The London sequence suggests that the new technology was adopted first in the London area itself, possibly by immigrant potters. The use of the wheel then spread to the SSW industry, possibly located just to the south-east of London, and sometime before the beginning of the 13th century the wheel had been adopted in north Middlesex and south Hertfordshire, where Hertfordshire reduced wares (SHER) were produced. Elsewhere in southern England the same sequence can be seen. The earliest wheelthrown pottery used in Wiltshire, for example, was of early 13th-century date and made at Laverstock, close to the royal palace at Clarendon. The Laverstock products, like London-type ware, included highly decorated glazed jugs, while the coarsewares used in the area continued to be made by hand. The Worcester industry presents a similar example in that there was already some pottery production in the 12th century, although there is little evidence for any connection between this production and the early 13th century industry, the main products of which were green-glazed roller-stamped jugs, decorated inside the rim with white slip. In that region too there is an appreciable lag between the introduction of the first wheelthrown, glazed wares and the general adoption of the techniques, even by potters working within 10km of Worcester, at Malvern Chase.

It is important to note that, whereas in the London area the changeover to wheelthrowing and the use of the kiln took place at the same time as the reduction in the number of sources supplying the City, the pattern found in the Severn valley is slightly different. There, the disappearance of small-scale industries took place in the second half of the 12th century, as in the London area, but the industries which replaced them did not use the wheel, which was only slowly introduced over the first half of the 13th century. This shows that the change in scale of the potting industry and the adoption of new techniques were not always as closely connected as in the London area.

The change in scale of the industry may have been a reflection of the growth of local markets. New towns such as Uxbridge sprang into existence during the 12th century, while Southwark may have grown from being a bridgehead settlement (although, as Domesday shows, of some size) to span the whole of Borough High Street. The adoption of the new technology may only have been possible following this change in market. It implies that there was a move towards full-time specialisation and more capital investment in production in the London area up to 50 years before similar changes in the south-west and west of England.

TYPE SERIES AND FABRIC DESCRIPTIONS

The photomicrographs printed in black and white on the following pages, pp.48–114, are reproduced in colour on the pull-out pages at the back of the book.

Very few of the wares used in late Saxon and early medieval London were made in centres which have been archaeologically investigated. Even where kilns have been found, as at Stamford and Ipswich, it is certain that further kilns remain to be discovered and quite likely that they will prove to lie some way away from previous discoveries. It is, therefore, not possible to attribute vessels from London to individual kilns and thus to groups of potters. Nevertheless, much of the pottery was made from clays containing distinctive inclusions which can be used both to show that a group of vessels was produced in a single 'industry' (discussed below) and, in favourable circumstances, to suggest their source.

To the naked eye, many of these fabrics are remarkably similar, and in some cases there appears to be a gradation from one fabric to another, so that precise classification is arbitrary. In order to achieve a classification with a petrological basis, from which the source of the pottery might be deduced, the pottery from several excavations (principally those between 1974 and 1978 at New Fresh Wharf) was examined in detail under the binocular microscope. This work was carried out principally by Clive Orton and Louise Miller. Sample sherds differing in the type or frequency of inclusions, or in details of firing or manufacture, were placed in the DUA fabric reference collection. A large proportion of this pottery has since been examined in thin-section and, using a combination of binocular microscope and thin-section analysis, the classification presented here has been produced.

While this work on the pottery fabrics was in progress, the remaining pottery from the sites included in this study was examined and classified. In cases where the results of the fabric analysis have occasionally altered the original conception of the fabric classification (which was based solely on binocular microscope study), the pottery has been re-examined and re-classified. However, it would be possible to continue this process ad infinitum, continually refining and redefining the fabrics. As knowledge of Saxon and early medieval pottery grows it will certainly be worthwhile re-examining these collections. Special care has been taken, however, to ensure that the illustrated vessels conform to the published fabric descriptions.

The wares are presented here in groups which reflect their sources. Firstly there are the shelly wares which originate in the Jurassic belt. Then follows a group of wares which, it is suggested here, probably come from an area to the southeast of London. After these are wares which have inclusions derived from Cretaceous deposits, further from London than the previous wares but from both north and south of the Thames. These wares are followed by quartz sand-tempered wares of 'Thetford ware' type (although none come from Thetford itself), and finally the various glazed and unglazed non-local and continental imports which, even in total, constitute a minute fraction of the total collection.

CHAF (**Chaff-tempered ware**)

All vessels are handmade. The fabric is soft, feels rough, and has a texture which can be either irregular, hackly or laminated. The surface is usually a very dark grey or dark brown colour (10YR 4/1, 3/1), with a similar core. The surface may also be abraded and have brown, oxidised patches (7.5YR 6/2, 6/4).

There are abundant impressions of organic inclusions (grass?) on the surface of the pot up to 10mm in length. In a freshly broken section the chaff survives as abundant burnt, black fragments. Moderate to abundant small grains of quartz, range from 0.1 to 0.2mm. Sparse rounded quartz can measure up to 2mm, and can be clear, milky, or iron-stained. Occasional larger grains up to 5mm protrude from the surface of the pot. Flint is sparse sub-angular and measures up to 1mm across. White mica is abundant and up to 0.3mm across.

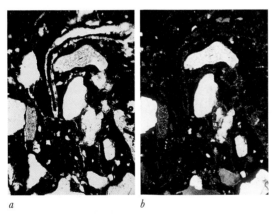

a *b*

2.20. Photomicrograph of chaff tempered ware; a, plain polarised light (p.p.l.) and b, cross polarised light (x.p.l.) Mainly quartz grains and one angular fragment of flint, bottom centre, and one large curved organic fragment (left).

The source of CHAF

The chaff-tempered sherds from the City of London have similar fabrics to those from the Strand sites and from Waltham Abbey. They may well all come from a single source. However, their inclusions are so undiagnostic that it is impossible to demonstrate this using petrology. At some stage this material would repay further analysis.

Corpus

There are no sherds from the City of London which can be usefully illustrated.

Dating and frequency

Analysis of the pottery from Mucking, Essex, by Dr H Hamerow has established that chaff-tempering, although present between the 5th and the 7th centuries (when the settlement was abandoned), only became dominant in the latest phase. Chaff-tempered pottery is also associated with a monastic site at Nazingbury apparently occupied between the early 8th and the late 9th centuries (Huggins 1978; Bascombe 1987). The fabric is also common on certain sites in the Strand, although it is rare at the Treasury site, which would appear to date to the late 8th century and later on the basis of sherds of Tating ware. The evidence from the City of London would support the view that chaff-tempered fabrics had ceased to be used for domestic pottery production by CP1 (late 9th to early 11th centuries). Very few sherds of chaff-tempered pottery have been found in the City of London, either in DUA excavations or previously. Only the sherds from the Riverside Wall excavations of 1974-5 (Rhodes 1980c) were found in contexts which could be contemporary with their use. These contexts were freshwater marsh levels which had developed behind the riverside wall from the 4th century onwards. Sherds from the Horn Tavern site in Knightrider Street were residual in medieval pits. Those from Peters Hill were found in late 9th to 10th-century and later deposits, the earliest being from a make-up deposit and therefore possibly imported to the site in the late Saxon period. A single sherd was found in an early 11th-century context at New Fresh Wharf, but is unlikely to be contemporary rubbish.

LSS (Late Saxon Shelly Ware)

The most distinctive aspect of the fabric of Late Saxon Shelly Ware is the presence of abundant fragments of shell, ranging from specks less than 0.25mm across to fragments in excess of 10mm. Some of this shell has been destroyed by chemical weathering and in other cases the firing has been sufficient to destroy the internal structure of the shell. Nevertheless the majority of sherds contain well-preserved shell. A sample of three sherds from Ironmonger Lane (context 298) was examined by John Cooper, Department of Palaeontology, British Museum (Natural History). He comments that the shell is mainly Gryphaea, a large oyster with a thick shell of flattened form. Ostracods, foramenifera, bryozoa and echinoid fragments, common inclusions in St Neots-type ware and late Roman shell-tempered ware, are conspicuous by their absence.

Carbonised wood fragments, containing some pyrite within the wood, are present in small quantities in the fabric. Rounded and angular fragments of quartz and flint/chert are sparse but sometimes several millimetres across. Sparse rounded quartz grains are found in virtually every sherd. The fabric has either a brown oxidised surface (5YR 6/6, 7.5YR 7/4, 6/4) with a grey, reduced core (2.5YR 4/0), or is reduced with a dark brown surface (10YR 5/1) and a dark grey core (N 4/0). Occasional vessels seem to be self-slipped (cf Fig 2.5).

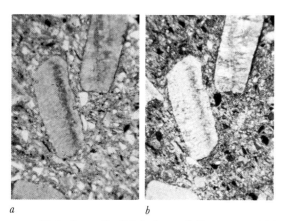

a   *b*

2.21. Photomicrograph of Late Saxon shelly ware; a, p.p.l b, x.p.l.

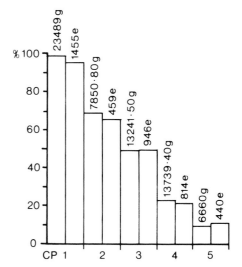

2.22. The percentage of Late Saxon shelly ware in stratified contexts, dated to CP1 to 5.

The source of LSS

Distribution evidence shows that LSS was traded over a large area centred on the Upper Thames Valley. The similarity in fabric, form and manufacture suggest a single source. Petrological examination of the clays does help to narrow down the potential source area but cannot pinpoint it.

The shell inclusions found in LSS have been identified as a Jurassic species by Dr John Cooper, who comments that the wood fragments are also likely to be of fossil origin. The quartz, flint/chert and rare freshwater shell fragments indicate that the clay is either an alluvial deposit containing abundant derived Jurassic material or a Jurassic clay contaminated by overlying alluvium. The absence of rounded Jurassic limestone fragments shows that the clay cannot have been overlain by the second Thames terrace gravels which in the Oxford area are characterised by fragments of these rocks. The higher terraces, however, do appear to be non-calcareous. A source in Oxfordshire, probably in the valley of a stream or river overlying or cutting through Jurassic shelly clays is likely.

Corpus (Figs 2.23-2.27)

Cooking pots form by far the largest class of vessels made in LSS. In the quantified sample of 55 eves from various sites excavated by the DUA, 83% of vessels were cooking pots. These are followed by open vessels of two basic shapes, here termed bowls (3%) and dishes (9%). The dish form is very similar to that of the late medieval 'frying pan'. Sooting is found on the outside of all these forms. Spouted pitchers (0.5%) and large storage jars (0.9%) are represented by numerous sherds but, given the size of these vessels, they were probably not a common form. Many sherds might be from either form (1.7%). A single sprinkler and a number of pedestal lamps (0.2%) complete the known corpus.

Cooking pots (Fig 2.23 Nos 1-10).

Bowls, some, if not all of which, have spouts (Fig 2.24 Nos 11-17).

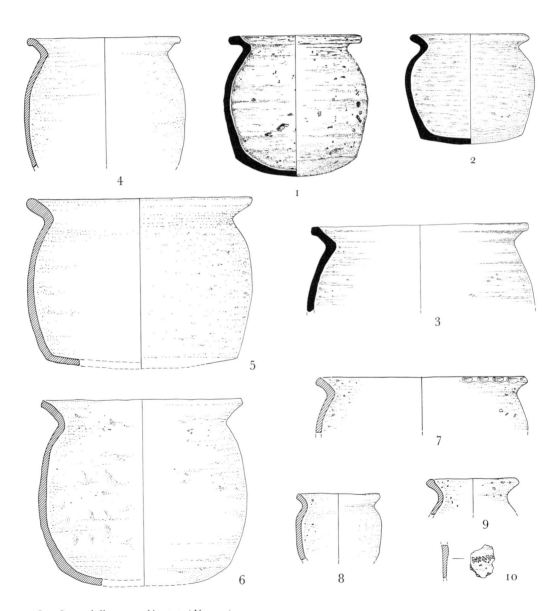

2.23. Late Saxon shelly ware cooking pots (No 1-10).

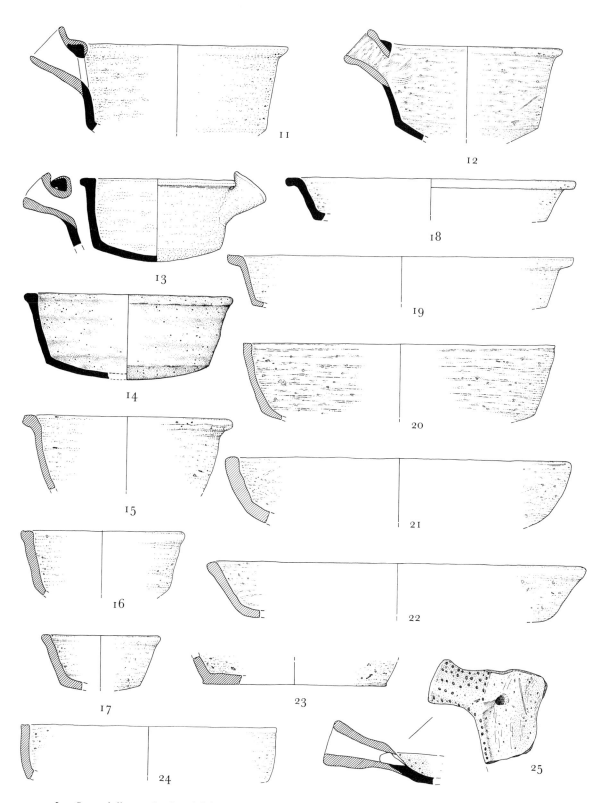

2.24. *Late Saxon shelly ware bowls and dishes (Nos 11-25).*

Dishes (Fig 2.24 Nos 18-25). No 23 appears to be a flat-bottomed dish. At least one of the dishes has a handle (Fig 2.24 No 25).

Spouted Pitchers (Fig 2.25 Nos 26-30). One vessel has a stamped handle (Fig 2.27) but this is unique within the DUA collection.

Storage Jars (Fig 2.26 Nos 31-34). No 34, with random wheel-stamps, appears to be too large to be a spouted pitcher.

Sprinkler (Fig 2.26 No 35). Only one example known.

Pedestal lamps (Fig 2.26 Nos 36-41).

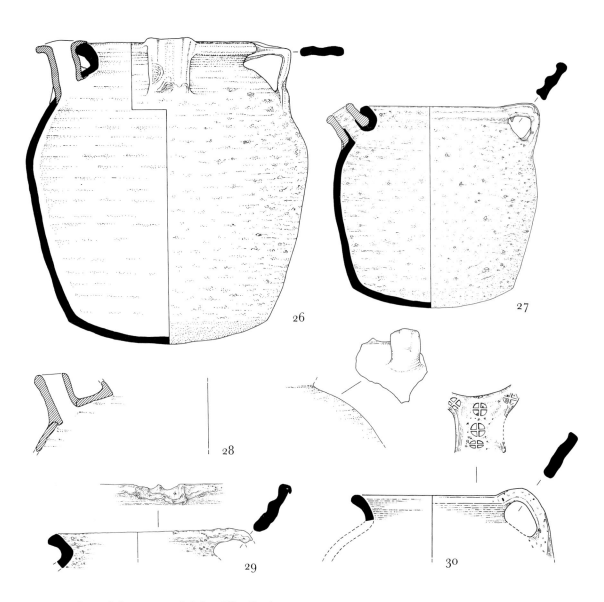

2.25. Late Saxon shelly ware spouted pitchers (Nos 26-30).

Dating and Frequency

LSS forms the main type of pottery found in the earliest late Saxon occupation of the City of London. The Billingsgate dendrochronologically-dated sequence shows that it was almost certainly still in use in 1039-40 but had ceased to be used by 1055 (Fig 2.22). These conclusions are in agreement with those arrived at from studying less well-dated assemblages in the City of London, but at Oxford what appears to be the same ware is thought to have been replaced by Oxford Fabric AC and St Neots-type ware (Oxford Fabric R) following the Viking sack of the borough in 1009 (Mellor 1980). If this historically-derived dating is correct at Oxford and if the two settlements

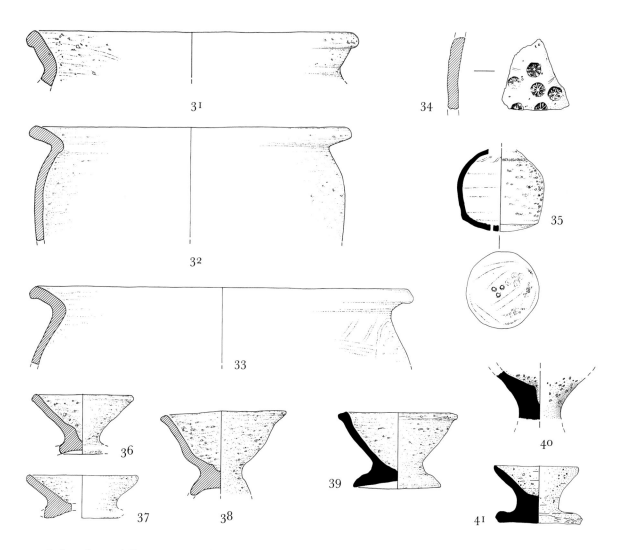

2.26. Late Saxon shelly ware storage jars (Nos 31-33), sprinkler (No 35) and pedestal lamps (36-41).

2.27. Late Saxon shelly ware spouted pitchers (Nos 26-30), showing individual stamps.

were being supplied by the same production centre then either the Billingsgate pottery is actually residual (which is a definite possibility in that particular deposit, considering the quantity of Roman sherds present), or the potters continued to supply London after loosing their market in Oxford, which was probably much closer to the source of the ware. Neutron Activation Analysis of sherds from the London area (Barking Abbey) and from Oxford is currently in progress (M Mellor and M Redknap pers comm).

NEOT (St Neots-type ware)

The term 'St Neots ware', later ammended to 'St Neots-type ware', was introduced by JG Hurst in his survey of the late Saxon pottery of East Anglia (Hurst 1955, 43-70). As used in this original paper, the term defined a regional ware sharing a distinct typology and with a characteristic fabric - abundant fine shell in a soapy clay matrix - but subsequently this term has been used for many shelly wares and the distinct grouping has been blurred. Further work on the ware includes a petrological and analytical study by Hunter (1979, 230-40), where it was noted that samples of the ware from Northampton contained bryozoa, a distinctive microfossil. This has subsequently been shown to be a characteristic of St Neots-type ware from the Severn Valley and the Middle to Upper Thames (Vince 1983a; Mellor 1980). It is therefore proposed to use the term in London to apply only to vessels in which abundant fine shell and bryozoa have been observed. As will be noted below, this St Neots-type ware fabric is found in vessels spanning a wide date and a further typological/technical division is needed to define products from a single industry since there is no apparent difference in fabrics.

St Neots-type ware usually has a dark grey or black core (N 3/0) but oxidized surfaces, usually a light brown colour (7.5YR 7/4). The ware is tempered with abundant fragments of bivalve shell, up to 2mm across. These include Gryphaea identified by Dr John Cooper, but other species are definitely present, although too fragmented for precise identification. Sparse brachiopod shell fragments are recognisable under the binocular microscope, because of the regular pattern of

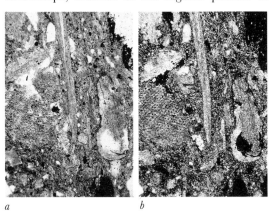

a   b

2.28. Photomicrograph of St Neots-type ware ; a, p.p.l. b, x.p.l. Showing fragments of bivalve shell and porous echinoid shell (bottom and centre).

holes through their shells. The bryozoa fragments are sparse to medium in abundance and a similar size to the shells. Again more than one species seems to be present, since they vary in the size and arrangement of holes. Sparse fragments of pyritized wood, up to 2mm long; shiny, opaque fossil fish fragments (possibly phosphatized?) up to 2mm long or, usually, smaller and sparse red iron-rich compounds and sparse sub-angular and rounded quartz up to 1mm across occur. The clay matrix is fine-textured but contains specks of brown iron-rich compounds.

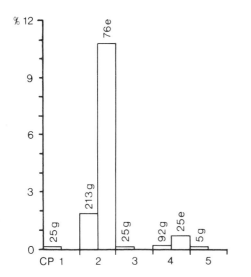

2.29. The percentage of St Neots-type ware in stratified contexts, dated to CP1-5.

The source of NEOT

Almost all the inclusions present in St Neot's-type ware might be expected in a natural shelly marl, such as occurs irregularly throughout the Jurassic clays. Dr John Cooper is of the opinion that the ware was produced from a naturally-occurring shelly facies of the Oxford clay. The distribution of the ware is concentrated in Bedfordshire, Huntingdonshire and Cambridgeshire and the source or sources must be within this area. However, the Oxford Clay outcrops in all three counties, but does slightly narrow the potential source area by excluding south Bedfordshire and the north of Cambridgeshire and Huntingdonshire. Hurst has suggested that the irregular firing noted on St Neots-type vessels indicates a bonfire firing and thus a dispersed industry. This remains to be demonstrated, perhaps by the plotting of distinct typological traits.

Corpus

St Neots-type vessels were wheelthrown and often have pronounced throwing ridges on the interior. The bases are invariably sagging and their formation has led to considerable smoothing of the lower surfaces.

Cooking pots (Fig 2.30 Nos 42-44)

Bowls (Fig 2.30 Nos 45-46)

Spouted pitcher(?) Fig 2.30 No 47, has the same form as the cooking pots, but also has a strap handle and may be part of a spouted pitcher.

2.30. St Neots-type ware; cooking pots (Nos 42-4) bowls (Nos 45-46) spouted pitcher(?) (No 47).

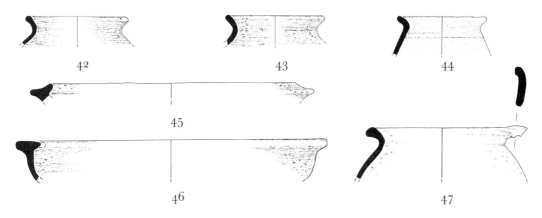

Dating

The ware is found so rarely in London that it is unclear whether it is present throughout the Saxon and early medieval sequence (CP1-6) or, as seems more likely, is essentially 11th century (CP3-4). The reason for the uncertain starting date is that so few groups can actually be dated to CP2 or earlier; most simply have a *terminus post quem*. The end date is uncertain because St Neots-type ware sherds have been found in late 12th century contexts (for example a bowl from Seal House) but there is always the possibility that single sherds like this may be residual. There are too few finds to produce a pattern (Fig 2.29). Recent work in the south-east midlands by Maureen Mellor and others suggests that this ware was in use in Hertfordshire and Buckinghamshire at the same time as LSS was used further south and west but that with the collapse of the LSS industry NEOT briefly found a wider market and is common in Conquest-period assemblages from Oxfordshire.

EMS (Early Medieval Sandy ware)

The visual characteristics of this ware are an abundant, well-sorted quartz sand and sparse to moderate flecks of a soft white to grey material, identified in thin-section as calcareous algae.

The most characteristic inclusions are abundant rose and clear quartz sand grains, up to 1 or 1.5mm across. Also present are: sparse grains of white quartz up to 5mm; sparse to moderate small white flecks of calcareous algae, up to 1mm across, and small pockmarks where the algae have weathered away; moderate black iron-rich compounds up to 1mm and sparse red iron-rich compounds up to 2mm. Other sparse inclusions

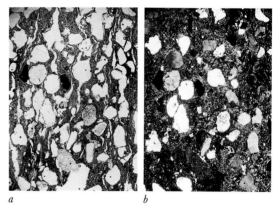

a   *b*

2.31. Photomicrograph of Early medieval sandy ware. a, p.p.l. b, x.p.l.

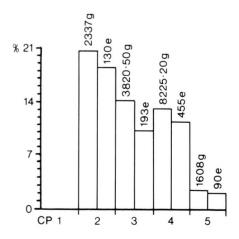

2.32. Percentage of Early medieval sandy ware in stratified contexts, dated to CP1-5.

include flint, shell fragments and carbonised organic inclusions, from 1mm to 13mm in length. Flecks of white mica up to 0.1mm in length are moderately common. Sherds tend to be reduced and/or burnt, and therefore have a grey to dark grey surface (N 3/0), sometimes with a lighter grey core. Orange/red oxidized sherds (2.5YR 6/6,6/8) with a light grey core also occur. The fabric is soft, feels rough, and has an irregular texture. All vessels are handmade.

Source

The origin of EMS should be considered alongside that of EMSS (see below), which is almost certainly composed of the same basic fabric with the addition of bivalve shell fragments. The quartz, flint and black iron-rich compounds are found in samples of local London Clay and the variations in clay matrix, from almost pure to slightly silty and micaceous, are to be found in the London Clay. The shell and algae fragments are probably indicative of a freshwater origin for either some of the inclusions or the clay. Since both are present in EMS and EMSS they seem to have a different origin from the fossil bivalve shell and phosphate

2.33. Early medieval sandy ware cooking pots (Nos 48-56).

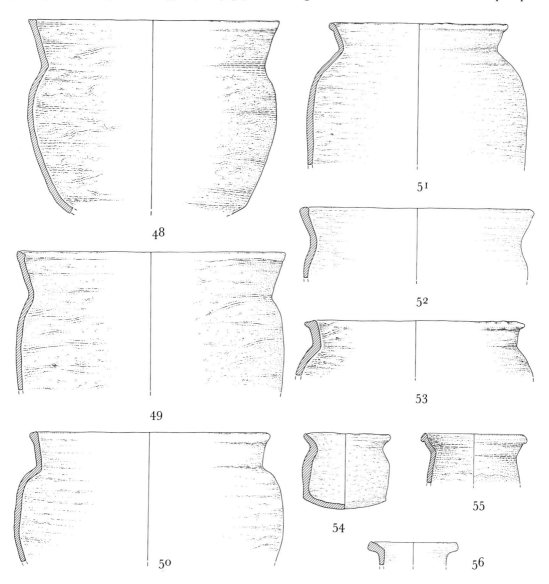

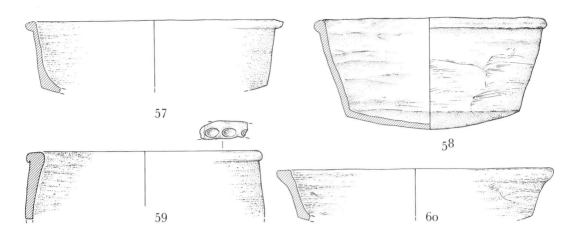

57

58

59

60

fragments, which only occur in EMSS. It is suggested, therefore, that EMS could have been made from a Tertiary clay with the addition of a Thames Valley alluvial sand and that either or both of these ingredients had been re-deposited in a freshwater stream, to account for the shell and algae inclusions.

Corpus

The majority of EMS vessels are cooking pots. In a sample of 14 eves, 87% are cooking pots. Shallow dishes, used in cooking, are the next most common form (6%), followed by bowls (3%). It is difficult to make a division between these two classes. Large storage jars (1%) and spouted pitchers (2%) are the only other common forms. Lamps are rare (0.3%).

2.34. Early medieval sandy ware bowls and dishes (Nos 57-60).

Cooking pots (Fig 2.33 Nos 48-56).

Bowls and dishes (Fig 2.34 Nos 57-60). Vessels ranging from bowl dimensions (No 58) to dish dimensions (No 60) are found.

Spouted pitchers (Fig 2.35 Nos 61-65). No 62 is very similar to the style of vessel made at Michelmersh, Hants (Addyman *et al* 1972) but is definitely in the EMS fabric.

Lamp (Fig 2.35 No 66)

2.35. Early medieval sandy ware spouted pitchers (Nos 61-65), and pedestal lamp (Nos 66).

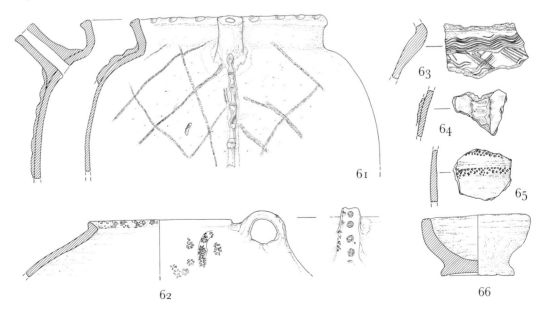

63

64

61

65

62

66

Dating and frequency

The appearance of EMS defines the start of CP2 (Fig 2.32) which is dated here to the late 10th to early 11th century. It quickly declines in favour of EMSS (Fig 2.40) although this is likely to represent the adoption of deliberate shell-tempering by a single group of potters rather than the replacement of one industry by another. The latest sherds of EMS which are likely to be contemporary with the deposits in which they were found are of mid-12th-century date.

2.36. Early medieval sandy ware showing diamond lattice roller stamping.

EMSS (Early Medieval Sand and Shell-tempered ware)

The visual characteristics of this ware are abundant quartz sand and sparse to abundant fragments of bivalve shell. There is often difficulty in separating sherds of this fabric from those of EMS and it is likely that the two fabrics are essentially the same with the addition of shell fragments to EMSS.

All vessels are handmade. The clay matrix varies between fine- and medium-grained, is soft, feels rough to abrasive, and has an irregular texture. The fabric contains abundant iron-stained, rose, clear, and white quartz grains, together with fragments of bivalve shell, varying from sparse to abundant, and ranging in size from tiny flecks up to 5mm. Calcareous algae, and small pockmarks, as in EMS, are also present. Other inclusions are sparse angular white flint up to 4mm, sparse red and black iron-rich compounds up to 1mm, and sparse organic inclusions. Irregular oxidization has resulted in an uneven surface colour, and most vessels are either oxidized on the surface and margins (7.5YR 5/4 & 6/4) with a grey core (N 4/0), or reduced and/or burnt (10YR 2.5/1).

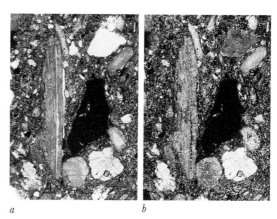

a   *b*

2.37. Photomicrograph of Early medieval sand and shell ware (EMSS).

Source

The similarity of fabric and appearance between EMS and EMSS vessels suggests that they were made in the same area. Distribution evidence suggests that the source lay close to the Thames and within

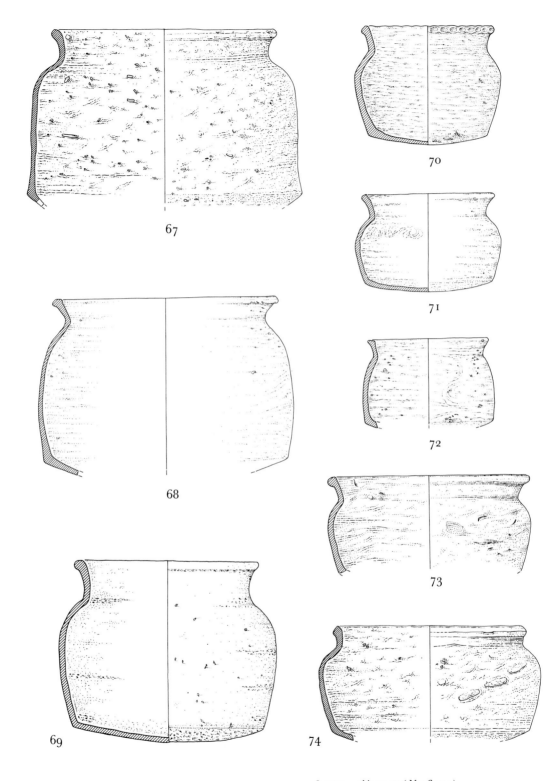

67

68

69

70

71

72

73

74

2.38. ᴇᴍss *cooking pots (Nos 67-74).*

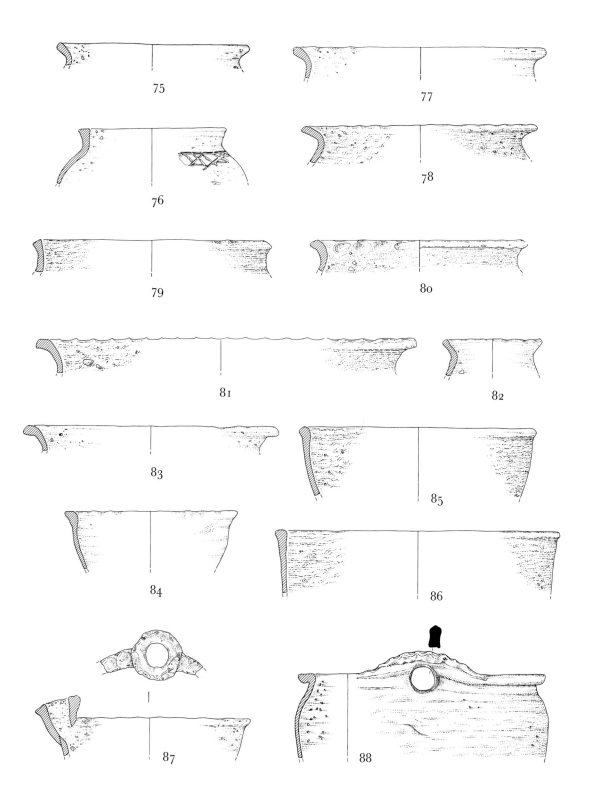

2.39. EMSS *bowls (Nos 84-88)*.

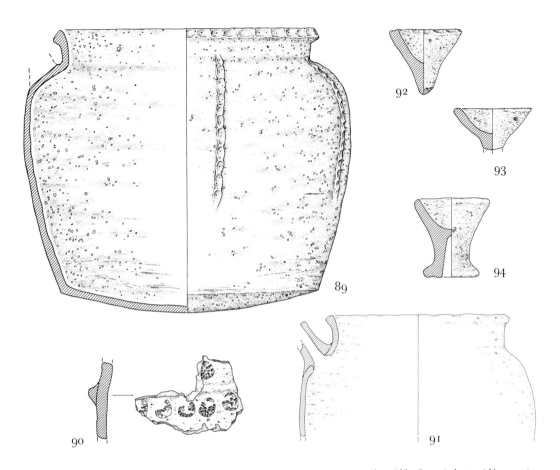

2.41. EMSS; *storage jars (Nos 89-91), lamps (Nos 92-4).*

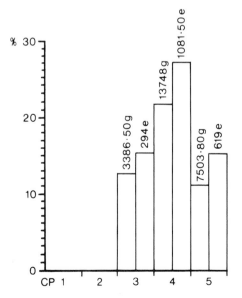

2.40. *The percentage of* EMSS *in stratified contexts, dated to* CP*1-5.*

*c.*10 miles of London. The presence of fossil shell as tempering suggests a source in the south east of this area, perhaps between Southwark and Greenwich.

Corpus

The majority of EMSS vessels found in London are cooking pots (91% out of a sample of 36 eves). Bowls (3%) and dishes (2%) are the next most common forms followed by lamps (1.4%), large storage jars (0.1%) and spouted pitchers (1.2%).

Cooking pots (Fig 2.38 Nos 67-74 and Fig 2.40 Nos 75-83).

Bowls (Fig 2.39 Nos 84-88). (No 87 is a spouted bowl. No 88 is a bowl or cooking pot form with, presumably, two handles for suspension over a fire.)

Spouted pitchers (Fig 2.41 Nos 89 and 91). Fig 2.41 No 90 is a stamped body sherd which may come from either a spouted pitcher or a storage jar.

Suspension lamp (Fig 2.41 Nos 92-93).

Pedestal lamp (Fig 2.41 No 94).

The date and frequency of EMS

The presence of EMSS sherds in a deposit is taken as the starting point of CP3. In absolute terms, the inception of this ware must be dated before 1039-40), but how much earlier is uncertain (Fig 2.38). EMSS vessels became more common in later 11th-century deposits and outnumber those of ESUR in deposits of CP4. There is a decline, relative to ESUR in the late 11th to mid 12th century but EMSS sherds are still common finds in these deposits (CP5). The ware had ceased to be used before the end of the 12th century (CP6).

EMSH (Early Medieval Shelly ware)

The most common inclusions in EMSH are abundant bivalve shells, varying in size from tiny flecks up to 12mm. Although always frequent, the degree of abundance varies. Other inclusions, which vary from sparse to moderate, are rounded quartz (up to 1mm), clear, opaque yellow, iron-coated and iron-stained, and moderate, red iron-rich compounds (up to 1.5mm). Sparse inclusions include angular flint (up to 4mm), clay pellets(?), and burnt out organic inclusions up to 2mm. The fabric has a rough feel, and a hackly texture. All vessels are handmade, with a soft, fine clay matrix. The surface of the pot is often slightly pockmarked, where the shell has been eroded, and the surface can be fairly worn and abraded.

EMSH often has a brown, oxidized surface and margins (5YR 5/6), although oxidization is often irregular resulting in an uneven surface colour. It usually has a light grey (N 7/0, 6/0) to dark grey (10YR 4/1) core, and is often reduced and/or burnt to a very dark grey on the surface (N 2.5/0).

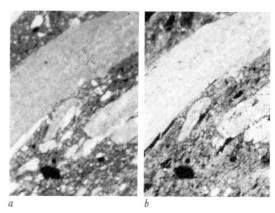

a   *b*

2.42. Photomicrographs of Early medieval shelly ware (EMSH) a, p.p.l. b, x.p.l.

Source

Vessels of identical appearance to EMSH form the majority of the pottery found on early medieval sites in northwest Kent. The identification of the shell inclusions as Tertiary fossils suggests that the ware was made from an outcrop, or outcrops, of the Woolwich Beds. This deposit extends as far as Southwark but is much more widespread in northwest Kent. The actual source is therefore unknown and unlikely to be pinpointed by

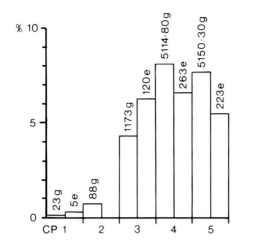

2.43. The percentage of EMSH *in stratified contexts, dated to* CP*1-5.*

petrological analysis. In the presumed source area wheelthrown vessels with squared rims similar to those found on SSW (12th–13th century Shelly Sandy ware) cooking pots are found. These show that manufacture continued into the later 12th-century, although none of these wheelthrown vessels are known from London.

Corpus

Most EMSH vessels are cooking pots (91% of a sample of 8 eves). Bowls (2%) and dishes (0.6%) are the next most common form, followed by storage jars (1%). In the quantified sample no spouted pitcher rims were present, although the form was made (as can be seen from Fig 2.48 Nos 123-6).

Cooking pots (Fig 2.44 Nos 95-102), Fig 2.45 Nos 103-111 and Fig 2.46 No 112 (No 112, although much larger than any other cooking vessel, is coated with soot, and must be similar in capacity to later medieval cauldrons).

Bowls and dishes (Fig 2.47 Nos 113-119).

Storage jars (Fig 2.48 Nos 120-122).

Spouted pitchers (Fig 2.48 Nos 123-126).

The date and frequency of EMSH

Compared with EMS and EMSS, EMSH is relatively rare. Sherds first occur in early to mid 11th-century deposits (CP3) but they are most common in late 11th to mid-12th-century groups (CP5), although never the major coarseware (Fig 2.43).

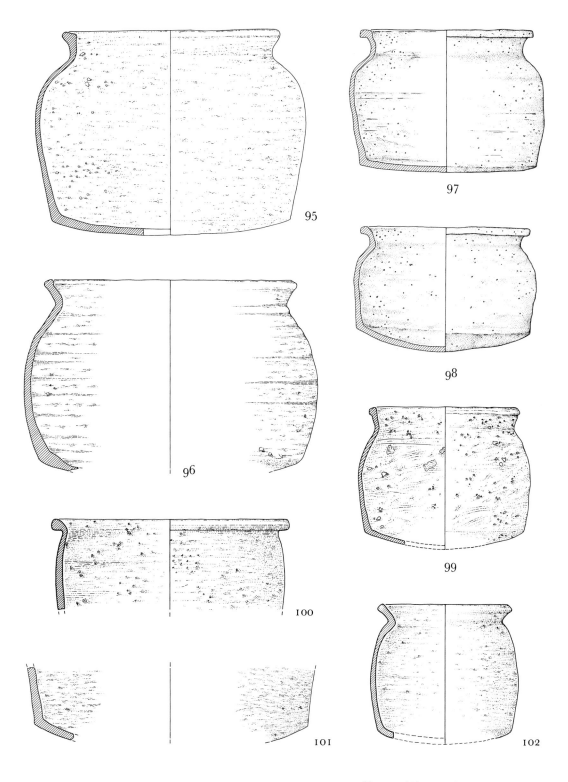

95

96

97

98

99

100

101

102

2.44. EMSH *cooking pots (No 95-102).*

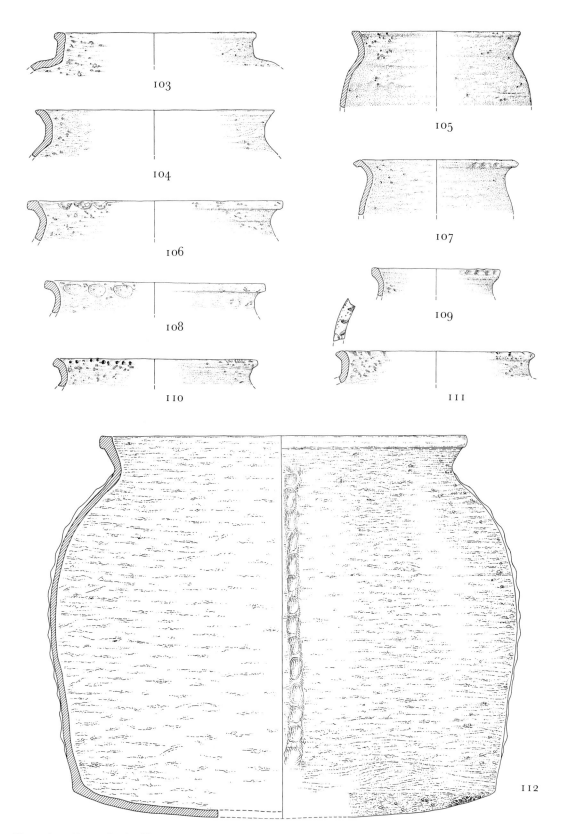

103

104

105

106

107

108

109

110

111

112

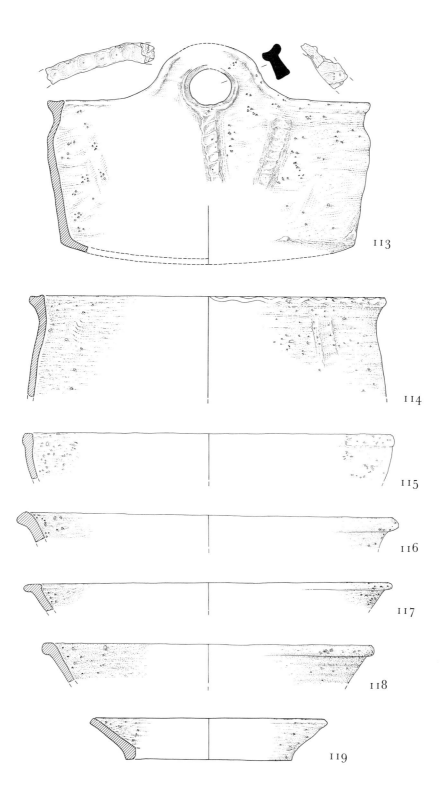

113

114

115

116

117

118

119

2.45. EMSH *cooking pots (No 103-111).*
2.46. EMSH *large cooking pot (No 112).*

2.47. EMSH *bowls and dishes (No 113-119).*

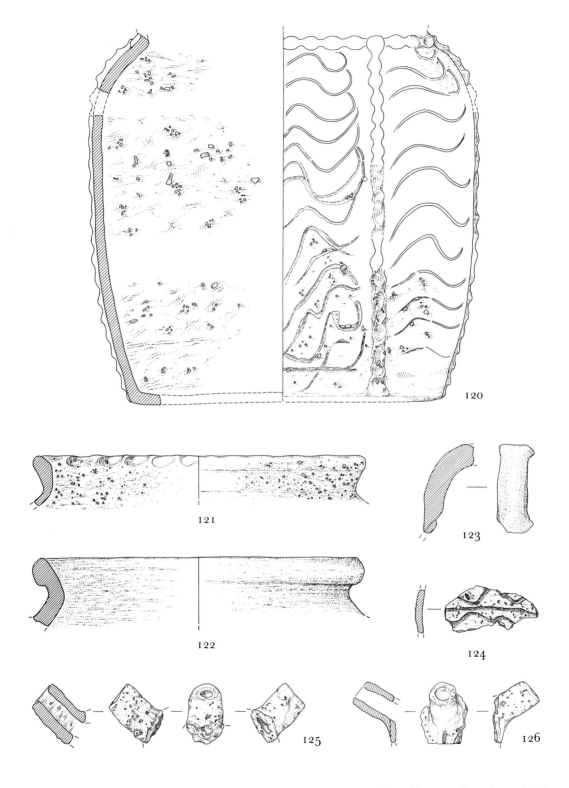

2.48. EMSH *storage jars (Nos 120-126), and spouted pitchers (No 120-126).*

EMFL (Early Medieval Flinty ware)

Early Medieval Flinty ware contains: abundant rounded milky, clear and iron-stained quartz grains up to 1mm across; abundant to moderate, angular black and white flint, up to 4mm across; sparse red and black iron-rich compounds up to 1mm, and sparse calcareous inclusions up to 2mm across.

Surfaces are usually dark grey (N4/0), or brown (7.5YR 6/4, 7.5YR 6/2), and can also be patchy. The core and margins can be both reduced and oxidised, resulting in a patchy orange (10R 5/8) and dark grey (N5/0, N4/0) colour, although most cores are reduced. The surface is also dark grey (N4/0). All vessels are handmade.

The source of EMFL

Flint is a common constituent of Thames Valley sands and gravels, mainly in the form of heavily battered, rounded pebbles. Relatively fresh fragments, such as those found in EMFL are less common, while the general appearance of the inclusions is different from those in most local wares. These features, together with the scarcity of the ware in London, suggest a source outside the immediate area. However, the ubiquity of flint and quartz-tempered wares in southern England makes even the approximate source uncertain.

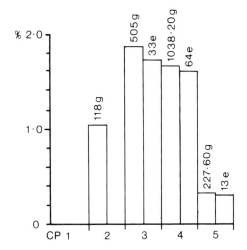

2.50. *The percentage of* EMFL *in stratified contexts, dated to* CP1-5.

Corpus

Only a small sample of EMFL sherds has been quantified (1.6 eves). It is therefore not surprising that the rims in this sample were all from cooking pots. Bodysherds of thick-walled storage jars or spouted pitchers have also been found.

Cooking pots (Fig 2.51 Nos 127-128).

Dating and frequency

Although always rare, EMFL sherds occur most frequently in early to mid 11th-century contexts (CP2 and CP3). Because of their rarity it is not possible to say how may of those sherds found in later contexts are residual (Fig 2.50).

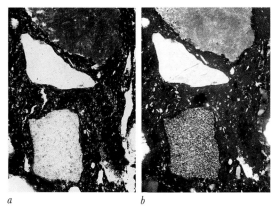

a   *b*

2.49. *Photomicrograph of Early medieval flinty ware (*EMFL*). a, p.p.l. b, x.p.l.*

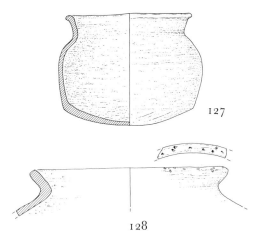

2.51. EMFL *cooking pots (Nos 127-128).*

EMCH (Early Medieval 'Chalky' ware)

EMCH has a rough feel and an irregular texture. The clay has a soft, fine-grained matrix, and the most distinctive characteristic is the presence of large pockmarks (up to 3mm) where chalk(?) and algal limestone have leached out (or partially leached out). A sherd was examined by Graham Elliott, British Museum (Natural History), who comments 'Cyanophyte thread-algae similar to those in present-day lakes and streams (Rivularia and its allies). Many pieces have lost structure, presumably in the firing, but NFW74 [97] shows it well. Cyanophytes are not confined to freshwater, but these look like and seem most likely to be freshwater. They are like known fluviatile and lacustrine material from Pleistocene and Recent deposits'. Characteristic inclusions consist of: calcareous algae and limestone (often large fragments up to 4mm); sparse ill-sorted rose and milky quartz, ranging from 1 to 3mm across; sparse, angular flint, up to 6mm long; sparse shell and abundant flakes of white mica, up to 0.3mm long. Sherds tend either to be reduced (or burnt) with a grey (5Y 6/1) to dark grey (10YR 6/1) surface, or oxidized brown on the surface (7.5YR 6/4) with a reduced core (N6/0).

Source

Distribution evidence suggests that the source of EMCH lay to the north-west of London. It is common, for example, in late 11th- or early 12th-century deposits at St Albans, mainly from excavations at the abbey directed by Martin Bid-

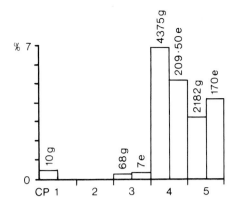

2.53. *The percentage of* EMCH *in stratified contexts, dated to* CP1-5.

dle, and has been seen in collections from Buckinghamshire. The presence of calcareous algae and freshwater molluscs indicate that the clay is riverine or lacustrine in origin while the silica-cemented sandstone and abundant white mica inclusions suggest that the inclusions and clay matrix are derived ultimately from Cretaceous deposits. Similar fabrics are known from Wiltshire and Berkshire. At Newbury in the Kennet valley a lacustrine deposit of mesolithic age contained abundant nodules of calcareous algae which could be shown to have formed around the stems of reeds.

Corpus

Cooking pots are the most common form in EMCH (78% out of a sample of 7 eves). However, spouted pitchers are much more common in this fabric than in many others. They form 20% of the quantified sample but this is due entirely to the presence of a smashed vessel on a floor of one of the Pudding Lane buildings and a complete rim from a robber-trench at Lime Street.

Cooking pots (Fig 2.54 Nos 129-135).

Spouted pitchers (Fig 2.54 Nos 136-137), Fig 2.55 No 138).

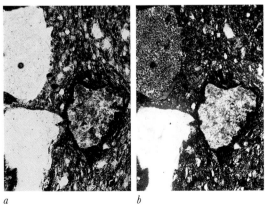

a   *b*

2.52. *Photomicrographs of Early medieval chalky ware* (EMCH). *a, p.p.l. b, x.p.l.*

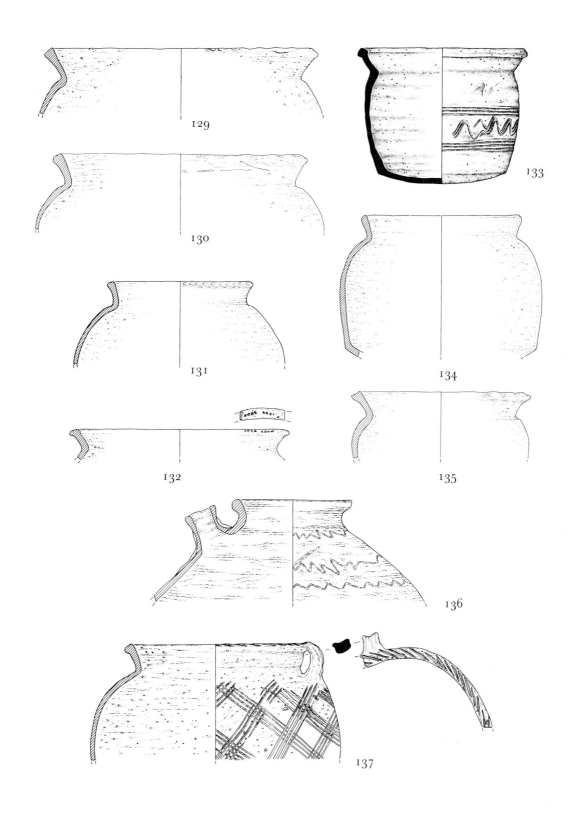

129

130

131

132

133

134

135

136

137

2.54. EMCH *cooking pots (Nos 129–135)*.

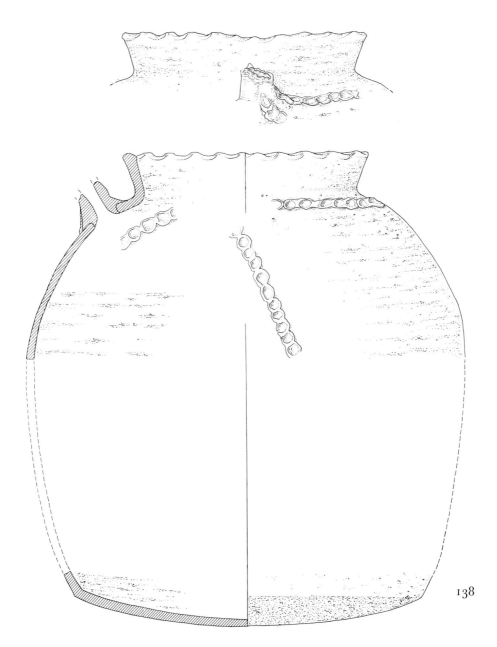

138

2.55. EMCH *spouted pitcher (No 138).*

Dating and frequency

Although never common, EMCH does briefly form a noticeable proportion of assemblages in London. It is absent from the New Fresh Wharf bank and silt deposits dated to the early to mid- 11th century but is present in slightly later deposits at Billingsgate Lorry Park and elsewhere. In mid- to late 11th-century deposits (CP4) it is almost as common as ESUR but by the late 11th to mid 12th century (CP5) it had declined and was about a fifth as common as ESUR (Fig 2.53).

ESUR Early Surrey ware and EMIS Early Medieval Iron-rich Sandy ware

Fabrics dominated by the presence of iron compounds and iron-coated quartz grains are divided here into coarse types (ESUR) with inclusions up to 2mm across, similar fabrics containing angular flint fragments (ESUR + FL) and fine types (EMIS) with inclusions up to 0.5mm across. It is possible that examples of EMIS have been missed, since in texture it is very similar to other sand-tempered wares, but ESUR is very distinctive. A few sherds contain the same quartz temper as ESUR but with sparse angular flint inclusions. The presence of ESUR has been taken to indicate the inception of CP4.

ESUR

The identifying feature of this fabric is abundant, rounded, iron-stained quartz. The surface colour can vary from a light brown (7.5YR 8/4) with a pale grey core (N 9/0), to brown (10YR 7/2) to dark grey or black (2.5Y 9/3), according to the firing and subsequent burning of the vessels. The fabric can be soft or hard, feels harsh and has an irregular texture.

ESUR is distinguished by its abundant, rounded, iron-stained quartz, up to 2mm. Grains may be either heavily coated with iron, or clear with iron-stained veins. White and grey grains are also present as are abundant red iron-rich particles up to 2mm across (appearing black where reduced). Sparse, sub-angular flint up to 1mm across is found. Abundant flecks of white mica up to 0.2mm are present in some sherds which also have a smoother fabric.

2.56. Photomicrographs of Early Surrey ware (ESUR). a, p.p.l. b, x.p.l. EMIS. c, p.p.l. d, x.p.l.

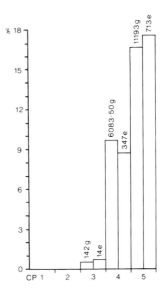

2.57. The percentage of ESUR in stratified contexts, dated to CP1-5.

EMIS

The external surfaces are either oxidised brown (10YR 6/2) with pink margins (5YR 8/4) and a dark grey/brown reduced internal surface (10YR 4/1), or dark surfaces (10YR 5/1) with pale grey core. The fabric is soft, feels rough, and has an irregular texture. EMIS contains abundant, ill-sorted, rounded iron-stained quartz grains up to 0.5mm across; sparse, large milky or grey grains up to 2mm across; abundant rounded red and black iron-rich compounds, which vary in size from 0.2mm to 2mm, but the majority of which are c.0.5mm across; and moderate flecks of white mica up to 0.3mm in length.

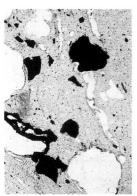
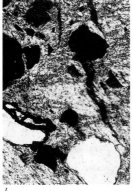
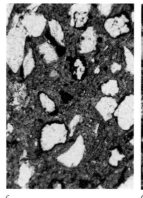
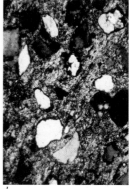

a

b

c

d

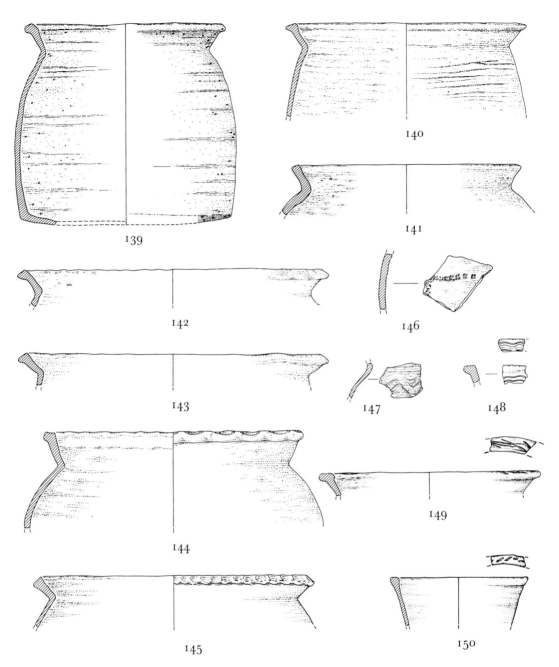

2.58. ESUR *and* ESUR + FL *(flint) cooking pots (Nos 139-149), and bowl(?) (No 150).*

Source

Both wares contain abundant fragments of iron-rich compound which in thin-section is identifiable as the cement from an iron-cemented sandstone. The clay matrix itself contains little quartz visible in thin-section and has a low iron content. In these respects it is similar to some late Roman pottery (Tilford ware alias Porchester D ware) made on the border of Surrey and Hampshire. It is also similar to some medieval Surrey Whitewares, especially Coarse Border ware which was made in a number of centres around Farnham. A difference between ESUR and Coarse

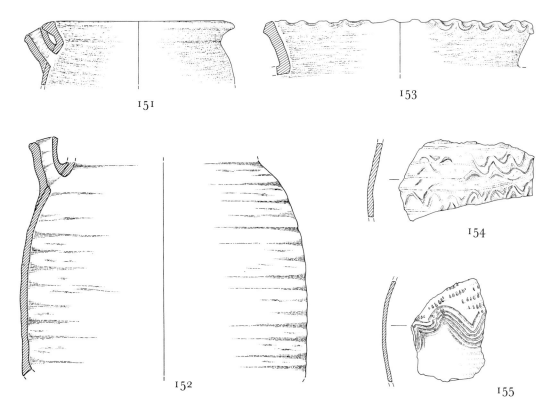

151

153

152

154

155

2.59. ESUR *spouted pitcher (Nos 151-152), and storage jar (No 153), and decorated sherds (Nos 154-5).*

Border ware is that the iron-rich cement grains in the later medieval ware are rounded, and there are occasional fragments of flint. These both indicate that the sandstone fragments have been worn and mixed with material from other sources. ESUR, on the other hand, must be tempered with material which had not been heavily weathered and was obtained close to the sandstone source. The few ESUR sherds which do contain flint also have rounded iron-rich cement grains and may be from a separate source, but in the same general area.

Corpus

Most ESUR vessels are cooking pots (98% of a sample of 27 eves) but a few bowls (1%) and dishes (0.4%) occur. Storage jars were represented by a single rim in the quantified sample (0.2%) while spouted pitcher body sherds but no rims were present.

Cooking pots (Fig 2.58 Nos 139-149). A characteristic feature of these vessels is the treatment of their shoulders, which appear to have had a rough

trimming with a broken piece of wood or similar tool (Fig 2.13).

Bowl(?) (Fig 2.58 No 150).

Spouted pitchers (Fig 2.59 No 151-152).

Storage jar (Fig 2.59 No 153).

Two sherds, Fig 2.59 Nos 154 and 155, are decorated with combing and may therefore be spouted pitchers, but in fact some decoration is found on cooking pots, such as Nos 146 and 147.

Dating and frequency

Sherds of ESUR are absent from early to mid 11th-century groups in London (CP3) and must therefore come into use between 1039-40 and 1055, since they are present at Billingsgate Lorry Park in a group of this date (Fig 2.57). They form a small fraction of mid to late 11th-century groups (CP4) but are more common in late 11th to mid 12th-century ones (CP5). Finds from later deposits are almost certainly residual, since there are some late 12th-century groups which contain no ESUR sherds at all.

LOGR (a Local Greyware)

LOGR is a sandy fabric with sparse to moderate freshwater shell fragments up to 4mm in size. The vessels were deliberately given a reduced surface. The fabric is usually a light or dark grey in colour (10YR 5/1, 7/1, or 2.5Y 9.5 N3/0, N4/0) with a similar core, but is occasionally oxidised light brown (10YR 7/4) or orange (5YR 6/6) with a grey core (7.5YR 9.5/5). The fabric is soft, feels rough and has an irregular texture.

LOGR is a sandy fabric containing: abundant rounded clear, grey, rose and iron-stained quartz grains up to 1mm across; sparse sub-angular flint, up to 2mm across; sparse to moderate freshwater shell fragments up to 4mm in length; sparse rounded calcareous inclusions up to 1mm across; abundant flecks of white mica; sparse to abundant red iron-rich compound up to 1mm across; and sparse voids/impressions left by organic inclusions up to 3mm across.

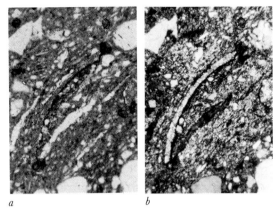

a   *b*

2.61. Photomicrographs of LOGR *; a, p.p.l. b, x.p.l.*

2.62. The percentage of LOGR *in stratified contexts, dated to* CP1-5.

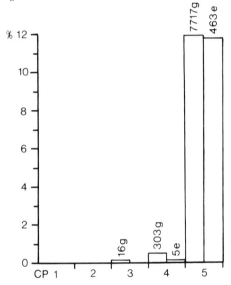

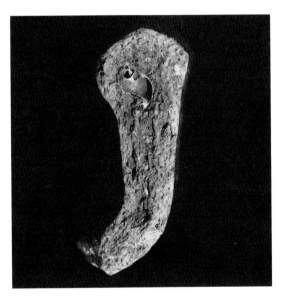

2.60. The broken edge of a LOGR *cooking pot showing a fragment of gastropod shell.*

Source

There is considerable variation in the texture and appearance of the fabric of different LOGR vessels but their petrology suggests that they could all have the same source area, an alluvial clay containing redeposited terrace sand. Except in firing and method of manufacture, LOGR vessels are very similar to LCOAR ones and it is likely that the two wares have a similar origin close to the City. It is quite possible that the LCOAR industry is a later development of the LOGR one.

Corpus

The majority of LOGR vessels are cooking pots (85% of a sample of 2.7 eves). Spouted pitchers are the next most common form (9%) followed by dishes (6%). Lamps were present in the sample but as body sherds only.

Cooking pots (Fig 2.63 No 156-168).
Spouted pitchers (Fig 2.64 No 169-178 (see also detail of vessel No 177, Fig 2.9) and Fig 2.65 No 178a.

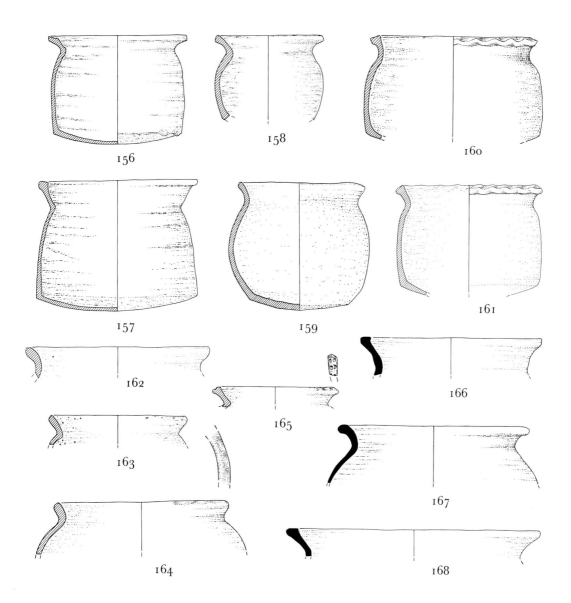

156

158

160

157

159

161

162

163

164

165

166

167

168

2.63. LOGR *cooking pots (Nos 156-168)*.

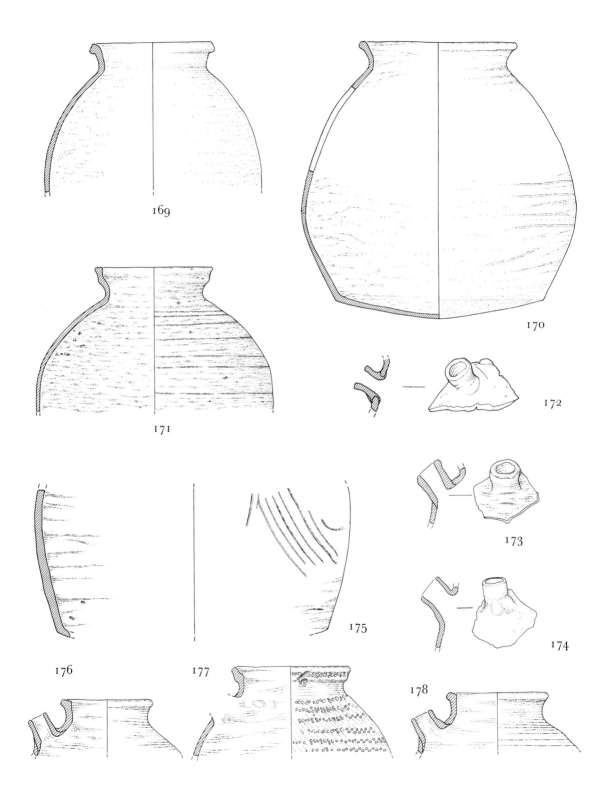

2.64. LOGR *spouted pitchers (Nos 169-178)*.

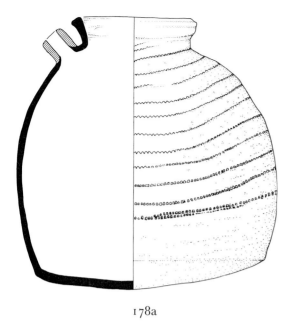

178a

2.65. LOGR *spouted pitcher (No 178a).*

Dishes (Fig 2.66 No 179-181).

Suspension lamps (Fig 2.66 No 182-184).

Fig 2.66 No 185 may either be a spout or handle, or possibly the neck of a bottle.

Dating and frequency

A few sherds of LOGR are present in late 11th-century contexts but the majority are of 12th-century date (Fig 2.62). In some early to mid-12th-century deposits (such as Baynards Castle 1975) LOGR vessels form between 25% and 33% of all vessels. There is very little LOGR recorded in late 12th-century groups (although this may partly be due to the similarity in appearance of these handmade greywares to wheelthrown Hertfordshire/North Middlesex greywares and their consequent mis-identification).

2.66. LOGR *dishes (Nos 179-180), spouted dish (No 181), lamps (No 182-4), spout/handle/neck of bottle (No 185).*

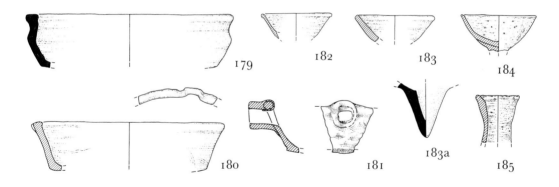

EMGR (Early Medieval Grog-tempered ware)

All EMGR vessels are handmade. The fabric is soft and fine, feels rough and has an irregular texture, although some sherds are finer than others. An uneven, blotchy surface colour is common, due to the conditions during firing (Fig 2.16). The surfaces and margins are usually a reduced, dark grey (N 2.5/0, 3/0) or light grey (5YR 5/1), while a few are oxidised and are light brown (5YR 5/4). The cores are usually light grey (N 7/0, 6/0).

Abundant grog is the most common inclusion, and is visible on the surface of the vessel, or just beneath the surface, as small lumps. The fragments of grog are angular/crushed, up to 4mm, and are both oxidised and reduced. (Some are oxidised around the edge of the grain and reduced in the core). Also present are moderate organic inclusions, (generally up to 2mm, although the largest is 22mm), sparse black and red iron-rich compound up to 1mm, sparse rounded quartz (rose, brown, clear and white), generally 0.5mm or 1mm, but one grain up to 2mm, sparse limestone or chalk(?), and sparse angular flint up to 6mm. There are also pockmarks where the calcareous inclusions have weathered away, and abundant tiny flecks of white mica.

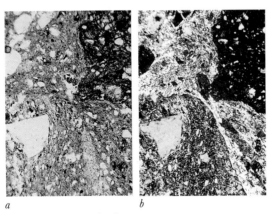

a   b

2.67. Photomicrographs of EMGR *; a, p.p.l. b, x.p.l.*

Source

The petrology gives no clue as to the source of EMGR, neither have sherds of this ware been noted in collections from surrounding areas. Since the ware is rare in London it need not have a local source although the forms found seem to have been restricted to south-eastern England.

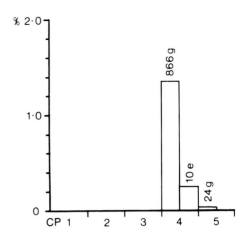

2.68. The percentage of EMGR *in stratified contexts, dated to* CP1-5.

Corpus

Both cooking pots and spouted pitchers are found in EMGR, although both occur in very small quantities. It is likely that spouted pitchers were the most common form.

Spouted pitchers (Fig 2.69 Nos 186-190). Since No 188 has a handle at right-angles to the spout, it is probably a three-handled vessel.

Dating and frequency

EMGR vessels first occur in mid- to late 11th-century contexts (CP4) but in very small quantities (Fig 2.68). They are also found in late 11th to mid-12th-century contexts (CP5) but are perhaps less common by then.

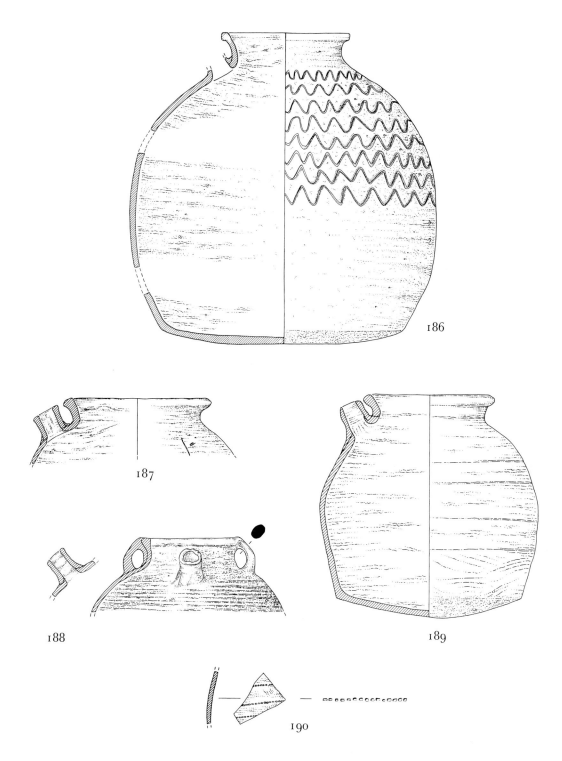

186

187

188

189

190

2.69. EMGR *spouted pitchers (Nos 186-190).*

NMDX (North Middlesex Coarseware)

NMDX is characterised by abundant, well-sorted rounded quartz sand, most of which has a white colour. The vessels are normally dark brown to black. All vessels are handmade.

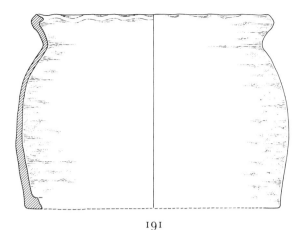

191

2.71. NMDX *cooking pot (No 191).*

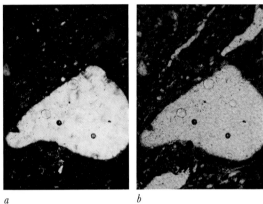

a　　　　　　　　*b*

*2.70. Photomicrographs of North Middlesex type ware (*NMDX*) ; a, p.p.l. b, x.p.l.*

Source

Similar fabrics have been noted from collections in north Middlesex and Hertfordshire and are distiguished from later fabrics from this area by their firing and method of manufacture as well as by their much coarser texture.

Corpus

Cooking pot (Fig 2.71 No 191).

Dating and frequency

A smashed NMDX cooking pot was found in a deposit at Billingsgate Lorry Park in a context which may have accumulated between *c.*1055 and *c.*1080. With this exception only isolated examples have been found in the City of London and the ware seems not to have been traded to London.

LCOAR (Coarse London-type ware)

The identifying features of this ware are a sandy, red-firing fabric with sparse, moderate or abundant fragments of freshwater shell and other calcareous inclusions. LCOAR has a soft fabric, a harsh or rough feel, and an irregular texture.

LCOAR contains: abundant rounded clear, red, pink, brown, yellow and iron-stained quartz grains up to 1.5mm, although the majority are smaller, c.0.5mm, and occasional large grains, up to 4mm across; sparse sub-angular and rounded flint up to 1mm; sparse, moderate or abundant freshwater shell, varying from tiny flecks to 3mm; moderate pockmarks where shell and other calcareous inclusions have leached out, and sparse calcareous inclusions up to 1mm across. Also present are organic inclusions up to 5mm, and visible in broken edges, pockmarks surrounded by black, burnt-out organic inclusions; sparse red iron-rich compound, varying from flecks to 1.5mm, although the majority are c.0.5mm; and flecks of white mica up to 0.1mm long.

Vessels were usually fired in oxidizing conditions and the surface and margins of sherds are usually varying shades of red (2.5YR 5/8, 6/8, 7/6, 6/6) or brown (10YR 6/2). A grey reduced surface is sometimes found (10YR 7/1). The core is usually dark grey or black (N7/0).

The lead glaze varies in quality from fairly smooth, glossy and well-covered, to thin, splashed and pitted. It is normally crazed. It can be coloured either with copper to produce a green (5GY 4/4) colour, or with iron to produce yellow (10YR 6/6, 6/8) or brown (10YR 4/4). The glaze is also used over a white slip (5Y 8/6 or 7.5Y 9/6).

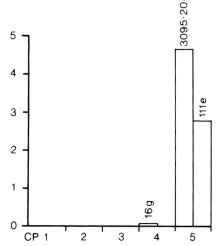

2.73. *The percentage of* LCOAR *in stratified contexts, dated to* CP1-5.

Source

This ware is thought to have been made close to London, mainly on distribution evidence. The petrological evidence does not conflict with this view, although it does not allow any greater precision.

Corpus

The majority of the LCOAR vessels are of late 12th-century date (CP6) and are published elsewhere (Pearce *et al* 1985). The only vessels published here are a distinctive variation on a known form, a pipkin, Fig 2.74 No 192, and two pitchers found together in a pit dated to CP5, Fig 2.74 Nos 193-194.

Dating and frequency

The presence of sherds of LCOAR is taken as the inception of CP5 (Fig 2.73). The absolute date of this event is given by the Billingsgate Lorry Park sequence, where sherds were absent from deposits dated c.1055 but present in a foreshore deposit associated with the use of the 1055 bank which also contained lead 'coins' of William I, dated 1080 or later. The succeeding waterfront, which sealed this deposit, was dated c.1080 or later by dendrochronology. LCOAR sherds are common in the mid 12th-century waterfront dump at Seal House but had been virtually replaced by LOND by the late 12th century.

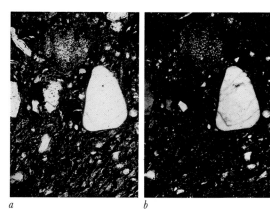

a   *b*

2.72. *Photomicrographs of Coarse London type ware (*LCOAR*);
a, p.p.l. b, x.p.l.*

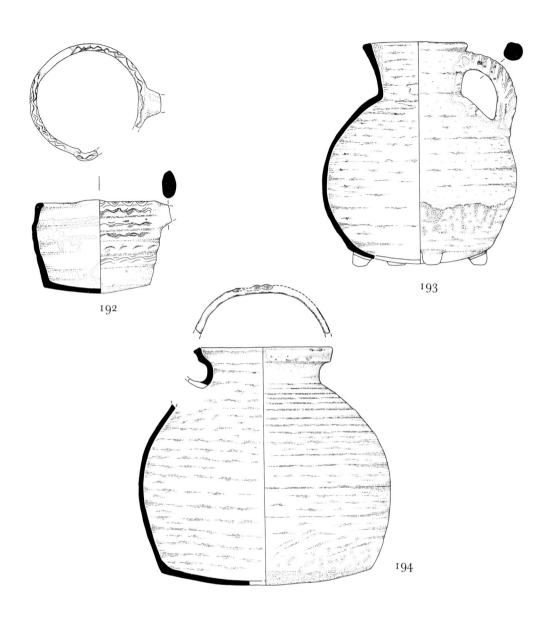

2.74. LCOAR *pipkin (No 192), tripod pitcher (No 193), and spouted pitcher (No 194).*

LCALC (Calcareous London-type ware)

A distinct variant of London-type ware contains moderate to abundant calcareous inclusions and has a lighter colour than LCOAR (Pearce *et al* 1985, 138-9). No examples are illustrated here.

Date and Frequency

Although rare, LCALC is found usefully stratified in some London contexts (Fig 2.75). Sherds were present at Pudding Lane in deposits associated with the final use of PDN5 and in several other early to mid-12th-century contexts on the site. Other sherds are mainly from late 12th-century deposits.

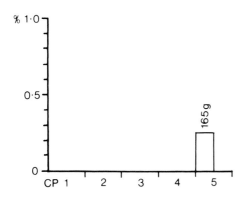

2.75. The percentage of calcareous London type ware (LCALC) in stratified contexts, dated to CP1-5.

LOND (London-type ware)

A corpus of LOND vessels from London has been published and the fabric described (Pearce *et al* 1985, 138-9). No further examples are illustrated here.

Date and Frequency

London-type ware is absent from the early to mid-11th-century waterfront deposits at New Fresh Wharf but present in the succeeding waterfront revetment dump (Period 3.2). The absolute date of this group is unknown but a timber thought to have been reused from this revetment was felled around the beginning of the 12th century. Clear-glazed body sherds, including one definitely from a spouted pitcher and one definitely from a tripod pitcher, were found at the neighbouring site at Billingsgate Lorry Park in deposits laid down in the mid-11th century (Period 4.4), *c.*1055. A single sherd was found stratified in a deposit on the same site associated with lead 'coins' of William I and earlier than a waterfront constructed in the late 11th century. It is likely that the first LOND vessels were in use in London at the end of the 11th century but even if this early date is eventually confirmed, it is not certain that these vessels were of the standard early rounded jug form and it is quite clear that local glazed wares were rare. By the late 11th to mid-12th century (CP5) LOND jugs are more common, although outnumbered by those in LCOAR, and by the end of the 12th century they had become one of the most common types used in the City.

MISC Miscellaneous wares

A small proportion of the sherds from late Saxon contexts from DUA excavations do not fit into any of the groups defined here. Some may be from residual Roman vessels, others may be atypical examples of defined wares and the remainder are presumably stray examples of late Saxon wares which do not normally occur in London. There would be little point in describing these sherds but eleven are illustrated in the hope that their form may eventually allow them to be identified (Figs 2.77-86 Nos 194-204).

A number of sherds of sand-tempered greywares were classified as MISC since LOGR, their most probable attribution, had not then been defined. It was not possible within the time allowed for the project to extract these vessels to re-identify them. This explains the apparent increase in the frequency of MISC sherds in CP3, CP4 and CP6 (Fig 2.76).

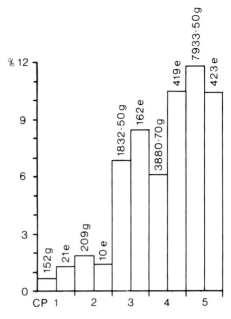

2.76. The percentage of miscellaneous (MISC) wares in stratified contexts, dated to CP1-5.

Following pages Figs 2.77 to 2.86.

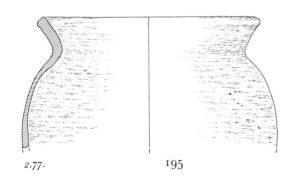

2.77.   195

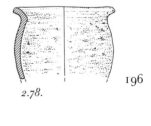

2.78.   196

2.79.   197

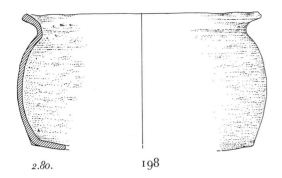

2.80.

198

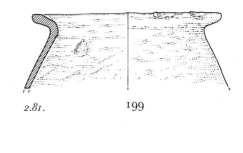

2.81.

199

2.82.

200

2.83.

201

2.84.

202

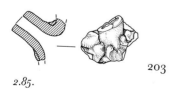

2.85.

203

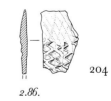

2.86.

204

IPS (Ipswich-type ware)

Most sherds of IPS are grey. Usual surface colours are grey to dark grey (N4/0, 6/0), with a core which is either a similar grey or a pale brown/beige (10YR 8/2) but may have dark grey surfaces, brown margins and a paler grey core. The fabric is soft, feels smooth, sometimes powdery, and has a fine texture.

Inclusions consist of abundant ill-sorted rounded, clear and white quartz, mainly between 0.2mm and 0.5mm, but with some larger grains, up to 2mm across and moderate flakes of white mica, up to 0.5mm long.

Small sherds of IPS appear to be wheel-thrown but on larger sherds it is clear that the vessels have been formed by hand and then rotated. It is occasionally burnished around the outside of the rim, and wiped and knife-trimmed inside.

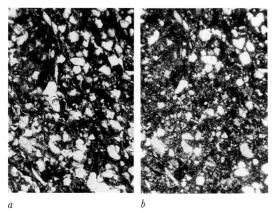

a   b

2.87. Photomicrograph of Ipswich Thetford type ware (IPS); a, p.p.l. b, x.p.l.

Dating and frequency

Both the starting and finishing dates of Ipswich-type ware are only roughly known. It is thought to have been made first in the early 7th century, although the evidence is as yet not conclusive and conflicts with the total absence of Ipswich-type ware both from pagan or 'transitional' burials and from the Anglo-Saxon settlement at Mucking, where the latest phase of occupation contained three *sceattas* of the late 7th century (Hamerow 1987). It was certainly being made in the 8th and 9th centuries but the end date is unclear. The traditional date has always been *c.*850, at around the time of the Viking invasion of East Anglia, but recent work in Ipswich suggests that the ware may have been made later, alongside the first wheelthrown Ipswich Thetford-type ware, in the late 9th and early 10th centuries (Wade and Blinkhorn forthcoming). The almost complete absence of Ipswich-type ware from sites within the walls of London and its ubiquity on sites along the Strand is remarkable but could either mean that the ware fell out of use earlier than now supposed or that the City was sparsely occupied until later. The only definitely-identified sherd of IPS from the City of London came from the Riverside Wall excavations (Rhodes 1980c, 97 and Fig 45 No 19).

THET Ipswich Thetford-type ware

Ipswich Thetford-type ware, THET, is a fine sandy wheelthrown greyware with moderate to abundant white mica. Vessels were often knife-trimmed on the interior (Fig 2.6) and the presence of wide thumbed strips with an asymmetrical cross-section is a distinguishing characteristic (Fig 2.14).

THET has a reduced grey surface (N4/0), and either a similar core, or brown oxidized (7.5YR 5/4) core and margins. The fabric is soft, feels smooth and has a fine texture.

Inclusions: abundant fine white and clear quartz sand is found, the majority range from 0.1mm-0.5mm, but sparse, rounded grains up to 1mm across are found; abundant to moderate white mica, from 0.1-0.5mm; and sparse iron-rich compound, up to 0.5mm are included.

Source

The petrology of the fabric is unremarkable, although the texture enables Ipswich Thetford-type ware to be separated from other Thetford-type wares (samples from the kilns at Thetford, Norwich, Grimston and Torksey have been examined in thin-section). The range of forms and decorations found on the London vessels is paralleled on material from Ipswich, although there are fewer plain cooking pots from London.

Corpus

Although THET cooking pots are found in London they only form 22% of a sample of 2 eves. The remaining vessels are mainly spouted pitchers (78%). A single jar (Fig 2.91 No 210) has no rim and is therefore not counted in the sample, although represented by an almost complete profile.

Storage jars/Spouted pitchers (Fig 2.90 Nos 205-206).

Spouted pitchers (Fig 2.90 Nos 207-208).

Fig 2.91 No 209 is a cooking pot form with traces of a handle attachment and applied strips around the neck.

Jar (Fig 2.91 No 210), with no sign of a handle or spout.

Cooking pots (Fig 2.91 Nos 211-213).

Dating and frequency

Body sherds of Thetford-type ware have been found in assemblages of CP1 dating between the late 9th to early 11th-century date (Fig 2.89). They are, however, very rare and in most cases could be contamination from later deposits. THET vessels are more common in early to mid-11th-century deposits (CP2 and CP3) and decline in the mid- to late 11th centuries (CP4). There are large assemblages dated to CP5 in which THET sherds are absent, suggesting that other examples in CP5 and later deposits are residual.

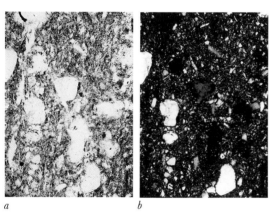

a   *b*

2.88. Photomicrographs of Thetford type ware (THET) a, p.p.l. b, x.p.l.

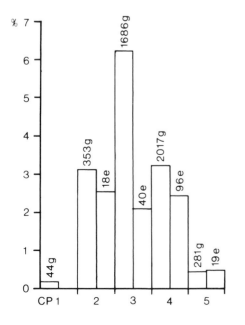

2.89. The percentage of THET *in stratified contexts, dated to* CP*1-5.*

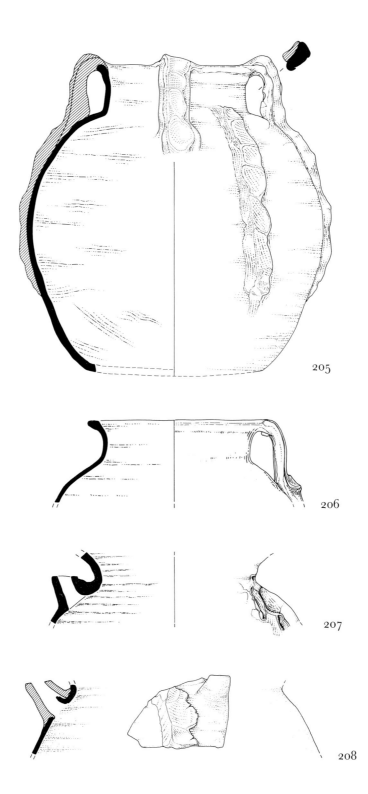

205

206

207

208

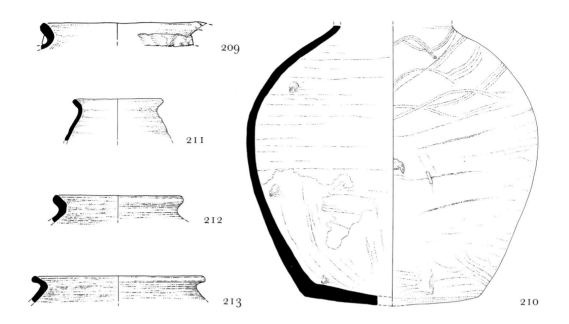

209

211

212

213

210

2.90. THET *storage jar/spouted pitcher (Nos 205-6), spouted pitchers (Nos 207-8).*

2.91. THET *cooking pot with handle (No 209), jar (No 210), cooking pot (Nos 211-213).*

SATH (Sandy Thetford-type wares)

A small number of wheelthrown greyware sherds have a rounded quartz sand temper which distinguishes them from Ipswich Thetford-type ware, which is essentially free of rounded inclusions. These vessels have been gathered together under one code but there are differences in texture and appearance which might eventually be used to distinguish sources.

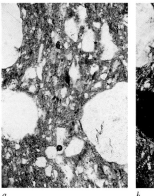

a   *b*

*2.92. Photomicrographs of Sandy Thetford type ware (SATH);
a, p.p.l. b, x.p.l.*

Source

The sherds grouped together as SATH are certainly much coarser than Ipswich Thetford-type ware (THET). There is, however, no convincing correspondence between SATH and samples of the products of some known Thetford-type ware kilns (Thetford, Norwich, Grimston, Torksey). An East Midlands or East Anglian source is, nevertheless, most likely.

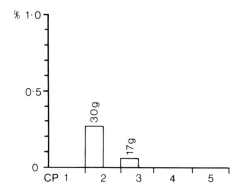

*2.93. The percentage of SATH in stratified contexts, dated to
CP1-5.*

Corpus

Cooking pot(?) (Fig 2.94 No 214), with horizontal roller-stamping on the shoulder (Fig 2.35).

Handled Storage jar (Fig 2.94 No 215), with bossing on the surface.

Handled Storage jar (Fig 2.94 No 216).

Cooking pot(?) (Fig 2.94 No 217).

Storage jar/Spouted pitcher (Fig 2.94 No 218).

Storage jars (Fig 2.94 Nos 219-220).

Cooking pot/Storage jar (Fig 2.94 No 221).

Dating and frequency

SATH sherds are very rare but have been found in contexts of early to mid-11th-century date (CP2 and CP3, Fig 2.93).

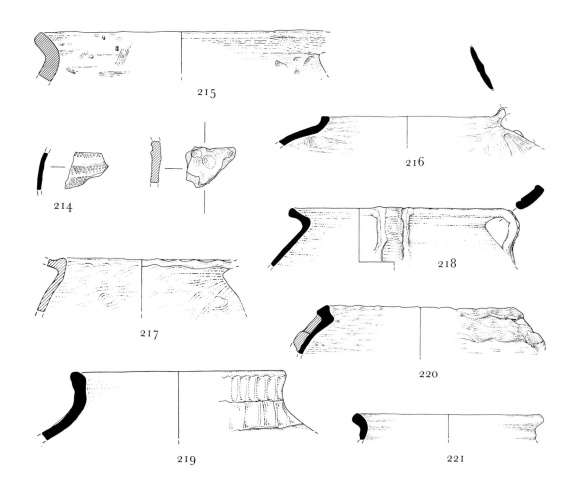

215

214

216

217

218

219

220

221

2.94. SATH *cooking pot (Nos 214 and 217), cooking pot or storage jar (No 221), storage jars (Nos 219-220), handled storage jars (Nos 215-6), storage jar/spouted pitcher (No 218).*

THWH (White Thetford-type ware)

Although termed a Thetford-type ware in this report, the main reason for this is the fact that THWH was wheelthrown and deliberately reduced and was often decorated with bosses. There is no other evidence to support an East Anglian or Midlands origin.

THWH is either reduced with a dark grey (N4/0) or lighter grey (10YR 6/1) surface, and a paler grey core (10GY N/8.5), or occasionally a darker grey core (N6/0), or it is an oxidised brown (7.5YR 7/4), with margins either the same or grey, or with a beige (10YR 8/2) surface and greyish beige margins and core. (10YR 8/1). It has a soft fabric, with a rough feel, and a fine or irregular texture.

Inclusions consist of : abundant rounded, yellow, grey, clear, rose and iron-stained quartz up to 0.5mm across; sparse red and black iron-rich compound, up to 0.5mm across; moderate flecks of white mica up to 0.1mm long; sparse sub-angular flint up to 1mm across; sparse organic inclusions, with black outlines surrounding voids up to 1mm across.

One near complete example in the Museum of London reserve collection (Fig 2.98 No 222 and Fig. 2.97) is handmade; but some sherds were possibly wheel-thrown. Vessels were scraped inside and knife-trimmed. They have flash marks around their sides.

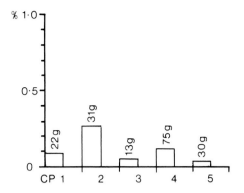

2.96. The percentage of THWH in stratified contexts, dated to CP1-5.

Source

The complete pitcher of THWH from Fenchurch Street (No 222) was thought by Dunning to be a Norman product (1959, 67-9). This is possible but unlikely in view of the difference in fabric between this ware and those of more definite Norman origin and the absence of other similar finds from the south coast (the parallels quoted by Dunning are only really similar in their method of decoration). The fabric offers no clues as to the source, although it is distinctive enough to date, no examples of THWH have been recognised from sites outside the City of London although there is no doubt that the ware is not locally made.

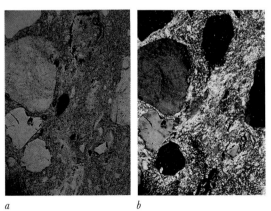

a   b

2.95. Photomicrographs of Thetford white ware (THWH) ; a, p.p.l. b, x.p.l.

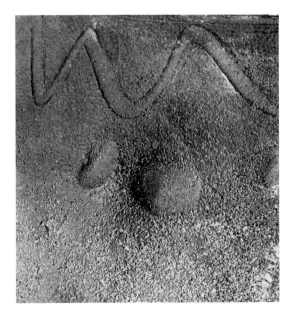

2.97. Detail of decoration on a THWH pitcher (No 222).

Corpus

The only vessel type certainly identified in this ware is the pitcher. Another virtually complete vessel has no spout, nor are spouts found as sherds. A few body sherds are sooted and therefore appear to be cooking pots.

Pitcher (Fig 2.98 Nos 222-223) Note the incised zig-zag and dot decoration around the shoulder of No 222 (see Fig 2.97)

2.98. THWH *storage jar (Nos 222-3).*

Dating and frequency

Although rare, THWH sherds have been found in groups of all dates from the late 9th to early 11th century (CP1) to the late 12th century (Fig 2.96). There is no apparent concentration in deposits of any date and the absence of sherds of this ware from the relatively large early to mid-11th-century levels at New Fresh Wharf and Billingsgate Lorry Park (CP3) suggest that sherds from other deposits of this date may be intrusive, or date the deposit to a later period. There is a sherd of THWH from St Nicholas Acon from a context dating before *c.*1084 and this is the earliest securely stratified example.

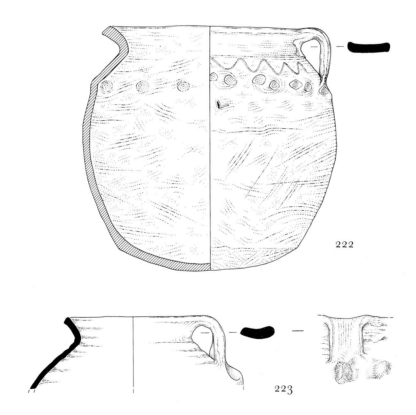

222

223

STAM (Stamford-type ware)

Although Stamford-type ware is well known it is often difficult to positively identify since it is a fine, white-firing fabric with a yellow glaze. Green-glazed examples are classified in the DUA system as Developed Stamford ware (DEVS) and belong to one of the wares whose appearance marks the beginning of CP6, *c.*1150. All STAM vessels are wheel-thrown. The fabric varies from soft to hard with a smooth feel, and a fine texture.

Inclusions consist of: abundant rounded quartz grains, mainly clear or milky up to 0.5mm across; sparse red and black iron-rich compound, up to 1mm across and organic inclusions or voids up to 1mm across.

STAM has a white-firing clay, the surface is beige (10YR 8/2, 2.5Y 8/2), or pale brown (10YR 7/4, 8/4), either with a pale beige (2.5Y 8/2) or grey core (N5/0).

STAM is usually well-glazed, although thin and slightly pitted, and crazed. The colour varies from yellow (2.5Y 7/8) to yellowish green (5Y 7/6) or green (10Y 6/4,5/4). The latter colours are due to reduction of naturally-present iron, not to the addition of copper.

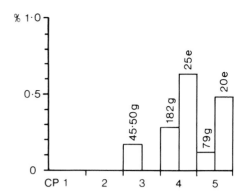

2.100. The percentage of STAM *in stratified contexts, dated to* CP*1-5.*

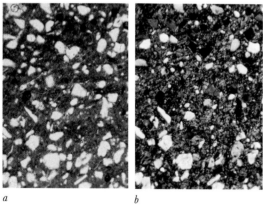

a   *b*

*2.99. Photomicrographs of Stamford-type ware (*STAM*). a, p.p.l. b, x.p.l.*

Source

Kilns and waste from kilns producing Stamford ware have been excavated at several sites in Stamford, Lincs. Following visual comparison of the London finds with those from Stamford there is little doubt that the former are products of the Stamford industry. This was confirmed by Dr Kilmurry (pers comm). No attempt has been made, however, to divide the London finds into fabric and glaze categories defined by Kilmurry (1980).

Corpus

The majority of STAM sherds are body sherds from externally glazed hollow ware vessels. These have been divided into several classes by Kilmurry but are here assumed to be from spouted pitchers. An almost complete storage jar (No 246a) demonstrates that body sherds of this form cannot be distinguished from those of pitchers. Out of a sample of 2 eves (which excludes the recently-discovered No 246a) 87% of identified rims are from pitchers and 13% from storage jars. Narrow-necked vessels, which may be costrels, jugs, bottles or sprinklers, are represented only by body sherds in the sample.

Pitchers (Fig 2.101 Nos 224-239). No 231 and 232 are much smaller than the rest and might possibly be bottles or sprinklers.

Tubular spouted jugs (Fig 2.101 Nos 240-242).

Fig 2.101 No 243: a narrow neck, possibly from a sprinkler, bottle or costrel.

Lid (Fig 2.101 No 244).

Costrel (Fig 2.101 No 245).

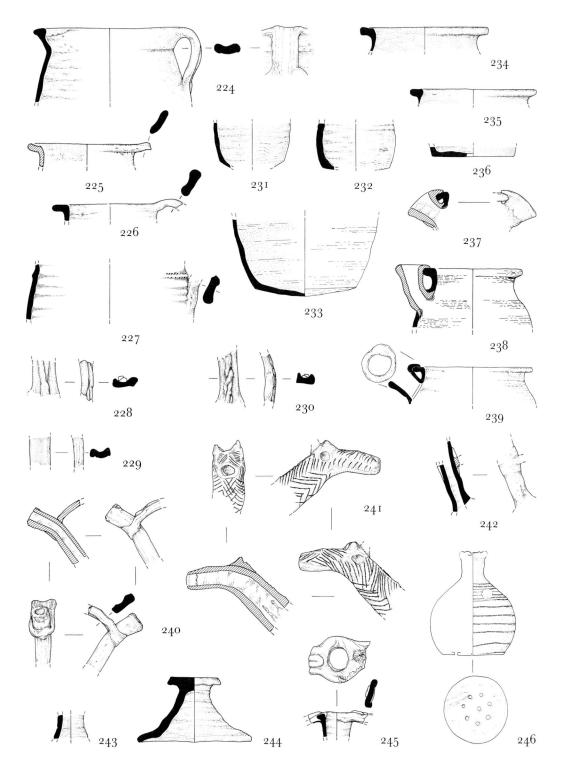

2.101. STAM *pitchers (Nos 224-6), pitcher/sprinkler/bottle (Nos 231-2), spouted pitchers (Nos 237-9), tubular spouted jugs (Nos 240-2), sprinkler/bottle/costrel (No 243), lid (No 244), costrel (No 245), sprinkler (No 246).*

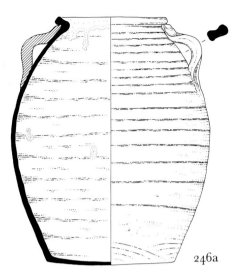

2.102. STAM *storage jar (No 246a).*

Sprinkler (Fig 2.101 No 246).

Storage jars (Fig 2.102 No 246a). Fragments of at least three storage jars have been found, including an almost complete vessel from Leadenhall Court. This vessel has two opposed handles and is decorated with a spiral grooved line.

Dating and frequency

A few of the STAM sherds from London are thought by Kilmurry to have been made in the early to mid-11th century, although only crucibles were found in contexts of this date. Most, however, were likely to date to the late 11th to early 12th century or early to mid-12th century (Fig 2.100). Many of these were stratified in groups of the appropriate date, including a context associated with the use of the *c.*1039-40 bank at Billingsgate Lorry Park and earlier than the *c.*1055 bank. There were no examples of types thought stylistically to be of later date occurring in earlier deposits. This seems to show that the Stamford ware chronology agrees with that erected for London and that the majority of sherds were recovered from contemporary groups. A storage jar rim from Watling Court was found in an early to mid-12th-century context (P44).

BADO (Badorf-type ware)

Badorf-type ware is the term given to whiteware Rhenish vessels fired at earthenware temperatures and made in a range of forms known from kilns at Badorf and probably also over a wide area of the middle Rhine.

Only four sherds of Badorf-type ware have been found in DUA excavations and one from an excavation by the Guildhall Museum at the Public Cleansing Depot. Although varying in texture and appearance the sherds have similar fabrics. The basic fabric appears quite fine but contains either abundant rounded clear and milky quartz grains, up to 1mm across, sparse white sandstone fragments with grains *c.*0.1mm across, and sparse rounded red iron-rich clay fragments up to 1mm across or abundant sub-angular clear and milky quartz. Voids caused by the burning out of organic debris, such as fine roots, are common in some sherds. The clay matrix contains abundant angular quartz and white mica laths, up to 0.1mm long, and, in one instance at least, sparse black mica laths of the same size. There appears to be an inverse relationship between the siltiness of the clay matrix and the size and abundance of the quartz sand.

Badorf-type ware is off-white, light brown to pale pink in colour.

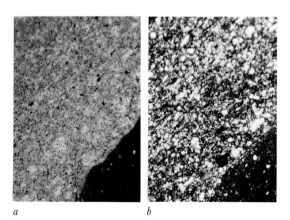

a   *b*

*2.103. Photomicrographs of Bardorf ware (*BADO*) ; a, p.p.l. b, x.p.l.*

Source

Badorf-type ware was produced on several sites in the middle Rhine.

Corpus

Large amphorae are the most distinctive form found. An example from Trig Lane is a narrow-necked vessel with a thumbed strip around the neck and vertical, roller-stamped strip running down from the neck (Fig 2.104 No 246b). What may be a splash of red paint is present on the interior. The Public Cleansing Depot sherd is a thin-walled vessel decorated with horizontal bands of roller-stamping. The remaining sherds are undecorated body sherds from thick-walled vessels. Two have knife-trimmed internal surfaces.

Date and Frequency

Badorf-type wares are thought to be principally of 8th- and 9th-century date and this is probably the date of vessels from the Strand and Waltham Abbey. Nevertheless, similar vessels were apparently made into the 12th century. This is shown by a sherd from Kings Lynn, which has produced no other evidence of pre-12th-century occupation (Clarke and Carter 1977, 230, Fig 102 No 30, found in a post-medieval context).

The few sherds from London are both scarce and sometimes residual. The most distinctive sherd, for example, is from a late 14th-century context at Trig Lane. The earliest stratified sherd is from Pit 3103 at Pudding Lane (CP1), that from St Peters Hill is from a mixed area of pitting. The Public Cleansing Depot sherd is associated with a group of mid- to late 11th-century coarsewares (CP4) and there is no earlier Saxon pottery in the group (although there is a large residual Roman assemblage). A sherd from Watling Court was found in Pit 48, dating to the late 11th to mid-12th-century (CP5) and here too there is no evidence for any residual earlier Saxon pottery. On balance, therefore, it is most likely that the sherds found in late 11th and 12th-century contexts were imported to London during that period.

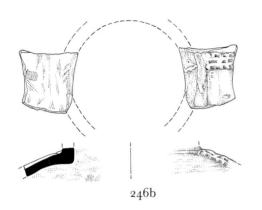

246b

2.104. BADO *ware (No 246b) and, below, the percentage of* BADO *in stratified contexts, dated to* CP1-5.

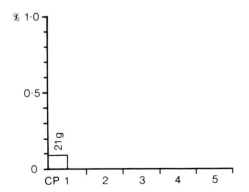

REDP (Rhenish Red-painted ware - Pingsdorf-type ware)

REDP can be either a sandy earthenware or a stoneware depending on the firing, with the colour of the fabric varying from a pale beige to a dark grey/brown (Ludtke 1985; 1989). The paint, which was probably applied with the fingers, can vitrify on the stonewares. Pingsdorf-type ware from Sleswig and Bergen has been divided into sub-fabrics based on the firing: a white fabric (Pingsdorf White), a yellow fabric (Pingsdorf Yellow) and an olive fabric (Pingsdorf Dark). An attempt was made to use this classification on the DUA finds but there were many intermediate and indeterminate sherds.

All vessels are wheelthrown. The fabric can vary considerably, from a soft to a hard, lower fired earthenware, to a very hard, highly fired stoneware.

The colour can also vary considerably - the lower-fired earthenwares are lighter in colour: pale beige outer surface (5Y 8.5/2), off-white inner surface (5Y 9/1), with brown paint 5YR 5/6,6/8), or an orange outer surface (5YR 7/6), or brown inner surface (7.5YR 7/2). The higher-fired wares are darker - grey/beige surfaces (2YR 7/2), with dark brown paint (5YR 3/2), or grey/brown (5YR 5/1) with very dark red paint (2.5R 3/2, 2.5/2). Cores can be oxidised (10YR 8/6) with reduced surfaces, surfaces and cores can be oxidised with reduced margins, or cores can be reduced with oxidised surfaces.

On highly-fired examples the red paint has vitrified into a glaze. This does not occur on the lower-fired examples, on some of which tiny particles are visible under the microscope.

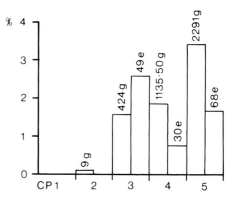

2.106. *The percentage of* REDP *in stratified contexts, dated to* CP1-5.

Inclusions consist of: abundant rounded and sub-angular clear, white, yellow and rose quartz, from 0.2-0.5mm across; sparse calcareous inclusions up to 2mm; sparse voids up to 0.5mm across and moderate red and black iron-rich compounds. In stonewares, the quartz and iron-rich compounds are still visible but in a hard, glassy matrix.

Source

Although there is a considerable variation in visual appearance, texture and firing within the London REDP sherds, they are probably all from the Meuse-Rhine area. Northern French red-painted wares are in general less highly-fired, do not have the thumbed bases of the Meuse-Rhine vessels, and contain inclusions characteristic of Cretaceous or later sediments (altered glauconite, rounded quartz grains and angular flint/chert). Although there have been attempts to subdivide Pingsdorf-type ware on the basis of firing, this classification does not separate vessels from different sources.

Corpus

The majority of REDP vessels are spouted pitchers (71% of a sample of 7 eves). Within this group the vessels can be split into those with between one and three handles and those which definitely do not have handles. There is a tendency for the handled vessels to be larger but this cannot be used to classify rim sherds which do not have

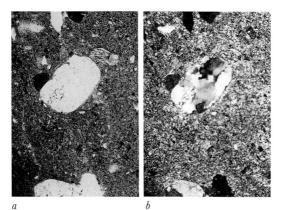

a   *b*

2.105. *Photomicrographs of* REDP *a, p.p.l. b, x.p.l.*

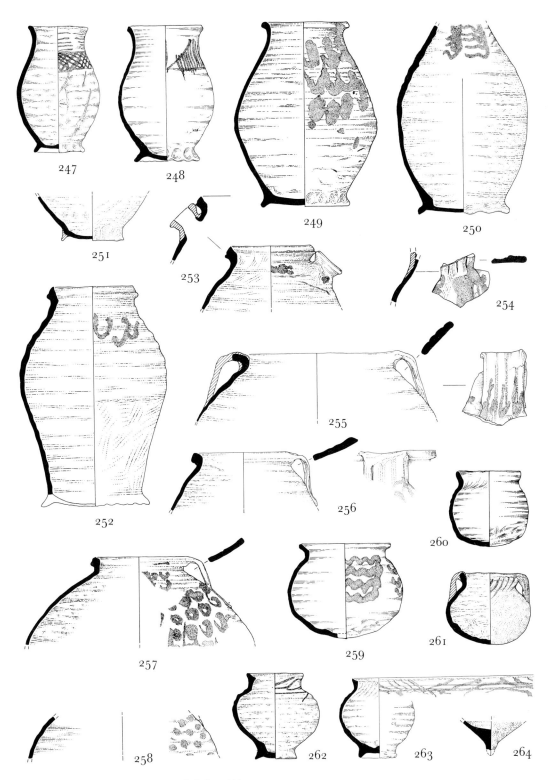

2.107. REDP *beakers (Nos 247-8), spouted pitchers (Nos 249 -253), handled pitchers (Nos 254-8), cooking pots (Nos 259- 61), globular jars (Nos 262-3), suspension lamp (No 264).*

handles attached. Small beakers are the next most common form (21%) followed by round bottomed cooking pots (8%). Apart from a single possible suspension lamp sherd, there are no other forms represented in the collection from London.

Jars or Beakers (Fig 2.107 Nos 247-248).

Pitchers (Fig 2.107 Nos 249-253).

Handled pitchers (Fig 2.107 Nos 254-258).

Cooking pots (Fig 2.107 Nos 259-261).

Globular jars (Fig 2.107 Nos 262-263).

Suspension lamp (Fig 2.107 No 264).

Dating and frequency

Isolated sherds of REDP occur in late 9th to early 11th-century contexts (CP1) but they start to occur more frequently in early to mid-11th-century deposits, including those at New Fresh Wharf (CP3, Fig 2.106). Both handled pitchers and beakers are represented in the latter groups, as are sherds exhibiting all variations in firing pattern and temperature but with few low-fired off-white sherds of Ludtke's Pingsdorf White sub-fabric. There was apparently a phase in Sleswig in which only this white fabric was common but the New Fresh Wharf finds should be of similar date to those from the earliest Sleswig deposits. A large deposit from the Public Cleansing Depot (4.2 eves) is probably datable to the late 11th to mid-12th century (CP5) and includes a handled pitcher (4%), several spouted pitchers (probably mainly without handles 55%), beakers (27%) and a number of indeterminate rims (15%). There is thus no clear difference between the Pingsdorf-type ware assemblages from groups differing in date by up to a century.

The cooking pot form does appear to be a relatively late introduction although never a common one. Three definite examples, the earliest from London, come from late 11th to mid-12th-century contexts (CP5) while two sooted body sherds, possibly from the same vessel, were found in late 12th-century contexts at Seal House (CP6).

Pingsdorf-type ware is found in late 12th- and early 13th-century contexts and may have been in use at that time. By the mid- 13th-century, however, it appears to have gone out of use, or to have developed into proto-stoneware (EGS).

BLGR (Paffrath-type or Blue-grey ware)

BLGR is a sandy fabric which can vary in colour from light to dark grey. The distinctive characteristic is the metallic blue-grey gloss found on the surface.

All vessels are handmade, in a grey sandy fabric, the surface of which varies from light to dark grey (N4/0, 10YR 6/1), or beige (10YR 8/1) on oxidised patches, with light grey cores. The fabric is soft to hard, feels rough and has an irregular texture.

Inclusions consist of: abundant rounded white, clear and pink quartz grains, up to 0.5mm across; sparse flecks of white mica up to 0.2mm long and sparse red and black iron-rich compound up to 0.5mm across.

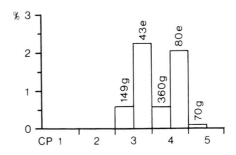

2.109. *The percentage of* BLGR *in stratified contexts, dated to* CP1-5.

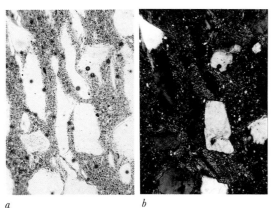

a   b

2.108. *Photomicrographs of Blue-grey ware (*BLGR*) a, p.p.l. b, x.p.l.*

Source

Paffrath-type ware was made in a number of centres in the middle Rhine valley. Thin-section analysis of a sample of seven sherds shows that all but one have a very similar fabric. The odd sample merely appears to be a coarse version of the others. There is therefore no obvious means by which sherds could be assigned to individual kilns.

Corpus

Almost all sherds of BLGR come from handled cooking vessels - better known as 'ladles' but of identical size and presumably function as later medieval pipkins. Apart from a single spout,

2.110. BLGR *ladles (Nos 265-7),* BLGR*(?) spouted pitcher (No 268), cooking pot (No 269).*

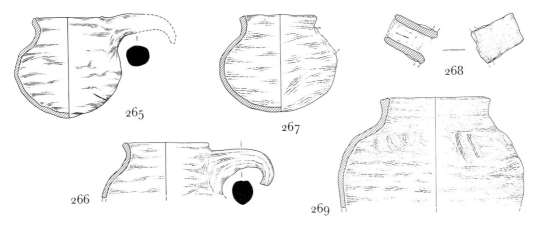

265

266

267

268

269

which may be made in another ware (the sherd is abraded and too small for certain identification), the only other form is a larger cooking pot, almost definitely without a handle.

Handled ladles (Fig 2.110 Nos 265-267).

Fig 2.110 No 268 - possibly not BLGR. Part of a spouted pitcher.

Cooking pot (Fig 2.100 No 269). A large number of sherds, with no sign of a handle.

Dating and frequency

The earliest stratified sherds of BLGR from London are two from Billingsgate Lorry Park, from a context dated c.1039-40, and two from New Fresh Wharf, from an early to mid-11th-century silt deposit (Period 2.3; Fig 2.109). They also occur in several mid- to late 11th-century groups (CP4), including St Nicholas Acon (pre-c.1084). There is no reason to doubt that these vessels were in use before the Norman Conquest although they were undoubtedly still used in the late 11th to mid-12th century (CP5), since examples were found in quantity at the Public Cleansing Depot, and quite probably into the early 13th century. After that time there was a sharp decline in the number of sherds found in London deposits, all of which are probably residual. Most finds are of featureless body sherds and there is no evidence for any change in typology through time. The illustrated cooking pot was found in a late 11th to mid-12th-century deposit.

ANDE (Andenne ware)

ANDE is made from a white-firing clay; the colour of the inner surface varies from off-white (5Y 9/1) and pale beige (2.5Y 7/2) to pale brown (10YR 8/4) and orange/brown (7.5YR 7/6). Some sherds are patchy due to partial reduction, eg grey/beige 10YR 8/2,6/1. The cores are generally oxidised, either orange/brown (7.5YR 8/6) or pale off-white (7.5YR 9.5/0). A few examples are grey (7.5YR 6/0).

Vessels are usually well-glazed (the glaze covers the outer surface of most sherds), with a thick, glossy glaze which is finely crazed and occasionally pitted. The glaze is usually orange in colour (7.5YR 6/10 or 10YR 7/10,6/10) or yellow (2.5Y 8/10,7/10), or occasionally green (7.5Y 5/6). Unglazed sherds, or those with a patchy glaze cover are common and probably come mainly from the the lower parts of the body and the base.

Inclusions consist of: abundant rounded and sub-angular white and clear quartz grains, ranging in size from 0.1-0.5mm across; and moderate red iron-rich compound up to 3mm across, which often combines with the fabric during throwing, producing orange streaks along the throwing marks in the fabric (usually very faint and best seen under a binocular microscope).

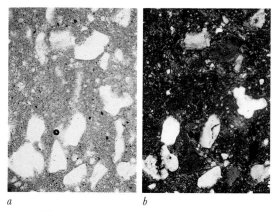

a   b

2.111. Photomicrographs of Andenne type ware (ANDE) a, p.p.l. b,x.p.l.

Source

The excavated kiln sites at Andenne have not produced vessels of the forms found in London. Furthermore, there is apparently a difference in the glaze cover (Titus Panhuysen pers comm). Never-

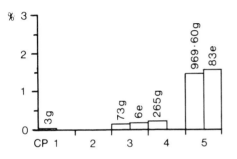

theless, vessels identical to those from London have been found on sites in the Meuse valley (eg. Maastricht, T. Panhuysen pers comm) as well as in north Germany (eg. Sleswig, Luedtke 1985, 63-5) and Norway (eg. Trondheim, I. Reed, pers comm). It is most likely that these finds represent an early phase of production either at Andenne itself or some other site within the Meuse valley. The petrology of the fabric is of no help in trying to characterise the ware.

2.112. The percentage of ANDE *in stratified contexts, dated to* CP1-5.

2.113. ANDE *spouted pitchers (Nos 270-274), costrel (No 275).*

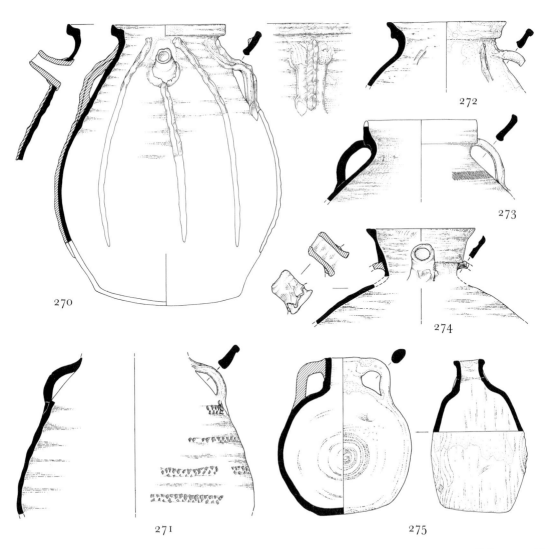

Corpus

The only vessel type recognised from excavated material from London is the pitcher. These vessels show very little variation in form apart from two distinct rim types; a collar rim (Nos 273-4) and a squared or rolled-out rim (Nos 270, 272). Decoration consists of horizontal bands of roller-stamping or vertical, triangular-sectioned strips or a combination of both (Fig 2.10). Vessels probably had at least two, possibly three handles. A single, complete, costrel is present in the Museum of London collection (Fig 2.113, No 275).

Pitchers (Fig 2.113 Nos 270-274).

Costrel (Fig 2.113 No 275).

Dating and frequency

A few sherds of ANDE have been recovered from deposits which would otherwise be dated to the early to mid-11th century (CP3; Fig 2.112). However, no ANDE was found in either the New Fresh Wharf or Billingsgate deposits of this date, although on both sites such sherds were found in the immediately succeeding levels, datable to the late 11th century (and at Billingsgate dated c.1055) and from St Nicholas Acon in deposits earlier than c.1084. They are most common in late 11th- to mid-12th-century deposits (CP5) but are quite likely to have continued to be used into the early 13th century. The finds in mid-13th-century and later deposits are so few as to suggest that the ware was by that time no longer used.

NFRE (North French unglazed ware) and NFRY (North French yellow-glazed ware)

The fabrics of north French unglazed and yellow-glazed vessels are identical, but the differences in form and perhaps date suggest that it may be worthwhile classifying the two separately. Obviously, small sherds from glazed vessels may therefore be classified as NFRE, given the incomplete glazing of many 11th- and 12th-century vessels. The pottery has a white-firing clay with abundant fine quartz and sparse grains up to 4mm in size.

Both wares are composed of the same white-firing clay, either buff (2.5Y 9/2), pinkish buff (7.5YR 8/2) or greyish buff (2.5Y 8/2) in colour. Cores are usually the same or slightly greyer. Surfaces are occasionally burnt. The fabric is soft to hard, feels rough and has a fine texture.

Inclusions consist of: abundant sub-angular white, clear, yellow and iron-stained quartz, up to 4mm across, but the majority are smaller; sparse to moderate red iron-rich compound, from tiny flecks up to 2mm across; sparse flecks of white mica up to 0.1mm long and in some examples, sparse, fragments of angular white flint up to 8mm long.

The greenish yellow (7.5Y 6/8, 7/6, 8/6) glaze can vary from glossy to thin and pitted, and is crazed. Some vessels have a thin reddish orange paint (7.5YR 8/6).

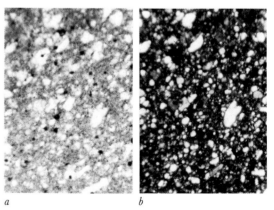

a   b

2.114. Photomicrographs of NFRE a, p.p.l. b, x.p.l.

Source

A northern French source for these wares is indicated by some aspects of the typology and the distribution evidence, which shows that similar wares are much more common in collections from south coast ports such as Southampton (Platt and Coleman-Smith 1975, 23-7, Figs 175-6). No attempt has been made to compare the London finds with finds from specific occupation or kiln sites in northern France but a sample has been compared in thin-section with two groups from Southampton, Beauvais Red-painted vessels and a north French whiteware of unknown source. No close parallels were found with the Beauvais fabrics but the second group was very similar to the London finds. This second group is more common than Beauvais wares in Southampton.

Corpus

Although some sherds can be indentified

2.115. NFRE *pitchers (Nos 276-281), cooking pots (Nos 282-5), pitcher/cooking pots (Nos 286-9), lid (No 290), unknown form (No 291).*

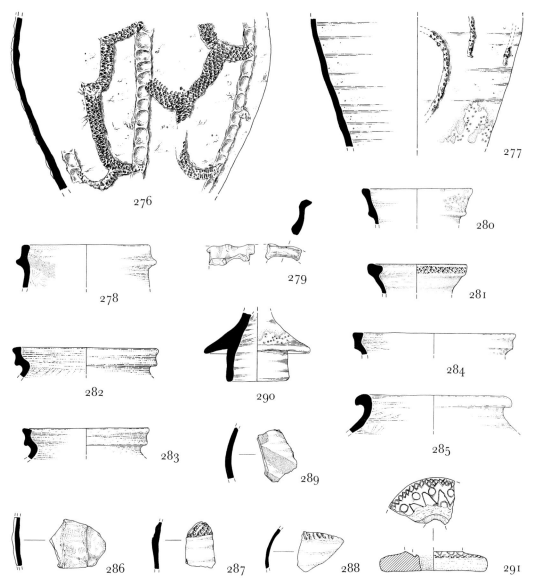

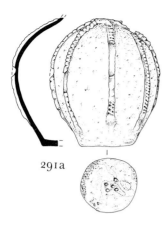

291a

2.116. NFRE *sprinkler (No 291a).*

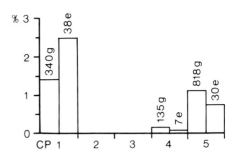

2.117. The percentage of NFRE *in stratified contexts, dated to* CP1-5.

positively as being from pitchers and others are definitely cooking pots there are a number which cannot be identified but are decorated with red paint or roller-stamping. Single examples have been found of lids, sprinklers and a pedestal base (from a lamp?).

Pitchers (Fig 2.116 Nos 276-281).

Cooking pots (Fig 2.116 Nos 282-285).

Pitchers/cooking pots (Fig 2.116 Nos 286-289).

Lid (Fig 2.116 No 290).

Fig 2.116 No 291: Pedestal base, complete form unknown, decorated with stamping and incised lines (Fig 2.19).

Sprinkler (Fig 2.117) decorated with thick applied strips under a crazed glossy glaze (Fig 2.18a and b).

Dating and frequency

A glazed pitcher and accompanying lid were found in a pit associated with LSS and presumably belonging to CP1. Three sherds of NFRE cooking pots were found in the New Fresh Wharf bank and silt levels datable to the early to mid-11th century. All three were reduced with black surfaces. One has a fine-textured fabric (SW1446) while the other two have a coarse texture and could be from the same vessel (SW1469 and SW1447).

Sherds become more frequent in mid- to late 11th-century contexts (CP4), although they are still rare (Fig 2.115). The NFRE vessels at this time are oxidized whitewares.

NORM (Normandy Glazed ware) and NORG (Normandy Gritty ware)

Most imports from Normandy are unglazed, coarse-textured whitewares (NORG) but a few yellow-glazed northern French vessels are coarser than the rest and are thought to be a glazed version of the gritty ware (NORM). Both are made from a white-firing clay, either with pale grey or cream surfaces and cores (10YR 8.5/1, 10YR 9/2), or dark grey or brown surfaces (10YR 5/1, 5/1,7/2,7/4,N5/0), with pale grey/pale brown cores (10YR 9/1,8/4). The fabric is soft, feels rough and has an irregular texture.

Inclusions consist of: abundant ill-sorted rounded quartz, mainly clear, white and iron-stained (the iron-staining can be very heavy and is very clear under the binocular microscope) the majority 0.5mm or 1mm, but larger grains up to 6mm across; moderate large white angular flint up to 4mm across; sparse to abundant red iron-rich compounds up to 1mm across (sparse up to 4mm across); sparse black iron-rich compound; sparse impressions of organic inclusions (grass?) up to 6mm long; sparse flecks of white mica up to 0.1mm long and abundant voids.

The glaze is a greenish yellow colour (7.5Y 6/6, 6/8, and 7.5Y 4/2, 4/4) with patches of brownish orange (10YR 6/8). It is glossy, slightly pitted, and crazed. Iron-rich compounds on the surface of the pot beneath the glaze produce reddish streaks in the glaze.

2.118. Photomicrographs of Normandy gritty ware (NORG) a, p.p.l. b, x.p.l.

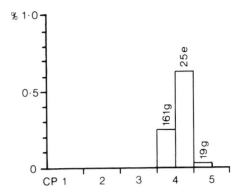

2.119. The percentage of NORM and NORG in stratified contexts, dated to CP1-5.

Source

The attribution of these wares to Normandy, as opposed to other areas of northern France or even Southern England, both of which would be possible source areas on the grounds of distribution, is based mainly on the high quantity of these wares from Southampton, the English port situated closest to Normandy. The quartz sand inclusions are very similar to those found in Coarse Border ware in the 13th to 15th centuries and in Early Surrey coarseware (ESUR) in the 11th and 12th centuries. The firing and manufacture distinguish the Norman sherds from ESUR whilst the possibility of intrusive sherds of CBW must always be conceded. Several sherds, however, occur with decoration not known on CBW vessels.

Corpus

Normandy gritty and glazed wares are very rare in London and mostly consist of body sherds which cannot be attributed to particular forms. However, a number of sherds are sooted and therefore probably from cooking pots.

NORG Jugs(?) (Fig 2.121 Nos 293).

NORM Pitchers (Fig 2.121 Nos 292 and 294). No 294 has an applied, roller-stamped strip.

NORG No 295: red painted - unknown vessel form.

NORM Lid: No 296.

NORG Handle: No 297.

2.120. NORG *cooking pot with roller stamping on the shoulder and traces of soot in the impressions.*

Dating and frequency

The earliest Normandy wares occur in late 11th to early 12th-century levels on a number of sites, including New Fresh Wharf, where both glazed and unglazed vessels were found in dump deposits datable to the second half of the 11th century (Fig 2.119). Only one unglazed storage jar (?) sherd has been found in an early to mid-12th-century context (at Billingsgate, associated with lead 'coins' of *c.*1080 and therefore possibly of very late 11th-century date) but isolated sherds have been found in late 12th (CP6) and early 13th-century contexts (CP7), so that it is probable that importation did continue. The quantity of finds is too low to say whether there really was a decline in importation in the early to mid-12th century.

NORG Jug or pitcher handle: No 298.

NORG Unknown form: No 299.

NORG Spouted pitcher: No 300.

2.121. NORG *pitcher (Nos 292-4), unknown (No 295), lid (No 296), pitcher handles (Nos 297-8), pitcher (No 299), spouted pitcher (No 300). See also next page.*

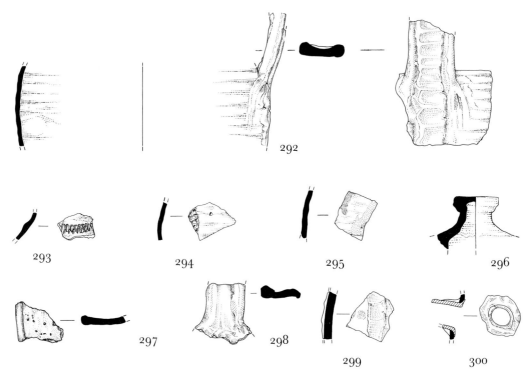

CROW (Crowland Abbey-type bowls)

Crowland Abbey-type bowls are named after a complete vessel found during clearance on the site of Crowland Abbey, Lincolnshire. This vessel was subsequently lost but small fragments of similar vessels are known from 11th- to 12th-century contexts in Oxford, Dublin, and Trondheim.

The fabric is oxidized, usually with a grey core. Inclusions consist of sparse rounded red clay or iron-rich pellets up to 2mm across and abundant fine quartz sand, up to 0.25mm across. The vessels are glazed inside and out with a glossy brown glaze. Pooling of glaze around the rim of a vessel from Ludgate Hill suggests that they were fired inverted. A vessel of the same, or very similar, type from the Library site, Kjopmannsgate 20-26, Trondheim (I. Read pers. comm.), also has a pool of glaze at the rim and was probably fired on its side. The glaze appears to have a deliberate brown colourant, presumably iron.

An unglazed bowl in an oxidized red fabric from the Museum of London collection may perhaps be a variant of this type.

2.122. Crowland Abbey (CROW) bowl sherd showing stamps.

Source

The source of Crowland Abbey-type bowls is unknown. The known findspots are scattered throughout north-west Europe and in particular at ports or coastal sites. The fabric gives no clue as to the source and the range of forms and techniques used distinguish these vessels from most other contemporary glazed wares. There is, however, a bowl of similar form, but undecorated, made in Stamford ware from the Flaxengate site in Lincoln (Adams Gilmour 1988, Fig 42 No 1).

Corpus

Bowls (Fig 2.123 Nos 301-5). The only vessel form recognised is a hemispherical bowl, decorated with large individual stamps (Fig 2.122). A zoomorphic handle in the Museum of London collection (Fig 2.123 No 302) may be from a similar bowl, although it is decorated by incision rather than stamping.

Date and Frequency

A sherd from Billingsgate Lorry Park was recovered from the first silting of the inlet, dating to the late 11th to early 12th century but including much earlier 11th-century pottery. That from Ludgate is from a fill of the City ditch which contains pottery of CP4 or 5 through to CP7. A later 11th- to 12th-century date is likely.

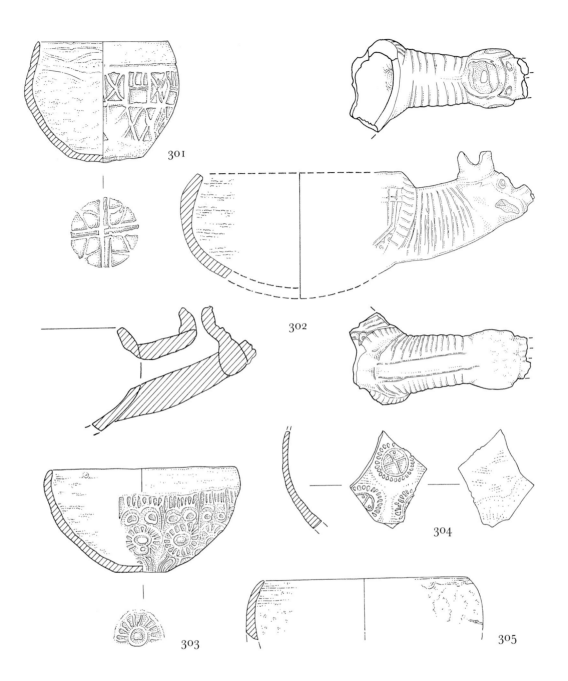

301

302

303

304

305

2.123. CROW bowls; stamped (No 301, 303, and 304) and plain (No 305). Scale 1:2.

Frankish imports

The three recognised Frankish imports from the City of London are described here (Fig 2.124 Nos 306-8). None was found in a recent excavation and they are typologically earlier than the imports from the same general source area found on sites in the Strand (Blackmore and Redknap 1988, 223–29).

No 306: The surface colour is pale pinkish buff or brown (7.5YR 7/4, 8/4, 6/2). The pot is almost complete, but the core and margin, where visible, are also pale pinkish buff (7.5YR 8/4). The fabric is soft, with a smooth or rough feel and an irregular texture. Inclusions consist of: abundant, ill-sorted white, milky, yellow and pink rounded and sub-angular quartz, up to 3mm across, but the majority are c.0.2-0.5mm; and moderate flakes of white mica up to 0.3mm long. The surfaces are smoothed and knife-trimmed. Published by Evison (1979, 38, Fig 15h, 3c9, Pl VIa).

No 307: The surface colour is brown to light brown (10YR 7/4, 6/4, 5/2). The vessel is almost complete, but the core seems to be the same colour. The fabric is soft, with a smooth or rough feel and a fine texture. Inclusions consist of: abundant, ill-sorted quartz measuring 0.1-0.5mm across, with sparse grains measuring up to 1mm across; sparse white mica up to 0.1mm long; sparse voids left by organic inclusions (grass?) up to 2.5mm long. The surfaces are smoothed and burnished. Published by Evison (1979, 37, Fig 14f, 3a6, Pl Xc).

No 308: The surface colour is dark brown (10YR 5/1, 4/1, 3/1), and the core and margins are the same. The fabric is hard, and feels rough, although the pot is almost complete and is heavily burnished. The texture seems fine, although there is no freshly broken edge. Inclusions consist of: abundant ill-sorted, sub-angular milky and yellow quartz, up to 0.5mm; and abundant flecks of white mica up to 0.2mm long. The surfaces are wiped, burnished, and knife-trimmed. Fingermarks are visible.

Source

The source of the decorated vessels is discussed by Evison (1979, 37, 38, 48, 54-7) but is certainly within present-day northern France or southern Belgium.

Corpus

Biconical jars (Fig 2.124 Nos 306-7).

Dish (Fig 2.124 No 308).

2.124. Frankish imports; biconical jars (Nos 306-7), dish (No 308). Scale 1:2.

307

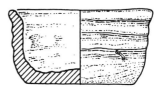

308

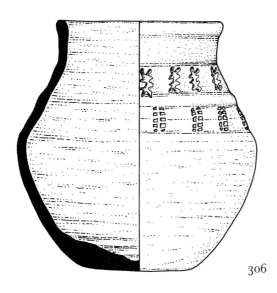

306

Dating and frequency

None of the illustrated vessels are from stratified contexts, nor have body sherds of similar vessels been found in DUA excavations. From their occurrence in pagan graves, both in England and on the continent, it seems likely that the biconical vessel is of late 6th- or early 7th-century date and the jar with the more rounded profile slightly later. The dish is thought to be of 6th-century date. To date, excavations on the site of the mid-Saxon settlement along the Strand have produced typologically later examples of the same types of decorated vessel but nothing comparable with these three finds.

DOMB (Domburg-type - a Low Countries Greyware)

A single vessel has been identified as a 9th to 12th-century Low Countries import on the basis of comparison with a vessel from Domburg (Hodges 1981, 71).

The external surface of the vessel is brown (5YR 4/1) and the internal surface is dark grey (N 4/0). The core is usually a slightly paler brown (10YR 6/2) and the margins are a reduced dark grey colour, similar to the internal surface (N 4/0). The vessel has a hard fabric, feels either rough or smooth, and has an irregular texture. Inclusions consist of: abundant, sub-angular white, milky and rose grains of quartz, up to 1mm across; abundant flecks of mica up to up to 0.2mm long; and sparse fragments of sub-angular flint, up to 3mm long. The surface and base are wiped, and the vessel has cross-hatched burnishing on the side.

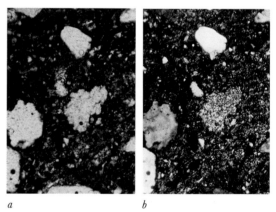

a   *b*

2.125. Photomicrographs of Domburg-type Greyware (DUMB) a, p.p.l. b, x.p.l.

Source

Thin-section analysis does not help to locate the source of this ware, which is thought at present to be somewhere in the lower Rhine valley.

Corpus

Pitcher (Fig 2.126 No 309).

Dating and frequency

The vessel was found in a pit at 87 Peters Hill (PET82 P453). This site has produced a quantity of poorly stratified late Saxon and early medieval finds.

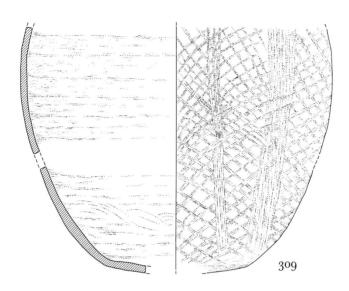

2.126. Domburg pitcher (No 309).

Acknowledgements

We would like to thank the very many people who have, over the years, helped to produce this report. In particular (in alphabetical order): Marsden Anderson, Lyn Blackmore, Bridget Brehm, Georgie Brine, John Cherry, John Clark, John Cotter, Julie Edwards, Barbara Hurman, Trevor Hurst and the staff of the photographic section, Phillip Jones, Guildford Museum, Maidstone Museum, Beverley Nenk (who prepared the original fabric descriptions), Clive Orton, Jacqui Pearce, Mark Redknap, Mike Rhodes and Peter Stott.

The photographs are the work of Louise Woodman.

The photomicrographs were taken by the authors, Beverley Nenk and Julie Edwards.

The illustrations are the work of Anne Jenner.

Appendix 2.1

Site code and context or Museum Accession Number of illustrated vessels

Fig	Cat	Name	Site [Context]	Mol Acc No
2.23	1	LSS	MLK [1214]	
2.23	2	LSS		A26275
2.23	3	LSS	37-9 Cheapside + 65 Friday St	12014C
2.23	4	LSS	PET [294]	
2.23	5	LSS	IRO [411]	
2.23	6	LSS	MLK [1374]	
2.23	7	LSS?	WAT [1135]	
2.23	8	LSS	PET [510]	
2.23	9	LSS	PET [534]	
2.23	10	LSS	PDN [450]	
2.24	11	LSS	IRO [777]	
2.24	12	LSS	PDN [3103]	
2.24	13	LSS	OLD GPO	11589
2.24	14	LSS		78.159/91
2.24	15	LSS	WAT [3565]	
2.24	16	LSS	WAT [1124]	
2.24	17	LSS	WAT [2650]	
2.24	18	LSS	PEN [500]	
2.24	19	LSS	PDN [416]	
2.24	20	LSS	PEN [702]	
2.24	21	LSS	PEN [289]	
2.24	22	LSS	WAT [2057]	
2.24	23	LSS	PET [1833]	
2.24	24	LSS	WAT [1194]	
2.24	25	LSS		C956
2.26	26	LSS		23112
2.26	27	LSS		29.9/5
2.26	28	LSS	WAT [2202]	
2.26	29	LSS	PET [1932]	
2.26	30	LSS	PEN [1682]	
2.27	31	LSS	WAT [1332]	
2.27	32	LSS	PEN [289]	
2.27	33	LSS	PET [355]	
2.27	34	LSS	GPO [4161]	
2.27	35	LSS		5685
2.27	36	LSS		12919
2.27	37	LSS	MLK [1276]	
2.27	38	LSS		12756
2.27	39	LSS	Princes St	299428
2.27	40	LSS		
2.27	41	LSS	PEN [635]	
2.30	42	NEOT	WAT [4260]	
2.30	43	NEOT	MLK [1092]	
2.30	44	NEOT	IRO [233]	
2.30	45	NEOT	LLO [236]	
2.30	46	NEOT	WAY [61]	
2.30	47	NEOT	MLK [29]	
2.33	48	EMS	WAT [2069]	
2.33	49	EMS	WAT [1099]	
2.33	50	EMS	MLK [2010]	

Fig	Cat	Name	Site [Context]	Mol Acc No
2.33	51	EMS	37-9 Cheapside + 65 Friday St	12014D
2.33	52	EMS	NFW [48]	
2.33	53	EMS	NFW [129]	
2.33	54	EMS?		A23547
2.33	55	EMS	IRO [148]	
2.33	56	EMS	NFW [129]	
2.34	57	EMS	PEN [382]	
2.34	58	EMS		6113
2.34	59	EMS	PET [450]	
2.34	60	EMS	PEN [261]	
2.36	61	EMS	GM144 ER112	18294
2.36	62	EMS	MLK [29]	Stamped
2.36	63	EMS	WAT [3533]	
2.36	64	EMS?	NFW [129]	
2.36	65	EMS	GDA [63]	
2.36	66	EMS	40 Lime Street	15200
2.39	67	EMSS	MLK [262]	
2.39	68	EMSS	MLK [1109]	
2.39	69	EMSS	MLK [54]	
2.39	70	EMSS	LLO [179]	
2.39	71	EMSS	MLK [2010]	
2.39	72	EMSS	GDH [228]	
2.39	73	EMSS		12014B
2.39	74	EMSS	MLK [3143]	
2.40	75	EMSS	PEN [500]	
2.40	76	EMSS	MLK [200]	
2.40	77	EMSS	WAT [4247]	
2.40	78	EMSS	PET [1930]	
2.40	79	EMSS	PET [1930]	
2.40	80	EMSS	WAT [4221]	
2.40	81	EMSS	PDN [421]	
2.40	82	EMSS	NFW [129]	
2.40	83	EMSS	NFW [123]	
2.40	84	EMSS	MLK [3050]	
2.40	85	EMSS	GM129 ER885	
2.40	86	EMSS	WAT [3763]	
2.40	87	EMSS		A16390
2.40	88	EMSS		C952
2.41	89	EMSS	MOL NN	
2.41	90	EMSS	FST [317]	
2.41	91	EMSS	MLK [211]	
2.41	92	EMSS		427
2.41	93	EMSS	112 Fenchurch St	11328
2.41	94	EMSS		424
2.44	95	EMSS	MLK [1007]	
2.44	96	EMSH	FMO [286]	
2.44	97	EMSH	GM29 ER115	24062
2.44	98	EMSH	GM29 ER115	24064
2.44	99	EMSH	GM29 ER115	24115
2.44	100	EMSH	PEN [635]	
2.44	101	EMSH	FST [232]	
2.44	102	EMSH	PET [452]	
2.45	103	EMSH	NFW [124]	
2.45	104	EMSH	SH [451]	
2.45	105	EMSH	SH [407]	

Fig	Cat	Name	Site [Context]	Mol Acc No
2.45	106	EMSH	SH [536]	
2.45	107	EMSH	WAT [4017]	
2.45	108	EMSH	MLK [3067]	
2.45	109	EMSH	WAT [3559]	
2.45	110	EMSH	NFW [129]	
2.45	111	EMSH	NFW [129]	
2.46	112	EMSH	FST [232]	
2.47	113	EMSH		25582
2.47	114	EMSH	IRO [119]	
2.47	115	EMSH	NFW [129]	
2.47	116	EMSH	BIG [3471]	
2.47	117	EMSH	WAT [3519]	
2.47	118	EMSH	SH [536]	
2.47	119	EMSH	GDH [1353]	
2.48	120	EMSH		24455A
2.48	121	EMSH	GM96 ER16	24958
2.48	122	EMSH	GM156 ER548	
2.48	123	EMSH	BIG [6974]	
2.48	124	EMSH	DEC	
2.48	125	EMSH	PDN [143]	
2.48	126	EMSH	St.Helens PBSGTE1964	26719
2.51	127	EMFL	Gracechurch St	A24131
2.51	128	EMFL	NFW [45]	
2.54	129	EMCH	NFW [59II]	
2.54	130	EMCH	NFW [129]	
2.54	131	EMCH	WAT [3953]	
2.54	132	EMCH	SM [104II]	
2.54	133	EMCH?	BIS [868]	
2.54	134	EMCH	NFW [48]	
2.54	135	EMCH	NFW [129]	
2.54	137	EMCH	CASS [9]	26356
2.55	138	EMCH	PDN [488]	
2.58	139	ESUR		20234
2.58	140	ESUR	35-9 Cheapside + 65 Friday St	12014A
2.58	141	ESUR + FL	ALG [11]	
2.58	142	ESUR	NFW [59II]	
2.58	143	ESUR	NFW [48]	
2.58	144	ESUR	MLK [27]	
2.58	145	ESUR	WAT [2529]	
2.58	146	ESUR	GDH : [IIII]	
2.58	147	ESUR	WAT [2584]	
2.58	148	ESUR	WAT [3559]	
2.58	149	ESUR	ALG [182]	
2.58	150	ESUR	WAT [4247]	
2.59	151	ESUR		14242
2.59	152	ESUR	ADM [73]	
2.59	153	ESUR	MLK [1100]	
2.59	154	ESUR	WAT [3905]	
2.59	155	ESUR	MLK [2202]	
2.63	156	LOGR	MLK [1089]	
2.63	157	LOGR	MLK [1082]	
2.63	158	LOGR	NFW [30]	
2.63	159	LOGR	IRO [194]	
2.63	160	LOGR	WAT [2091]	
2.63	161	LOGR	WAT [3901]	
2.63	162	LOGR	PET [1042]	
2.63	163	LOGR	PET [341]	
2.63	164	LOGR	WAT [3901]	
2.63	165	LOGR	NFW [89]	
2.63	166	LOGR	PET [561]	
2.63	167	LOGR	WAT [3901]	
2.63	168	LOGR	PET [549]	
2.64	169	LOGR	WAT [3901]	
2.64	170	LOGR	MLK [1107]	
2.64	171	LOGR	GDH [36]	
2.64	172	LOGR	WAT [3901]	
2.64	173	LOGR		78.159/44
2.64	174	LOGR	MLK [1015]	
2.64	175	LOGR	MLK [205]	
2.64	176	LOGR		2893
2.64	177	LOGR		A13639
2.64	178	LOGR		12933
2.65	179	LOGR	WAT [2661]	
2.66	180	LOGR	WAT [3512]	
2.66	181	LOGR	WAT [4260]	
2.66	182	LOGR	MLK [1056]	
2.66	183	LOGR	MLK [1056]	
2.66	183A	LOGR	GM156 ER548	
2.66	184	LOGR	GDH [697]	
2.66	185	LOGR	MLK [1015]	
2.69	186	EMGR	PET [153]	
2.69	187	EMGR		A28172
2.69	188	EMGR		18464
2.69	189	EMGR		A27530
2.69	190	EMGR	PEN [680]	
2.71	191	NMDX	BIG [6936]	
2.74	192	LCOAR	WAT [180]	
2.74	193	LCOAR	GDH [36]	
2.74	194	LCOAR	GDH [36]	
2.77	195	MISC		17720
2.78	196	MISC	PET [455]	
2.79	197	MISC	PET [640]	
2.80	198	MISC	FMO [210]	
2.81	199	MISC	GM131 ER1180	
2.82	200	MISC	ALG [501]	
2.83	201	MISC	PET [401]	
2.84	202	MISC	PET [442]	
2.85	203	MISC	PET [448]	
2.86	204	MISC	MLK [1056]	
2.90	205	THET		
2.90	206	THET		18417
2.90	207	THET	WAT [2684]	
2.90	208	THET	WAT [1134]	
2.91	209	THET	WAT [1634]	
2.91	210	THET	PDN [276]	
2.91	211	THET	MLK [1061]	
2.91	212	THET	PDN [436]	
2.91	213	THET	PET [1099]	
2.94	214	SATH	MLK [1056]	
2.94	215	SATH	PEN [524]	
2.94	216	SATH	PET [1507]	

Fig	Cat	Name	Site [Context]	Mol Acc No	Fig	Cat	Name	Site [Context]	Mol Acc No
2.94	217	SATH	PET [1507]		2.107	263	REDP		5818
2.94	218	SATH	WAT [3953]		2.107	264	REDP	MLK [3061]	
2.94	219	SATH	PET [126]		2.110	265	BLGR		A24998
2.94	220	SATH	NO PROV. CITY		2.110	266	BLGR	GM157 ER268D	23303
2.94	221	SATH	PEN [1401]		2.110	267	BLGR	GDH:	357
2.98	222	THTW		12708	2.110	268	BLGR?	SM [150]	
2.98	223	THTW		21498	2.110	269	BLCR	TR [306]	
2.101	224	STAM	MIL [463]		2.113	270	ANDE		21903
2.101	225	STAM	WAT [2005]		2.113	271	ANDE	NFW [45]	
2.101	226	STAM	BIG [5851]		2.113	272	ANDE		5850
2.101	227	STAM	PET [549]		2.113	273	ANDE	WAT [3665]	
2.101	228	STAM	SWA [3015]		2.113	274	ANDE	ALG [182]	
2.101	229	STAM	LIM [673]		2.113	275	ANDE		85.59/36
2.101	230	STAM	BIG [2614]		2.116	276	NFRE	IME [155]	
2.101	231	STAM	BIG [5961]		2.116	277	NFRE	PDN [294]	
2.101	232	STAM	PET [138]		2.116	278	NFRE	BIG [7005]	
2.101	233	STAM		21226	2.116	279	NFRE	BIG [4756]	
2.101	234	STAM	SM [109]		2.116	280	NFRE	BIG [7078]	
2.101	235	STAM	BIS [428]		2.116	281	NFRE	BIG [4584]	
2.101	236	STAM	BIG [4208]		2.116	282	NFRE	NFW [124]	
2.101	237	STAM	BIS [723]		2.116	283	NFRE	NFW [124]	
2.101	238	STAM		18410	2.116	284	NFRE	WAT [3953]	
2.101	239	STAM	MLK [2008]		2.116	285	NFRE	BIG [7064]	
2.101	240	STAM	GDH [1241]		2.116	286	NFRE	BIG [6762]	
2.101	241	STAM		A5604	2.116	287	NFRE	WAT [2584]	
2.101	242	STAM	BIS [172]		2.116	288	NFRE	BIG [7595]	
2.101	243	STAM	SM [407]		2.116	289	NFRE REDP	WAT [4096]	
2.101	244	STAM	MIL [464]		2.116	290	NFRE	PDN [294]	
2.101	245	STAM	GDH MUSEUM		2.116	291	NFRE	WAT [1040]	
2.101	246	STAM	MAIDSTONE		2.117	291a	NFRE	??	
2.102	246A	STAM	LCT [4100]		2.121	292	NORM	BIG [7078]	
2.104	246b	BADO	TL		2.121	293	NORM	SM [101]	
2.107	247	REDP		2980	2.121	294	NORM	NFW [59]	
2.107	248	REDP		A10305	2.121	295	NORM	SM [101]	
2.107	249	REDP		A16420	2.121	296	NORM	NFW [59]	
2.107	250	REDP	WAT [202]		2.121	297	NORG	BIG [4542]	
2.107	251	REDP	NFW [59II]		2.121	298	NORG	WAT [3953]	
2.107	252	REDP		22014	2.121	299	NORG	BIG [6936]	
2.107	253	REDP		22014	2.121	300	NORG	PEN [583]	
2.107	254	REDP	MLK [3050]		2.123	301	CROW		4066
2.107	255	REDP	WAT [3953]		2.123	302	CROW		5576
2.107	256	REDP	MLK [3067]		2.123	303	CROW	BM DEPOSIT REG	
2.107	257	REDP	FMO [63]		2.123	304	CROW	BIG [7005]	
2.107	258	REDP	WAT [4017]		2.123	305	CROW	LUD [1150]	
2.107	259	REDP	WAT [525]		2.124	306	MISC IMP		4068
2.107	260	REDP	SWA [2053]		2.124	307	MISC IMP		A19828
2.107	261	REDP		10614	2.124	308	MISC IMP	CHRISTS HOSP EC1	10368
2.107	262	REDP	CUMING C15000		2.125	309	DOMB	PET [534]	

Appendix 2.2

Museum of London Accession Number or Site code and context of vessels illustrated by photography in Section 2.

Fig 2.5	MOL Acc No A26275
Fig 2.6	PSN81 [276]
Fig 2.7	MOL Acc No 85.59/36
Fig 2.8a	FST85 [317]
Fig 2.8b	PDN81 [160]
Fig 2.8c	PDN81 [651]
Fig 2.8d	LBT86 [516]
Fig 2.8e	MLK76 [29]
Fig 2.8f	FEN83 [499]
Fig 2.9	MOL Acc No A13639
Fig 2.10	SM75 [78]
Fig 2.11	IME83 [155]
Fig 2.12	PET81 [534]
Fig 2.13	MOL Acc No 20233
Fig 2.14	MOL No Acc No
Fig 2.15	MOL Acc No 5850
Fig 2.16	MOL Acc No A27530
Fig 2.17	MOL Acc No 85.59/36
Fig 2.18	MOL Acc No 18472
Fig 2.19	MOL Acc No 18472
Fig 2.25	PEN79 [1680/1682]
Fig 2.35	MLK76 [1056]
Fig 2.60	MLK76 [1056]
Fig 2.97	MOL Acc No 12708
Fig 2.120	SM75 [101]
Fig 2.122	BIG82 [7005]

Appendix 2.3

Photomicrographs

Fig No.	Common name code	Potstore ref.	DUA Thin Section No.	Site Code	Context Number
2.20	CHAFF	CISY679	863	BC75	402
2.21	LSS	CHILMY1769	533	CS75	0
2.28	NEOT	HY949	27	NFW74	129
2.31	EMS	SY968	976	SM75	101
2.37	EMSS	HSY780	876	TL74	292
2.42	EMSH	HY2378	10	SH74	467
2.49	EMFL	FSW1001	849	NFW74	45
2.52	EMCH	LMSY952	866	NFW74	104
2.56 a and b	ESUR	ISY511	604	ACW74	D2
2.56 c and d	EMIS	ISW923	1101	SM75	192
2.61	LOGR	ISY3533	1213	MLK74	205
2.67	EMGR	GY2941	1160	FST85	659
2.70	NMDX	SY3511	1279	CAT86	49
2.72	LCOAR	ISGW558	258	ACW74	5
2.87	IPS	IMSW677	1272	BC75	401
2.88	THET	IMSW1321	1029	SM75	192
2.92	SATH	SY2982	1156	PDN81	276
2.95	THWH	NO.NO	710	PDN81	544
2.99	STAM	SKW1062	1350	NFW74	75
2.103	BADO	ISY3569	1296	PET81	977
2.105	REDP	ISY1398	950	SM75	150
2.108	BLGR	SW1331	1100	TR74	306
2.111	ANDE	SKW818	877	MFW74	129
2.114	NFRE	SKW2972	1146	PDN81	294
2.118	NORG	SKNOW2285	1025	CUS73	28
2.125	DOMB	ISY3562	1207	PET81	534

3. SMALL FINDS

Frances Pritchard

In 1927 the first of the London Museum catalogues, *London and the Vikings*, was published, followed eight years later by *London and the Saxons*. Both catalogues were landmarks in the study of early medieval artefacts in England and demonstrated the range of the Museum's collections. The objects described were, however, mainly acquired as a result of chance discovery, particularly through the dredging of the Thames to rebuild London Bridge in 1824-31, the construction of Victorian sewers and commercial redevelopment in the years both before and after the First World War. Findspots were frequently recorded by antiquaries and local observers but, apart from the depth below ground level, the stratigraphy was largely ignored. Thus, the great majority of artefacts, other than coins and associated finds, were dated on stylistic and typological grounds. The need to establish a sound chronological framework has been a guiding tenet of subsequent fieldwork, and the meticulous recording techniques adopted by the Department of Urban Archaeology now enables this new catalogue of Saxon and Norman artefacts from dated deposits to be placed beside the earlier reference books. This does not mean that the dating of previous finds has been resolved or that the chronology of new finds is beyond dispute. Many past discoveries remain unique, while all too often the most notable new pieces have been found in later medieval rubbish dumps. The sequences produced for certain groups of organic material, particularly the leather shoes and cloth, nevertheless provide invaluable fresh evidence of a kind not considered in the earlier catalogues.

Most of the artefacts described come from sites listed in Fig 1.1 (see p.11) but similar items from other sites are included to provide a more comprehensive survey. Thus, the catalogue of motif-pieces contains five which were recovered from two sites excavated since 1985. Where such recently discovered material is presented in the catalogue, the dating is restricted to the ceramic phase established from an examination of the pottery. Occasionally the absence of pottery means that even this information is lacking; for example, two loomweights were found alone in a pit beside Gracechurch Street and, consequently, their date can only be inferred from the stratigraphy.

Material recovered by metal detector enthusiasts from the foreshore of the Thames and from dumps of soil removed from building sites in the City is excluded, since it lacks an archaeological context. The latter is a severe loss since much important metalwork has been found in this manner, among which may be singled out a copper *cloisonné* enamel disc (Buckton 1986, 14), a silver-gilt ball-headed dress pin and various lead alloy disc brooches. However, a silver nummular brooch portraying William I is included in the section on coinage as it can be dated intrinsically from its die type (see p.315). Sadly, therefore, one has to turn to places other than London to establish the dating evidence for most of this material.

Retrieval by archaeological methods tends to be very variable because of the soil conditions prevailing in the City, which are generally hostile to the preservation of organic materials and metalwork. Where anaerobic deposits are present, for example beside the Thames, in the Walbrook valley and in pits dug close to the watertable, the range and quantity of finds increase considerably, yielding valuable assemblages of leather and cloth as well as more robust metalwork. The low survival rate in most areas of the City can be assessed by the fact that many sites with early medieval deposits produce only one or two artefacts to be placed alongside a plethora of ceramic wares. Hence, analysis of artefact distribution within the City, other than for pottery, is subject to severe limitations.

The imbalance of preservation makes even the most fragmentary item worthy of scrutiny and, consequently, many hundreds of objects were examined for this study. This revealed that in common with other former Roman towns, such as Lincoln, there is a high degree of residual Roman material within Saxon and Norman deposits. A number of objects are therefore included whose attribution is open to question. Nevertheless, by drawing attention to such pieces, it is hoped that fresh evidence concerning their date and origin may be produced. Similarly, a proportion of 10th- and 11th-century artefacts has been recovered from more recent deposits. Where such pieces have been recognised, they are catalogued, although they offer no useful dating information.

The catalogue is arranged by material, rather than function, in chronological order begining with metalwork, followed by stone, ceramic and glass artefacts and concluding with organic remains. Where an item is composed of two or more materials, it is cross-referenced under one number. Thus an ivory-handled knife found in its sheath is catalogued under ironwork, ivory and leather but not under copper alloy, although the sheath was bound together with copper alloy wire, since this was an incidental feature of its construction. Unidentified objects, which are sufficiently preserved to suggest that they may be recognised by future scholars, are described at the end of each section but small, undiagnostic fragments are listed only in the site catalogues. The textiles are not catalogued within this monograph since they were the subject of a separate article (Pritchard 1984, 46-76). They are, however, included in the site concordances so that their dating and context can be correlated (see Appendix 1). Methods of analysis are explained under the headings of the separate materials.

Only rarely do the finds from Saxon and Norman deposits in London throw much light on the function of a particular site, but this can be seen to be a result of intensive urban redevelopment over many centuries which has destroyed most of the material evidence, rather than a general reflection on the living and working habits of the period. The overall impression, consequently, differs from that of well-preserved towns, such as Dublin, where the degree of disturbance has been less severe and where soil conditions are more favourable, thereby accounting for the greater range and quantity of artefacts on all types of site. One is, therefore, left in London mainly with glimpses of the household utensils, tools and personal possessions that formed part of daily life.

Sufficient artefacts are preserved for changes in style over a period of time to be observed among some classes of objects, for example footwear, for which there is a continuous, albeit patchy, sequence from the 10th to the 12th centuries. The sequence shows that shoes of increasing complexity were made in the 11th century, which would have demanded more labour and presumably also expense than those represented from 10th-century London. The range of styles similarly appears to have widened in the 11th century, and a consciousness of fashion evidently developed among Londoners. This can be seen most clearly from shoes embroidered with silk thread (Nos 327-337) and those with long, curling toes (Nos 338-340) recovered from deposits dating to the second quarter of the 12th century, which occur on more than one site and imply that more than one household was affected by the desire to wear conspicuous footwear in emulation of court styles. However, although changes can be identified from the archaeological evidence, the dating is as yet insufficiently precise to pinpoint exactly when they occurred in relation to political events.

The direction of cross-cultural influences also remains to be determined for many ordinary artefacts as opposed to highly decorated metalwork and carved stone, since the similarity of a wide variety of the London finds, including cloth, shoes, wooden utensils and antler combs, with those from towns and settlements of northern Europe is a persistent feature of the material. Where the source of materials, such as stone, can be identified, supply routes and distribution patterns can be more easily established. Thus, it can be perceived that trade with Norway was a crucial factor in the switch to the import of Norwegian Ragstone for hones, which began in the 10th century (No 122) and continued during the 11th century (Nos 123-126). Furthermore, the economic advantages of importing such stone was evidently not affected by the change in England's political allegiance in 1066. Hones made from Norwegian Ragstone and Blue Phyllite played no part in Roman London when the market was largely monopolised by supplies of Kentish Ragstone (Rhodes 1986, 240-1), but other stone commodities, particularly basalt lava querns from quarries at Mayen in Germany, were a feature of London's everyday life in the Roman, Saxon and Norman periods. This probably reflects the highly organised character of the industry located in an area served by good communications with southern and eastern England, which outlived the withdrawal of Roman administration and which met an essential domestic need for grinding corn, and perhaps other plant matter such as madder roots from which the dye was prepared. It should not, however, be discounted that some of the querns could have been shipped to London as ballast, particularly as two (Nos 155-156) were found incorporated into the foundations of a building near to the waterfront and had apparently never been used for grinding.

Another artefact known in the north west provinces of the Roman empire, which reappears in 10th-century London was the linen-smoother or calender made from glass (No 186). Their presence in Scandinavian female graves is well attested, and it is difficult to deny that the spread of Viking influence caused calenders to become more popular, although again they persisted in use far beyond the period of subjection to Danish rule. Other items whose distribution suggests Scandinavian influence, for example a bone implement or pin with a zoomorphic head (No 226), were more ephemeral in London probably because they were affected by changes in fashion rather than practical considerations of utility, while certain raw materials, such as amber and soapstone, which were popular in Anglo-Scandinavian York and Lincoln, have yet to be recorded from 10th or 11th-century London.

The links that London maintained with north west Europe in the 9th century are reflected in three new finds of brooches from the City. They are two copper alloy equal-armed brooches (Nos 94-95) and an enamelled saint-brooch (*Heiligenfibel*) (No 96). Such personal jewellery falls outside the ambit of trade but it provides tangible evidence of traffic across the English Channel undertaken by merchants, pilgrims and immigrants. Another feature of presumed 9th-century artefacts from the City is that almost without exception they are recovered from more recent levels, particularly from rubbish dumps beside the Thames, indicating that medieval urban development and rubbish clearance was responsible for at least some redeposition of earlier material. A possible exception is a handled comb from a pit at Plough Court, Lombard Street (Marsden 1968, 36, Pl 1) but unfortunately no other artefacts were found in association with it to help clarify the date of the deposit.

Although it is suggested below that London was affected by a recession in long-distance trade during the 10th century (see p. 433), the supply of luxury goods does not seem to have suffered. Silks first appear in the archaeological record of the City at this period and among other exotica is a double-sided comb of ivory. The small silken goods found at Milk Street, including part of a headdress; two ribbons, one sewn from a strip of unpatterned cloth and the other purpose-made partly from grège (gummed) silk; a cord plied from thread dyed yellow and a braid (Pritchard 1984, 59-63, Nos 34-35, 38 and 39), need not be considered as possessing an inordinately high prestige value. They were probably fairly easy to obtain and the cord and braid could have been fabricated locally from imported thread, which was chiefly in demand for embroidery. The resumption in supplies of silk being brought into England from the 7th century (following a lapse after the 4th century) is, indeed, comparatively well documented, although most references are to diplomatic gifts or to isolated purchases by pilgrims in Rome, Pavia, and less frequently Constantinople and Jerusalem (Dodwell 1982, 154-7), rather than to merchandise. The red, white and blue patterned silk (Eastwood and King in Pritchard 1984, 61, No 37), woven in Central Asia or perhaps further east, is, however, of a very different character to the other silken items and is a remarkable find to encounter in a fill of a 10th-century domestic rubbish pit as opposed to a tomb or cathedral treasury. Such a cloth would have been beyond the resources of most local inhabitants unless it was a recycled scrap, which was sufficient to be used as a garment trimming or as a small bag for a relic.

Leatherwork from early 12th-century London also offers a new insight into English embroidery of the period for it is apparent that leather shoes and girdles were frequently embellished with stitching worked in coloured thread. Furthermore, there is evidence in the form of an earlier shoe style decorated with two stripes on its vamp (No 281) to suggest that embroidered leatherwork belonged to a long Anglo-Saxon tradition as, indeed, might be expected from a country acclaimed throughout Europe for its needlework.

An ivory comb (No 224) from a 10th-century pit fill likewise has an interest extending beyond its present unprepossessing appearance. Its double-sided form contrasts with most of those worked from antler and the high status accorded to ivory at the time perhaps stimulated the output of double-sided combs of horn, of which one was found in a 10th-century pit at Milk Street (No 219). The occurrence of ivory-handled knives (Nos 10, 18 and 19) in late 11th and early 12th-century deposits is another feature that analysis of the archaeological material has established but this has only been possible by using sophisticated equipment, which was unavailable earlier this century.

The value of archaeological material in helping to date art styles of the 9th to 11th centuries has been emphasised by scholars. Unfortunately, this is not an area where new material from London is able to provide much assistance. Items of decorated metalwork, especially a 'Winchester-style', copper alloy strap-end (No 97) and a 'Ringerike-style', lead-alloy buckle (No 121) come from an unstratified deposit and a late 14th-century waterfront dump respectively. Thus, their contribution lies in supplementing the corpus of existing material and emphasising the popularity of both these art styles in London.

Artists active, at least temporarily, in London probably played a part in the dissemination of both these art styles and new evidence for the presence in the City of highly skilled craftsmen comes from the excavation of nine bone motif-pieces (Nos 198-206). One of these motif-pieces (No 203) is inscribed with an Old English name, ælfbeorht or ælfburh, and there is a strong possibility that this could be the name of the engraver of the piece. Furthermore, the concentration of these pieces in the neighbourhood of Cheapside, suggests that a workshop was situated in the locality. The earliest stylistically of the motif-pieces appears to date to the late 9th century (No 206), while others from London have been recovered from 10th and early 11th-century contexts. Consequently, the method was probably of longstanding use here and, as in other English and Irish centres, the practice of producing motif-pieces appears to have begun before the era of Scandinavian influence. However, despite the early occurrence of some motif-pieces, their concentration in late 10th and 11th-century London and Dublin is a coincidence that warrants further investigation and forms part of Uaninin O'Meadhra's current research. The study of archaeological material from both towns has, indeed, already established that close cultural links existed between London and Dublin in the early 11th century, thereby adding substance to the historical record of political alliance between Cnut and Sihtric Silkbeard (Wallace 1987, 224-5).

London's role as a centre of artistic activity is glimpsed again in archaeological evidence preserved from the 12th century, for among the more unusual finds are two artists' palettes (Nos 184-185) bearing traces of vermilion, a pigment particularly associated with manuscript illumination at this period.

It is common to find odd pieces of manufacturing debris in pits or along the Thames waterfront but the sites of specific workshops dating to the 10th, 11th and early 12th centuries have so far eluded detection in London. A large assemblage of waste from the production finger rings made from shale and cattle metatarsals was, however, recovered from the fill of a pit behind Wood Street (Figs 3.38 and 3.56). The workshop producing the finger rings appears to have been poorly equipped, lacking the use of a lathe, and the trinkets could only have satisfied the lower end of the consumer market. The unexpected character of this material, therefore, provides a fascinating new insight into 11th-century jewellery and reveals how common it must have been to wear plain finger rings at this period, whether made of metal, amber, jet, glass, shale, bone or antler. It also shows that some craftworkers specialised in particular products rather than basing their output on one type of raw material.

Like many other English towns, London was producing high-lead glass in the late 10th century and, as well as making finger rings, the industry appears to have supplied inlays to jewellers working in metal and carvers of walrus ivory. At the same period an increasing amount of potash glass was produced with the result that window glass was to be seen in a few secular buildings in the City during the 11th century (Nos 192-196). While most alkali glass of this character may have been produced in the countryside close to beech woodland, giving it the name of forest glass, evidence of a glass furnace from late 9th-century York indicates that rural production was not necessarily usual at this date (Bayley 1982, 494; Hall 1984, 43-4). There is, however, at present nothing to suggest that potash glass was made in London during the 10th or 11th centuries.

Other crafts, which appear to have been, at least partly home-based in 10th and 11th-century London were the dyeing and processing of wool and the weaving of cloth. This is indicated by the wide distribution in the City of sherds of pots used as dyebaths (Fig 3.52); a woolcomb and the tooth of another (Nos 27-28); spindlewhorls made from pot-sherds (Nos 181-183), bone (Nos 262-263), and a particular variety of imported limestone (Nos 170-174); loomweights (Nos 176-180); and pin-beaters (Nos 232-234). There is no concentration of these textile-related items in any one part of the City and it may be supposed that output was chiefly domestic. Nevertheless, the long distance import of stone spindlewhorls, and perhaps also dyestuffs, indicates that commercial factors affected the production of cloth and clothing and not only the supply of raw wool.

Spectacular pieces of jewellery like the gem encrusted gold brooches from Dowgate Hill and St Mary-at-Hill, which illustrate the wealth that London attracted in the years before and just after the Norman Conquest, have not been encountered in recent excavations. Significant new information about the material culture of Saxon and Norman London can, nevertheless, be culled from recent finds. The promise offered by future excavations is that more artefacts and evidence will be brought to light to enrich our understanding of the structure of London's everyday life.

Contents

Abbreviations of the names of specialists referred to in the catalogue:

PLA	Philip L. Armitage
GE	Glynis Edwards
RG	Rowena Gale
CM	Carole Morris
DTM	David T. Moore
DJR	D. James Rackham
VRS	Vanessa R. Straker
IGT	Ian G. Tyers
AGV	Alan G. Vince
BW	Barbara West
JW	Jacqui Watson

Other abbreviations used in the text:

AML	Ancient Monuments Laboratory
BM	British Museum
BM(NH)	British Museum (Natural History)
DUA	Department of Urban Archaeology
GMC	Guildhall Museum Catalogue
IMS	Industrial Methylated Spirits
MOL	Museum of London
NMI	National Museum of Ireland
VCH	Victoria County History

IRONWORK

All the ironwork, apart from what appeared to be nails and a small number of rivets, was x-radiographed. This was perhaps unnecessarily restrictive and a policy of x-radiographing all the iron might have resulted in a few further artefacts such as awls and loose teeth from woolcombs being singled out from among the nails. Poor preservation and the small size of each artefact group limited metallurgical analysis except for one knife, which formed part of a larger pilot study undertaken in 1985 by Paul Wilthew of the Ancient Monuments Laboratory on the composition of 12th- to 15th-century knives from London (Wilthew 1987a). A fracture across the blade of a pattern-welded knife enabled it to be examined in cross-section, while scanning electron microscopy allowed the handles of a pattern-welded knife and two knives with reversible blades to be identified. Inlays and tin coatings were identified by spot tests. Nails and rivets are omitted from this study and horse equipment is catalogued but not discussed, since it is to form the subject of a separate monograph (Clark forthcoming).

Knives

Knives are, as one would expect, the most common iron artefact, after nails and rivets, from Saxon and Norman London, with a sequence spanning the 10th to 12th centuries. A few are distinctive and merit particular attention; for example a 10th-century knife with twisted wire inlay, a late 11th-century knife decorated with a narrow band of circles cut from copper alloy wire, two knives with pattern-welded blades from 11th- and 12th-century deposits and two knives with pivoting blades and ivory handles.

A small knife with twisted wire inlay (Figs 3.1-3.3, No 1) is the best preserved of the seven 10th-century knives discussed here, perhaps because of its structural composition, although no metallographic examination has been undertaken to show if this assumption is correct. The knife is of classic late Saxon form (Wheeler's Type IV) with a straight cutting edge running parallel to its back, which bends at an angle to meet the point of the blade. The front face of the blade is embellished with inlay carried out in fine bichrome wires, one red (a copper alloy) and the other yellow (probably brass) (Fig 3.2). Each line of inlay

3.1. Tenth-century knife with twisted wire inlay, No 1.

3.2. Detail of twisted wire inlay on knife No 1.

is composed of a pair of alternately twisted wires, laid side by side in prepared grooves and hammered to produce a herringbone effect. The direction of the herringbone spine changes once along both lines of inlay and the two lines run in opposing directions. Three small pendent loops made from short lengths of red and yellow z-twisted wire lie immediately below the upper line of inlay. The combination of these coloured wires corresponds with findings elsewhere in England,

which show that red wire was often twisted with white or yellow wire but never white and yellow together (Evison 1964, 33). Further evidence of a common workshop tradition can be seen in the pattern layout, the pendent loops on the Peninsular House knife recalling those on the 'OSMHND' knife found on the Thames foreshore at Putney (Clark 1980b, 348). The restriction of the decoration to the front face of the blade may have been influenced by the knife's size, although it is only slightly smaller than a knife of this type from Wicken Bonhunt, Essex, which has twisted wire inlay on both sides of its blade (Musty *et al* 1973, 287). A date range of the late 9th to early 11th century has long been proposed for this group of

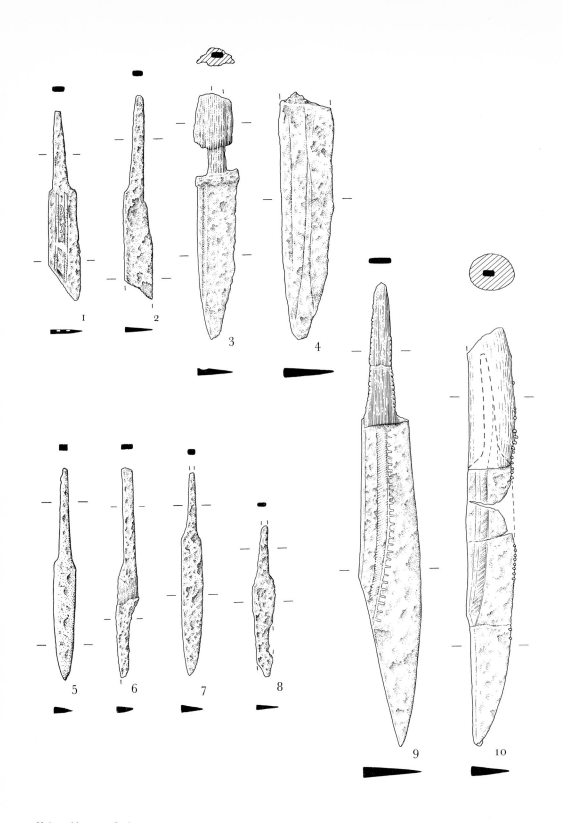

3.3. Knives, Nos 1–10. Scale 1:2.

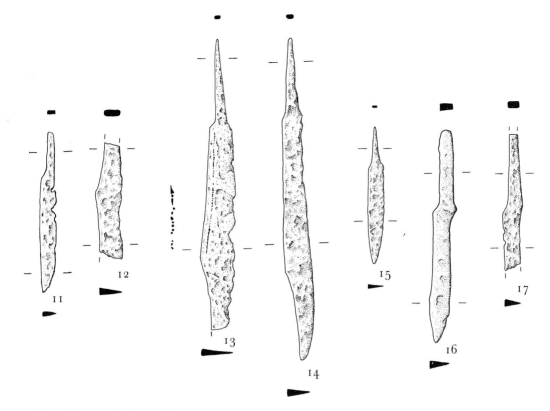

3.4. Knives, Nos 11-17. Scale 1:2; inlay 1:1.

high quality English knives (Wheeler 1935, 179; Evison 1964, 34). This fresh example, therefore, furnishes further proof of their prevalence in 10th-century London, where their distribution is concentrated.

The remaining six knives from London contexts of the 10th century outwardly lack diagnostic features to distinguish them from knives of other periods (Fig 3.3, Nos 2-7). They have straight or slightly sloping backs curving gently down to the blade tip. Three of the smaller examples have drooping shoulders marking the junction of the tang and the blade, while the length of the tang in proportion to the blade shows a lack of uniformity. None have a tang greater than the blade in length, common elsewhere in 10th-century England, but this absence probably reflects the small size of the London sample. Two knives bear traces of wooden handles, of which one was probably either maple or a fruitwood (Fig 3.3, No 3).

The two largest of the 13 knives recovered from London deposits dating to the 11th and 12th centuries have blades which were strengthened by pattern-welding (Figs 3.3, Nos 9-10; 3.6; and 3.8; see pp.131-34). Both are of similar form with an angled back and a convex cutting edge (Wheeler's Type III), a type that is frequently claimed as pre-Conquest and which can be paralleled by many examples retrieved from the Thames (Wheeler 1935, Pl XV, Nos 17, 19 and 22). One, the Pudding Lane knife was, however, recovered from a 12th-century pit fill and other pattern-welded knives persist in London riverside rubbish dumps to the middle of the 13th century (Cowgill *et al* 1987, 16). The earlier character of the Pudding Lane knife is, nevertheless, reflected in the style of its leather sheath, which is 'stapled' with wire along one edge rather than being butt-seamed up the back (see p.133), and it is probable that the knife was kept for a long time before being discarded. The ivory handle of the Pudding Lane knife provides a further indication of its value. The handle of the second pattern-welded knife, by contrast, was made from a fine-grained wood, probably box.

Two smaller knives (Fig 3.4, Nos 13 and 14), are of a longer lived form and have a rather similar profile to the pattern-welded knives, although the back bends with a more pronounced concave curve down to the tip of the blade. The more angular of the two knives, which was recovered from a deposit dating to the second half of the 11th century, is decorated along the upper part of its back on both sides with a 1mm wide band of copper alloy wire arranged in the form of continuous tiny circles (No 13), a pattern that was described by the German Benedictine monk, Theophilus, in his early 12th-century manual, *De Diversis Artibus* (Hawthorne and Smith 1979, 186). Two other knives with this type of decoration from London came from deposits dating to the 13th century, both are, however, characterised by the use of silver wire and the form of the blade is different (Cowgill *et al* 1987, 16 and 80, Nos 14 and 25). A knife from the same 12th-century pit as knife No 14 has two notches cut into the back of its blade near the shoulder (Fig 3.4, No 17). The explanation for this feature is not readily apparent but it is not an isolated English example (Patrick Ottaway pers comm).

There are also two knives with reversible blades from the late 11th-century waterfront at Billingsgate, while a further example from the same site, and which appears to be residual, is included for comparison (Fig 3.5, Nos 18-20). Only No 19 preserves both of its blades but the other two fragments reproduce details of its form. The shorter blade at the pivot end slopes gently towards its point; the longer blade, by contrast, has a pronounced shoulder. Both these characteristics distinguish the three London knives from other English examples, notably those from Canterbury (Graham-Campbell 1978, 130; Graham-Campbell 1980, 135, No 473), Little Paxton, Cambridgeshire (Addyman 1969, 86, Fig 16, No 4), Thetford (Goodall 1984, 83, Fig 122, Nos 48 and 49) and Winchester (Biddle 1990), which have a short pivoting blade with a sharply angled back and no shoulder on the longer one. A reversible knife from Northampton is a hybrid of the two types with a sharply angled back to the short blade and a longer blade with an angled back and convex cutting edge (Goodall 1979, 268, Fig 118.31). A knife from Dorestad in the Netherlands is, however, the closest in form to those from London (Van Es and Verwers 1980, 184–5, Fig 137, No 11). This suggests that the shape of the knives was modified during their period of production in the 10th and 11th centuries, the

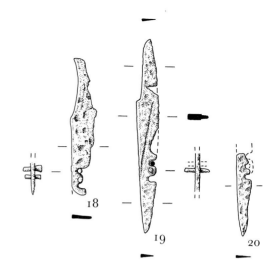

3.5. Reversible knives, Nos 18-20. Scale 1:2.

Canterbury knife representing the prototype, with the London examples being the latest in the sequence.

The handles of these reversible knives are also of interest, since they demonstrate the re-emergence of scale-plates in Britain after an interval of four centuries. The intricate Borre-style carving on the Canterbury bone handle further singles it out as an item of high quality. The handles on the reversible knives from London are too vestigial for any decoration to be apparent; nevertheless, scanning electron microscopy of the two better preserved knives indicates that the scale-plates were cut from a tooth tissue, probably ivory (Watson 1986), and thus would have possessed considerable scope for embellishment. The specialised function of these knives remains a matter of conjecture, although Martin Biddle has recently mooted that they may have been used as manuscript scalpels (Biddle 1990) and, indeed, the portrayal of St Luke the Evangelist in the Hereford Gospels, dating to the middle of the 11th century (Turner 1984, 86, No 70), depicts a knife bearing a striking resemblance to a pivoting-bladed knife both in size and in outward appearance.

Many of the knives discussed here have very worn cutting edges, and have undergone a considerable amount of resharpening. It seems unlikely that they were hardened with steel to improve their quality but this has not been tested scientifically due to the disadvantages of destructive sam-

a

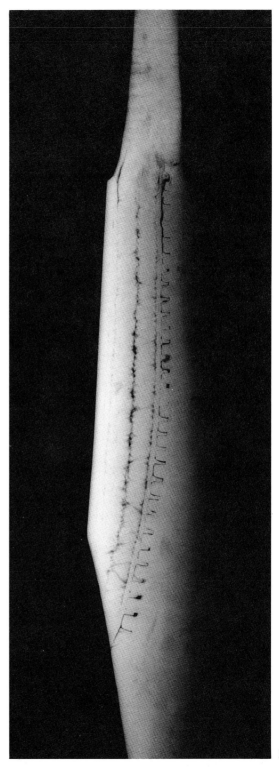

b

3.6. *Wooden-handled knife with a pattern-welded blade, No 9: a) photograph; b) x-radiograph.*

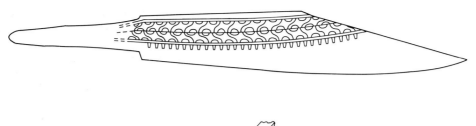

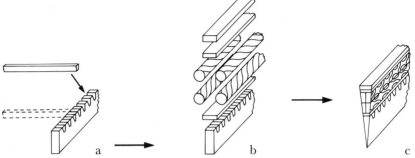

3.7. Diagram of knife No 9 showing the disposition of the pattern-welding on the blade, and a) the construction of the serrated edge of the pattern-welding; b) the components of the pattern-welded blade; and c) reconstruction of the finished structure of the blade. Scale 1:2.

3.8. Ivory-handled knife with a pattern-welded blade in its leather sheath, No 10: a) photograph; b) x-radiograph, the white spots are copper alloy wire, which bound the sheath.

pling and the small number of knives which are adequately preserved. Metallographic analysis of a small, 12th-century knife from Billingsgate (Figs 3.4, No 15 and 3.11-3.12), indicated that it was forged from a single piece of metal with a low hardness value (see p.134), but more intensive investigations have shown that blacksmiths employed a variety of methods to produce knives at this period (Tylecote 1981, 46-8).

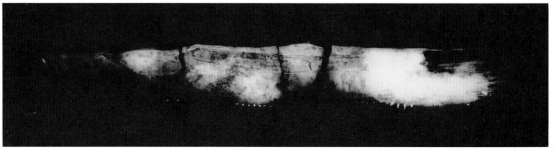

A pattern-welded knife (Fig 3.7)

Brian Gilmour

The blade of this knife (No 9) survived in remarkably good condition, no doubt due to anaerobic burial conditions in the ditch where it was found. The surface of the blade was covered in a dark greenish-black patina, which was slightly lumpy and pitted over parts of the surface. Elsewhere the patina appeared to preserve the original surface of the blade. Within this, along a band parallel with the back, or spine, of the blade, traces of a complex pattern-welded design can be seen (Fig 3.6a).

X-radiography of the blade showed the main structural elements that make up the pattern-welded design, which would have been visible on either side of the blade (Fig 3.6b). This design consists of two adjacent twisted pieces flanked by two narrow bands (Fig 3.7). A separate strip forms the spine of the blade. Against the inner narrow band a series of 'teeth' give a serrated edge to the pattern. Along the pattern-welded zone the x-radiograph shows a rather confusing superimposition of criss-crossing and distorting lines suggesting that a double layer of twisted rods is present. The rest of the structure of the patterned area is fairly clear and on this basis the reconstruction shown in Fig 3.7c was made.

The four rods forming the central part of the pattern-welded design would have been twisted and then welded together. The twisted design appears to have been etched differentially suggesting that each of the rods was made from a piled bar consisting of alternate laminations (possibly six or eight in all) of two different alloys of iron, containing varying amounts of carbon and phosphorus. The main part of the design was completed by welding two plain strips, one on top and one underneath, to the welded bundle of four twisted rods. A separate spine was added (Fig 3.7b).

The cutting edge with the toothed part of the design was prepared separately and then added. The bar of metal that was to form the cutting edge was given a series of notches, probably while hot, using a set or chisel of the correct profile. The 'teeth' of the design would appear to have been created by successively welding in and cutting off the end of a narrow bar of rectangular section as shown in Fig 3.7a. The completed cutting edge would then have been welded onto the rest of the blade. The blade must then have been forged out more or less to its eventual shape. This process caused part of the pattern-welded design nearest the cutting edge to become curved whereas near the spine it is still fairly straight. After final forging, the blade was ground down, removing the upper part of the pattern-welded design and resulting in the distorted wavy pattern (Fig 3.7), which would have become visible after final polishing and etching treatments. The pattern itself is a variant of a general form of pattern-welded design which is very common on scramasaxes or larger knives of the late Anglo-Saxon period.

Little further can be said about either the construction or metallurgy of the blade without metallographic examination. The cutting edge part may have been made from one or more pieces and examinations of other similar blades would suggest that it probably conforms to one of a series of knife blade types (Tylecote and Gilmour 1986, 6, Fig 1 and 140-4).

A leather-sheathed, pattern-welded knife (Fig 3.8)

Helen Ganiaris and Brian Gilmour

During excavations at Pudding Lane a knife (No 10) was found complete with its handle and leather sheath in the fill of a 12th-century pit. It has a pattern-welded blade with an angled back, and a whittle tang set into a handle, seemingly of ivory (Fig 3.8a). The sheath is bound along one edge with metal wire; on the x-ray image, where the binding was first detected, it appears as a series of white dots along the cutting edge of the blade (Fig 3.8b). The organic components survived by mineral replacement, (ie by corrosion products from the iron blade). Although substantially changed and degraded, each component of the knife could be identified and examined.

The blade

The shape and main structure of the blade were determined by x-radiography together with the visual examination of a break across the blade. It consisted of six main components, as shown in the reconstruction diagram (Fig 3.9a). Two twisted rods, possibly of composite manufacture, were welded side by side and sandwiched between two plain strips thus forming the pattern-welded

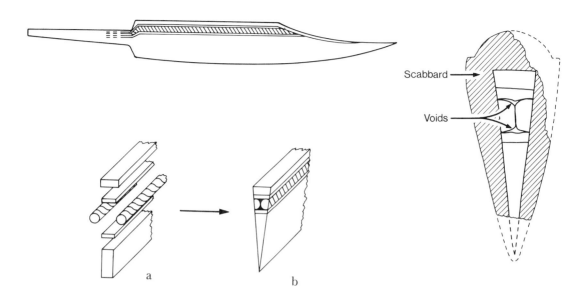

3.9. *Diagram of knife No 10 showing the disposition of the pattern-welding on the blade, and a) the components of the pattern-welded blade; b) reconstruction of the finished structure of the blade. Scale, knife 1:2 ; a) and b) 1:1.*

3.10. *Diagram of knife No 10 from the cross-section of a break in the blade. Scale 2:1.*

part of the blade. This was forge-welded onto the cutting edge piece and then, except for the tang, the blade forged out to roughly its final shape. Finally the back piece was added. This was welded on top of the pattern-welded part and extended round the angle of the back nearly to the tip of the blade (Fig 3.9). After this the final forging was carried out, including the forging out of the tang. The x-radiograph (Fig 3.8b) shows all the main components of the blade continuing into the tang, including the pattern-welding in very elongated and distorted form.

Figure 3.9b gives an idea of how the main components of the blade were combined. The voids (shaded black in Fig 3.9b) were clearly visible in cross section at a break in the blade (Fig 3.10). This was the part of the structural detail that showed up best in the corrosion products and indicates the imperfect nature of the internal welding of the pattern-welded part of the blade. The voids were probably originally filled with hammerscale (iron oxides) trapped inside this part of the blade during forging. It, therefore, would appear that the twisted rods were little more than tack-welded together before being sandwiched between the two plain strips. When these four components had been welded together this combined piece was more extensively forged out to the desired shape. The x-radiograph

appears to show that the finished blade resulted from forging and owed little of its form to abrasive processes, although the edge is likely to have been ground down.

Although the general structure of the blade could be deduced, the metallurgy could not be determined as no uncorroded metal appeared to survive. Metallographic analysis of similar weapons has shown them to vary greatly in quality and to the extent and ways in which steel was incorporated and heat treatments employed (Tylecote and Gilmour 1986, 243-50). The Pudding Lane knife clearly was elaborately constructed; it is fairly likely to have had steel incorporated, and may also have been heat treated.

The sheath

The sheath (220mm long as preserved) covers the handle but its original length is not known because neither the end of the handle nor of the sheath have survived. It is narrow, hugging the blade closely along its entire length (29mm at its widest point). Unlike some late Saxon sheaths, there is no flange or shoulder where evidence of suspension points might be expected (Thornton 1979, 28; MacGregor 1978, 53; Tweddle 1982,

142-3). It is possible that it was suspended from the handle end, but this area is missing.

The sheath is bound along one edge with metal wire, unlike later sheaths which usually have a seam up the centre of the back. Descriptions of other Anglo-Saxon sheaths mention holes for rivets, or stitching along one edge, but no references to late Saxon sheaths have been noted which mention surviving bindings. (Some continental publications show sheaths with rivets; see, for example, Blomqvist 1938, 146; Arbman 1943, Abb 183, No 47, Abb 253.6, Abb 408). On the Pudding Lane sheath, the bindings are very close (approximately 2mm apart) and resemble staples, rather than rivets, pinching the two faces of the leather together. The x-radiograph shows a knot of wire at the point of the sheath which might suggest that the wire was continuous. No evidence survives for connections between the individual bindings, however, and although there seem to be no precedents for staple-like bindings, this is how they appear. They seem to have gripped tightly, as can be seen from the puckering between each binding, a feature that survives in spite of the fragility of the mineralised leather.

The corroded metal of the wire bindings is distinguishable from the surrounding leather only by its dark grey colour. Analysis by x-ray fluorescence showed that the wire is essentially copper with some lead and tin. Although this was only a qualitative analysis, it was clear that the readings for lead and tin were considerably higher than would be expected for a copper alloy. Two explanations may be suggested for this: the wire could be copper or bronze with a lead-tin coating to give it a white metal appearance; alternatively, copper, being more reactive than lead or tin, could have been preferentially leached in burial.

The sheath is very degraded so that its full thickness is preserved in a few areas only. Enough of the grain pattern of the original surface has survived to identify the leather as ox or cattle hide. Sheaths were often decorated and some of the examples cited earlier from York have elaborate interlace patterns. It was also common for decoration to indicate the positions of the handle and blade of the knife. Over the handle of this knife the sheath is plain, but in the region of the blade the leather is too degraded for decoration to be seen by visual inspection. However, in several places on the x-ray image there are markings which look significant but do not correspond to any feature on the blade. It is possible that these

marks are traces of an interlace design on the sheath, which now appear only as slight changes in density on the x-radiograph.

Handle

The remains of the handle measure 74mm long; its diameter is 18-20mm and it is slightly curved. The tang is visible where the end of the handle is lost. Due to poor survival, it is difficult to determine the material of which the handle is made. Examination of the end (where broken) shows conical-splitting, parallel grooves, and a white colour at fractures, all of which suggest ivory. Examination by scanning electron microscopy showed evidence of dentinal tubules, also associated with ivory. It is not possible to identify the type of ivory: the most probable would be walrus since this was the main source at the time (MacGregor 1985a, 40-1).

Metallographic examination of a knife

Paul Wilthew

Two sections from the blade of this knife (No 15) were examined (Fig 3.11a), according to the method described in Wilthew 1987a, which showed that the blade consisted of a piled structure including areas of ferrite and of ferrite and pearlite (Fig 3.11b). There were no clear weld lines between the ferrite and pearlite regions and the different structures probably resulted from variations in carbon content in a single piece of metal, possibly due to phosphorus segregation. The latter possibility is supported by the high hardness of the ferrite region ($mHV500 = 227$), as the presence of phosphorus would harden the ferrite.

The knife was, therefore, forged from a single piece of metal with a piled ferrite and ferrite and pearlite structure. The low hardness of the metal ($mHV500 = 193$, 227, and 283; Fig 3.12) suggests that it would not have retained a sharp cutting edge and would have been of poor quality.

Area	Structure	mHV500
Blade	Ferrite	227
Blade	Ferrite + Pearlite (mainly ferrite)	193
Blade	Ferrite + Pearlite (mainly pearlite)	283

3.12. Table of microhardness test results for knife No 15.

3.11. Diagram of knife No 15 showing a) the positions at which sections were obtained; and b) composite diagram showing the main features present in sections, s1 and s2. Scale a) 1:2; b) 12.5:1. F = ferrite; P = pearlite.

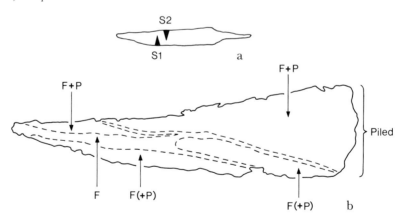

Tools

A variety of iron tools suggest that certain crafts were practised in the City, although few offer clues as to the location of workshops and none indicate activity on more than a domestic scale. A small pair of tongs from an 11th-century building at Pudding Lane (Fig 3.13, No 21) cannot be precisely classified, since both jaws are broken, but the wide bow would have made them suitable for lifting crucibles. The short length of the handle, however, suggests that their use may have been confined to working cold metal. The only other pair of tongs from this period in London was found in the Thames among a reputed cache of battle-axes and spearheads dated stylistically to the early 11th century (Fig 3.13; Wheeler 1927, 23, Fig 1). They have long slender handles and scissor-like jaws indicating that they could have been used for cutting hot sheet metal. A punch from the late 11th- or early 12th-century waterfront at Swan Lane (Fig 3.13, No 22) is another standard metalworker's tool which has scarcely altered over the centuries. An iron rod (Fig 3.13, No 23) and wires (Nos 24-25) may, in addition, represent minor items of a blacksmith's stock.

Several of the pits at Milk Street also yielded examples of discarded tools. The most impressive is a T-shaped carpenter's axe with a haft of oak held in place with an iron wedge, neither of which, surprisingly, was removed before the broken axehead was thrown into the pit (Fig 3.14, No 26). The wedge would have enabled the axehead to be turned for left-handed as well as right-handed use, a supposition reinforced by a representation on the Bayeux Tapestry, which shows a shipbuilder wielding a similar shaped axe in his left hand. This type of carpenter's axe with a long slender neck was discussed by the late Sir Mortimer Wheeler, who argued that the form, modelled on a Frankish prototype, was in widespread use from the 9th century to the middle of the 14th century (Wheeler 1927, 24; Wheeler 1935, 58). The conspicuous absence of this type of axe from pagan Anglo-Saxon graves (Wilson 1976, 255-7) offers a contrast with later Anglo-Saxon settlements where they have a wide distribution, and an 8th-century or later date for their first appearance in England can now be more fully substantiated.

Another tool of importance to the domestic economy was the woolcomb, which was used for processing long-stapled wool from which a high grade worsted yarn was spun. A woolcomb from Milk Street, in common with others recorded from Saxon England, has two rows of teeth embedded in a wooden base, probably of oak, which is capped with a sheet of iron (Fig 3.15, No 27). The roots of the teeth were fitted into the iron binding, thus resulting in a stronger and more elastic tool than if the wood had not been reinforced (Ling Roth 1909, 4). The handle is not preserved but it would have run at an angle of between 80° and 90° to the teeth.

This type of woolcomb represented an improvement on those of the Roman period, which consisted of a flat piece of iron with teeth welded in place at one or both ends (Wild 1970, 25; Manning 1976, 148, Fig 251). At present no woolcombs with two rows of teeth at one end are known to date earlier than the 7th century in England, a set of three combs in a 7th-century grave of a young woman at Lechlade (Grave 50) apparently being the earliest. Although the evidence is inconclusive, wooden-handled woolcombs may have been introduced at the same time as annular loomweights, which also represent a modification of the previous Romano-British technology. Grave finds from Harrold (Bedfordshire) (Evison 1970, 42) and Lechlade (Gloucestershire) show that, as in Norway, both men and women were accustomed to combing wool, and it was evidently not confined to rural, sheep-farming estates, as the comb from London and others from York (Hall 1984, 79, Fig 107) and Thetford (Goodall 1984, 79, Fig 119) demonstrate.

The woolcomb from Milk Street has square-sectioned teeth of a length in excess of 78mm. A single tooth was, in addition, recovered from the 12th-century waterfront at Billingsgate (Fig 3.15, No 28). It retains traces of its iron binding, showing that it was set into a base to a depth of 18mm. Its length of 86mm accords with the range recorded for the teeth of native woolcombs, the shortest complete examples from Shakenoak, Oxfordshire, measuring approximately 63mm (Brown 1973, 134) and the longest from Thetford over 154mm (Goodall 1984, 79). This variety suggests that the teeth were graded into different lengths for each row, as became the practice in modern times (Baines 1977, 34). The positioning of the teeth in each row and the number inserted appears not to have been significant; a woolcomb binding from Thetford indicated that it had sixteen teeth in one row and seventeen in the other (Goodall 1984, 80, Fig 119, No 20) and a tendency to stagger the placing of the teeth is apparent from the Milk Street example.

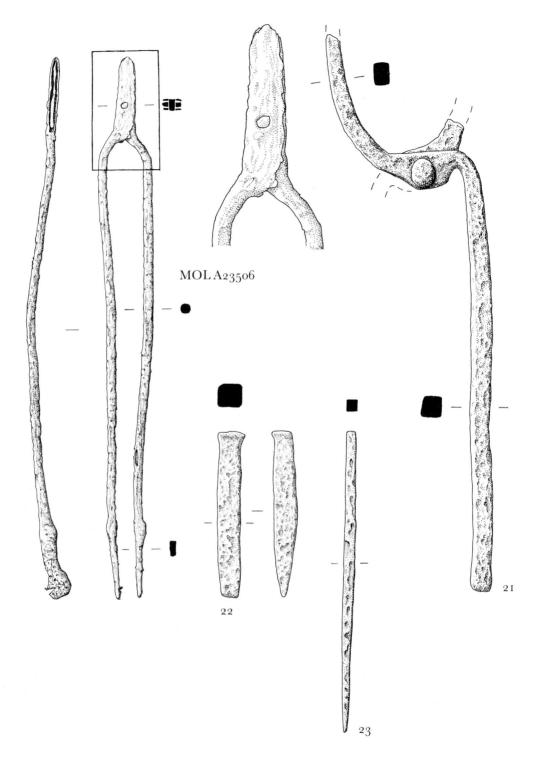

MOL A23506

22

23

21

3.13. *Iron tools associated with metalworking: tongs, No 21 and MOL A23506; punch, No 22; and rod, No 23. Scale Nos 21-23, 1:2; MOL A23506, 1:4, except for detail of the blades of the tongs which is at 1:2.*

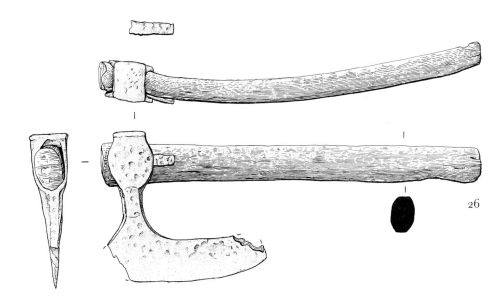

26

3.14. Carpenter's axe with iron wedge, No 26. Scale: drawing, 1:4.

Four awls have been identified from deposits in London dating from the 10th to the early 12th centuries (Fig 3.16, Nos 29-32). They are diamond-shaped in section and may, therefore, have been used in leatherworking.

The fishhooks recovered from the Thames waterfront are distinguishable from Roman ones because they were made from iron and not copper alloy, although an iron fishhook from the river silt at New Fresh Wharf is considered to be Roman (Rhodes 1986, 238). Roman fishhooks also frequently have two barbs, one at either end (GMC

1908, 36, Pl XXVIII, Nos 13-17). All the 11th- and 12th-century fishhooks from London have single barbs. The small examples have flat heads, which were hammered into shape (for example, Fig 3.17, Nos 34, 37 and 43), while the large fishhook (Fig 3.17, No 33) has a looped head, to help support the weight of a larger fish. The latter is a formidable size for a fishhook but a near contemporary example of similar dimensions was excavated at Lund in Sweden (Blomqvist and Mårtensson 1963, 163, Fig 163). Most freshwater fish caught with a hook and bait, including those listed in Aelfric's *Colloquy*, would only have needed hooks of the smaller size and, as one would expect, these are the type usually found in Eng-

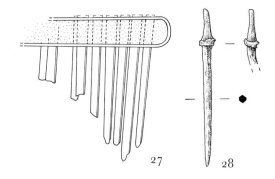

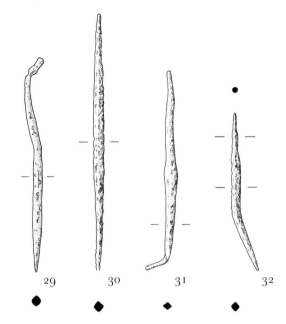

27   28

3.15. *Woolcomb (shown diagrammatically) and a woolcomb tooth, Nos 27 and 28. Scale 1:2.*

29   30   31   32

3.16. *Awls, Nos 29-32. Scale 1:2.*

land. Fish remains from a Saxo-Norman well in Lower Thames Street suggest that London was mainly supplied by fish from the North Sea and it is probable that hooks and lines were used to catch some species of marine fish, such as haddock, mackerel, whiting, and thornback ray (Wheeler 1980, 162). Another feature of interest is that the smallest fishhook, recovered from an early 12th-century riverside revetment at Seal House (Fig 3.17, No 44), appears to have been made from a length of drawn wire rather than from a square-sectioned metal rod.

3.17. *Fishhooks from the 11th and 12th-century London waterfront, Nos 33-34, 36-37 and 43-44. Scale 1:2.*

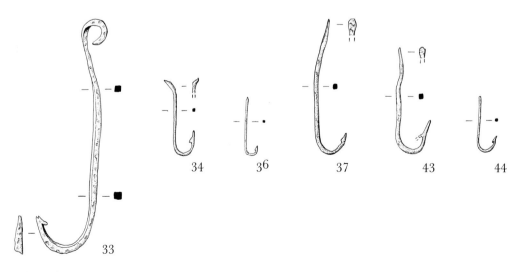

34   36   37   43   44

33

Miscellaneous ironwork

The change from copper alloy to iron in the Anglo-Saxon period for particular items of metalwork is also illustrated by the Milk Street bell (Fig 3.18, No 45). It was made from a rectangular sheet of iron, which was bent in half, the short sides were then made by folding the sheet iron inwards at an angle and the overlapping edges brazed together. Two iron staples were inserted in each of the top corners for attaching a handle and the bell was plated on both sides with copper alloy to prevent it from rusting, and perhaps also to improve its tone and resonance. It is similar in form, although larger in size, to two four-sided iron bells from the 6th-century cemetery at Kingston Down, Kent, and to one from a 9th-century farmstead at Ribbleshead, Lancashire (Evans 1983, 894-5). These mark a departure from the circular bells, often cast in two halves, of Roman Britain. By the 11th century, four-sided bells made from sheet metal had probably become widespread, although very few English examples are preserved, the closest parallel in this country being a small bell from Coppergate, York, which retains its semi-circular suspension loop (Roesdahl *et al* 1981, 127). Handbells of this form are depicted in the Bayeux Tapestry, where child mourners are shown ringing them at the funeral of King Edward, but the Milk Street bell is more likely to have been strapped to the neck of an animal, perhaps a sheep or horse.

A small fragment of an iron strainer from a 12th-century deposit at Billingsgate (No 46) provides further evidence of the switch from copper alloy to iron that occurred in early medieval England. Iron was also used as a cheap substitute for copper alloy, and the four 12th-century mounts, coated in tin to improve their appearance as well as their durability (Fig 3.19, Nos 47-50), and a strap-end (Fig 3.19, No 51) are, consequently, similar to contemporary examples in copper alloy.

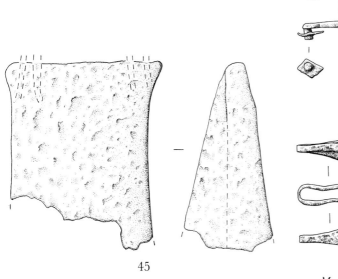

45

3.18. Bell plated with copper alloy, No 45. Scale 1:2.

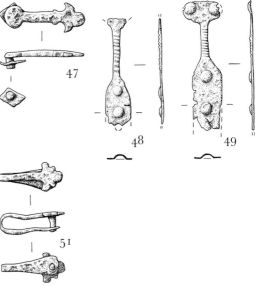

3.19. Mounts and strap-end of the late 11th to early 12th centuries, Nos 47-49 and 51. Scale 1:2.

Locks, door furniture and domestic fittings

Other items made from sheet iron include a key from a late 11th-century waterfront deposit (Fig 3.20, No 52). Similar keys were common in Scandinavia during the 10th and 11th centuries (Blomqvist and Mårtensson 1963, 125, Fig 107;

Richardson 1959, 83) but in England, where examples have been recorded from York, Thet-

3.20. Lock and door furniture of the 10th to mid-12th centuries: key, No 52; padlock bolt, No 53; hasp, No 54; hinges, Nos 55-56 & 58-59; bolt, No 61. Nos 59 and 61 were fitted to the same door. Scale 1:2.

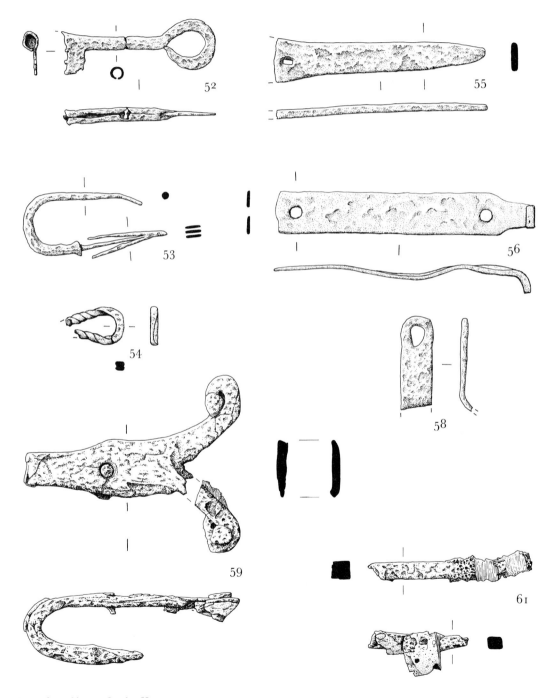

ford and Northampton, it is not clear whether they were introduced before 1000. Keys made from sheet metal were obviously not made to last as long as cast types with solid shanks, nor were they as ornate. Examples from Bush Lane and Wood Street in London, acquired by the British Museum from C.Roach Smith and G.F.Lawrence, have openwork bows and small suspension loops set at right angles to the bow (Wilson 1964, 147 and 153, Nos 38 and 46), in contrast to the very simple form of the New Fresh Wharf key. Other items of lock furniture, includ-

ing part of a barrel padlock (Fig 3.20, No 53) and a hasp with a characteristic spiral twist (Fig 3.20, No 54), were recovered from late 11th or 12th-century deposits and are typical examples of post-Conquest ironwork (Goodall 1981, 60). The remaining iron fittings, namely strap-hinges, pintles and staples are unexceptional, although a pair of bifurcated hinges and a bolt or latch-lifter (Fig 3.20, Nos 59-61) were found *in situ* on an oak door recovered from the demolition debris of Building 5 at Pudding Lane (Horsman *et al* 1988, 89-91, Figs 84 and 86).

3.21. Pintles, Nos 62 and 65; u-shaped staples, Nos 66-69; rectangular staples, Nos 71-72, and 75. Scale 1:2.

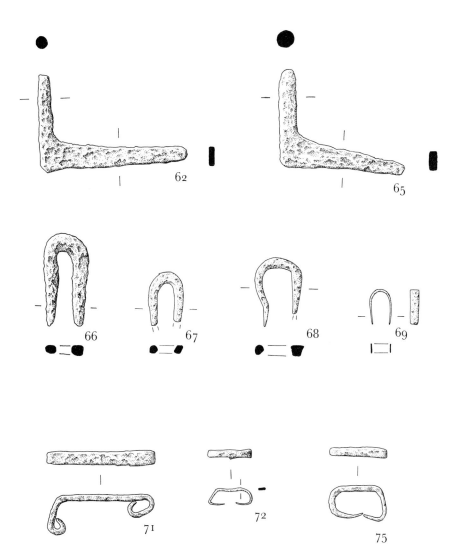

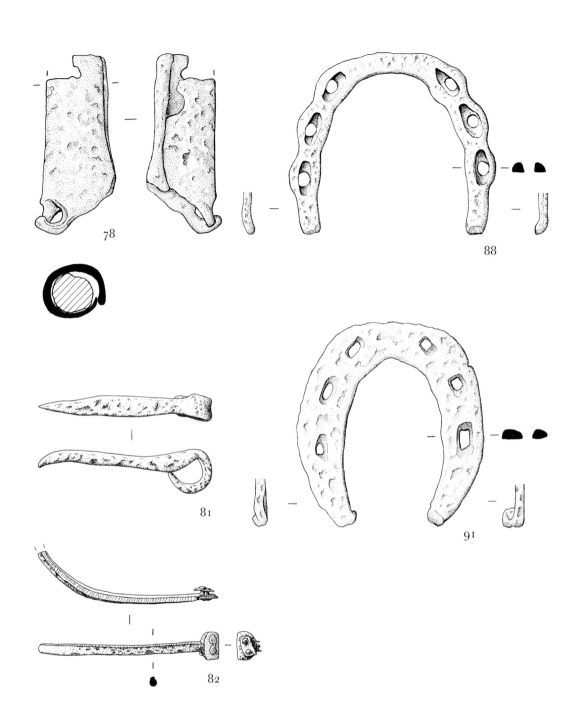

3.22. Miscellaneous ironwork: ferrule, No 78; tin-coated buckle-pin, No 81; spur, No 82; horseshoes, Nos 88 and 91. Scale 1 :2.

Equal-armed brooches

Among the more significant new discoveries of metalwork are two equal-armed 'caterpillar' brooches (Fig 3.23, Nos 94-95). One, which was recovered from the debris of an 11th-century building at Well Court, has eight protruding lobes and is stamped along its bow with a repeating ring-and-dot pattern. The other, decorated with grooved transverse bands, was found in an early 13th-century waterfront revetment at Swan Lane. Both belong to the twilight of this long-lived form of female dress ornament, until recently classified as Merovingian (Hubener 1972). Comparable brooches have been recorded from Domburg, situated at the mouth of the Rhine (Capelle 1976, 10, Taf 2, Nos 7-14 and 16, Taf 8, Nos 100-102), and the Swan Lane brooch is also similar to one from Fishergate, Norwich (Ayers 1988, 9) and another from St Denis, France (Meyer et al 1985, 40, No 8). They add to the increasing number now known from Britain, concentrated in settlements facing across the Channel and North Sea, and extending from Southampton and Old Erringham, near Shoreham, Sussex, in the south, to York in the north and as far inland as Totternhoe, Bedfordshire (Wilson in Addyman and Hill 1969, 71; Evison 1966, 149; Hall 1984, 102, Fig 115). Their distribution raises new questions concerning the style of women's dress in southern and eastern England at a time when brooches were no longer a prominent item of female jewellery (Owen-Crocker 1986, 91), although they were sometimes

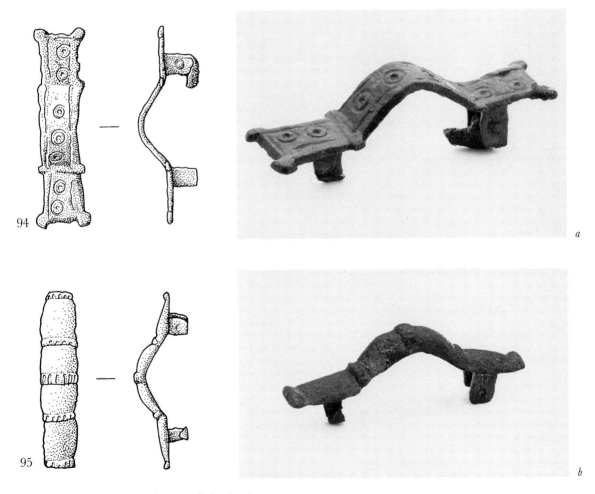

3.23. Equal-armed brooches, Nos 94-95. Scale: drawing, 1:1.

used to secure items other than clothing; one from Emmen in Holland fastened a cloth purse (Evison 1966, 150). The poor standard of craftsmanship exhibited by the two London examples makes it unlikely that these ornaments were trade imports and without further evidence it is not possible to attribute their wear to a particular ethnic minority. Two brooches of this type from York have, nevertheless, been tentatively claimed to provide tangible proof of the 9th-century colony of Frisian merchants in the city (Roesdahl *et al* 1981, 126).

Enamelled disc brooch

David Buckton, British Museum

An enamelled disc brooch, made from brass containing a trace of lead (Bayley 1985), was cast in the form of a 2mm-thick disc 27mm in overall diameter with a 1.5mm rebated flange all round (Fig 3.24, No 96). Six depressions in the obverse define a schematic human bust: hair or halo, face (cheeks and the area between nose and chin), throat, the Y-shaped yoke and front of a garment, and two upper sleeves. The depressions contain the remains of glass which had apparently been fused into place: that in the hair, or halo, cell is a glossy opaque red (Munsell 10R 3/8), and that in the face and throat cells was evidently off-white, while the glass in the three cells representing the clothing has lost all trace of its original colour or colours. On the reverse of the brooch survive a single lug, which acted as a hinge, and the remains of a catch, showing that the pin, now missing, ran horizontal to the bust on the obverse.

Recovered from a late 13th or early 14th-century waterfront rubbish dump at Billingsgate, the brooch had apparently lain buried in strongly reducing conditions, parts of its surface having been stripped and other parts obscured by a crusted deposit (Bayley 1985). The drawing consequently relies heavily on an x-radiograph of the object (Fig 3.24c).

The brooch belongs to a well-known continental group of enamelled artefacts, the so-called *Heiligenfibeln* (saint-brooches). These have been found all over the territory of the present-day Federal Republic of Germany and just outside its borders: findspots range from the Jutland peninsula in the north to the Swiss Alps in the south, and from west of the Rhine to just east of the Iron Curtain. This distribution has been interpreted as consistent with a Carolingian date up to about 900 (Vierck 1984, 405, Abb 193); at the earlier end of the sequence a *Heiligenfibel* has been found in a grave of the second half of the 8th century, at Maschen (Kreis Harburg), near Hamburg (*Sachsen und Angelsachsen*, 1978, No 44, colour Pl N).

Enamelled copper-alloy *Heiligenfibeln* are of two basic types: the first, which includes the example from Maschen, has details rendered in the labour-intensive *cloisonné* technique, while the second type, to which the Billingsgate find belongs, is to all intents and purposes *champlevé* and may well have been mass-produced. (If it is cast, of course, it is not strictly *champlevé*, since the fields for the enamel, the *champs*, have not actually been lifted out, *levés*). Brooches of the first type are either completely *cloisonné*, but with the area between the perimeter of the brooch and the silhouette of the bust filled with molten metal before the details within the silhouette were enamelled (eg a brooch at Darmstadt, West Germany: Rosenberg, 1922, Fig 84), or hybrids in which a single *champlevé* cell defines the outline of the bust, within which the details are in *cloisonné* enamel (eg the brooch from Maschen, and two recently-discovered examples from near Thetford, Norfolk). In practice the totally *cloisonné* brooch can be distinguished from the commoner hybrid by the existence of copper strip round the perimeter of the brooch and the outline of the bust.

The *champlevé* type of *Heiligenfibel* exhibits various degrees of stylization in the representation of the human half-figure. The Billingsgate brooch lies towards the more naturalistic end of the range, and other examples (eg Fig 3.25) support the view that this new find was mass-produced. Examples of a more stylized version have recently been found at Barham and Wetheringsett-cum-Brockford in Suffolk.

A more numerous group of enamelled base-metal disc brooches with cruciform motifs, of Carolingian date and with a similar distribution to *Heiligenfibeln* (Vierck 1984, Abb 193), is better represented by English finds. These *Kreuzemailfibeln* have been found, for example, in East Anglia (Atkin 1978, 134; Goodall 1984, 68, No 7, Fig 109), but unless the present publication is instrumental in prising out of public and private collections further - previously unidentified - examples, the Billingsgate and the Barham, Thetford and Wetheringsett-cum-Brockford finds appear to be the only *Heiligenfibeln* so far recovered from English soil.

Strap-ends

A tongue-shaped strap-end from St Peter's Hill (Fig 3.26, No 97) reveals the high quality of much English metalwork even when working in base metal. Although unstratified and heavily worn, its 'Winchester-style' decoration places it alongside examples from Winchester, Ixworth (Suffolk), Buccombe Down (Isle of Wight), Wilbury Hill (Herts), and York (Backhouse *et al* 1984, 96-7, Nos 81-84; Wilson 1975, 202, Fig 25; Kendrick 1938, Pl LXXIV; MacGregor 1982, 87, Fig 46, No

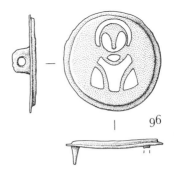

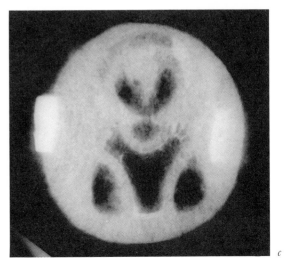

3.24. *Enamelled disc brooch showing the bust of a saint, No 96: a) drawing; b) photograph; c) x-radiograph. Scale: drawing, 1:1.*

3.25. Heilegenfibel *from Mainz (?), Landesmuseum Mainz, N 5856.*

451, Pl IIIa and b). The majority of this group of strap-ends employ openwork patterning, a feature absent on the London example, whereas those carved from bone and ivory are unpierced. A strap-end in the British Museum once considered as possessing a London provenance, although this has now been refuted, is, however, similarly cast in low relief (Wilson 1964, 207, No 148, Pl XLIII). The symmetrical arrangement of the animal and plant ornament, which was designed to be viewed either way up, the little lion

3.26. Copper alloy strap-end, No 97. Scale: drawing, 1 : 1.

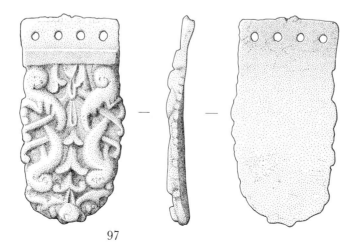

97

3.27. Brass strap-end, No 98. Scale 1:1.

or cat mask and the continuation of the pattern to the edge of the tongue, bear a strong resemblance to a strap-end from Lower Brook Street, Winchester, which has been dated stratigraphically to the first half of the 10th century (Backhouse *et al* 1984, 96, No 82). The ornament on a bone strap-end from Highcross Street, Leicester (Backhouse *et al* 1984, 128-9, No 133), and the copper alloy censer cover from London Bridge (Wilson 1964, 151-2, No 44, Pl XXIV) are also stylistically close and, since they are considered to be late products of a workshop employing this style (Backhouse *et al* 1984, 89), it would be unwise to rule out a date in the second half of the 10th century for the manufacture of the St Peter's Hill strap-end. The degree of surface wear to the strap-end makes it difficult to detect whether any punched decoration was used to delineate details of the four animal bodies or whether there was originally any silver inlay, patches of which remain preserved on the example from Ixworth (Hinton 1974, 23-4, No 17).

The strap-end would probably have been mounted on a leather belt of a single thickness and a reconstruction of an example from a man's grave at Birka in Sweden provides an indication of how it might have been worn (Grave 478, Arbman 1943, 138, Abb 83).

A smaller, rectangular strap-end made from brass was recovered from a waterfront deposit dating to the middle of the 13th century at Swan Lane (Fig 3.27, No 98). Its surface has been adversely affected by the conditions in which it lay buried and, although it appears as though it may have been inlaid, analysis undertaken at the Ancient Monuments Laboratory revealed no trace of any enamel or niello, and the shiny black substance adhering to the front is in fact a sulphide corrosion product (see Duncan and Ganiaris 1987, 109ff). The pattern consists of a contorted animal or animals enclosed within a plain frame but the outline is difficult to distinguish. The style suggests that the piece may be dated within the 9th century but it remains isolated from the mainstream of English ornament, which is epitomised by the decorated objects in the Trewhiddle hoard (Wilson 1964, 24-5).

Strap-distributors

A different form of strap-fitting, a strap-distributor with a three spoked construction, was recovered from a mid-11th century waterfront at New Fresh Wharf (Fig 3.28, No 99). It is incomplete and abraded, with the result that the pattern on the centrepiece cannot be fully distinguished, and, in addition, the edge has been hacked. It is, nevertheless, a rare and important piece, which finds few parallels in Britain, although a second example is known from London. The latter was found 'at a depth of about ten feet in the Temple' in 1878 and was illustrated in the London Museum Medieval Catalogue, where it was attributed to the 16th century (Ward Perkins 1940, 197, Fig 63, No 5; Figs 3.29-3.30). Its identity was, however, recognised by Ingmar Jansson on a visit to London in 1980. The ensemble is exceptionally well preserved and includes a three-spoked distributor in bronze, two bronze articulated clasps each enclosing a leather strap, and a series of tin-coated, bronze double-sided mounts, through which the straps slot. The straps are a single thickness of leather, folded double where the rivets were inserted, and the rivets heads are unusual in having a central groove (visible on the underside of the clasps).

The ornament was designed to match the form of each piece resulting in a varied but harmonious composition. The three spokes of the distributor terminate in tear-shaped lobes with globular insets made in imitation of cabochons. The clasps, patterned only on the upper portion, feature symmetrical acanthus-leaf ornament in low relief enclosed within a plain frame, and stylised animal heads, seen from above with long ears curving back to the edge of the frame, grip the distributor with their mouths; while the mounts are patterned with pointed quatrefoils, which are contained within square fields edged with a billeted border. The decoration, therefore, draws on familiar elements of the English metalworker's repertoire and may be considered to be of insular origin. The streamlined acanthus foliage of the clasps, reminiscent of that on a quatrefoil 'mount' from Southampton (Wilson in Addyman and Hill 1969, 69, Fig 27, No 5), can be assigned stylistically to the late 10th or 11th century. A more detailed study of the strap-distributor is, nevertheless, desirable in order to place it more precisely within the artistic development of the period and to understand its relationship to similar objects on the continent.

Strap-distributors of a three-spoked form have chiefly been recorded from the Baltic region of Scandinavia and, where preserved, all three clasps tend to be of identical form, as for example, from Leikkimäki, Satakunda in Finland (Nordman 1931, 194, Fig 26) and Gotland (Wilson 1964, Pl xd). A further set of three clasps with a small strap-distributor was recovered from the late 9th-century boat-grave at Kiloran Bay, Colonsay (Shetelig 1940, 53, Fig 30). An exception is a strap-distributor from a Viking grave at Cronk Moar on the Isle of Man, where a buckleplate was apparently placed between two clasps (Bersu and Wilson 1966, 74, Fig 43). The Cronk Moar suite was associated with a man's belt but other strap-distributors have been interpreted as items of horse-harness, including that from the Kiloran Bay boatgrave, where a skeleton of a

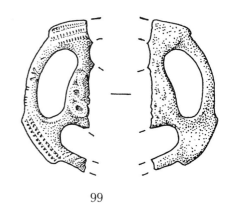

99

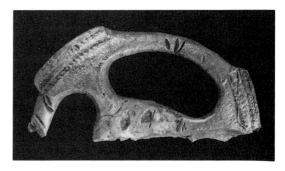

3.28. Copper alloy strap distributor, No 99. Scale: drawing, 1:1.

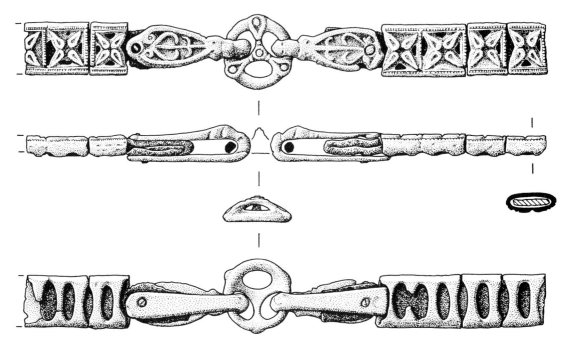

3.29. Bronze strap distributor with leather straps and bronze fittings, MOL A17992. Scale 3:4.

3.30. Bronze strap distributor, MOL A*17992.*

3.31. Hooked tags, No 100 and MOL *3896. Scale 1:1.*

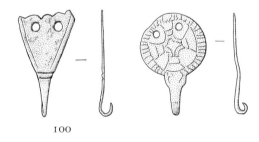

100

horse accompanied the burial, and it is to the latter function that the Temple ensemble probably belongs. The animal head modelled on each clasp may, indeed, have been intended to represent the head of a horse, as can be asserted for other strap-fittings of the period, for example a buckle-plate from Lyveden, Northamptonshire (Cherry 1975, 106, Pl 28). It could be a coincidence that finds from the Temple include both a strap-distributor and a sword of Petersen's type S, the latter embellished with 'Jellinge-style' animal ornament (Read 1887, 530-1; Shetelig 1940, 77-8, Fig 45), and that the only other site in the British Isles with comparative examples is the Viking grave at Cronk Moar (Bersu and Wilson 1966, 72-5). They, nevertheless, reflect the importance of the Temple area of London throughout the period of Viking incursions and Danish sovereignty.

Hooked tags

A hooked tag recovered from a late 12th-century waterfront revetment at Billingsgate (Fig 3.31, No 100) is one of only three made from copper alloy recorded from London. All differ from one another in form, but they find parallels among the growing corpus of material in England (see Graham-Campbell 1982, 146-8). The triangular plate of the Billingsgate tag has a scalloped butt end and a lightly incised border. No sign of wear

is evident round either of the two holes, in contrast, for example, to the strap-end from Swan Lane. Hooked tags of this form were common both in copper alloy, for example from North Elmham (Norfolk), Portchester and Whitby (Goodall 1980, 500, Fig 263, No 11; Hinton and Welch 1976, 207, Fig 137, No 50; Peers and Radford 1943, 60, Fig 12, No 12), and in silver, the latter, not surprisingly being more elaborately decorated. Another hooked tag from Billingsgate, in the ownership of a private collector, is altogether cruder in form and shows no attempt to imitate those fashioned from silver.

The third hooked tag from London entered the collection of the Guildhall Museum in the late

19th century and has no precise findspot (Fig 3.31; GMC 1908, 121, No 84). It has a circular plate decorated with an Anglian cross, a pattern which emphasises the tags' original association with Christianity, for like many other personal ornaments their introduction into England in the 7th century was intertwined with the spread of the 'new' faith. The billeted frame to the cross resembles the decoration on a hooked tag from either Hamwic or Southampton (Wilson 1969, 69-70, Fig 27, No 6) but the plate of the London tag is pierced with two holes rather than having lugs for the purpose. In this respect it is closer to a hooked tag decorated with an Anglian cross excavated in Glastonbury and a pierced disc similarly embellished from Portchester (Hinton and Welch 1976, 217, Fig 139, No 60).

Pins

Only one metal dress-pin has been recovered from recent excavations, a plain form made from a single length of wire, the solid globular head being constructed by twisting the wire in a s-direction and then hammering it smooth (Fig 3.32, No 101). Previous London finds have included ring-headed pins from London Wall (GMC 1908, 121, No 87, Pl LI, No 13), St Helen's Place, Bishopsgate (Wheeler 1927, 45-6, Fig 25), and the Temple (GMC 1908, 121, No 86); various pins with faceted heads and ring-and-dot ornament in the Charles Roach Smith collection (Roach Smith 1859, Pl XXXVI, Nos 18 and 27); and another in the same collection with a lozenge-shaped head finished with three projecting knops (Roach Smith 1859, Pl XXXVI, No 26), which closely resembles two pins from York (Waterman 1959, 78-9, Fig 11, No 15; MacGregor 1978, Fig 28, No 26) and others from Ireland (Armstrong 1922, 85 and Pl XIII, Fig 4 Nos 9–10). In addition, three small silver pins with gilded, spherical heads cast in two halves and decorated with filigree ornament have been recorded from London, which makes it the largest concentration of ball-headed pins in England. One was recovered from beside the Thames at London Bridge (MOL 83.344/1); another, from Chamberlain's Wharf, Thames Street (MOL A2964), was formerly in the Hilton Price collection and is very similar to a pin from Goathurst Common, Kent (Robinson 1981, 157, Fig 3); while a third example, which is now in the British Museum, lacks a precise find spot (Robinson 1981, 157, Fig 2). None of these latter pins has any dating evidence associated with it.

Finger rings

Two finger rings, which were recovered from deposits dating to the first half of the 12th century, were made from a strip of thin sheet metal rolled and hammered to make them more solid, but with the seamline remaining visible on the inside of the hoop (Fig 3.33, Nos 102-103). One has been analysed as brass and the other, visually similar, is probably the same. The penannular form of the finger rings with tapering ends copied Viking

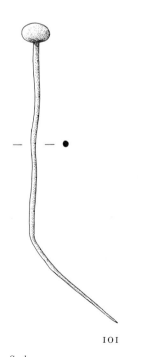

101

3.32. Pin, No 101. Scale 1:1.

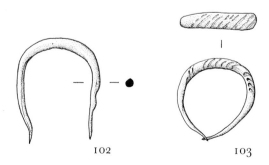

102   103

3.33. Brass finger rings, Nos 102-103. Scale 1:1.

examples made from precious metal, often comprising twisted or plaited rods. A gold ring of penannular form with punched dot decoration was included in a coin hoard hidden in the late 11th century at Soberton, Hampshire (Roesdahl *et al* 1981, 75, E17), suggesting that finger rings of this style were worn in England at least up to the time of the Norman invasion. Plain examples made from silver and copper alloy have been recorded from late Saxon deposits at Norwich (Margeson and Williams 1985, 27, No 1 and 29, No 6) and, on the Continent, Bernold, Bishop of Utrecht (d. 1054) was buried with a gold ring of this form (Aartsbisschopelijk Museum 1972, No 34). The manufacture of finger ring hoops from rolled sheet metal continued beyond the 12th century but with the two ends soldered to a bezel in accordance with a change in popular taste (Egan and Pritchard forthcoming).

Mounts

Fragments of a gilded strip mount (Fig 3.34, Nos 105-106), from a waterfront rubbish deposit at Seal House dating to the first half of the 12th century, are typical of casket fittings of the period and, although such mounts have chiefly been recorded from castle and manor sites (Jope and Threlfall 1959, 267-8; Goodall 1981, 70) indicating that the caskets were owned by people of fairly high social rank, they are also found in towns, for example in Ipswich and Norwich (West 1963, 276-7, Fig 56; Margeson and Williams 1985, 30-1, Fig 26, No 12) as well as in London. Another strip mount, from New Fresh Wharf, is wider and has a flat, round end (Fig 3.34, No 104). There is, however, a possibility that it may be a late Roman piece, since the waterfront deposit from which it was recovered included Roman artefacts among which was a group of offcuts from a bronzesmith's workshop (Chapman 1986, 235).

Two other 'mounts' with stylised animal heads are more unusual and it is, therefore, unfortunate that they appear to be residual coming from late 12th- and early 13th-century deposits. It is uncertain how the ring-mount functioned or for what it was originally made (Fig 3.34, No 107), although it could have been sewn or hinged into place. A similar ring-mount with opposing animal heads was recovered at Jarrow but without any associated dating evidence (Rosemary Cramp pers comm). The pierced mount which has an animal head at one end could represent the end

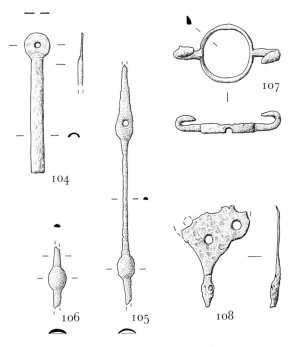

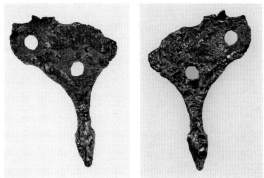

3.34. Mounts: Nos 104-108. Scale: drawings, 1:1.

of a loop or tag to which a plate may have been fixed. Although different from technical and stylistic standpoints, the form of the mount resembles that of an object found at Letchworth in the 1930s, and which, it has been suggested, was a 9th-century book clasp (Westell 1935, 350-1). It can similarly be compared with an 11th-century bronze openwork mount in the form of a coiled ribbon animal with a projecting head, which may have been found in London, and is now in the British Museum (Wilson 1964, 203-4, No 141; Backhouse *et al* 1984, 112, No 109).

Miscellaneous

Among the miscellaneous finds are a number of nails, of which one has a domed head, and which may be Roman (Fig 3.35, Nos 109-111), although evidence from the continent shows that a cauldron in a double grave at Birka had at least nine dome-headed rivets (Arbman 1943, 307, Abb 253.24), and similar rivets were sometimes used to secure the edges of leather sheaths (Menghin 1983, 190, Abb 100). Similarly, the three buckle pins may belong to an earlier epoch (Nos 112-114). A strip of sheet metal with a clip (Fig 3.35, No 115) is a type of find that recurs along the foreshore of the Thames throughout succeeding centuries, although the preservation of the clip *in situ* is unusual (Geoff Egan pers comm). A handle from New Fresh Wharf decorated with a simple pattern of incised lines is, by contrast, anomalous (Fig 3.35, No 116). Lengths of wire, including a coil of very fine wire (No 117), and a flat, hammered strip (No 120) from waterfront rubbish dumps, supplement the slim archaeological evidence for local copper alloy and bronze-working gained from the crucibles (see Chapter 6) and lumps of pitch which were present in pits 7, 25, and 20 at Milk Street and which could have temporarily supported a metal disc or sheeting while it was being decorated.

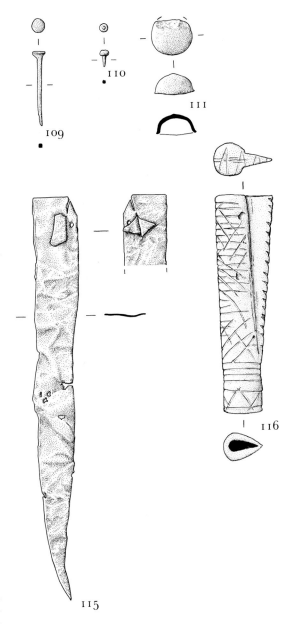

3.35. Miscellaneous artefacts made from copper alloy: nails, Nos 109-111; strip of sheet metal with a clip, No 115. Scale 1:2; handle, No 116, Scale 1:1.

LEAD ALLOY

Buckle

Dress ornaments made from lead alloy became increasingly popular in the late 10th and 11th centuries. The most important group of jewellery in this metal from London is the hoard found on the north side of Cheapside, between Milk Street and Honey Lane, in 1838 (VCH 1909, 160), which consists of unfinished brooches, beads and finger rings simulating forms in precious metals. Isolated examples of lead alloy brooches and beads have subsequently been recovered from various findspots in the City, including Cloak Lane and Cheapside as well as the Thames foreshore and from Billingsgate spoil tips. Despite this distribution and the evidence that at least some were locally made only one 11th-century lead alloy dress ornament has come from DUA excavations, and it is dated stylistically since the deposit in which it lay formed part of the late 14th-century waterfront at Billingsgate.

The ornament is a buckle-loop decorated with two outward facing animal masks positioned on each side at the point where the loop bends back to join the bar, to which the pin would have been attached. From the back of each animal head springs a lobed tendril, which curves towards the centre of the loop (Fig 3.36, No 121). The form of the frame resembles that of an openwork loop cast in copper alloy, which was recovered from a grave at Winchester dating to the first half of the 11th century, although the buckle is considered to be in a late 10th-century style (Backhouse et al 1984, 104, No 97). The animal heads and elongated lobed tendrils of the London buckle are closer to Ringerike-style ornament, and thus an early 11th-century date for the buckle seems plausible. If this interpretation of the Billingsgate buckle is accepted, it forms an important comparative link with the Ringerike-style bronze buckle-loop in the Charles Roach Smith collection in the British Museum (Wilson 1964, No 34, 143–4, Pl xxi), which was almost certainly retrieved from spoil dredged from the bed of the Thames at Old London Bridge.

121

3.36. Lead alloy buckle-loop with Ringerike-style decoration, No 121. Scale 1:1.

STONE ARTEFACTS

The absence of suitable local stone in London limited its use to essential functions such as grinding and sharpening, where other types of material were inappropriate, or to those symbolising status, for example architectural decoration, monumental slabs and crosses. Choice was determined by the availability of supplies and the selection of particular types of stone for specific purposes can be shown very clearly. Recent finds are chiefly items of practical use: hones, querns, lamps and spindlewhorls; artefacts not discussed in Wheeler's studies of London in the Saxon and Viking periods.

The discovery of ornately carved slabs of late Saxon date from the churchyards of St Paul's Cathedral and St Benet Fink in the 19th century and from All Hallows Barking in 1960 have not been repeated in recent investigations and they remain of significance not only for their stylistic qualities but also because they provide evidence for the exploitation of oolitic limestone in London during the late 10th and early 11th century. The identification of two fragments of a gable slab decorated with Ringerike ornament as sandstone or a sarsen (VCH 1909, 168) is no longer upheld (Fuglesang 1980, 190, No 89; Roesdahl et al 1981, 163, No 120) and probably arose from the smooth, flat finish given to the piece, which is characteristic of the Ringerike group of stone carvings. Re-examamination of the slab from All Hallows Barking, which has been described as a reddish brown sandstone (Fuglesang 1980, 188, No 87), showed that it likewise is an oolitic limestone. Professor Jope rightly advised caution in accepting all oolitic limestone as being freshly quarried (Jope 1964, 91) and in London where its popularity in the Roman period is well attested, the likelihood of re-use is very strong. One of the four decorated pieces, a grave slab from the churchyard of St Benet Fink (Fig 3.37), was probably not locally carved and its traditional, English interlace ornament links it to a school operating within East Anglia, particularly around Peterborough and Cambridge (VCH 1909, 170; Fox 1921, 23), which was an area served by a good network of waterways with easy access to stone quarries at Barnack, which is the likely source of the stone. By contrast, there is little doubt that the Ringerike ornament of the other London pieces, was the work of Scandinavian craftsmen based in the City, whose products were commissioned by the ruling elite during the first half of the 11th century (Fuglesang 1978, 212). Fragments of a cross-shaft and inscribed cross-head from All Hallows Barking provide further evidence of stone sculptors working in London during the first half of the 11th century (Kendrick and Radford 1943, 14 and 16; Okasha 1967, 249)

Evidence for local workshops can also be inferred from the presence of imported goods, such as basalt lava querns and hones of Norwe-gian Ragstone, in a semi-finished state, although some pieces could represent ships' ballast. The recent discovery in a pit beside Wood Street of waste from the manufacture of finger rings in shale, probably either from Kimmeridge or Whitby (identified by Robin Sanderson, Institute of Geological Sciences) (Fig 3.38), and dated pro-visionally to the late 11th or early 12th century, adds a further dimension since the shale finger

3.37. Grave slab from the churchyard of St Benet Fink. Scale 1:4.

rings appear to have been made in a workshop that also produced rings of a similar style sawn from the metatarsals of cattle (see p.175).

Hones

Re-use of Roman building stone included foreign marbles, for example a hone, found in a 12th-century pit at Watling Court, was made from a small piece of *cipollino* marble (Figs 3.39 and 3.43, No 147). This is a white and green banded marble quarried only on the island of Euboea off the east coast of Greece. Its popularity plummeted after the collapse of the Roman empire and green porphyry replaced it in Byzantine taste (Lambraki 1980, 57). *Cipollino* was widely used in Roman Britain and it occurs in London in 3rd- and 4th-century deposits (Pritchard 1986, 184, Fig 13). Other exotic stones and marbles, such as *pavonazzetto* from Asia Minor, green porphyry from Sparta, and Imperial porphyry from Egypt, all of which have been recorded from Roman London (*ibid*, Fig 13), occur in 10th and 11th-century deposits in the City, where they usually bear signs of weathering or burning. Thus, although their colourful appearance probably attracted the fascination of the local English populace, there is no firm evidence that they were souvenirs of pilgrimages to Rome as has been suggested more convincingly for pieces of green porphyry recovered from 11th-century deposits in Dublin (Lynn 1984, 21-2 and 24-7), and for which there is support from English literary sources (Dodwell 1982, 35 and 195).

Three of the London hones have been thin-sectioned by David T Moore, Department of Mineralogy, BM(NH) (Nos 132, 135 and 142), while the remainder have been identified visually and with a binocular microscope. Two of the thin-sectioned hones proved to be Blue Phyllite, of which one was recovered from a late 10th-century deposit (Fig 3.42, No 132). The source, or sources, of this stone remains uncertain with a recent survey favouring the Norwegian Caledonides on the basis of isotopic age studies of the stone and the geographic distribution of these hones (Crosby and Mitchell 1987, 502). The other varieties of phyllite found in London (Nos 136-138) were probably also imported from abroad, perhaps from the same region in Norway, together with Norwegian Ragstone, since it has often been observed that hones made from Blue Phyllite and Norwegian Ragstone have a very similar pattern of distribution.

The earliest dated hone of Norwegian Ragstone from London was recovered from a 10th-century pit at Watling Court (Fig 3.39-3.40, No 122), but it was not until after the Norman Conquest that such hones began to dominate the London market, a pattern which continued until the 14th century. Both the 10th-century Norwegian Ragstone hone from Watling Court and a grey schist hone from a 10th-century deposit at Milk Street (Fig 3.41, No 129) have a smooth oval profile, in contrast to the rectangular cross-sections of most of the other hones, suggesting that the earlier hones were water-worn pebbles rather than cleaved from freshly quarried blocks. A large block of a pale coloured phyllite from another pit at Watling Court (Fig 3.42, No 138), however, points to the import by the late 11th century of unfinished stone into London for manufacture into hones, a practice that was widespread throughout North Sea coastlands.

An aspect of the hones used in London during the 10th to early 12th centuries, which should not be underestimated, is the variety of types of stone that were used in contrast with certain other towns in eastern England, such as Thetford and Lincoln, where hones of Norwegian Ragstone and Blue Phyllite form a larger proportion of the hone assemblages (Moore and Ellis 1984, 107; Mann 1982, 27). Although it is not possible to determine the sources of many of the stones used for hones in London, at least one (Fig 3.43, No 142) appears to have come from the Isle of Purbeck in Dorset or perhaps from a source further south west, thus providing slight corroborative evidence for a trading link between London and the Dorset coast suggested by the occurrence of shale waste from the production of finger rings.

There was apparently no preference as to what type of hone-stone was pierced but the wear on small perforated hones indicates that blades sharpened on them were held flat as they passed across the stone thus causing the hone to become thinner in the course of time (eg Figs 3.39 and 3.41, No 130). By contrast, V-sectioned grooves are confined to larger, unpierced hones showing that care was paid to personal safety when carrying out sharpening.

3.38. Waste associated with the production of shale finger rings.

3.39. Pierced hones made from a variety of different types of stone: Norwegian Ragstone, No 122; schist, Nos 130-131; *Blue Phyllite, No 135; calcareous siltstone/mudstone, No 140; Cipollino marble, No 147.*

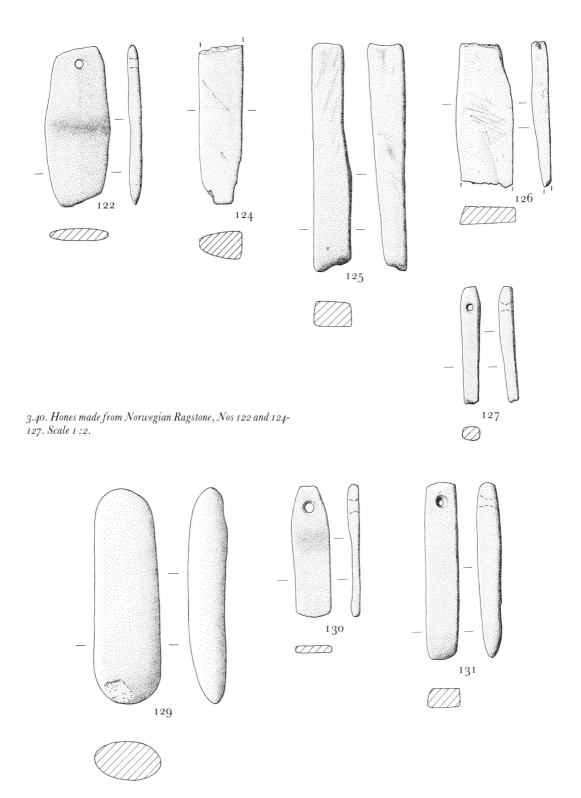

3.40. Hones made from Norwegian Ragstone, Nos 122 and 124-127. Scale 1:2.

3.41. Hones made from other types of schist, Nos 129-131. Scale 1:2.

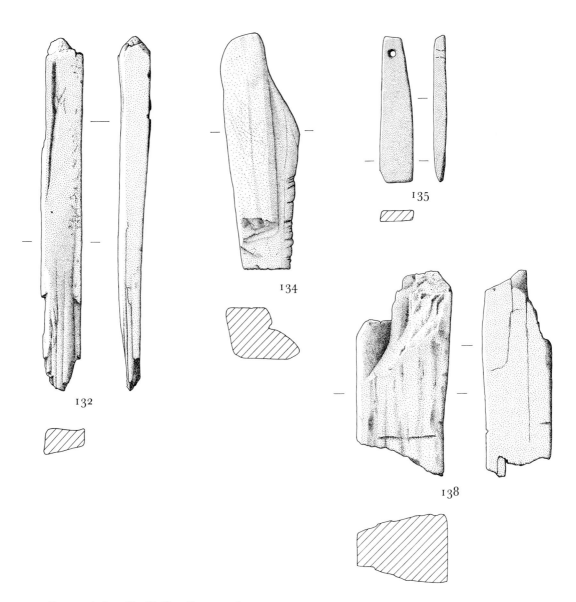

3.42. Hones made from Blue Phyllite, Nos 132 and 134-135;
and another type of phyllite, No 138. Scale 1:2.

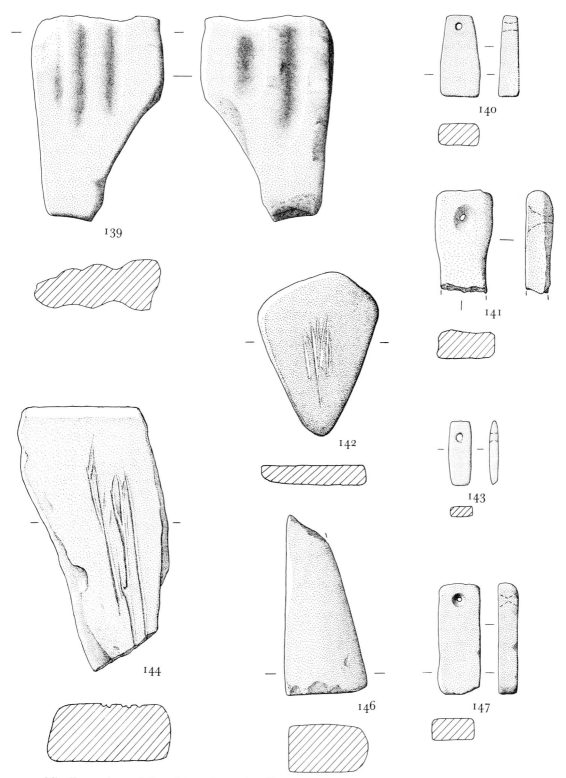

140

139

141

142

143

144

146

147

3.43. Miscellaneous hones of the 10th to 12th centuries, Nos 139-144 and 146-147. Scale 1:2.

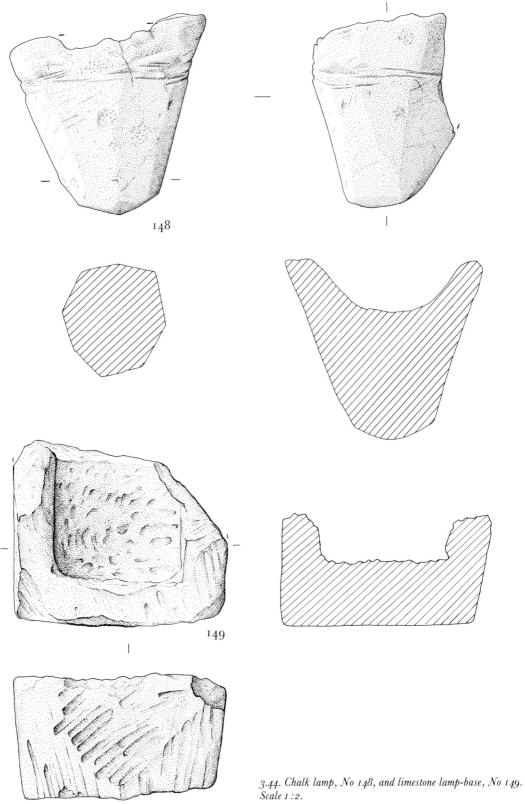

148

149

3.44. *Chalk lamp, No 148, and limestone lamp-base, No 149.*
Scale 1 : 2.

Lamps

The lamp and lamp-base add to the variety of lighting utensils recorded from 11th- and 12th-century London. The faceted chalk lamp appears to have been suspended or lashed to a post rather than being placed in a stable container (Fig 3.44, No 148), and in this respect it may be compared to one from Gwithian in Cornwall dated between the 7th and 10th centuries, which has a series of grooves below its rim (Adams 1967, 51 and 55, Fig 13, No 3). The top-heavy character of many stone lamps led to the production of solid block bases (Knight 1972, 132) and it is into this category that the limestone lamp base from Building 6 at Milk Street falls (Fig 3.44, No 149).

Mortar

A different type of fine-grained limestone was used for a mortar (Fig 3.45, No 150), which appears to match stone quarried near Caen. The pit fill from which the mortar handle was recovered is dated by the associated pottery to the middle of the 11th century, thus hinting, albeit tentatively, at pre-Conquest trade in the stone into London. The handled form of the mortar (Dunning Type 1) has a wide distribution in southern and eastern England (Dunning 1977, 332, Fig 152), and the early date of this example bears out Dunning's suggestion that mortars with pierced handles preceded the development of those with solid handles within the medieval period (*ibid*, 321).

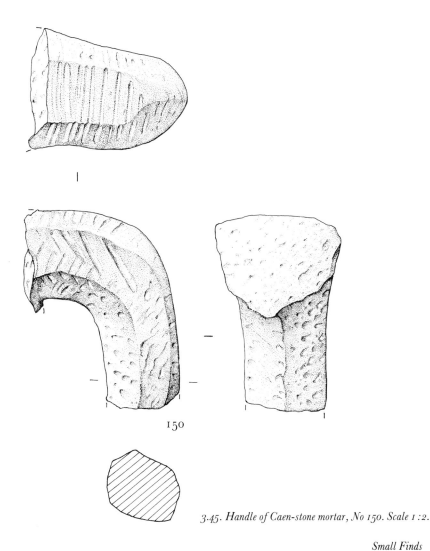

150

3.45. Handle of Caen-stone mortar, No 150. Scale 1 :2.

Rotary querns

The querns from London dating from the 10th to mid-12th centuries are without exception fashioned from imported basalt lava, the traditional stone supplied to the City for grinding in both the Roman and medieval periods. Consequently, it is not possible with many of the smaller fragments to be certain to which period they belong. Where diagnostic features remain, such as tooling and thickness, it appears that all pieces are from upper stones, a pattern also observed at Cheddar (Rahtz 1979, 234). The range in size was evidently considerable; one example is estimated to have had a diameter of 1.5m (No 152), while the smallest was approximately 390mm in diameter (No 155). A quernstone, which was recovered from an 11th-century building at Well Court, has a flanged central hopper (Fig 3.46, No 153), which is very similar to one that was found in a late 11th-century well at Billingsgate Buildings, London (Rhodes 1980b, 144-5, No 743). Two unfinished quernstones were used in the foundations of Building 3 at Pudding Lane (Fig 3.47-3.48, Nos 155-156), indicating that not all quernstones were imported for the ostensible purpose of grinding cereals, and the likelihood is that these two stones arrived in London as ship's ballast.

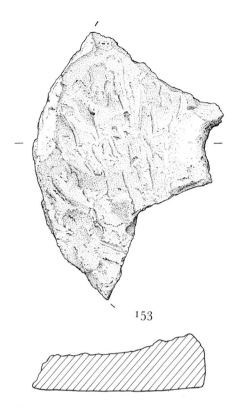

153

3.46. Part of an upper-stone from a rotary quern with a hopper made from basalt lava, No 153; Scale 1:4.

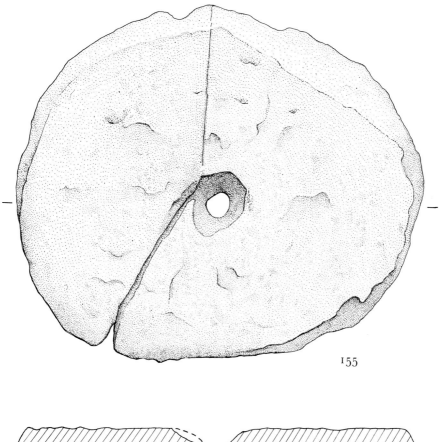

155

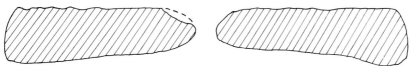

3.47. Unfinished basalt lava quernstone, No 155. Scale 1 : 4.

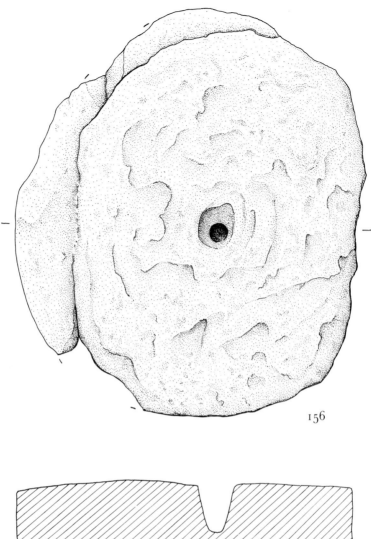

156

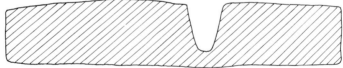

3.48. Unfinished basalt lava quernstone, No 156. Scale 1 :4.

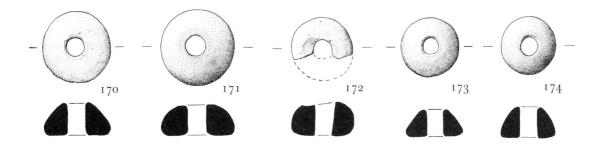

3.49. *Stone, lathe-turned spindlewhorls of the 10th to early 12th centuries, Nos 170-174. Scale 1:2.*

Spindlewhorls

Consistency in the type of stone is similarly a feature of spindlewhorls found in London for they were all made on a lathe from a hard, fine-grained calcite mudstone (Fig 3.49, Nos 170-174). Although the source of the stone has not been narrowed down to a particular place, other examples of spindlewhorls in the same type of limestone have been recorded as far apart as Gloucester (Heighway 1979, 201), Hereford (Vince 1985c, 14) and Thetford (Rogerson and Dallas 1984, 111-2, Fig 148, No 4). Their production may thus have formed part of a specialised, small-scale industry with a good distribution network, for there is no stone-working debris of this kind in London from which to infer local manufacture.

The use of a lathe meant that the size of each spindlewhorl could be regulated fairly easily. Accordingly, the diameter of the hole, where the spindle would have been inserted, varies very little between the five whorls, whereas the weight range is greater, presumably to allow different grades of yarn to be spun.

CERAMIC ARTEFACTS (other than purpose-made vessels)

Mould

The enormous quantity and durability of Roman tile, which remained in Saxon London, led to its reuse in a variety of ways. Perhaps the most unusual was to adapt a broken tile into an 'open' mould by hollowing out a T-shaped depression into which molten metal could be poured (Fig 3.50, No 175). Scientific analysis was not able to determine how many times the mould was used or with what metal it was associated but the shape of the matrix suggests that dress ornaments, particularly pendants, in the form of Thor's hammer could have been worked up from the cast blanks.

Part of a Roman tile from an Anglo-Scandinavian level at Coppergate, York, was similarly used as a mould (Hall 1984, 56, Fig 55), and at Haithabu, Schleswig-Holstein, an imported stamped tile of the *Legio I Minervia* had an ingot mould cut into its sanded underface (Ruger 1970, 74, Abb 1). Other materials were sometimes recycled as moulds in the Viking empire; thus broken soapstone artefacts were often adapted locally into moulds in Dublin (Wallace 1987, 218) and, indeed, a double-sided soapstone mould found among 10th-century material from High Street, Dublin, included a matrix for casting Thor's ham-

3.50. Part of a Roman tile re-used as a mould, No 175. Scale: drawing, 1:2.

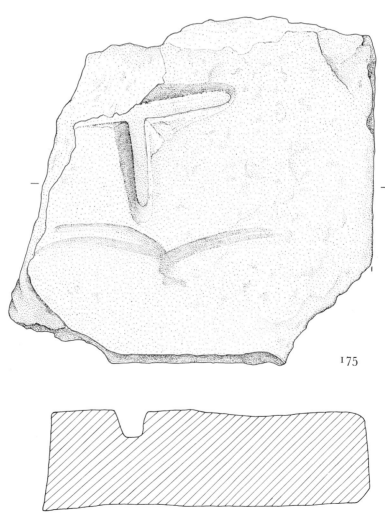

175

mer symbols (O'Riordain 1971, 79, Fig 21d; NMI 1973, 30, No 51a). It has also been suggested that a stone mould from Whitby Abbey with a т-shaped matrix, which is very similar to the example from London, is Viking (Wilson 1976, 395; Graham-Campbell 1980, 8, No 2). The late 11th-century date of the pit fill into which the London mould had been thrown after breakage accords with the use of the mould in the town during the period of Danish supremacy.

Loomweights

Loomweights appear to have had a wider distribution throughout the City than any other artefact associated with a manufacturing process, although few have been recorded from recent excavations. Unlike many other types of find, these weights have not been recovered from late medieval revetment dumps beside the Thames. Consequently, their distribution is probably a fairly accurate reflection of where warp-weighted looms were at times erected, although, in contrast, for example, to the site of the Adelphi in the Strand in London and another at Back Street, Winchester, where over 100 weights and 23 weights repectively were found (British Museum Accessions Register; Hedges 1978, 33), none apparently marked the spot where a loom col-

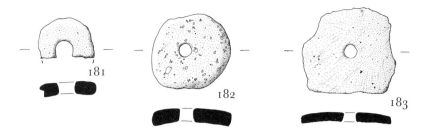

3.51. Spindlewhorls of the 11th and 12th centuries made from re-used pot sherds, Nos 181-183. Scale 1 :2.

lapsed. There is, unfortunately, little dating evidence associated with the loomweights from the City to assist in establishing how long the warp-weighted loom continued in use in medieval London (Pritchard 1984, 66). One fragment from behind the skull of a teenage boy in a grave dating to the late 11th or early 12th century in the cemetery at St Nicholas Shambles (No 177; Pritchard 1984, 65, Fig 17, No 7; White 1988, 64), however, implies that it was discarded sometime earlier.

Spindlewhorls

Three spindlewhorls, each made from a pot sherd of a different ceramic fabric common in London in the 11th and 12th centuries, complement those made from bone and stone both in weight and in the size of hole made to fit the spindle (Fig 3.51, Nos 181-183).

DYEPOTS

During pottery analysis, a number of sherds were identified as having a pinkish-red residue (Munsell 2.5R, value 3 to 5, chroma 2 and 4) adhering to the inside surface. Twenty-three sherds were, consequently, sent to George Taylor, dye consultant, who concluded that the sherds were, with two exceptions, stained with the dyestuff madder (see p.170). Further sherds with a visually similar residue were subsequently found among the DUA collections of pottery dating from the 10th to 12th centuries, which indicated that the vessels con-

taining madder were distributed throughout the City rather than being concentrated solely in a few localities.

The range of sherds show that there was no predilection for a particular ceramic ware or size of vessel, although all were unthrown forms of cooking pot made in southern England in common use in London (Fig 3.52). A contemporary sherd of a Thetford ware (?) bowl, recovered from excavations in Thetford, was similarly found to retain traces of madder (Rogerson and Dallas 1984, 167). The variety of fabric types makes it unlikely that madder, reduced to its powdered state, was being traded commercially in the pots. Furthermore, a heap of partly used madder roots recovered from Anglo-Scandinavian levels at Coppergate, York (Hall *et al* 1984, 58-9) reveals that processing of the raw material did take place in urban centres.

To prepare madder for use, the roots which contain the dye need to be dried. They may then be chopped up and steeped in warm water, but, to maximise the crop and to obtain the best results, the roots should be ground or pounded into a powder (Grierson 1986, 194-5). Madder roots are still ground with a rotary quern in a few villages in Turkey (Thompson 1986, 16), but, according to Theophilus, mortars were used for the purpose in 12th-century Germany (Hawthorne and Smith 1979, 188). Finally, the powder is added to water and heated slowly for over an hour in order to release the main colouring agent, alizarin, after which the dyebath is ready. Therefore, since dyeing is not a quick process and the dye liquid has to be heated, the reason why the sherds are permanently stained and the choice of cooking pots as the vessel for the dyebath becomes clearer. The lack of standard-sized containers reflects the domestic scale of the activity, since to own a large metal cauldron is likely to have been beyond the resources of most local inhabitants, nor was it an essential utensil.

Cloth, for which madder was the most popular red dyestuff in Saxon England, was not usually dyed in the piece before the late 12th or 13th century, when growing industrialisation and the increased division of labour led, in London, to dyeing establishments becoming concentrated in premises close to the Thames. Instead, wool was either dyed as fleece or in the skein, which meant that a small dyebath was practical. Garments, furnishings and trimmings could thus be woven with or without colour effects, such as stripes and checks, as seen on contemporary textiles from London (Pritchard 1984, 58).

Madder, however, was not limited to the dyeing of fibres; it could be used to colour leather and, as Theophilus described, for staining ivory and antler (Hawthorne and Smith 1979, 189). A tau-cross crozier, now in the British Museum, carved from madder-stained walrus ivory in an English workshop during the first half of the 12th century confirms that this method was adopted in England as well as on the continent (Lasko 1984, 219, No 194), but the practice was unlikely to have been as widespread domestically as the number of dyepots from London might imply. It seems reasonable, therefore, to assume that the pots were mainly used for dyeing fleece or yarn, while the apparent absence of madder-stained sherds from late medieval deposits would also be consistent with changes in dyeing cloth as described above.

Dyepots - method of analysis

George Taylor

All sherds were tested by 'basting' with hot IMS/ acid. The coloured extracts were then treated in the usual way: IMS evaporated off and the aqueous residue extracted with ether. The sherds were rinsed under the tap and allowed to dry. (No pieces were broken off for testing). The ether extract was divided into two parts, for paper chromatography (IMS/water, 1/1 by volume, develop by painting with methanolic potassium hydroxide solution), and for spectroscopy. For the latter, the ether was evaporated, and the residue taken up in sufficient methanol to fill a microcell. In most cases, magne-

Site	Context	Acc. No.	Ceramic phase	Ceramic fabric	Tested for madder
MIL72	161/12A	325	CP4	EMFL	Positive
MIL72	161/12C		CP4	?	Negative
MLK76	1019	1692	CP2	EMS	—
MLK76	1210	1691	CP2	EMS	—
MLK76	1210	1689	CP2	LSS	—
MLK76	1211	1690	CP2	EMS	—
MLK76	1061	1697	CP4	LSS	—
MLK76	1092	1693	CP4	EMS	—
MLK76	1092	1694	CP4	LSS	—
MLK76	2224	1699	CP4	EMSS	—
MLK76	2226	1696	CP4	EMFL	—
MLK76	3104	1700	CP4	EMFL	—
MLK76	3111	1688	CP4	LSS	—
MLK76	2014	1701	CP4/6	SHEL	—
MLK76	1056	1698	CP5/6	EMS	—
WAT78	502	1130	CP4	EMSS	Positive
WAT78	663	1131	CP4	EMCH	Positive
WAT78	692	1128	CP4	EMCH	Positive
WAT78	824	133	CP4	EMCH	Positive
WAT78	3891	1134	CP5	LSS	Positive
PEN79	1632	523	CP2	EMS	Negative
PEN79	1013	524	CP5/6	EMS	Positive
PDN81	1977	2054	CP1	LSS	Positive
PDN81	2008	2053	CP1	LSS	Positive
PDN81	2041	2048	CP1	LSS	Positive
PDN81	427	2050	CP2	LSS	Positive
PDN81	428		CP5	EMS	Positive
PDN81	407	2051	CP3	EMFL	Positive
PDN81	407		CP3	EMFL	Positive
PDN81	407	2054	CP3	LSS	Positive
PDN81	1470	2049	CP3	EMFL	Positive
PET81	1756	1158	CP1	LSS	Positive
PET81	355	1159	—	EMS	Positive
PET81	488	1160	PMED?	EMSS	Positive
GDH85	409	63	—	LSS	Positive
ABS86	108	932	—	LSS	—
ABS86	311	937	—	EMS	—
ABS86	438	938	—	EMS	—
ABS86	450		CP4	LSS	—
ABS86	522	933	—	LSS	—
ABS86	665	934	CP2	EMS	—
ABS86	777	935	—	LSS	—
ABS86	777	939	—	EMCH	—

3.52 Table of 10th-to 12th-century dyepots fom eight sites in London

sium acetate crystals were added before spectroscopy to enhance test sensitivity.

All the sherds, with the exception of MIL 72 [161/12C] and PEN 79 [1632] <523>, seemed to be stained with alizarin, which is a major component of the colorant in madder. Purpurin, another major colorant, was only occasionally seen, and only when the sensitivity of detecting it was enhanced by the presence of a relatively large amount of dye extracted from the sherd. However, the proportions of the minor components, such as xanthopurpurin and munjistin, appeared to be 'normal' for a madder dyeing.

The sherds, therefore, appeared to have been exposed to a dye of the madder type, either madder itself or a close relative. To further identify the dye, one of the sherds showing no dye MIL 72 [121/12C] was refluxed in a dyebath containing modern madder root (*Rubia tinctorum* L. ex Colorcraft) for one hour and then allowed to stand in the cold bath for one week. The sherd, which appeared to be stained purple, was removed from the bath and rinsed thoroughly with cold water, with a final rinse in warm water. The dried sherd was then basted with hot IMS/acid in the usual way. The extracted colorant was identical with that from the sherds previously shown to have been stained with the dye, that is, essentially alizarin (spectroscopy and chromatography).

To check whether the high proportion of alizarin in the extracted colorant from the sherds was not simply produced by the 'basting' technique, a sherd MIL 72 [161/12A] was refluxed with IMS/acid in the standard way used for textile samples. The analytical results were identical with those obtained using the 'basting' technique.

The conclusion is that the sherds had indeed been exposed to a madder dyebath and had selectively soaked up alizarin, possibly because of some chemical peculiarity of the pottery fabric. The behaviour of the fabric (presumably rich in alumina-like material) is, of course, analogous with the action of alum mordant in textile dyeing.

OYSTER-SHELL PALETTES

Two oyster-shells containing traces of a bright red pigment were recovered from two pits situated on the western side of the City (Fig 3.53). One came from the fill of a pit dating to the first half of the 12th century (No 184) and the other from a fill dating to a few decades later (No 185). Optical microscopy and micro-chemical tests carried out on small samples of each pigment by Helen Ganiaris indicated it was probably vermilion (red mercuric sulphide), and this identification is supported by the brilliant pillar-box red of the ground pigment (Munsell 7.5R 5/12).

The 12th century saw a rise in the use of vermilion as knowledge of how it was manufactured spread (Thompson 1956, 105), but it remained expensive and, therefore, the lavishness of its application depended upon the wealth of the patron. This is apparent from church wall-paintings of the early 12th century where, for example, vermilion was only sparingly used for the series of wall-paintings in St Botolph's church, Hardham, Sussex, whereas it formed a larger part of the colour scheme for the wall-paintings in the apse in St Gabriel's chapel, Canterbury Cathedral, which were probably commissioned by Prior Ernulf, *c*.1130-1140 (Tristram 1944, 82 and 104). A preference for strong, vibrant colours, especially royal blue, bright red and green, also came to the fore in English manuscript illumination during the 12th century, influenced by the style of Master Hugo in the Bury bible, *c*.1135 (Alexander and Kauffmann 1984, 108, No 44), and the increased colour intensity of the palette has been attributed to the wider availability of vermilion (Thompson 1956, 107).

Shell palettes had a long tradition of use (Gettens and Stout 1966, 310), and, as oysters were a popular delicacy in London throughout the medieval period, empty oyster shells would have been easily obtained. Other examples of shell palettes from medieval England include a pecten shell containing azurite from Clarendon Palace, Wiltshire (Hughes and Lewis 1988) and an oyster shell, with gold and red and blue pigments, reputedly associated with a 14th-century tombchest in Boyton Parish church, Wiltshire (Alexander and Binski 1987, 391, No 440). Since little is known about 12th-century painting in London, the recovery of the two palettes containing ground vermilion from among domestic rubbish adds a significant new dimension to our knowledge of the subject.

3.53. Oyster-shell palettes containing traces of ground vermilion pigment, Nos 184-185.

Most glass found in Saxon and Norman levels in London derives from the Roman occupation. It is generally both fragmentary and abraded, with nothing to suggest that the sherds were the redeposited souvenirs of Scandinavian settlers, comparable to pieces recovered from contemporary deposits in Dublin, or used as cullet for the manufacture of beads. The absence of glass dating to the 5th- to 9th-centuries from the City reinforces the impression of a low population density within the old Roman town, particularly as other settlements within south-east England, including the nearby abbey at Barking and the Jubilee Hall site, Covent Garden, have yielded a variety of Carolingian glass. An anomaly from the City, a cup in greenish coloured glass (MOL 5492 M.VIII.147), reputed to have been found in Lime Street and claimed as a 5th- or 6th-century import from the Rhineland, is now not considered to be an authentic Saxon piece.

Tenth- to early 12th-century glass recovered from recent City excavations was analysed qualitatively by x-ray fluorescence at the Ancient Monuments Laboratory with the exception of some window glass (Nos 192 and 194-197). A finger ring from the Poultry, acquired by the London Museum in 1925, was similarly analysed (Vince and Bayley 1983, 93) but the remaining pieces from the collection of the former London Museum and the British Museum are identified as soda-rich alkali glass on the basis of visual appearance rather than scientific evidence. The distinction between soda and potash glass among the analysed pieces also rests upon appearance, especially the way the pieces have weathered, as the analyses were of weathered surfaces which have very different alkali contents to those of the glass when made.

Even adopting a cautious approach to the identification of the glass and despite the very limited amount preserved, the London material is notable for its range, since soda, lead and potash glass all appear to be represented, thus providing a contrast with mid-Saxon towns such as Hamwic where neither lead or potash glass have been recorded (Hunter 1980). The pieces also illustrate the different uses to which these types of glass were put, soda glass being associated with imported tableware, lead glass with English-made trinkets, and potash glass with items of utilitarian character.

No further pieces of soda-rich glass that could have been used in London in the 10th or 11th century have been recovered since those already described in print by Donald Harden. These consist of the bases of three wine-coloured phials with opaque-white marvered trails from the Bank of England site excavations in 1928-34 and Holborn Viaduct in 1866, together with part of the body and base of a similarly coloured, vertical ribbed flask or narrow mouthed bowl from the Roach Smith collection, and a complete, pale green globular flask from 34, Great Tower Street (Harden 1970, 9-10; Harden 1956, 155-6). All are considered to be Islamic although some doubt remains as to the antiquity of the phials, which scientific analysis could perhaps resolve. The globular flask lacks any surface decoration by which to attribute it to a particular country or production centre but the ribbed bowl decorated with horizontal opaque white trails, which change to pale green threads towards the rim, is typical of Fatimid Egypt (969-1171) and closely resembles a complete example in the Ashmolean Museum (Pinder-Wilson 1976, 146, No 144). An example of a beaker or jar in a similar fabric but with white dashes on a green ground was recovered from a pit at Porchester, considered to be of mid-Saxon date (Harden 1976, 232-4, Fig 145, No 9). However, since the manufacture of such vessels continued into the Ayyubid period (1171-1250) a date before the 11th century cannot be established for the bowl found in London.

Difficulty in obtaining supplies of suitable marine plant ash led to experiments with other types of alkaline flux in 10th-century Europe (Charleston 1984, 18). Lead oxide was used as a flux for small items, such as beads, bangles and finger rings, where low working temperatures were an advantage and no special furnace, or glass-blowing skills were required. Debris from Gloucester, Lincoln and York indicates that production was located in a number of urban centres in different parts of the country (Bayley 1979, 201-2; Bayley 1982, 493-5; Colyer and Jones 1979, 60; MacGregor 1978, 42; Bayley in Tweddle 1986, 226-7). The only example of lead glass identified from London is a plain finger ring found at the Poultry (Vince and Bayley 1983, 93). It has a yellow hue, rather than the attractive dark green for which copper was added as a colorant, recorded from York and Lincoln (Roesdahl et al 1981, 138). It is probable that the glass settings preserved in three of the six types of brooches, included in the 11th-century Cheapside hoard, are composed of lead glass but this remains to be confirmed. Similarly, glass inlays in late Anglo-Saxon walrus ivory carvings, for example a 'pen-case' found in London and dated to the middle or late 11th century (Backhouse *et al* 1984, 127-8, No 132) and a small plaque recovered from a late 10th-century deposit in Dublin (Backhouse *et al* 1984, 126, No 130) appear to be lead glass. It may be that the increased use of lead-alloy jewellery in the 10th century played an influential role in this flirtation with lead glass, which continued in England into the 12th century, and perhaps a little longer (Henderson 1986, 226). High-lead glass was not, however, a purely English phenomenon. Theophilus recommended its use for finger rings in his treatise on glassmaking (Hawthorne and Smith 1979, 73-4), and analyses of medieval glass from East European countries have led to its identification from sites in Poland and Russia, where it apparently continued in production from the 9th to 13th centuries (Besborodov 1957, 168; Henderson 1986, 224; Thompson 1967, Fig 91).

Textile implements

Potash glass was used as an alternative to soda glass particularly for items that were created by blowing. It predominates among recent discoveries from London, which comprise four calenders, or linen smoothers, part of a spindlewhorl, fragments of a vessel and window glass. Calenders required little technical skill to make since they are composed of merely a single 'gather' of glass (Fig 3.54, Nos 186-189). Their function was to impart a gloss or lustre in the finishing of cloth, primarily linen but fine worsteds also responded to the same treatment. This was accomplished by warming the glass hemisphere and then vigorously sliding it over the cloth. Such smoothers made from glass rather than stone were introduced into Britain no later than the 3rd century AD (Wild 1970, 84-5), but no Roman example has yet been subjected to analysis in order to determine whether the composition of the glass was different from those of the medieval period. It is possible that their renewed popularity in the Viking period was initially associated with a particular type of material or fashion in dress, for example fine worsted lozenge twills or pleated linen, but their long term success as a domestic tool is demonstrated by their use throughout succeeding centuries, for it was not until the 17th century that were they superseded by hot metal plates and heavy wooden rollers in England, while they continued to be produced in glass factories in Norway until the late 19th century (Noss 1976, 6).

The biconical shape of the spindlewhorl, made by winding molten glass round a rod or stick (Fig 3.55, No 190), distinguishes it from those made from bone and stone recovered from 10th to 12th-century deposits in London, which are conical. The form was not, however, a new departure since biconical whorls in stone were common elsewhere in England, and even occasionally in bone as demonstrated by an example from a pit at Harrold, Bedfordshire (Evison 1970, 45, Fig 14). Glass was also not a new medium for spindlewhorls; a few examples in greenish-blue glass have been excavated from Roman deposits in London, where there is evidence for their local manufacture (John Shepherd pers comm), while in the 6th and 7th centuries large glass beads often decorated with marvered trails, found in association with textile implements in women's graves, have been interpreted as whorls, although it is acknowledged that they could equally have served a variety of other functions (Evison 1955, 171). It is of particular interest that the spindlewhorl from Watling Court was made from potash glass rather than lead glass, suggesting that its manufacture was not closely associated with bead-making.

Vessel and window glass

Forest glass (ie potash glass) vessels dating to *c.*10th century are increasingly being recognised from urban sites, for example at Thetford, Northampton and Winchester (Harden 1984, 116; Oakley and Hunter 1979, 298; Hunter 1990), but because of the non-durable nature of the glass only small sherds are usually preserved and the range of vessel forms awaits a full assessment. The base of a vessel, perhaps a small jar (No 191), from a pit fill dating to the late 11th century is a typical, severely weathered sherd, whose precise character is more likely to be determined by future discoveries. The fragments of window glass from the cellar of a late 11th-century building and three nearby pits at Watling Court are similarly heavily weathered (Nos 192-197). Their importance rests on the fact that they appear to have come from secular rather than ecclesiastical establishments and that they are the earliest fragments of medieval window glass preserved from the City.

3.54. *Potash glass calenders, Nos 186-188. Scale: drawings,
1:2.*

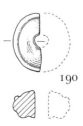

190

3.55. *Potash glass spindlewhorl, No 190. Scale 1:2.*

Mammal bone and ivory were used as the raw material for a wide variety of artefacts in Saxon and Norman London, as in the Roman town. Antler and horn, by contrast, were used mainly for combs, although this does not exclude the possibility that some knives, for example, could have had horn handles which have decayed in the soil; and a similar fate could have befallen other items made from horn such as dress pins and spoons.

Evidence for the working of these materials in the City is limited but a comprehensive survey of offcuts and waste has not proved possible since most of the material is stored with unworked bone, which has yet to be examined. It has, however, been noted that sawn tines from red deer antler occur on a number of sites, whereas sawn beams and burrs are more scarce since they could be shaped into a variety of products leaving very little waste behind. Despite the apparent lack of material evidence for antler-working in London, there are some hints that activities such as comb-making were pursued in the town. For example, a small unfinished broken plaque, 35mm wide and 2-3mm thick, which was presumably intended for the tooth-plate of a comb or perhaps a square weaving-tablet was recovered from a late 11th-century waterfront deposit. While most antler used for artefacts was naturally shed and gathered from the annual moult, a red deer antler from an 11th-century context by the London waterfront retains part of the skull showing that the deer had been killed, probably for its meat. Consequently, this antler escaped being utilised for artefacts.

Bone waste from London, likewise, appears rarely to consist of more than one or two offcuts per site. An exception is a group of cattle metatarsals from a late 11th or early 12th-century pit at St Alban's House, Wood Street, which is associated with the manufacture of undecorated finger rings made from shale as well as from bone. The discarded bones illustrate each stage of making the finger rings (Fig 3.56), and the presence of such a comprehensive range of offcuts and waste suggests that a workshop (even if only a temporary one) was situated in the locality. There is no indication that the craftworker diversified his output by producing other artefacts, and it appears that the workshop specialised in a single commodity. The shaft of a horse metatarsal sawn with a series of circular markings was also found in a 10th-century pit at Watling Court but the method of sawing the bone was not the same as that employed for the finger rings made from cattle metatarsals and it is uncertain for what product the horse bone was being used.

The evidence for ivory-working is tenuous and consists of a single wedge-shaped piece (probably sawn from an elephant's tusk) recovered from the early 12th-century waterfront at Seal House. The deposit contained Roman material as well as medieval and, therefore, the ivory waste is not securely dated.

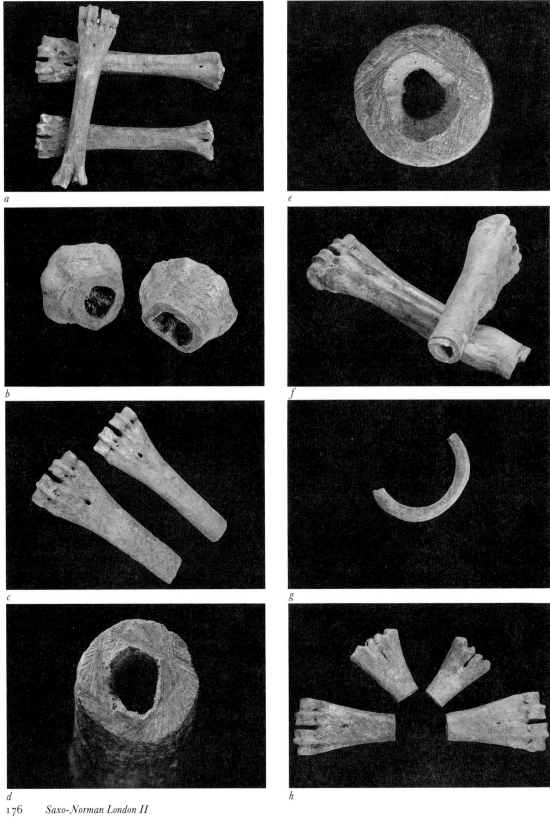

a

e

b

f

c

g

d

h

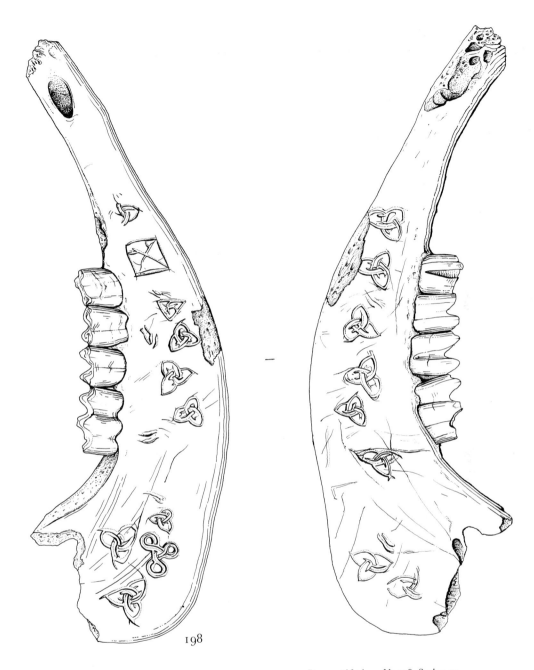

198

3.57. *Bone motif-piece, No 198. Scale 1:2.*

3.56. *Stages in the production of finger rings from cattle metatarsals.*

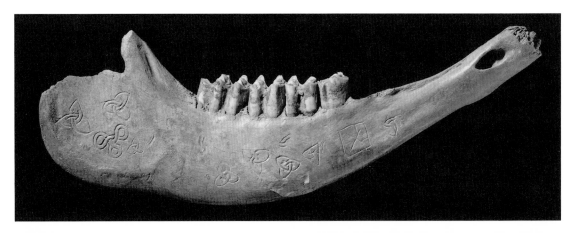

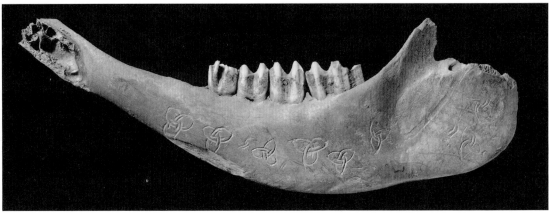

3.58. Bone motif-piece, No 198.

Motif-pieces

The bone artefacts are generally very similar to those from contemporary settlements in England and northern Europe, but one class of objects is exceptional for this country, at least. This is a group of motif-pieces, which have been recovered from four sites in the City in recent years, namely Milk Street, Guildhall House, St Alban's House (Wood Street) and Seal House (Nos 198-206). The first three sites, which account for eight motif-pieces, cluster closely together in the western sector of the City, north of Cheapside, whereas a single motif-piece from a late 12th or early 13th-century waterfront at Seal House is residual and must have been dumped as rubbish from another part of the City. The choice of bone differs from that of many artefacts since the need for a large and relatively flat surface area on which the pat-

terns could be carved was a prime consideration. Thus innominate bones of a pig and a horse were used (Nos 201-202) as well as cattle and pig mandibles (Nos 198-199), cattle-sized rib-bones (Nos 200 and 203-205) and a cattle femur (No 206). Many of the bones bear marks of having been broken or chopped and were presumably used as a source of meat before they reached the hands of a craftsman.

The recently excavated motif-pieces complement eight examples from London recorded in earlier publications, of which two were excavated on the north side of Cheapside close to Milk Street (Wheeler 1935, 183 and 194). Six of these motif-pieces are illustrated here for comparison (Figs 3.69-3.70 and 3.73-3.74). One motif-piece of bone, which was recorded as coming from the corner of Lawrence Lane, Cheapside, and was acquired by the London Museum in 1928 (MOL 28.86; Wheeler 1935, 183 and 194) cannot now be located and no drawing or photograph appears to exist of it. In addition, a polished bone cylinder from St Martin-le-Grand decorated in Ringerike

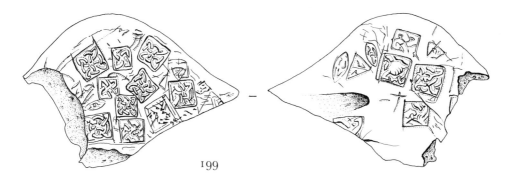

199

3.59. Bone motif-piece, No 199. Scale: drawing, 1:2.

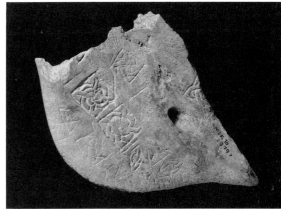

style with the head of a 'great beast' in profile and a serpent with prominent eyes and an interlaced body ending in a lobed tail, which is often described as a 'trial-piece' (eg VCH 1909, 169; Wheeler 1927, 54; Fuglesang 1979, 194, No 99, Pl 61A and B; and Graham-Campbell 1980, 148, No 500), is not illustrated here. This piece is stylistically distinct and the presence of three holes bored into the side of the cylinder suggests that it was used as an artefact, comparable to other pierced bone cylinders such as examples decorated with interlace from Sawdon, Yorkshire (Waterman 1948, 182-3; Roesdahl *et al* 1981, 75) and from London (GMC 1908, 122, No 116, and Pl LI, No 16).

Where the deposits from which the motif-pieces were found can be dated, they range from the 10th century to the middle of the 11th century, with the single exception of a late 12th- or early 13th-century waterfront rubbish dump where the motif-piece was clearly redeposited. Redeposition probably also accounts for why one motif-piece

was found in the City Stone Yard in Southwark in 1847 (Cottrill 1935, 69). The pieces do not, however, reflect a stylistic progression, although the squatting beast with a collared head and long snout appears to derive from the Trewhiddle tradition and can thus be considered the earliest of the London motif-pieces, dating perhaps to the late 9th or early 10th century. Other motif-pieces, including examples from 10th and 11th-century deposits, bear geometric patterns tried out repeatedly until the complicated sequence of intersecting lines was mastered when the motif was worked deeper into the surface of the bone (eg Fig 3.59, No 199A). Only occasionally can the order in which the motifs were sketched on a piece be reconstructed, although this was possible with a motif piece from York where a series of interlace animals were incised within a polygonal frame (Tweddle 1980, 24). Certain geometric motifs appear to have particularly preoccupied the London artisans. The pattern of a quadriloop interlacing with a circle in square field lines occurs

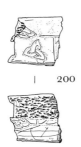

3.60. *Bone motif-piece, No 200. Scale: drawing, 1:2.*

on seven of the pieces (Figs 3.71-3.74, Nos 199, 201, 204, 205, MOL 4001, BM 56 7-1, 1482 and the City Stone Yard piece), and a triquetra interlacing with a circle in triangular field lines is present on four (Figs 3.72-3.74, No 202, MOL 4001; BM 56 7-1, 1482 and the City Stone Yard piece). Cord plaits of various lengths; a duplex in square field lines; pointed knots in lentoid field lines; and an assortment of triquetrae also appear to have been assiduously practised, for this does seem to have been the principal function of the motif-pieces found in London, in contrast to some of the motif-pieces from Ireland. Indeed, few of the patterns are complete, which would have caused them to be unsatisfactory for impressing foils or wax models, or for use as 'pattern-books' when works of art were commissioned.

The patterns on the London motif-pieces can be compared with similar ones on English metalwork of the 10th century. Thus the pattern of a quadriloop interlacing with a circle, particularly the example carved on a rib-bone from Wood Street (Figs 3.67 and 3.73, No 205), resembles that used for the four inner fields of the King's School Canterbury disc brooch, which is dated stylistically to the early 10th century (Wilson 1964, 42 and 127). However, as David Wilson points out, this ornament both lacks chronological significance and is a feature of various decorative styles in Europe (Wilson 1960, 22). Indeed, a similar quadriloop knot inlaid in niello on a silver sword pommel, which it has been argued was made in Scandinavia in the middle of the 9th century (Müller-Wille 1976, 77), offers another close parallel to the pattern in metalwork.

The triquetra and duplex were similarly employed as patterns on metalwork and other artefacts in England and the continent over a long

period, although L. R. A. Grove felt able to assert that a motif-piece carved with triquetra, duplex and plait patterns which was excavated in the precincts of York Castle in 1938 could be dated to the middle of the 10th century on stylistic grounds (Grove 1940, 285-7). Similar triquetra and duplex patterns are also extremely common among the motif-pieces excavated in Dublin, where they apparently range in date from the 10th to the 12th century (O'Meadhra 1979, Nos 22, 40, 43-4, 47, 52, 54 and 60-1).

More unusual are a trilobe knot (Figs 3.57 and 3.71, No 198) and an equal-armed cross with trefoil terminals interlacing with a circle and saltire (Figs 3.67 and 3.73, No 205). A cross of similar form occurs on a late Anglo-Saxon *cloisonné* enamel disc brooch from Coventry (Buckton 1986, 12, Fig 4, No 9) and, although the motif can be interpreted as a simplified example of a foliate corner boss which frequently formed part of the page border in English illuminated manuscripts of the later 10th and 11th centuries, these patterns must chiefly have embellished mass-

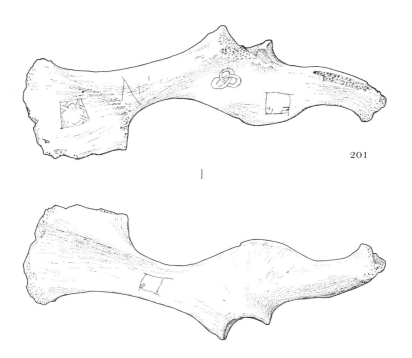

3.61. Bone motif-piece, No 201. Scale: drawing, 1:2.

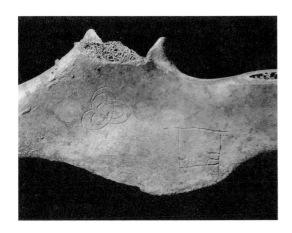

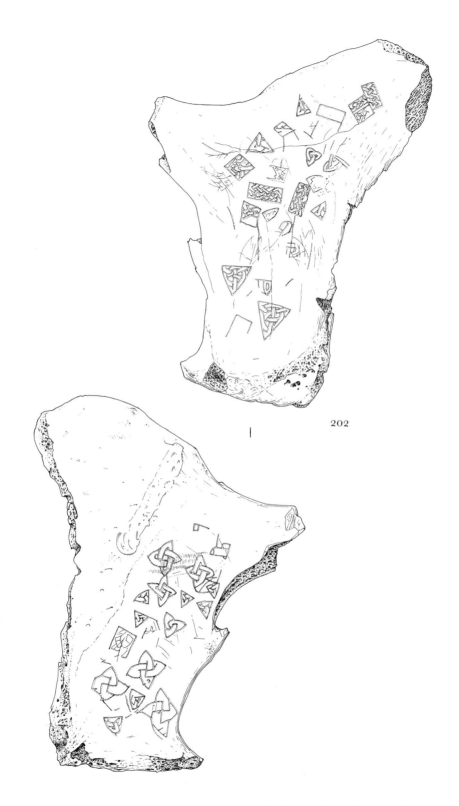

202

3.62. Bone motif-piece No 202. Scale 1:2.

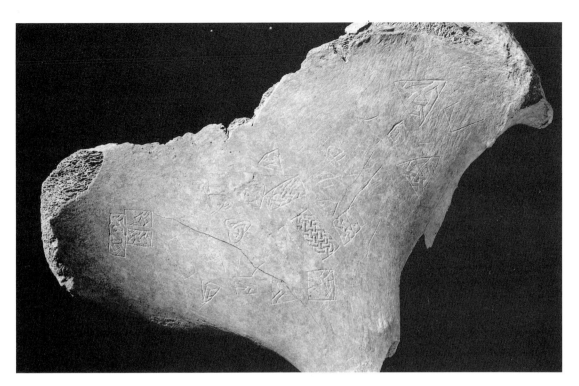

3.63. Detail of motifs on motif-piece, No 202.

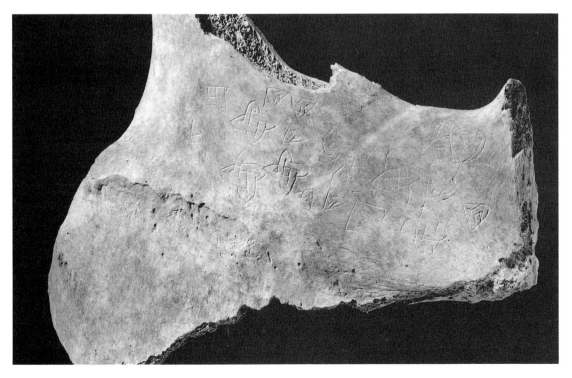

3.64. Detail of motifs on motif-piece, No 202.

produced ornaments very few of which have survived to the present.

The City Stone Yard motif-piece is the most useful stylistically of the London pieces since it combines plant and animal ornament alongside geometric patterns that are comparable to those incised on some of the pieces from dated contexts. While it has been suggested that this piece dates to the latter part of the 10th century (Cottrill 1935, 71), an early to mid-11th-century date for it is also tenable as the motifs depicted, including an interlace knot nestling beside an acanthus leaf, an upright sprouting acanthus leaf, and an animal, perhaps a dog or fox, with a stumpy tail and three-toed paws, are common in English art of this period.

One motif-piece is particularly important since it has a name, which is possibly that of the artist, inscribed in Old English on both faces of the rib-bone. Elisabeth Okasha examined and read the inscription and her report on it follows.

An inscribed motif-piece (No 203)

Elisabeth Okasha

The text on face (a) is legible but probably incomplete. It is incised without panels or framing lines and reads horizontally from wide to narrow end. Letter height 4-7mm.
Reading: AELVBRH-

The letters A, L and V are inverted.

The text on face (b) is legible and complete. It is incised without panels or framing lines and reads horizontally from wide to narrow end (i.e. upside down in relation to text A). Letter height 4-6mm.
Reading: AELVBRH |
The letters L and V are inverted; R is insular not capital in form.

System of transliteration (see further Okasha 1971, 45)
A = legible letter A
A̱ = letter A, damaged but legible
– = text lost
| = end of text

(Figs 3.66 and 3.72)

Both texts contain what is probably a form of the Old English personal name *ælfbeorht*. This name is likely to be that of the engraver. The name *ælfbeorht* may be recorded, for example in the form *ælbriht*, a London moneyer of Cnut (see Smart *SCBI* 28, indexed however under *æthelbeorht*); certainly both *ælf-* and *-beorht* are recorded Old English name-elements. In Domesday Book, *ælu-* is recorded as a spelling of *ælf-* (Feilitzen 1937, 172) and *-beorht* is recorded with spellings *-berht*, *-ber*, *-briht* etc (Feilitzen 1937, 193). The script and spelling of both texts are consistent with the mid-11th-century date provisionally suggested by the archaeological context.

The texts may have been two attempts at the same text or one may be a copy of the other. They are clearly roughly contemporary. If one is a copy then the copier understood his text sufficiently to transpose capital and insular R (the sixth letter). Text (b) is slightly less carefully executed with respect to letter-shape and stroke-formation; the letters are also slightly smaller. If this text was incised first, text (a) might have been an attempt to improve on it. In this case text (a) would be complete. If text (a) was incised first and text (b) was a copy, then either text (a) is complete or else text (b) was copied from text (a) after the final letter(s) had flaked off.

Additional note on the inscription

Kevin Gosling

It is perhaps better to assume that text (a) is complete, and to read the name as a female one: *Ælfburh*. Although this name seems not to occur elsewhere (John Insley pers comm), it is a perfectly regular formation, comprising two common elements. It may confidently be added to the corpus of known Old English names.

The form of some of the letters calls for comment. In text (a) the letter B is interesting because its triangular bows do not meet in the middle, a feature suggestive of the equivalent runic character. The next letter in text (a), at first sight a closed R, could also indicate that the carver was familiar with runes; the broad groove which closes the letter could well be the result of accidental flaking. This would make the intended form a runic-looking, open one (Ray Page pers comm). It is worth noting, too, that the inverted forms of L and V in both texts also suggest runic influence, although the inverted A in text (a) does not.

That these Roman forms should apparently be influenced by their runic counterparts is perhaps not such a surprise; the magnificent stone from St Paul's churchyard shows that the runic script, in its Danish form at least, was in use in 11th-century London (Moltke 1985, 322–5).

This inscription is discussed in more detail in Gosling forthcoming.

3.65. Inscribed bone motif-piece, No 203. Scale: drawing, 1:2; inscriptions, 1:1.

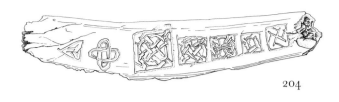

204

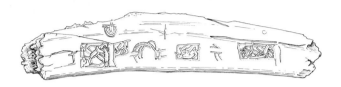

3.66. Bone motif-piece, No 204. Scale: drawing, 1 :2.

205

3.67. Bone motif-piece, No 205. Scale: drawing, 1:2.

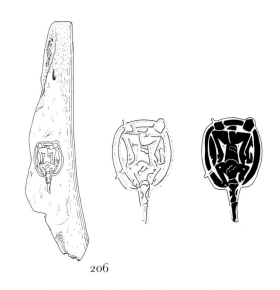

206

3.68. Bone motif-piece, No 206. Scale: drawing, 1:2; detail, 1:1.

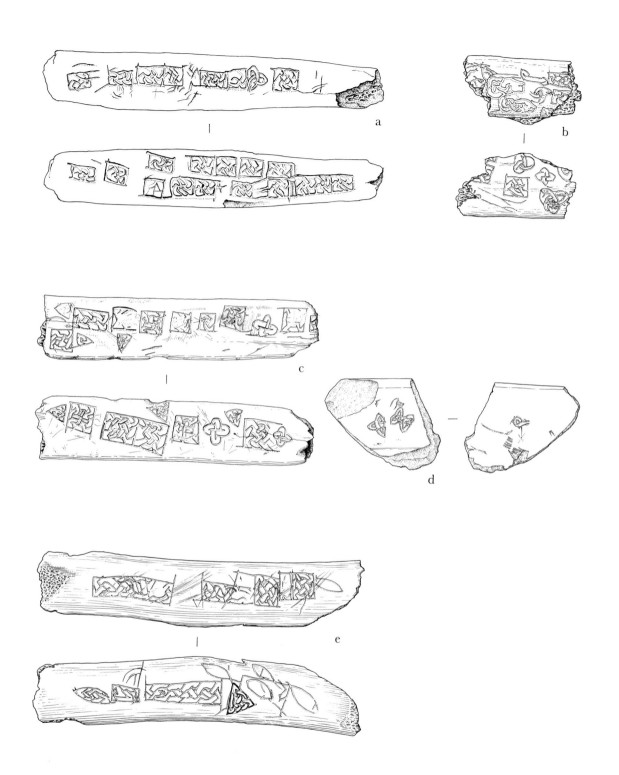

3.69. Other motif-pieces from London: a)-b) St Mary Woolnoth, Lombard Street, MOL 32.169/1 and 2; c) London Wall, MOL 4001; d) 99, Cheapside, MOL 11676; e) BM 56 7-1, 1482. Scale 1:2.

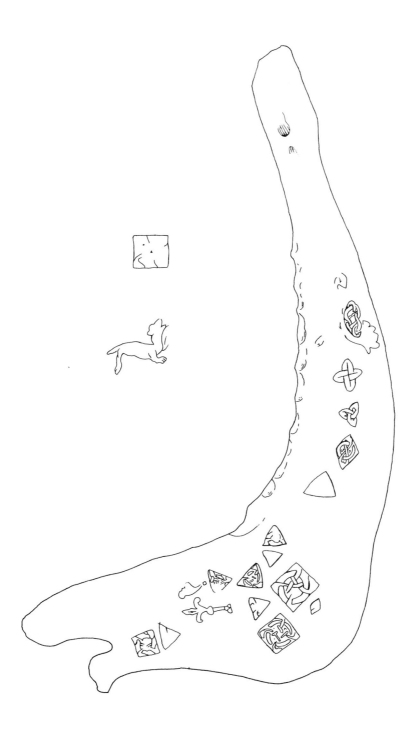

3.70. Motif-piece found in the City Stone Yard, based on drawings by A. H. Burkitt and F. Cottrill. Scale 1:2.

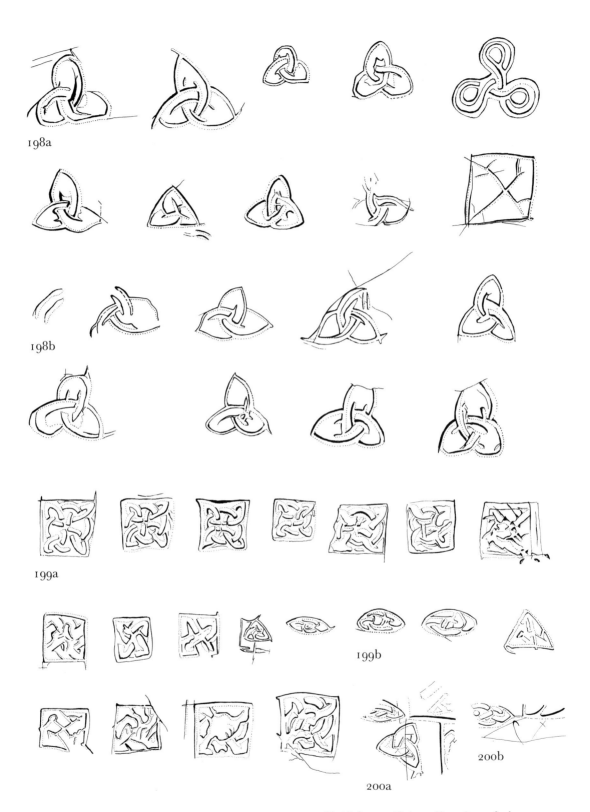

198a

198b

199a

199b

200a

200b

3.71. Motifs from motif-pieces, Nos 198-200. Scale 1:1.

201a 201b 202a

202b

203

204a

204b

3.72. Motifs from motif-pieces, Nos 201-204. Scale 1:1.

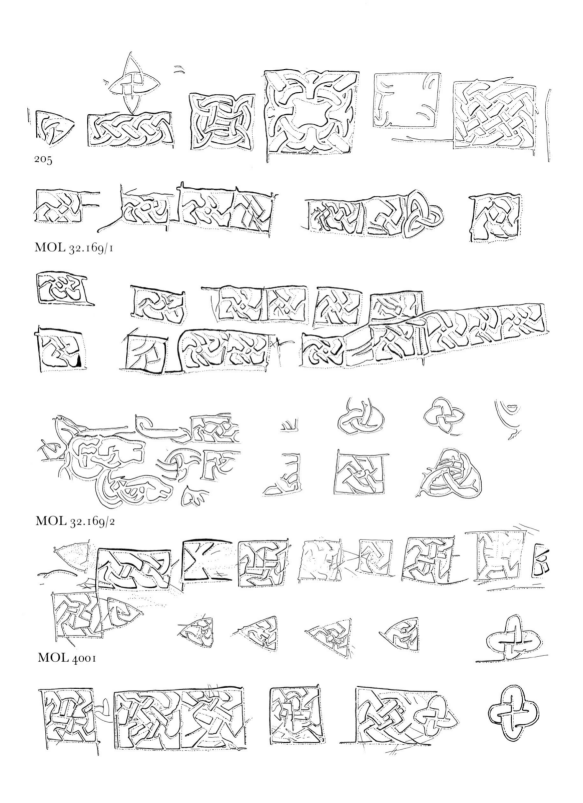

205

MOL 32.169/1

MOL 32.169/2

MOL 4001

3.73. Motifs from motif-pieces; No 205; MOL 32.169/1 and 2; and MOL 4001. Scale 1 : 1.

MOL 11676

BM 56 7-1, 1482

3.74. Motifs from motif-pieces, MOL 11676; BM 56 7-1, 1482; and the City Stone Yard. Scale 1:1.

Combs

Combs are among the most common artefacts from early medieval London, reinforcing the impression gained from other settlements and cemeteries that they were regarded as an essential item of daily life. Apart from side-plates made from split rib-bones being used with sheets of horn, no examples of composite combs employing mixed materials were recorded from London in contrast, for example, to Lincoln where a combination of antler connecting plates and bone tooth plates was apparently prevalent (Mann 1982, 7). The range of forms is, however, considerable, and it is of particular interest that double-sided combs of horn, ivory and antler were apparently used contemporaneously with antler single-sided composite combs in 10th-century London. In view of the variety of the combs, single-sided composite combs are discussed first followed by simple and composite double-sided types, but it must be understood that this does not reflect a chronological distinction. The terminology follows that defined by Patricia Galloway (Galloway 1976, 154-6) as modified by Arthur MacGregor (MacGregor 1985a, 75, Fig 43).

Single-sided composite combs

Single-sided composite combs form the largest group of combs represented and several different styles can be distinguished from among them. One form conspicuous by its absence is the handled comb, which was usually, but not invariably, single-sided (MacGregor 1985a, 91-2), and English in origin (Riddler forthcoming). An example, reportedly made from bone and decorated on one side, at least, with three bands of transverse lines, was recovered from a pit at Plough Court, Lombard Street in the mid-1950s (Marsden 1968, 36, Pl 1). The comb, however, can only be dated typologically since no other artefacts were found with it in the pit to help clarify the date of the deposit. Its simple linear decoration, apparently utilising a display side, and its construction from bone rather than antler suggest a 7th to 9th century date (Ian Riddler pers comm).

An unusual comb to be found in England comes from a 12th-century deposit at St Peter's Hill. It has relatively broad, thin connecting-plates decorated with lines and ring-and-dot ornament (Fig 3.75, No 207). No other combs of

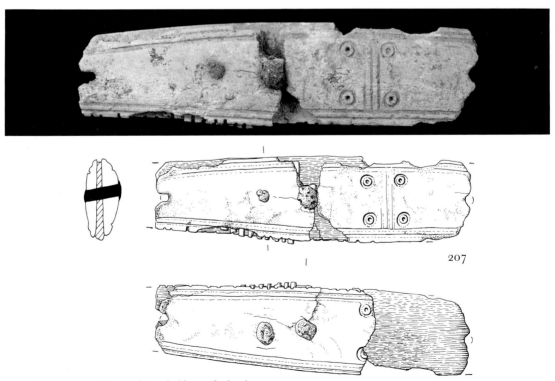

3.75. Antler single-sided composite comb, No 207. Scale: drawing, 1:1.

this character have been recorded from southern England but a fragment which, like the London comb, has both terminals missing, was recovered from a grave of the 'Viking period' at Lyking in the Orkneys (Shetelig 1940, 80, Fig 44). The absence of the terminals on the connecting-plates means that the London comb cannot be precisely classified but the general style conforms to examples distributed among trading centres and settlements throughout northern Europe, ranging from Staraja Ladoga, north Russia, and Birka in the east (Davidan 1970, Fig 6, E1; Arbman 1943, Taf 160, Nos 5 and 7; Tempel 1969, Taf 16, No 9; Tempel 1972, Taf 8, No 8) to Dorestad, on the mouth of the Rhine, in the west (Holwerda 1930, Afb 72, No 91), and also including examples from Haithabu and Elisenhof, in northern Germany (Tempel 1969, Taf 18, No 15; Tempel 1979, Abb 5, Nos 30-32). The dating of these combs suggests that the one from London was not made before the second quarter of the 9th century or later than the early 10th century (Ambrosiani 1981, 25-9, Figs 9 and 10) and therefore the context of the London comb shows it to be residual. The comb can be regarded as an import, otherwise more could be expected to have been recorded in England, although this absence could in part reflect the sparse number of contexts dating from the middle of the 9th to the early 10th century that have been excavated in this country. The recovery of the comb from London is of particular importance since it has been argued that the absence of combs of this general type from southern England implies that they were not traded across the Channel, and has been put forward as a reason why they were unlikely to have been made in Frisia (Ambrosiani 1981, 32-4). Although the centres of production for such combs remain uncertain, the difference in distribution between combs of this form decorated with simple linear and ring-and-dot ornament and those with zones of interlace pattern and zoomorphic terminals, which are especially common in areas with strong Scandinavian connections and are better represented in Britain, continues to be pertinent. Kristina Ambrosiani has also pointed out the influence of elk antler upon the distinctive shape of the connecting-plates, which she sees as an indicator of the Scandinavian origin of the combs (Ambrosiani 1981, 34-7). An examination of the comb from St Peter's Hill, however, proved inconclusive with regard to the type of antler from which it was made and the precise whereabouts of its manufacture thus remains enigmatic, although it is evidently not English.

The only single-sided composite comb excavated from a 10th-century deposit in London in recent years is a comb of exceptional length (241mm), which was recovered from a pit at Pudding Lane (Fig 3.76, No 208). It includes fifteen tooth-plates with a total of ninety-two teeth and has angular end-plates. Iron rivets were inserted between alternate tooth-plates, with an extra one inserted between the second and the third tooth-plates, and through each end-plate. The decoration on the connecting-plates, which consists of a saltire partly infilled and bounded with bands of transverse lines arranged in five zones, conforms to a stock repertoire of pattern elements. Similar pattern elements are extremely common among the combs at Haithabu, for example (Tempel 1969, Tafs 20-23), and a comb fragment from Northampton also provides a close parallel (Oakley 1979, 310, Fig 137, No 35). The angularity of the end-plates is likewise reproduced on examples from both these towns as well as at York (Waterman 1959, Pl XVIII, No 1) and Thetford (Rogerson and Dallas 1984, 169, Fig 187, No 9), and it is apparent that the form was generally associated with long combs, thus resulting in an aesthetically more pleasing outline.

Another long comb, which has many features in common with that excavated at Pudding Lane, was recorded by an antiquary, Sir John Morland, as coming from a deep trench between the Mansion House and the Royal Exchange in the middle of the 19th century. The comb has lost an end-plate but, when complete, it would have been only slightly shorter than the one from Pudding Lane. It can also be observed that both the style of the decoration and the riveting sequence bear a close resemblance to the Pudding Lane comb (Fig 3.76, MOL 50.9). While it cannot be asserted that these two combs from London were the product of the same comb-maker, since it appears that combs of this general character were produced as a seasonal activity in many centres throughout northern Europe (Ambrosiani 1981, 38), it is significant that the riveting sequence employed is apparently rare, if not unknown, on combs recorded from the continent.

The chronology of composite combs of the type found at Pudding Lane, based on evidence from graves and settlements throughout northern Europe, has established that the form was common throughout the 10th century (Ambrosiani 1981, 24-9, Figs 9-10). The 10th-century date of

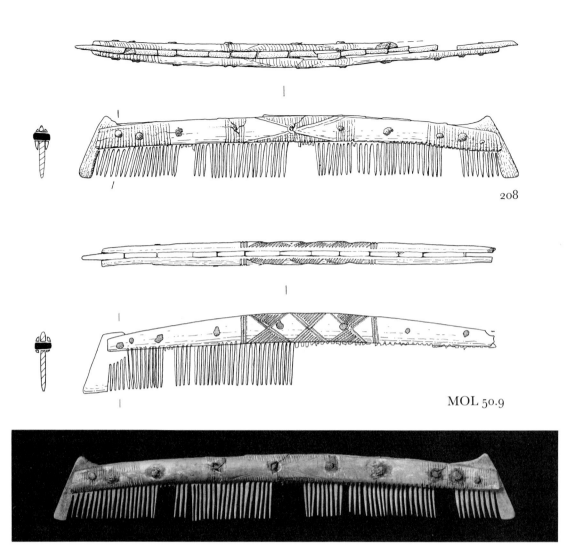

208

MOL 50.9

3.76. Antler single-sided composite combs, No 208 and MOL *50.9. Scale: drawing, 1:2.*

the pit fill from which the Pudding Lane comb was recovered is, therefore, consistent with the wider European chronology. It also seems probable that the Mansion House comb dates to the 10th century.

A further nine composite, single-sided combs were recovered from late 11th- and 12th-century deposits in London, principally from domestic pits situated some distance from the waterfront, and with one possible exception (No 213) all were made from antler (Figs 3.77-3.78). A limited repertoire of linear ornament was employed on the connecting-plates, either in the form of transverse bands (Nos 209-210 and 215) or a

repeating sequence of saltire crosses scored with double lines (Nos 211 and 212), but their fragmentary character means that they cannot be fully reconstructed. Similar pattern elements, which had a long duration of use, have again been recorded from many north European towns, particularly Haithabu (eg Tempel 1969, Taf 23), York (MacGregor 1982, 49, Nos 526-7) and Wolin, in northern Poland (Wilde 1953, Taf vb).

A distinctive feature of one of these London combs is that the connecting-plates are thick and trapezoidal in cross-section (Fig 3.77, No 211a). In addition, the teeth for this comb appear to have been graded into two sizes, since the teeth on one tooth-plate, which is no longer riveted in position (Fig 3.77, No 211b), are almost twice as compact as the others that remain. Both these characteristics suggest that this comb was orig-

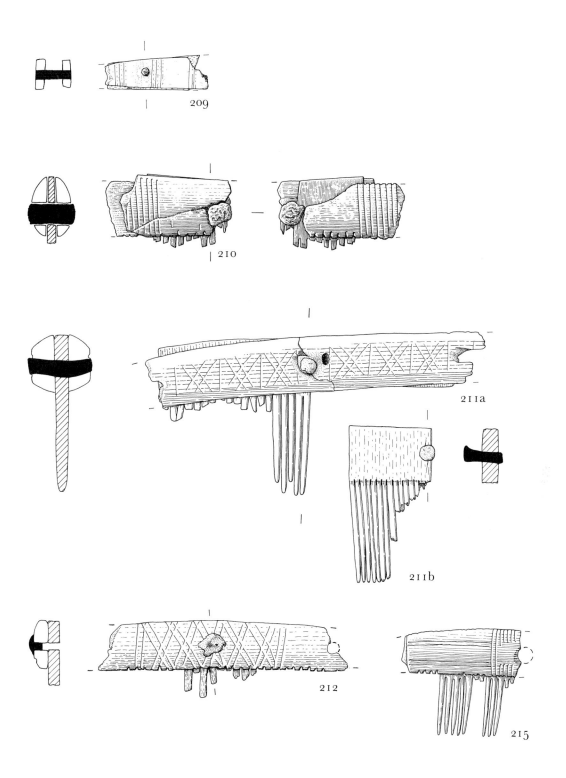

3.77. Antler single-sided composite combs, Nos 209-212 and 215. Scale 1:1.

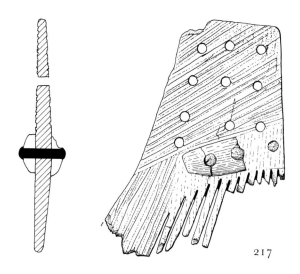

216

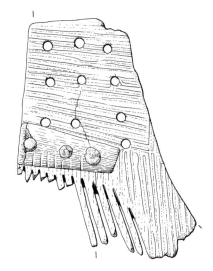

217

inally a long one. Combs with a similar trapezoidal cross-section occur at Wolin (Wilde 1953, Taf vb, Nos 14 and 22) and Haithabu (Tempel 1969, 100), where they have been dated to the 10th and 11th centuries, and further examples have been recorded from York (Waterman 1959, 88, Fig 16, No 2), Dublin and Aberdeen (MacGregor 1985a, 90). The distribution of combs with this form of cross-section has led to the proposition that they were produced in the lands bordering the south Baltic (Ambrosiani 1981, 23). While it has been argued by some scholars that decoration should not be used as a criterion for distinguishing between combs trapeze-shaped in section (Jankuhn 1943, 150), the London comb clearly exhibits a different style of ornament singling it out from the combs of supposed south Baltic make. Thus, instead of the decoration being divided into longitudinal zones, which emphasise the faceted form of the connecting-plates, the London comb merely has a single band of repeating saltire crosses.

A gradual change in single-sided composite combs took place during the 11th century characterised, for example, by more finely sawn teeth, or by teeth graded into fine and coarse types (eg No 211). Another feature was the re-introduction of ornate end-plates epitomised in London by a comb with stylised animal-heads, which was recovered from Cheapside in 1927 (Wheeler 1935, 190, Pl xx), and decorated tooth-plates projecting above the back of the connecting-plates. Significantly, although the end-plates of only two combs among those recently excavated from 11th- to 12th-century deposits in London are preserved (Nos 216 and 217), they demonstrate the change from the plain terminals of 10th-century combs to a more florid style featuring drilled holes and elaborate edges, which has been attributed to an increasing use of metapodial bones (MacGregor 1985a, 90-1), although both examples catalogued here were made from antler. The decoration on the end-plate of comb No 217 is particularly poorly executed and the need for three rivets to hold it in place is unusual and suggests the comb was the product of an inexperienced craftsman.

Double-sided combs made from antler were far less common than single-sided composite combs during the 10th century, but they continued to be made in England where the tradition of production and use stretched back to the late Roman period. Part of a double-sided composite comb of antler (Fig 3.79, No 218) was recovered from a building at Milk Street amid household debris of the late 10th century. The comb's connecting-plates are not preserved but they have left a faint impression on the surface of the remaining end-plate. It is also apparent that a hole piercing the end-plate was drilled after the comb was assembled. A lack of any diagnostic features, except for the hole which is not common, curtails comparison between this comb and others of a similar date. It is, nevertheless, apparent that this 10th-century comb is unlike a double-sided comb from Threadneedle Street in the City, which has ring-and-dot decoration on its end-plates as well as along both connecting plates, and slotted into a case embellished with similar ornament (VCH 1909, 165, Fig 25). The Threadneedle Street comb has been described as 'probably late Saxon' (Wheeler 1935, 190), but recent evidence from towns in northern Europe suggests that it is unlikely to have been made much before the end of the 11th century.

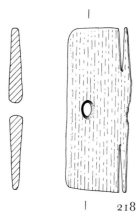

3.79. Antler double-sided composite comb, No 218. Scale 1:1.

Double-sided combs of horn were also popular in London during the 10th to 12th centuries, but unlike composite combs of antler they appear to have altered very little throughout the period. The best preserved comb of this type was recovered from a 10th-century pit at Milk Street (Fig 3.80, No 219). This comb is made from a flat sheet of horn with side-plates cut from a split cattle-sized rib-bone, and it was assembled with three iron rivets, one rivet being positioned in the centre and the others close to each end. The bone side-plates are undecorated and they were presumably added for practical reasons to help stabilise the horn in a flat state, although this was strictly unnecessary as later medieval simple double-sided horn combs demonstrate (eg Ulbricht 1984, Taf 24, Nos 3-5; Persson 1976, 328, Fig 293, No 50). Other combs of this composite form from recent excavations in London come from deposits of the late 11th and early 12th century and preserve only their side-plates held together with either two or three iron rivets (Fig 3.81, Nos 220-223). These plates do not always bear marks from the sawing of teeth along their sides and as a result many examples of side-plates have failed to be correctly identified, although they occur extensively throughout England.

The number of rivets used to assemble these combs was influenced by the length of the side-plates, in contrast to composite combs made from antler where the positioning of the tooth-plates was the chief determining factor. Thus among the bone side-plates from recent excavations in London, the longest examples (161mm, 153mm and 119mm) have three rivets (Nos 219 and 220), whereas the shorter ones, ranging in length from 73mm to 105mm, only have two (Nos 221-223). Other pairs of side-plates from London include longer plates with only two rivets (MOL A16884, A16885 and 4005), and it, therefore, appears that no standard practice applied.

The use of side-plates shaped with either perpendicular or angular ends was equally haphazard and one comb has plates with differently shaped ends on each side (MOL A16884). This implies that the plates were not modelled in pairs as was customary with antler composite combs. Furthermore, the rough edges of the ends of many of the side-plates (eg Fig 3.81, No 221) suggests that they were not always sawn and provides another indication of their cheap quality. The use of decoration on side-plates was also extremely

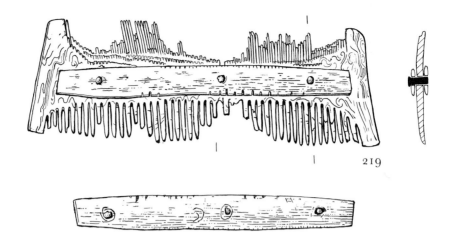

219

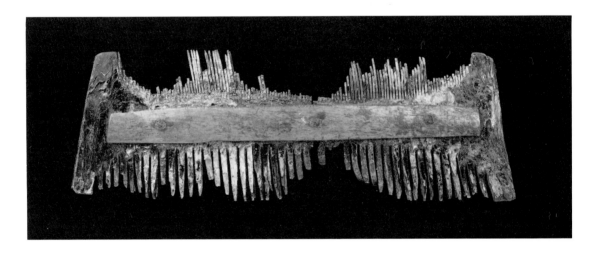

3.80. Horn double-sided comb with bone side-plates, No 219.
Scale : drawing, 1 :2.

limited in contrast to connecting-plates on other forms of composite combs. Thus the only embellishment on a side-plate recovered from recent excavations is a saltire lightly incised on one of a pair of plates (Fig 3.81, No 221). Among other comb side-plates in the collection of the Museum of London, one has a saltire bounded with transverse bands on one plate and a less carefully arranged pattern of saltires on the other (MOL A16884). Indeed, only one pair of side-plates from London is decorated with a matching pattern, namely mutliple ring-and-dot ornament (GMC 1908, 122, No 103, Pl XXXIV, 10 and 11).

Double-sided ivory comb

An ivory comb (Fig 3.82, No 224) is fragmentary and in a poor state of preservation. The entire comb appears to have been made in one piece with teeth sawn along each side, and the spacing of the remaining teeth suggests that they represent the finer set. Despite its condition, the London comb was evidently not of the diminutive size familiar from three examples made from walrus ivory and elephant ivory, which are considered to date to the 10th and 11th centuries (Wilson 1960, 17-19; MacGregor 1985b, 38-9). Consequently, the typological range of ivory combs in 10th and 11th-century England is probably greater than is at present known and their domestic use more common than is often supposed.

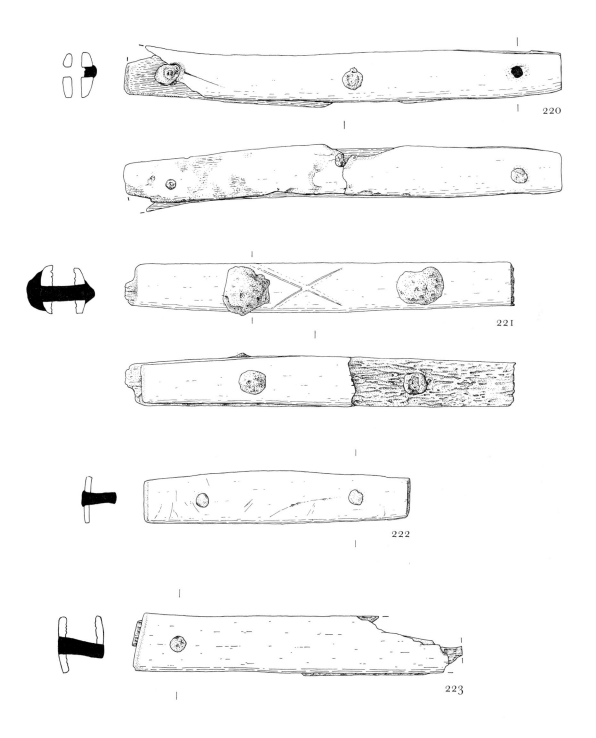

3.81. Bone side-plates from double-sided composite combs, Nos 220-223. Scale 1:1.

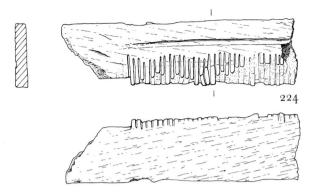

3.82. *Ivory comb, No 223. Scale 1 : 1.*

3.83. *Part of a comb-case, No 225. Scale 1 : 1.*

Comb-case

Part of a comb-case (Fig 3.83, No 225) was recovered from a site in the City in the 1950s. No details of its context were recorded but other comb-cases from northern Europe indicate that this case from London probably dates to the late 11th or 12th century. The height of the side-plate (21mm) and the presence of two rivet holes at each end indicate that the case would have consisted of a single pair of plates. This form of comb-case appears to have been less common than those with two pairs of plates, although one was found with its comb from Cloak Lane, London (GMC 1908, 122, Nos 104 and 108, Pl LIV, Nos 15 and 16), and a number have been recorded from York (Waterman 1959, Pl XIX, Nos 2, 4, and 7).

The pattern incised on the comb-case, which consists of two bands of chevrons separated by a pair of lines, and framed by a further pair of lines, cannot be precisely paralleled but similar pattern elements are present among the large assemblage of comb-cases dating to the 11th and 12th centuries from Schleswig, north Germany. There is

one, for example, which is partly decorated with chevrons and another combines chevron and linear ornament (Ulbricht 1984, Taf 74, No 8, and Taf 30, No 9).

Ivory knife handles

Apart from the simple double-sided ivory comb, the only ivory artefacts represented from recent excavations in the City are knife handles. One is fitted to a pattern-welded knife with a whittle tang (Fig 3.3, No 10), and the other two are scale plates which formed the handles of reversible claspknives (Fig 3.5, Nos 18–19). Previous finds have included carved walrus ivory items of high status; the head of a tau-cross crozier found at Water Lane in 1893 (Beckwith 1972, 131, No 57; Backhouse *et al* 1984, 119–20, No 121), and a so-called pen-case with a sliding lid (Beckwith 1972, 128, No 46; Backhouse *et al* 1984, 127–8, Pl XXV; Lasko 1984, 215, No 185), both made in English workshops during the 11th century.

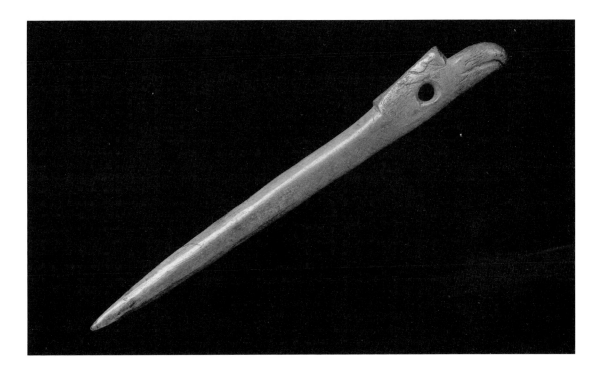

Longbone implements

Longbones, particularly those of cattle and horses, were used for a variety of implements, and among those represented from 11th- and 12th-century London are weaving tools, a spoon and two dice. There are, in addition, four pierced implements, one of which has a head shaped into that of a bird of prey (Figs 3.84 and 3.85, No 226), and the simple elegance of the carving can be compared with that employed on similar implements with zoomorphic heads, for example one resembling the head of a swan or goose from Dublin (NMI 1973, 27, No 31, Pl 6). The classification of these implements remains open to question, although in recent years they have generally been interpreted as dress pins that fastened thick outer garments such as mantles, which could have withstood the strain on the cloth that the thick pin shanks would have caused (Wilson 1983, 343 and 348, Fig 146). It is, nevertheless, possible that some were used in the hair and in this context it is perhaps worth noting that among the terms used for hair pins in Old English glossaries is the compound *haer-neadl* (Owen-Crocker 1986, 145).

Three pierced implements (Fig 3.85, Nos 227-229) have worn tips, which is where one of them has snapped (No 228). Similar signs of wear occur across the tip of a double-ended unpierced imple-

3.84. Pierced implement made from a longbone and carved with the head of a bird of prey, No 226.

ment (No 234). The narrow head of one suggests that it could have served a different function from those with expanded or zoomorphic heads, and one possibility put forward for similar implements found elsewhere in northern Europe is that they may have been used as single needles for making stockings, mittens or milk-sieves in *nålebinding* (looped needle-netting) (Lindström 1976, 275-8; Hald 1980, 278-9; Tweddle 1986, 227).

The presence of decoration on other implements with expanded heads of this general type from London ensured that at least a number of them were collected in the past (VCH 1909, 164, Fig 24; Wheeler 1927, 49-50, Fig 28, Nos 1-4). The style of the ornament also enabled them to be dated to the late 10th and 11th centuries, which accords fairly closely with the dating evidence of the more recent City finds, which were recovered from deposits of the late 11th or early 12th centuries.

The identification of those unpierced longbones, which are characterised by blunt ends and smooth, polished surfaces (Fig 3.85, Nos 232–234), as weaving tools is similarly debatable

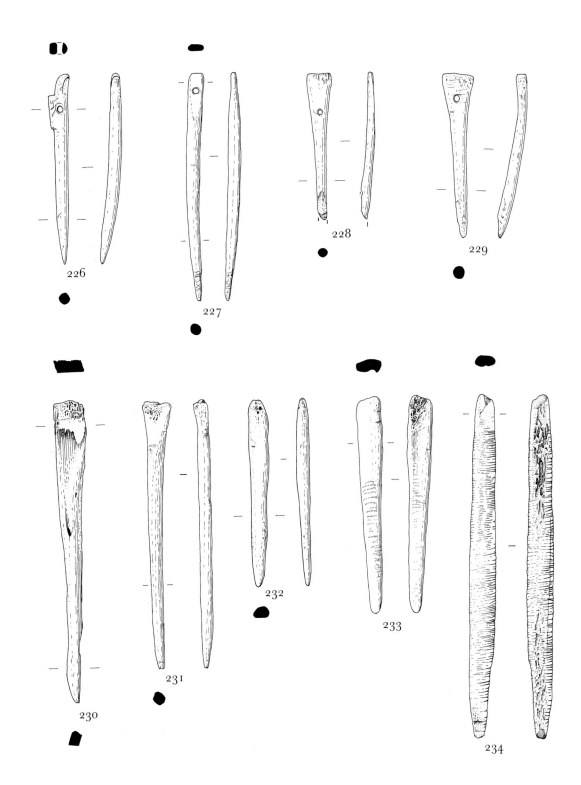

3.85. Implements made from longbones: pierced, Nos 226-229; unfinished, Nos 230-231; single-ended, Nos 232-233; double-ended, No 233. Scale 1:2.

since they could equally have functioned as burnishers (Waterman 1959, 85). This controversy partly stems from the change in form that weaving tools underwent during the 10th and 11th centuries, which coincided with a decline in use in England of the warp-weighted loom.

Thus the cylindrical, round-sectioned pin-beater, which is common from Anglo-Saxon settlements up to the 10th century, and is known from findspots in London, particularly in the eastern half of the City, including Lombard Street (MOL 17001 and 17117) and Gracechruch Street (MOL A10626) (Pritchard 1984, Fig 1 and Fig 18, Nos 9–10 and 12), appears to have been superseded by an asymmetrical double-ended tool which often has a slight concavity at the broader end (Fig 3.85, No 233).

Marta Hoffmann demonstrated through her study of weaving traditions in western Scandinavia the important role that the pin-beater played in producing cloth on upright looms tensioned by weights (Hoffmann 1964, 126–7 and 135–6). Similar tools would also have been necessary for weaving on a vertical two-beamed loom, on which it is argued many three-shed twills could have been produced (Crowfoot 1983, 442). Cloth with this weave construction became increasingly common in England after the 10th century and this may account for why the form of the beater was modified.

Two further implements are unfinished (Fig 3.85, Nos 230–231), and it is uncertain whether they were intended to be pierced or not. However, they demonstrate that implements made from longbones were being produced in London in the 11th century.

Spoon

A bone spoon with a shallow oval bowl and long slender handle was recovered from a late 11th-century deposit at Watling Court (Fig 3.86, No 235). Its simple form is closely paralleled by an undated example from Middle Brook Street, Winchester (Collis and Kjølbye-Biddle 1979, 384-5, Fig 4a).

Dice

Two dice were recovered from pit fills in London, the earlier dating to the first half of the 11th century and the other to the late 11th or early 12th

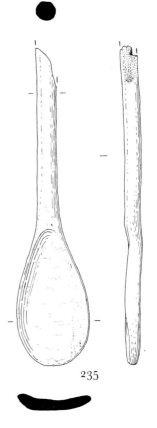

3.86. Bone spoon, No 235. Scale 1 : 1.

century (Nos 236-237). Both are approximately cube shaped with ring-and-dot markings that add up to seven on opposing faces. The smaller example was stamped with a die only 2mm in diameter consisting of two rings round a dot, while the larger die has a pattern unit of one ring and dot 3mm in diameter (Fig 3.87, No 236).

Gaming pieces

Six gaming pieces are included in the catalogue, although one was found in a post-medieval pit (No 242) and another was recovered from a late 12th-century waterfront deposit (No 243). The earliest two pieces here date to the late 11th or early 12th century thus providing support for the longheld view that they were a Norman introduction. The smallest gaming piece (diameter 31mm) was made from a cattle-sized longbone (Fig 3.87, No 238); four, which range from 44mm to 54mm in diameter, were produced from cattle-sized

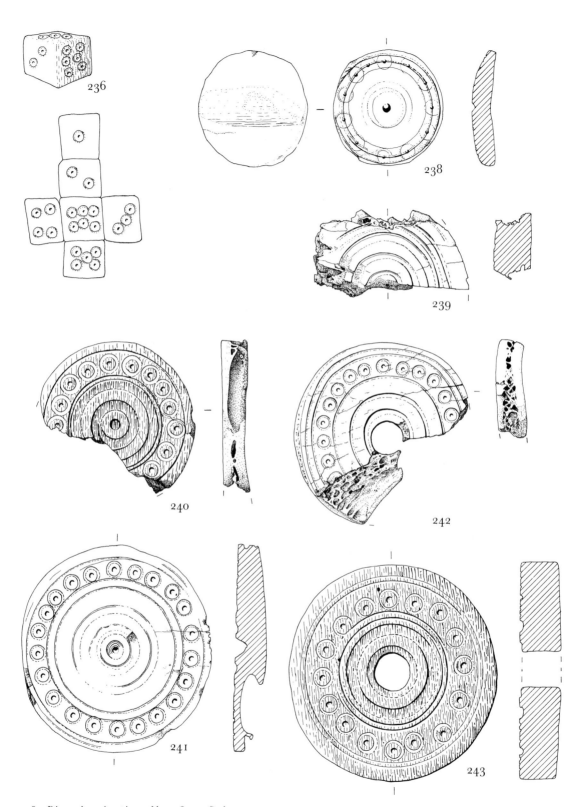

3.87. Dice and gaming-pieces, Nos 236-243. Scale 1:1.

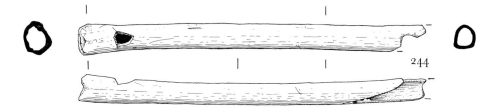

3.88. Birdbone flute, No 243. Scale 1:2.

mandibles (Fig 3.87, Nos 239-242); while the sixth and largest (diameter 57mm) was made from cetecean bone (Fig 3.87, No 243). All are decorated on just one face and have compass drawn grooves. Five are embellished further with a circle of repeating ring-and-dot ornament and two are perforated in the centre. They complement the large number of examples previously recorded from the City (Wheeler 1927, 47-8) and their wide distribution suggests that gaming was a popular pastime in Norman London.

Flute

A flute made from the ulna of a large bird, probably a goose or swan, is a form of musical instrument which had a long ancestry in north west Europe (Megaw 1960, 9–11). They appear to have been popular in medieval England up to the 13th century, and the London example fits well into this chronological sequence since it was recovered from a late 11th or early 12th-century deposit. The voicing lip and blow hole are intact but the flute has broken across the first finger hole (Fig 3.88, No 244), with the result that the total number of holes cannot now be determined. A further feature of the London flute is that the holes have been cut into the concave, posterior surface of the bone; the effect that this would have had on the sound has not been investigated. Other flutes with this feature have been recorded, including examples from Haithabu and York (Brade 1978, 26, Abb 1, No 3; Waterman 1959, 92, Fig 19, No 11).

Pig fibula pins

Five implements, probably dress pins, made from pig fibulae come from deposits of the 10th to 12th centuries (Fig 3.89, Nos 245-249). Each has been pierced at the distal end of the bone with a hole approximately 4mm in diameter. The rest of the head was deliberately narrowed, while the proximal end was shaped into a point. Although these pig fibula implements from London are less robust than pierced longbone implements, they are of very similar length. Thus pig fibula pins from recent excavations in the City range in length from 98mm to c.120mm compared with pierced longbones which range from 86mm to 121mm.

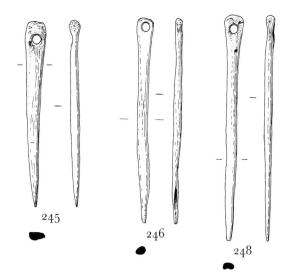

3.89. Pig fibula pins, Nos 245-246 and 248. Scale 1:2.

Perforated pig metapodia

There are three examples of perforated pig metapodia from London deposits of the late 11th or early 12th century and all have two holes bored through the shaft (Fig 3.90, Nos 250-252). Further examples have been recorded from recent excavations in the City but they were recovered from later deposits and are not included in this survey. Although similar pierced bones have been found throughout northern Europe, their function remains uncertain. It seems unlikely that they were worn as dress fasteners or used to close drawstring pouches, and the suggestion that they were an early type of whirligig toy is more attractive (Hruby 1957, 195, Fig 29). By contrast to most bone artefacts which used the bones of mature animals, the metapodia of juvenile pigs appear to have been preferred for these items; a selection which reflects the fact that pigs were kept as livestock for a shorter period than other domestic animals. However, among the three bones here, the only one that can be fully identified is that of an adult pig (No 251).

Skates

A large number of skates have been recorded from London (MacGregor 1976, 65; West 1982, 303). Six examples from 11th and early 12th-century deposits are catalogued here and the seventh is almost certainly contemporary although the

deposit from which it came lacked any associated finds by which to date it. There are also skates from later medieval deposits in London which are not included in this survey.

The bones used for the skates comprise four horse metatarsals (Nos 253, 254, 255 and 257), two horse metacarpals (Nos 258–259), and a cow metatarsal (No 256); a selection which accords with findings from other studies. Worked features including shaping to the toe, holes drilled through the toe and heel to help fasten the skate to the foot, and transverse cuts along the upper surface to improve the foothold, recorded elsewhere (MacGregor 1976, 59), are similarly represented. One skate made from a horse metatarsal has a vertical hole through its heel as well as its toe (Fig 3.91, No 253), and although it has been shown that similar perforated bones were sometimes fixed to wooden sledges as runners (Clason 1980, 244–6, Fig 171), this item here could equally have served as a skate.

Socketed points

Another type of artefact for which the metatarsals of cattle were selected are socketed points. Two have been recovered from late 10th-century deposits in London (Fig 3.92, Nos 260–261) and they are common from other towns in England at this period. However, despite their wide distribution their function remains uncertain (MacGregor 1982, 96–7).

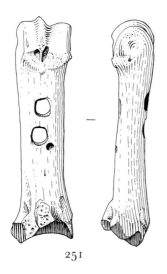

251

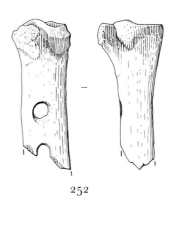

252

3.90. Perforated pig metapodia, Nos 251-252. Scale 1 : 1.

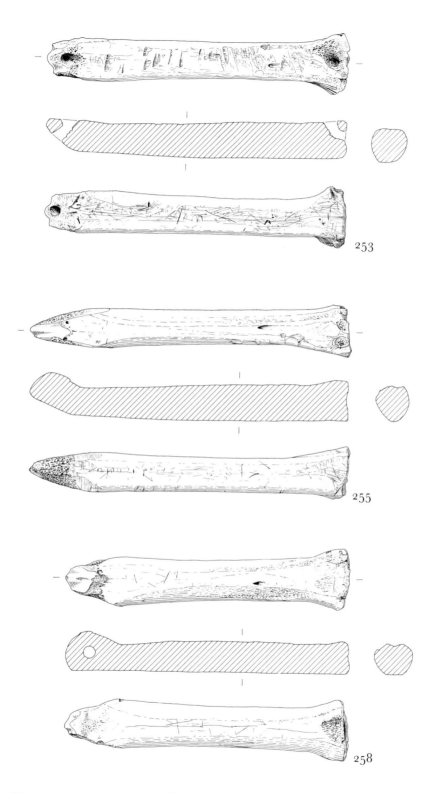

3.91. Skates, Nos 253 and 255 are horse metatarsals and No
258 is a horse metacarpal. Scale 1 : 3.

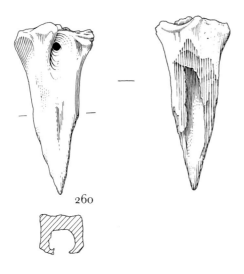

3.92. Socketed points, Nos 260-261. Scale 1:2.

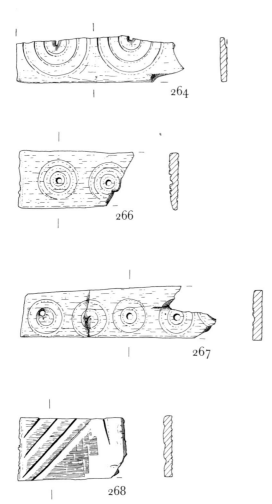

Spindlewhorls

The practice of using femur heads of cattle for spindlewhorls in antiquity appears to have continued in London until the 12th century, although whorls made from imported limestone were by this time beginning to become popular (see p. 165). Two spindlewhorls made from bone are catalogued here (Nos 262–263); the former was knife trimmed so that it was lighter as well as more angular, while the latter was left in its natural hemispherical form.

Mounts

Five thin mounts made from split cattle-sized ribs were recovered from late 11th- and 12th-century deposits in the City (Nos 264–268). Like the bone side-plates of composite horn combs, the mounts were cheaply produced with the ends being partly snapped rather than sawn and the ring-and-dot patterns often stamped with a lack of precision (eg No 265). Three of the London mounts have rivet holes by which they could be fixed to a casket (Fig 3.93, Nos 264, 266 and 267), but the other two, which are relatively short, do not and it is possible that they were glued into place or, perhaps, are waste material.

3.93. Bone mounts, Nos 264 and 266-268. Scale 1:1.

Leather artefacts of 10th- to mid 12th-century date from excavations in London mainly consist of footwear, but two scabbards and seven straps are also among the finds excavated in recent years. Offcuts from leatherworking were present in many of the same pits as the shoes at Milk Street but the quantity is minimal; in addition, some shoe uppers had been deliberately cut, presumably for reuse in cobbling. There is nothing, however, to foreshadow the pre-eminence in leatherworking that the lanes off Cheapside, particularly Lawrence Lane, were to attain in the 13th century (Keene 1985, 18). The amount of scrap leather and offcuts from the waterfront, particularly that at Seal House dating to the second quarter of the 12th century, is much greater than that from the Milk Street pits, but it is still inconsiderable when compared with what a workshop in regular production would generate; a deposit one metre thick of leather at High Street, Dublin, providing an indication of what might be expected (NMI 1973, 16). The type of animal skins used for the leather of the scabbards and a sample of the footwear and straps was identified by Glynis Edwards of the Ancient Monuments Laboratory, but no offcuts were examined.

Scabbards

The distinctive cut and styling of the two scabbards make them valuable additions to the small number recorded from England for the 10th to

early 12th centuries. They were made for knives, of which one with a pattern-welded blade is preserved intact inside its sheath (Figs 3.3 and 3.8, No 10; see p.131). The shape of the other knife remains outlined in the leather indicating that the knife had a short blade (c.60mm in length) and a cylindrical handle. To form the scabbards a piece of leather was folded double and joined along the raw edge, the method, however, of securing the seam differed for the two examples catalogued here. One, a plain 10th-century sheath from Milk Street, was sewn with overcast stitches spaced at intervals of 7mm (Fig 3.94, No 269), while the other, the scabbard for the Pudding Lane knife, was clipped together with 'staple-like bindings' of copper alloy wire (Fig 3.8, No 10; see p.133). These methods differ also from those evident on two scabbards of 10th- or 11th-century date previously recorded from the City; a scramasax sheath from Cheapside having been secured with a row of at least nineteen metal rivets (Fig 3.95; Waddington 1927, 526-7, Pl LXV) and an incomplete scabbard from the site of Blossom's Inn, Lawrence Lane, with a line of (?) running stitches or metal clips, indicated by pairs of holes, set in 5mm from the edge (Fig 3.94; Dunning 1932, 177).

A wide diversity in finishing leather scabbards is similarly apparent from the roughly contemporary assemblage at Haithabu, in what is

3.94. Leather scabbards of the 10th and 11th centuries from London: No 269, from Milk Street; and MOL 12516 from the site of Blossom's Inn, Lawrence Lane. Scale 1 :2.

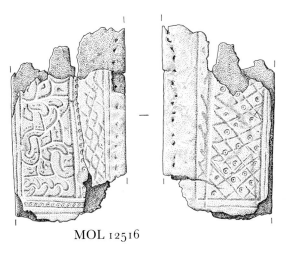

269

MOL 12516

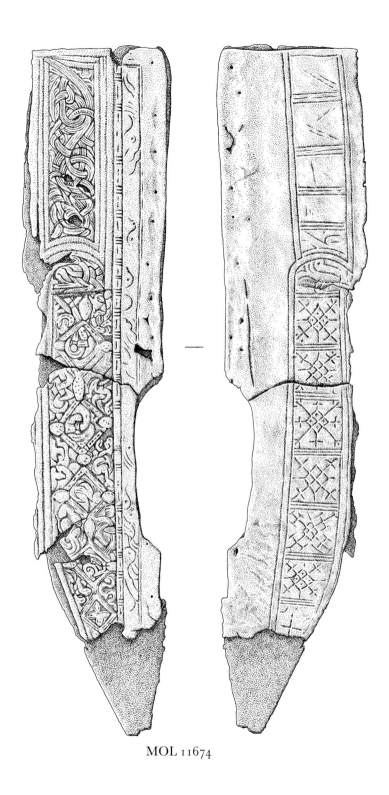

MOL 11674

3.95. Leather scabbard MOL *11674 from 99, Cheapside. Scale 1 :2.*

now northern Germany (Waateringe 1984, Tafs 20-22), and this variety contrasts strongly with the standardisation of construction evident on knife scabbards found in London from the 13th century and later (Cowgill *et al* 1987, 34–5). The use of calf and cattle hide for the Milk Street and Pudding Lane sheaths, however, is consistent with later craft practice. The absence of decorated scabbards from Haithabu highlights an important aspect of English leatherworking since intricate, interlace patterns divided into panels, such as those present on the scabbards from Cheapside and Blossom's Inn, appear to have been a native English speciality, a supposition strengthened by the occurrence of personal names inscribed in Old English on two sheaths decorated in this style (Tweddle 1986, 240 and 279, note 9; Okasha 1981, 47-8, Fig 6).

It is possible that the scabbard from Milk Street tore along the leather where a slot was cut for a thong to be inserted. However, none of the other three scabbards from London exhibit evidence of any such slot and it is probable that they were fitted at the opening with a metal binding and a ring, or tab, for attachment to a belt or other dress accessory (MacGregor 1978, 53; Roesdahl *et al* 1981, 106; Tweddle 1982, 142).

Footwear

The terminology used in this section is based on a glossary of shoe terms compiled by the late John Thornton (Thornton 1975). The drawing conventions follow those adopted for later medieval shoes from London (Grew and de Neergaard 1988) with the flat patterns showing the flesh side of the leather. Exceptions are a decorated vamp (No 285) and top-bands (Nos 348 and 352-359) where the grain face is depicted.

The footwear forms part of an impressive sequence of medieval shoes from London. All were made by the turnshoe method but they demonstrate that considerable changes in pattern-cutting and styling took place in the 11th and 12th centuries, shoes becoming a particularly conspicuous item of dress in the early decades of the 12th century.

Tenth-century footwear

Tenth-century shoes were recovered from five pits at Milk Street (pits 12, 17, 42, 45 and 57), of which one intercut another. Thus the fact that they are all low-cut shoes reaching to just below the ankle-bone may have little significance, although they offer a contrast to the London footwear of the two succeeding centuries, when ankle-boots predominate (Fig 3.96). The most consistent feature of 10th-century footwear from London is the pattern of the sole. This consists of a rounded toe with the sides broadest across the tread tapering to a point (v-back) at the heel, while the slightly asymmetric cut of the forepart enables the right foot to be distinguished from the left (Fig 3.98, No 272). Only one 10th-century sole deviates from this basic pattern, a child's shoe with a symmetrical sole which ends in a squared-

Ceramic phase	Low-cut shoe	Ankle boot	Boot
CP1	7	—	—
CP2	1	—	—
CP3	1	2	1
CP4	—	12	—
CP5	—	28	—

3.96 Table of London footwear dating from the 10th to the middle of the 12th century

3.97. Two 10th-century shoes, Nos 272 and 274.

off heel tunnel-stitched to the upper (Fig 3.99, No 274), thereby achieving a better fit for a small foot.

The pattern of the upper shows greater variation. The simplest pattern was cut in one piece, folded double and stitched at the heel with a diverging seam into which the raised v-back of the sole fitted. The v-back sometimes extends to the full height of the quarters (No 276) but on other shoes the quarters meet above it (eg Fig 3.98, No 272). It is not clear whether one-piece uppers were cut as a long continuous strip and then shaped when damp (Fig 3.99), which was the method favoured for a low-cut shoe with a drawstring fastening from Southgate Street, Gloucester (Pritchard forthcoming), or whether they were partly shaped in the course of cutting (Fig 3.98). It is possible that both methods were employed but further investigation into this aspect of shoe-making is required.

A different style of upper, which was similarly economical in its use of leather, was a one-piece wrap-round pattern seamed at the side rather than at the back of the heel. This style belonged to an older tradition, as far as can be judged from the limited range of footwear preserved from Anglo-Saxon England, and was the pattern used for two pairs of shoes recovered from the ship burial at Sutton Hoo (East 1983, 803, Fig 574). Shoes with a side-seam are uncommon among 10th-century footwear from London but there are at least two which hint at a continuity of the wrap-round construction, although neither shoe is complete (Nos 278 and 312). The better preserved of these two shoes had its vamp removed before it was thrown away but sufficient remains for a reconstruction to be attempted (Fig 3.100). The pattern shows that the prevailing custom of having a v-back sole was satisfied by cutting a triangular section out of the back-part of the upper, and since the upper could not be cut from a single skin, a rectangular insert was added at the side. The insert was sewn to the vamp wing with a thong of leather and to the quarters with a fine, linen thread, of which traces are preserved in the stitch holes. Wear on the heel indicates that the insert was probably placed on the outside and, therefore, that the shoe was worn on the right foot. The interpretation of wear marks, however, needs to be treated cautiously since a shoe shaped for the left foot recovered from the same pit fill at Milk Street (No 277) shows heavy wear on the inside of the heel, contrary to what is considered

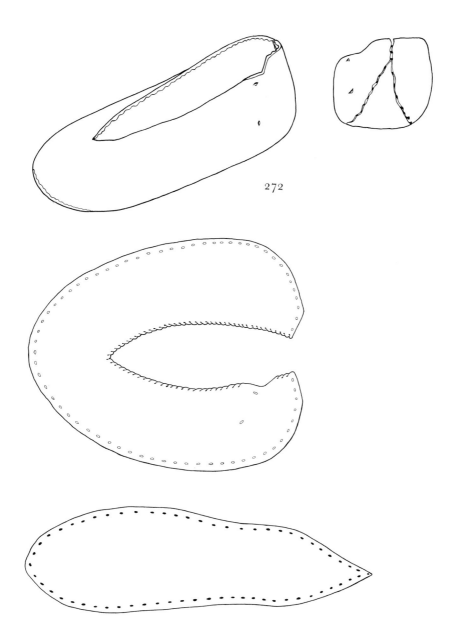

272

to be the normal pattern (Swallow 1975, 28, Fig 1).

Another shoe with a two-piece upper was recovered from Poultry (the eastern extension of Cheapside) and purchased by the London Museum in 1925. The pattern of its two-piece upper with a complete join at the heel, in addition to a single, leather thonged side-seam (Fig 3.101, MOL A28033) is similar to the slip-on style of most of the 10th-century shoes from Milk Street, which suggests that although unstratified it could have been contemporary.

3.98. Tenth-century shoe from Milk Street, No 272: shoe as preserved and pattern of the upper and sole. The sole has a lasting margin with edge/flesh stitch holes. Scale 1:3.

A feature common to all the shoes of the 10th century, and which continued to be prevalent for many generations, is the presence of stitch holes round the top edge of the upper. Ankle-boots from the 11th and 12th centuries show that such stitch holes held in place a top-band or binding, which varied considerably in size and style. It is probable that a similar practice was adopted in the

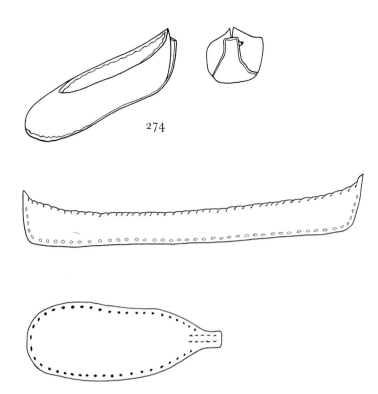

274

3.99. Child's shoe from the 10th century, No 274: shoe as preserved and pattern of the upper and sole. The sole was tunnel-stitched at the extension to the heel. Scale 1 :3.

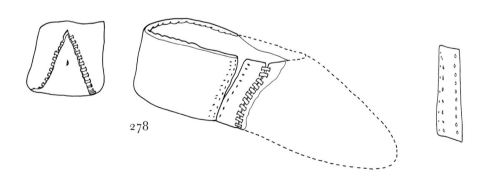

278

3.100. Tenth-century shoe from Milk Street, No 278: shoe as preserved with reconstructed toe and vamp, and pattern of side insert. Note that the backseam does not extend to the top edge of the back-part. Scale 1 :3.

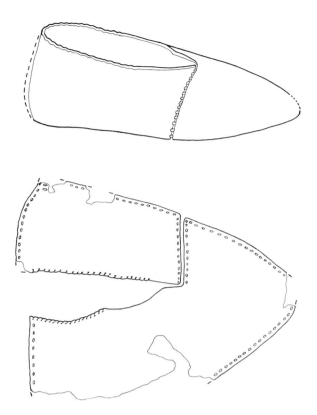

3.101. Shoe from the Poultry, MOL A28033: reconstructed and pattern of the upper. Scale 1 :3.

10th century, thus causing the shoes to have fitted higher at the ankle than is now apparent. Additionally, or alternatively, the stitching may have helped to secure a lining in place, as was suggested by Richardson in his report on a group of 'Anglo-Danish' shoes from Hungate in York (Richardson 1959, 90). An additional hypothesis put forward by MacGregor, in relation to a low-cut shoe of similar pattern to many of those from Milk Street, was that the stitching at the throat may have been for attaching a tongue or gusset (MacGregor 1982, 139-40, Fig 71, No 545), and in this respect it may be observed that St Aldhelm and two nuns at Barking are shown wearing shoes with tongues in a late 10th-century manuscript drawing (London, Lambeth Palace Library MS 200 f.68v; Temple 1976, 62-3, No 39, PL 132).

The practice of sewing the upper to the sole with a narrow leather thong is an important chronological feature, since the footwear from London shows it to have been commonplace in the 10th century, but of declining popularity in the following century, and present only on one shoe from a 12th-century deposit; the pattern of the latter shoe also indicates that it belonged to an earlier era of shoemaking (No 280). When stitched with leather the edge of the sole was pared ('skived') with a knife and the margin then pierced with edge/flesh stitch holes, spaced at intervals of c.5mm, while the thong passed through the entire thickness of the leather upper (eg Figs 3.97-3.99, Nos 272 and 274). Two 10th-century shoes from Milk Street sewn in this manner also appear to include a thin rand (Nos 271 and 279), a detail which can also be seen on the shoe from Poultry and two from deposits of a slightly later date along the waterfront (Fig 3.102, No 280; and No 283). The purpose of a rand was to keep a shoe watertight and there may have been a long tradition in England as a stitched shoe with a rand was among those recorded from the ship burial at Sutton Hoo (East 1983, 793, Fig 569, a and b). Rands have also been recorded on shoes sewn with leather from Little Paxton, Cambridgeshire (Thornton 1969, 91), which are in a similar style to some 10th-century shoes from London. However, on the London shoes, the presence of narrow strips of

3.102. *Detail of a shoe upper joined to the sole with a leather thong, No 280. The sole leather has laminated along the lasting margin leaving behind a narrow strip.*

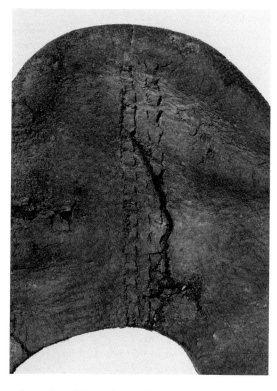

leather (10mm or 11mm in width) along the lasting margins can be explained by the sole leather laminating along the line of the stitching.

Three 10th-century London shoes, including one with a side-seam (No 312), have soles with a different type of lasting margin. The margin here takes the form of a channel of tunnel-holes, which penetrate the flesh side of the leather but not the grain except at the v-back where the tunnel-holes change to grain/flesh holes piercing the full thickness of the leather (Nos 311-313). As described below, this method is more prevalent among the 11th-century footwear from London and the modification of the margin appears to be associated with a change in the sewing medium, namely from leather to a thread of wool (see p.221), a supposition reinforced by the absence of any leather thonging in the margin of soles of this type from London, despite the presence of repair patches attached by leather on one example (No 312). By contrast, leather sewing thongs are invariably preserved on soles with the more common form of lasting margin from London. Footwear from Oxford with similar tunnel-stitched lasting margins was, nevertheless, sewn with leather thongs (Thornton 1977, 160) so that the method cannot be considered exclusive to one type of thread.

One shoe with the upper joined to the sole with leather preserves evidence of decoration. This takes the form of two vamp-stripes indicated by four rows of incisions on the grain side of the fairly stout calfskin upper (Fig 3.103, No 285). The shoe was recovered from a watching brief at Swan Lane in association only with sherds of Roman pottery and consequently it is not possible to give it an accurate date. It is clearly not a Roman shoe style, and its rounded toe and thonged lasting

3.103. *Shoe upper decorated with vamp-stripes from Swan Lane, No 285. Scale: drawing, 1:3.*

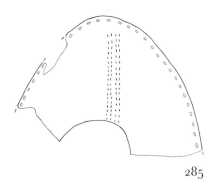

285

margin point, on present evidence, to the 10th century. English figurative art of the 10th century provides many examples of shoes with vamp-stripes worn by both men and women, for example the representations of Pope Sixtus II, Gregory the Great and their deacons, Laurence and Peter, embroidered on the maniple of St Cuthbert made between 909 and 916 (Battiscombe 1956, Pls xxv and xxiv), and the drawing of Philosophy on the frontispiece to a manuscript of *c*.970 (Cambridge, Trinity College MS 0.3.7, f.1; Temple 1976, 47, No 20, Pl 44). It is evident, nevertheless, that this form of decoration had a long tradition, since one pair of shoes from Sutton Hoo, was also decorated in this manner (East 1983, 809 and Figs 520 and 573).

Eleventh-century footwear

There is only a scant amount of footwear from deposits in London which date to the first half of the 11th century (Fig 3.96) so that any development or transition in styles during the century is difficult to trace or to attribute to a particular continental source with any degree of authority. Deposits of late 11th-century date yielding leatherwork are, however, more numerous in London and, therefore, shoe styles can be more clearly perceived. The principal group of late 11th-century leather was recovered from the waterfront at New Fresh Wharf. Footwear from a waterfront bank at Billingsgate also dates to this period. There are, in addition, two ankle-boots from pit 55 at Milk Street (Nos 302-303) and a leather-stitched shoe from pit 62 at Watling Court (No 279), which are assigned to ceramic phase four and which are described in the section on footwear of the late 11th century.

1000-1050

One of the few examples of footwear from a deposit dating to the first half of the 11th century is the toe section of what was probably an ankle-boot with a side-seam (No 280). The upper was attached to the sole with a leather thong but the shape of the toe is slightly more pointed than for footwear of the 10th century (Fig 3.102). Incomplete though it is, the pattern this shoe most closely resembles is an ankle-boot shaped for a left foot excavated at King Street, off Cheapside, in 1927, which was later purchased at auction by the London Museum (Fig 3.104, MOL 73.104/1). Such

ankle-boots with a flap over the instep fastened with a T-shaped leather toggle, which interlocked with a tab secured at the side by a knot hidden on the inside of the quarter, have also been recorded from Oxford (Thornton 1977, 156, Fig 35, No 11, and 160) and a number of sites in York (Thornton and Goodfellow 1958, 526, Fig 6, No 5; Richardson 1959, 88, Fig 22, Nos 7-10; MacGregor 1982, 141, Fig 72, No 627), showing that the style was a common one of the period. It is fortunate, therefore, that the example from New Fresh Wharf helps to place the style within the London sequence. An early 11th-century date for such ankle-boots would also help to explain why animal fibre thread, probably wool, was sometimes used in place of leather to join the upper to the sole, as on an example from York (Mac Gregor 1982, 138). Indeed, it is probable that an incomplete boot, which has a wide tunnel-stitched lasting margin (No 286), and was recovered from a deposit dated 1039-1040, was another shoe of this style sewn with wool thread. Low boots fastened in a similar manner with a leather toggle are considered to date to *c*.9th century on the continent, where examples have been recovered from beneath the foundations of the abbey at Middelburg on the island of Walcheren in Zeeland (Hendriks 1964, 115, Abb 25). Further evidence, however, is needed to prove that any English examples can be dated so early.

There are also pieces of an ankle-boot in a wrap-round pattern with a side-seam cut from thick leather (No 295). The shoe apparently fastened with a drawstring, which passed through a slot on each side of the throat. This is another style not encountered among 10th-century shoes from London and the closest parallels from England appear to be two ankle-boots from Hungate, York (Richardson 1959, 87, Fig 21, Nos 1 and 2), although the damaged condition of the London example makes the comparison tentative.

Other fragments of footwear from London of this date include two side inserts for ankle-boots (Nos 306-307), of which one has slots for a drawstring (Fig 3.105) and is similar in style to an insert forming part of an ankle-boot with a centre front opening recovered from a contemporary deposit in Lund, southern Sweden (Blomqvist and Mårtensson 1963, 183, Fig 194). There are, in addition, fragments of two top-bands. One is a plain strip (No 347) and would have been lined, while the other was folded along one side and finished with a double row of decorative stitching

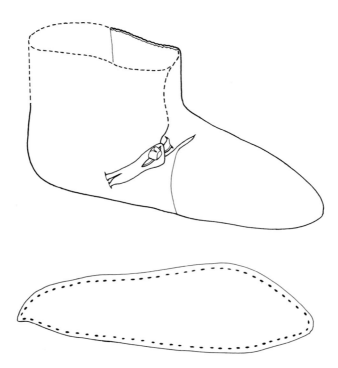

3.104. Ankle-boot with a latchet fastening from King Street, MOL 73.104/1 : ankle-boot as preserved with the quarters partly reconstructed and pattern of sole showing it was shaped for a left foot. Scale 1 :3.

(Fig 3.122, No 353). These four items offer a fore-taste of the ankle-boots, which predominate among the footwear of the late 11th century and show that styles which demanded a greater amount of cutting and stitching were already being worn in the City early in the century. By contrast, a low-cut shoe from Milk Street (No 278) looks back to a 10th-century style and, indeed, is probably residual since it was recovered from a pit which intercut an earlier one.

1050-1100

Typical traits of London's late 11th-century foot-wear are easier to identify. Ankle-boots, most of which appear to have opened at the side and been fastened with a drawstring, became common-place. This resulted in uppers no longer being cut as one-piece. Inserts were added both in the form of a flap at the side to conceal the gap where the opening lay, and at the throat, which was cut squarer to add height above the instep. The side

flap was seamed to the vamp wing (eg Nos 288 and 298), or the vamp side of a slit cut in the quarters (eg No 287), while the throat insert was stitched to the throat on three sides (Figs 3.111-3.112). Side-seams became customary and the pattern of the sole, which basically remained unchanged, caused a triangular piece to be removed from the upper to accommodate the v-back, a feature also apparent on side-seamed shoes in London during the 10th century. The only minor alteration to the shape of the sole was

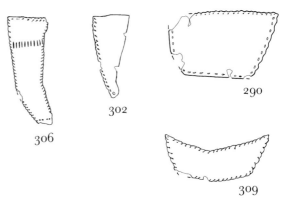

3.105. Inserts from 11th-century ankle-boots: side insert, No 306; side flap, No 302; throat inserts, Nos 290 and 309. Scale 1 :3.

that the tail of the heel became slightly more asymmetrical to help lessen the strain on the leather when the shoe was being worn (Fig 3.114), and the margin was fractionally cut away at the waist to achieve a better fit (Fig 3.112). These two observations, however, are based on a very limited amount of evidence since no complete soles are preserved. The lasting margin of the sole was usually tunnel-stitched and coarse two-ply thread, 2.5mm to 3mm in diameter, tended to supplant narrow strips of leather for attaching the upper to the sole, although leather thongs continued to be used in cobbling soles. Traces of fibre thread are preserved in some lasting margins, especially those of two ankle-boots from pit 55 at Milk Street (Nos 302-303), which show the thread was s-plied from two z-twisted yarns and sewn continuously in one direction (Fig 3.114), rather than having two threads stitched in opposite directions as might have been anticipated. A sample of thread from No 303 was submitted to Michael Ryder to identify whether the fibre was wool or goat-hair and he comments that, 'the sample is certainly [a] true hairy [fleece-type] with a continuous distribution from 13 to 87 microns with a hair at 121 microns. The mean is 43.6 ± 21.8 microns and the mode 41 microns

with 24% medullated fibres and 2% pigmented fibres. Since this fleece-type is used in carpets rather than clothing you do not get many [examples] and, although it could be goat, I think on balance that this is sheep'. Similar wool thread is preserved in some slots cut in the top-bands of ankle-boots (Fig 3.122, No 302).

Before the end of the 11th century, a further development took place with the lasting margin on some shoes being reduced in width and edge/flesh stitch holes, spaced at intervals of c.3mm, replacing tunnel-stitching on soles with v-backs (Fig 3.115, No 322). The reason for this change appears to have been a switch from thick wool thread to a finer thread made from a plant fibre, most probably flax. Why this happened is difficult to understand since linen thread had been in use for generations for sewing side-seams and bindings on shoes. The elongated character of the stitch holes on the uppers also suggests that two threads were introduced for sewing the upper to the sole, which resulted in the threads entering each hole from opposite directions (Waateringe 1984, Abb 7.1-3)

Another feature of late 11th-century footwear was that the toe probably increased in length, at least to judge by the negative evidence that none

3.106. Two late 11th-century ankle-boots, Nos 287 and 298.

Ceramic phase	Uppers of low-cut shoes	Ankle boot uppers				Soles				Top-bands			Drawstrings		
	Calf	Calf	Cow	Sheep/goat	Too worn	Calf	Cow	Calf/Cow	Too worn	Calf	Sheep/goat	Too worn	Calf	Sheep/goat	Too worn
CP1	6	—	—	—	—	1	2	1	2	—	—	—	—	—	—
CP2	—	—	—	—	—	—	—	—	—	—	—	—	—	—	—
CP3	1	1	—	—	—	—	—	—	—	—	(1)	—	—	—	—
CP4	—	6	—	2 (2)	1	—	—	1	—	1 (4)	1	2	(1)	(2)	3
CP5	—	1 (1)	—	2	—	—	—	1	—	—	—	—	—	—	1

*KEY: ( ) species not positively confirmed

3.107. *Table showing the types of leather used for footwear in London in the 10th to mid-12th centuries based on a sample of the total assemblage.*

of the London shoes preserves the toe intact.

Several factors may have been responsible for the new pattern of ankle-boot, which can be seen to have been worn in many towns throughout northern Europe, including Haithabu (Waateringe 1984, Taf 13) and Lund (Blomqvist and Mårtensson 1963, Figs 187-189), by the middle of the 11th century. One factor revealed from an examination of the leather used for nine ankle-boots of the late 11th century from London was that goatskin or sheepskin was being used as well as calfskin for uppers, whereas the sample tested showed that earlier styles were exclusively cut from calf-leather (Fig 3.107). The percentage of goatskin uppers was even greater among the shoes from Haithabu (Waateringe 1984, Abb 15), but more sampling is required to determine how widespread the phenomenon was in Europe at this period.

A further characteristic of the ankle-boots was to finish the top edge with a leather band also cut from either calfskin or sheep/goatskin (Fig 3.107). At least seven styles of top-bands were produced, of which five types were cut with rows of tiny vertical slots to take decorative stitching. Occasionally, a top-band was folded over to expose the ankle (Fig 3.113, No 303) but more frequently it remained upright against the leg (Figs 3.106 and 3.108, No 287).

There are at least five styles present among the ankle-boots, distinguishable by the manner in which they were finished once the basic pattern had been cut. One style, represented by five examples (Nos 287-291), has a series of closely spaced thong slots on each quarter. Two thongs were inserted through these slots and each thong was cut with tiny horizontal slits so that the thongs could be pulled through one another at the junction of the thong slot on the shoe to produce a decorative effect (Figs 3.106 and 3.108, No 287). An additional detail retained by one ankle-boot is its top-band, made from a narrow strip of leather folded double to a height of only 8mm and cut, after it was folded and sewn into position, with a single row of small slots, which penetrate the leather on each side of the band. Below the row of vertical slots is a horizontal slot which, when the band was sewn in place, would have been positioned on the inside quarters, and probably helped to secure the side flap and keep the side opening of the shoe closed. One ankle-boot of this type was cut without a slit at the quarters, so that a larger flap would have been necessary to conceal the gap at the side of the ankle (Fig 3.109, No 288).

Another contemporary style of ankle-boot was also characterised by intricate patterning carried out with two thongs, which were inserted through alternate slots front and back to create a 'chequered' effect (Fig 3.110, No 292). The three ankle-boots from London displaying this characteristic (Nos 292-294) are less well preserved than those of the style previously described and the reconstruction illustrated is consequently less certain.

A third style of ankle-boot with a side opening was fastened with a single drawstring, which was inserted through slots spaced further apart than

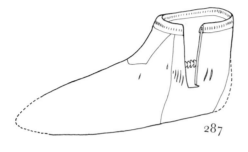

287

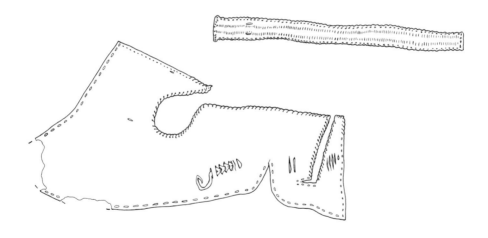

those with decorative thonging. One example, which preserves part of its sole shaped for a right foot, proves that the side-seam and side opening were placed on the inside of the ankle (Fig 3.111, No 296). A child's ankle-boot was made to a similar pattern but the smaller size of the upper meant that no slit was cut in the quarters and instead the side flap was sewn to the vamp wing (Fig 3.106 and 3.112, No 298). A top-band preserved in association with another of these ankle-

boots has, instead of being folded double, a narrow hem along the top sewn with two rows of decorative stitching, resulting in a finished height of 22mm (Fig 3.122, No 302).

The fourth style of ankle-boot from late 11th-century London is limited to one example, which was recovered from pit 55 at Milk Street (Fig 3.113, No 303). It appears, from the pattern of the sole, to have been shaped for the right foot with a side-seam on the outside quarter. The side-seam was sewn together with a 2mm wide thong of leather, although wool thread was used to join the upper to the sole. An ankle-strap, which passed over the instep was stitched to the vamp wing, while a small triangular insert was sewn to the throat side of the strap, which seems to have been matched by a corresponding insert on the opposite side of the throat. Whether the throat inserts overlapped one another is conjectural. Passing through the throat insert, the lower part of the strap and quarters of the ankle-boot is a drawstring, while sewn to the top edge round the heel opening was a plain band, which folded over to reveal the ankle. The pattern of this ankle-boot

appears to be unparalleled, although the style can be compared to roughly contemporary shoes fastened with drawstrings ('leash shoes') from Borgund on the west coast of Norway where a top-band (rather than an ankle strap) was sewn to a slit cut in the quarters and along the edge of the side opening before passing round the throat and the rest of the top edge (Larsen 1970, 24-7, Pls IV and V). These shoes, therefore, did not require a side flap.

The fifth style of ankle-boot is represented by four examples, of which the earliest was recovered from a deposit dating no later than 1080. The pattern consists of a wrap-round upper cut either

3.109. Late 11th-century ankle-boot with a side opening, No 288: reconstructed and pattern of upper. The pattern of the inside quarters should be contrasted with No 287, Fig 3.108. Scale 1:3.

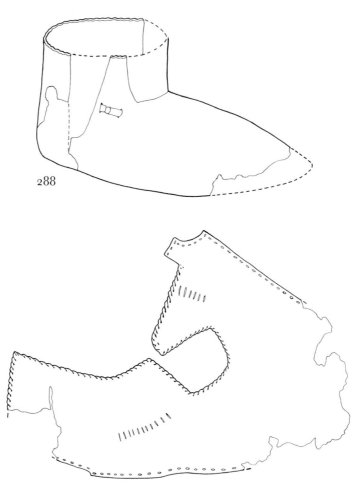

288

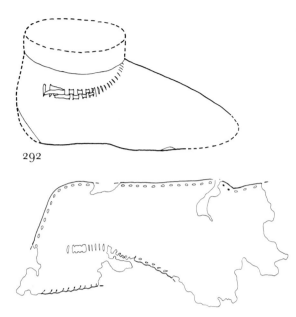

292

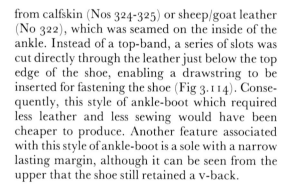

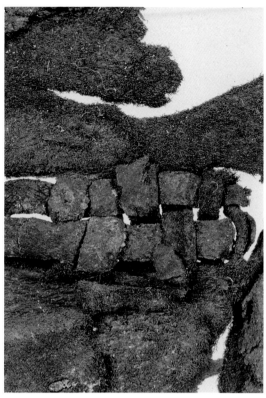

3.110. Late 11th-century ankle-boot with two drawstrings inserted through alternate slots, No 292. Scale: drawing, 1:3.

from calfskin (Nos 324-325) or sheep/goat leather (No 322), which was seamed on the inside of the ankle. Instead of a top-band, a series of slots was cut directly through the leather just below the top edge of the shoe, enabling a drawstring to be inserted for fastening the shoe (Fig 3.114). Consequently, this style of ankle-boot which required less leather and less sewing would have been cheaper to produce. Another feature associated with this style of ankle-boot is a sole with a narrow lasting margin, although it can be seen from the upper that the shoe still retained a v-back.

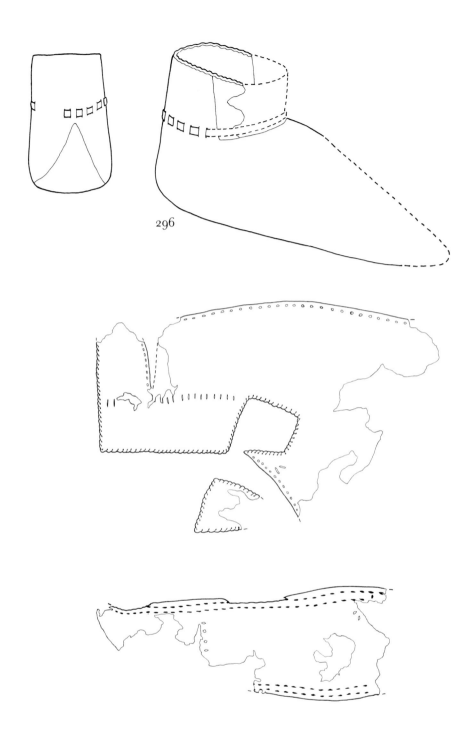

3.111. *Late 11th-century ankle-boot with a drawstring fastening, No 296: reconstructed and pattern of upper, throat insert and sole. The sole has a tunnel-stitched lasting margin and was repaired across the forepart and heel-seat. Scale 1 :3.*

296

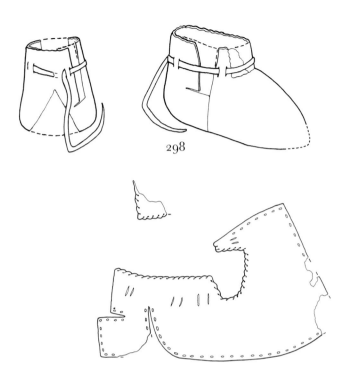

298

3.112. Child's ankle-boot with a side opening and drawstring fastening from the late 11th-century, No 298: reconstructed and pattern of upper and throat insert. Scale 1 :3.

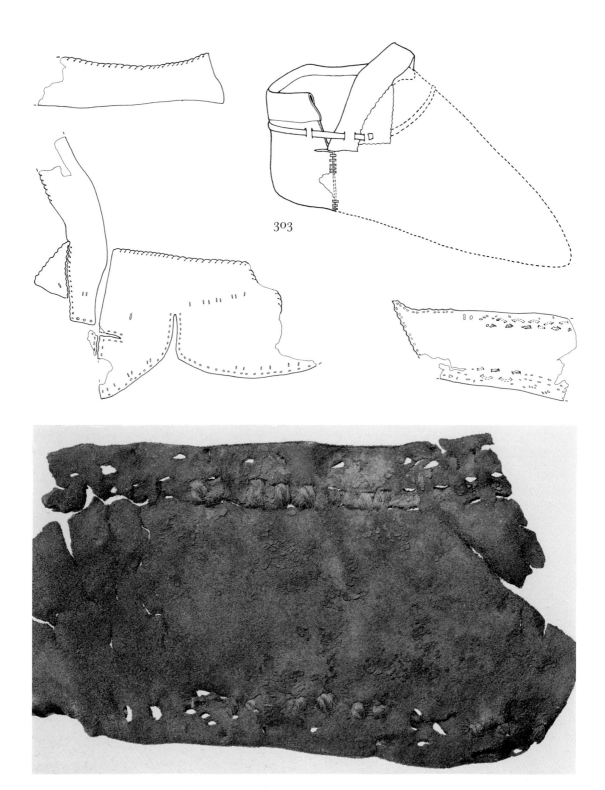

303

3.113. Late 11th-century ankle-boot with a strap over the instep, a folded top-band and a drawstring fastening, No 303: reconstructed and pattern of upper with a triangular insert, instep strap, and top-band; and sole. Scale: drawing, 1:3. Detail of lasting margin sewn with a single thread of two-ply wool.

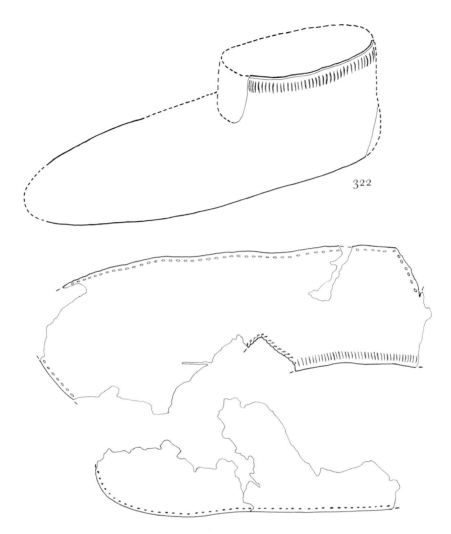

3.114. *Late 11th-century ankle-boot with a drawstring fastening along the top edge, No 322: reconstructed and pattern of upper and sole. The sole has a narrow lasting margin with edge/flesh stitch-holes. Scale: drawing, 1:3. Detail of lasting margin.*

Further changes had taken place in footwear by the middle of the 12th century. The main break with the past was to abandon the v-back sole, influenced by the new emphasis placed on the shape of the toe. This was epitomised at the court of William Rufus in the decade before 1100 by the fashion for shoes with pointed toes curled like scorpions' tails and rams' horns, which were castigated by contemporary chroniclers (Barlow 1983, 104). Orderic Vitalis, in particular, bewailed the aping of the style among the lower classes and the truth of his claim is here illustrated by three ankle-boots with exaggerated toes from deposits dating to the second quarter of the 12th century (Figs 3.117-3.119, Nos 338-340). Blunt, pointed toes are more usual among excavated footwear of this period but a wider turnover of toe styles can be perceived by the presence in the same dump at Seal House of an ankle-boot with a round toe (Fig 3.121, No 342).

The rejection of the v-back sole led to new ways of reinforcing the heel. One method favoured was the use of a heel-stiffener, which was whip-stitched to the inside of the upper at the heel. The earliest shoes from London with this feature are two ankle-boots from the waterfront at Seal House (Nos 332 and 342). A more alluring solution was the addition of a triangular *appliqué* patch sewn to the outside but since this only occurs on a shoe with a distinctive low-cut vamp, it was presumably intended chiefly as a form of decoration rather than as a reinforcement (Fig 3.121, No 343).

The upper was also restyled at this period but the preference for ankle-boots remained. Side openings and side flaps disappeared and various small inserts were added to complete the wrap-round pattern when necessary, for example adjoining the back-part at the heel (Fig 3.119, No 340), or at the ankle (Fig 3.120, No 342), or alongside the vamp wing (No 344). The square throat was replaced by a small flap cut all in one with the upper; a second flap was then stitched along two sides of the throat, which either crossed in front or more probably behind the flap of the upper. Drawstring fastenings remained usual but the number of thong slots was reduced to generally just one pair on each wing or quarter, although occasionally pairs of slots were positioned above one another indicating that the drawstring was wound round the ankle more than once (Nos 326 and 333). Patterned thonging on

the quarters, a feature associated with side-opening ankle-boots, also disappeared since to be effective a series of closely spaced slots was essential. In its place the vamp-stripe embroidered in silk became the most popular form of decoration (Nos 327-337). Less common was geometric openwork decoration, which is represented by one ankle-boot from Seal House with a circle cut out on the ankle-bone (Fig 3.120, No 342), and appliqué work, which is likewise limited to one example, namely a shoe with an ankle-fastening and low-cut vamp (Fig 3.121, No 343).

The developments outlined above are examined in the following section by looking at five shoe styles from London dating to the first half of the 12th-century, all of which were cut to a basic wrap-round pattern with a side-seam.

An ankle-boot from Billingsgate, of which only a small part of the upper is preserved, illustrates the change in the styling of the throat to include a flap cut as part of the upper (Fig 3.115, No 326). This particular ankle-boot is characterised by a drawstring, which was wound twice round the ankle, and a seam up the centre of the vamp, the latter feature being more prevalent among footwear on the continent, including examples from north Germany and Antwerp, Belgium (Hald 1972, 69-75; Waateringe 1984, Abb 13; Walle 1961, Pl XVIIIc). The vamp seam on the shoe found in London is the work of an experienced hand for the edge of the leather was skived so that the overlapping leather lay smooth and the top of the seam at the throat was reinforced with five tunnel-stitches to prevent it splitting open (Fig 3.115). The seam, itself, consists of tiny horizontal slots, through which a thread would have been drawn resulting in a decorative finish. The origin of this type of seam was constructional since it evolved from shoes cut entirely in one-piece with the vamp open at each end, which consequently required to be sewn up the centre of the vamp (eg Hald 1972, 72 and 74, Figs 75-76, 79 and 80; Waateringe 1984, Tafs 1-2 and 8).

As stated above a more common form of vamp decoration on the London footwear of the 12th century was the vamp-stripe, which consisted not of a seam but of rows of embroidery stitches, which penetrated only the grain side of the leather leaving the inside smooth and, therefore, more comfortable to wear. There are at least eleven examples of ankle-boots decorated in this manner from deposits at Billingsgate and Seal House dating to the first half of the 12th century and a further one of similar date from the waterfront at

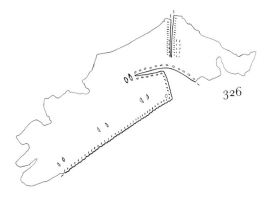

326

3.115. Part of upper from a late 11th- or early 12th-century ankle-boot with a vamp-seam and slots for a draw-string fastening, No 326. Scale: drawing, 1:3. Detail of vamp seam: a) grain side; b) flesh side.

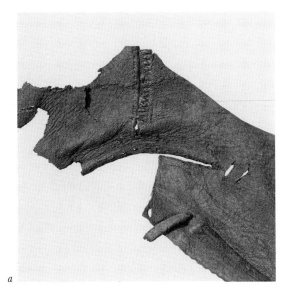

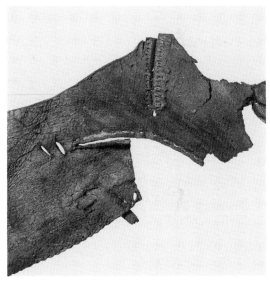

a

b

Baynard's Castle (Rhodes 1980d, 112, No 143, Pl 17; note the dating has been refined as a result of recent work, see Appendix I). This latter shoe has four stripes, whereas among the other eleven, seven have three stripes (Nos 327-331, 333 and 335), three have two stripes (Nos 332, 334 and 337), and one has a single stripe (No 336). An ankle-boot of this character from Seal House retains most of its embroidery showing that single-stranded silk thread, undyed and dyed red and (?)green, was used (Fig 3.116, No 328). Silk thread of this type lacking in twist had several advantages over plied silk thread since it would have been cheaper to obtain, more lustrous in appearance and less likely to tear the leather. The stitch employed, plait-stitch, was also well chosen since most of the thread remains visible on the sur-face, while the reverse consists of a hidden row of horizontal tunnel-stitches. This is the only type of embroidery stitch evident from the early 12th-century group from London, although vestiges of silk thread are also preserved in the vamp-stripe of the shoe from Baynard's Castle. A contemporary group of 12th-century shoes from Bergen, Norway, reveals a greater variety of silk embroidery showing the repertoire of stitches to have included cross-stitch and satin-stitch, in addition to plait-stitch, and a wider range of colour effects (Pedersen in Larsen forthcoming), and it is probable that a similar variety was current in London. Vamp-stripes persist on footwear recovered from later 12th-century deposits in London (Pritchard in Grew and de Neergaard 1988, 77). In the first half of the 12th century,

Small Finds 231

3.116. *Detail of vamp stripe embroidered in plait-stitch using red, white and (?) green silk. The two stripes on the left were sewn from the throat to the toe and the one on the right from the toe to the throat. Ankle-boot, No 328.*

however, such embellishment appears to have been principally confined to wrap-round ankle-boots with a throat flap and drawstring fastening.

It may be observed that none of the embroidered ankle-boots from London have exaggerated toes, although the decoration focussed attention on the vamp. This evidence contrasts with examples from Bergen (Larsen forthcoming) and that portrayed by a small, copper alloy figure of a soldier wearing armour of mid 12th- century design in the Wallace Collection, whose pointed shoes with a pronounced outward curl, are decorated with a vamp-stripe (Mann 1931, S151, Pl 38). London's archaeological record, therefore, probably does not reflect the full extent of the fashion but it does emphasise the popularity of the vamp-stripe in the 12th century and shows in part, at least, how the decoration was accomplished.

The pronounced shape of the toe that developed at the court of William II in the decade

before 1100 is reflected in three ankle-boots from London fastened with drawstrings. Two examples from Seal House have uppers cut in one-piece from finely-dressed sheep or goat leather (Figs 3.117 and 3.118, Nos 338-339). The pattern of No 338 is a particular *tour de force* in its simplicity of cut, and, since the opening for the foot is not stitched, the ankle-boot apparently had no binding round the top to divert attention away from the toe. A third example was less skilfully cut and required a horizontal insert at the lower edge of the back-part (Fig 3.119, No 340), another feature associated with the disappearance of the v-back sole.

The 'scorpion's tail' character of the toe is distinctive and entirely different in form from that which developed in the 14th century (Grew and Neergaard 1988, 29). Also, in contrast to 14th-century piked shoes, no moss or moss impressions remain on the inside of the upper or the sole, which suggests, albeit negatively, that tow could have been used as a stuffing material in the early 12th century as literary sources imply. The strain such a toe style could have induced on a foot with a bunion joint (*hallux valgus*) may account for the stitched slit or dart present on the upper of the Billingsgate ankle-boot (Fig 3.119, No 340), and lends some credence to the claim of Orderic Vitalis that the fashion was designed to conceal the bunions on the feet of Count Fulk of Anjou (Barlow 1983, 104). The toe style, however, is evident as early as 1080 in the remarkable portrayal of Rudolf, King of Swabia on his bronze tomb-cover in Merseburg Cathedral, East Germany (Beckwith 1969, 175, Fig 164). Thus while it has been suggested that contact with the orient during the First Crusade could have inspired the eccentric shape of the toe (Harris 1987, 10), the fashion evidently appeared in the west before the crusaders reached Constantinople in 1097.

The style of the ankle-boot with openwork decoration (Fig 3.120, No 342) closely resembles that of other early 12th-century shoes from London, and it is only the form of decoration and shape of toe that is different. Similarly, it is the low-cut opening over the instep with the ankle-fastening above it, and the *appliqué* work decoration at the heel, which singles out another ankle-boot (Fig 3.121, No 343). Both styles, nevertheless, show a new concern for the nature of hose worn beneath the shoe, a fact vividly illustrated by contemporary manuscript illuminations, such as the Winchester Psalter (London, British Library, MS Cotton, Nero C.IV; Wormald 1973).

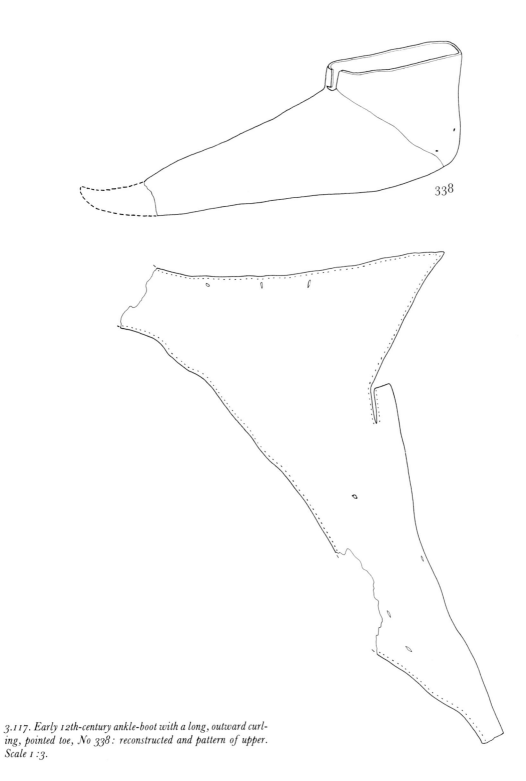

338

3.117. *Early 12th-century ankle-boot with a long, outward curling, pointed toe, No 338: reconstructed and pattern of upper. Scale 1 :3.*

3.118. Early 12th-century ankle-boot with a long, outward curling, pointed toe and a drawstring fastening round the ankle, No 339: reconstructed and pattern of upper sole. The sole was repaired across the forepart and and heel-seat. Scale 1:3.

339

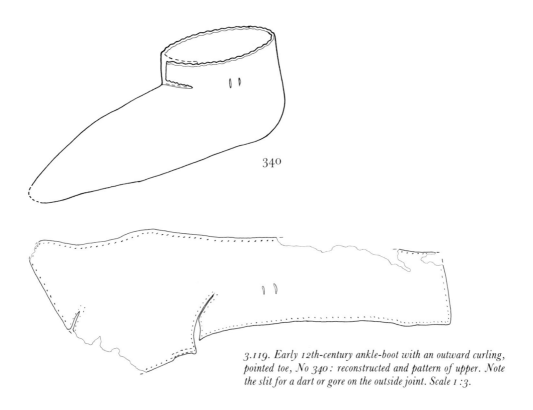

340

3.119. Early 12th-century ankle-boot with an outward curling, pointed toe, No 340: reconstructed and pattern of upper. Note the slit for a dart or gore on the outside joint. Scale 1:3.

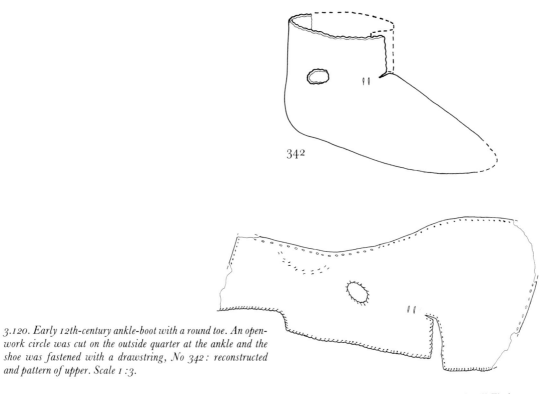

342

3.120. Early 12th-century ankle-boot with a round toe. An openwork circle was cut on the outside quarter at the ankle and the shoe was fastened with a drawstring, No 342: reconstructed and pattern of upper. Scale 1:3.

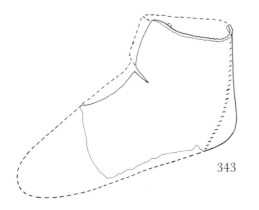

343

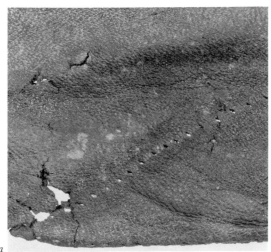

a

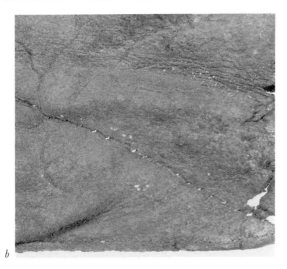

b

3.121. Early 12th-century ankle-boot with a low cut vamp and stitching for an appliqué patch at the heel, No 343: reconstructed. Scale: drawing, 1:3. Detail of the awl-holes and stitch impressions associated with the appliqué patch: a) grain side; b) flesh side.

Shoe top-bands

Evidence for bindings occur on most shoes from London of the 10th to 12th centuries, but only three have been found in direct association with ankle-boots (Nos 287, 302, and 303). Loose examples, however, are fairly numerous especially from 11th-century deposits, which perhaps suggests that in the 10th century shoes were more often trimmed with fur or cloth, which have suffered more severely from decay or from being recycled.

Top-bands were fashioned in a variety of ways of which the most common consisted of a strip of leather ranging from 13mm to 34mm in width lined with a similar strip of leather (Type A; Fig 3.122, No 348), or, since both pieces are rarely preserved, either the lining or the outside may have sometimes been cut from cloth of a contrasting colour. One example (No 350) has three ragged holes along the centre of the band suggesting that gemstones or imitation baubles could have been attached to it, which were removed before the leather strip was discarded. A style which required less sewing since it only had to be stitched to the top edge of the upper was a plain strip that folded over like a collar (Fig 3.113, No 303). There is only one example of this type from London and the style may have lacked popular appeal. Some of the lined wider bands could, however, have been folded over to create a similar effect, such as seen on an example from Lund (Blomqvist and Mårtensson 1963, 185, Fig 196).

It was more usual for the top edge of a band to be folded inwards to form a narrow hem, which was then cut with either one or two rows of closely-spaced, vertical slots and sewn with coloured thread (Types B and C; Fig 3.122, Nos 352-354). Top-bands from London of this type were made from leather strips of between 30mm and 37mm in width giving a finished height of 20mm to 28mm (Nos 302, and 352-354).

A stiffer finish to a top-band was achieved by folding the leather double and interlining it with another strip (Fig 3.123, No 356). Such bindings were sewn in place by stitching one side of the band to the top edge of the upper, the leather was then folded over and the second side oversewn on the inside of the shoe. The side of the top-band stitched first to the upper has grain/flesh stitch holes penetrating right through the leather, while that stitched to the inside of the upper pierced only the edge of the leather band and, indeed, sometimes wandered off the leather altogether in

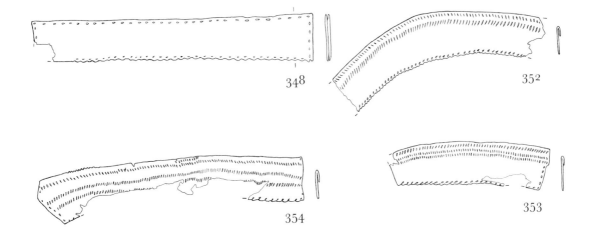

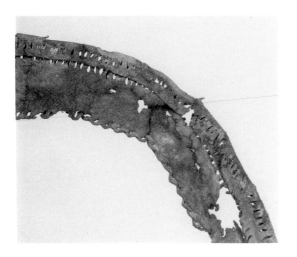

3.122. *Top-bands from 11th-century ankle-boots: two strips formerly sewn together with the grain side outer-most, No 348; band folded along the top and cut with a single row of slots, No 352; band folded along the top and cut with two rows of slots, the narrow width of the hem resulted in only the top row of slots piercing the folded thickness of leather, Nos 353 and 354. Scale: drawing, 1:3. Detail of slots on top-band of ankle-boot No 302 showing traces of wool thread.*

the effort to keep the stitches concealed (eg Fig 3.123, Nos 355 and 358).

Top-bands which were folded double (Types D-G) tend to have been made from wider strips of leather measuring between 40mm and 58mm (Nos 355-359) but one example is only 16mm wide (No 287). Such bands are associated with shoes of more than one style, the narrow binding, for example, was sewn to an ankle-boot with a side flap and has a characteristic horizontal slot for securing the flap, which is apparent also on another top-band (Fig 3.123, Nos 357-358), which has three slots to help adjust the fit. A top-band cut with a v-shaped notch, which enabled it to bend at an angle of 90° (Fig 3.124, No 357), could have come from an ankle-boot with a centre front opening, similar to several examples from Lund dating to the second quarter of the 11th century (Blomqvist and Mårtensson 1963, Figs 192,

194, and 199-200). It can, however, be observed that some side-opening shoes on the continent had top-bands cut with a notch to enable the binding to be sewn to one edge of the quarters as a means of finishing the opening (Larsen 1970, Pls IV and V). The long length of leather needed for these top-bands resulted in some being cut in two strips to complete the edging. An example of one such short strip cut in this instance with three rows of slots was recovered from Swan Lane (Fig 3.124, No 359). Another example of a top-band with three rows of slots was recovered from Parliament Street, York (Tweddle 1986, 254, Fig 117, No 859), although in the report it is described as a strap. Also like some of the bindings from London it was cut from sheepskin rather than from calf leather. Where fibre remains in the slots of the London top-bands, it appears to have been wool (Fig 3.122, No 302), but an unstratified example

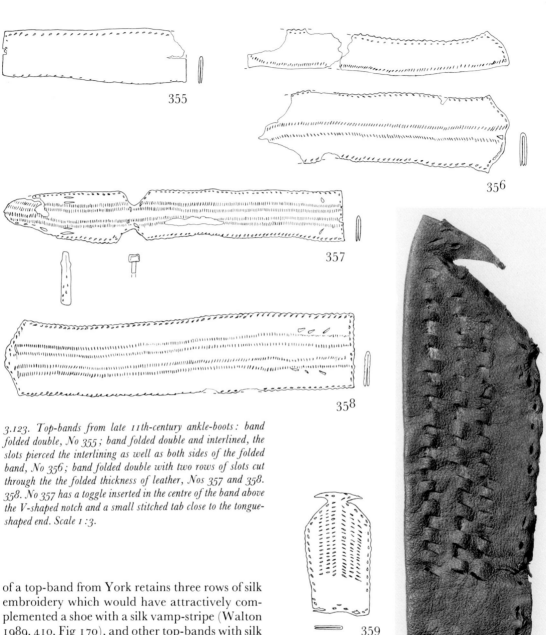

3.123. *Top-bands from late 11th-century ankle-boots: band folded double, No 355; band folded double and interlined, the slots pierced the interlining as well as both sides of the folded band, No 356; band folded double with two rows of slots cut through the the folded thickness of leather, Nos 357 and 358. 358. No 357 has a toggle inserted in the centre of the band above the V-shaped notch and a small stitched tab close to the tongue-shaped end. Scale 1 :3.*

of a top-band from York retains three rows of silk embroidery which would have attractively complemented a shoe with a silk vamp-stripe (Walton 1989, 410, Fig 170), and other top-bands with silk embroidery have been recorded among 12th-century shoes from Bergen, Norway (Pedersen in Larsen forthcoming).

The wide variety of top-bands from London is particularly notable since only two styles were identified at Haithabu from a group of 105 bindings (Waateringe 1984, Abb 198). These two styles correspond to Types B and D from London, although it can be seen that the Haithabu assemblage also included a few strip bindings of the kind which would have been lined (ie Type A) (Waateringe 1984, Taf 17, Nos 6 and 9).

3.124. *Top-band from a late 11th-century ankle-boot folded double with three rows of slots piercing the leather, No 359. Scale: drawing, 1 :3. Detail of slots.*

Straps

Fragments of seven straps were recovered, thus forming a small but important group in view of the sparse numbers recorded from the whole of England at this period. They vary in size and style, although, from those sampled, the use of calfskin was constant. One method of making straps from a single strip of leather was to fold the leather along each side, securing the hems down the centre with a butt-seam so that the grain side was exposed on each face. Three of the four straps from London made in this manner were strengthened with stitching along each side, helping the hems to lie flat and adding a decorative flourish (Fig 3.125, Nos 360-362). The tongue-end was carefully shaped on two 11th-century straps of this type (Nos 360-361), neither being styled for strap-ends, which generally appear to have been

3.125. Leather straps, Nos 360-366. Scale 1 :2.

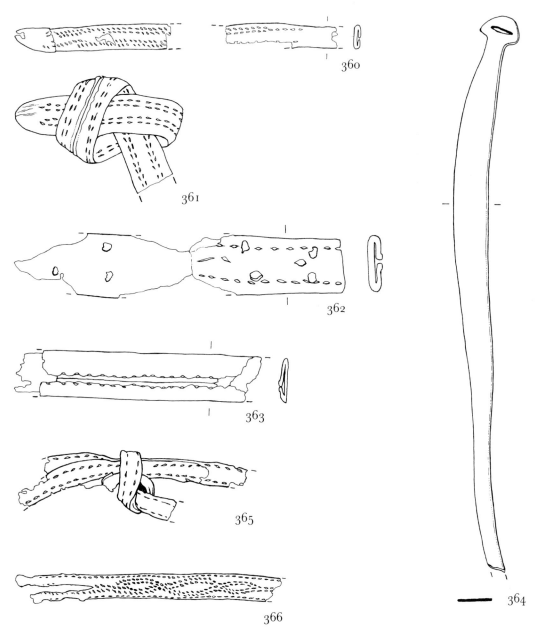

associated with leather of a single thickness. Pairs of holes positioned along part of another of these straps (No 362) suggest that they could be rivet holes from metal mounts. However, the holes are rather large for rivets and a strap of similar dimensions and date from Gloucester has a leather thong passing through the holes (Watkins 1983, 210-1, No 5).

Two other straps, probably girdles, are decoratively stitched (Fig 3.125, Nos 365 and 366). They are relatively narrow and were made from only a single thickness of leather. The latter has a pattern of simple interlace, a motif that was also sewn on a strap of this type from York (Tweddle 1986, 254, Fig 117, No 850), and which can be seen to better effect on a tablet-woven braid dating approximately to the 8th century from Elisenhof, north Germany (Hundt 1984, 69, Taf 1, No E417). This suggests that the practice of stitching patterns onto leather girdles may have been inspired by tablet-weaving. Such stitching on leather probably would have been worked in coloured thread to enhance the pattern and, together with the silk embellished vamp-stripes on a number of the shoes (see p.230), points to the popularity and importance of embroidered leatherwork in 12th-century England.

WOODEN ARTEFACTS

incorporating comments by Carole Morris

Wooden artefacts were recovered from pits at Milk Street, a well at Watling Court and from the Thames waterfront at New Fresh Wharf; all deposits where anaerobic conditions prevailed. They include household utensils, an assortment of pegs and handles and a variety of isolated items, attesting to the random nature of survival. The species of wood used for each artefact was identified wherever possible. Where no species is stated in the catalogue positive identification could not be made. The work of botanical identification was undertaken by Rowena Gale, Carole Morris, Vanessa Straker, Ian Tyers and Jacqui Watson.

Evidence for local woodworking is slight but this may be due to the lack of material preserved. A maplewood waste core from a vessel (Fig 3.126, No 367) made on a reciprocating pole-lathe (Morris 1982, 251-3) and found in a 10th-century pit at Milk Street, indicates that a wood-turning workshop may have existed somewhere in the neighbourhood of Cheapside, and a carpenter's axe was also recovered from an 11th-century pit on the same site (see p.135). Another 10th-century pit yielded fragments of a turned cup made from ash (Fig 3.126, No 368). The cup has straight sides decorated round the rim with three grooves, a common form which can be paralleled, for example, from 10th-century York (Hall 1984, Fig 82). A handled maplewood bowl or ladle can be identified from its angular handle with the grain of the wood running lengthwise (Fig 3.126, No 370) comparable to examples from Elisenhof, Novgorod and Haithabu (Szabo *et al* 1985, Abb 73-74; Schietzel 1970, 83, Abb 5), including one from the latter town which terminates in a stylised animal head (Graham-Campbell 1980, 19, No 61). The bowl was probably lathe-turned and the projecting handle finished afterwards by hand. The propensity of the handle to break is shown by this example from London and another from Winetavern Street, Dublin, where the bowl but not the handle is preserved (NMI 1973, 45, No 208). Two thicker-walled vessels, one hemispherical (No 371) and the other a rectangular trough with a lip handle at one end (Fig 3.126, No 372) were hollowed out of the trunks of ash with an adze. They would have served everyday culinary purposes, the bowl perhaps for mixing food ingredients and the trough, a traditional bread-making utensil in north west Europe, for knead-

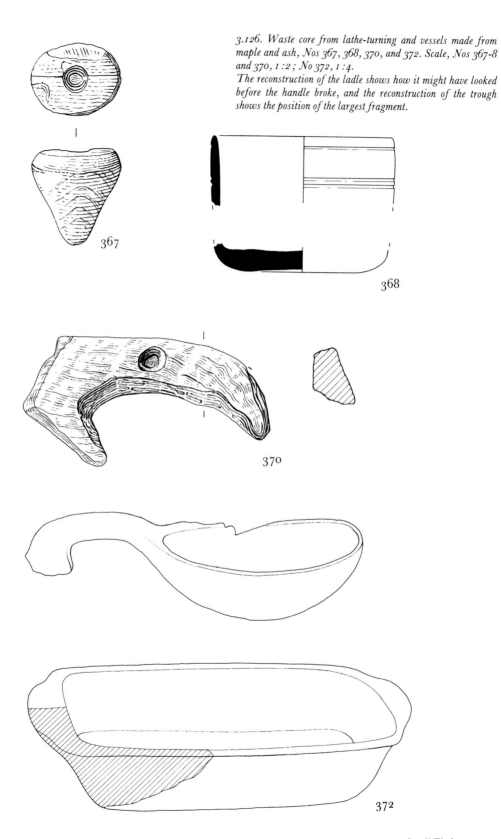

3.126. Waste core from lathe-turning and vessels made from maple and ash, Nos 367, 368, 370, and 372. Scale, Nos 367-8 and 370, 1:2; No 372, 1:4.
The reconstruction of the ladle shows how it might have looked before the handle broke, and the reconstruction of the trough shows the position of the largest fragment.

367

368

370

372

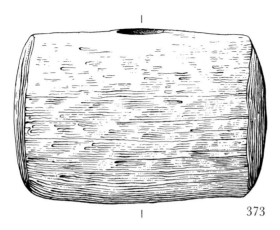

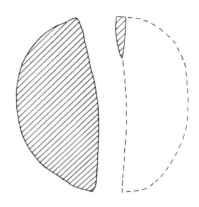

3.127. *Maplewood mallet-head and finial, Nos 373 and 374. Scale 1 :2.*

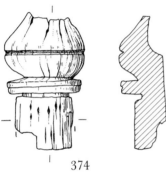

ing dough (Brøgger and Shetelig 1928, 142). Since it was considered worthwhile to repair the bowl with an iron staple, wooden vessels may not have been so cheap or plentiful in London as to be discarded immediately they cracked and examples from York show that a similar practice was adopted for wooden tableware (Richardson 1959, 85-6, Fig 20).

Ash, despite its acclaimed flexibility, was only identified otherwise for a plank of uncertain function (No 388). Maplewood, by contrast, had been selected for a wider range of artefacts including a mallet-head (Fig 3.127, No 373), part of an item of (?) furniture (Fig 3.127, No 374) and probably for the handle of a knife (Fig 3.3, No 3). The mallet-head dates to the 11th century and, since it shows little sign of wear, may have split soon after manufacture. At least three of the knives had wooden handles and, in addition to the one made from maple or fruitwood, another was probably made from box (Fig 3.2, No 9). These species

remained the most popular for knife handles during the later medieval period, since as they were fine-grained they were comfortable to hold and did not easily splinter (Cowgill *et al* 1987, 25 and Table 6).

Stave-made artefacts

Oak was used for objects which required long planks of split wood such as stave-built vessels and roof shingles. An almost complete oak pail was recovered from an 11th-century well in the City at Billingsgate Buildings (Rhodes 1980b, 144, No 144). It was bound with ash and birch hoops, an important distinction from stave-built buckets of the pagan Anglo-Saxon era which had hoops of iron or bronze (Wilson 1976, 254). A semi-circular base stave from a smaller container was recovered from the late 11th-century waterfront at New Fresh Wharf (Fig 3.128, 375). Such pails were characteristic of daily life in 11th-century towns and parallels can be cited, for example, from Lund and Dublin (Graham-Campbell 1980, 15, Nos 35-36). The bases of smaller vessels were cut from a single stave; two examples of very similar dimensions were recovered from a late 11th-century pit at Milk Street (Fig 3.128, Nos 376-377). The lower section of a cask was excavated at Watling Court, where it had been rammed into the ground (Fig 3.128, No 378). It was probably a wine cask, such as that depicted in the Bayeux Tapestry, although like other 11th-century casks

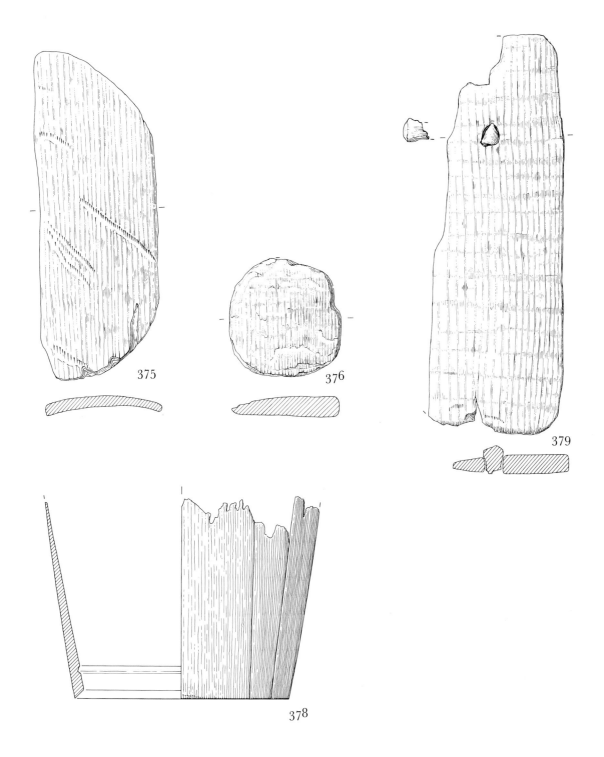

3.128. Base staves cut from oak, Nos 375-376, shingle, No 379.
Scale 1 :3. Reconstruction of cask, No 379. Scale 1 :16.

recorded from England, the vent hole, from which the liquid flowed, was cut through a side stave rather than at one end (Dunning 1958, 214).

Oak roof shingles appear to have been an early feature of City buildings since a fragment was found in a 10th-century pit at Milk Street (Fig 3.128, No 379) making it the earliest example recorded from England. Its length of 310mm is shorter than the late 11th-century shingles from Winchester (Biddle and Quirk 1962, 194) and those from a 13th-century pit at Cuckoo Lane, Southampton (Platt and Coleman-Smith 1975, 235-6, Fig 232, Nos 1670-1671). Ceramic roof tiles, however, introduced into London during the 12th century, ranged in length between 305mm and 314mm showing their legacy from wooden prototypes, whereas later standard London peg tiles were reduced in size to only c.260mm (Armitage et al 1981, 359; Pritchard 1982).

Patten

A 12th-century patten or sandal (Fig 3.129, No 380) is a another rare survival from Norman London. The sole was made from alder, a light, straight-grained, water-resistant wood, which does not split easily and has been favoured for clog-making in England right up to the present day (Vigeon 1977, 2). The leather upper was attached to both sides of the sole with dome-headed iron nails. The exact style is uncertain, but from the positioning of the nails the patten may have had more than one strap; perhaps a toe strap and a second strap running diagonally over the instep. It offers a contrast to a 13th-century patten from London, which has iron fittings at the heel and a wedge below the ball of the foot to lift the wearer at least two inches off the ground (Grew and de Neergaard 1988, 91-3, Figs 125-126).

3.129. Twelfth-century alderwood patten, No 380. Scale 1 :3.

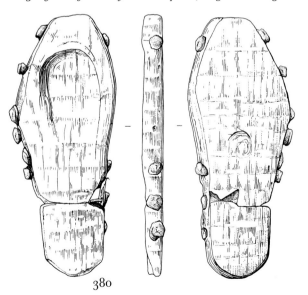

380

3.130. Miscellaneous wooden artefacts: pegs of oak and hazel, Nos 381-382; trenail, No 383; wedge, No 384; unidentified objects, Nos 385, 389, 390, 392 and 393. Scale 1 :2.

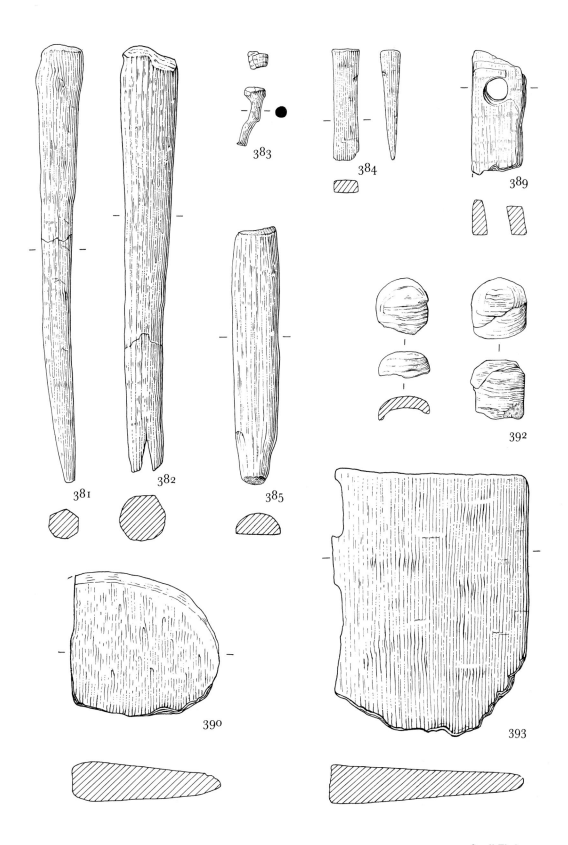

381

382

383

384

385

389

392

390

393

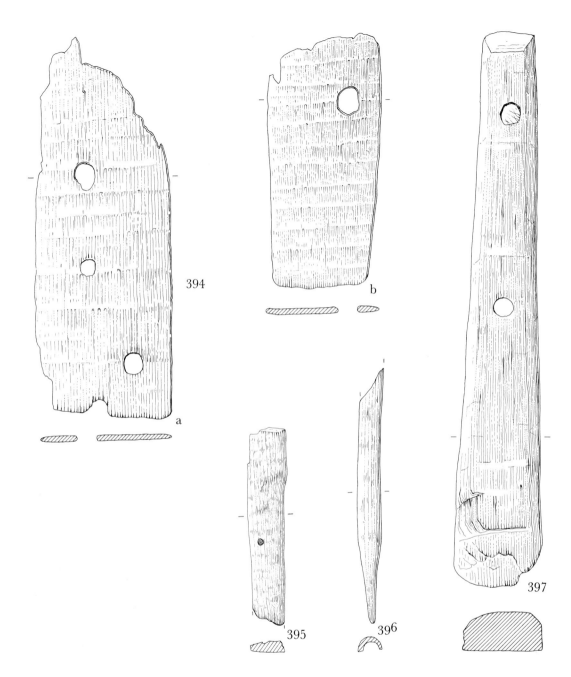

394

a

b

395

396

397

*3.131. Miscellaneous woodwork : Nos 394, 395 and 397, oak ;
No 396, elder. Scale 1 :3.*

CORDAGE

A piece of cord was recovered from waterfront silt at New Fresh Wharf, which is dated to the first half of the 11th century (Fig 3.132, No 398). When first recorded the total length of the cord measured *c*.1.4m (Michael Rhodes archive report), but it is now in fragments. A sample was submitted to Rowena Gale at the Jodrell Laboratory, Kew Gardens, who identified it as a woody material on the evidence of vestigial rays, rather than stem fibres from a herbaceous plant.

Fragments of similar twisted cord from a roughly contemporary pit at Pevensey, Sussex, were tentatively identified as willow, and it was suggested that they could have formed part of a basket (Dunning 1958, 217). Such a use is less likely for the considerably longer length of cord from London, and although most types of cordage prevalent in northern Europe at this period appear to have been produced from bast fibres, including a piece from a well in London (Rhodes 1980b, 144-5, No 741), the subject merits further investigation for which large assemblages, such as that now existing in Dublin, will afford the raw data.

3.132. Pieces of plied cord made from a woody material, No 398. Scale 2:1.

Acknowledgements

Many people have been instrumental in the compilation of this section on small finds and particular thanks go to the specialists, who wrote reports or identified material, credited in the text.

The finds were processed by a changing team of staff with the continuous support of Penelope MacConnoran. Conservation was principally undertaken by Helen Ganiaris, Suzanne Keene, Rose Johnson, Marilee Parrott and Kate Starling, while scientific back-up was supplied by Justine Bayley, Glynis Edwards, Jacqui Watson and Paul Wilthew of the Ancient Monuments Laboratory.

Most of the finds drawings are by Nick Griffiths, Susan Mitford and Terry Shiers. Their observations enabled the study of the artefacts to progress further than would otherwise have been possible. Other drawings are by Michael Bentley, Angelika Elseback, Jennifer Harding, Sally Myer, Redenta Soprano, Ann Sutton and Mark Thacker. The diagrams of the knives with pattern-welded blades, Figs 3.7, 3.9 and 3.10, were based on drawings by Brian Gilmour and the diagram of knife No 15, Fig 3.11, was based on a drawing by Paul Wilthew. The drawing of the motif-piece from London Wall, Fig 3.69, appears by permission of the British Museum. The photographs are by Jon Bailey, Jenny Bewick, Trevor Hurst, Jan Scrivener and Louise Woodman with the exception of Fig 3.25 which is published by permission of the Landesmuseum, Mainz.

The artefacts from New Fresh Wharf were initially prepared for publication by Michael Rhodes. Archive reports by John Clark on the metalwork and bonework, Arthur MacGregor on a bone skate, and Carole Morris on the wooden artefacts were also consulted. Jo Groves catalogued the material from the Milk Street pits and Barbara West the bone skates.

The staff of the Medieval Department of the Museum of London, especially John Clark, patiently answered innumerable questions and provided access to objects. Useful comments on the artefacts were also proffered by Justine Bayley, Jane Cowgill, Geoff Egan, Vera Evison, James Graham-Campbell, Francis Grew, Patrick Ottaway, Ian Riddler, and Leslie Webster.

Helen Ganiaris and Brian Gilmour would like to thank Justine Bayley, Philip Armitage, Glynis Edwards, Don Claugher, Jonathan Thornton and Jacqui Watson for help with analysis of the different components of the knife from Pudding Lane.

David Buckton acknowledges the help of Justine Bayley, Mavis Bimson, Torsten Capelle, Barbara Green, Elizabeth James, Dafydd Kidd, Sue Margeson, John Newman, Andrew Oddy, W Selzer and Hayo Vierck.

CATALOGUE OF FINDS

Ironwork

Knives

1. PEN 79 [1675] ⟨82⟩, Building 10
Date of deposit: 10th century (CP1)

Knife with a straight cutting edge and a parallel back sharply angled towards its tip. The front face of the blade is ornamented with a zone of inlay carried out in fine twisted wires of two different metal alloys, one red and one yellow, partly set in a herringbone pattern. Tang, offset from blade, tapering with squared off terminal. Length of knife 101mm; length of blade 59mm; length of tang 42mm. (Figs 3.1-3.3)

2. WAT 78 [1159] ⟨1166⟩, Pit 15 use
Date of deposit: 10th century (CP1)

Part of a knife, blade broken, tang offset from blade, tapering with squared off terminal. Length of tang 51mm. (Fig 3.3)

3. WAT 78 [94] ⟨337⟩, Pit 18
Date of deposit: 10th century (CP1, contaminated)

Part of a knife with a broad blade, the back of the blade curves gradually down to its tip. Tang, offset from blade, with part of wooden handle, possibly maple or a fruitwood (identified by Jaqui Watson, AML). Length of blade (tip broken) c.90mm. (Fig 3.3)

4. PEN 79 [1288] ⟨71⟩, Building 2
Date of deposit: 10th century (CP1)

Part of a knife with a broad blade, no tang is preserved. (Fig 3.3)

5. MLK 76 [1214] ⟨1564⟩, Pit 45 use
Date of deposit: 10th century (CP1)

Knife with a slightly sloping back and a tapering tang, offset from blade. Length of knife 111mm; length of blade 58mm; length of tang 53mm. (Fig 3.3)

6. IRO 80 [298] ⟨85⟩, Building 1 use
Date of deposit: 10th century (CP1)

Part of a knife with no cutting edge preserved. Straight tang, offset from blade, broken; traces of wooden handle at junction of tang and blade. (Fig 3.3)

7. IRO 80 [278] ⟨36⟩, Building 1 disuse
Date of deposit: 10th century (CP2)

Knife with a slightly sloping back; tang, offset from blade, slightly tapering with a squared off terminal. Length of knife c.108mm; length of blade 74mm; length of tang c.34mm. (Fig 3.3)

8. MLK 76 [1210] ⟨1526⟩, Pit 45 disuse
Date of deposit: Early to mid-11th century (CP3, contaminated)

Part of a knife with a slightly sloping back and a tapering tang, offset from blade. The tip of the blade is broken and the cutting edge very worn. Length of tang c.26mm. (Fig 3.3)

9. ALG 84 [588] ⟨381⟩, Ditch
Date of deposit: 11th to early 12th century (CP3 or later)

Knife with a slightly convex cutting edge and an angled back; pattern-welded blade. Tang, offset from blade, slightly tapering with file marks along each edge; traces of wooden handle, probably box (identified by Jacqui Watson, AML). Length of knife 248mm; length of blade 176mm; length of tang 72mm. (Figs 3.3 and 3.6-3.7)

10. PDN 81 [570] ⟨134⟩, Pit 21
Date of deposit: Early to mid-12th century (CP5)

Knife with a slightly convex cutting edge and an angled back; pattern-welded blade. Tang, offset from blade, with a cylindrical ivory handle. Length of knife c.208mm; length of blade 158mm; length of tang c.58mm. (For sheath see **Leatherwork**) (Figs 3.3, and 3.8-3.10)

11. SM 75 [103] ⟨83⟩, Waterfront dump 3.2
Date of deposit: Late 11th century (CP4)

Small knife with a straight back and a very worn cutting edge. Tang, offset from blade, slightly tapering with a squared off terminal. Length of knife 84mm; length of blade c.60mm; length of tang 24mm. (Fig 3.4)

12. WAT 78 [502] ⟨1121⟩, Building 4 disuse
Date of deposit: Late 11th to early 12th century (CP4)

Part of a knife, tang offset from blade, no cutting edge preserved. (Fig 3.4)

13. BIG 82 [7076] ⟨3789⟩, Waterfront bank 4.4 construction 2
Date of deposit: 1055 to c.1080 (CP4)

Knife with a slightly convex cutting edge and an angled back, which dips in a concave curve towards the broken tip; very little cutting edge preserved. The blade is decorated on both faces with a narrow line of copper alloy wire arranged in a pattern of continuous circles, which runs parallel to the back from the shoulder to the angled bend. Tang, offset from blade, tapering to a point. Length of knife 153mm; length of blade 109mm; length of tang 46mm. (Fig 3.4)

14. PEN 79 [189] ⟨83⟩, Pit 75
Date of deposit: 12th century (CP5/6)

Knife, of similar form to No 13, but not decorated. Length of knife 170mm; length of blade 130mm; length of tang 40mm. (Fig 3.4)

15. BIG 82 [6978] ⟨3409⟩, Foreshore 4.6 disuse
Date of deposit: Post 1080 to early 12th century (CP5)

Knife with a slightly sloping back and a tapering tang, offset from blade. (Forged from a single piece of metal with a piled ferrite and ferrite and pearlite structure, Paul Wilthew, AML Report No 4538.) Length of knife 72mm; length of blade 52mm; length of tang 20mm. (Figs 3.4 and 3.11-3.12)

16. SH 74 [578] ⟨688⟩, Waterfront I dump
Date of deposit: Early to mid-12th century (CP5, contaminated)

Knife with no cutting edge preserved. Tang, slightly tapering, offset from blade; both blade and tang broken. Length of knife c.112mm. (Fig 3.4) (Cowgill *et al* 1987, 78, No 3, Fig 54)

17. PEN 79 [189] ⟨233⟩, Pit 75
Date of deposit: 12th century (CP5/6)

Part of a knife with two notches on the back of the blade, no cutting edge preserved. Tang, offset from blade, slightly tapering with squared off terminal. (Fig 3.4)

18. BIG 82 [7013] ⟨3748⟩, Waterfront bank 4.4 construction 2
Date of deposit: 1055 to c.1080 (CP4)

Knife with two reversible blades along one side. One blade has a slight shoulder while the opposite one has a rivet passing through it and a notch on either side of the rivet hole. A second rivet, which acted as a stop for the pivoting blade, is preserved in the inner notch. Both blades are broken. The scale plates for the handle were made from a tooth tissue, possibly ivory (identified by Jacqui Watson, AML Report No 29/86). (Fig 3.5)

19. BIG 82 [7073] ⟨4996⟩, Waterfront bank 4.4 construction 2

Date of deposit: 1055 to c.1080 (CP4)

Knife with two reversible blades along one side, of similar form to No 18. The outline of scale plates are visible in the corrosion products on either side of the knife, the material is apparently a tooth tissue, possibly ivory (identified by Jacqui Watson, AML Report No 29/86). Length of knife 108mm; length of short blade 27mm; length of longer blade 68mm. (Fig 3.5)

20. BIG 82 [7275] ⟨5088⟩
Date of deposit: -

Short blade from a double-bladed reversible knife, with a rivet hole and one notch preserved. Length of blade 29mm. (Fig 3.5)

Tools

21. PDN 81 [1908] ⟨550⟩, Building 1 use
Date of deposit: Early to mid-11th century (CP3)

Part of a pair of tongs, both jaws and one handle are broken. Surviving length 300mm. (Fig 3.13)

22. SWA 81 [384] ⟨4128⟩, Waterfront bank construction
Date of deposit: 11th to early 12th century (CP3/4)

Punch with a head burred from hammer blows. Length 89mm. (Fig 3.13)

23. BIG 82 [7336] ⟨5072⟩, Waterfront bank 4.4 construction 2
Date of deposit: 1055 to c.1080 (CP4)

Square-sectioned rod tapering to a point. Length 159mm. (Fig 3.13)

24. BIG 82 [7013] ⟨4110⟩, Waterfront bank 4.4 construction 2
Date of deposit: 1055 to c.1080 (CP4)

Bent fragment of wire, round-sectioned. Length 34mm; diameter 1mm.

25. BIG 82 [7005] ⟨3374⟩, Foreshore in 4.5
Date of deposit: Post 1080 to early 12th century (CP5)

Bent fragment of wire, square-sectioned. Length 125mm; width 2.5mm.

26. MLK 76 [1064] ⟨57⟩, Pit 55
Date of deposit: 11th to early 12th century (CP4)

Carpenter's axe with T-shaped head, broken at one end; blade sharpened on both sides. Offset oakwood haft held in position by a small iron wedge. (Fig 3.14)

27. MLK 76 [3081] ⟨1347⟩, Pit 32
Date of deposit: Early to mid-11th century (CP3)

Part of a woolcomb with ten teeth preserved set in a wooden base in two rows and bound with a sheet of iron. The teeth are square in section. Thickness of wooden base 12mm. (Fig 3.15)

28. BIG 82 [7005] ⟨4633⟩, Foreshore in inlet 4.5
Date of deposit: Post 1080 to early 12th century (CP5)

Woolcomb tooth with part of iron binding attached. The tooth is square in section above the binding but rounded below it, bent into a S-shape. Length 86mm. (Fig 3.15)

29. MLK 76 [1214] ⟨675⟩, Pit 45 use
Date of deposit: 10th century (CP1)

Awl, diamond-shaped in section, bent at one end. Length 118mm. (Fig 3.16)

30. BIG 82 [6180] ⟨3235⟩, Waterfront bank 4.1 construction
Date of deposit: 1039 to 1041 (CP3)

Awl, diamond-shaped in section with central expansion. Length 138mm. (Fig 3.16)

31. BIG 82 [7013] ⟨4061⟩, Waterfront bank 4.4 construction 2
Date deposit: 1055 to c.1080 (CP4)

Awl, diamond-shaped in section with central expansion, bent at one end. Length 112mm. (Fig 3.16)

32. BIG 82 [7338] ⟨5105⟩, Waterfront bank 4.4 construction 2
Date of deposit: 1055 to c.1080 (CP4)

Awl, diamond-shaped in section, short tang, bent mid-shank. Overall length 87mm; length of tang 21mm. (Fig 3.16)

33. SM 75 [37] ⟨23⟩, Waterfront dump 3.2
Date of deposit: Late 11th century (CP4)

Fishhook with looped head, square-sectioned. Length 175mm; width 4mm. (Fig 3.17)

34. BIG 82 [7073] ⟨4874⟩, Waterfront bank 4.4 construction 2
Date of deposit: 1055 to c.1080 (CP4)

Fishhook, complete except for broken tip of flattened head, square-sectioned shank. Length 60mm; width 2mm. (Fig 3.17)

35. BIG 82 [7073] ⟨4848⟩, Waterfront bank 4.4 construction 2
Date of deposit: 1055 to c.1080 (CP4)

Fragment of fishhook, both ends broken, square-sectioned shank. Width 2.5mm.

36. BIG 82 [7073] ⟨4993⟩, Waterfront bank 4.4 construction 2
Date of deposit: 1055 to c.1080 (CP4)

Part of fishhook, flattened head broken, square-sectioned shank. Width 1.5mm. (Fig 3.17)

37. BIG 82 [7073] ⟨5097⟩, Waterfront bank 4.4 construction 2
Date of deposit: 1055 to c.1080 (CP4)

Fishhook with flattened head, square-sectioned shank. Length 90mm; width 2.5mm. (Fig 3.17)

38. BIG 82 [7073] ⟨5470⟩, Waterfront bank 4.4 construction 2
Date of deposit: 1055 to c.1080 (CP4)

Fragment of fishhook, both ends broken, square-sectioned shank. Width 2mm.

39. BIG 82 [7336] ⟨5071⟩, Waterfront bank 4.4 construction 2
Date of deposit: 1055 to c.1080 (CP4)

Part of fishhook, flattened head broken, square-sectioned shank. Width 2.5mm.

40. BIG 82 [7336] ⟨5075⟩, Waterfront bank 4.4 construction 2
Date of deposit: 1055 to c.1080 (CP4)

Fragment of fishhook with flattened head, square-sectioned shank. Width 2.5mm.

41. BIG 82 [7005] ⟨5307⟩, Foreshore in inlet 4.5
Date of deposit: Post 1080 to early 12th century (CP5)

Part of fishhook with flattened head, square-sectioned shank. Width 2.5mm.

42. BIG 82 [6936] ⟨5178⟩, Foreshore 4.6 disuse
Date of deposit: c.1080 (CP5)

Part of fishhook with flattened head, barbed end broken, square- sectioned shank. Width 3mm.

43. BIG 82 [6978] ⟨3402⟩, Foreshore 4.6 disuse
Date of deposit: c.1080 (CP5)

Fishhook with flattened head, square-sectioned shank. Length 82mm; width 2.5mm. (Fig 3.17)

44. SH 74 [514] ⟨383⟩, Waterfront foreshore
Date of deposit: Early to mid-12th century (CP5)

Fishhook, round-sectioned shank. Length 40mm; diameter 1.5mm. (Fig 3.17)

Miscellaneous

45. MLK 76 [274] ⟨1672⟩, Pit 30
Date of deposit: Late 11th to early 12th century (CP4)

Bell made from sheet iron plated with copper alloy on both sides. The clapper is missing and there is no indication of how it was attached. Width 85mm; height 75mm. (Fig 3.18)

46. BIG 82 [7336] ⟨5077⟩, Waterfront bank 4.4 construction 2
Date of deposit: 1055 to c.1080 (CP4)

Fragment of a strainer. Thickness 1mm; c.7 holes per sq cm.

47. BIG 82 [7073] ⟨4994⟩, Waterfront bank 4.4 construction 2
Date of deposit: 1055 to c.1080 (CP4)

Mount, wrought and hammered, with a round riveted head and a fleur-de-lis terminal, tin coated. The rivet has a small lozenge-shaped rove. Length 45mm. (Fig 3.19)

48. BIG 82 [7073] ⟨4998⟩, Waterfront bank 4.4 construction 2
Date of deposit: 1055 to c.1080 (CP4)

Part of a mount decorated with transverse gadrooning and two bosses, sheet metal, tin coated. (Fig 3.19)

49. BIG 82 [7393] ⟨5309⟩, Waterfront bank 4.4 construction 2
Date of deposit: 1055 to c.1080 (CP4)

As preceding but with four bosses. (Fig 3.19)

50. BIG 82 [7384] ⟨5210⟩, Waterfront bank 4.4 construction 2
Date of deposit: 1055 to c.1080 (CP4)

Small fragment of mount, sheet metal, tin coated.

51. BIG 82 [6978] ⟨3412⟩, Foreshore 4.6 disuse
Date of deposit: Post 1080 to early 12th century (CP5)

Strap-end, wrought and hammered, folded double and riveted. The upper face has a degenerate, acanthus terminal. Finished length 35mm. (Fig 3.19)

Locks, door furniture and domestic fittings

52. SM 75 [103] ⟨24⟩, Waterfront dump 3.2
Date of deposit: Late 11th century (CP4)

Key with an oval bow and hollow stem rolled from sheet metal. The bow is flat in section, the end fitting into the top of the stem. The bit is broken. (Fig 3.20)

53. SH 74 [627] ⟨327⟩, Waterfront I dump
Date of deposit: Early to mid-12th century (CP5)

U-shaped padlock bolt from a barrel padlock, single-spined with a double-leaf spring. (Fig 3.20)

54. BIG 82 [7073] ⟨5000⟩, Waterfront bank 4.4 construction 2
Date of deposit: 1055 to c.1080 (CP4)

Part of a spiral twisted, figure-eight shaped hasp. (Fig 3.20)

55. WAT 78 [804] ⟨1114⟩, Building 4.2 use
Date of deposit: Late 11th to early 12th century (CP4)

Part of a strap hinge fitting with a small rectangular hole. (Fig 3.20)

56. BIG 82 [7013] ⟨4103⟩, Waterfront bank 4.4 construction
Date of deposit: 1055 to c.1080 (CP4)

Strap hinge originally secured by two rivets. The eye is broken. Width 22mm. (Fig 3.20)

57. BIG 82 [7013] ⟨4137⟩, Waterfront bank 4.4 construction 2
Date of deposit: 1055 to c.1080 (CP4)

Fragment of strap hinge, one rivet preserved.

58. BIG 82 [7393] ⟨5322⟩, Waterfront bank 4.4 construction 2
Date of deposit: 1055 to c.1080 (CP4)

Part of a strap fitting with an oval hole at one end. Width 17.5mm. (Fig 3.20)

59. PDN 81 [584] ⟨135⟩, Building 9 construction
Date of deposit: Early to mid-12th century (CP5)

Bifurcated hinge with U-shaped eye secured by three rivets. (Fig 3.20)

60. PDN 81 [585] ⟨136⟩, Building 9 construction
Date of deposit: Early to mid-12th century (CP5)

As for No. 59.

61. PDN 81 [586] ⟨137⟩, Building 9 construction
Date of deposit: Early to mid-12th century (CP5)

Part of bolt, square-sectioned. Width 9mm. (Fig 3.20)

62. MLK 76 [3177] ⟨1537⟩, Building 1 phase 3 disuse
Date of deposit: Late 10th century (CP2)

Part of pintle, guide arm broken. Length of shank 81mm. (Fig 3.21)

63. WAT 78 [502] ⟨672⟩, Building 4 phase 2 disuse
Date of deposit: Late 11th to early 12th century (CP4)

Part of pintle bent out of shape with traces of wood preserved on the guide arm.

64. PDN 81 [513] ⟨145⟩, Building 5 construction
Date of deposit: Late 11th to early 12th century (CP4)

Part of pintle, both guide arm and shank broken.

65. WAT 78 [1060] ⟨1164⟩, Pit 41
Date of deposit: Early to mid-12th century (CP5)

Part of pintle, guide arm broken. Length of shank c.69mm. (Fig 3.21)

66. MLK 76 [2010] ⟨1335⟩, Pit 86
Date of deposit: 11th to early 12th century (CP4)

U-shaped staple with slightly out-turned arms, square in section. Length 110mm. (Fig 3.21)

67. BIG 82 [6978] ⟨3871⟩, Waterfront bank 4.4 construction 2
Date of deposit: 1055 to c.1080 (CP4)

Part of U-shaped staple with straight arms, square in section. (Fig 3.21)

68. BIG 82 [7338] ⟨5109⟩, Waterfront bank 4.4 construction 2
Date of deposit: 1055 to c.1080 (CP4)

Part of U-shaped staple, one arm out-turned, the other broken, square in section. (Fig 3.21)

69. BIG 82 [6980] ⟨3753⟩, Waterfront bank 4.4 use
Date of deposit: Post 1080 to early 12th century (CP5)

U-shaped staple with thin, straight arms, rectangular in section. Length 50mm. (Fig 3.21)

70. WAT 78 [774] ⟨1275⟩, Pit 47
Date of deposit: Late 11th to 12th century (CP4)

Fragment of rectangular staple, both arms broken.

71. BIG 82 [7013] ⟨4141⟩, Waterfront bank 4.4 construction 2
Date of deposit: 1055 to c.1080 (CP4)

Rectangular staple, both arms clenched, rectangular in section. Length 135mm; width 7.5mm. (Fig 3.21)

72. BIG 82 [7073] ⟨4999⟩, Waterfront bank 4.4 construction 2
Date of deposit: 1055 to c.1080 (CP4)

Rectangular staple, both arms inturned, rectangular in section. Length 60mm; width 4mm. (Fig 3.21)

73. BIG 82 [7073] ⟨5964⟩, Waterfront bank 4.4 construction 2
Date of deposit: 1055 to c.1080 (CP4)

Fragment of rectangular staple, one arm inturned, the other broken. Width 5mm.

74. BIG 82 [7336] ⟨5074⟩, Waterfront bank 4.4 construction 2
Date of deposit: 1055 to c.1080 (CP4)

Rectangular staple, both arms inturned, rectangular in section. Length 70mm; width 3.5mm.

75. BIG 82 [7384] ⟨5235⟩, Waterfront bank 4.4 construction 2
Date of deposit : 1055 to c.1080 (CP4)

As preceding. Length 92mm; width 4mm. (Fig 3.21)

76. BIG 82 [7384] ⟨5236⟩, Waterfront bank 4.4 construction 2
Date of deposit: 1055 to c.1080 (CP4)

Fragment of rectangular staple, one arm inturned, rectangular in section. Width 5mm.

77. BIG 82 [7414] ⟨5100⟩
Date of deposit: Late 11th to early 12th century (CP4)

Rectangular staple, both arms inturned, rectangular in section.

78. BIG 82 [7005] ⟨3373⟩, Foreshore in inlet 4.5
Date of deposit: Post 1080 to early 12th century (CP5)

Fragment of rectangular staple, one arm broken, rectangular in section. Max width 7mm.

Other ironwork, mainly horse tack

79. BIG 82 [7464] ⟨4101⟩, Waterfront bank 4.4 construction 2
Date of deposit: 1055 to c.1080 (CP4)

Ferrule rolled from sheet metal with a hole at its base. Max length 95mm; diameter 30mm. (Fig 3.22)

80. WAT 78 [2650] ⟨1380⟩, Pit 38
Date of deposit: 10th century (CP1)

Buckle with circular frame and pin. Diameter c.28mm.

81. SH 74 [620] ⟨379⟩, Waterfront I dump
Date of deposit: Early to mid-12th century (CP5)

Buckle pin, tin coated, rectangular in section. Finished length 47mm. (Fig 3.22)

82. SH 74 [627] ⟨393⟩, Waterfront I dump
Date of deposit: Early to mid-12th century (CP5)

Part of prick spur with straight sides, round in section. Squared off terminal, with two rivets and a small retaining plate for securing the spur leather. Thin strips of copper alloy decorate the terminal and outside edge of the spur, the latter embellished with incised hatching. (Fig 3.26)

Horseshoes with countersunk nail holes and a lobate profile

83. IRO 80 [410] ⟨153⟩, Building 1 use
Date of deposit: 10th century (CP1)

Branch fragment with three nail holes; nails are preserved in two of the holes.

84. PET 81 [1245] ⟨420⟩, Phase 5.7
Date of deposit: 10th century (CP1)

Fragment.

85. BIG 82 [7073] ⟨4997⟩, Waterfront bank 4.4 construction 2
Date of deposit: 1055 to c.1080 (CP4)

Branch fragment with two nail holes.

86. BIG 82 [7462] ⟨4054⟩, Waterfront bank 4.4 construction
Date of deposit: 1055 to c.1080 (CP4)

Complete, six nail holes, three on each branch; one fiddle-key type nail.

87. SH 74 [578] ⟨269⟩, Waterfront I
Date of deposit : Early to mid-12th century (CP5, contaminated)

As for No. 86, except no nail; two calkins.

88. SH 74 [620] ⟨328⟩, Waterfront I dump
Date of deposit: Early to mid-12th century (CP5)

As for No 86, except no nail; one calkin. (Fig 3.22)

89. SH 74 [620] ⟨454⟩, Waterfront I dump
Date of deposit: Early to mid-12th century (CP5)

One branch with three nail holes.

90. BIG 82 [6980] ⟨3416⟩, Waterfront bank 4.4 use
Date of deposit: Post 1080 to early 12th century (CP5)

Branch fragment with three nail holes.

Horseshoes with countersunk nail holes and a plain rim

91. MLK 76 [1101] ⟨222⟩, Pit 50
Date of deposit: Late 11th to early 12th century (CP4)

Complete; six nail holes, three on each branch and part of one calkin. (Fig 3.22)

92. PDN 81 [609] ⟨260⟩, External surface
Date of deposit: Early to mid-12th century (CP5)

Two branch fragments; six nail holes, three on each branch.

Horseshoe of uncertain form

93. BIG 82 [7336] ⟨5079⟩, Waterfront bank 4.4 construction 2
Date of deposit: 1055 to c.1080 (CP5)

Heel tip with calkin.

Copper alloy artefacts

Equal-armed brooches

94. WEL 79 [1090] ⟨21⟩, Building 3 disuse
Date of deposit: Late 11th to early 12th century (CP4)

Rectangular equal-armed ansate brooch with eight protruding lobes, decorated with a stamped ring-and-dot pattern. On the reverse of one arm is a pair of lugs to which is attached the remains of an iron pin, held in position with a rivet of copper alloy, on the other arm is a simple catch. Length 53mm. (Fig 3.23)

95. SWA 81 [2279] ⟨2174⟩
Date of deposit: Early 13th century (CP7)

Cast, equal-armed brooch with five transverse mouldings. On the reverse, on opposite arms, is a pair of lugs for the pin attachment and a simple catch. Length 45mm. (Fig 3.23)

Enamelled disc brooch

96. BWB 83 [290] ⟨203⟩
Date of deposit: Late 13th to mid-14th century (CP9)

Brass (AML) *champlevé* enamel disc brooch showing the bust of a saint facing front in a circular frame with a rebated flange. Little enamel is preserved but three or four colours were originally present. The nimbus is opaque red and the face and throat white; the glass in the remaining three cells has discoloured. On the back is a single lug for attaching the pin and traces of a catch; the pin is missing but its axis ran horizontal to the figure on the obverse. Diameter 27mm; thickness of brass plate 2mm. (Fig 3.24)

Strap-ends

97. PET 81 ⟨7⟩, unstratified

Cast, tongue-shaped strap-end with a symmetrical design in relief. At the butt end, the attachment plate is pierced with four, countersunk rivet holes and a transverse bar separates it from the main field of ornament. Immediately below the bar, a foliate stem and two side shoots spring from a debased palmette. Two inward facing, long-tailed beasts sit on the side shoots and mirroring them are two similar beasts, whose tails intertwine with the first pair. At the tongue end, the central stem issues from the mouth of an animal mask. The surface is worn and the back plain. Length 54mm; width 27mm. (Fig 3.26)

98. SWA 81 [2273] ⟨2280⟩
Date of deposit: Mid-13th century (CP8)

Cast, rectangular strap-end made from brass (AML) with a stylised animal pattern; the attachment panel has two rivet holes and the back is plain. Length 30mm; width 19mm. (Fig 3.27)

Strap-distributors

99. SM 75 [195] ⟨78⟩, Waterfront silt 2.3
Date of deposit: Mid-11th century (CP3)

Part of a cast strap distributor with a three-spoked construction, decorated round sections of the rim with billeted ornament arranged in two tiers. The edge has been hacked. Diameter *c*.40mm. (Fig 3.28)

Hooked tag

100. BWB 83 [173] ⟨3497⟩
Date of deposit: Late 12th century (CP6)

Hooked tag with a triangular plate made from sheet metal. The butt end has two holes and a scalloped edge. A lightly incised border runs along two sides of the plate. The back is plain. Length 28mm; thickness 0.36mm. (Fig 3.31)

Pin

101. BIG 82 [7353] ⟨3246⟩, Waterfront bank 4.4 construction 2
Date of deposit: 1055 to *c*.1080 (CP4)

Pin with a solid round head and a long shank, which is bent. Length 90mm; diameter of head 7.5mm; diameter of shank 1-1.5mm. (Fig 3.32)

Finger rings

102. BIG 82 [7452] ⟨3419⟩, Waterfront foreshore 4.5
Date of deposit: Post 1080 to early 12th century (CP5)

Finger ring with a penannular hoop and tapering open ends; bent out of shape. Internal diameter 19mm; external diameter 22mm. (Fig 3.33)

103. OPT 81 [81] ⟨284⟩
Date of deposit: Early to mid-12th century (CP5)

Brass (AML) finger ring, as preceding, upper part of hoop decorated with diagonal grooves. Internal diameter 17mm; external diameter 20mm. (Fig 3.33)

Mounts

104. SM 75 [220] ⟨105⟩, Waterfront bank 2.3
Date of deposit: Early to mid-11th century (CP3)

Part of a strip mount, D-shaped in section, terminating in a flat, round plate pierced to accommodate a rivet. (Fig 3.34)

105. SH 74 [451] ⟨168⟩, Waterfront I dump
Date of deposit: Early to mid-12th century (CP5)

Fragment of a gilded binding strip, D-shaped in section, with two bosses, of which one has a rivet hole. (Fig 3.34)

106. SH 74 [451] ⟨169⟩, Waterfront I dump
Date of deposit: Early to mid-12th century (CP5)

As preceding, but only with one boss. (Fig 3.34)

107. BIG 82 [5113] ⟨2826⟩
Date of deposit: Late 12th century (CP6)

Ring mount, triangular in section, with two hooks, one on either side, terminating in animal heads. Two tiny semi-circular grooves have been cut on opposing sides of the ring. Length 30mm; external diameter of ring 15mm. (Fig 3.34)

108. SWA 81 [2267] ⟨2534⟩
Date of deposit: Early 13th century (CP6)

Part of a small mount with a stylised animal head terminal, pierced with at least three holes. (Fig 3.34)

Miscellaneous

109. MLK 76 [1011] ⟨1349⟩, Pit 46
Date of deposit: Late 10th century or later (CP2+)

Nail with a flat-topped head; shank slightly bent and broken at the tip, square in section. Surviving length 39mm; diameter of head 7mm. (Fig 3.35)

110. MLK 76 [1091] ⟨478⟩, Pit 60
Date of deposit: Early to mid-11th century (CP3)

Part of a nail with a flat-topped head and a square-sectioned shank. Diameter of head 5mm. (Fig 3.35)

111. BIG 82 [7384] ⟨5194⟩, Waterfront bank 4.4 construction 2
Date of deposit: 1055 to *c*.1080 (CP4)

Domed nail head. Diameter 22mm. (Fig 3.35)

112. GM 129 [879] ⟨1⟩, Dark earth over pit 3
Date of deposit: Late 11th to early 12th century (CP4)

Buckle pin round in section. Length 47mm.

113. NFW 74 [129] ⟨268⟩, Waterfront dump 3.2
Date of deposit: Late 11th to early 12th century (CP4)

As preceding. Length 48mm.

114. NFW 74 [129] ⟨269⟩, Waterfront dump 3.2
Date of deposit: Late 11th to early 12th century (CP4)

As for No 112. Length 48mm.

115. SH 74 [514] ⟨227⟩, Waterfront foreshore
Date of deposit: Early to mid-12th century (CP5)

Strip of sheet metal tapered at one end. A clip of similar sheet metal is inserted through a slit at the opposite end. Length 215mm; thickness 0.47mm. (Fig 3.35)

116. SM 75 [109] ⟨1⟩, Waterfront dump 3.4
Date of deposit: Late 11th to early 12th century (CP4)

Cast handle of cylindrical form with an angular projection, pierced longitudinally for about two-thirds of its length by a hole, which is of narrow triangular form at its mouth; incised linear decoration. Length 58mm; weight 32gm. (Fig 3.35)

117. BIG 82 [6936] ⟨5266⟩, Foreshore 4.6 disuse
Date of deposit: Post 1080 to early 12th century (CP5)

Coil of round-sectioned wire. Diameter 0.1mm.

118. SH 74 [407] ⟨317⟩, Waterfront I dump
Date of deposit: Early to mid-12th century (CP5)

Fragment of round-sectioned wire. Length 170mm; diameter 0.8mm.

119. SH 74 [451] ⟨228⟩, Waterfront I dump
Date of deposit: Early to mid-12th century (CP5)

Fragment of round-sectioned wire. Length 590mm; diameter 0.5mm.

120. SH 74 [627] ⟨305⟩, Waterfront I dump
Date of deposit: Early to mid-12th century (CP5)

Hammered strip. Length 102mm; width 4mm; thickness 0.86mm.

Lead alloy

Buckle

121. BWB 83 [330] ⟨2863⟩
Date of deposit: Late 14th century (CP11)

Part of a cast buckle-loop with two stylised animal heads facing outwards and from behind each of which a lobed tendril extends towards the centre of the loop. Wear marks from the buckle-pin are present on the loop, slightly off-centre. Length 40mm. (Fig 3.36)

Stone artefacts

Hones

Norwegian Ragstone

122. WAT 78 [90] ⟨57⟩, Pit 18
Date of deposit: 10th century (CP1)

Hone, oval in section, with suspension hole. Length 83mm; width 35mm; max thickness 3.5mm; diameter of hole 5mm. (Figs 3.39-3.40)

123. NFW 74 [59] ⟨53⟩, Waterfront dump 3.2
Date of deposit: Late 11th to early 12th century (CP4)

Part of hone, rectangular in section, broken at one end. Surviving length 83mm; width 20mm; thickness 10mm.

124. NFW 74 [129] ⟨112⟩, Waterfront dump 3.2
Date of deposit: Late 11th to early 12th century (CP4)

Part of hone, D-shaped in section, broken at one end. Surviving length 82mm; width 23mm; max thickness 17mm. (Fig 3.40)

125. WAT 78 [736] ⟨767⟩, Building 4 disuse
Date of deposit: Late 11th to early 12th century (CP4)

Part of hone, rectangular in section, tapering, broken at both ends. Surviving length 122mm; max width 18mm; max thickness 18mm. (Fig 3.40)

126. BIG 82 [7403] ⟨5285⟩
Date of deposit: Late 11th to 12th century (CP4)

Part of hone, rectangular in section, broken at both ends; considerable transverse wear on one face and a single shallow groove. Surviving length 75mm; max width 30.5mm; max thickness 9mm. (Fig 3.40)

127. IRO 80 [119] ⟨10⟩, Pit 27
Date of deposit: Early to mid-12th century (CP5)

Part of a hone, rectangular in section, with suspension hole, broken at one end; worn across both faces. Surviving length 62mm; max width 10mm; max thickness 7mm; diameter of hole 4mm. (Fig 3.40)

128. IRO 80 [119] ⟨13⟩, Pit 27
Date of deposit: Early to mid-12th century (CP5)

Part of a hone, broken at both ends and in section; possibly unfinished. Surviving length 96mm; max width 14mm; max thickness 26mm.

Other schists

129. MLK 76 [1095] ⟨569⟩
Date of deposit: Late 10th century (CP2)
Dark grey schist, provenance not known (AGV)

Hone, oval in section, with surface worn smooth. Length 120mm; max width 27mm; max thickness 19mm. (Fig 3.41)

130. IRO 80 [407] ⟨68⟩, Building 1 disuse
Date of deposit: Late 10th century (CP2)
Grey schist with white vein of ? calcite, large inclusions 0.5mm now iron stained voids, provenance not known (AGV)

Hone, rectangular in section, with suspension hole at narrow end; very worn from use below hole. Length 69mm; max width 20mm; max thickness 6mm; diameter of hole 6.5mm. (Figs 3.39 and 3.41)

131. BAR 79 [337] ⟨21⟩
Date of deposit: Late 11th to mid-12th century (CP4/5)
Purple schist/sedimentary rock (AGV)

Hone, rectangular in section, with suspension hole; worn at lower end. Length 90mm; max width 18mm; max thickness 12mm; diameter of hole 3mm. (Figs 3.39 and 3.41)

Blue Phyllite

132. IRO 80 [233] ⟨35⟩, Building 2 disuse
Date of deposit: Late 10th century (CP2?)

Part of hone, rectangular in section, with V-sectioned sharpening grooves on one face; broken at both ends. Surviving length 186mm; width 20mm; max thickness 19mm. (Fig 3.42)

133. GM 129 [879] ⟨2⟩, Dark earth over pit 3
Date of deposit: Late 11th to early 12th century (CP4)

Fragment of hone, broken at both ends and in section. Surviving length 48mm.

134. SM 75 [85] ⟨42⟩, Waterfront dump 3.2
Date of deposit: Late 11th to early 12th century (CP4)

Part of hone, irregular profile, broken at one end, with V- sectioned sharpening groove along one face. Surviving length 125mm; width 42mm; max thickness 37mm. (Fig 3.42)

135. BIG 82 [7469] ⟨5411⟩, Phase 3.2
Date of deposit: Late 11th to early 12th century (CP4)

Hone, rectangular in section, with a suspension hole at narrow end; lower end very worn from use. Length 77mm; max width 17mm; max thickness 7.5mm; diameter of hole 5mm. (Figs 3.39 and 3.42)

Other phyllites

136. WAT 78 [2132] ⟨753⟩, Pit 23
Date of deposit: 10th century (CP1)
Light coloured quartz-muscovite bearing phyllite, provenance not known (AGV)

Part of hone, probably originally rectangular in section. Surviving length 55mm; max width 37mm.

137. SM 75 [101] ⟨47⟩, Waterfront dump 3.4
Date of deposit: Late 11th to early 12th century (CP4)
Quartz and muscovite bearing phyllite, provenance not known (DTM)

Part of hone, probably originally rectangular in section, broken at one end; very worn on one face. Surviving length 80mm; width 29mm.

138. WAT 78 [3074] ⟨903⟩, Pit 35
Date of deposit: Late 11th to early 12th century (CP4)
Light coloured phyllite, provenance not known (AGV)

Part of a rectangular block, scored with a cutting line, broken at both ends. Surviving length 110mm; width 50mm; max thickness 37mm. (Fig 3.42)

Miscellaneous

139. IRO 80 [308] ⟨53⟩, Building 1 use
Date of deposit: 10th century (CP1)

Glauconite-quartz-muscovite >0.25mm in silica cement, similar to Kentish Rag (AGV)

Part of hone, irregular in section, wide grooves worn at one end all four faces. Surviving length 109mm; max width 73mm; max thickness 31mm. (Fig 3.43)

140. WAT 78 [2120] ⟨140⟩, Pit 20
Date of deposit: 10th century (CP1)
Banded, calcareous siltstone/mudstone with quartz muscovite in light coloured bands, clay minerals in darker ones, provenance not known (AGV)

Hone, rectangular in section, with suspension hole at narrow end. Length 41mm; max width 21mm; max thickness 11.5mm; diameter of hole 4mm. (Figs 3.39 and 3.43)

141. PEN 79 [1263] ⟨72⟩, Building 5
Date of deposit: Late 10th century (CP2)
Quartz, silt, ? glauconite (some fossil replacement) in calcareous matrix, provenance not known (AGV)

Part of hone, waisted, rectangular in section, with suspension hole pierced from one side only. Surviving length 54mm; max width 28mm; max thickness 14mm; diameter of hole 3.5-12mm. (Fig 3.43)

142. SM 75 [195] ⟨203⟩, Waterfront silt 2.3
Date of deposit: Mid-11th century (CP3)
Quartz-muscovite-tourmaline (?glauconite) calcareous grit, Isle of Purbeck or SW England (DTM)

Hone, originally rectangular in section, worn smooth; shallow grooves on two faces. Length 87mm; max width 65mm; max thickness 10mm. (Fig 3.43)

143. SM 75 [192] ⟨31⟩, Waterfront silt 3.3
Date of deposit: Late 11th to early 12th century (CP4)
Micaceous sandstone, provenance not known (DTM)

Part of hone, rectangular in section, with suspension hole, broken at one end. Surviving length 34mm; max width 12mm; max thickness 5mm. (Fig 3.43)

144. MLK 76 [1068] ⟨1319⟩, Pit 47
Date of deposit: 11th to early 12th century (CP4)
Greyish-brown stone containing glauconite-quartz-muscovite >0.1mm in calcareous cement, provenance not known (AGV)

Part of hone, rectangular in section, sharpening grooves on one surface only, burnt along one edge. Surviving length 142mm; surviving width 74mm; thickness 27mm. (Fig 3.43)

145. WAT 78 [3074] ⟨904⟩, Pit 35
Date of deposit: Late 11th to early 12th century (CP4)
Muscovite, thin-walled bivalves, quartz silt >0.1mm in calcareous cement, provenance not known (AGV)

Part of hone, rectangular in section. Surviving length 112mm; width 74mm; max thickness 18mm.

146. SWA 81 [2206] ⟨3170⟩, Waterfront foreshore 1
Date of deposit: Late 11th to early 12th century (CP4)
Sandstone with sparse flakes of muscovite (AGV)

Part of hone, rectangular in section, with smooth, worn surfaces; broken at narrow end. Surviving length 96mm; max width 43mm; thickness 25mm. (Fig 3.43)

147. WAT 78 [4312] ⟨643⟩, Pit 96
Date of deposit: Early to mid-12th century (CP5)
Cipollino marble

Hone, rectangular in section, with suspension hole bored from both sides. Length 58mm; width 22mm; thickness 11mm; diameter of hole 7mm. (Figs 3.39 and 3.43)

Lamps

148. SM 75 [114] ⟨27⟩, Waterfront dump 2.4
Date of deposit: Early to mid-11th century (CP3)
Chalk

Part of lamp, carved in the form of an inverted cone with nine faceted sides, eight of which appear to have met at a base. The sides were chiselled into shape while a hollow in the top was gouged out to a depth of *c*.38mm. A groove runs around the outside of the lamp *c*.30mm below the top edge, which could have been used to hold a suspension cord in position. Traces of burning remain round the top of the object, in the hollow and along a broken edge. Height 110mm. (Fig 3.44)

149. MLK 76 [2097F] ⟨653⟩, Building 6 construction
Date of deposit: Late 11th to early 12th century (CP4)
Fine-grained limestone, provenance not known (AGV)

Part of a square lamp base with slightly outward sloping walls; interior roughly tooled, exterior and underside chisel-dressed. Base 167mm sq; height 64mm. (Fig 3.44)

Mortar

150. MLK 76 [3083] ⟨355⟩, Pit 31
Date of deposit: Early to mid-11th century (CP3)
White, fine-grained limestone probably from Caen

Handle from a mortar, the top and outer surface were chisel-dressed and the inner face roughly pecked. (Fig 3.45)

Rotary querns

151. IRO 80 [352] ⟨51⟩, Building 2 use
Date of deposit: 10th century (CP1)

Edge fragment from an upper stone, tool marks run vertically along the edge and tangentially as a border to the upper face; abraded. Estimated diameter 450mm: average thickness 28mm.

152. SM 75 [114] ⟨296⟩, Waterfront dump 2.4
Date of deposit: Early to mid-11th century (CP3)

Edge fragment from an upper stone. Only *c*.3% of the original circumference is present, although enough remains to suggest that the original diameter was *c*.1.5m. Tangential tool marks run along both the edge and the upper face. The lower surface is worn. Thickness 80mm.

153. WEL 79 [1186] ⟨128⟩, Building 3 construction
Date of deposit: Early to mid-11th century (CP3)

(a) Edge fragment from an upper stone with a central hopper, encircled by a broad flange, now mostly broken. The underside is flat and worn; the upper face is parallel to it and, although much abraded, shows a series of tool marks running tangentially across the surface. Diameter *c*.460mm; diameter of hopper *c*.80mm; average thickness 43mm. (Fig 3.46)

(b) Two small fragments, probably from an upper stone, tangential tool marks run across the upper surface. Average thickness 35mm.

154. PDN 81 [1297] ⟨459⟩, Building 3
Date of deposit: Early to mid-11th century (CP3)

Two small fragments from an upper stone including part of an edge. Tangential tool marks run across the upper face and round the edge. Thickness *c*.65mm.

155. PDN 81 [1634] ⟨490⟩, Building 3
Date of deposit: Early to mid-11th century (CP3)

Unfinished quernstone with hole worked from both sides, tangential tool marks round the edge. Diameter *c*.390mm; thickness 60-65mm; diameter of hole *c*.30mm. (Fig 3.47)

156. PDN 81 [1634] ⟨611⟩, Building 3
Date of deposit: Early to mid-11th century (CP3)

Unfinished quernstone, roughly circular with hole through the centre, tangential tool marks round the edge. Diameter 365- 430mm; thickness 40-65mm; diameter of hole 20-25mm. (Fig 3.48)

157. SM 75 [103] ⟨428⟩, Waterfront dump 3.2
Date of deposit: Late 11th century (CP4)

Edge fragment from an upper stone. The underside is worn smooth but tool marks remain visible round the edge. A small socket with a rounded base is positioned *c*.55mm from the original edge. Thickness 60mm.

158. WEL 79 [1067] ⟨23⟩, Building 3 disuse
Date of deposit: Late 11th to early 12th century (CP4)

Seven small fragments from an upper stone. The form and tooling are similar to No 153 above and it is possible that they were part of the same stone as (b), although no joins have been noted. On one fragment there is an oblique handle-hole and on another a raised area, possibly part of a flange around the hopper. Thickness c.31mm-36mm.

159. WEL 79 [1109] ⟨22⟩, Building 6 disuse
Date of deposit: Late 11th to early 12th century (CP4)

Small fragment probably from an upper stone but too little survives for certain identification of the form. Thickness c.33mm.

160. PDN 81 [506] ⟨406⟩, Building 3.2 construction
Date of deposit: Late 11th to early 12th century (CP4)

Two fragments with no original features remaining.

161. PDN 81 [1279] ⟨460⟩, Building 4 construction
Date of deposit: Late 11th to early 12th century (CP4)

Fragment with no original features remaining.

162. PDN 81 [1280] ⟨461⟩, Building 4 construction
Date of deposit: Late 11th to early 12th century (CP4)

Two small fragments, only part of the underside remains.

163. BIG 82 [7517] ⟨5306⟩, Waterfront bank 3.4 construction 1
Date of deposit: 1049 to 1071 (CP4)

Fragment.

164. BIG 82 [7395] ⟨5437⟩, Waterfront bank 3.4 construction 2
Date of deposit: 1055 to c.1080 (CP4)

Fragment, very abraded.

165. WAT 78 [1098] ⟨227⟩, Pit 41
Date of deposit: Early to mid-12th century (CP5)

Edge fragment from an upper stone, tangential tool marks run across the upper face and round the edge. Diameter c.320mm; thickness 100mm.

166. PDN 81 [643] ⟨1064⟩, External surface
Date of deposit: Early to mid-12th century (CP5)

Two small fragments, no edges; very abraded.

167. PDN 81 [682] ⟨486⟩, Building 5 disuse
Date of deposit: Early to mid-12th century (CP5)

Fragment with no original features remaining.

168. BIG 82 [7595] ⟨5761⟩, Foreshore in inlet 3.3
Date of deposit: 1039 to early 12th century (CP5)

Fragment.

169. MLK 76 [2084] ⟨1169⟩, Pit 89
Date of deposit: Late 11th century or later (CP4, contaminated)

Fragment, no edges.

Spindlewhorls

170. PEN 79 [1450] ⟨101⟩, Building 11
Date of deposit: Late 10th century (CP2)
Calcite mudstone (AGV)

Conical spindlewhorl, lathe-turned. Weight 23gm. External diameter 37mm; diameter of hole 10-13mm. (Fig 3.49)

171. NFW 74 [134] ⟨256⟩, Waterfront dump 2.4
Date of deposit: Early to mid-11th century (CP3)
Calcite mudstone (AGV)

Subconical spindlewhorl, lathe-turned. Weight 29gm. External diameter 39mm; diameter of hole 11mm. (Fig 3.49)

172. BIG 82 [6179] ⟨3234⟩, Waterfront bank 3.1
Date of deposit: 1039 to 1040 (CP3)
Calcite mudstone (AGV)

Part of subconical spindlewhorl, lathe-turned. External diameter 32mm; diameter of hole 11-13mm. (Fig 3.49)

173. NFW 74 [124] ⟨267⟩, Waterfront dump 3.2
Date of deposit: Late 11th to early 12th century (CP4)
Calcite mudstone (AGV)

Conical spindlewhorl, lathe-turned. Weight 15gm. External diameter 30mm; diameter of hole 10-14mm. (Fig 3.49)

174. GPO 75 [538] ⟨1124⟩, Pit
Date of deposit: Late 11th century (provisional)
Calcite mudstone (AGV)

Conical spindlewhorl, lathe-turned. Weight 15gm. External diameter 32mm; diameter of hole 9mm. (Fig 3.49)

Ceramic artefacts

Mould

175. MLK 76 [33] ⟨1685⟩, Pit 6
Date of deposit: Late 11th century or later (CP4, contaminated)

Part of Roman tile re-used as a mould. The matrix in the form of a T was cut into the upper face; broken. (Fig. 3.50)

Loomweights

176. GPO 75 [1336] ⟨1684⟩
Date of deposit: -

Fragment of bun-shaped loomweight.

177. GPO 75 [5193] ⟨1508⟩, Grave
Date of deposit: -

Fragment of bun-shaped loomweight with 'brand' mark. (Pritchard 1984, 65, Fig 17, No 7)

178. ace 83 [38] ⟨57⟩, Pit 69
Date of deposit:-

As for No 176.

179. ace 83 [38] ⟨57⟩, Pit 69

As for No 176.

180. htp 79 [87] ⟨71⟩, Backfill of foundation trench
Date of deposit: Post 12th century

As for No 176.

Spindlewhorls

181. wel 79 [1057] ⟨13⟩, Building 5 construction
Date of deposit: Late 11th to early 12th century (cp4)

Part of spindlewhorl made from a sherd of an ems cooking pot. Diameter of hole 10mm. (Fig 3.51)

182. gm 4 [1069] ⟨10⟩, Building disuse
Date of deposit: Early to mid-12th century (cp5)

Spindlewhorl made from sherd of an emsh cooking pot. Weight 16gm; diameter of hole 7–9mm. (Fig 3.51)

183. gm 3 [1226] ⟨2⟩, Pit
Date of deposit: Early to mid-12th century (cp5)

Spindlewhorl made from a sherd of esur ware. Weight 16gm; diameter of hole 7–9mm. (Fig 3.51)

Oyster-shell palettes

184. gm 131 [1183] ⟨2⟩, Pit 23
Date of deposit: Late 11th to early 12th century (cp4)

Part of an oyster-shell valve containing ground red pigment, probably vermilion. (Fig 3.53)

185. mlk 76 [1015c] ⟨40⟩, Pit 54
Date of deposit: Late 12th century (cp6)

Oyster-shell valve containing ground red pigment, probably vermilion. (Fig 3.53)

Glass

Textile implements

186. wat 78 [1147] ⟨758⟩, Pit 9 use
Date of deposit: 10th century (cp1)

Complete calender enveloped in a thin, weathered crust. Diameter 80mm; weight 331gm. (Fig 3.54)

187. wat 78 [2550] ⟨645⟩, Pit 69
Date of deposit: Late 11th to early 12th century (cp4)

Complete calender, dark coloured glass, irregular in shape. Diameter c.80mm; weight 331gm. (Fig 3.54)

188. pen 79 [519] ⟨49⟩, Building 7
Date of deposit: Late 11th to early 12th century (cp4)

Fragment of a calender, burnt and heavily weathered. (Fig 3.54)

189. cle 81 [245] ⟨264⟩
Date of deposit: Late 11th to early 12th century (cp4, contaminated)

Fragment of a calender, dark coloured glass with a thin weathered crust.

190. wat 78 [2138] ⟨393⟩, Pit 23
Date of deposit: 10th century (cp1)

Part of biconical spindlewhorl, heavily weathered. External diameter 30mm; diameter of hole 6mm. (Fig 3.55)

Vessel and window glass

191. wat 78 [2678] ⟨472⟩, Pit 31
Date of deposit: Early to mid-11th century (cp3)

Fragment of vessel base, heavily weathered. Max thickness 4.41mm.

192. wat 78 [824] ⟨1146⟩, Building 4.1 use
Date of deposit: Late 11th to early 12th century (cp4)

Tiny fragments of window glass, severely weathered. Thickness c.3mm.

193. wat 78 [825] ⟨843⟩, Building 4.1 use
Date of deposit: Late 11th to early 12th century (cp4)

Small fragments of window glass representing quarries of two different thicknesses, severely weathered. Thickness 2.53mm and 3.20mm.

194. wat 78 [804] ⟨1147⟩, Building 4.1 use
Date of deposit: Late 11th to early 12th century (cp4)

As for No 192.

195. wat 78 [2536] ⟨1141⟩, Pit 65
Date of deposit: Late 11th to early 12th century (cp4)

Fragment of window glass with bubbly surface, severely weathered. Maximum length 57mm; thickness 3-3.5mm.

196. wat 78 [2536] ⟨1144⟩, Pit 65
Date of deposit: Late 11th to early 12th century (cp4)

As preceding. Thickness 3mm.

197. wat 78 [3540] ⟨1150⟩, Pit 125
Date of deposit: Early to mid-12th century (cp5)

As for No 195. Thickness 2.5mm.

Worked antler, bone, horn and ivory

Motif pieces

198. MLK 76 [1095] ⟨519⟩, Dark earth
Date of deposit: Late 10th century (CP2)
Cattle mandible (BW)

Motif-piece; both ends of bone broken, patterns and tool-scrapes present on both sides:-

A. 1 trilobe knot
6 complete triquetrae of varying size and shape of loop
1 pointed triquetra in triangular field-line
1 square field-line with radial markings, unfinished
1 unfinished triquetra

B. 9 triquetrae in various stages of layout
(Figs 3.57-3.58 and 3.71)

199. MLK 76 [1091] ⟨379⟩, Pit 60
Date of deposit: Early to mid-11th century (CP3)
Mandible, probably pig (BW)

Motif-piece; bone broken, patterns and tool-scrapes present on both sides:-

A. 5 quadriloops, each interlacing with a circle, in square field-lines (one is broken) and 3 similar quadriloops in square field-lines in various stages of layout. (Traces of red (?) haematite present on a number of the motifs appear to have resulted accidentally during deposition).
1 angular duplex interlace in square field-line
1 unfinished angular duplex in square field-line
1 triquetra in triangular field-line
1 double pointed knot in lentoid field-line
1 roughly marked out lentoidal motif
Assorted compass drawn lines

B. 4 quadriloops, each interlacing with a circle, in square field-lines in various stages of finish (one is broken)
Unfinished duplex band interlace in square field-line
2 double pointed knots in lentoid field-lines
1 triangular field-line with rough layout for triquetra
1 unfinished triquetra in sub-triangular field-line
Various lightly incised intersecting lines
(Figs 3.59 and 3.71) (MacGregor 1985, 196, Fig 106)

200. MLK 76 ⟨749⟩, unstratified
Cattle-sized rib (BW)

Part of a motif-piece; bone broken on all but one natural edge; both sides polished and carved with various patterns:-

A. 1 triquetra
1 double pointed knot in lentoid field-line (broken)
1 corner of square field-line (broken)

B. 1 double pointed knot in lentoid field-line (broken)
1 corner of square field-line containing an indeterminate motif (broken)

(Figs 3.60 and 3.71)

201. GDH 85 [980] ⟨176⟩
Date of deposit: 10th century (CP1, provisional)
Pig innominate bone (DJR)

Motif-piece; bone slightly broken on some edges, patterns present on both sides:-

A. 1 triquetra with rounded loops
Square field-line containing unfinished quadriloop interlacing with a circle
1 square field-line with start of layout for a quadriloop interlacing with a circle
Various lightly incised lines

B. Square field-line with start of layout for a quadriloop
(Figs 3.61 and 3.72)

202. GDH 85 [980] ⟨177⟩
Date of deposit: 10th century (CP1, provisional)
Innominate bone of adult horse, right side (DJR)

Motif-piece; bone broken or chopped along two edges, patterns and tool-scrapes present on both sides:-

A. Two 4 x 8 cord plaits with pointed loops in rectangular field-lines and another unfinished cord plait in an adjoining rectangular field-line
Two 6 x 10 cord plaits in rectangular field-lines
Square field-line divided into two rectangular field-lines one with a 4 x 6 cord plait and the other with an unfinished cord plait
Square field-line with unfinished quadriloop motif
Square field-line with unfinished duplex
3 pointed triquetrae in triangular field-lines
2 unfinished triquetrae, one in triangular field-lines
1 triquetra
2 unfinished (?)triquetrae
Two triquetrae each interlacing with a circle in triangular field-lines
3 sides of a rectangular field-line
Various other lines and tool-scrapes

B. 3 angular duplex with very closely interlaced bands
3 duplex interlace with pointed bends
1 triquetra
6 pointed triquetrae in triangular field-lines
1 unfinished triquetra in triangular field-line
1 unfinished square field-line containing lightly incised tooling
Various other intersecting lines
(Figs 3.62-3.64 and 3.72)

203. GDH 85 [86] ⟨61⟩
Date of deposit: Unphased
Cattle-sized rib

Motif-piece; bone broken at both ends, patterns and inscription present on both faces:-

A. Unfinished knot motif, centrally grooved band, in square field-line (broken)
Irregular knot interlace in rectangular field-line

B. Four intersecting lines (broken) (Fig 3.65)

204. GDH 85 [1183] ⟨208⟩
Date of deposit: Unphased
Cattle-sized rib

Motif-piece; bone broken at both ends, both sides polished, particularly side B; patterns and tool-scrapes present on both sides:-

A. Pointed triquetra in triangular field-line
Duplex interlace with rounded bends
Angular duplex interlacing with 2 circles in square field-line
Unfinished quadriloop interlacing with circle in square field-line
Quadriloop interlacing with circle in square field-line
Unfinished angular duplex band interlace in square field-line
Outline of angular duplex band interlace in square field-line

B. Unfinished rectangular field-line
Unfinished quadriloop interlacing with a circle in a square field-line
Part of duplex with rounded bends (broken)
Paired knot in rectangular field-line
Two intersecting loops forming part of unfinished motif
4 x 6 cord plait with pointed loops in rectangular field-line
Linear tool marks forming start of motif
Rough layout for cord plait in rectangular field-line
(Figs 3.66 and 3.72)

205. ABS 86 [607] ⟨430⟩
Date of deposit: Early to mid-11th century (CP3, provisional)
Cattle-sized rib

Motif-piece; both ends of bone broken, patterns present on one side only:-

Edge of motif (broken)
1 pointed triquetra in triangular field-line
4 x 10 cord plait with pointed loops in rectangular field-line (deep set)
1 duplex with pointed bends
1 quadriloop interlacing with a circle (deep set)
1 quatrefoil with lobes at the cardinal points interlacing with a circle and saltire in a square field-line (deep set)
1 square field-line with the initial markings out of a quadriloop interlacing with a circle
8 x 8 cord plait in a square field-line
1 line
(Figs 3.67 and 3.73)

206. SH 74 [483] ⟨276⟩, Waterfront II-III
Date of deposit: Late 12th century to early 13th century (CP6/7)
Cattle femur (DJR)

Motif-piece; broken shaft of longbone. Single motif

depicting an aerial view of a squatting beast with a collared head and a long, protruding snout, partly contained within an oval frame. There are also a few tool-scrapes and light incisions on the surface of the bone. (Fig 3.68)

Combs

207. PET 81 [1726] ⟨510⟩, Phase 5.4
Date of deposit: Early to mid-12th century (CP5)
Antler (DJR)

Part of a single-sided composite comb with a slightly curved back and shallow convex cross-section; one tooth-plate preserved. Held together with iron rivets; one rivet pierces the tooth-plate and another is positioned between the tooth-plate and the next one. Both connecting-plates similarly decorated with two parallel grooves along each edge and a zone of ring-and-dot ornament divided by a band of three transverse grooves. Max width of connecting-plates 21mm; 4 teeth per cm. (Fig 3.75)

208. PDN 81 [3103] ⟨596⟩, Pit 20
Date of deposit: 10th century (CP1)
Antler (PLA)

Single-sided composite comb with a curved back and splayed end-plates; 15 tooth plates, of which 14 are preserved. Held together with ten iron rivets, positioned between alternate tooth-plates and through each end-plate. Both connecting-plates similarly decorated with a saltire in the central zone partly infilled and bounded by bands of transverse grooves with further bands of transverse grooves at either end. Length 241mm; max width of connecting-plates 15mm; 4-5 teeth per cm. (Fig 3.76)

209. MLK 76 [218] ⟨107⟩, Pit 2
Date of deposit: Late 11th to early 12th century (CP4, contaminated)
Antler (DJR)

End portion of connecting-plates from single-sided composite comb held together with iron rivets. Both connecting-plates similarly decorated with two bands of three transverse grooves and one band of two transverse grooves. Max surviving width of connecting-plates 9mm. (Fig 3.77)

210. PDN 81 [641] ⟨315⟩, Building 5
Date of deposit: Late 11th to early 12th century (CP4)
Antler (PLA)

Part of single-sided composite comb. One tooth-plate preserved with iron rivet inserted between two tooth-plates where the comb has since broken. The rivets appear to have been positioned between alternate tooth-plates. Both connecting-plates similarly decorated with a zone of at least eight transverse lines. Burnt. 5 teeth per cm. (Fig 3.77)

211. FST 85 [937] ⟨86⟩ and ⟨160⟩
Date of deposit: Late 11th to early 12th century (CP4)
Antler (DJR)

Part of single-sided composite comb, trapezoidal in cross-section, with a curved back and long teeth, which are sawn in two different sizes; three tooth-plates preserved. The finer spaced teeth are confined to a loose tooth-plate but its size and the polish along the top edge indicate it belonged to the same comb. Held together with iron rivets positioned between alternate tooth-plates. One hole pierces the centre of the comb but was probably wrongly placed since it appears not to have held a rivet. Both connecting-plates similarly decorated with a zone of repeating saltire crosses divided by single, transverse lines. Max width of connecting-plates 15mm; 4 coarse teeth per cm 4; 7 fine teeth per cm. (Fig 3.77)

212. GPO 75 [1381] ⟨789⟩, Graveyard soil
Date of deposit: Late 11th to 12th century (provisional)
Antler (DJR)

Fragment of single-sided composite comb with a slightly curved back; part of one connecting-plate is preserved and a single tooth-plate. Held together with iron rivets; one rivet preserved which pierces the tooth-plate. Connecting-plate decorated with a central zone of saltire crosses, which intersect along the top edge, bounded by double transverse lines. Max width of connecting-plate 12mm; 3-4 teeth per cm. (Fig 3.77)

213. GPO 75 [1381] ⟨750⟩, Graveyard soil
Date of deposit: Late 11th century to 12th century (provisional)
(?) Bone (BW)

Tooth-plate from single-sided composite comb. Grooves worn at either end from rivets positioned between the tooth-plates. 6 teeth per cm.

214. WAT 78 [78] ⟨94⟩, Pit 54
Date of deposit: Early to mid-12th century (CP5)
(?) Antler (BW)

Tooth-plate from single-sided composite comb with iron staining at one end from rivet positioned between the tooth-plates. 3 teeth per cm.

215. GM 29 [1159] ⟨4⟩

Part of single-sided composite comb with slightly curved back; one tooth-plate preserved. Held together with iron rivets, which appear to have been positioned between alternate tooth-plates. Both connecting-plates similarly decorated with a central zone bounded by a pair of transverse lines and flanked by a zone with two pairs of horizontal lines. 5-6 teeth per cm. (Fig 3.77)

216. PDN 81 [651] ⟨375⟩, External surface
Date of deposit: Early to mid-12th century (CP5)
Antler (PLA)

End section of single-sided composite comb. The end-plate, which is perforated, projects above and beyond the connecting-plates and possibly terminated in a serrated edge. Held together with iron rivets; one rivet preserved, which pierces the end-plate. Broken at the point where the second rivet was inserted. 3 teeth per cm. (Fig 3.78)

217. GPO 75 [178] ⟨373⟩
Date of deposit: 12th century (provisional)
Antler (DJR)

End section of single-sided composite comb. The end-plate projects above and beyond the connecting-plate and is crudely decorated with incised lines and four rows of holes. Slightly curved connecting-plate held in position with iron rivets, of which three pierce the end-plate. 3 teeth per cm. (Fig 3.78)

218. MLK 76 [3000] ⟨83⟩, Building 2.4
Date of deposit: Late 10th century (CP2)
Antler (DJR)

End-plate of double-sided composite comb with one tooth preserved on either side of solid zone. The comb has broken where the first rivet was positioned. A small hole is pierced through the end and the outline of the connecting-plates is visible showing the hole was cut after the comb was assembled. Max height 43mm (Fig 3.79)

219. MLK 76 [1041] ⟨41⟩, Pit 57
Date of deposit: 10th century (CP1)

Trapezoidal double-sided composite comb with teeth sawn from a single sheet of horn, and side-plates made from split cattle-sized rib-bones. The side-plates have angular ends and are held in place with three iron rivets spaced 45mm and 62mm apart. On one side-plate, circles were roughly inscribed around each rivet and there are also two semi-circular scratches not associated with a rivet on the same side-plate. The finer grade of teeth were sawn along the shorter side of the sheet of horn, which has split in two along the line of the centre rivet. Several strands of hair were found between the teeth of the comb. Max length 190mm; max height 64mm; length of side-plates 153mm and 161mm; max width of side-plates 17.5mm and 15mm. No of teeth: (i) coarse grade, 3 per cm; total no 46 (ii) fine grade, 8 per cm; total no 120. (Fig 3.80)

220. WAT 78 [2584] ⟨212⟩, Pit 69
Date of deposit: Late 11th to early 12th century (CP4)
Split cattle-sized rib (BW)

Side-plates from composite comb held together with three iron rivets spaced 42mm apart; perpendicular ends. Length of side-plate 119mm; max width 12.5mm. (Fig 3.81)

221. PUB 80 [19] ⟨15⟩, Pit 196
Date of deposit: Late 11th to early 12th century (CP4)
Split cattle-sized rib

Side-plates from composite comb held together with two iron rivets spaced 45mm apart. One plate has a cross incised on it, the other is broken; perpendicular ends, snapped off rather than cut right through the bone. Length of complete side-plate 105mm; max width 13mm. (Fig 3.81)

222. BIG 82 [7013] ⟨5010⟩, Waterfront bank 3.4 construction 2
Date of deposit: 1055 to c.1080 (CP4)
Split cattle-sized rib

Side-plate from composite comb with two iron rivets spaced 38mm apart; perpendicular ends, which were marked out before being cut. Length 73mm; max width 14mm. (Fig 3.81)

223. BIG 82 [7509] ⟨3959⟩, Waterfront bank 3.4 construction 2
Date of deposit: 1055 to c.1080 (CP4)
Split cattle-sized rib

Side-plates from composite comb held together with two iron rivets spaced 67mm apart; angular ends. Length 93mm; max width 16mm. (Fig 3.81)

223. WAT 78 [101] ⟨146⟩, Pit 17
Date of deposit: 10th century (CP1)
Ivory (DJR)

Part of a double-sided simple comb with a shallow horizontal groove incised above the teeth on one side. Surviving length 63mm; 8 teeth per cm. (Fig 3.82)

225. GM 29 [1159] ⟨1⟩

Side-plate from the case of a single-sided composite comb pierced at each end with two holes. Decorated with two rows of chevrons and pairs of lines along the centre and both sides. Length 122mm; max width 20mm. (Fig 3.83)

Ivory knife handles

10. PDN 81 [570] ⟨134⟩, Pit 21
Date of deposit: Early to mid-12th century (CP5)
Tooth tissue, probably ivory (SW)

Part of the cylindrical handle of a whittle tang knife. (Fig 3.3)

18. BIG 82 [7013] ⟨3748⟩, Waterfront bank 4.4 construction 2
Date of deposit: -
Tooth tissue, possibly ivory (SW)

Outline of scale plates forming the handle of a reversible knife visible in iron corrosion products. (Fig 3.5)

19. BIG 82 [7073] ⟨4996⟩, waterfront bank 4.4 construction 2
Date of deposit: 1055-c.1080 (CP4)
Tooth tissue, possibly ivory (SW)

As for No 18. (Fig 3.5)

Longbone implements

226. NFW 74 [124] ⟨216⟩, Waterfront dump 3.2
Date of deposit: Late 11th century (CP4)
Cattle-sized longbone shaft (DJR)

Implement with a head in the form of a bird's head and a hole for its eyes. Length 100mm; diameter of hole 5mm. (Figs 3.84-3.85)

227. PET 81 [190] ⟨58⟩, Pit 241
Date of deposit: Late 11th to early 12th century (CP4)
Cattle-sized longbone (BW)

Implement with a flat, pierced head and a blunt, pointed tip; polished; groove worn close to tip. Length 121mm; diameter of hole 3.5mm. (Fig 3.85)

228. NFW 74 [48] ⟨171⟩, Waterfront dump 3.2
Date of deposit: Late 11th to early 12th century (CP4)
Cattle-sized longbone shaft (DJR)

Implement with a splayed head pierced by hole; tip broken; polished shank. Diameter of hole 2.5mm. (Fig 3.85)

229. NFW 74 [124] ⟨172⟩, Waterfront dump 3.2
Date of deposit: Late 11th to early 12th century (CP4)
Cattle-sized longbone shaft (DJR)

As for No 228 with wear marks confined to the blunt, pointed tip. Length 86mm; diameter of hole 4mm. (Fig 3.85)

230. MLK 76 [1053] ⟨108⟩, Pit 55
Date of deposit: Late 11th to early 12th century (CP4)
Cattle-sized longbone

Unfinished implement with partly trimmed shank. Length 160mm. (Fig 3.85)

231. GPO 75 [1373] ⟨1071⟩, Graveyard soil
Date of deposit: 12th century (provisional)
Cattle-sized metapodial (BW)

Blunt, single-pointed implement with roughly trimmed shank, possibly unfinished. Length 142mm. (Fig 3.85)

232. EST 83 [51] ⟨1⟩, Pit 62
Date of deposit: Late 11th to early 12th century (CP4)
Cattle-sized longbone

Blunt, single-pointed implement with a high polish. Length 100mm. (Fig 3.85)

233. GPO 75 [86] ⟨749⟩
Date of deposit: 12th century (provisional)
Cattle-sized longbone

Blunt, single-pointed implement, oval in section. The other end is less highly finished and some cancellous tissue is apparent. File marks visible along polished shank. Length 104mm. (Fig 3.85)

234. GPO 75 [538] ⟨756⟩, Pit
Date of deposit: Late 11th century (provisional)
Cattle-sized longbone (BW)

Blunt, double-pointed implement with both ends broken, oval in section. File marks are visible along most of the shank, which is polished although some cancellous tissue remains apparent. Shallow groove worn at one end. Surviving length 181mm. (Fig 3.85)

Spoon

235. WAT 78 [824] ⟨614⟩, Building 3.1
Date of deposit: Late 11th to early 12th century (CP4)
Cattle-sized longbone (BW)

Part of spoon with shallow oval bowl, undecorated. Handle broken in antiquity. Width of bowl 20mm. (Fig 3.86)

Dice

236. WAT 78 [150] ⟨145⟩, Pit 55
Date of deposit: Early to mid-11th century (CP3)
Cattle-sized longbone shaft (DJR)

Roughly cube-shaped die, each unit is represented by a ring-and-dot arranged with the units on opposite faces totalling seven. Dimensions 12mm x 11mm x 10mm. (Fig 3.87)

237. MLK 76 [3169] ⟨580⟩, Pit 36
Date of deposit: Late 11th to early 12th century (CP4))
Cattle-sized longbone shaft

As for No 236 except that the pattern unit consists of two rings encircling dot. Dimensions 8mm x 9mm x 9mm.

Gaming pieces

238. PET 81 [415] ⟨68⟩, Pit 607
Date of deposit: 11th to early 12th century (CP3/4)
Cattle-sized longbone (BW)

Gaming piece decorated on one face with five concentric grooves of varying width and depth surrounding central dot. Ring-and-dot pattern round edge, superimposed over three of the grooves. Natural bone cavity apparent on reverse. Diameter 31mm. (Fig 3.87)

239. IRO 81 [141] ⟨6⟩, Pit 26
Date of deposit: Late 11th to early 12th century (CP4)
Cattle-sized mandible (BW)

Part of gaming piece decorated on one face with six concentric grooves of varying width. Diameter c.50mm. (Fig 3.87)

240. GM3 [1226] ⟨1⟩, Pit
Date of deposit: Early to mid-12th century (CP5)
Cattle-sized mandible (BW)

Part of gaming-piece decorated on one face with five concentric grooves of varying width and a circle of repeating ring-and-dot units. Burnt. Diameter 44mm. (Fig 3.87)

241. WAT 78 [3901] ⟨370⟩, Pit 121
Date of deposit: Early to mid-12th century (CP5)
Cattle-sized mandible (BW)

Gaming piece decorated on one face with five concentric grooves of differing width and a circle of repeating ring-and-dot units. Diameter 54mm. (Fig 3.87)

242. WAT 78 [5157] ⟨386⟩
Date of deposit: Residual in post-medieval pit
Cattle-sized mandible (BW)

Part of gaming piece with hole in centre, decorated on one face with five concentric grooves and a circle of repeating ring-and-dot units. Diameter 49mm; diameter of hole 10mm. (Fig 3.87)

243. BIG 82 [6507] ⟨3351⟩
Date of deposit: Late 12th century (CP6, contaminated)
Cetacean bone (BW)

Gaming piece with hole in centre, decorated on one face with six concentric grooves of varying width and a circle of repeating ring-and-dot units. Diameter 57mm; diameter of hole 10mm. (Fig 3.87)

Flute

244. BIG 82 [7595] ⟨5268⟩, Foreshore in inlet 3.3
Date of deposit: Post 1080 to early 12th century (CP5)
Ulna of large bird, possibly goose or swan (BW)

Part of a flute, broken at one end, with a triangular blow-hole and one or more finger-holes. Surviving length 190mm. (Fig 3.88)

Pig fibula pins

245. IRO 80 [298] ⟨83⟩, Building 1 use
Date of deposit: 10th century (CP1)
(?) Pig fibula (BW)

Pin with perforated head, shank trimmed and polished. Length 98mm; diameter of hole 3.5mm. (Fig 3.89)

246. MLK 76 [1210] ⟨1527⟩, Pit 45 disuse
Date of deposit : Early to mid-11th century (CP3, contaminated)
Pig fibula (DJR)

Pin with perforated head and polished shank, tip broken. Surviving length 109mm; diameter of hole 4mm. (Fig 3.89)

247. PET 81 [457] ⟨318⟩, Pit 453
Date of deposit: 11th to early 12th century (CP3/4)
Pig fibula (BW)

Part of pin with perforated head, both head and tip broken. Surviving length 96mm.

248. PET 81 [457] ⟨319⟩
Date of deposit: 11th to early 12th century (CP3/4)
Fibula of juvenile pig (DJR)

Part of pin with perforated head, tip broken. Surviving length 120mm; diameter of hole 3.5mm. (Fig 3.89)

249. FMO 85 [138] ⟨145⟩
Date of deposit: Early to mid-12th century (CP5)
Pig fibula (DJR)

Part of pin with perforated head, tip broken. Surviving length 50mm; diameter of hole 3.5mm.

Perforated pig metapodia

250. NFW 74 [77] ⟨64⟩, Waterfront dump 3.4
Date of deposit: Late 11th to early 12th century (CP4)
Metapodial of pig

Part of 'whirligig', broken at both ends, with two holes bored through shaft.

251. SM 75 [101] ⟨41⟩, Waterfront dump 3.4
Date of deposit: Late 11th to early 12th century (CP4)
Pig metacarpal III (PLA)

'Whirligig' with two holes bored through shaft, a third hole was started, but abandoned. (Fig 3.90)

252. WAT 78 [709] ⟨741⟩, Building 3.2 disuse
Date of deposit: Late 11th to early 12th century (CP4)
Metatarsal of pig (BW)

Part of 'whirligig', broken at proximal end, with two holes mid-shaft, one of which is broken; worn around edge of hole. (Fig 3.90)

Skates

253. BIG 82 [5961] ⟨4190⟩, Waterfront bank 3.1 use
Date of deposit: 1039 to 1041 (CP3)
Horse metatarsal (BW)

Skate, pointed upswept toe with vertical hole; hole at proximal end also vertical. Posterior surface only slightly flattened with rough transverse cuts to improve grip. Anterior surface highly polished and flattened with wear. Length 240mm. (Fig 3.91)

254. PDN 81 [276] ⟨40⟩, Pit 61
Date of deposit: Early to mid-11th century (CP3)
Horse metatarsal (BW)

Part of skate, toe chopped and broken, with axial hole at the proximal end; anterior surface highly polished and flattened with wear. Surviving length 240mm.

255. NFW 74 [48] ⟨519⟩, Waterfront dump 3.2
Date of deposit: Late 11th to early 12th century (CP4)
Horse metatarsal, right leg (PLA)

Skate with pointed upswept toe and no holes at either end; hardly worn. Length 255mm. (Fig 3.91)

256. WAT 78 [1137] ⟨1279⟩, Pit 43
Date of deposit: Late 11th to early 12th century (CP4)
Cattle metatarsal (BW)

Skate with pointed upswept toe and no holes at either end; worn. Length 190mm.

257. TAV 82 [69] ⟨122⟩
Date of deposit: Late 11th to early 12th century (CP4)
Horse metatarsal (BW)

Skate with pointed, upswept toe and no holes at either end. The anterior surface is so flattened with wear that the medullary cavity is exposed at the proximal end. Length 200mm.

258. LLO 78 [V 50] ⟨15⟩
Date of deposit: 11th or 12th century (provisional)
Horse metacarpal (BW)

Skate, flat pointed toe with transverse hole and axial hole at proximal end; moderately worn. Length c.224mm. (Fig 3.91)

259. WOW 79 [35] ⟨4⟩
Date of deposit:-
Horse metacarpal (BW)

Skate with pointed upswept toe and no holes at either end; hardly worn. Length 230mm.

Socketed points

260. PDN 81 [402] ⟨117⟩, Pit 44
Date of deposit: Late 10th century (CP2)
Cattle metatarsal (PLA)

Bone cut to a point at proximal end. Length 90mm. (Fig 3.92).

261. ILA 79 [158] ⟨27⟩, Pit 150 disuse
Date of deposit: 10th century or later (CP2 +)
Cattle metatarsal (PLA)

As for No 260. Length 107mm. (Fig 3.92)

Spindlewhorls

262. WAT 78 [2160] ⟨232⟩, Pit 63
Date of deposit : Late 11th to early 12th century (CP4)
Cattle femur head (PLA)

Spindlewhorl with knife trimmed sides. Weight 12gm; diameter of hole 10mm.

263. GPO 75 [431] ⟨1136⟩
Cattle femur head (PLA)

Spindlewhorl, slightly broken along one edge. Weight slightly in excess of 15gm; diameter of hole 10-11mm.

Mounts

264. IRO 80 [140] ⟨48⟩, Pit 18
Date of deposit: Late 11th to early 12th century (CP4)
Split cattle-sized rib (BW)

Fragment of mount; one end and one side broken. Decorated with row of repeating ring-and-dot units, consisting of three rings encircling dot; two rivet holes pierced through dots. Surviving length 46mm. (Fig 3.93)

265. GM 131 [1133] ⟨1⟩, External dump
Date of deposit : Late 11th to early 12th century (CP4)
Split cattle-sized rib

Rectangular mount with no rivet holes. Decorated with two rows of repeating ring-and-dot units consisting of three rings encircling dot, some overlapping of pattern units. Length 38mm.

266. MLK 76 [2084] ⟨570⟩, Pit 89
Date of deposit : Late 11th to late 12th century (CP4/6)
Split cattle-sized rib (BW)

Fragment of mount with one end broken. Decorated with row of repeating ring-and-dot units consisting of three rings encircling dot, on both pattern repeats present, the outer ring is weakly scribed. Surviving length 31mm. (Fig 3.93)

267. MLK 76 [2030] ⟨75⟩, Pit 91
Date of deposit: Early to mid-12th century (CP5)
Split cattle-sized rib (BW)

Fragment of mount slightly tapering towards one end, which was cut at a slight angle; one rivet hole preserved. Decorated with row of repeating ring-and-dot units consisting of two rings encircling dot. Surviving length 53mm. (Fig 3.93)

268. MLK 76 [1131] ⟨574⟩, Pit 51
Date of deposit: Late 11th to early 12th century (CP4)
Split cattle-sized rib (BW)

Small rectangular mount with both ends cut at slight angle, no rivet holes. Decorated with four diagonal grooves. Length 30mm. (Fig 3.93)

Leatherwork

Scabbards

269. MLK 76 [70] ⟨415⟩, Pit 12
Date of deposit: 10th century (CP2)
Calfskin (GE)

Lower part of scabbard; leather folded double and oversewn along raw edge, which is shouldered where the handle met the knife blade; grain/flesh stitch holes. Probably undecorated but the shape of the knife is preserved showing that the scabbard was made to accommodate the handle as well as the blade. Surviving length 134mm (shrinkage during treatment *c*.5.4%). (Fig 3.94)

10. PDN 81 [570] ⟨134⟩, Pit 21
Date of deposit: Late 11th to early 12th century (CP4)
Cowhide (GE/PLA)

Part of scabbard; leather folded double and bound with copper alloy wire along raw edge. The leather is too degraded for any surface decoration to be discernible. Surviving length 220mm. (Figs 3.3 and 3.8)

Footwear

Shoes with V-back soles attached to upper with leather

270. MLK 76 [60] ⟨511⟩ and ⟨1663⟩, Pit 17
Date of deposit: 10th century (CP1)
Calfskin upper (GE)

Part of shoe, one-piece upper with backseam; edge/flesh stitch holes along top edge. The sole continues up the heel to a point below the top edge of the quarters.

271. MLK 76 [60] ⟨49⟩, Pit 17
Date of deposit: 10th century (CP1)

Fragments of sole with a V-back, very worn with thonged repair patches on the forepart and heel-seat.

272. MLK 76 [1118] ⟨729⟩, Pit 42
Date of deposit: 10th century (CP1)

Shoe, right foot, with rounded toe. One-piece upper with backseam, the inside quarter has two small holes vertically aligned; edge/flesh stitch holes along top edge. The sole continues up the back of the heel to a point below the top edge of the quarters, worn, particularly the heel and tread. Length of sole 290mm; length of shoe 230mm (shrinkage 12%). (Figs 3.97-3.98)

273. MLK 76 [1373D] ⟨260⟩, Pit 42
Date of deposit: 10th century (CP1)
Leather too worn for identification (GE)

Sole, right foot, with rounded toe and V-back, very worn with repair patches attached by thonging on forepart and heel. Length of sole 230mm; length of shoe 200mm.

274. MLK 76 [1041] ⟨725⟩, Pit 57
Date of deposit: 10th century (CP1)
Calfskin upper; calfskin sole, 3mm thick (GE)

Shoe, right foot, with rounded toe, child's size. One-piece upper with backseam; edge/flesh stitch holes along top edge. The sole continues up the heel covering the backseam and is squared off below the top edge of the quarters, evenly worn sole. Length of sole 168mm; length of shoe 130mm. (Figs 3.97 and 3.99)

275. MLK 76 [1214] ⟨258⟩, Pit 45 use
Date of deposit: 10th century (CP1)
Calfskin upper, 3mm thick; cow sole (GE)

Shoe, (?) left foot, with rounded toe. One-piece upper with backseam; edge/flesh stitch holes along top edge. The sole continues up the heel to the top edge of the quarters, repair patches attached by thonging on forepart and heel. Length of sole c.280mm; length of shoe c.230mm

276. MLK 76 [1214] ⟨259⟩, Pit 45 use
Date of deposit: 10th century (CP1)
Calfskin upper, 3mm thick; cow sole (GE)

Part of shoe, upper fragment with backseam; edge/flesh stitch holes along top edge. The sole continues up the back of the heel to the top edge of the quarters. Both quarters were deliberately cut.

277. MLK 76 [1215] ⟨733⟩, Pit 45 use
Date of deposit: 10th century (CP1)

Shoe, left foot, with rounded toe. One-piece upper with back seam; edge/flesh stitch holes along top edge. The sole continues up the back of the heel to a point immediately below the top edge of the quarters, worn particularly on the inside heel. Length of sole 225mm; length of shoe 180mm (shrinkage 9.3%).

278. MLK 76 [1215] ⟨753⟩, Pit 45 use
Date of deposit: 10th century (CP1)
Calfskin upper; sewing thong possibly calfskin; calfskin/cow sole (GE)

Part of shoe, (?) right foot. Two-piece upper including a side insert sewn to the vamp wing seam with leather; pairs of grain/flesh stitch holes along side-seam on outside quarter, matched by edge/flesh stitch holes along corresponding insert side-seam; edge/flesh stitch holes along top edge of quarters. The sole continues up the back of the heel to a point just below the top edge of the back-part, small hole at centre back; heel very worn. (Fig 3.100)

279. MLK 76 [48] ⟨1670⟩, Pit 12
Date of deposit: Late 10th century (CP2)

Shoe, upper fragments including part of backseam for a V-back sole.

280. SM 75 [256] ⟨627⟩, Waterfront silt 2.3
Date of deposit: Early to mid-11th century (CP3)
Calfskin upper (GE)

Part of ankle-boot with blunt, pointed toe. Upper with side-seam, edge/flesh stitch holes along vamp wing seam and throat. (Fig 3.102)

281. MLK 76 [1147] ⟨1110⟩, Pit 45 disuse
Date of deposit: Early to mid-11th century (CP3, contaminated)
Calfskin upper (GE)

Part of shoe, with rounded toe. One-piece upper with backseam for a V-back sole; edge/flesh stitch holes along top edge.

282. WAT 78 [2201] ⟨1203⟩, Pit 62 disuse
Date of deposit: Late 11th to early 12th century (CP4)

Part of shoe or ankle-boot. Upper with butted side-seam sewn with leather; edge/flesh stitch holes along top edge. Sole very worn.

283. SWA 81 [2200] ⟨4768⟩, Waterfront foreshore 2
Date of deposit: Late 11th to early 12th century (CP4)

Fragments of upper, including lasting margin.

284. SH 74 [400] ⟨891⟩, Waterfront I dump
Date of deposit: Early to mid-12th century (CP5)

Part of shoe or ankle-boot, (?) right foot, with rounded toe. Upper with butted side-seam sewn with leather. Sole, only part of lasting margin preserved.

285. SWA 81 [2167] ⟨4710⟩
Date of deposit: -
Calfskin upper (GE)

Part of shoe with rounded toe. Upper decorated with two vamp stripes; vamp deliberately cut. Forepart of sole repaired. (Fig 3.103) Grew and de Neergaard 1988, Fig 112c

Boot with a V-back sole

286. BIG 82 [6289] ⟨5922⟩, Waterfront bank 4.1 construction
Date of deposit: 1039 to 1040 (CP3)

Part of boot, upper fragment with edge/flesh stitch holes along top edge; sole fragment with tunnel-stitched lasting margin, forepart and heel-seat repaired. The forepart repair patch is preserved and was formerly attached with leather thonging.

Ankle-boots with a side-opening and a V-back sole

(a) Interlaced drawstrings

287. SM 75 [192] ⟨357⟩, Waterfront silt 3.3
Date of deposit: Late 11th to early 12th century (CP4)
Sheep/goatskin upper; top-band and drawstrings too worn for identification (GE)

Ankle-boot, right foot. Upper with seam for V-back sole which stops just above the level of the thong slots; slit on inside quarter for side flap ending in horizontal cut with three grain/flesh stitch holes on either side. Edge/flesh stitch holes on side-seams where inside quarter was joined to flap. Both sides of upper meet in a side-seam, grain/flesh stitch holes on inside quarter except for the top few stitches where they change to edge/flesh stitch holes, and edge/flesh stitch holes on vamp wing; edge/flesh stitch holes along top edge. Slots for ankle thong on both quarters, eight on outside quarter, and seven inside quarter, part of thong preserved, comprised of two strips of leather slotted through one another to create a 'plaited' effect. Top-band, folded double lengthwise with single row of slots cut through both thicknesses of leather; the sides stitched to the top edge of the upper have grain/flesh stitch holes. Width of thongs 4-5mm; top-band length 205mm; width 16mm; finished width 8mm; 4-5 pairs of slots per 10mm. (Figs 3.106 and 3.108)

288. BIG 82 [7095] ⟨6019⟩, Waterfront bank 4.4 construction 2
Date of deposit: 1055 to c.1080 (CP4)
Upper and drawstrings too worn for identification (GE)

Part of ankle-boot, left foot. Upper, side-seam along vamp wing ending in a curved cut out section immediately above the lasting margin, insert missing; edge/flesh stitch holes along both side-seams except the lower edge of the vamp wing where they change to grain/flesh stitch holes. Edge/flesh stitch holes along top edge and vamp throat. Two thongs slotted through one another as for No 287 on both vamp wings, eleven slots on outside wing and six slots on inside wing. Width of thongs 6mm. (Fig 3.109)

289. BIG 82 [6980] ⟨4588⟩, Waterfront
Date of deposit: Post c.1080 to early 12th century (CP5)

Part of ankle-boot, right foot. Upper with seam for V-back sole, which stops just below the level of the drawstring; inside quarter slit to accommodate a side flap; grain/flesh stitch holes on inside quarter, formerly joined to vamp wing, except for the top third where they change to edge/flesh stitch holes; edge/flesh stitch holes along side-seams for attaching flap, top edge and throat; eight thong slots on outside quarter and five thong slots on inside quarter in front of the insert both with two thongs slotted through one another as for No 287; also two thong slots on the heel side of the inside quarter. Width of thongs c.4mm.

290. BIG 82 [7005] ⟨5791⟩, Foreshore in inlet 4.5
Date of deposit: Post 1080 to early 12th century (CP5)

Part of ankle-boot, left foot. Upper fragments, grain/flesh stitch holes along vamp wing seam; edge/flesh stitch holes at throat and top edge; six thong slots on outside quarter with two thongs slotted through one another as for No 287. Throat insert with grain/flesh stitch holes on three edges and edge/flesh stitch holes along top edge. Width of thongs 4mm and 5mm. (Throat insert Fig 3.105)

291. BIG 82 [7005] ⟨7135⟩, Foreshore in inlet 4.5
Date of deposit: Post 1080 to early 12th century (CP5)

Part of ankle boot, right foot. Upper fragment, edge/flesh stitch holes along top edge; five thong slots on outside quarter with two thongs slotted through one another as for No 287. Width of thongs 5mm and 6mm.

(b) Two drawstrings inserted through alternate thong slots

292. SM 75 [192] ⟨353⟩, Waterfront silt 3.3
Date of deposit: Late 11th to early 12th century (CP4)
Calfskin upper, drawstrings too worn for identification (GE)

Part of ankle-boot, right foot. Upper fragment, edge/flesh stitch holes along side-seam and top edge. Fragments of two thongs preserved threaded through alternate slots front and back. Width of thongs 3mm and 3.5mm. (Fig 3.110)

293. BIG 82 [7005] ⟨7136⟩, Foreshore in inlet 4.5
Date of deposit: Post 1080 to early 12th century (CP5)

Part of ankle-boot, (?) left foot. Upper fragment, edge/flesh stitch holes along side-seam, top edge and throat; six thong slots on vamp wing with two thongs preserved threaded through alternate slots front and back. Width of thongs 3mm and 4mm.

294. BIG 82 [6984] ⟨4376⟩, Phase 6.6
Date of deposit: Late 12th century (CP6)
Upper sheep/goatskin; drawstring too worn for identification (GE)

Part of ankle-boot, left foot. Upper, vamp fragment with butted side-seam; slit cut in vamp with edge/flesh stitch holes on either side. Vamp wing has eight thong slots with two thongs preserved threaded through alternate slots back and front. Length of vamp slit 21mm; width of thongs 3mm.

(c) Single drawstring

295. SM 75 [220] ⟨473⟩, Waterfront bank
Date of deposit: Early to mid-11th century (CP3)

Part of ankle-boot, (?)left foot. Three fragments of upper, the vamp has one thong slot on each side of the throat; edge/flesh stitch holes along edge of throat and side-seam; part of (?) insert with drawstring secured by being folded through on itself at one end; edge/flesh stitch holes along insert side-seam. Max width of drawstring 7mm.

296. NFW 74 [48] ⟨190⟩, Waterfront dump 3.2
Date of deposit: Late 11th to early 12th century (CP4)
Calfskin upper and throat insert (GE)

Ankle-boot, right foot, with slightly pointed toe. Upper, with seam for V-back sole, which stops just below the level of the drawstring, edge/flesh stitch holes along side-seam overlapping side flap; grain/flesh stitch holes at vamp wing seam; part of throat insert is preserved with butted seams; edge/flesh stitch holes along top edge of upper, including top edge of throat insert. Part of drawstring and nine pairs of thong slots preserved. Sole with V-back heel and wide lasting margin with tunnel-stitches; forepart and heel-seat repaired. Width of drawstring 5mm. (Fig 3.111)

297. NFW 74 [124] ⟨143⟩, Waterfront dump 3.2
Date of deposit: Late 11th to early 12th century (CP4)

Part of ankle-boot, left foot, child's size. Upper fragment with edge/flesh stitch holes along vamp wing seam and throat.

298. NFW 74 [129] ⟨181⟩, Waterfront dump 3.2
Date of deposit: Late 11th to early 12th century (CP4)
Sheep/goatskin upper and throat insert; drawstring possibly sheep/goatskin (GE)

Ankle-boot, left foot, child's size. Upper with seam for V-back sole, which stops just below the level of the drawstring. Small, horizontal slit cut on inside quarter with grain/flesh stitch holes on either side, above this point the leather was cut away to the top edge to accommodate a side flap. Grain/flesh stitch holes along side-seams, which stop short of the top edge; edge/flesh stitch holes along top edge. Part of throat insert preserved with edge/flesh stitch holes along all sides including top edge. Leather drawstring passes round throat and probably tied at heel, two pairs of thong slots preserved on each side of boot. Width of drawstring 4mm. (Fig 3.106 and 3.112)

299. NFW 74 [129] ⟨182⟩, Waterfront dump 3.2
Date of deposit: Late 11th to early 12th century (CP4)
Upper possibly sheep/goatskin (GE)

Ankle-boot, right foot, child's size. Upper with small, horizontal slit cut on inside quarter with three grain/flesh stitch holes on one side and three edge/flesh stitch holes on the other. Edge/flesh stitch holes along side-seams, which were butted together below the point of the slit and at throat. Four pairs of thong slots preserved, two on each quarter. (This ankle-boot probably forms a pair with No 298)

300. SM 75 [192] ⟨152⟩, Waterfront silt 3.3
Date of deposit: Late 11th to early 12th century (CP4)
Calfskin upper; drawstring possibly calf (GE)

Part of ankle-boot. Upper fragment, edge/flesh stitch holes along top edge, part of drawstring and three pairs of thong slots preserved. Width of drawstring 7-8mm.

301. SM 75 [192] ⟨364⟩, Waterfront silt 3.3
Date of deposit: Late 11th to early 12th century (CP4)
Calfskin upper (GE)

Part of ankle-boot, (?) right foot. Upper fragment, edge/flesh stitch holes at throat; four pairs of slots for drawstring; no stitching along top edge.

302. MLK 76 [1053] ⟨543⟩, Pit 55
Date of deposit: Late 11th to early 12th century (CP4)
Calfskin upper; drawstring possibly sheep/goatskin (GE)

Part of ankle-boot, right foot. Upper with seam for V-back sole, which stops just below the level of the drawstring; edge/flesh stitch holes along top edge and throat; eight thong slots on outside quarter with thong preserved. Side flap has edge/flesh stitch holes along side-seam; the opposite edge and top edge were not sewn, slot for thong at bottom margin. Top-band, slightly torn at one end, folded along one edge with double row of slots only the top row piercing both thicknesses of leather; grain/flesh stitch holes along the side sewn to the upper and at both ends. Sole with V-back, tunnel-stitched lasting margin; very worn. Traces of two-ply wool sewing thread preserved in the lasting margin of both the upper and sole, and in the slots of the top-band. Top-band length 200mm; width 30mm; width of hem 6mm; finished width 22m; 3 pairs of slots per 10mm. (Side flap Fig 3.105; top-band Fig 3.122)

303. MLK 76 [1064] ⟨518⟩, Pit 55
Date of deposit: Late 11th to early 12th century (CP4)
Calfskin upper; drawstring possibly different (GE)

Part of ankle-boot, right foot. Upper, with seam for V-back sole, which stops just below the level of the drawstring, composed of at least four pieces, including a triangular insert, an ankle-strap and top-band. A side-seam below the strap was sewn with a narrow leather thong. The quarters have a drawstring threaded through a row of slots, continuing through the strap and insert; edge/flesh stitch holes along top edge and on the throat side of the ankle-strap. Pairs of slots immediately above the lasting margin for a repair patch extending across the heel-seat. Sole with V-back and tunnel-stitched lasting margin; worn. Traces of two-ply wool sewing thread are preserved in the lasting margin of both the upper and the sole. Width of drawstring 4mm. (Fig 3.113)

304. BIG 82 [7005] ⟨4454⟩, Foreshore in inlet 4.5
Date of deposit: Post 1080 to early 12th century (CP5)

Part of ankle-boot, right foot. Upper with inside quarter slit to accommodate a side flap, grain/flesh stitch holes along both side-seams; edge/flesh stitch holes along top edge; eight thong slots on outside vamp wing with drawstring preserved passing round the throat; one thong slot on inside quarter. Side flap has edge/flesh stitch holes along side-seam, opposite edge and top edge not sewn, two grain/flesh stitch holes at bottom margin; two thong slots on level with those on quarters with drawstring, also two thong slots above one another further up flap, which extends above the top edge of the quarters. Width of drawstring 6mm.

305. BIG 82 [7005] ⟨7137⟩, Foreshore in inlet 4.5
Date of deposit: Post 1080 to early 12th century (CP5)

Part of ankle-boot, right foot. Upper fragment, edge/flesh stitch holes along side-seam and throat; two thong slots on vamp wing.

Inserts for ankle-boots

306. SM 75 [150] ⟨407⟩, Waterfront silt 2.3
Date of deposit: Early to mid-11th century (CP3)
Leather too worn for identification (GE)

Side insert, with six slots for a narrow drawstring; edge/flesh stitch holes along side edges and top edge, grain/flesh stitch holes along bottom margin. (Fig 3.105)

307. NFW 74 [137] ⟨134⟩, Waterfront dump 2.4
Date of deposit: Early to mid-11th century (CP3)

Part of side insert, top edge torn; edge/flesh stitch holes on each side and along bottom margin. Part of sewing thong preserved at bottom corner.

308. NFW 74 [48] ⟨702⟩, Waterfront dump 3.2
Date of deposit: Late 11th to early 12th century (CP4)

Part of side flap, bottom margin torn; edge/flesh stitch holes along one side, opposite side and top edge not sewn.

309. NFW 74 [106] ⟨214⟩, Waterfront dump 3.2
Date of deposit: Late 11th to early 12th century (CP4)
Possibly calfskin (GE)

Throat insert, edge/flesh stitch holes along top edge and three sides. (Fig 3.105)

310. MLK 76 [1094] ⟨1649⟩, Pit 64
Date of deposit: Late 11th to early 12th century (CP4)

Part of throat insert with edge/flesh stitch holes along top edge and two sides, the third side is torn.

Soles with wide tunnel-stitched lasting margins

311. MLK 76 [40] ⟨27⟩, Pit 17
Date of deposit: 10th century (CP1)

Part of sole with tunnel-stitched lasting margin, very worn.

312. MLK 76 [60] ⟨48⟩, Pit 17
Date of deposit: 10th century (CP1)
Calfskin upper, 3mm thick; sole too worn for identification (GE)

Part of (?)shoe, right foot. Upper fragment with side-seam; edge/flesh stitch holes along vamp wing seam and top edge. Sole, very worn, tunnel-stitched lasting margin, forepart and heel-seat repaired, the latter with thonging preserved.

313. MLK 76 [48] ⟨1555⟩, Pit 12
Date of deposit: Late 10th century (CP2)

As for No 311.

314. NFW 74 [48] ⟨701⟩, Waterfront dump 3.2
Date of deposit: Late 11th to early 12th century (CP4)

Part of sole, left foot, with V-back, child's size; tunnel-stitched lasting margin; worn at heel and tread.

315. NFW 74 [129] ⟨638⟩, Waterfront dump 3.2
Date of deposit: Late 11th to early 12th century (CP4)

Sole fragment with oval toe and part of lasting margin, very worn.

316. NFW 74 [129] ⟨700⟩, Waterfront dump 3.2
Date of deposit: Late 11th to early 12th century (CP4)

Part of sole with V-back and tunnel-stitched lasting margin, small slot at back of heel.

317. SM 75 [192] ⟨410⟩, Waterfront silt 3.3
Date of deposit: Late 11th to early 12th century (CP4)

As for No 311.

318. BIG 82 [7005] ⟨5794⟩, Foreshore inlet 4.5
Date of deposit: Post 1080 to early 12th century (CP5)

Part of sole with V-back, tunnel-stitched lasting margin; very worn.

319. BIG 82 [7005] ⟨7138⟩, Foreshore in inlet 4.5
Date of deposit: Post 1080 to early 12th century (CP5)

As for No 318, slightly shaped at the waist.

Shoe repair patches

320. NFW 74 [48] ⟨141⟩, Waterfront dump 3.2
Date of deposit: Late 11th to early 12th century (CP4)

Repair patch, one edge torn, formerly held in place with leather thong.

321. MLK 76 [103] ⟨36⟩, Pit 27
Date of deposit: Late 11th to late 12th century (CP4-6)

Part of a repair patch for sole formerly held in place with leather thong.

Side-seamed ankle-boots with a drawstring along the top edge and a V-back sole

322. BIG 82 [7464] ⟨4828⟩, Waterfront bank 4.4 construction 2
Date of deposit: 1055 to *c*.1080 (CP4)
Upper possibly sheep/goatskin; calfskin/cow sole (GE)

Part of ankle-boot, left foot, with rounded toe. Upper cut with a row of thong slots immediately below the top edge; edge/flesh stitch holes at throat for insert. Sole, part of lasting margin with edge/flesh stitch holes, very worn; forepart repaired with patch formerly attached with thread. Two pairs of thong slots per 10mm. Length of shoe *c*.260mm (Fig 3.114)

323. BIG 82 [6980] ⟨4589⟩, Waterfront
Date of deposit: Post *c*.1080 to early 12th century (CP5)

Part of ankle-boot. Upper fragment, top edge styled as for No 322. Three pairs of thong slots per 10mm.

324. BIG 82 [6779] ⟨4788⟩
Date of deposit: -
Upper possibly calfskin (GE)

Part of ankle-boot, left foot. Upper fragment, top edge styled as for No 322; edge/flesh stitch holes along vamp wing seam, grain/flesh stitch holes at seam on inside quarter; edge/flesh stitch holes at throat for insert. Part of the vamp has been deliberately cut. Two pairs of thong slots per 10mm.

325. BIG 82 [7520] ⟨5830⟩, (Phase 2.4)
Date of deposit: -
Calfskin upper (GE)

Part of ankle-boot. Upper, top edge styled as for No 322; edge/flesh stitch holes at throat for insert. One pair of thong slots per 10mm.

Ankle-boot with vamp-seam

326. BIG 82 [7005] ⟨5836⟩, Foreshore in inlet 4.5
Date of deposit: Post 1080 to early 12th century (CP5)
Upper probably calf; drawstring too worn for identification (GE)

Part of ankle-boot, (?) right foot. Upper with two rows of thong slots and part of a drawstring; edge/flesh stitch holes at top edge; grain/flesh stitch holes at throat. The vamp was partly slit down the centre, and seamed with a running-stitch; throat end strengthened with five tunnel-stitches. Width of drawstring 3mm. (Fig 3.115) (Grew and de Neergaard 1988, Fig 112a-b)

Side-seamed ankle-boots decorated with vamp-stripes

327. SH 74 [451] ⟨206⟩, Waterfront I dump
Date of deposit: *c*.1140 (CP5)

Part of ankle-boot, right foot. Upper fragment, edge/flesh stitch holes at vamp wing seam and throat; decorated with three vamp-stripes running from toe to throat. Vamp deliberately cut.

328. SH 74 [451] ⟨207⟩, Waterfront I dump
Date of deposit: *c*.1140 (CP5)

Part of ankle-boot, right foot, with blunt, pointed toe. Upper fragment, edge/flesh stitch holes at vamp wing seam and throat; decorated with three vamp-stripes embroidered in silk thread running from toe to throat. (Fig 3.116) Grew and de Neergaard 1988, Fig 114.

329. SH 74 [451] ⟨723⟩, Waterfront I dump
Date of deposit: *c*.1140 (CP5)
Calfskin upper (GE)

Part of ankle-boot, left foot, with blunt, pointed toe. Upper fragment, edge/flesh stitch holes at throat; decorated with three vamp-stripes running from toe to throat.

330. SH 74 [451] ⟨902⟩, Waterfront I dump
Date of deposit: *c*.1140 (CP5)

Part of ankle-boot, right foot. Upper fragment with edge/flesh stitch holes at throat, throat flap and along top edge; decorated with three vamp-stripes.

331. SH 74 [513] ⟨645⟩, Waterfront foreshore
Date of deposit: *c*.1140 (CP5)

Part of ankle-boot, left foot, with blunt pointed toe. Upper fragment, edge/flesh stitch holes at vamp wing seam, throat, throat flap and top edge; double row of stitch holes on inside joint of lasting margin; one pair of thong slots on outside quarter. Decorated with three vamp-stripes running from toe to throat.

332. SH 74 [513] ⟨646⟩, Waterfront foreshore
Date of deposit: *c*.1140 (CP5)

Part of ankle-boot, left foot. Upper fragment, edge/flesh stitch holes at vamp wing seam, throat, throat flap and top edge; one pair of thong slots on throat flap, a second pair of slots on the outside quarter and a single slot beside the side-seam to take a lower drawstring; tunnel-stitch holes on flesh face for small heel stiffener. Decorated with two vamp-stripes.

333. SH 74 [620] ⟨603⟩, Waterfront I dump
Date of deposit: *c*.1140 (CP5)

Part of ankle-boot with blunt, pointed toe. Upper decorated with three vamp-stripes running from toe to throat.

334. SH 74 [620] ⟨904⟩, Waterfront I dump
Date of deposit: c.1140 (CP5)

Part of ankle-boot, left foot. Upper fragment, edge/flesh stitch holes at vamp wing seam, throat, throat flap and top edge. Decorated with two vamp-stripes running from toe to throat.

335. SH 74 [620] ⟨905⟩, Waterfront I dump
Date of deposit: c.1140 (CP5)

Part of ankle-boot, right foot, with blunt, pointed toe. Upper fragment, edge/flesh stitch holes at throat and top edge. Decorated with three vamp-stripes running from toe to throat.

336. BIG 82 [7064] ⟨4829⟩, Foreshore in inlet 4.5
Date of deposit: Post 1080 to early 12th century (CP5)

Part of ankle-boot, left foot, with blunt, pointed toe. Upper fragment, edge/flesh stitch holes at vamp wing seam and throat; single thong slot on outside vamp wing with drawstring preserved. Decorated with vamp stripe running from toe to throat. Width of thong 3mm. Grew and de Neergaard 1988, Fig 112d

337. BIG 82 [7064] ⟨4830⟩, Foreshore in inlet 4.5
Date of deposit: Post 1080 to early 12th century (CP5)

Part of ankle-boot, left foot, with blunt, pointed toe. Upper fragment, edge/flesh stitch holes at throat, throat flap and top edge; one pair of thong slots on each vamp wing. Decorated with two vamp-stripes. Grew and de Neergaard 1988, Fig 112f

Side-seamed ankle-boots with long, curling pointed toes

338. SH 74 [451] ⟨184⟩, Waterfront I dump
Date of deposit: c.1140 (CP5)
Sheep/goatskin upper (GE)

Part of ankle-boot, right foot, with long, outward curling pointed toe. One-piece upper with a butted side-seam cut on the diagonal; edge/flesh stitch holes at throat; no stitch holes along top edge; one thong slot on each quarter and one at the heel at the top of the back-part. Three slots along the inside joint for a repair patch, which would have extended across the forepart of the sole. (Fig 3.117) Grew and de Neergaard 1988, Figs 6 and 84

339. SH 74 [513] ⟨635⟩, Waterfront foreshore
Date of deposit: c.1140 (CP5)
Sheep/goatskin upper; calfskin/cow sole (GE)

Ankle-boot, right foot, with toe styled as for No 338. Upper with butted side-seam; edge/flesh stitch holes at throat, throat flap and top edge; one pair of thong slots on inside wing. Part of sole with rounded heel-seat and narrow lasting margin with edge/flesh stitch holes; both forepart and heel-seat repaired. (Fig 3.118) Grew and de Neergaard 1988, Figs 5 and 83

340. BIG 82 [6979] ⟨6013⟩ (Phase 4.6)
Date of deposit: Post c.1080 to early 12th century (CP5)

Part of ankle-boot, left foot, with toe styled as for No 338. Upper with butted side-seam, the seam margin on the vamp wing includes five tunnel-stitches; edge/flesh stitch holes at throat, throat flap, top edge; slit on outside joint with edge/flesh stitch holes; one pair of thong slots on outside quarter. (Fig 3.119)

Other side-seamed ankle-boots

341. SH 74 [451] ⟨240⟩, Waterfront I dump
Date of deposit: c.1140 (CP5)

Part of ankle-boot, right foot, with blunt, pointed toe; edge/flesh stitch holes along vamp wing seam.

342. SH 74 [451] ⟨900⟩, Waterfront I dump
Date of deposit: c.1140 (CP5)

Part of ankle-boot, right foot, with rounded toe. Upper with circle cut-out on outside quarter encircled with edge/flesh stitch holes; tunnel-stitch holes on flesh-face for small heel stiffener; edge/flesh stitch holes at throat and top edge; one pair of thong slots on each quarter. All seams butted. Length from toe to heel c.160mm. (Fig 3.120)

343. SH 74 [451] ⟨903⟩, Waterfront I dump
Date of deposit: c.1140 (CP5)

Part of ankle-boot, left foot. Upper with a low cut vamp; grain/flesh stitch holes round vamp opening; edge/flesh stitch holes round throat flap and top edge. Diagonal row of awl holes from bottom of outside quarter to top of heel continuing down on the inside quarter where the upper was later deliberately cut. (Fig 3.121) Grew and de Neergaard 1988, Fig 10

344. SH 74 [513] ⟨889⟩, Waterfront foreshore
Date of deposit: c.1140 (CP5)

Part of ankle-boot, right foot, with blunt, pointed toe. Upper with edge/flesh stitch holes along side-seam and seams attaching a small rectangular insert to inside quarters and vamp; tunnel-stitching on flesh-face at top edge; two pairs of thong slots on inside quarters; vamp deliberately cut. Sole with rounded heel-seat, edge/flesh stitch holes along lasting margin, very worn across heel-seat with stitch holes for a repair patch.

345. SH 74 [620] ⟨620⟩, Waterfront I dump
Date of deposit: c.1140 (CP5)

Part of ankle-boot, left foot. Upper fragment, edge/flesh stitch holes along side-seam, throat, throat flap and top edge; one thong slot on outside quarter.

346. BIG 82 [7064] ⟨1085⟩, Foreshore in inlet 4.5
Date of deposit: Post 1080 to early 12th century (CP5)

Part of ankle-boot, left foot, with blunt, pointed toe. Upper fragment, edge/flesh stitch holes along vamp wing seam. Sole, very worn, forepart and heel-seat repaired with thread.

Shoe top-bands

Single or single strips sewn together with no slots (Type A)

347. SM 75 [220] ⟨355⟩, Waterfront bank
Date of deposit: Early to mid-11th century (CP3)

Part of top-band, one end torn, grain/flesh stitch holes along both sides and intact end. Surviving length 75mm; width 33mm.

348. NFW 74 [129] ⟨192⟩, Waterfront dump 3.2
Date of deposit: Late 11th to early 12th century (CP4)

Top-band comprised of two strips originally sewn together with the grain side outermost; grain/flesh stitch holes along both sides and both ends. Length 225mm; width 34mm. (Fig 3.122)

349. NFW 74 [129] ⟨196⟩, Waterfront dump 3.2
Date of deposit: Late 11th to early 12th century (CP4)
Sheep / goatskin (GE)

Top-band with grain/flesh stitch holes along both sides, and one end. Length 160mm; width 18-22mm.

350. MLK 76 [1094] ⟨1550⟩, Pit 64
Date of deposit: Late 11th to early 12th century (CP4)

Part of top-band, torn both ends; edge/flesh stitch holes on one side and grain/flesh stitch holes along the other; three holes, 20mm apart, along centre of band. Surviving length 95mm; width 25mm.

351. MLK 76 [1094] ⟨1648⟩, Pit 64
Date of deposit: Late 11th to early 12th century (CP4)

Part of top-band, both ends torn; edge/flesh stitch holes along one side, grain/flesh stitch holes along the other. Surviving length 120mm; width 13mm.

Folded along one side with single row of slots (Type B)

352. NFW 74 [129] ⟨195⟩, Waterfront dump 3.2
Date of deposit: Late 11th to early 12th century (CP4)
Probably calfskin (GE)

Part of top-band, with slots cut through both thicknesses of leather; both ends torn. Edge/flesh stitch holes along side formerly seamed to upper. Surviving length 180mm, width 33-37mm; width of hem 6-7mm; finished width 20-27mm; 3 pairs of slots per 10mm. (Fig 3.122)

Folded along one side with two rows of slots (Type C)

353. NFW 74 [137] ⟨135/1⟩, Waterfront dump
Date of deposit: Early to mid-11th centry (CP3)
Possibly sheep/goatskin (GE)

Part of top-band with a double row of slots, only the top row piercing both thicknesses of leather; one end torn and the other cut diagonally. Edge/flesh stitch holes along side formerly seamed to upper, and grain/flesh stitch holes along the intact end. Surviving length 135mm; width 32-33mm; width of hem 4-5mm; finished width 27-28mm; 3 pairs of slots per 10mm. (Fig 3.122)

354. NFW 74 [108] ⟨140⟩, Waterfront dump 3.2
Date of deposit: Late 11th to early 12th century (CP4)
Calfskin (GE)

Top-band with a double row of slots partly piercing both thicknesses of leather; one of the two ends is cut diagonally. Edge/flesh stitch holes along side formerly seamed to upper, and grain/flesh stitch holes along both ends. Length 230mm; width 34mm; width of hem 9mm; finished width 25mm; 3-4 pairs of slots per 10mm. (Fig 3.122)

(See also ankle boot No 302)

Folded double with no slots (Type D)

355. NFW 74 [129] ⟨193⟩, Waterfront dump 3.2
Date of deposit: Late 11th century (CP4)
Leather too worn for identification (GE)

Top-band, folded double lengthwise. Grain/flesh stitch holes along both ends and one side; edge/flesh stitch holes along opposite side. Length 150mm; width 43mm; finished width 21-22mm. (Fig 3.123)

Folded double with single row of slots (Type E)

356. NFW 74 [129] ⟨194⟩, Waterfront dump 3.2
Date of deposit: Late 11th to early 12th century (CP4)
Probably calfskin (GE)

Part of top-band folded double lengthwise with a single row of slots cut through both thicknesses of leather; one end cut diagonally and the other torn. The end and both sides have grain/flesh stitch holes. A single thickness of leather interlined the band pierced with corresponding slots and stitch holes. Surviving length 220mm; width 58mm; finished width 28mm; 3 pairs of slots per 10mm; width of lining 25-27mm. (Fig 3.123)

(See also ankle-boot No 287)

Folded double with two rows of slots (Type F)

357. NFW 74 [48] ⟨191⟩, Waterfront dump 3.2

Date of deposit: Late 11th to early 12th century (CP4)
Possibly calfskin (GE)

Part of top-band folded double lengthwise with a double row of slots cut through both thicknesses of leather; one of the two ends tapers to a point, and a V-shaped cut enabled the band to bend 90°. Fragments of two thongs are preserved, one, which slotted through a hole above the V-shaped cut, was secured by being folded through on itself at one end. The other thong, positioned 29mm from the end, has two rows of grain/flesh stitch holes. Further slots are preserved at both ends. Sewn to the upper along one side with grain/flesh stitch holes and along the other with edge/flesh stitch holes. Surviving length 290mm; width c.40mm; finished width 20mm; 5 pairs of slots per 10mm. (Fig 3.123)

358. BIG 82 [7095] ⟨5961⟩, Waterfront bank
Date of deposit: 1055 to c.1080 (CP4)
Possibly calfskin (GE)

Top-band, folded double as for No 357; one of the two ends is cut diagonally. There is a vertical slot at the angular end and three horizontal slots near the vertical end. Grain/flesh stitch holes along both ends and along one side formerly sewn to the upper; edge/flesh stitch holes along the other side. Length 280mm; width 58mm; finished width 29mm; 4 pairs of slots per 10mm. (Fig 3.123)

Folded double with three rows of slots (Type G)

359. SWA 81 [427] ⟨345⟩, Waterfront foreshore 1
Date of deposit: Late 11th to early 12th century (CP4)

Top-band, folded double lengthwise with three rows of slots; V-shaped slit at one end. The sides and ends have grain/flesh stitch holes. Length 95mm; width 51mm; finished width 23-26mm; 2-3 pairs of slots per 10mm. (Fig 3.124)

Straps

360. MLK 76 [54] and [55] ⟨1666⟩ and ⟨410⟩, Pit 20
Date of deposit: Early to mid-11th century (CP3)
Calfskin (GE)

Part of strap, tongue-end preserved, buckle torn off opposite end. Made from a single thickness of leather folded lengthwise along both sides and sewn with two rows of stitch holes, which stop short of the buckle; the hems were butt-seamed together along the centre back. Surviving length 410mm; finished width 13-17mm; 4 pairs of stitch holes per 10mm (shrinkage 9.5%). (Fig 3.125. Note the central portion of the strap is not shown in the drawing.)

361. WAT 78 [776] ⟨1327⟩, Building 4.2 use
Date of deposit: Late 11th to early 12th century (CP4)
Calfskin (GE)

Part of strap, tongue-end preserved, buckle-end cut. Made from a single thickness of leather, sewn and seamed as for No 360; knotted. Surviving length 420mm; finished width 22mm; 2-3 pairs of stitch holes per 10mm. (Fig 3.125)

362. SH 74 [407] ⟨238⟩, Waterfront I dump
Date of deposit: c.1140 (CP5)

Part of strap, both ends cut away. Made from a single thickness of leather, seamed as for No 360 and sewn with a single row of stitches along a section on each side. Four pairs of holes at irregular intervals and two (?) buckle-pin holes. Surviving length 175mm; finished width 30mm. (Fig 3.125)

363. BIG 82 [7005] ⟨4455⟩ Foreshore in inlet 4.5
Date of deposit: Post 1080 to early 12th century (CP5)
Calfskin (GE)

Part of strap, both ends torn. Made from a single thickness of leather, seamed as for No 360, very worn. Surviving length 125mm; finished width 24-25mm. (Fig 3.125)

364. MLK 76 [1118] ⟨1646⟩, Pit 42
Date of deposit: 10th century (CP1)
Possibly calfskin (GE)

Part of strap, tongue at one end cut with a slit for slotting through the opposite end, made from a single thickness of leather. Length 296mm. (Fig 3.125)

365. MLK 76 [1053] ⟨418⟩, Pit 55
Date of deposit: Late 11th to early 12th century (CP4)
Cow/calfskin (GE)

Part of strap, both ends torn, made from a single thickness of leather with a row of stitch holes along each side; knotted. Surviving length c.300mm; width 12mm; 2-3 stitch holes per 10mm. (Fig 3.125)

366. SH 74 [514] ⟨896⟩, Waterfront foreshore
Date of deposit: c.1140 (CP5)

Part of strap, one end bifurcated possibly for attaching a buckle, both ends torn. Single thickness of leather with a row of stitch holes along both sides and a simple interlace pattern. Surviving length 145mm; width 13mm. (Fig 3.125)

Wooden artefacts

367. MLK 76 [60] ⟨2⟩, Pit 17
Date of deposit: 10th century (CP1)
Acer sp, Maple (VRS)

Turned core from a bowl or cup. (Fig 3.126)

368. MLK 76 [60] ⟨1⟩ and ⟨6⟩, Pit 17
Date of deposit: 10th century (CP1)
Fraxinus excelsior, Ash (IGT)

Fragments of a turned cup, including part of rim and base. Decorated externally below the rim with three shallow concentric grooves. Rim diameter *c*.120mm. (Fig 3.126)

369. MLK 76 [76] ⟨1551⟩, Pit 7
Date of deposit: Late 11th to early 12th century (CP4)
(?)*Fraxinus excelsior*, Ash (IGT)

Two tiny fragments of a turned (?) bowl.

370. NFW 74 [102] ⟨220⟩, Waterfront silt
Date of deposit: Early to mid-11th century (CP3)
(?) *Acer campestre*, Field maple (IGT)

Handle with a hooked end, broken from a bowl or ladle. Turned and carved from a radially split plank. Surviving length 130mm. (Fig 3.126)

371. MLK 76 [1193D] ⟨989⟩, Pit 80
Date of deposit: Late 11th to late 12th century (CP4 or 6)
Fraxinus excelsior, Ash (IGT)

Part of a hemispherical bowl hollowed out with an adze from a split half trunk of ash with sides up to 15mm thick. Repaired with an iron staple.

372. NFW 74 [48] ⟨411⟩, Waterfront dump 3.2
Date of deposit: Late 11th century (CP4)
Fraxinus excelsior, Ash (CM)

One end and three wall fragments of a large, rectangular trough hollowed out with an adze from a split half trunk of ash. The bark still adheres to the external surface in places. The end fragment has the remains of a horizontal everted lip handle with a rounded edge, which was carved all-in-one piece with the end. Width *c*.350mm; height *c*.150mm. (Fig 3.126)

373. MLK 76 [1131] ⟨495⟩, Pit 51
Date of deposit: Late 11th to early 12th century (CP4)
Acer sp, Maple (VRS)

Part of a cylindrical mallet-head, with an oval socket for the handle. Length 138mm; diameter 84mm; diameter of socket 21-26mm. (Fig 3.127)

374. NFW 74 [59] ⟨223⟩, Waterfront dump 3.2
Date of deposit: Late 11th century (CP4)
(?) *Acer campestre*, Field maple (CM)

Fragment of a spindle-turned object, possibly a finial, made from a full stem branch. The upper part is globular with a wide lathe-cut groove round its girth; below the globular part is a circular collar, also decorated with a lathe cut groove. The lower part is broken, but was originally cylindrical and there are traces of seven or eight small nail holes just below the collar, one still retaining part of an iron shank. These could possibly have held a leather covering, especially since the cylindrical part seems to be unturned and unde-

corated. The globular section is partly hollowed from the top, while a small circular augered hole leads from the bottom of the hollow down the length of the object. Surviving length 73mm; max diameter 47mm. (Fig 3.127)

3. WAT 78 [94] ⟨337⟩, Pit 18
Date of deposit: 10th century (CP1)
Maple or a fruitwood (JW)

Part of the handle of a whittle-tang knife. (Fig 3.3)

9. ALG 84 [588] ⟨381⟩, Ditch
Date of deposit: 11th century or later (CP3+)
Probably *Buxus* sp, Box (JW)

Part of the handle of a whittle-tang knife. (Fig 3.3)

27. MLK 76 [3081] ⟨1347⟩, Pit 32
Date of deposit: Early to mid-11th century (CP3)
Probably *Quercus* sp, Oak (IGT)

Part of a woolcomb base and handle. (Fig 3.15)

26. MLK 76 [1064] ⟨57⟩, Pit 55
Date of deposit: Late 11th to early 12th century (CP4)
Quercus sp, Oak (VRS)

Curved haft of carpenter's axe, round in section. (Fig 3.14)

Stave-made artefacts

375. NFW 74 [137] ⟨294⟩, Waterfront dump 2.4
Date of deposit: Early to mid-11th century (CP3)
Quercus sp, Oak (CM)

Part of a semi-circular stave of a caskhead or bucket base, cut from a radially split plank. The rounded edge is chamfered on one side only for fitting into a V-sectioned groove on the upright vessel staves. One flat side has linear cuts in no apparent pattern, and could possibly indicate re-use as a trencher or cutting board. Diameter 255mm. (Fig 3.128)

376. MLK 76 [83] ⟨29⟩, Pit 15
Date of deposit: Late 11th to early 12th century (CP4)
Quercus sp, Oak (VRS)

Roughly circular stave cut from a radially split plank. Possibly a lid or base of a small vessel but the edge shows no sign of having been chamfered. Diameter 97mm. (Fig 3.128)

377. MLK 76 [83] ⟨23⟩, Pit 15
Date of deposit: Late 11th to early 12th century (CP4)

Roughly circular stave, similar to No 376 above. Diameter 95mm.

378. WAT 78 [1158] ⟨296⟩, Pit 46 construction
Date of deposit: Late 11th to early 12th century (CP4)
Quercus sp, Oak (VRS)

Fifteen staves from an 18 staved cask. The staves vary in width and have a sloping chime. The bottom of each stave is chamfered to accommodate the base and each has a V-sectioned croze groove. One of the staves has a circular vent hole, in which are the remains of a wooden bung. Max surviving height 640mm; internal diameter of base c.680mm; diameter of vent hole 14mm. (Fig 3.128)

379. MLK 76 [48] ⟨781⟩, Pit 12
Date of deposit: 10th century (CP2)
Quercus sp, Oak (VRS)

Part of a shingle cut from a radially split plank with one peg-hole, but possibly a two peg hole form. The remains of a trenail was found in association with the shingle. Length 310mm; width 107mm; diameter of peg hole 17mm. (Fig 3.128)

Patten

380. SM 75 [192] ⟨356⟩, Waterfront silt 3.3
Date of deposit: Late 11th to early 12th century (CP4)
Alnus glutinosa, Alder (CM)

Sole of patten made from a single block of wood, shaped for a left foot. At least twelve iron dome-headed nails were fixed into the side of the clog for securing the leather upper, but only ten now remain. The underside, particularly the heel, is very worn. Length 202mm; width of forepart 80mm; width of heel seat 54mm. (Fig 3.129)

Pegs

381. NFW 74 [48] ⟨234⟩, Waterfront dump 3.2
Date of deposit: Late 11th century (CP4)
Quercus sp, Oak (CM)

Long peg with a battered head and a rounded, blunt point, whittled from a full stem branch; oval in section. Length 230mm; max diameter 22mm. (Fig 3.130)

382. MLK 76 [2208] ⟨276⟩, Pit 90
Date of deposit: 10th to mid-12th century (CP1-5)
Corylus avellana, Hazel (IGT)

Long peg with a battered head and broken tip, whittled from a branch, oval in section. Surviving length 225mm; max diameter 29mm. (Fig 3.130)

Trenail

383. MLK 76 [1108] ⟨419⟩, Pit 53
Date of deposit: Late 11th to early 12th century (CP4)

Part of a trenail with a rectangular head, the shank is round in section. Surviving length 30mm; diameter 5mm. (Fig 3.130)

Wedge

384. SM 75 [37] ⟨391⟩, Waterfront dump 3.2
Date of deposit: Late 11th century (CP4)
Quercus sp, Oak (CM)

Small rectangular wedge, tapering to a point in longitudinal section. The thin end is broken. Surviving length 60mm. (Fig 3.130)

Unidentified woodwork

385. MLK 76 [1041] ⟨414⟩, Pit 57
Date of deposit: 10th century (CP1)
Alnus glutinosa, alder (IGT)

Artefact, polygonal at one end, whittled from a sapling or young branch. Length 148mm. (Fig 3.130)

386. MLK 76 [1041] ⟨308⟩, Pit 57
Date of deposit: 10th century (CP1)
Quercus sp, Oak (IGT)

Trapezoidal shaped piece, sawn at both ends, cut from a radially split plank. Width 85mm.

387. MLK 76 [48] ⟨782⟩, Pit 12
Date of deposit: 10th century (CP2)
Featureless fragment, possibly part of shingle. Thickness 13mm.

388. NFW 74 [124] ⟨499⟩, Waterfront dump 3.2
Date of deposit: Late 11th century (CP4)
Fraxinus excelsior, Ash (CM)

Two pieces, possibly part of the same object. One is a small, rectangular plank cut from a quarter of a half split trunk and pierced with a circular hole. It is now very twisted but probably originally had straight, parallel sides. The second piece is also twisted and much smaller, with both ends broken. (a) Surviving length 283mm; (b) surviving length 228mm.

389. SM 75 [108] ⟨390⟩, Waterfront dump 3.2
Date of deposit: Late 11th century (CP4)
Quercus sp, Oak (CM)

Fragment, pierced by a circular hole with traces of a smaller second hole along one broken edge; cut from a radially split plank. Surviving length 67mm. (Fig 3.130)

390. SM 75 [37] ⟨405⟩, Waterfront dump 3.2
Date of deposit: Late 11th century (CP4)
Quercus sp, Oak (CM)

D-shaped object cut from a radially split plank; sub-rectangular in cross-section, but slightly compressed towards one edge, which is broken. Surviving length 80mm; max thickness 21mm. (Fig 3.130)

391. SM 75 [71] ⟨392⟩, Waterfront dump 3.2

Date of deposit: Late 11th century (CP4)
Betula sp, Birch (CM)

Several fragments of a (?) pin, D-shaped in cross section. Total surviving length 55mm.

392. MLK 76 [76] ⟨369⟩, Pit 7
Date of deposit: Late 11th to early 12th century (CP4)
Acer sp, Maple (VRS)

Several small cap-like shavings, possibly lathe-turning waste. Diameter 20mm-25mm. (Fig 3.130)

393. MLK 76 [87] ⟨4⟩, Pit 15
Date of deposit: Late 11th to early 12th century (CP4)
Quercus sp, Oak (VRS)

Fragment, cut from a radially split plank, sawn along one edge. Surviving length 130mm. (Fig 3.130)

394. MLK 76 [1108] ⟨445⟩ and ⟨544⟩, Pit 53
Date of deposit: 11th to early 12th century (CP4)
Quercus sp, Oak (VRS)

Two pieces cut from a radially split plank probably originally part of the same object. The larger piece has four unaligned dowel holes, while the smaller piece has a single dowel hole. Max surviving width 110mm; thickness *c*.5mm; diameter of holes 12-18mm. (Fig 3.131)

395. MLK 76 [1064J] ⟨1081⟩, Pit 55

Date of deposit: Late 11th to early 12th century (CP4)
Quercus sp, Oak (IGT)

Fragment, sub-rectangular in cross-section. One face has a small dowel hole and various tool marks. Surviving length 153mm. (Fig 3.131)

396. MLK 76 [1064J] ⟨1082⟩, Pit 55
Date of deposit: Late 11th to early 12th century (CP4)
Sambucus sp, Elder (VRS)

Part of artefact whittled from stem branch split longitudinally and hollowed out; the broader end is burnt. Surviving length 195mm. (Fig 3.131)

397. MLK 76 [1191] ⟨551⟩, Pit 80
Date of deposit: Late 11th to late 12th century (CP4 or CP6)
Quercus sp, Oak (IGT)

Two conjoining pieces with tenon at broader end and two dowels holes; one dowel preserved. Length 440mm; width 45-70mm. (Fig 3.131)

Cordage

398. SM 75 [195] ⟨530⟩, Waterfront silt 2.3
Date of deposit: Early to mid-11th century (CP3)
Woody material (RG)

Fragments of cord s-plied from three strands. Diameter, *c*.11mm. (Fig 3.132)

4.i SAXON AND NORMAN COINS FROM LONDON

Peter Stott

As our knowledge of single finds of Saxon and Norman coins accumulates and is added to the evidence of hoards and mint production, a picture is emerging of monetary circulation in England during this period (Blunt and Dolley 1977, Blackburn 1983, Blackburn and Bonser 1984 and 1985, Pirie 1986). It is clear, moreover, that single finds from archaeological sites in urban centres should be viewed in total and not merely in the context of individual sites if they are to provide an indication, if not necessarily a direct measure, of the changing commercial fortunes of a town and its position within the monetary system of the kingdom as a whole. In a recent analysis which compared Saxon coin evidence from certain towns (Hinton 1986), London was conspicuous by its absence. From the first post-Roman evidence of its re-emergence as a viable urban entity, London has been regarded as a major commercial centre which perhaps exceeded in importance other towns in England, but in the absence of a complete listing of single coin-finds, and of the gauge to the town's commercial health which such information would offer, there has been a significant gap in the evidence by which this view might be tested. Published work on Saxon and Norman single finds from London has been limited because it has concentrated only on specific periods (Metcalf 1980 and 1981, Rigold and Metcalf 1984). It is hoped that in some measure the present survey will overcome this deficiency. The single finds provide the central element, but an attempt has also been made to place them in the context of other numismatic studies already undertaken on hoards and on the evidence of mint output. On the interpretation of hoards from Saxon and early-Norman London the work of the late Michael Dolley should be consulted (Dolley 1960) together with the relevant sections in the work that was to be his *festschrift* (ASMH). In the present essay, additions are made to the tally of hoards (Appendix 2) (Appendices referred to relate to this chapter unless prefixed by another chapter number.) together with some refinement of the description of 11th-century hoards from the City.

Information has been gathered from as many sources as are known on coins found within the area which, until 1 April 1986, came under the administration of the Greater London Council. Thus, this section on coins is broader in its geographical scope than other chapters in the present volume, but it does ensure, for example, the recognition of distribution patterns relevant to the problem of identifying the position of the mid-Saxon *emporium*.

The quality of provenances varies, the best being those discovered as a result of controlled archaeological excavation. By contrast, some of the antiquarian records are frustratingly imprecise. Undoubtedly the most important of such sources are the catalogues, notes and journals of Charles Roach Smith. Roach Smith's list of Anglo-Saxon coins contained in his 1854 *Catalogue* assigns findspots of any precision to only a limited number of discoveries, and otherwise confines itself to the fact that coins were discovered 'during the progress of recent extensive alterations made in the city of London'. The problem here is deciding whether Roach Smith was referring to the modern City of London, or more specifically to the area within the Roman and later walls, or whether he intended his reader to understand that the term 'city' indicated the more generalised notion of central London. In view of this it is worth remarking that all those pieces with known provenances were found in the City, and the work of Michael Rhodes on Roach Smith's journals and notebooks has revealed finds additional to those listed in the 1854 *Catalogue* which in all but a very few cases were found in the City or in the City's Thames foreshore (Appendix 4). There is some reason to suppose, therefore, that those coins in the *Catalogue* without a provenance were found in the City or in that stretch of the Thames which forms the City's southern border.

A significant position amongst our sources is occupied by the stray finds of recent years. Their discovery has primarily involved the use of metal detectors by individuals searching the Thames foreshore and spoil removed from City sites, and the resulting finds are now for the most part in private collections. Recognition by professional numismatists of the need to harness this activity to their own requirements has already borne fruit (Blackburn and Bonser 1984 and 1985). In London, the dividends of co-operation between publicly-funded archaeologists and privately-motivated metal-detector users have been apparent for some years and the substantial group of material found in spoil removed from Billingsgate Lorry Park is particularly remarkable in this respect. This area of Billingsgate fish market was the subject of a well-publicised archaeological excavation and a subsequent watching-brief between 1982 and early 1984. However, the great bulk of finds, including the coins, were discovered by metal detector users in spoil transported by contractors from the site to widely scattered dumps, mostly in Kent and Essex. Inevitably, the contextual relationships of finds from this source are, to say the least, difficult to determine. Nevertheless, without the collaboration which made this material available for study, the quality of information from this prime waterfront site would have been considerably poorer (Egan 1985/6).

Without doubt we must accept that the completeness of our record is open to question. Public appreciation of the archaeologist's need to examine stray finds is not universal and it is more than likely that an unknown number remains unrecorded. Equally, we can only ponder from the experiences of the Billingsgate site what pieces the archaeologist has been unable, for a number of reasons, to uncover. Nevertheless, the collection of material presented here may be regarded as sufficiently complete to suggest the patterns of coin-loss and thus document the changes in the economy of London from mid-Saxon times to 1158, a terminus chosen for its numismatic importance as the end of the Saxon system of coinage.

COINS FROM PRE-ALFREDIAN LONDON

The location of Pre-Alfredian London

The central issue which has for some years exercised the mind of the student of pre-Alfredian London is the failure of archaeology to corroborate sources which tell of a town busy with commerce and highly estimated by contemporaries. Such has been the apparent paucity of archaeological remains from the intramural City that some have been moved to question the significance of London before its development under Alfred in the late 9th century. The validity of the recently proposed solution - that we have been looking in the wrong place (Biddle 1984, Vince 1983 and 1984) - is demonstrated by the evidence of coin discovery presented in Fig 4.3. It seems clear that during the period 700-886, there was indeed a settlement of some kind to the west of the intramural City, which equally clearly was discontinued after 886 when the former Roman walled city once again became the core of the community (Figs 4.4-6). How extensive an area this western settlement covered has not been determined although the concentration of finds stretches along the north bank from Fleet Street upstream to Lambeth Bridge. At the same time, the tally of finds from the City itself has proved more substantial than might previously have been expected so that if, as has been suggested, the western settlement was the commercial element in a city consisting of two parts, this cannot be demonstrated on the basis of numismatic evidence. The map of pre-Alfredian coin-loss rather gives the impression that London may have been a scattered series of settlements as opposed to two units with distinct functions.

Professor Biddle was justified in stating the urgency of the need for a listing of single coin-finds from mid-Saxon London (Biddle 1984): the present listing provides, at least for the period of the sceattas, an impression of a town which closer than hitherto approximates to the kind of *emporium* noted by Bede. Even without this knowledge, however, evidence of mint activity would already have given some indication of the town's importance. The London mint was active during the thrymsa period and was apparently responsible for the transitional 'Vanimundus' group and for sceatta series B in addition to series L (Grierson and Blackburn 1986, 164-5). A series T sceat apparently reading 'De Lundonim' was included in the Hallum hoard (ibid, 181). The inclusion of a mint name on this, on two of the three thrymsa series, and amongst series L sceattas is a unique distinction at this period.

Thrymsas and sceattas

The earliest discoveries with which we are concerned are the 'Witmen' thrymsa found in the Thames at Blackfriars (Appendix 1,1) and two further thrymsas noted by Roach Smith as having been 'found in London' (Appendix 1, 2 and 3). As there appears to be some doubt whether thrymsas may be regarded as a form of regular currency (Stewart 1978, 144-5), there is perhaps some difficulty in accepting these finds as evidence of monetary circulation in London. Most known specimens of the native form of this early gold coinage derive from the hoards found at Crondall and Sutton Hoo. Single finds are very rare and perhaps only the late debased types, which blend into the ensuing silver coinage of the late 7th century, may be thought of as the constituents of a monetary economy. These three finds from London, which probably cover an extensive period, offer no firm reason to dispute this view.

By contrast, the numbers of discoveries of sceattas, or as some would prefer, denarii,[1] are such that it is inconceivable that they were intended for any purpose other than as a general medium of exchange. London finds of sceattas, apart from the few additions recorded here, have been listed in the recent comprehensive survey (Rigold and

4.1. Coin finds from London AD600-1158.

Horizontal scale : date range by decade.
Vertical scale : single finds.
Hoards included at base of diagram.

Finds have been placed on the chronological scale within the decade which corresponds to their earliest known or suggested date of minting. A more realistic picture may have been presented had the arrangement been by currency range or period of issue, but in most cases, such information is not available or is at best conjectural. The histogram does, however, serve the purpose of demonstrating in general terms the comparative rates of loss, and thus probably of production and circulation, between different periods.

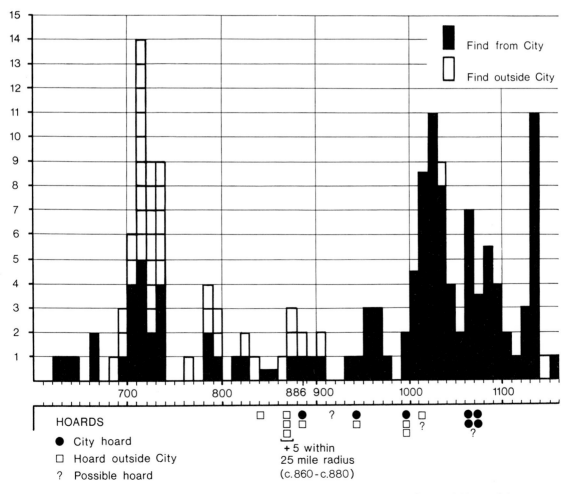

Metcalf 1984). The large volume of finds from London and elsewhere indicate the extent to which this coinage, and indeed coinage as a medium of exchange, became established; more so, it would seem, in comparison to the later broad flat penny after its introduction in the late 8th century. Coin finds from London do not occur in comparable quantities until those for the 11th century (Fig 4.1), and this comparison between the currency rates of the sceattas and of the penny during its first two centuries would appear to apply also to the rest of the country, or at least to the south and east where the sceattas were current (Hinton 1986, 15 ff.).

There are several indications of London's position as an important centre within the sceatta currency. It has one of the heaviest concentrations of finds and its mint was active during all phases of this coinage. It appears to have been a pivotal point in the currency flow from Kent into Mercia, and perhaps to some extent also into Wessex and Essex (Metcalf 1984, 32, 56-7), London, however, did not dominate the money market to quite the same extent as, apparently, did Southampton (Hamwic) or the East Kent triangle formed by Canterbury, Reculver and Richborough (Rigold and Metcalf 1984). It was in East Kent that the great bulk of the minting took place and this area was most suitably positioned to benefit from the Frisian market. Furthermore, it seems clear from the scale of finds that Southampton and East Kent underwent substantial commercial development during the secondary phase of the sceatta coinage (Metcalf 1984, maps on pp.33 and 35), a development, the evidence appears to indicate, in which London did not share. By comparison with the major centres, the proportion of finds of secondary phase sceattas seems to suggest that London enjoyed a respectable, though not outstanding, volume of trade. Why this should be is not clear, although for a variety of reasons, geographical position not least among them, London may have functioned largely as an entrepôt and rather less as an international port directly at the receiving end of the major mercantile activities.

There may be some merit in arguing that the numbers of finds are artificially low due to irretrievable loss during the course of building works, in particular the excavations preparatory to the construction of deep basements during the 19th century (Biddle 1984, 25). But even if future archaeological excavation in London were to result in numerous additions to the body of finds,

these would be unlikely to alter the impression of shortfall compared, in particular, to Southampton where the volume of recent finds has continued to reflect Hamwic's dominant position (Hinton 1986, 11). In any case, even if works of demolition and construction have not always been the subject of close archaeological scrutiny, they have often in the past attracted antiquarian interest, and it was precisely this kind of operation which resulted in the discovery of the largest concentrations of sceattas in London, reported mostly by Roach Smith. It is a distinct possibility that the single finds in this group were discovered in the intramural City or its Thames foreshore (Appendix 4) but not as a hoard as was once thought. The 'Thames Hoard' is a separate find and though its City provenance is even less assured than that of the Roach Smith pieces, Rigold and Metcalf (Rigold and Metcalf 1984, 254) state that the hoard was acquired by the British Museum from Roach Smith which, by implication, albeit tenuous, suggests a City findspot.

Appendix 1 includes all known finds of sceattas, updating the catalogue in Hill and Metcalf (1984) by 18 discoveries. A very worn series K from Billingsgate spoil reveals enough detail to be identified as similar, if not certainly identical, to another London find catalogued as number 30 in Metcalf and Walker's survey of the 'Wolf' sceattas (Metcalf and Walker 1967) (Appendix 1, 19). A find from excavations at Bermondsey Abbey (Appendix 1, 20) carries a series K reverse closest in style to numbers 7 and 41 in the same survey, but is otherwise unknown. The obverse is less clear but a design representing three berries on a stalk may be distinguished, indicating that the whole design might be a derivative of the 'bird and branch' of series U. In the absence of any parallel, this piece is perhaps best interpreted for the moment as an imitation. A further discovery at Bermondsey Abbey is of series G and displays irregular stylistic features recognised on examples elsewhere. Whether this is a series of imitations or the work of a single individual operating under official auspices it is difficult to say. The distribution of finds of series G offers no reliable clues as to its origin (Appendix 1, 17).

In the past three years, archaeological excavation has provided physical evidence to support the propositions of Vince and Biddle (Vince 1983 and 1984, Biddle 1984) on the location to the west of the present City of mid-Saxon London. The discovery of six sceattas at four of the sites involved has attracted considerable interest. In 1985 a series V sceat was discovered at Jubilee Hall in Covent Garden (Appendix 1, 46) (Whytehead 1985). The distribution of this type is concentrated in East Kent, the only previous exceptions to this being finds from Reading and Southampton (Metcalf 1984, map on p.45). The present example is the only one to have been discovered north of the Thames, although this findspot is hardly sufficient to give credence to any suggestion that the design on this series is a visual pun on the dynastic name of the Wuffingas (Metcalf 1984, 44). At the nearby site of Maiden Lane excavated in 1986, a series D sceat was discovered (Appendix 1, 10) (Cowie 1987, 30-34). This series, it has been suggested, may be of Frisian origin although the possibility that it was manufactured in England or in Merovingian territory cannot be ignored (Stewart 1984, 19). In 1987, the site at the National Gallery produced a series T sceat (Appendix 1, 43) (Cowie 1987, ibid). One example of this type bears a legend interpreted as reading 'DE LUNDONIM' (Grierson and Black-

burn 1986, 181) although, in the opinion of the present writer, this requires considerable imagination and the present specimen is consistent with others in the series in carrying a legend which does not clarify the matter. London has more finds of this series than elsewhere in England but the distribution does not necessarily favour a mint there (Metcalf 1984, 39).

In terms of finds of sceattas, the most productive of these sites to the west of the City has been that at Bedfordbury. The three sceattas found there include a series L (Appendix 1, 27). In comparison with series T, there is greater assurance that much of this series is likely to have been produced by a mint in London, but the present example is worn and no legend indicating its origins can be detected (Grierson and Black-

4.2. Coin finds before c.680. Five mid-Saxon coins of this category are known from London (Appendix 1, 1-5), only no. 1 has a known findspot.

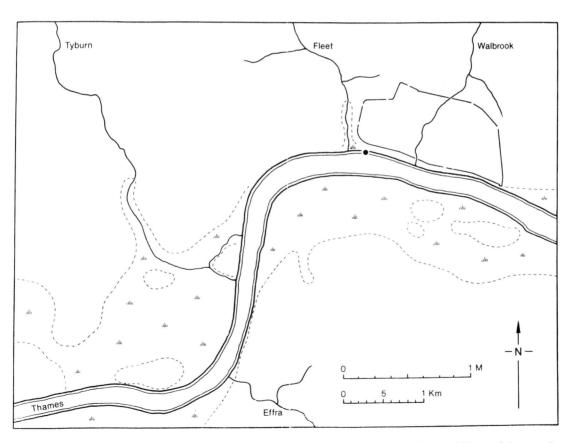

burn 1986 178-9). The second coin from the site is a series M (Appendix 1, 30). The finds of this series have a southerly distribution with a concentration at Reculver suggesting a Kentish origin (Metcalf 1984, 44).

The third sceat from Bedfordbury is of series S, one of two of this series found in London in recent years, the other being from Rotherhithe (Appendix 1, 39 and 40). Metcalf has suggested an East Saxon origin for series S, and also for series Z (Metcalf 1984, 56), an example of which was discovered in Billingsgate spoil (Appendix 1, 49). It is likely that London had an important monetary relationship with Essex during this period, as the major centre in East Anglia was at Ipswich whose monetary influence over Essex appears to have been slight (Metcalf 1984, Fig.6, series E and R). If finds of 'sphinx' sceattas in London illustrate persistent East Saxon influence there after Aethelbald's time, the Bedfordbury and Rotherhithe finds may be regarded as a small addition to the still slight evidence for this. Another discovery at Rotherhithe is an example of series X (Appendix 1, 47) with the beard on the 'Woden' bust presented as a series of vertical lines, perhaps indicating that this example is a local imitation of the original Frisian or Danish model. Apart from these two discoveries of sceattas, no other material evidence exists for mid-Saxon activity at Rotherhithe, although the Old English element 'hyd' in the name suggests a naval significance.

Six sceattas discovered recently during excavations at Barking Abbey have been included in the catalogue. They will receive more extensive consideration in a future publication (Appendix 1, 15, 21, 22, 33, 44 and 45).

After the latest of the sceattas the rate of coin loss in London apparently suffered an abrupt and complete reduction. A similar reduction is evident in Southampton (Addyman and Hill 1968, 76) and the finds from both places probably reflect the widespread decline in coinage in south-east England in the second half of the 8th century. Although production of the great majority of sceattas ceased before the mid-century, it appears that some continued in use, mostly in a debased form, through to the first extensive issues of the new style of coinage introduced in the time of Offa (Blackburn 1984, 168). It should be understood that the construction of the histogram in Fig 4.1 is based approximately on suggested or established dates of issue and not on periods of currency, so that some of the sceattas found in London may have been deposited anything up to fifty years after their date of issue.

The earliest broad pennies

London's commercial opportunities, it may be assumed, provided the Mercians with an incentive to maintain control of the town and the port may have been central to Offa's design of enhancing his prestige on the continent. It may be stretching the evidence somewhat to interpret the comparative peak in the histogram representing finds of Offa's coins as reflecting London's role in his foreign policy, but when it is considered that the circulation of the new style coinage seems in general to have been at a lower rate than that of the sceattas (Hinton 1986, 15 ff.), these finds may go some way to consolidating the suggestion that London enjoyed some kind of commercial success during Offa's reign. Further indications of this have emerged in a recent analysis of Offa's coins which demonstrates the possibility that London, at least before 790, was Offa's principal mint (Stewart 1986).

It is believed in some quarters that the broad silver penny was introduced under Frankish influence not by Offa but by two contemporary Kentish kings, Heaberht and Ecgberht (Blunt 1961, 39). It is not intended that the respective merits of the Mercian and Kentish candidates should be reviewed here. Instead, mention of Ecgberht is used to draw attention to the discovery early this century of a penny of this king at Stamford Hill in north London (Appendix 1, 51).

Two coins of Offa and a possible third, all of the light coinage, are known from London. The earliest in terms of type was found in the Thames at Wandsworth in 1980. It is a group I coin of the moneyer Eoba (Appendix 1, 52). A group II portrait coin of the moneyer Ethelwald is now in the Fitzwilliam collection (Appendix 1, 53). Said to have been found in the City of London, it can only be assumed once again that the term 'City' here applies to the administrative unit which now bears that name and not to the general geographical area of central London. The coin about which there is some doubt is a group II portrait coin of the moneyer Pendred (Appendix 1, 54). It was published by Lockett in 1920 but the record that it was 'found in the Thames' was not discussed in any further detail.

In addition to these coins of Offa, a coin of his queen, Cynethryth, was discovered in Billingsgate spoil in 1984 (Appendix 1, 55). As with all coins in the name of Cynethryth, the moneyer is Eoba and the dies appear to be the same as those used to produce the specimen held by Reading University. (On coins of Cynethryth, see Blunt 1961, 46-7 and Stewart 1986, 41.)

The first half of the 9th century

It is over twenty years since the work of Blunt and others overcame the problem of the absence of mint signatures and established a pattern of mint production, based on an analysis of moneyers' names, the coins they produced and their stylistic features, in south-east England in the first half of the 9th century (Blunt, Lyon and Stewart 1963). London was, during this period, predominantly under Mercian control. After Offa, coins appear to have been struck in London for Coenwulf, Ceolwulf and Wiglaf, the mint being closed under Wiglaf's predecessors Beornwulf and Ludica. In 829, Ecgberht of Wessex seized control of Mercia from Wiglaf and minted his own coinage in London which bore the mint signature, probably as propaganda. On regaining power, Wiglaf resumed production in London but closed the mint soon thereafter in the 830s. Beorhtwulf seems to have minted an extensive coinage in London after 843 (Pagan 1986, 47) but after his death in 852, there is no evidence to suggest that London minted again until what appears to have been a dramatic revival under Burgred during the 860s.

Even if London was the main centre of coin production during the early stages of Offa's coinage, its development thereafter seems to have been inconsistent. As we have seen, it was closed for a considerable time. If mint representation in the Delgany and Middle Temple hoards offers any indication, Canterbury emerges as the principal mint for both Mercian and West Saxon kings, while London's output diminishes between 828 and 842 (respectively the deposit date of each hoard) and is overall less than that of the other two south-eastern mints included, Rochester and an as yet unidentified East Anglian town (Blunt, Lyon and Stewart 1963, 44-45.) Except during the brief interlude of Ecgberht's takeover, London remained in Mercian hands and as such was probably affected by an overall Mercian decline, particularly after the battle of Ellendun in 825.

The early 9th century coins from London were thus probably deposited against a background in which economic development was adversely affected by the political climate. The pattern of coin loss for this period is generally similar to that of Southampton - both indicate a decline in the rate of loss - although the volume of losses recorded so far in the southern port suggest that the commercial activity there continued to be healthier than that of London.

Blunt, Lyon and Stewart's article of 1963 included a corpus of known coins for the period 796-840. Two coins from London were recorded, one of Coenwulf found in Fleet Street in 1914 (Appendix 1, 56) and one of Ceolwulf in the Roach Smith collection, found possibly in the City (Appendix 1, 59). A coin of Archbishop Wulfred was found in March 1824 at London Bridge and a record was made at the time in *Archaeologia* (Appendix 1, 60). From the legend provided, the coin may with confidence be identified according to the typology established in 1963 as Group III, moneyer Saeberht. The corpus does not record any discoveries of coins of Wulfred from London Bridge, but it is possible that one of those mentioned may represent this coin after it had found its way into a public or private collection.

Three recent discoveries should be added to the corpus. During excavations at Maiden Lane, near Covent Garden, in 1986 a coin of Coenwulf Group I of the moneyer Ibba was discovered (Appendix 1, 57). The context of this find was a pit containing domestic refuse which included fragments of Ipswich-type pottery dated c.650-850, and the site as a whole is of significance to the question of the topographical extent of mid-Saxon London. Another specimen of this type has been found at Breedon-on-the-Hill while another was probably found in Shropshire, and the obverse of the Maiden Lane find was produced from the same die as the latter. Another coin of Coenwulf has been reported as being found in Billingsgate spoil, but no further information was available at the time of going to press (Appendix 1, 58).

A coin of Baldred of Kent found in the Thames at Lambeth Bridge in 1973 has been discussed by Christopher Blunt (Appendix 1, 61.).

Coins of Ecgberht of Wessex were not included in the 1963 survey but were covered by Christopher Blunt in a separate article (Blunt 1955-7). A coin of this king was found during excavations at Westminster Abbey (Appendix 1, 62) in a series of dumped deposits overlying a late Saxon quarry pit, and was associated with material including Roman residual artefacts, Ipswich-type pottery,

Badorf-type pottery and late Saxon shell-tempered pottery. In view of the assessment of the latest of this pottery as 10th-11th century, it would appear that the coin was deposited at this spot some 200 years after it was minted, and so presumably it ought to be regarded as a secondary deposit. It is a portrait type of the moneyer Ethelmod, a moneyer placed by Blunt in his Group IV, who is noted by North as working at the Rochester mint (North 1980, 87). This is of a previously unknown variety. The design of the reverse cross is new, as is the spelling of the king's name (EGBEOR(H)T). The letter O is crudely represented by a circular blob.

From the first Viking attacks to 886

In his journal for 14 September, 1837, Roach Smith recorded the discovery in the Thames of a coin of Aethelwulf of Wessex (Appendix 1, 63): no further information was provided. With the exception of this discovery, coins of the mid-9th century are otherwise unrepresented amongst London finds. This corresponds to the period of decline and closure of the London mint, apparently reversed only temporarily during the reign of Beorhtwulf. As we have seen, local rivalry was probably at the root of the mint's misfortunes (Pagan 1965, 12), but account should also be taken of instability caused by Viking attacks, which had become regular features of Londoners' lives by the middle of the century.

The Middle Temple hoard is reckoned to have been deposited in c.842, the date at which the *Anglo-Saxon Chronicle* records a highly destructive descent upon the town. If, after this, Beorhtwulf minted successfully in London, it was probably in a climate of improved relations with Wessex arising from the need for mutual support in the face of the new series of encroachments (Dolley 1970, 17). Thereafter, hoards from the London area chronicle the intensification of Danish incursions, particularly from the 860s. Those found at Croydon Palace and Dorking may have been deposited during an assault on southern England in c.861.[2] In 865, a new phase of Danish involvement in England commenced with the landing in East Anglia of the *micel here*, or 'great army', which heralded the beginnings of substantial Viking settlement. In the winter of 870/1 an army occupied London and the hoards from Wandsworth (Appendix 2b), Waterloo Bridge, Westminster Bridge, Gravesend and possibly Barking may be in some way associated with this event. Another cache hidden at Croydon probably in 872 has been interpreted as a Viking's hoard, perhaps a sample of tribute collected during the occupation of London (Brooks and Graham-Campbell, 1986).

The Vikings may have left London after 872, although the *Anglo-Saxon Chronicle* is by no means clear on this. Equally, a body of opinion might claim that the town of which Alfred took possession in 886 had probably been continuously a Danish colony since 871 (Pagan 1965, 27). Indeed, it was once widely thought that the Danes were so established in London that they could afford the luxury of producing their own coinage (Stenton 1971, 250). The pennies and halfpennies issued in the name of 'Alfdene', a figure identified with the Halfdan who commanded the occupying army, were taken as evidence for this. The obverse of the penny bears the Two Emperors design used by Alfred and Ceolwulf II on their coinages from c.875, while the London monogram occupies the reverse. Two moneyers are recorded. One, Tilewine, is credited as the sole moneyer of Alfred's own monogram coinage. However, in more recent years, numismatists have been of the opinion that the monogram made its first appearance under Alfred in association with his occupation of London in 886 and not before. The historical Halfdan appears to have left London for good in 872 and was probably dead by 877 (Stenton 1971, 253), a date held to be unacceptably early for the production of a monogram coinage, although it is not too early for an imitative coinage to have adopted the Two Emperors design. Nevertheless, it has been preferred to group the Alfdene coins with the many Viking imitations of Alfredian types and to suggest that Alfdene must be a later figure, unknown to history and whose coins were issued in quite another part of the country (Dolley and Blunt 1961, 82-3, 89-90).

If coin was not produced in London before 886 under the auspices of the Danes, it is likely that the native authorities presided over their own output which displayed a greatly improved performance over previous years. Indeed it has been proposed that London was continuously the principal south-eastern mint in the two decades before 886, the period of the most intense Viking activity in south-east England (Pagan 1965, 12-4, 26-7; Dolley 1970, 18-9.), producing coins for both Mercia and Wessex in at least the two major designs, the Lunette and the Cross-and-Lozenge, common to both kingdoms. According to this theory, Viking attacks, after an initially disruptive effect, may have ultimately strengthened local resolve and, continuing whatever arrangement had existed between Beorhtwulf and Aethelwulf, Mercia and Wessex may have been obliged to operate in unison, perhaps in political terms as well as over money matters. The circulation of coin seems to have increased during this period and was, moreover, concentrated on London - the countrywide distribution of hoards of the 860s and 870s is suggestive of the volume of coinage available in the various areas as much as of the danger of the times (Brooks and Graham-Campbell 1986, 107). Perhaps the immediate need for all this money was to meet the exaction of tribute - when the *Anglo-Saxon Chronicle* speaks of 'making peace' we can be sure this involved no small financial consideration. If so, this would not be the last time that Scandinavians were responsible for stimulating local money supply and circulation (see p.296).

The study of moneyers, their types and stylistic features, have provided the evidence for the proposition that London was at this time the prime centre of coin production. Also of importance in this respect is the lead weight which was discovered in St Paul's Churchyard in 1838 (Appendix 1, 69). It carries the Cross-and-Lozenge design with an obverse of Alfred, and the moneyer whose name is included, Ealdulf, is known for Burgred and for the Two Emperors type of Ceolwulf II (Pagan 1965, 14). The very nature of the piece suggests local minting, while the combined evidence of moneyer and type may indicate that this took place in an almost uninterrupted sequence from the time of Burgred through to 886, not least because Pagan has put forward the idea that the Cross-and-Lozenge design may have been discontinued only at the time of Alfred's capture of London and not, as noted elsewhere, in about 880 (Pagan 1965, 26-7, cf North 1980, 92).

How far we may take the numbers of single finds of this period to reflect an increased volume of coinage in London must be a matter for some caution. In addition to the St Paul's find there have been three further discoveries. One is the Burgred coin from Northumberland Avenue catalogued by Pagan, another is an Alfred penny of 'Burgred' (Lunette) type which was found 60 feet upstream of Lambeth Bridge in 1974; while another of this type was reported by Roach Smith in his journal for December 1837 (Appendix 1,

65, 67-8). Another coin of Burgred is noted as having been discovered in the Thames at Westminster Bridge (Appendix 1, 66) and may be from the Westminster Bridge hoard. These finds hardly constitute spectacular contributory evidence and the most that can be said is that they do not collectively contradict the findings of research undertaken elsewhere on London's money market in the twilight years of Mercian control.

The idea that London achieved a position of pre-eminence in the years before the Alfredian occupation has not been accepted without question. Much doubt concerns the role of the Danes. In order to be consistent with the argument favouring a resurgence under native auspices, it has been felt necessary to suggest that, although the increased output of coin may have been due to a transitory Danish presence around the coast and inland, a Danish settlement in London during the period 871-886 would have been detrimental to any minting developments (Pagan 1965, 27). The converse of this view is that London did not undergo any revival, due primarily to the total disruption caused by Danish colonists. Several arguments in favour of this have been put forward. For example, why, if the mint's production was so extensive, could Alfred muster only one moneyer to produce the monogram issue in London? The impression this arrangement gives is of a coinage issued *pro tempore* until the conditions neccessary to produce a substantial output could be established (Lyon 1968, 237). Some commentators have therefore toyed with the idea that another mint, for example Rochester, may have been responsible for producing much, if not all, of the supposed London coins (Lyon 1968, 234; Metcalf 1977, 353).

It will be appreciated that the evidence on which such arguments are based is insufficient to support firm conclusions, and further research is likely to heighten the debate rather than solve the problem. Certainly no solution will be offered in these pages. On the matter of the role and status of the Danes in London, perhaps the suggestion that they were in joint occupation of a species of 'open city' offers an acceptable compromise (Dolley and Blunt 1961, 81). In any case, perhaps it is time to dispense with the notion that the presence of Vikings automatically involved the complete cessation of daily life and communications. On the contrary, the evidence would suggest, and not only in this instance, that wherever they were established for any length of time, they were, even if initially disruptive, instrumental in vitalising the money market and perhaps also in establishing their adopted localities in an active trading network.

FROM 886 TO EADGAR'S REFORM

However long the Danish army/community had been in London by 886, its influence was decisively eclipsed in that year by Alfred's assumption of control. About this at least there seems little dispute. Also generally accepted is the notion that his monogram coinage was minted to celebrate the achievement. In spite of the shortage of available moneyers it seems to have been a popular issue. In London it is comparatively well represented by two single finds (Appendix 1, 70 and 71) and two hoards - those from Bucklersbury and Erith. Both hoards consisted apparently exclusively of monogram coins (Dolley 1960, 41 and 43; Dolley and Blunt 1961, 81.). In the case

of the single finds, the date of deposition might possibly have been at any time into the early 10th century (Dolley and Blunt 1961, 82), while it has been suggested that the hoards were concealed contemporaneously in c.888 (Dolley 1960, 48; Blackburn and Pagan 1986, 294 where c.890 is proposed), a time for which no event of the magnitude likely to have occasioned such simultaneous hoarding has been recorded. The Danish assault of 892 should be considered too late, because if the hoards had been deposited then, we should expect them to have included Alfred's Two Line type and of this there is no evidence. The only other major insecurity and destruction recorded at this time is the occupation of 886 itself. To associate the hoards with this would, of course, require the minting date of the monogram coinage to be moved to some point in the years before 886, which is not an absolute impossibility in view of the suggestion that minting took place in London during this time.

4.3. Coin finds c.680-886.

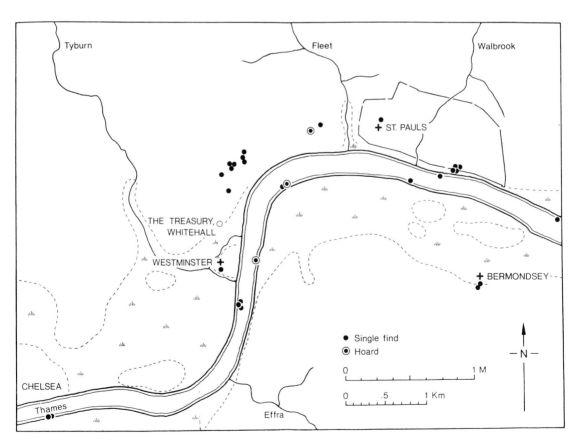

The use of the monogram itself also raises a question about the usual interpretation of this coinage. Coins of the issue presumably circulated in some quantity among the Danish community in England, which would account for the repeated use by them of the monogram as a device, not only on London imitations but also on some of their coinages issued at other mints (North 1980, 77-85). By contrast, the monogram as a means of denoting the mint is used only once again in the English coinage on a London halfpenny of Eadgar. If, therefore, a monogram was used by Alfred on a coinage which celebrated victory over the Danes, why was the device thereafter so popular, particularly amongst the population of the Danelaw?

These questions notwithstanding, the idea that Alfred's monogram coinage was a propaganda issue in honour of military glory is attractive. The inclusion of a mint signature at a time when it was not the practice to do so bears comparison with the occasion when Alfred's predecessor Ecgberht produced an issue carrying the legend LUNDONIA CIVIT, probably to mark his capture of the City in c.829. The unique departure in style and the apparently short duration of the monogram issue further lend it something of the distinction of a 'limited edition'.

Even if the precise history of the coinage around 886 is uncertain, the topographical result of the occupation is clear. There could be no better illustration of the re-organisation of London in the area within the Roman walls than the distribution of coin finds. The contrast between finds of pre- and post-886 coins is remarkable, with all but a very few of the latter emanating from the intramural City (Figs 4.3 and 4). The apparent desertion of the Strand settlement, at least for commercial purposes, is equally striking.

The silence of the *Anglo-Saxon Chronicle* over London in the 10th century, coupled with the comparative absence of hoards from the vicinity (Dolley 1960) appear to indicate that London was, for most of the following century, allowed to develop in peace. The mint may now have been continuously in production and the Grateley Decrees of c.926-c.930 show that it was then regarded as the most important in Aethelstan's kingdom, with eight moneyers to Canterbury's seven and Winchester's six. In spite of this, a major feature of the numismatic history of the period from Alfred to Eadgar is a shift in the emphasis of minting away from the south-east to

the north of the country, as if mirroring the historical sources' focus of attention upon English activity in the Danelaw (Metcalf 1986). The prime example of this development is the mint at Chester which, during Edward the Elder's reign, achieved a position of prominence in terms of output and the number of moneyers working there, a position it was to maintain until the Scandinavian attack on the town in 979/980. Other northern mints, for example York and Lincoln, both towns whose populations appear to have increased in the late 9th/early 10th century (Sawyer 1986, 193), were also playing a more prominent role. After the conquest of the Danelaw this northern emphasis was accompanied by a concentration of hoards in the area of the greatest Scandinavian activity in Ireland, the Isles and north-west Britain. In contrast to this and to the picture for late-9th century Britain, hoards from southern England are relatively few in number (SCBI 8, maps on pp.24 and 35).

Thus it is reasonable to assume that Scandinavians were responsible for attracting a significant amount of silver towards the north and that the output of the northern mints was increased in order to cater for the expanded market. Whatever the reasons for this new direction in the flow of coin - a trade in slaves has been suggested (Metcalf 1986, 135) - London's status as a mint seems relatively to have diminished, although its production levels were perhaps maintained, and Chester in particular was proving to be a major rival. Insofar as we can accept the evidence of coin finds as a monitor of trade, London does not appear to have been attracting commerce to any outstanding extent either. Certainly the number of discoveries for the period between Alfred and Eadgar is not significantly greater than that for Lincoln, and while this does demonstrate that London was commercially viable, it does not reflect its primacy in the Grateley Decrees (Blackburn 1983, 9, Fig 13).

The earliest finds for this period from London are two coins found during construction work in Cornhill in the 1850s, whose whereabouts are now unknown (Appendix 1, 72 and 73). One is a specimen of the Viking Northumbrian *Cunnetti* series which the contributor of 1858 mistook for a type of Cnut the Great and suggested Marlborough as the mint. The bewildering comment included in the note remarks that the find 'is looked upon as one of the hoard of coins discovered at Cuerdale, in Lancashire, in May 1840.' It is no secret that some of the Cuerdale coins were dispersed before the Crown's seizure of the hoard (Lyon and Stewart 1961, 96), but unless it can be envisaged that this coin was reinterred in the middle of London within 18 years of its discovery, the comment must surely be taken to mean that the find was of a type discovered at Cuerdale. Few specimens of *Cunnetti* coins are known outside the Cuerdale hoard (Lyon and Stewart 1961, 118, n2) which implies that the type enjoyed for the most part only a short life predominantly within the confines of Viking Northumbria. Any further discoveries must therefore enhance our understanding of its circulation and as there is elsewhere reason to think that Viking Northumbrian issues were not unknown within the currency of southern England (see p.291), the present coin may be regarded as an illustration of commercial contacts between London and the Scandinavian communities of Britain in the late 9th/early 10th century. Some verification of this view is provided by the other coin of similar date from the same provenance—an Edward the Elder Type II of the moneyer Deorwald. Both coins could constitute

the remnant of a hoard but in the absence of detailed information concerning the circumstances of their discovery, it is impossible to conclude that their deposition was simultaneous.

Also found during the same excavations were coins of Aethelred, Cnut, and Edward the Confessor (see below and Appendix 2c). At least some of these seem likely to have been part of a hoard also, but one which ought not to have included the two coins already discussed. Even allowing for the most extended period of currency of these coins up to 973, the *Cunnetti* and the Edward the Elder should not have survived in circulation after the reform of that year.

Two further coins of Edward the Elder, one of Aethelstan and one of Plegmund, Archbishop of Canterbury have in recent years been recorded from the southern foreshore of the Thames opposite the City. Southwark appears to have

4.4. Coin finds 886-973.

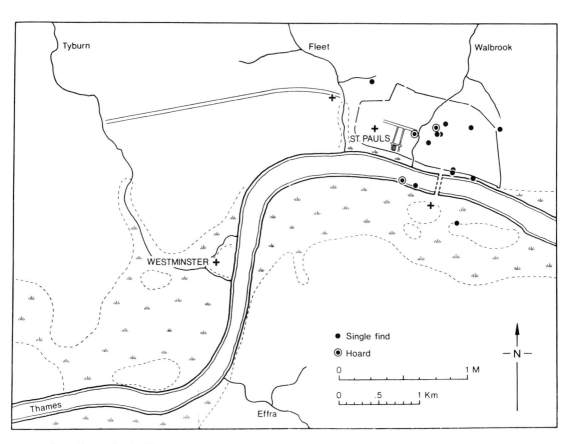

been fortified at a date approximate to that of these coins (Dyson 1980, 85 and 91), but it would be difficult to associate them directly with any developments in Southwark, the importance of which was such that by the time of Aethelred II it was capable of supporting its own mint. One would be entitled to expect that such continuous improvement might be reflected in a corresponding series of finds. The fact is, however, that these four coins, which as we shall see constitute two deposits, are all that has been found on the Southwark foreshore for our period and thus should not be regarded as signifying the growing importance of the southern bridgehead.

It has recently emerged that one of the Edwards, the Aethelstan and the Plegmund, although reported at different times by different correspondants and at more than one museum, were discovered at the same findspot in the foreshore near Cannon Street Railway Bridge. In addition, an unknown quantity of coins of Edward and Aethelstan were found in the same confined area although the whereabouts of these have not been determined. There was no evidence of a container but the indications are that these are what remains of a hoard which, in the absence of coins of Eadmund, may have been deposited around 940 (Appendix 2c). A series B sceatt was also found in association with these coins (Appendix 1, 7) but, with this exception, the homogeneity of the group suggests a hoard rather than a scatter. The discoveries were made in a thin layer of surface silt containing artefacts from a very broad range of dates and which was probably formed as a result of some disturbance, very likely dredging of the river bed, or of foreshore dumping. The other coin of Edward was found on a completely separate occasion under Southwark Bridge and may be regarded as an independent deposit. It is a Type III of late London style. The moneyer, Grimwald, minted in London for Aethelstan (Appendix 1, 74).

Previously, the only hoard from London known to have been deposited in the earlier 10th century was that from Threadneedle Street, discovered in 1924 (Appendix 2b). However, in addition to this and the above-mentioned Cannon Street Railway Bridge hoard, it was announced early in 1986 that another hoard had been discovered, apparently on the Thames foreshore in London (Appendix 2c). It consists of 3 coins of Edward the Elder, 2 St Eadmund Memorial, and one St Peter York and was probably concealed in about 915. If the London provenance of this hoard could be established beyond doubt, its inclusion of Viking coinage would provide evidence, additional to that from Cornhill, of London's trade with England's Scandinavian communities during the early stages of the re-conquest of the Danelaw. Enquiries have, however, not yet revealed its provenance and it is essentially from the appearance of the coins themselves - they carry a patina thought to be characteristic of London river finds - and from the fact that the chain of sales along which they passed took place in London that a London findspot has been inferred.

Without doubt this is flimsy information and not of great use as a basis for constructing a background to its deposition. Nevertheless, the other two hoards might suggest the need for a review of the condition of London just before the middle of the century. The silence of documentary sources has been understood to imply a time of peace and the Threadneedle Street hoard has been interpreted as a concealment under essentially local circumstances (SCBI 8, 30). In the absence of historical information there may admittedly be limited returns from any speculation but, potentially, the accepted view may be open to some revision.

Of the remaining single finds of 10th century coins, an irregular type of Aethelstan, a Type V with double obverse, was discovered at Aldgate in 1919 and is now in the collection of the Museum of London (Appendix 1, 75). Also discovered in that year, but in Leadenhall Street, was what appears to be an Eadmund Type I of the moneyer Wulfgar with a blundered obverse legend (Appendix 1, 76). A recent report on a similar discovery suggests that such pieces may be Danelaw imitations, a view expressed with reference to the findspot of the coin in question (Blackburn and Bonser 1984, 67-68). A London find might therefore cast doubt on this interpretation, but in view of the likelihood that Anglo-Danish coins did circulate, or at least were known in London, it remains a reasonable assumption. Three coins of Eadred are known, all of Type V. The first, of the moneyer Albert, was found in the Thames and its sale to the British Museum in 1836 was apparently the cause of some annoyance to Roach Smith (Appendix 1, 77). The second is of the moneyer Wilebert and was recorded in Roach Smith's catalogue of 1854 (Appendix 1, 78), whilst the third was found in more recent years on the northern foreshore of the Thames at Custom House (Appendix 1, 79). The moneyer's name is not clear although it may be Mannecin.

It was during Eadgar's reign that the history of England's coinage reached one of its major junctions. The reform of 973 established the basic pattern of coin production until the 12th century (Dolley and Metcalf 1961) and also abolished the halfpenny denomination which, apart from a brief re-appearance under Henry I, was not to be established as a permanent feature of the coinage until the late 13th century. Dolley has suggested that the similarity of Eadgar's London and Winchester halfpennies to Alfredian types may have been a deliberate commemoration of the denomination's imminent abolition (Dolley 1970, 24), and it is ironic that, in an age which has witnessed the halfpenny disappear once again from the coinage, a specimen of Eadgar's London halfpenny should emerge (Appendix 1, 80). The coin was discovered during the 1982 excavations on the site of Billingsgate Lorry Park, but was residual to its context, a waterfront dump of mid-12th century date. The obverse is struck in a peculiar manner, as though from an incomplete die, the profile bust of the face represented only by an outline of the nose and eye. In comparison with the similar piece from the Chester hoard, the execution of the monogram is thinner, the flan is broader and the weight slightly less (Chester = 0.70g, Billingsgate = 0.63g). Another Eadgar halfpenny found in London was exhibited by Roach Smith to the Numismatic Society in 1841 (Appendix 1, 81). The coin, with a Winchester mint mark, was found at St Bartholomew's church just outside the north-west wall of the City. Roach Smith tells us that the coin disintegrated while entrusted to the care of Mr Cuff, a noted numismatist of the time, and one suspects from Roach Smith's explicit reference to the accident that his feelings towards the unfortunate Cuff, who had died by the time of Roach Smith's publication, were not entirely charitable.

Roach Smith also notes in his journals the discovery of a coin of Eadgar in St Swithin's Lane (Appendix 1, 83). The fact that it was purchased by the British Museum after it had broken whilst in their possession is mentioned, but no description of the coin is offered.

EADGAR'S REFORM TO 1158

Post-reform and 11th century hoards

The most complete list to date of late Saxon hoards is in the recent publication *Anglo-Saxon Monetary History*, which adds the Chelsea Reach hoard (*c*.988) to Dolley's original listing (Blackburn and Pagan 1986). A further small hoard from the southern shore of the Thames at Chiswick Bridge must now be added (Appendix 2c). The Museum of London received word of the hoard, although the record is incomplete, and it appears to have been discovered in 1982 and consisted of six or more coins, including cut halves, all of Aethelred's Last Small Cross issue, three of which were of the Lincoln, Stamford and Dorchester mints. In view of the hoard's composition, it may be thought that the background to the deposit was Edmund Ironside's defence of London against the Danes (Dolley 1960, 39).

The group of coins found in Cornhill in the 1850s seems to have included more than one parcel, and eight of those coins recorded may have been from a single hoard (Appendix 2c). The chronological isolation of the coins of the Confessor might suggest that they do not belong to the same hoard as the Cnut element and, ideally, multiple-type hoards are incompatible with the theory, now well established, of regular and comprehensive re-coinage in the period after Eadgar's reform. Certainly for the period between 973 and 1042 single type hoards would appear to have been the norm and examples from London are provided by those found at Chiswick Bridge and Chelsea Reach. However, late Saxon multiple type hoards are by no means unknown (Archibald 1974, 247-8), but even if the group of eight late Saxon pieces from Cornhill incorporates several individually deposited items, the homogeneity in date displayed by the Cnut pieces would suggest that they at least ought to be regarded as a hoard.

Of the remaining known late Saxon hoards from London, there is reason to think that some reconsideration of their number and provenances may be necessary. This applies to those once housed in the Guildhall Museum and which now form part of the collection of the Museum of London; namely, the St Martin-le-Grand, Gracechurch Street and Walbrook hoards. The first two were discussed by Dolley in the 1950s (Dolley 1952/4; Butler and Dolley 1958/9) but it appears that he overlooked a register in the manuscript catalogue of the Guildhall Museum (Appendix 3) which throws some light on any consideration of all three hoards. The coins listed were part of an inventory of items in the John Walker Baily collection which were found in the City between 1863 and 1872, and acquired by the Museum after Baily's death in 1881.

For our present purposes, the important information to note is a 'heap' of silver coins and a list referring to 230 coins, two elements of what is stated to be a single composite find of coins and which can be recognised as that part of the so-called Walbrook hoard(s) (Dolley 1960, 40) which was acquired by the Guildhall Museum.

We will examine first the 63 coins of Aethelred. Of the 58 coins of this king in the Guildhall collection, 57, all Last Small Cross, were shown by Dolley to be part of a hoard found in St Martin-le-Grand. In 1870, Baily exhibited to the British Archaeological Association 25 silver coins of unstated type of Aethelred II which were recorded as having been found in St Martin-le-Grand (JBAA 26 1870 379). Dolley suggested that the group of Aethelreds in the Guildhall Museum, which at the time he wrote had not been assigned a provenance, contained these 25 coins and that 32 of the remaining 33 were also from that hoard. But the only record relating to the acquisition of coins of Aethelred by the Guildhall Museum is Baily's MS inventory, and according to this the Museum's Aethelreds should not be regarded in isolation from those coins which make up the Walbrook group. This is not to suggest that a St Martin-le-Grand hoard never existed; it did, for it is recorded that Baily had at least part of it in his possession in 1870, but from the evidence supplied by the MS inventory, it must be supposed that it no longer exists intact. It should be noted that Baily exhibited the 25 coins in 1870 in order to demonstrate the success of a cleaning method devised by him. They had been, it was said, 'in such a state of dirt and decomposition that it had been pronounced impossible to make anything of them.' Over 11 years later, it should be noted, the 63 Aethelreds acquired by the Guildhall Museum were still 'not cleaned', but the grime cannot have been so bad as to prevent their being identified, unlike those from St Martin-le-Grand before cleaning. It should be concluded therefore that the 25 cleaned coins from St Martin-le-Grand cannot have been amongst the 63 Aethelreds acquired by the Guildhall, and the latter must instead be equated with the 58 coins of Aethelred remaining in the collection which, with one exception, must be regarded as belonging to the Walbrook hoard.

However, as all the coins are of the Last Small Cross issue, such integral consistency would suggest that the group is comparable with the norm of single-type hoards of the post-reform period.

On these grounds it may be objected that the 63 Aethelreds perhaps ought to be thought of as independent of the Walbrook material and that they represent a hoard deposited in connection with the defence of London in 1016. Nevertheless, Thompson's *Inventory* did include coins of the Last Small Cross type amongst the Walbrook coins and, moreover, it has been suggested that the Walbrook hoard may have been a deposit of bullion reserve, and as such could not be treated as an example of coins circulating at the time of concealment (Dolley 1960, 40). It is just possible, therefore, that a prominent element of Last Small Cross coins may be explained as an accumulation of tribute - it was during this type's currency that the heaviest recorded payments were made - which never reached the hands of the intended recipients and which remained until the time of deposit as part of a reserve stock of silver.

The Guildhall and London Museum collections were amalgamated to form that of the Museum of London and with the exception of those coins from the London Museum and the very few single finds from other known provenances, the list of the Museum of London's collection of coins of Aethelred - William I presented below is, allowing for a few re-identifications and losses since 1881, substantially the same as that which appears in the MS inventory:

	pennies	cut fractions
Aethelred	58	–
Edward the Confessor	184	22
Cnut	11	–
Harold I and II	16	5
William I	5	1

The major difference is that there are now 50 more coins of Edward the Confessor, and Dolley suggested that these were what remained of the 56 or more coins of Edward discovered in Gracechurch Street (Dolley 1952/4). The only reference to a hoard ever having been found in Gracechurch Street is contained in the 1908 printed catalogue of the Guildhall Museum where the entry reads 'Hoard of silver coins of Edward the Confessor. Gracechurch St.' (Guildhall Catalogue, 124, no 169). It should be noted that Baily's address, given in the MS catalogue, was 71 Gracechurch Street, so it is possible that the compiler of the printed catalogue confused the address with the findspot and that these 50 coins are that part of the Baily acquisition otherwise unrepresented in the present collection of the Museum, namely the 'heap' noted in the MS inventory and containing an unspecified number of coins. Dolley noted the poor condition of what he took to be the Gracechurch Street coins, very different from that of the other Baily pieces, but this difference may have resulted from their being left untreated for some time after the others had been cleaned. As the majority of those coins from the hoard listed in the MS catalogue are of Edward the Confessor, the difficulty of accepting the suggestion that the 'heap' could have consisted entirely of coins of this king might be diminished somewhat. It may have been the case, as it was with the Aethelred coins, that the dirt on the heaped coins was not so extensive as to prevent an initial identification, and as they were so well represented amongst the cleaned coins, it was probably felt that a group of the Confessor's coins would be the most suitable to display in the condition in which they were discovered, although if their identification were known, one would expect

it to have been recorded. Nevertheless, there is some reason to think that the Gracechurch Street hoard was never an independent entity and that the coins of which it consisted were also from the Walbrook hoard.

Taking the MS inventory at its word, it would seem that we ought not to distinguish the Conquest and post-Conquest elements in the Walbrook hoard identified by Dolley (Dolley 1960, 40). There may be some difficulty in accepting this, and indeed the aforementioned consequences of a literal reading of the MS inventory. The reasons for recognising several distinct parcels in this material are indeed sound, so it would not be unreasonable to regard the information it has to offer as spurious on the grounds that it was compiled after Baily's death and because the compiler may not have had access to all the necessary details of discovery. It should also be appreciated that the find would by no means have received the closest archaeological scrutiny and that, for example, no distinction will have been

4.5. Coin finds 973-1050.

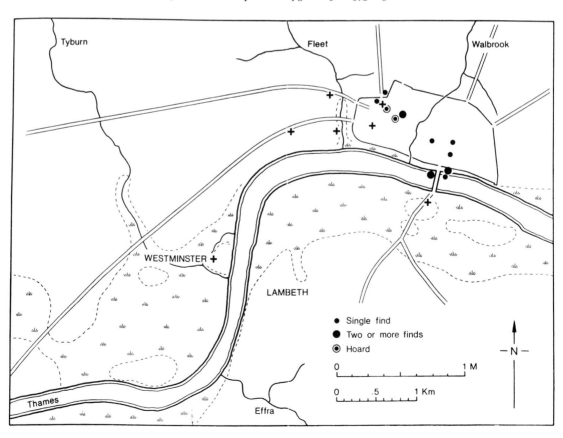

drawn by Baily's informants between hoard coins and loose finds. Nevertheless, it is sufficient for the moment that attention should be drawn to the existence of this record and that it should be included in any consideration of the composition of the Walbrook hoard.

Single finds: Eadgar's reform to Edward the Confessor

The first find of the post-reform period is a cut halfpenny of Eadgar's reform issue (Appendix 1, 82.). Cutting coins as a means of producing halfpenny and farthing denominations dates from 973, in which year the round halfpenny was abolished, and if we are to judge from this example, the practice was adopted very quickly in London. From this date onwards, a large proportion of the city's finds consist of cut fractions, with the amount increasing under Cnut and still further after the Conquest.

The Eadgar halfpenny was found in spoil removed from Billingsgate lorry park, the source of the great bulk of late Saxon and Norman coins from London. The difficulties of determining the circumstances of deposition of coins from this source should again be noted. What can be said is that it is likely that a good deal of them were incorporated in rubbish dumped at Billingsgate after having been collected elsewhere in the City. This dumping was not simply the humdrum process of refuse disposal, but part of the development of harbour facilities to cope with the demands of trade, and the volume of coins may be seen as one demonstration of the extent of this development. This does mean, however, that many of the coins, even if they were originally deposited during their period of currency, may have long since terminated their useful life by the time they reached their Billingsgate resting place. Indeed, those two coins of the period from the controlled excavations on the site show that they can be residual to their Billingsgate context by as much as 200 years (Appendix 1, 80 and 86). So, while they may be some use in chronicling the commercial development of the City as a whole, the information they have to offer in this respect on Billingsgate itself may be limited, although it may be no accident that all but a very few of the coins are of post-1000 date. The first documentary reference to Billingsgate occurs in 1000, implying that its assumption of the position of major international port on the seaward side of London Bridge had

begun or was recognised about this time (Dyson 1985, 20).

The next finds in terms of date are two Crux types of Aethelred II, one originally part of the Roach Smith collection and now in the British Museum, the other a cut farthing found in Billingsgate spoil and reported as recently as December 1986 (Appendix 1, 84 and 85) The absence of single finds of Aethelred's first two substantive issues may be contrasted with finds from Lincoln and York, where the First Hand is well represented. In the north-east, where mints appear to have produced very few Second Hand pennies, the First Hand may have continued to circulate after it was demonetised elsewhere (Blackburn 1983, 16-17). This, together with the London evidence, need not imply that the Second Hand issue was not generally circulated. Contrary to what was once supposed, the Chelsea Reach hoard, which consisted entirely of Second Hand pennies from a wide geographical selection of mints, demonstrated that this issue was at least intended to be substantive (Dolley and Grover 1983). The paucity of finds of both Hand issues from London may therefore indicate a certain deficiency in the money market there. There is in general a low survival of post-reform issues (Metcalf 1986, 153), but as far as London is concerned, the study of Scandinavian material also suggests that the output of the mint was comparatively low during the post-reform coinage and the early stages of Aethelred's coinage, whereas the output of Winchester, York and Stamford appears to have been on a larger scale (Metcalf 1980, 33). Perhaps, therefore, London was during this period going through the final stage of the recession it seems to have experienced during much of the 10th century. Presumably much of the currency flow was still in a northerly direction, where acquisitive Scandinavians dominated the market and where, in spite of Chester's abrupt decline in 980, other mints were still operating successfully and would continue to do so until after the Norman Conquest (Metcalf 1980, 33).

During the excavations at Billingsgate Lorry Park in 1982, a Helmet type penny of the Chichester mint was found (Appendix 1, 86). It is partly broken but exhibits very little wear although, as the coin was residual to its context, its condition is of little interpretative value as far as the Billingsgate site is concerned. The context was a late 12th century waterfront dump so it is possible that it somehow intruded into a consignment of rubbish from the interior of the City.

The most aesthetically remarkable coin of Aethelred found in London is a specimen of the Agnus Dei issue (Appendix 1, 87). The London provenance of this coin was narrowed by Dolley to Gracechurch Street, although no further information on the circumstances of its discovery appears to be available.

Four single finds of Aethelred's last issue are known from London: two are from the Roach Smith collection, a very fragmentary specimen now in the Museum of London was found in Eastcheap, although the date of its discovery seems to be unknown, whilst another was found in 1979 during excavations at the site of the General Post Office near St Martin-le-Grand (Appendix 1, 88-91). In addition to these single finds, the hoards from Walbrook/St Martin-le-Grand, Chiswick Bridge and Cornhill suggest that, in comparison to previous types of Aethelred, there was a greater availability of the Last Small Cross. Here again a contrast may be made with Lincoln and York where there have been no finds of coins from Aethelred's later issues (Blackburn 1983, Pirie 1986).

As far as Lincoln at least is concerned, it has been suggested that an explanation for this absence is to be found in the high representation of Last Small Cross pennies of the Lincoln mint in the Systematic Collection in Stockholm and in the apparent peace in Northumbria and Lindsey during the first two decades of the 11th century. In other words, the reason appears to be that much of the currency of the period was removed from the north-east in the form of tribute, but perhaps also as a result of trade with Scandinavia (Blackburn 1983, 19-20). However, in contrast to the situation obtaining before c.1000, the London mint has by far the largest number of Last Small Cross pennies in the Systematic Collection and it was during the period of this issue, after 1010, that Danish pressure on London was at its most persistent and that a number of recorded payments of tribute took place. Can we therefore suggest that the same explanation of tribute and possibly trade with the Scandinavians lies behind the favourable representation of the Last Small Cross issue amongst single finds in London and of London mint specimens of the type in Scandinavia? The superficial explanation may be the same but there was perhaps a difference in the degree to which the exchange of coin, by whatever means, took place. In Lincoln, the background of peace may have ensured that transactions were to some extent automatic, whereas the insecurity of London possibly created an atmosphere of far greater intensity. Perhaps there is something to be gained from a comparison with cities threatened with military takeover in modern times, where the greater an individual's command of financial resources, the greater his capacity to escape peril.

Whatever this evidence indicates, it seems clear that London during these years underwent a considerable monetary revival. From this point on, the numbers of single finds from London are greatly in excess of those of previous centuries with the exception of the sceattas (Fig 4.1). This to some extent reflects the situation apparent elsewhere for, generally speaking, the circulation of coinage appears in the 11th century to have been more rapid than in the 10th and so, in consequence, was coin wastage (Metcalf 1986, 157), but London's monetary growth appears to have been such that it now achieved a position of pre-eminence over other centres. The outstanding representation of London mint Last Small Cross pennies in Scandinavia has already been noted and it may be thought that London's leading position in terms of coin production was from now on generally unchallenged (Metcalf 1980, 33) (although see p.299). By 1066, moreover, die-production and distribution was probably centralised there (Blackburn and Lyon 1986, 223-5).

It seems a reasonable assumption that this resurgence is best understood in the context of Scandinavian activities in Britain, as indeed should the major geographical orientations in monetary affairs over the preceeding two centuries. It is clear that London by the end of Aethelred's reign had become the key to the control of the kingdom (Brooke C, 1975, 22), and a revival of the mint and an increased volume of coin passing through the town may have been corollaries to political and military development. Undoubtedly, a central reason for monetary expansion would have been the need to produce and pay the several tributes demanded, but Scandinavian trading interests should not be ruled out as a probable influence on the revival. In London, there was a Scandinavian community before the Conquest and probably before 1000 (Sawyer 1986, 191-2; Dolley 1960, 41), which was very likely instrumental in developing the town's commerce, particularly with regard to overseas trade (Brooke C, 1975, 261-265).

Seven finds of Aethelred pennies are of unknown type. Two, discovered at London

Bridge in March 1824, were reported in *Archaeologia* at the time; another, of the London moneyer Godric, was found in Aldersgate Street and reported to the BAA in 1883; while four others were recorded in Roach Smith's journals (Appendix 1, 92-98.).

Cnut inherited without alteration the monetary system developed during his predecessor's reign; a system in which London now seemed fully established as the prime mint and major trading port in the country. During a peaceful reign these arrangements were maintained. 15 singly-found coins of Cnut are known from London. Of the Quatrefoil types, one was discovered in the 1820s during excavations for the construction of St Katherine's Docks and was illustrated in the *Mechanic's Magazine* for 1827-8 (Appendix 1, 99). We may be confident that the correspondent's description of this coin as having been minted in Antrim on the authority of a king Eric was the result of a mis-reading of the legend. Another Quatrefoil was found in an 11th/12th century pit in Milk Street in the course of excavations there in 1976 (Appendix 1, 101). The moneyer, Aelfwi, is known for this type and the style of his name may be an abbreviation for Aelfwig, although another moneyer who produced this type, Aelfwi Spencel, probably demonstrates by the inclusion of his surname that a distinction from a moneyer Aelfwi was required. The coin was found in a fragmented state and was mounted in a perspex frame before any idea of its weight could be obtained. Another fragmented Quatrefoil was discovered on the site of St Nicholas Acon and its condition was so poor that it seems to have disintegrated altogether (Appendix 1, 100). An identification was however achieved previously, but only to the extent that it was a Quatrefoil. The third Quatrefoil, of the Winchester moneyer Wine, was discovered in April 1984 in Billingsgate spoil (Appendix 1, 102).

Of Cnut type XIV (Pointed Helmet), a cut halfpenny of the Hertford mint was found in Billingsgate spoil in February 1985 (Appendix 1, 104). Roach Smith records another find of this type of the London moneyer Edwine and one of a Short Cross coin with a reverse legend recorded as LOD.ON.LUNDEN (Appendix 1, 103 and 105). The name of the moneyer is a misreading of 'God', perhaps an abbreviation for one of the several London moneyers whose names began with these three letters. The coin is not included in the 1893 catalogue of Anglo-Saxon coins in the British Museum, the ultimate resting place for much of

the Roach Smith material (Grueber and Keary 1887/93). Two further coins of Cnut are included in the Roach Smith catalogue of 1854 which, although the entry does not make it entirely clear, are of the Short Cross type (Appendix 1, 106 and 107). They are of the moneyer Boga at Dover and Wulfred at London. The other Short Cross coin from London, of the London moneyer Swan, was found in Billingsgate spoil in December 1984 (Appendix 1, 108).

The remaining six coins of Cnut are of unknown types. Five were discovered at London Bridge in March 1824 while the sixth, of the London mint, obtained from river workmen and therefore most likely from the Thames, was noted by Roach Smith in his journals under 17 and 31 October 1835. This last coin may or may not be one of those recorded in Roach Smith's 1854 catalogue (Appendix 1, 109-114). Definitely not included in the 1854 catalogue are the three coins of Harold I noted under the same dates in the journals and acquired under similar circumstances (Appendix 1, 115-117).

Harold ruled jointly with his half-brother Harthacnut from 1035 to 1037 and then as sole King 1037-40. On Harold's death, Harthacnut, who was at the time preparing an expedition against England to claim his inheritance, was invited to succeed. His short reign ended in Lambeth in 1042 when, at the age of 25, he died 'as he stood at his drink'. To the period of joint rule belongs the Jewel Cross type issued in the names of Cnut, Harold and Harthacnut. The fleur-de-lys type, although it occurs in the name of Harthacnut, is the coinage principally associated with Harold. The Arm-and-Sceptre type was issued in the names of Cnut and Harthacnut and those of the former king have been regarded either as a posthumous issue or as a type issued by Harthacnut but preserving the name of Cnut as an abbreviation. One such coin was discovered on the Thames foreshore at Billingsgate in May 1986 (Appendix 1, 118.). The reverse legend reads LE(A?)STAN ON SNOTI and because the name, as it appears here, occurs nowhere else on late Saxon coinage, it may be intended to represent the name, familiar amongst moneyers, of Leofstan, who is not, however, recorded as working at the Nottingham mint. The coin was discovered in association with 17th century material so that little can be suggested about the circumstances of its deposition beyond the possibilities of its having reached its findspot as a result of dredging or dumping.

Perhaps the most significant event which took place in London during the reign of Edward the Confessor was the episode in 1052 when the fleets of Edward and Godwin, manouevering in the Thames, narrowly avoided an outbreak of hostilities. This demonstrates the central strategic role of London in the kingdom's politics and, as a faction of Londoners were instrumental in persuading Edward to reach a compromise with Godwin, the power of the citizens in influencing their course (Brooke C, 1975, 25-6). The king's relationship with the Londoners may have been at the root of the removal of the royal residence from the City to Westminster, although the decisive factor is not known. But if there was in this an element of exile or protest, the split was not so drastic as to divorce the seat of royal power, which Westminster was to become, from the country's commercial centre.

Billingsgate accounts for six of the ten finds of the Confessor's coins, all six being discovered in spoil removed from the site. The earliest is a Trefoil/Quadrilateral of the London moneyer Brunman (Appendix 1, 119). There follows a specimen of the Expanding Cross (light coinage)

type (Appendix 1, 121). The mint is Lincoln and the obverse displays the light coinage style of bust favoured by north-eastern mints. The reverse legend is partly obscured by wear so that the only letters distinguishable with any certainty are GOD... at the beginning and ...INCO at the end with probably eight letters in between. A reverse of the moneyer Godric reading GODRIC ON LINCO is known for this and other types (Grueber and Keary 1887/93, No 701), but the present legend includes more letters. Nevertheless, judging from what can be seen, and allowing perhaps for some inconsistency in the style of representing names on coins, this die probably was the responsibility of a Godric working at Lincoln. The single example of the Sovereign/Eagles type among these finds would appear to be a copy (Appendix 1, 122). The legends on both sides are blundered, as is the obverse design, although the annulets on the reverse would suggest a York or at least northern origin. Unfortunately, the weight of this piece was not recorded. The other three Billingsgate

4.6. Coin finds 1050-1158.

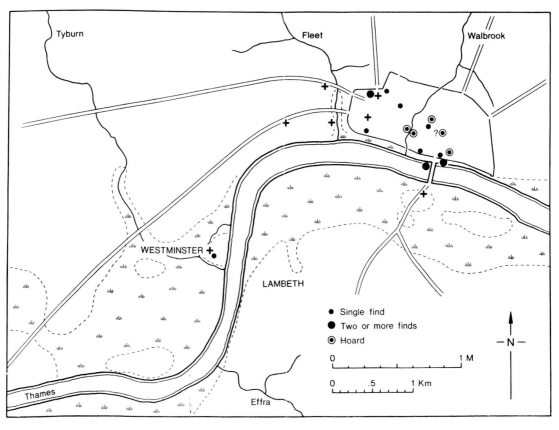

spoil pieces are cut halfpennies. Two are of the Hammer Cross type, one of the London mint and one of the Hastings moneyer Duning, while the third is a Pyramids type of the London mint (Appendix 1, 124, 123 and 128).

Of the four coins not found in Billingsgate spoil, one is of the Small Flan issue, the type introduced to alleviate the drain of silver used to pay the Heregeld, and the other three are of the Bust Facing issue. The Small Flan specimen has been noted by Metcalf (Appendix 1, 120) and appears to be from the Roach Smith collection. The earliest of the Bust Facing specimens from the point of view of discovery date was found in the graveyard of All Hallows, Lombard Street during excavations there in 1940 (Appendix 1, 125). The style of the legend and of the initial letter of the moneyer's name are represented in the British Museum catalogue (Grueber and Keary 1887/93, No 1059). A more recent find, a cut halfpenny, comes from the 1981 excavations in Pudding Lane, the immediate context being the ground outside a domestic building otherwise dated to the late 11th/early 12th century (Appendix 1, 126). Even if the coin had not been residual, and the pottery dating would suggest that it is, its use as a precise dating tool would have been open to qualification as there is quite a clear indication that coins of Edward the Confessor did not adhere as rigidly as those of his predecessor to their official currency periods (Archibald 1974, 247-8). One notable feature of this piece is the single pellet in place of a cross as the obverse initial mark. All that can be distinguished of the mint name are the first two letters HE..., so the mint is presumably either Hertford or Hereford. Finally, the discovery of another Bust Facing penny has been reported (Appendix 1, 127). It was found in the outskirts of East London in spoil removed from a site in the centre of the city, possibly one on the Thames waterfront in Southwark.

For the period after Eadgar's reform, which required all coins to carry the appropriate mint signature, a survey such as the present one can provide some illustration of the influence of the subject town by the representation of mints among single finds. As expected, the mint representation from Eadgar to Edward the Confessor demonstrates the focal position of London in the kingdom's flow of coin. The mints involved cover a geographical area whose boundaries are formed by points ranging from Dover in the south-east, perhaps as far as Hereford in the west and to Lincoln in the north. The London mint itself accounts for about 50% of the coins, whereas, by contrast, coins of the same period found in Lincoln and York are almost totally dominated by coins from the mints at these towns. Winchester, from what information has been published, also appears to have catered for a currency of predominantly local orientation (Blunt and Dolley 1977).

There are two coins apiece from the mints at Winchester and Lincoln; otherwise all other mints outside London are represented by a single coin each. Of the other Five Boroughs, Leicester, Nottingham and Derby are included and Lincoln occurs again in the immediate post-Conquest period. The output of the northern mints continued to be large and indeed appears to have been increasing during the first half of the 11th century. Only William's harrying of the north would seriously impair their development (Metcalf 1980, 33). Lincoln in particular was very strong and in the Stockholm Systematic Collection its coins of the period 1053-65 outnumber even those of London which, if this is acceptable as a measure of its true output and trading capacity, would suggest that Lincoln at this time dominated English trade with the Baltic (Blackburn 1983, 22-3). If the finds of Lincoln coins in London provide any indication, a proportion of Lincoln's trade passed in a southerly direction whereas the complete absence of single finds of the York mint, which before Lincoln's dramatic development was the second largest in the country, is perhaps symptomatic of that town's greater degree of independence from southern influence. Also absent are coins from East Anglian mints which, like York, are well represented in the Walbrook hoard. This may indicate the deficiency of single finds in indicating the prime trade routes in and out of London, but equally it may suggest that the Walbrook hoard, which has been interpreted as a bullion reserve (Dolley 1960, 40), is of limited merit in reflecting trading in London's streets and markets. It does, certainly, demonstrate the necessity of considering all available numismatic evidence before any conclusions are drawn.

One further feature to note is the representation of mints on or near the south coast, for example, Chichester, Dover, Hastings, Lewes and Lympne. A period of intense activity at the Dover mint between 1030 and 1040/5 has been noted elsewhere (Metcalf 1980, 33) and, collectively, the smaller southern ports had presumably assumed a large part of Southampton's role in south coast trade. Hamwic's own commercial position by this time appears to have diminished to virtually nothing. There are no coin finds from there for this period, and numismatic evidence from the late Saxon port which replaced Hamwic documents an unremarkable monetary turnover, to say the least (Addyman and Hill 1968, 77; Hinton 1986, 17.).

It is more difficult to assess London's post-Conquest currency pattern on this basis owing to the high number of cut farthings and the consequent impossibility in most cases of identifying the mint.

Single finds: the Normans

On Christmas Day, 1066, the acclamation given to William the Conqueror by the Londoners on the occasion of his coronation was so vigorous that Norman troops, mistaking the tumult for a riot, were panicked into a violent attack on some of the citizens. The incident was symptomatic of the acute tensions following William's acquisition of power after Hastings. The Londoners, even if they were in good voice on Christmas Day, had in the preceeding months good reason to be apprehensive. After the victory at Hastings, and having recuperated at Dover, William's progress towards London, pillaging as he went, and the threats he issued as he occupied Westminster, left little room for doubting his readiness to gain the Londoners' submission by force. It was very likely against this background that the Walbrook I hoard (if such a distinction can be made. See p.294) and the probable hoard from Cornhill were concealed, while Walbrook II (possibly) and that from St.Mary-at-Hill (more certainly), both deposited within a decade of the Conquest, testify to a continuing atmosphere of insecurity (Dolley 1960, 39-40).

William, however, was shrewd enough to recognise the necessity of preserving London's power and wealth intact and of harnessing them to his own ends, and thus of effecting a takeover with the minimum of destruction. The rate of coin loss in London gradually diminishes from the beginning of the Norman period (Fig 4.1) (with the exception of an anomalous peak at the beginning of the 12th century. See p.301), but this does not signify any commercial decline of the town. It is rather to be expected because, with the exception of the Conqueror's last type, the coins of the first four Norman kings are in general of greater rarity than those of their late Saxon predecessors.

William showed no inclination to alter the monetary system in any radical sense. Adjustments were mainly of a minor character, for example the regular adoption of a full-face obverse bust instead of the profile preferred by the Saxons. Also, the currency period of each issue was tightened, probably by the introduction of a triennial cycle (Archibald 1974, 249). One significant change, however, appears to have been in the geographical pattern of minting. Metcalf has shown that a study of mint representation in the Conqueror's PAXS type, his last issue, suggests that the hitherto high output of northern mints, for example York, Lincoln and Stamford, was reduced, while the emphasis in minting shifted southwards, with Winchester in particular improving its performance (Metcalf 1980, 32-3). William's harrying of the north must account for the decline, while the emphasis on the south coast was probably due to new cross-Channel contacts, as well as to William's distrust of the Danelaw's inhabitants and his desire to remove from them any source of influence, commercial as well as political. For London, the result of this appears to have been that it too suffered a relative decline in coin output although its commanding position overall does not seem to have been under any serious threat.

Ten coins of William I are known as single finds from London. The earliest was found in June 1984 in Billingsgate spoil (Appendix 1, 129). It is a mule with an obverse of Edward the Confessor's Pyramids type and a reverse of William's first issue, the Profile/Cross Fleury, of the Lincoln moneyer Garvin and is thus a good example of the Norman willingness to perpetuate the Saxon monetary system. There is perhaps some political significance in the fact that this is a Norman coin displaying the face of Edward the Confessor and not the immediately preceeding Harold II, although there may be a more practical explanation in that the dies of Edward the Confessor were more readily available owing to the brief time allowed for the production and distribution of dies of Harold's single type. A moneyer of this name is also recorded for the Confessor's Lincoln coinage (North 1980, 145; Brooke 1916, No 396) although there the spelling is 'Garfin', but because the name Garvin occurs nowhere else in either Edward's or William's coinage, it is more than likely that the two spellings refer to the same individual.

The second of our two finds of William Type I, discovered very close in time to the previous coin and from the same provenance, is in fact a brooch (Appendix 1, 130.). It is furnished with a copper alloy pin and the fittings are made from folded sheets of copper alloy which appear to have been soldered onto the obverse of the coin. Coin-brooches are not unknown - there is an example in the Museum of London's collection from the time of Henry I (*English Romanesque Art*, No 468), but whereas that is little more than a copper alloy disc bearing a coin design on one face only and thus could never have passed as a coin, the present example is made of silver, is complete in all details on both faces, carries the name of a moneyer known for William in London and, although no die-duplicate has been located, appears to have been manufactured from official dies. The coin is however very thick and probably accounts for the greater part of the overall weight, far in excess of any regular coin. In addition, the condition of the coin is such as to suggest that it never circulated so that, all in all, it is reasonable to suppose that the original intention behind its manufacture was that it should function not as a coin but as a brooch, albeit one which doubled as a source of wealth.

A cut halfpenny of the Canopy type was discovered during excavations in Noble Street (Appendix 1, 131). The reverse legend appears to be blundered but an attempt at a London mint signature may be detected. A late 11th/early 12th century pit in the 1976 Milk Street excavations yielded a much fragmented example of the Two Stars type (Appendix 1, 132), the condition of which does not permit any further information to be extracted.

Of the other six coins of William I found in London, one is an unknown type of the Canterbury moneyer Alfred which was discovered at London Bridge and recorded in Roach Smith's journal for 1839 (Appendix 1, 138), while the remainder are all of the PAXS type. Of all the Conqueror's issues, only this type is common. This has long been thought to be due to the discovery of the Beauworth hoard in 1833 which contained 6,439 specimens of the type. It has recently been argued however, that the PAXS type was produced in much higher quantities than William's previous issues, principally in order to accommodate a Danegeld raised after 1083 to stave off an invasion threatened by Denmark's King Cnut, son of Svein Estrithsson (Blackburn 1983, 30). Work on Scandinavian collections has also demonstrated the dominance there of the PAXS amongst William's types. It is therefore probably no accident

that over half the London single finds of the Conqueror's pennies belong to this type and this implies that, in London at least, there may have been more coin circulating at the end of the reign than at any time in the previous 20 years.

One of the finds of this type, a cut farthing revealing nothing further than its type, was discovered in a mid-12th century road surface during excavations at St Peter's Hill in 1981 and thus must be regarded as residual to its context (Appendix 1, 135). Two examples found in Billingsgate spoil are of the Canterbury mint and, together with the find from London Bridge above, perhaps reflect the southern emphasis in minting at this point in the reign (Appendix 1, 136 and 137). Metcalf noted another in the British Museum's collection, a Thetford mint coin of Folcaerd or Godred, apparently from the Roach Smith collection (Appendix 1, 134). Finally, Roach Smith's journal for 1839 notes an example discovered at London Bridge (Appendix 1, 133). The moneyer is Siferth who, although the mint was not identified by Roach Smith, is recorded in the Beauworth hoard as one of only two moneyers active at the Lincoln mint during this issue, such was the recession suffered by that mint by the period of the PAXS issue (Blackburn 1983, 31; Brooke 1916, Nos 747-757).

The rarity of William II's coins is reflected in the comparatively small number of finds (four) from London. A mule with a Cross-in-Quatrefoil obverse and Profile reverse was discovered during excavations at the GPO site, near St Martin-le-Grand, in 1975 (Appendix 1, 139). Mules between types I and II are known (SCBI 20, No 1477; Brooke 1916, Nos 66 and 67) although these have the obverse and reverse types arranged alternatively to the present example. The other three coins of William II were all found in Billingsgate spoil. They are a Cross-in-Quatrefoil type of an uncertain mint, but which is probably Gloucester or Ilchester, a cut halfpenny of the Cross-Pattee-and-Fleury type of a completely unidentifiable mint, and another of this type of the Bristol moneyer Snedi (Appendix 1, 140-142). This last example is irregular - the sword on the obverse is borne over the king's left shoulder instead of the right as normal.

Of those finds dating from the 12th century, there is a high number of coins of Henry I (13) and Stephen (six) and coins of the period *c.*1130-*c.*1140 are particularly prominently represented. This peak of discovery is abnormal considering the generally low volume of coinage during this period. All except four are from Billingsgate spoil and a likely explanation is that some at least of this group belong to a hoard. Henry's last issue and Stephen's first account for the highest number of coins in the group. Indeed all the coins of Stephen are of his first type with the exception of two pieces, one probably and one certainly unconnected, so that, if there were a hoard here, the likely *terminus post quem* for its deposit would be *c*.1141. As it happens, the circumstances under which a hoard might have been concealed did exist at this time, because London in 1141 became the ground on which the power struggle between Stephen's party and that of Empress Matilda was fought. After the battle of Lincoln and Stephen's capture, the Londoners intended to plead for the king's release, but their support waned with the entry into the City of Matilda in the company of a large army. During preparations for her coronation, her arrogant treatment of the citizens incited them to a demonstration of armed defiance and, as Stephen's queen with her own army had arrived on the outskirts of the town, the Empress was obliged to make a hasty departure, thus missing her major opportunity to take the throne of England. Once again, Londoners were responsible for directing the course of English political history (Brooke C 1975, 36-8).

There are difficulties in fully accepting this group as a hoard. They were not discovered in close association but in spoil dumped at a number of locations, so their relationship with each other and the nature of the immediate archaeological contexts is now impossible to determine. The group also contains a very high proportion of cut fractions. Indeed, of the 15 coins under consideration, only six are not cut fractions. Other hoards deposited during Stephen's reign do contain cut coins and in the Lincoln hoard the proportion is quite high (Mack 1966, 101-7). Nevertheless, a hoard in which cut fractions predominate is unusual to say the least, but in view of the improbability of there being such a concentration of individual finds for this period, it is not unreasonable to suspect that amongst these coins there lurks a deposit perhaps representing the loss of a purse of small change, caused accidentally or in consequence of the disturbances in the City in 1141. The general background to any hoard lost in the City would have been one of small-scale commerce, which might help to explain the high proportion of cut fractions.

The coins from this group are described in Appendix 1 amongst the single finds, as distinguishing which of them might have a hoard provenance and which not would be difficult. For the most part they are uninformative beyond revealing their type. Worth drawing attention to is the pair of Henry I type XV coins which were discovered bent double and placed one inside the other (Appendix 1, 151-2). Bending coins to test their quality was a common practice in Scandinavia and an example of an Edward the Confessor penny so treated was discovered in Lincoln (Blackburn 1983, 28). Such pieces might also denote devotional practices. Bent coins were presented at shrines as votive offerings but the evidence for this is mostly of a much later date than the present example (Finucane 1977, 94-5).

Two of the four coins not from Billingsgate spoil were found on the site itself. One, a very worn example of a Henry I type XV, emerged during the watching brief on the site in the winter of 1983/4 and may be part of the suggested hoard (Appendix 1, 150), although it must again be stressed that there is no concordance between the material investigated on the site, much of which had in any case been disturbed by contractor's work, and that examined at spoil tips outside London. The other Billingsgate piece is a Stephen type VII cut halfpenny of the London moneyer Rogier, found during excavations at the lorry park in 1982 (Appendix 1, 161). The coin was intrusive to layers featuring a Roman quay, the disturbance having been caused by modern piling operations. Again the problem of contextual relationships with material from the spoil tips should be taken into account, although this piece is later than the main group of coins which form the nucleus of the probable hoard and its chronological isolation suggests that it should be regarded as a separate loss.

The two remaining pieces are a Henry I type VI of the London mint found on the GPO site in 1979, and a Stephen type II cut farthing found during excavations at Gardiner's Corner in London's East End (Appendix 1, 145 and 160). The moneyer of this latter coin, Adelard, has not previously been recorded for this type.

Single finds: foreign coinage

From Offa's time, England appears to have been very successful in excluding foreign pieces from its currency (Spufford 1963, 127; Dolley and Morrison 1963, 86). Foreign coins found in England do not in general represent a tendency for infiltration but are isolated instances of circulation, perhaps by accident, within the native currency. The finds from London do nothing to alter this picture. To reflect the town's position as an international port some evidence of the loss of foreign coin might be expected from riverside areas and indeed, five of the six pieces in question are from waterfront sites. In the main, they may be viewed as by-products of cross-Channel contacts.

The earliest coin, discovered during the Billingsgate watching brief of 1983/4, dates from the first half of the 11th century and has been identified as a denier minted in the area now occupied by Belgium (Appendix 1, 162). The discovery of a Netherlandish imitation of a coin of Emperor Conrad II at Westminster Abbey has been the subject of a report which also mentioned a similar find from Seal House in 1974 (Appendix 1, 163 and 165). The Seal House coin is again a Netherlandish copy, this time of Emperor Henry IV, Duisberg, dated c.1080-90 and, like the Westminster find may be regarded as having been deposited at a date much later than that at which it was minted, as it was discovered in the context of a waterfront dated by pottery to the mid-12th century. If we add to these the pfennig of Henry III (1039-56) included in the Walbrook hoard, then considering the rarity of such pieces from England as a whole, London would appear to have had more than its fair share. The fourth continental piece, found in Billingsgate spoil, is a Normandy denier of the late 11th/early 12th century (Appendix 1, 166).

An exception to the cross-channel character of these finds is the discovery of a penny of the Norwegian king Olaf Kyrre (1067-93) reported in December 1986 (Appendix 1, 164). This coin is of a type which has been found in Lincoln and also in America (Blackburn 1983, 32). In terms of comparative interest, the London find may be rather more prosaic than that from America, which deserves to be greeted with some excitement as material support for the evidence of a Viking presence across the Atlantic, but rather more remarkable than the find from Lincoln, a town whose Scandinavian character in the 11th century is well established elsewhere. The suggestion that London should have been part of the Scandinavian North Sea trading empire, even after the Norman Conquest, need not merit much surprise, but in view of the sketchiness of the evidence, this coin may be regarded as a valuable indicator.

England's island status will have played no small part in the kingdom's success in maintaining a homogeneous currency. The land-bound kingdoms of the continent could not avoid contamination to the same extent. But England, of course, shared a land-border with Scotland which in c.1136 started to produce its own coinage at the captured English mint of Carlisle, and in time 'small and irritating quantities' (Spufford 1963, 127) of Scottish coin would infiltrate the system with enough frequency to offend English insular sensibilities. An illustration of this is perhaps provided by a coin found in the Thames foreshore at London Bridge in 1982 (Appendix 1, 167). It is a cut halfpenny of the Cross-Crosslet design minted, probably at Bamborough, by Stephen and by Henry, son of David I of Scotland. Both issuing authorities employed a moneyer by the name of Willelm and if, as appears to be indicated by Commander Mack, the style of the reverse legend supplies the distinguishing feature, then this specimen should be thought to belong to the Scottish prince. If so, then it is the earliest Scottish coin to have been found in London. Further isolated examples occur for the late 12th and earlier 13th century, but Scottish currency only becomes to any degree persistent in the London monetary scene in the late 13th century.

SUMMARY AND CONCLUSION

In the light of recent studies, it is apparent that the body of single finds of Saxon and Norman coins from any urban centre should be treated as a whole, in order that the comparative economic performance of towns may be assessed and some idea of the distribution of wealth may be gained. As no attempt has previously been made to record all single finds of this period from London, it has been with some justification that the present survey has gone to some extent beyond the scope of the volume in which it is contained by including as many finds as possible from Greater London. Some interesting observations have emerged.

Coin finds have given clues to the geographical position of mid-Saxon London which is now being clarified by archaeological excavation. The availability and circulation of sceattas emerges as greater than that of coinages of the ensuing centuries up to the 11th, with London as a major centre of monetary activity during their currency, although its secondary position in relation to Southampton and towns in East Kent is to be noted. Studies based on the attribution of coins to mints have suggested that London was the prime mint in the earlier stages of Offa's reign, that it suffered a decline in the first half of the 9th century and a revival after c.860. The falls and rises in the numbers of single finds from London during this 100-year period do generally reflect these fluctuating fortunes although in view of the low numbers of finds, it is difficult to be confident of the accuracy of this information.

The geographical distribution of finds for the period after Alfred's capture of London shows how the area of the intra-mural City became the focus of urban development and how the area to the west was reduced in importance - a change which was apparently abrupt and planned. The continuation in the comparatively low level of finds during the 10th century may be seen in relation to the Scandinavian-inspired monetary development in the north of the country. This situation apparently continued beyond Eadgar's reform and until the end of Aethelred's reign, at which point single finds and evidence of mint output combine to show a marked revival in London's money market, demonstrably another result of Scandinavian activity. Thereafter, London's predominance in monetary matters appears to have suffered no serious challenge. After the Norman Conquest, there seems to have been a reduction in the numbers of coins lost in London, reflecting a general decline in the availability of coinage under the Norman kings, the exception being the PAXS type of William I. An anomalous peak comprising coins of Henry I and Stephen is perhaps best explained as a hoard.

Michael Dolley, in a survey of Saxon hoards from London, covered a period broadly similar to that of the present survey (Dolley 1960). His concern was to use the evidence to illustrate London's pre-eminence in the kingdom during the period and also to correct a number of omissions in Thompson's *Inventory* (Thompson 1956) which included only those hoards of post-1000 date from London, thus giving the impression that the town developed at a late stage. During the period as a whole, the proportion of London hoards to those in the country as a whole is undoubtedly impressive, but setting the evidence in such a wide framework does ignore fluctuations. It is hoped that the present survey, by adding the evidence of single finds to the work of others on hoards and mint activity, has shown that there is, after all, some truth in the impression unintentionally conveyed by Thompson's work, that London's pre-eminence was assured and consistent only after c.1000, and that this distinction had only limited application during the foregoing period.

NOTES

1. Stewart 1978, 144. The recent major publication on this coinage, Hill and Metcalf 1984, is content to refer to the coins as 'sceattas' so this practice is continued here.

2. The Croydon Palace hoard has recently been dated c.857 (Blackburn and Pagan 1986, 294.). The list compiled by Blackburn and Pagan adjusts the supposed date of deposit of many Saxon hoards from Britain.

PHOTOGRAPHS

As far as possible, photographs of all recent finds have been included. Omissions have occurred either because the condition of a coin is very poor, or because, in the case of finds reported as a result of the use of metal-detectors, the circumstances of recording have not permitted the taking of photographs.

Appendix 4.1:

CATALOGUE OF SINGLE FINDS

c.600-1158

Order of information (not all
details recorded in each case):
    Issuing authority
    Type
    Details of obverse (o)
    Details of reverse (r)
    Mint and moneyer
    Comparative published
    specimens
    Weight and die axis (DA)
    Provenance
    Location
    Accession number (Museum of
    London specimens)
    Previous publication

1. Tremissis
   'Witmen' group
   Thames, Blackfriars, 1848
   Sutherland 1948, 90, No 62a.

2. Tremissis
   Uncertain type
   'Found in London'
   Blunt 1962, 45, No 4.

3. Tremissis
   Merovingian
   Gunricus, Cormes, Sarthe
   Provenance as 2
   British Museum
   Blunt 1962, 45, No 3.

4. Sceat
   Series PA
   Ex-Roach Smith 1852/4
   British Museum
   Rigold and Metcalf 1984, 254.

5. Sceat
   As 4.

6. Sceat
   Series A
   Thames, Wapping, 1982/3
   Private collection
   Stott 1984, 243.

7. Sceat
   Series B
   Thames, Cannon Street
   Railway Bridge, 1974
   Rigold and Metcalf 1984, 255.

8. Sceat
   Series B
   Brentford?
   Rigold and Metcalf 1984, 247.

9. Sceat
   Series C
   Ex-Roach Smith 1852/4
   British Museum
   Rigold and Metcalf 1984, 254.

10a

10b

10. Sceat
    Series D
    o: Cross with letters
    r: Standard
    1.20g
    Maiden Lane
    Museum of London
    MOL, DOGLA (North London
    Unit), MAI 86 77 8.

11. Sceat
    Series E
    Ex-Roach Smith 1852/4
    British Museum
    Rigold and Metcalf 1984, 254.

12. As 11.

13. As 11.

14. Sceat
    Series E
    Thames, Battersea, 1982/3
    Private collection
    Stott 1984, 243.

15. Sceat
    Series E
    o: Porcupine, CIII below
    r: Devolved standard
    0.69g
    Excavation at Barking Abbey
    1987
    Passmore Edwards Museum.

16. Sceat
    Series F
    Thames, Battersea, 1982/3
    Private collection
    Stott 1984, 243.

17a

17b

17. Sceat
    Series G
    o: Bust right
    r: Standard
    1.10g
    Bermondsey Abbey 1987
    Museum of London
    MOL, DOGLA (Southwark and
    Lambeth Unit), BA 84 1368
    (2752)
    Comments Dr Metcalf.

18. Sceat
    Series H/U
    Ex-Roach Smith 1852/4
    British Museum
    Rigold and Metcalf 1984, 255.

19. Sceat
    Series K
    o: Bust right
    r: Wolf's head

cf. Metcalf and Walker 1967,
No 30
0.69g.
Billingsgate spoil 1985
Museum of London
MOL 85.291.

20a

20b

20. Sceat
Series K, imitative
R: Wolf's head right
0.86g
Bermondsey Abbey, in soil pre-
dating Abbey foundation
Museum of London
MOL, DOGLA (Southwark and
Lambeth Unit), BA 84 559
(1652)
(Identification and comments
by Dr Metcalf).

21. Sceat
Series K
O: Diademed bust right
R: Curled wolf
1.11g
Excavations at Barking Abbey
1987
Passmore Edwards Museum.

22. Sceat
Series K?
O: Stag left, looking back to
right, tree behind
R: Elaborate cross
0.97g
Provenance and location as 21.

23. Sceat
Series L
Ex-Roach Smith 1852/4
British Museum
Rigold and Metcalf 1984, 255.

24. Sceat
As 23.

25. Sceat
Series L
Thames
Rigold and Metcalf 1984, 255;
SCBI 20, No 340.

26. Sceat
Series L
Thames 1976
Rigold and Metcalf 1984, 258.

27a

27b

27. Sceat
Series L
O: Bust right
R: Figure standing on crescent
with cross in right and bird in
left hand
0.48g
Excavations at Bedfordbury,
1987
Museum of London
MOL, DOGLA (North London
Unit), PEA 87 009 7.

28. Sceat
Series M
Thames 1976
Rigold and Metcalf 1984, 255.

29. Sceat
Series M
Rigold and Metcalf 1984, 255.

30a

30b

30. Sceat
Series M
O: 'Hound' right
R: Spiral branch
0.76g
Excavations at Bedfordbury,
1987
Museum of London
MOL, DOGLA (North London
Unit), PEA 87 + 47.

31. Sceat
Series N
Ex-Roach Smith 1852/4
Rigold and Metcalf 1984, 255.

32. Sceat
As 31.

33. Sceat
Series N
O: Two standing figures facing
each other, holding a cross
between their heads
R: Fantastic animal left,
looking back to right
1.12g
Excavations at Barking Abbey
1987
Passmore Edwards Museum.

34. Sceat
Series Q
Found in London?
Rigold and Metcalf 1984, 255.

35. Sceat
Series R
Ex-Roach Smith 1852/4
British Museum
Rigold and Metcalf 1984, 255.

36. Sceat
Series R
Found Deptford? 1977
Rigold and Metcalf 1984,
250-1.

37. Sceat
Series s
Ex-Roach Smith 1852/4
Rigold and Metcalf 1984, 255.

38. Sceat
As 37.

39a

39b

39. Sceat
Series s
o: Sphinx
R: Wolf-whorl
0.72g
Thames, Rotherhithe 1980s
Private collection.

40a

40b

40. Sceat
Series s
o: Sphinx
R: Wolf-whorl
0.81g
Excavations at Bedfordbury,
1987
Museum of London
MOL, DOGLA (North London
Unit), PEA 87 97 192.

41. Sceat
Series T
Ex-Roach Smith 1852/4
Rigold and Metcalf 1984, 255.

42. Sceat
Series T
Thames, Lambeth Bridge
Stewart collection
Rigold and Metcalf 1984, 255.

43. Sceat
Series T
o: Porcupine
R: Bust right, legend: LCLV
0.89g
National Gallery excavations,
1987
Museum of London
MOL, DOGLA (North London
Unit), NAG 87 34 17.

43a

43b

44. Sceat
Series U
o: Man facing left, holding two
crosses and standing in ship
R: Bird pecking at branch
0.95g
Excavations at Barking Abbey
1987
Passmore Edwards Museum

45. Sceat
Series U
o: Man facing right, holding
two crosses and standing on
curved line
R: Bird pecking at branch
0.80g
Provenance and location as 44.

46. Sceat
Series v
o: Bird and vine
R: Wolf and twins
1.17g
Fill of well, excavations at
Jubilee Hall, Covent Garden,
1985
Museum of London
MOL, DOGLA (North London
Unit), JUB 85 SF2 39.

47. Sceat
Series x
o: Facing head
R: Beast motif
1.04g
Thames, Rotherhithe, 1987
Private collection
Information from Dr Metcalf.

47a

47b

48. Sceat
Series z
London
Rigold and Metcalf 1984, 255.

49. Sceat
Series z
O: Facing head
R: Beast right
1.22g
Billingsgate spoil? 1986
Information from Dr Metcalf.

50. Sceat
Uncertain type
Waterloo Bridge, 1882
Rigold and Metcalf 1984, 255.

51. Ecgberht of Kent (c.765-c.780)
BMC I
Udd
Stamford Hill, 1906
Information from the British
Museum

52. Offa
Group I (c.784-c.787)
Eoba
cf.Blunt 1961, no.17
0.57g.; 180°
Thames, Wandsworth, 1980
Blunt collection.

53. Offa
Group II Portrait (c.787-c.792)
Ethelwold
cf.Blunt 1961, no.57-8
'Found in the City of London'
SCBI 1, No 391.

54. Offa
Group II Portrait
Pendred
Thames, London
NC, 1920, pl.XI, 14.

55a

55b

55. Cynethryth
O: EOBA
R: +CINEÐRÐÐ REG
Eoba, Canterbury
cf.Blunt 1961, No 123; SCBI 11,
No 7 (same dies)
0.59g; 270°
Billingsgate spoil, 1984
Private collection.

56. Coenwulf
Group I (796-c.805)
Fleet St., 1914
Blunt, Lyon and Stewart 1963,
51, no 11.

57. Coenwulf
Group I
O: M in centre
COENVVLFREX

57a

57b

R: Tribrach moline of 3 lines
IB./:B:/:A.
Ibba, London or Canterbury
cf.Blunt, Lyon and Stewart
1963, Cn16, same obv. die as
Shropshire find, p.51
1.09g; 225°
Pit of domestic refuse, Maiden
Lane, 1986
Museum of London
MOL, DOGLA (North London
Unit), MAI 86 (241) SF68.

58. Coenwulf
Billingsgate spoil
No further inf.

59. Ceolwulf (821-823)
BMC 109
Werbald
Found in City
Roach Smith 1854, 108; Blunt,
Lyon and Stewart 1963, 62,
No 29b.

60. Wulfred, Archbishop of
Canterbury
Group III (c.810-823)
Saeberht

cf.Blunt, Lyon and Stewart
1963, Wu4-6
London Bridge, March 1824
Archaeologia, XXV, 600.

61. Baldred of Kent (*c*.823-825)
Group II
O: Cross crosslet
BELDRED REXCAN
R: Long cross fourchee
DI/OR/MO/DM
Diormod
1.12g; 180°
Thames, Lambeth Bridge,
1973
Blunt 1974a.

62a

62b

62. Ecgberht of Wessex
Portrait type (*c*.825-*c*.828)
O: Bust right
+EGBEOR(H)TREX
R: Cross design
+EDELM(O)D·:·
Ethelmod, Rochester?
0.17g; 270°
Late Saxon dump at
Westminster Abbey, 1986
MOL, DOGLA (North London
Unit), WST 86 SF43 379.

63. Aethelwulf (839-858)
Thames
Roach Smith journals, 14
September 1837.

64. Aethelwulf
BMC I, Phase 3 (*c*.845-55)
O: Monogram of DORIB in
centre
+EDELV...
R: Monogram of CANT in centre
+.....ONETA
Canterbury
0.56g; 0°. Broken fragment
Excavations at Barking Abbey
Passmore Edwards Museum.

65. Burgred (852-874)
Hugered
Northumberland Avenue
Pagan 1965, 22.

66. Burgred
Wulferth
Westminster (probably
Westminster Bridge Hoard)
SCBI 30, No 207.

67. Alfred
BMC I (Lunette or 'Burgred'
type), (871-75)
Hebeca
0.98g, 180°
Thames, 6oft upstream of
Lambeth Bridge, 1974
Information from the British
Museum.

68. Alfred
BMC I
Dunn
Barnes, ex-City (see appendix
4.4)
Roach Smith journals, 5 May
1839.

69. Alfred
Lead weight, BMC V (Cross-
and-lozenge), (875-880/6?)
Ealdulf
St Paul's churchyard, 1838
British Museum
Roach Smith 1854, 107; Blunt
1962, 45.

70. Alfred
BMC VI (London monogram),
886
Found 'between Old Broad
Street and the French
Protestant Church'
(Threadneedle Street)
British Museum
Roach Smith 1854, 108; Blunt
1962, 45.

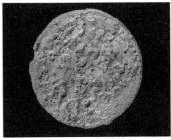

71a

71b

71. Alfred
Halfpenny, (London
monogram)
R: Londonia monogram
0.68g, 270°
From a ditch of Saxo-Norman
date, 11-19 St.Thomas Street,
1977.
Museum of London
MOL, DOGLA (Southwark and
Lambeth Unit), St.Thomas
Street 27 94.

72. Northumbrian Viking
Cunnetti (*c*.897)
O: Archiepiscopal cross
CVNET R
R: Small cross with two pellets
CVNNETTI
'Exhumed in making a sewer in

one of the courts in Cornhill'
JBAA, XIII, (1858), 237.
(From a hoard?)

73. Edward the Elder (899-924)
BMC II (Two Line)
O : EADVVEARD REX
R : DEORVVALD MO
Deorwald
Provenance as 72.

75a

76a

74a

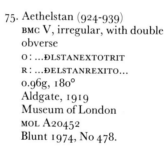
75b

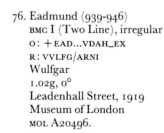

76b

74b

74. Edward the Elder
BMC III (Portrait)
O : + EADVVEARD REX
R : GRIMP/ALDMO
Grimwald
cf.SCBI 11, No 48 (different
dies)
0.84g, 225°
Thames, Southwark Bridge,
south side, 1980.
Private collection
Information from
M.Blackburn.

75. Aethelstan (924-939)
BMC V, irregular, with double
obverse
O : ...ÐLSTANEXTOTRIT
R : ...ÐELSTANREXITO...
0.96g, 180°
Aldgate, 1919
Museum of London
MOL A20452
Blunt 1974, No 478.

76. Eadmund (939-946)
BMC I (Two Line), irregular
O : + EAD...VDAH_EX
R : VVLFG/ARNI
Wulfgar
1.02g, 0°
Leadenhall Street, 1919
Museum of London
MOL A20496.

77. Eadred (946-955)
BMC V (Crowned Bust)
Albert
City of London
British Museum
Roach Smith journals, 25 July
1836; *Gentleman's Magazine*,
September 1836.

78. Eadred
BMC V
R : WILEBERT MONE
Wilebert
Acquired Barnes, ex-City
British Museum
Roach Smith 1854, 108; Roach
Smith journal, 25 February
and 10 March 1839.

79. Eadred
BMC V
O : EADRED R...
R : Λ...HICᴖM°ll
Mannecin?
0.49g, 135°
Thames, Custom House, 1980s
Private collection.

79a

79b

80a

80b

80. Eadgar
Halfpenny, pre-reform (prior to 973)
O: Vestigial bust right
EADGARRE
R: Londonia monogram
London
0.63g, 0°
Mid-12th century waterfront dump, Billingsgate Lorry Park, 1982
Museum of London
MOL, DUA, BIG 82 [7595] ⟨3423⟩.

81. Eadgar
Halfpenny, pre-Reform
Winchester
St Bartholomew's Church
Roach Smith 1854, 108; Blunt 1962, 44.

82. Eadgar
Cut halfpenny (Reform Portrait) (973-5)
R: AE....OLINE
Same dies as BM specimen 1891-4-4-77
Aethestan, Lympne
1.30g, 0°
Billingsgate spoil, reported December 1986
Inf. J. Bispham.

83. Eadgar
Unknown type
St Swithin's Lane
Roach Smith's journal, 28 July and 4 August 1836.

84. Aethelred II
BMC IIIa (Crux) (991-997)
O: +AEDELRED REX ANGLOR
R: +BYRHTLAF MO LVN
Byrhtlaf, London
Found in the Thames along the City foreshore
British Museum
Roach Smith 1854, 108; Roach Smith's journal No 2, final pages.

85. Aethelred II
Cut farthing, BMC IIIa
O: .....GLOX
R: .....RMER
0.34g
Billingsgate spoil? 1986
Inf. J. Bispham.

86. Aethelred II
BMC VIII (Helmet) (1003-9)
O: ......EDREXANGL
R: +AEÐ.......OCISICI
Aethelm, Chichester
0.53g, 315°, broken
Late 12th century dump on site of Billingsgate Lorry Park, 1982
Museum of London
MOL, DUA, BIG 82 [4064] ⟨2778⟩.

87. Aethelred II
BMC XI (Agnus Dei) (1009)
Blacaman, Derby
Found in London, Gracechurch Street?
Dolley 1960, 44; Dolley and Talvio 1977, 131.

88. Aethelred II
BMC I (Last Small Cross) (1009-17)
R: +ALFWOLD ON WINCST (as published)
Aelfwold, Winchester
Found in Thames, City
British Museum
Roach Smith 1854, 108; Roach Smith's journal No 2, final pages.

89. Aethelred II
BMC I
R: LEOFNOTH ON LEPE (as published)
Leofnoth, Lewes
Found in City?
British Museum
Roach Smith 1854, 108.

90. Aethelred II
BMC I
Coin fragmented
Plantation House, Eastcheap
Museum of London
MOL 300.

91. Aethelred II
BMC I
O: +AE....EDEXANGL:
R: .....IØFPØLDN $\tilde{n}$ ØNLV..
Liofwold, London
cf.SCBI 7, no 901, same die?
0.53g, 270°, broken
Excavation at the site of the GPO building, City, 1979
Museum of London

MOL, DUA, POM 79 [1311]
⟨279⟩.

91a

91b

92. Aethelred II
Unknown type
R : GODRIC NO LVNDENE
Godric, London
Aldersgate Street
JBAA, XXXIX, (1883), 86.

93-94. Aethelred II
Unknown types
London Bridge, March 1824
Archaeologia, XXV, 600.

95. Aethelred II
Unknown type
Leofred, London
Thames
Roach Smith's journal No 2,
final pages.

96. Aethelred II
Unknown type
Found in London?
Roach Smith's journals, 2
January(?) 1838.

97. Aethelred II
Unknown type
Aethelnoth, Lincoln
London Bridge
Roach Smith's journal, 9 April
1840.

98. Aethelred II
Cut halfpenny, unknown type
Leofwine
Acquired Barnes, ex-City (see
appendix 4)
Roach Smith's journal, 21
August 1840.

99. Cnut
BMC VIII (Quatrefoil),
(1018-24)
Leofwine, Canterbury?
St Katherine's Dock
Mechanic's Magazine, 1827-8,
409.
Inf.Alex Werner.

100. Cnut
BMC VIII
St Nicholas Acon
Marsden 1967, 219.

101. Cnut
BMC VIII
O : + CNVTREXANGLO
R : + AELFPI(ONL)VND
Aelfwi, London
cf.SCBI 14, No 2052 (different
dies)
wt. not recorded, 0°
11th/12th century pit,
excavations at Milk Street,
1976
Museum of London
MOL, DUA, MLK 76 [1043] 60.

102. Cnut
BMC VIII
O : + CNVTREXANGLORUM
R : + P(INN)EONPINCSTR
Wine, Winchester
0.84g., 180°
Billingsgate spoil, April 1984.

103. Cnut
BMC XIV (Pointed Helmet)
(1024-30)
O : + CNVT RECX
R : EDPINE ON LVNDE
Edwine, London
Found in the City?
British Museum
Roach Smith 1854, 108.

102a

102b

104a

104b

104. Cnut
Cut halfpenny, BMC XIV
O: ....EX:
R: ....ONHERT
Hertford?
0.48g, 180°
Billingsgate spoil, February
1985.

105. Cnut
BMC XVI (Short Cross) (1030-
35/6)
O: CNVT RECX AN
R: LOD ON LUNDEN (as
published)
God, London
Found in the Thames (City?)
British Museum
Roach Smith 1854, 108;
Roach Smith's journal No 2,
final pages.

106. Cnut
BMC XVI
R: BOEA ON DOFRA (as
published)
Boga, Dover
Found in the City?
British Museum
Roach Smith 1854, 108.

107. Cnut
BMC XVI
O: +CNVT REX
R: WVLFRED ON LVND (as
published)
Wulfred, London
Found in the Thames (City?)
British Museum
Roach Smith 1854, 108;
Roach Smith's journal No 2,
final pages.

108. Cnut
BMC XVI
O: +CNVTREX
R: +SPANONLVND
Swan, London
cf. SCBI 14, Nos 2918 and 2921
(same reverse die?)
0.75g, 0°
Billingsgate spoil, December
1984.

109-113. Cnut
Unknown types
London Bridge, March 1824
Archaeologia, XXV, 600.

108a

108b

114. Cnut
Unknown type
From the Thames at the City
Roach Smith's journal, 17
and 31 October 1835.

115. Harold I
Unknown type
Provenance as 114
Roach Smith's journal, 17
October 1835.

116-117. Harold I
Unknown types
Provenance as 114
31 October 1835.

118. Harthacnut or Cnut
posthumous
BMC XVII (Arm and Sceptre)
(1040-42)
O: +CNVTRECX
R: +LE(A)STANONSNOTI
Leofstan, Nottingham
0.79g, 180°
Thames foreshore,
Billingsgate, May 1986.

118a

118b

119a

119b

119. Edward the Confessor
   BMC III (Trefoil
   Quadrilateral) (1046-48)
   O: +EDPERDREX
   R: +BRVMMANONLVND
   Brunman, London
   0.96g, 180°
   Billingsgate spoil, December
   1984.

120. Edward the Confessor
   BMC II (Small Flan) (1048-50)
   Canterbury
   Ex-Roach Smith?
   Metcalf 1980, 40.

121. Edward the Confessor
   BMC V (Expanding Cross)
   (1050-53)
   O: +EDPARDRE....
   R: +GOD.....ONLINCO
   Godric?, Lincoln
   0.99g, DA not recorded
   Billingsgate spoil, October
   1984.

122a

122b

121a

121b

123a

123b

122. Edward the Confessor
   Contemporary copy?, BMC IX
   (Sovereign Eagles) (1056-59)
   Blundered designs and
   legends
   wt. and DA not recorded
   Billingsgate spoil, April 1984.

123. Edward the Confessor
   Cut halfpenny, BMC XI
   (Hammer Cross) (1059-62)
   O: ....RDRE
   R: ......INGONH...
   Duning, Hastings
   cf.SCBI 17, Nos 443 and 444
   wt. not recorded, 270°
   Billingsgate spoil, June 1984.

124a

124b

124. Edward the Confessor
   Cut halfpenny, BMC XI
   R: ....NLVND
   London
   0.45g, 270°
   Billingsgate spoil, June 1984.

125. Edward the Confessor
   BMC XIII, (Bust Facing)
   (1062-65)
   O: +EADPARDREXANG:
   R: +∞PETMAN'ONLVN
   Swetman, London
   0.91g, 0
   All Hallows, Lombard Street.,
   1940
   Museum of London
   MOL 554.

125a

125b

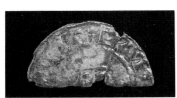

126a

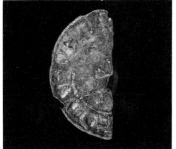

126b

126. Edward the Confessor
Cut halfpenny, BMC XIII
O : EAD.......NG
R : ....EONHE...
Hertford?
0.15g, 180°
Late 11th/early 12th century
context, excavations at

Pudding Lane, 1981.
Museum of London
MOL, DUA, PDN 81 [644]
⟨382⟩.

127a

127b

127. Edward the Confessor
BMC XIII
O : EADPRDREX
R : +AEGLPINEONLEA
Aegelwine, Leicester
0.58, 180°
Found in spoil from
?Southwark, January 1987.

128a

128b

128. Edward the Confessor
Cut halfpenny, BMC XV
(Pyramids) (1056-66)
O : ED............
R : +PVLF......NDE
Wulf...., London
wt. not recorded, 135°
Billingsgate spoil, May 1984.

129a

129b

129. Edward the Confessor/
William I mule
O : (EC XV) EADDARDREX
R : (WI) GAR..NONLIIIC
Garvin, Lincoln
0.73g, 0°
Billingsgate spoil, June 1984.

130. William I
Coin-brooch, BMC I (Profile/
Cross Fleury) (1066-68?)
O : ......ILLE...MVSRE
R : +PVLGARONLVDAO
Wulfgar, London
3.31g, 270°, 1mm thick
Billingsgate spoil, June 1984.

130a

130b

131a

131b

131. William I
Cut halfpenny, BMC III
(Canopy) (1070-72?)
O: +P..........
R: .....ONOIEONŁIIN..
Lincoln/London?
0.44g, 315°
Noble Street
Museum of London
MOL 558.

132. William I
BMC V (Two Stars)
(1074-77?)
Fragmented
Late 11th/early 12th century
pit during excavations in
Milk Street, 1976
Museum of London
MOL, DUA, MLK 76 [3039]
⟨426⟩.

133. William I
BMC VIII (PAXS) (1083-86?)
R: SIFERDONI....(as recorded)
Siferth, Lincoln
London Bridge
Roach Smith journals,
catalogue at end of journal
No 3.

134. William I
BMC VIII
R: .....D ON TH....(as
published)
Folcaerd or Godred, Thetford
Ex-Roach Smith?
Metcalf 1980, 40.

135. William I
Cut farthing, BMC VIII
0.14g, DA?
Mid-12th century road
surface, excavations at
St Peter's Hill, 1981.
Museum of London
MOL, DUA, PET 81 [1078]
⟨118⟩.

136. William I
BMC VIII
O: + PILLELMREX
R: + PINEDIONCNT'L
Winedi, Canterbury
1.14g, 315°
Billingsgate spoil, June 1984.

136a

136b

137a

137b

137. William I
BMC VIII
O : + PILLELMREX
R : + IELFREDONCNTII
Aelfred, Canterbury
1.20g, 0°
Billingsgate spoil, July 1984.

138. William I
Unknown type
Aelfred, Canterbury (CNTI)
London Bridge
Roach Smith's journal No 3,
at the end.

140a

140b

139a

139b

139. William II
BMC II/I mule (1089-92?)
O : (II) + PILLELMR...
R : (I) + SIPEG....NCOL...
Swigen, Colchester
0.75g, 0°
Excavations at the site of the
GPO building, 1975
Museum of London
MOL, DUA, GPO 75 [222] ⟨13⟩.

140. William II
Cut halfpenny, BMC II (Cross
in Quatrefoil) (1089-92?)
O : .....ILLELM....
R : + ...ONGHI
Gloucester/Ilchester?
0.51g, 170°
Billingsgate spoil, July 1984.

141. William II
Cut halfpenny, BMC IV (Cross
pattee and fleury)
(1095-98?)
O : ....MRE
R : ......CON...
0.55g, DA?
Billingsgate spoil.

142. William II
BMC IV
O : + P.......EXA (Sword over
left shoulder)
R : ......DIONBR...
Snedi, Bristol
1.13g, DA not recorded
Billingsgate spoil, March
1984.

143. Henry I
Cut halfpenny, BMC II
(Profile/Cross Fleury)
(1101-4?)
O : .....RIREX
R : .....N VI....
London
0.43g, 45°
Billingsgate spoil, July 1984.

143a

143b

144a

144b

144. Henry I
Cut halfpenny, BMC IV
(Annulets and Piles)
(1107-8?)
R : ......A.....
0.50g
Billingsgate spoil, July 1984.

145a

145b

147a

147b

151

152

145. Henry I
Cut halfpenny, BMC VI
(Pointing Bust and Stars)
(1113-6?)
O : +hE......
R : ....PINEONLV....
London
0.48g, 270°
Excavations on the site of the
GPO building
Museum of London
MOL, DUA, POM 79 [656]
⟨122⟩.

146. Henry I
Cut farthing, BMC X (Full
Face/Cross Fleury) (1124-5?)
O : ......E.....
R : +GOD......
0.20g
Billingsgate spoil.

147. Henry I
BMC X
O : ......ENRIC...
R : .....EXEL...?
Duning, Exeter
1.28g, 315°
Billingsgate spoil, June 1986
Inf. J.Bispham.

148. Henry I
Cut farthing, BMC XIII (Star
in Lozenge Fleury)
(1128-31?)
0.24g
Billingsgate spoil, July 1984.

149. Henry I
Cut farthing, BMC XIV
(Pellets in Quatrefoil)
(1131-4?)
R : . +.L.....
0.18g
Billingsgate spoil, July 1984.

150. Henry I
BMC XV (Quatrefoil in Cross
Fleury) (1134-5?)
0.39g
Watching brief on site of
Billingsgate Lorry Park,
1983/4
Museum of London
MOL, DUA, BWB 83 [298]
⟨1071⟩.

151-152. Henry I
BMC XV

Two coins, complete, folded
in half and placed one
inside the other
wts. and DAs not recorded
Billingsgate spoil, May 1984.

153. Henry I
Cut halfpenny, BMC XV
R : ......OV....
0.61g
Billingsgate spoil.

154. Henry I
Cut halfpenny, BMC XV
O : hEN........
R : .....hEI...
0.57g
Billingsgate spoil.

155. Henry I
Cut farthing, BMC XV
0.25g
Billingsgate spoil.

156. Stephen
BMC I (Watford)
(c.1135-c.1141)
Gefrei, Thetford
wt. and DA not recorded
Billingsgate spoil?, July 1985
Inf. British Museum.

157a

157b

157. Stephen
  Cut halfpenny, BMC I
  R : ....ISVLT...
  0.49g
  Billingsgate spoil, May 1984.

158a

158b

158. Stephen
  BMC I
  Billingsgate spoil, May 1984.

159a

159b

159. Stephen
  BMC I
  O : +STIEFNEREX
  R : +A......DE
  London?
  1.40g, 270°
  Billingsgate spoil, July 1984.

160a   160b

160. Stephen
  Cut farthing, BMC II (Cross
  voided and Mullets)
  O : .....IEFN....
  R : .....LARD....
  Adelard
  0.26g, 270°
  Excavations at Gardener's
  Corner, 1980

DOGLA (North London Unit)
GDC 80 164 (27).
Whytehead 1984, 49.

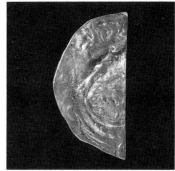

161a

161b

161. Stephen
  Cut halfpenny, BMC VII
  (Awbridge) (c.1150-8)
  O : +ST......
  R : +R....R.....
  Rogier, London?
  0.57g, 20°
  Intrusive to Roman context,
  excavations at Billingsgate
  Lorry Park, 1982
  Museum of London
  MOL, DUA, BIG 82 [7007]
  ⟨3619⟩.

Foreign Coins

162. Belgium area, first half of the
    11th century
    Denier
    0.75g
    Watching brief on the site of
    Billingsgate Lorry
    Park 1983/4
    Museum of London
    MOL, DUA, BWB 83 [298]
    ⟨994⟩.
    Identification Prof.P.
    Berghaus, Munster.

162a

162b

163. Imitation of Duisberg,
    Emperor Conrad II (1027-39)
    Minted in the Netherlands
    Mid-11th century ditch,
    Westminster Abbey
    Black 1977, 200.

164. Olaf Kyrre, Norway,
    (1067-93)
    0.53g, Broken
    Billingsgate spoil, December
    1986
    Inf. J.Bispham.

165a

165b

165. Imitation of Duisberg,
    Emperor Henry IV
    Minted in Lower Rhineland?
    (1080s-90s)
    0.64g
    Mid-12th century waterfront,
    Seal House 1974
    Museum of London
    MOL, DUA, SH 74 [620] ⟨292⟩.

166. Normandy, late 11th/early
    12th century
    Denier
    O :
    R : (+NORM)A(N)NA)
    cross with pellet in each angle
    cf.Luneau No 18 (Pl XIII, 7);
    Dumas, Group C
    (Pl XX, 10).
    Billingsgate spoil

167. Henry of Northumberland,
    Scotland?
    Cut halfpenny
    R : .....EL :.....
    Bamborough?
    cf.Stewart 1967, Type 3;
    Mack 1966, 288/9
    wt. not recorded, 0°
    London Bridge, September
    1982.

Appendix 4.2a:

LONDON HOARDS c.700-1158

(For further information, see
Appendices 4.2B and 4.2C (Nos.10,
13, 14, 15, 20, 23, 26), or
Blackburn and Pagan 1986.)

1.	Thames Hoard	c.740
2.	Middle Temple	c.842
3.	Croydon Old Palace	c.857
4.	Dorking	c.862
5.	Barking	c.870
6.	Gravesend	c.871
7.	Waterloo Bridge	c.872
8.	Croydon (Whitehorse)	c.872
9.	Westminster Bridge	c.872
10.	Wandsworth	c.873
11.	Bucklersbury	c.890
12.	Erith	c.890
13.	London? (C.Blunt)	c.915
14.	Cannon Street Railway Bridge	c.940
15.	Threadneedle Street	c.945
16.	Chelsea Reach	c.988
17.	Isleworth	c.991
18.	Honey Lane	c.1000
19.	St Martin-le-Grand?	c.1008 (see above)
20.	Chiswick Bridge	c.1016
21.	Gracechurch Street?	c.1062 (see above)
22.	Walbrook I	c.1066
23.	Cornhill	c.1066
24.	Walbrook II	c.1075
25.	St Mary-at-Hill	c.1075
26.	Billingsgate?	c.1141

Appendix 4.2b:

WANDSWORTH AND THREADNEEDLE
STREET HOARDS

The existence of both of these
hoards, the remains of which
are in the Museum of London,
has been widely known since
Dolley's survey of London
hoards (Dolley 1960). Their
contents, however, have not
previously been published in
their entirety.

Wandsworth (pre-1913)
c.873
4 coins of Burgred, type A (lunettes
    unbroken)

2a

4a

2b

4b

1a

3a

2. O: BVRGREDREX
   R: ∴O :MON ∴/CUDULF/ ˙.˙ ETA ˙.˙.˙
   CETHEWULF?
   1.03G, 270°
   MOL A5883

3. O: BVRGREDREX
   R: :MON./BEAGSTA/::ETA
   Beagstan
   0.86g, 270°
   MOL A5884

4. O: BVRGREDREX
   R: MON/BEAGSTA/ ˙ ˙ ETA ˙.˙
   Beagstan
   0.72g, 35°
   MOL A5885

1b

1. O: BVRGREDREX
   R: . .MON ∴ /CENRED/ ˙.˙ ETA ˙.˙.˙
   Cenred
   0.88g, 0°
   MOL A5882

3b

Threadneedle Street (1924)
c.945
5 coins

1. Aethelstan (924-39)
   BMC I (Two Line)
   O : /EÐELSTANRE....
   R : /ELFFR/....MO
   Aelfred
   cf. Blunt 1974, No 9 and Cannon
   Street Railway Bridge hoard
   No 3 (Infra. Appendix 4.2c),
   different dies
   0.95g, 0°
   MOL 55.20/2

2a

4a

1a

2b

4b

3. Eadmund (939-46)
   BMC I (Two Line)
   O : +EVDMVNDRE
   R : BACI/AGER
   Baciager
   1.21g, 180°
   MOL 55.20/3.

4. Eadmund
   BMC I
   O : +EADMVNDREX
   R : DIARE/MMO
   Diarelm
   0.93g, 0°, Broken
   MOL 55.20/4.

1b

3a

2. Aethelstan
   Mule BMC V/I, irregular
   O : + \EÐEL ̇ ̇ZTAƷHEXTOR
   R : EIƷ_IO/EENBb
   1.10g, 270°
   MOL 55.20/1
   Blunt 1974, no.454.

3b

5a

5b

5. Eadmund
BMC I
O: EADMVN....
R: DOMEN/....ESM...
Domences
0.79g, Fragment
MOL 55.20/5.

Appendix 4.2c:

NEW AND PREVIOUSLY UNRECORDED
HOARDS

Thames, London? (1986)
c.915
6 coins (3 Edward the Elder, 2 St
Eadmund Memorial, 1 St Peter,
York.
See above p.291. Blunt forthcoming
(My thanks to Mr Blunt for
permitting mention of this
hoard.)

Cannon Street Railway Bridge
(1974/5)
c.940
7 + coins, of which three recorded:

1a

1b

1. Plegmund, Archbishop of
Canterbury
Class II (910-23?)
O: +PLEGMVNDARCHIEP
R: SIGEHE/LMMON
Sigehelm
0.95g, 90°
Museum of London
MOL 76.53.

2a

2b

2. Edward the Elder (899-924)
BMC II (Two Line)
O: +EADVVEARDREX
R: ÆÐER/EDMO
Aethered
1.63g, 170
Museum of London
MOL 75.1/40

3. Aethelstan (924-39)
BMC I (Two Line)
O: +EDELSTANREX
R: ÆLFR/EDMŌ
Aelfred
cf.Blunt 1974, No 9, same dies
1.47g
Inf.British Museum

+ plus at least 3 further coins of
Edward, 1 of Aethelstan and 1 of
Plegmund.

Chiswick Bridge (1982)
c.1016
6 coins? all Aethelred, BMC I (Last Small Cross) (1009-17)

1. PVLFNOÐONDO
   Wulfnoth, Dorchester

2. LEOFPINEMΩSTAN
   Leofwine, Stamford

3. Cut halfpenny
   ...ONLINCO...
   Lincoln

plus 3-4 cut halfpennies

Cornhill (c.1855)
c.1066
8 coins (possibly not all from hoard)
JBAA, XIII, (1858), 236-7
Legends as published:

1. Aethelred II
   BMC I (Last Small Cross) (1009-17)
   O: ETHELRED REX
   R: LEFPINE M-O EOFRP
   Leofwine, York

2. Cnut
   BMC VIII (Quatrefoil) (1018-24)
   O: CNVT REX ANGLO
   R: EGELPINE O(N) LVN
   Aegelwine, London.

3. Cnut
   BMC XIV (Pointed Helmet) (1024-30)
   O: CNVT REX ANG
   R: PVLFPINE NO LINCO
   Wulfwine, Lincoln.

4. Cnut
   BMC XIV
   O: CNVT REX A
   R: BRVNGNC ON LVND
   Bruninc, London.

5. Cnut
   BMC XIV
   O: CNVT REX A
   R: GODRICE ON LVND
   Godric, London.

6. Cnut
   BMC XIV
   O: CNVT REX A
   R: POLRMER ON ORDPI
   Wulfmaer?, Norwich

7. Edward the Confessor
   BMC II (Small Flan) (1048-50)
   O: EDPERD RES
   Described as a forgery of a halfpenny

8. Edward the Confessor
   BMC XIII (Bust Facing) (1062-5)
   O: EADPARD REX ANG
   R: DVLF ∽I ON LVNDE
   Dulfsi?, London.

Billingsgate? (1984)
c.1141
Uncertain number of coins
See Appendix 4.1, large number of coins of Henry I (especially type XV) and Stephen type I (and William II?) from Billingsgate spoil may constitute part of a hoard.

Appendix 4.3

Extract from the catalogue of the John Walker Baily collection transferred to the Guildhall Museum, compiled after Baily's death in 1881. All items are noted as having been discovered in the City between 1863 and 1872.

'A heap of Silver coins, part of a large 'find', preserved as a specimen to show the state in which they were discovered; a portion of the bowl containing them.

The following 230 coins forming part of that 'find', cleaned and mounted between glass plates:

  63 Ethelred, 979 (not cleaned)
134 Edward the Confessor, 1042
  14 Cnut, 1016
  14 Harold I and II, 1035-1066
   5 William the Conqueror 1066
  ———
230

  30 halves of the same kind of coins also cleaned and mounted between glass
   1 of Emperor John Zimisces 969'

Appendix 4.4

NOTE ON THE COINS RECORDED BY CHARLES ROACH
SMITH

Michael Rhodes

A number of Saxon coins are known only from unpublished records by the 19th century London archaeologist Charles Roach Smith (1806-90). These have been incorporated in Appendix 1 as Nos 63, 68, 83, 95-98, 114-117. The coins are recorded in Smith's manuscript journals, now in the British Museum's Department of Medieval and Later Antiquities. The relevant entries date from October 1835 to August 1840. The inclusion of coins which have not survived and whose identification therefore cannot be verified may be justified as follows:

Although Smith's interest in City antiquities commenced at the beginning of 1835, his passion for coin-collecting and numismatics had begun about ten years previously, when he was apprenticed to a chemist and druggist in Chichester. By 1835 Smith had acquired a good knowledge of the subject, and would have been familiar with Ruding's *Annals of the Coinage of Britain* (1817), a landmark of numismatics, which contains many plates of late Saxon coins and is generally reliable with regard to basic identifications. Smith's ability was recognised in January 1837 when he was elected to the newly-formed Numismatic Society. In 1840 he was elected to its council, and in 1841 became the Secretary. Smith's numismatic competence during the 1830s may also be demonstrated by the survival of a number of Saxon coins described in his journals.

A number of coins seen or purchased by Smith were obtained from bargees at various places along the Thames upstream of London. These almost certainly came from the City. Following the rebuilding of London Bridge in 1824-31, the old bridge was removed, and for several ensuing years there were repeated dredging operations along the line of the old bridge to clear and deepen the channel. Numerous antiquities were recovered as mud and ballast was heaved into the barges. Others were spotted when the ballast was used to repair the banks of the Thames upstream of the City. Antiquities not purchased by Smith were generally sold without record. His journals describe how in 1836 he obtained or recorded Roman coins from gravel dumped on the river-bank at Battersea and along the Surrey Canal. In January 1837, he ascertained that ballast was now being used to repair the tow-path between Hammersmith Bridge and Barnes. Thereafter, Smith made regular visits to this part of the river, making many purchases (Parsloe 1928, 194).

ACKNOWLEDGEMENTS

Work on this survey has been greatly dependent on discussion with and help from Marion Archibald, Mark Blackburn, John Clark and Alan Vince and the generosity of Joe Bispham, Christopher Blunt, Michael Metcalf and Michael Rhodes has also been appreciated.

The following have provided information on some of the more recent finds:
A.Allen, K.Bellringer, P.Bone, M.Butcher, P.Connolly, S.Cornelius, D.Elliot, B.Farrow, A.Freeman, G.Grant, J.Hedges, T.Letch, A.McGoldrick, D.Miller, N.Mills, M.Moran, S.Myrtle, H.Norris, A.Pilson, D.Rogers, A.Stewart, E.Taylor, S.Wheeler.

I am also grateful for the indulgence of my colleagues John Clark and Brian Spencer at the Museum of London, to Tony Dyson, who read and suggested amendments to the text and to Nick Griffiths, who drew the maps and histogram.

4.ii ANGLO-SAXON AND NORMAN LEAD OBJECTS WITH OFFICIAL COIN TYPES

Marion M Archibald

Among the finds from Billingsgate are a large number of pieces which look like early medieval coins but are made of lead, not silver. A few of them came from the excavations, but most were found by metal-detecting on spoil from the site dumped at various places in Essex. It should be emphasized that the material termed 'Billingsgate' came from a site later to be occupied by St Botolph's wharf. As I had been collecting information on these and other lead monetiform pieces, the Museum of London and the director of the excavations, Steve Roskams, generously invited me to publish the Billingsgate finds. I am grateful to the editor Alan Vince for allowing examples known to me from elsewhere to be included here, so that the discussion of the rôle of this group of material might be as comprehensive as possible. I am particularly indebted to Peter Stott for passing on information about lead pieces shown at the London Museum and for so readily offering to exclude them from his otherwise comprehensive account of London numismatic finds published in this volume. Many other people have taken great trouble to ensure that finds of these items were properly recorded and have discussed them with me; they are listed with my warmest thanks under Acknowledgements below.

Details of sixty-one pieces appear in the Corpus, to which the numbers in brackets in the discussion refer. Two additional pieces were reported as this paper went to press. They are included in the statistics and in the tables but, as full details were not available, they could not be added to the corpus or the plates. Both are monetiform; the first, an Æthelred II Last Small Cross type of the Worcester mint found in excavations at Worcester, mentioned by kind permission of the director, Charles Mundy, and the second, a Henry I in a private collection in the United States - and possibly from the Billingsgate spoil - about which there is at present no more information.

The great majority of these lead pieces are monetiform, but cognate non-monetiform lead pieces are also included in this review. To make reference easier, all categories are listed together in a single chronological sequence. It is their official character which sets these objects apart from other lead artifacts such as pseudo-coin brooches and the various classes of para-numismatic items such as tokens. The latter groups are excluded from this survey, as are coin-forgeries and the by-products of forgery made of lead. One unofficial piece (60) has been included since it is from Billingsgate and would not otherwise have been recorded. The material ranges in date from the second quarter of the eighth century to the early 1150s. The representation of reigns and types is summarized in Fig. 4.7.

There are eight pieces from London excavations: seven from Billingsgate (19, 26-7, 29 and 57-9) and one from Aldersgate Street (15). Twenty-six are from the Billingsgate spoil heaps (14, 16, 18, 20-4, 28, 30-42, 47, 52, 56, and 60). The additional Henry I may also be from the Billingsgate spoil. One nineteenth-century find (6) is certainly from London and another (51) is almost certainly so, making a total from the capital of thirty-six, or possibly thirty-seven, in all. Twenty-one specimens are from other places, and the findspots of five are unknown. The known provenances of the material are summarized in Fig. 4.9.

Technique

These lead pieces fall into two main technological groups: the small, early, series with incuse types and inscriptions, and the main series where types and inscriptions are in relief as on the coinage.

The incuse series comprises only the four earliest pieces (1-4) datable between *c.*720 and

Period or reign	Type	B'gate	London ex B'gate	other sites	total
Sceat	East Anglian	-	-	I	I
Coenwulf of Mercia/ Eadwald of East Anglia	East Anglian	-	-	2	2
Athelstan I of East Anglia	Cross and pellets	-	-	I	I
Burgred of Mercia	Lunette (a)	-	-	I	I
Alfred of Wessex	BMC V	-	I	-	I
St Edmund Memorial type		-	-	I	I
Athelstan	BMC IV	-	-	I	I
,,	BMC V	-	-	I	I
Regnald Guthfrithsson / Anlaf Sihtricsson	Circumscription Cross	-	-	I	I
Eadwi	BMC Id (HR3)	-	-	I	I
Edgar	Reform type	-	-	I	I
Aethelred II	Long Cross	-	-	I	I
,, (not in Corpus)	Last Small Cross	-	-	I	I
Edward the Confessor	Trefoil Quadrilateral/ Expanding Cross	I	-	-	I
,,	Expanding Cross	I	I	-	2
,,	Pointed Helmet	-	-	I	I
,,	Pyramids	I	-	-	I
Edward the Confessor / Harold II	Pointed Helmet / Pax	I	-	-	I
William I	BMC II	I	-	-	I
,,	BMC IV	2	-	I	3
,,	BMC V	2	-	I	3
,,	BMC IV/VI	I	-	-	I
,,	BMC VI	3	-	-	3
,,	BMC VII	13	-	(4)	17
,,	BMC VIII/VII	I	-	-	I
,,	BMC VIII	-	-	I	I
,,	uncertain type	-	-	(2)	2
William II	BMC II	I	I	-	2
,,	BMC III	-	-	I	I
,,	BMC V	-	-	I	I
Henry I (not in Corpus)	no details	?I	-	-	I
Stephen	BMC I	-	-	I	I
,,	BMC VII	I	-	-	I
Blanks		3	-	-	3
Pseudo-coin type based on William I, BMC VIII		I	-	-	I
		34	3	26	63

In the 'other sites' column (which includes the five unknown findspots) the numbers in brackets denote pieces found in a single group. The associations of the Billingsgate finds are discussed in the text.

4.7 Summary of finds by reign and type.

c.840. They were made by using silver pennies in the rôle of positive dies to impress their designs and inscriptions onto a lead sheet or blank. This technique gives incuse and mirror-image impressions on the lead. Both single-sided (4) and double-sided (1-3) pieces exist. The former could be produced using only one coin; the latter required the lead blank to be placed between two coins. As both coins could be positioned with either side towards the lead blank, double-obverses (1 and 2) and double-reverses (not yet noted) might arise. Some sort of cushioning would have been desirable to protect the coin or coins when the 'sandwich' was squeezed or hit with a hammer to create the impressions. Leather, say, or lead could have served equally well for this purpose, but lead would have maximized output by producing additional uniface pieces, if such were acceptable, in the one operation.

In view of the acknowledged incompleteness of the record of dies preserved on surviving pennies of this period, it is hardly surprising that none of the dies represented on the few incuse examples has yet been matched on the silver coins. The identity of both type and style between the pieces in the two metals leaves no doubt that currency coins were being used to make the lead pieces. Numbers 2 and 3, pairing types of Eadwald who reasserted East Anglian independence on the death of Offa in 796, and Coenwulf who soon restored Mercian supremacy, show that they were made from the range of coins in general circulation rather than produced exclusively from coins of the type currently in issue, and also that coins of the local king continued to circulate after his overthrow.

The incuse technique seems, on present evidence, to have been employed only and exclusively in the early period. This pattern is probably chronological, but it just might be geographical since all four early pieces are of East Anglian or Essex types. The Merovingian monetiform lead pieces, which probably inspired the use of such things in a similar context in England, were apparently struck in relief from coinage dies from the very beginning (see Fillon 1850, 216-7; Fillon 1858, 91-3; Prou 1886, 210-11; and Prou 1890, 346). The incuse English ones are unlikely however to have been forgeries of an official class which was already struck from coinage dies, as no struck ones at all survive among finds from three different places, and no such pieces are found later. An incuse technique may in fact have been deliberately chosen at first to differentiate

the lead pieces clearly from coins, so that they could not be passed off into circulation as silver pennies. It had disadvantages however in that it was a rather cumbersome process and could itself be easily counterfeited by anyone with a penny. It may be assumed that it was therefore abandoned in favour of striking the lead directly with official coinage dies, access to which was strictly controlled, not least by the self-interest of the moneyers.

None of this earliest group so far recorded is derived from coins believed to have been produced in London. This may well be fortuitous, but it should be borne in mind that nearly all the London finds have come from Billingsgate which was not in operation at this time. Lead pieces with London-sceatta types and late-eighth and early-ninth century broad-penny prototypes are potential from extra-mural Lundenwic.

The earliest extant English lead piece struck in relief is the Burgred of Mercia, 851-74, found at Tilbury (5). Like all the coins of this period, it is not mint-signed, but it belongs to a group attributed to London. There can be no doubt that the pieces in this series were struck and not cast, as the outline of the die is visible on several pieces which are either mis-struck badly off-centre or are on wide flans extending well beyond the outer circle of the coin-type. On some the outline is circular (the York examples 8, 9 and 11), but more characteristically it is rectangular with rounded corners (eg 6, 13 and 24), a shape which would facilitate the production of coins with a regular die-axis. The round form on the extant tenth-century pieces, both lead strikings and dies (Pirie 1986 pls V - X) is both preceded and followed by a rectangular form, but all the pieces from this period are from York or Chester, and the shape used may well have been a matter of regional practice or tradition rather than one of chronology. This would certainly be understandable in the tenth century when the English coinage itself was organized regionally, and before a unified nationwide system was instituted *c*.973. There is a continental parallel for this, for although the one surviving Carolingian die is round in outline (Pirie 1986 pl Xa), two large uniface lead pieces found at Dorestadt were struck with coinage dies of these same two different shapes (Volkers 1965, pl. G III, 202-3). One shows overlapping impressions of a rectangular die with rounded corners of a Christiana Religio temple design without mint signature which was the last issue of Louis the Pious, 814-40, but continued into the reign of his son Charles the Bald, 840-77. The other, from the earliest years of Charles the Bald, was struck with a single impression from a die of round outline from the mint of Paris. The issues of the first period of the coinage of Charles the Bald, like that of tenth-century England, was marked by a greater diversity of regionally-grouped types.

Excluding the irregular piece (60), the style of all the dies is, with the sole exception of the reverse of 16, that of the regal silver coinage and official dies were obviously being used. The obverse of 16 is from an official die, and this emergency - or illegally cost-saving - use of a home-made upper (reverse) die is also found occasionally in the coinage. Sometimes it is possible to match the dies with those of surviving coins (10, 17, 22a, 27, 48, 53 and 55), and it is likely that this list would have been longer had the lead pieces been in good enough condition for identities to be established with certainty. In two cases (27 and 55) a flaw appears in a more developed state on the lead piece showing that it was a later striking than the silver coin from the same die. The reverses of 27 and its silver die-duplicate BMC 417 are shown x2 in fig. 1; note that the flaw at the right-hand side of the lower limb of the cross is more developed on the lead piece. Some of the lead pieces are mules, eg between Edward the Confessor's Helmet type and Harold II (19), and between William I types IV and VI (26). Mules are found in the coinage but there the dies are usually from consecutive - or next but consecutive - types; a gap of four types, as in the case of the Edward/ Harold piece, is unheard of on coins of the Anglo-Saxon or Norman periods, although greater intervals between paired dies are known in the later medieval period.

The poor condition of many of the lead pieces makes it difficult to determine their original outline. A few (eg 53) seem to have been chopped out with a ring-punch after striking, following normal late Anglo-Saxon and early Norman coinage practice. More of them exhibit an angularity - characteristically, rectangular with the corners removed echoing the shape of the dies - which shows that they were cut out with a chisel or shears (22, 37, 47 and 56). It is possible that this shape was intended to differentiate them from the round silver pennies. Another feature of the lead pieces which was probably also designed to prevent confusion with coins, is that they are consistently both wider and heavier than contemporary pennies (see Fig 4.8). Pieces whose diameter

lead

silver

4.8. Comparison of silver and lead pieces struck with the same die.

has been enlarged by corrosion are discounted. Although many have lost weight by damage or corrosion, almost ninety per cent of them weigh above the coinage standard of their time. This is true even of the earliest of them, the sceat type (1) which weighs 1.33g at a period when the standard was about a gramme. A few are, at least as they survive, on flans smaller than those of contemporary pennies (eg 32 and 33).

In a number of instances, obverse and reverse are seriously out of register (34 and 56), suggesting that they were cut out after striking following the design of the upper side; in others, parts of several impressions from the same die are visible on both sides showing that the blank had been turned over between blows (15), and cut out in the same way after striking. Individual small pieces of lead or lead sheet could both have been used in the manufacturing process.

Metal

Eleven of these pieces have been analysed by XRF: ten from Billingsgate (15, 19, 24, 26-7, 29, 38 and 57-9) by Michael Cowell of the British

Museum Research Laboratory, and one from York (25) by the University of Bradford. All were found to be lead, with no alloying metals being detected. It should be noted that the composition of these pieces is different from that of the cores of silver-plated cliché forgeries which are not made of lead but of a tin, or tin-lead alloy, solder (Archibald and Oddy 1979).

Chronological Pattern

The bias in the provenances of the material, more than half of which come from Billingsgate, distorts the chronological pattern. Table 1 shows that, after allowing for this, the lead pieces occur fairly regularly throughout the period from their earliest known appearance in the second quarter of the eighth century until the early 1150s when they cease abruptly. It is noteworthy that one of the pieces (10) is from the Viking kingdom of York, emphasizing the continuity there from the examples in the name of Athelstan (8 and 9). The absence of examples from the reigns of Cnut and his sons could just be coincidental, but numbers do start to show a perceptible increase from the middle of the reign of Edward the Confessor, when the weight of the penny was raised and other administrative and design changes were being made in the coinage, and reach their highest representation in the later years of William I.

The earliest lead pieces from Billingsgate belong to the heavy issue of Edward the Confessor's Expanding Cross type usually dated to 1052-3, about half a century after the date once attributed to the first documentary reference to the site. The absence of earlier lead pieces might have been thought fortuitous, but the dendro-chronological evidence shows that the first timber structure on the wharf must be dated as late as 1039-40, in the reign of Harthacnut, and the revetment to c.1055, in the middle of the reign of Edward the Confessor. This fits very well with the numismatic evidence, given the greater rarity of issues of Harthacnut in terms of the coinage at least, and suggests a later start for the systematic use of the site than was formerly believed. The latest type from Billingsgate, the Stephen type VII, is the latest from anywhere, but Billingsgate continued to function after these lead pieces had ceased to be used.

The concentration of the Billingsgate material in types V, VI and - especially - VII of William I is particularly marked, but it is necessary to ask whether this represents a real increase in their use there in excess of the slight rise noted more generally at this time, or whether these figures are distorted by a group or groups deposited together. The seven pieces from the archaeological excavations were not individual finds: six (three of this

4.9. Summary of lead objects by findspot and mint.

Findspot	Total	Local mint	No	Other mint	No
Aveley, near Greys, Essex	4			uncertain	4
Canterbury, Kent	1	Canterbury	1		
Canvey Island, Essex	2	East Anglia	2		
Ipswich, Suffolk	1	East Anglia	1		
London, Aldersgate Street	1	London	1		
,,　　 Billingsgate	34	London	24	uncertain	10
,,　　 St Paul's churchyard	1	London ?	1		
,,　　 uncertain	1	London	1		
Richmond, Yorkshire	1			'Castle Rising'	1
Thetford, Norfolk	1	Thetford	1		
Tilbury, Essex	2	Essex	1		
		London (?)	1		
Winchester, Hants.	2	Winchester	1	East Anglia	1
Worcester	1	Worcester	1		
York, Coppergate	3	York	2	Chester ?	1
,,　　 Clifford's Castle area	3	York	1	uncertain	2
	58		39		19

period plus the group of three blanks) came from the same context and the remaining, earlier, piece was found in residual material whose origin is uncertain. The site context of the many pieces found on the spoil dumps is not known. Although the question cannot be fully answered, what we seem to have at Billingsgate is a series of individual losses over the century from 1052 to the early 1150s, with, in addition, a group of pieces deposited together during William I's type VII which may have included, like a contemporary coin hoard, a smaller number of pieces of the previous one or two types. The involvement of a dispersed group is the more likely since three moneyers including Edwi are represented on the lead pieces of type VI, but he alone is present on the more numerous type VII pieces among which there is also a high number of die-duplicates. Even allowing for this, there does seem to be a perceptible increase in volume during the later part of the reign of William I. It would also have been useful to know if the other apparently isolated losses from different periods were concentrated on parts of the Billingsgate site, even in one area, as this might have been indicative of their function, but there is no evidence on this.

Provenance

There is a strong correlation between the mint named on the fifty-eight provenanced lead pieces and the place where they were found, as shown in Table 2. Let us look at the apparent exceptions to this rule. The two Coenwulf pieces from Canvey Island were made from coins struck in East Anglia at a time when Essex appears not to have had a mint and when the whole area was subject to the Mercian king. In the case of the Athelstan I of East Anglia found at Winchester, the findspot is not certain, although it seems likely. A connection between the two places may not be so implausible as appears at first sight as there is a possibility, too complicated to discuss here, that the Athelstan of East Anglia, known to history only from his prolific coinage, may have been the documented West-Saxon prince of the same name who was sub-king of Kent under Æthelwulf, king of greater Wessex. Modern findspots along the Thames must always be somewhat equivocal as there has been so much dredging and transference of soil over the years, but the London coin of Burgred found at Tilbury - assuming it to have been an original deposit there - is apparently an exception. While London was Mercian, Essex is believed to have been in the control of Wessex at this time, although the case for continuity of West Saxon control might bear re-investigation.

The Aveley group are all virtually illegible although one of them might bear the name of Edwi, the London moneyer of the many Billingsgate finds of the same type. Accepting that this is a genuinely independent deposit despite the coincidence, it may be noted that London was the nearest operating mint to this findspot at the time, but a possible explanation for the group will be discussed with their function below. The non-local origin of the York lead strip will be considered there also.

The attribution of the Stephen type I coins by Bertold, where the mint-signature never gets beyond RI, to the Castle Rising mint is not beyond doubt. Wishing to avoid multiplying mints unnecessarily, students have assumed that these coins were struck at the same place as the pennies of Stephen type VII whose readings of RIS and RISINGE allow them to be attributed with confidence to Castle Rising. Bertold however is known only in type I. The discovery of the present lead piece on the river bank below the castle at Richmond (see note to 55 in the Corpus), a place beginning with RI which had been a borough since the time of Henry I, suggests that the possibility of attributing Bertold's coins to Richmond rather than Castle Rising should be considered. The coincidence of mints and findspots remains on any reckoning much closer than is normal among isolated coin-finds, and can only be a consequence of their function to which we must now turn.

Function

A number of possible functions have been proposed for examples of these lead pieces. The first is that they are simply forgeries of the current silver pennies made for circulation. They are certainly not further examples of the cliché-type forgeries (Mitchiner and Skinner 1985, nos 50-1), since they have now been shown to be struck pieces in lead, invariably without any trace of silvering, unlike the forgeries made by the cliché technique which have cast cores - a tin, or tin-lead, solder in the examples tested - covered by a repoussé silver-foil skin (Archibald and Oddy 1979). Another reason for rejecting the forgery theory is that the lead pieces under discussion were struck from official dies at several mints, and so it would be necessary to postulate that many moneyers, or people with access to their dies, were producing forgeries at all of them, and that at London Edwi, or a user of his dies, was able to produce forgeries with impunity in four successive types. It is also inconceivable that forgeries would be found so consistently only at the place named on them. The obvious physical differences between most of the lead pieces and coins as discussed above - their distinctive shape, and/or wider flans and higher weights - argue against the possibility of their being produced as forgeries for currency. The struck lead pieces may reasonably be assumed to have followed in the same rôle as the earlier incuse pieces which, as discussed above, are not themselves plausible as coin-forgeries. Finally, a forgery theory cannot explain why these lead pieces suddenly cease while other types of counterfeit continue unabated. The possibility that the lead pieces could have been used, or adapted for use, as forgeries if an opportunity presented itself to the unscrupulous, does not invalidate the argument that they were not made for that purpose.

Other rôles which have been proposed for examples over the years are trial pieces or record pieces (Dolley 1953 and Stewart 1978). The monetiform ones at least cannot be identified as pieces used to test the dies during their manufacture and before any coins were struck from them, as there are now several groups of duplicates, and in two instances the lead striking is demonstrably later than a silver penny from the same die (27, fig.1, and 55). The idea that they might have been made to record dies for archival purposes may be dismissed for similar reasons. The rejection of these rôles for the monetiform lead pieces has wider implications. If the Winchester piece, for example, is not a trial piece, then with it falls the evidence for a die-cutting centre at Winchester as late as the mid-1050s (Dolley 1953, 177-8). Whatever the interests of the family of the hereditary die-cutters in Winchester (Biddle et al 1976, 409-10) the testimony of Domesday Book that it was to London that the moneyers had to send for their dies when the money was changed may be accepted at face value, with its corollary that it was in London that the dies for the coinage were cut.

The York strip (11) has also been identified as a trial piece (Pirie 1986), but it has not been possible to explain why a trial piece struck from dies which are of West Mercian (Chester ?) type

should be found in York. This piece will be discussed later after the rôle of the other pieces has been considered.

Another possible function for the monetiform pieces is as predecessors of the later medieval jettons used with a chequer-board for accounting purposes. It is unlikely because there is no evidence of continuity in this field: the lead pieces stop abruptly in the 1150s and the first of the English jettons, in different metal, do not appear until the end of the thirteenth century. The evidence of the *Dialogus de Scaccario* (Johnson 1950, 25) suggests that in the twelfth century actual coins were used for this purpose.

As we have seen, these lead pieces were struck from official dies and so their function itself must have been official. This function must have been carried out in places all around the country and must also have been, for the most part, initiated and completed in the same town or city. These conditions would be satisfied if the lead pieces were a form of receipt given to those who had paid their royal dues, in particular customs dues, to one official so that they could demonstrate this fact to others. Before testing this hypothesis, it is helpful to look at the later evidence for customs receipts in both England and France.

In England, a written receipt known as a *visus compoti* (view of account) or more popularly as a cocket was given. The Oxford English Dictionary says that although its origin is obscure, the word cocket is a corruption of *quo quietus est* (by which he is quit). The cocket was a small piece of parchment with an official seal attached to it, detailing the total amount of customs received by the collector, and a statement of any sum still outstanding (discussed by Gras 1918, 157-8).

The French evidence is particularly instructive. There is a lead piece dated to the thirteenth century, not struck from coinage dies but similar to the early English examples in being rectangular in shape with the corners cut off, which has the explicit inscription, *aquite sui* (I am quit). Another lead piece of about the same date, again uniface but round, has the inscription *lesco liberes* (meaning something like, pay the tax). Both were found on the banks of the Seine in Paris (Forgeais 1866, 128-30). There seems no impediment to accepting French opinion that these are *méraux fiscaux*, tax or customs tickets. French students have, on analogy, attributed a similar function to the earlier lead monetiform objects struck from coinage dies dating from Merovingian times onwards.

There is also French documentary evidence which bears upon the question. A charter of the future Henry II of England given to Rouen *c.*1150 includes the provision *quod nullus eorum a vicecomite intersignia accepiat ad barrarium, sed ipse affidet barrario quod consuetudinem non debet* (that none of them - the citizens of Rouen - takes from the Vicount - the ruler's financial officer - intersignia for the [city] bar, but declares on oath at the [city] bar that he does not give - is not subject to - the [customs] charges (quoted by Beaurepaire 1878, 399-400); my attention was first drawn to this charter by a reference in a general article by M. Jacques Labrot shown to me by Dr Marcus Phillips, and I am grateful to them and to Madame Françoise Dumas, Librarian of the Institut de France for sending me a copy of the published text). Although French commentators have identified the *intersignia* with lead tickets, it has to be acknowledged that the context does not actually require them to be metal, and that the acceptance of the identification by the editor of Du Cange (vol. III, 3rd edn, 1844, 869) was no doubt influenced by the numismatistic opinion of his own day. Metal tickets were however certainly used for a closely similar purpose in France as is shown by a charter of 1167 to the Count of Nevers which referred specifically to tokens which conferred on those who possessed them the right to carry and cry their merchandise. This and other sources are discussed by Mitchiner and Skinner 1983, 33. In the light of these references and of the two very specific inscriptions on the two later lead pieces, it seems reasonable to suppose that the *intersignia* were lead tickets.

While written tax receipts survive from the Roman period in Egypt, certain lead tesserae have also been identified as such (Mitchiner 1984) although these did not use coin dies or reproduce their types. Examples of lead strikings from coinage-type dies in the Byzantine series are also recorded (Grierson 1982, as listed in the index, 409; Hendy 1985, 730, pl.30 and Oikonomides 1986,64-5) and have been characterized as emergency issues in place of other base-metal coins (Morrisson 1981). The latter explanation is not tenable for the English examples and their existence may prompt a wider reconsideration of the evidence.

To return to the early English lead pieces, we shall look first at the significance of their provenances. Billingsgate, the most prolific site by far, was the wharf in London where foreign merchants were obliged to show their merchandise and pay landing and customs dues. The Anglo-Saxon Billingsgate Tolls record in detail the grounding charges on ships of various sizes and import and export dues are set out on a wide range of goods. Another London find is significantly from Aldersgate Street, near one of the city gates where tolls were also collected. A number of other coastal or river-front sites including Ipswich and Worcester have also produced local examples. Two findspots were almost certainly, and one more very probably, at or near the places where these lead pieces and cognate coins were struck: at Coppergate in York the lead pieces were found in association with dies for other coins; Clifford's Castle, York, was the site of the later medieval mint and so a mint was probably in operation there in Norman times also (Hall 1983, 285), and Richmond Castle too might well have housed the local mint. The majority of the findspots are likely sites for either mints, customs or royal tax activities, with possibly more than one of these functions being carried out in the same place. No lead pieces have been recorded from *Hamwic* (Southampton) but, significantly, the waterfront area on the River Itchen has not so far been excavated.

Ancient secondary features displayed by some of the lead pieces support the view that they were used as receipts, and would be hard to reconcile with the other proposed functions. One specimen (23) has had a small wedge cut out of the edge, and another (58) has two such clips which appear to be signs of inspection or cancellation in the manner of a modern railway ticket. This second piece (58) also has a small hole, possibly so that it could be attached to the goods to which it referred.

The Billingsgate Tolls are silent about how the customs payments were actually collected and monitored, and there is no other early written evidence, but it is perhaps worth trying to suggest how the system might have worked. We may hypothesize that when a ship landed, the king's financial officer assessed the merchandise *in situ*, exacted what was due and gave the trader an official lead ticket as a receipt. The trader then had to present it as proof of his having paid the prescribed charges at some check point - at the exit from the port area, in the local market or at the city gates if he was taking his goods outside for sale. The ticket was inspected if he was going further or, if not, retained there, possibly being returned to the port area for re-use or passed back to the apparently restricted group among the moneyers with this side-line in lead ticket production as scrap for re-working. It is not known at this early period whether there was a retail market at Billingsgate to the north of the port area as there was later, or whether the goods landed were transported to other places in the city for sale (Archer *et al* 1988). The existence of such a market would have kept many tickets within the Billingsgate area, but their collection at a market elsewhere in the city or further afield is possible. It is again a matter for regret that the precise find-spots of all these Billingsgate pieces, which would have a bearing on this point, are not known. The lead pieces may thus be viewed as cockets before they had acquired documents as might have been appropriate in an earlier, more illiterate, period. It is possible however that they could have been accompanied by written receipts in the way it is known that loose seals were sometimes carried as authentication of a message and its bearer. This system seems to have been brought to an abrupt end, and presumptively succeeded by one based on cockets, by a reform of Henry II.

In the later middle ages, persistent attempts were made by the king to restrict initial imports to specific major ports in order to prevent evasion of customs. It was intended that appropriate charges would be exacted there and the merchant could then go on, armed with his cocket, to some smaller port to off-load finally. This system of a 'port' and its 'ports adjacent' or 'members' is discussed by Gras 1918, 105. Henry I forbade that any ship should ply at any hythe in Cambridgeshire except the hythe of the borough of Cambridge (Britnell 1978, 194), and Henry II gave similar orders for Lincoln, adding that this was to be done as in the time of his grandfather 'so that my reeves of Lincoln may not lose my customs' (Ballard 1913, 168). Carolingian kings had imposed similar restrictions. We may postulate the operation of such a system at an early period in England also on the strength of the discovery of London-struck lead pieces at Tilbury (Burgred) and probably at Aveley (William I), suggesting that the goods to which they referred had been shown at London, customs had been charged on them, and then their owners had gone off to land them on the Essex coast. We may therefore expect to find some of these lead pieces at sites other than the principal toll-points at which they were struck although the majority would not have passed outside these places. This model of a series of major regional centres with satellites is also found in other areas of Anglo-Saxon administra-

tion eg very early in the military arrangements of the Burghal Hidage, and later in the die-cutting centres for the supply of coinage-dies to minting places in the early eleventh century.

The royal officials concerned with the collection of the customs were the portreeves. From an early period, identities of name occur between the few portreeves who are recorded and contemporary moneyers. Although there is no proof that the same persons are involved, the coincidence is striking for the reign of Edward the Confessor at London. The names of all three of the known portreeves, Wulfgar, Leofstan and Ælfsige are also found as moneyers on the coinage; so is that of Ælfgæt the sheriff. (The names of these officials are taken from Brooke 1975, 193-7 and Appendix II.) This apparently places moneyers in a customs context closely related to that being proposed for them here in connection with the lead pieces, although so far the names of none of the few known portreeves have appeared on these objects. Unfortunately the names of no portreeves are recorded from later William I and William II when the lead pieces are at their most plentiful. The only portreeve known from these reigns, Gosferth who appears *c*.1067, has a name not found on the coinage. While the tally of both portreeves and makers of lead pieces is small, it may be significant that in London a maximum of two or three portreeves are known at any one time and a maximum of only three moneyers are named on the extant lead pieces in any one type. Much more evidence will be needed before the implications of this can be fully evaluated, but that there is some connection seems likely.

The cut-quarter (20) appears to indicate a requirement for the smaller denominations (eg to acknowledge payment of the standing dues of a halfpenny on small boats prescribed in the Billingsgate tolls at a time when the only denomination struck was the silver penny) and prompts the question whether there are any deliberate multiple denominations among the lead pieces? The poor condition of many of them reduces the number that can be used as evidence in this context and makes histograms of the weights thinner and more difficult to interpret, especially in view of the changing weight standards involved. Although there is a concentration at just above the weight of the penny, there is no evidence of low multiples. The weights vary widely and apparently randomly according to the thickness of the sheet from which they were cut.

Three pieces however stand apart from the

others in their markedly higher weight. The Alfred piece from St Paul's Churchyard (6) at 163.1g is quite accurately half a Roman pound, the equivalent of 120 silver pennies. The Æthelred II piece from Thetford (13) at 44.9g, is roughly the weight of thirty contemporary pennies, the equivalent of one gold mancus, also found as a common unit of value in contemporary financial transactions. The Edward the Confessor piece from Winchester (17) at 37.6g is again approximately on the same thirty-penny / mancus standard. Are these really weights, albeit more or less inaccurate, or are they too customs receipts, denominational or otherwise?

In an original charter dated to 1018 Eadnoth, bishop of Crediton, says that he has borrowed *XXX mancsa goldes be leadgewihte* - thirty mancuses of gold by lead-weight (Napier and Stevenson 1895, 9 and 77-8). The natural understanding of this passage is that the gold was weighed in a balance using a lead weight or weights. In the code of laws known as IV Æthelred the king orders under article 9.2 that market weights shall be the same as those at which his money is received. As the text has been transmitted in several differing twelfth-century Latin versions, there are considerable problems in arriving at a satisfactory reading of the original clause (Lyon 1969, 214), but it seems clear that the weights were to be stamped that fifteen ores make a pound. No such weights are yet known. A simple way of authenticating weights and at the same time keeping a check on their makers would have been to have them produced by the moneyers and impressed with coinage dies. The only possible candidates for this category of weights among the extant material are these heavy lead strikings from coinage dies.

Any discrepancies in the weights of the three lead objects under discussion need not necessarily be fatal to their being intended as weights, as later medieval objects which are certainly weights are often highly inaccurate. All three have deliberate cancellation marks of a sort not found on any of the smaller examples: cuts across the obverse on the Alfred, a score across the obverse and gouging on the reverse of the Æthelred, and gouging on the obverse of the Edward the Confessor. It might be supposed that since the weight-standards of consecutive coin types were not always the same, the practice grew up that each time the coin type was changed the weights of the old type were defaced and replaced by ones on the new standard struck with dies of the new type. The Alfred and the Edward pieces are beautifully finished but the Æthelred is very rough, and possibly explicable as an uncompleted 'waster' rejected because it was inaccurate. Lead objects found in Viking levels at Hedeby have been identified as weights and the two lead pieces found at Dorestadt have also been accepted as such by continental students. There is however a hole at the edge the Paris piece found in Dorestadt, and although this could be explained in a weight, its findspot so far from its place of issue might suggest that it had arrived attached to some merchandise. The very wide and thin discoid shape of these French pieces is also rather unusual for weights. While it is perhaps preferable to accept that these heavy pieces, especially the English ones, are indeed weights, they could also fit into a receipts system as proof of payment of higher amounts of customs or other regal taxation, reckoned in mancuses, marks or pounds. (The general run of the lead pieces cannot be weights, not least because their own weights are so erratic.)

We must now consider the two lead strips, one from Billingsgate (52) and the other from York (11). The Billingsgate piece is only about 10mm across at its widest point and the coin impression overlaps the edges. A narrow piece of metal this shape would have been an unlikely choice as a tester for a coin die. It had been bent double and narrows to a hook at one end which probably went through a slot, only a broken part of which survives at the wider end, and by this means, it is suggested, it was secured to the goods to which it referred as proof that dues had been paid on them. The York piece, although larger, appears to belong to the same category. It too had been bent double and narrows sharply at one end into a tag which has been broken off but which would have been used to secure it to its merchandise. This function would explain the West Mercian (Chester?) origin of a piece found in York. The trader arrived in Chester from, say, Ireland, was duly charged on his imported goods, and as he was not going to sell them locally, an official tag was attached to them to prove that he had paid. He then travelled to York, proved that he had already paid his dues and the tag was broken off and retained by the king's officer to prevent its being fraudulently re-used. The Coppergate site may have been the moneyer's workshop to which used lead pieces were taken as scrap for re-forming. Lead was a valuable commodity, sought after as a royal gift (Loyn 1962, 102-3), and would not have been just thrown away when it had served its purpose. Unlike the monetiform class of these lead pieces which were intended principally for local use, these customs tags were a different category employed for goods to which receipts could be attached and which were to be taken beyond the port of entry for sale elsewhere in the country.

The preference for another function for the York strip does not of course rule out the possibility of lead trial-plates elsewhere. Although there are no other English candidates, larger sheets of lead - one struck with multiple impressions of a reverse die of Svend Estridsen dated *c.*1070-4 found at Lund (Jensen 1983) and another rougher lump of lead from Hungary (Gedai 1986) have been proposed as trial pieces. The impressions on the first example appear, at least from the published illustration, to be struck in a ordered way and it may be that it represents a stage in the manufacture of such tickets. As these pieces were made by the moneyers also responsible for striking coins, it is predictable that they should be found in a known minting area or in the company of minting tools.

I hope to have made out a case for identifying most of these lead objects as customs receipts. If this interpretation is accepted, it offers a new type of evidence for the customs system in Anglo-Saxon and Norman England, and for the sophistication of its administration from an early date, not least in the City of London.

CORPUS

The lead pieces listed below are 'pennies' unless stated otherwise. The designs follow the standard coin-types and are not described unless they are abnormal. Inscriptions on all coins are given; illegible portions - enclosed by square brackets - are supplied from die-duplicates in better condition where possible. Each of the pieces has been compared with the others of its type, mint and moneyer in the corpus and the dies are different unless they are explicitly said to be the same as the obverse or reverse of another piece, or are uncertain or illegible. References are given to silver pennies struck from the same dies. The present maximum diameter or diagonal measurement is given for round, or nearly round, pieces; dimensions are quoted for those which are irregularly-shaped. The present location of pieces in publicly accessible collections is indicated; pieces cited from recent excavations may be expected to be acquired in due course by the local museum. Pieces marked by a star are illustrated in Figs 4.4-7 where they are given the same numbers as in the corpus. All the finds from London (except 23, 41 and 42 of which no photographs are available) appear on the plates. Even pieces in poor condition are illustrated to record them, since lead is such an unstable material that further deterioration is likely, and also to prevent the same pieces being noted as 'new' examples when they next re-surface. References are given to illustrations of pieces which have been published elsewhere if they are not included in the plates. For acknowledgments and bibliography of references see below.

A Impressed Type

Abbreviations used in the text:
d. = diameter
r. = radius
w. = width
o = obverse
R = reverse

1. Sceat*
Essex type, Rigold 1977 Series S (BMC type 47) *c.*720-30; double obv.
o: Female centaur (incuse and retrograde)
R: Female centaur (incuse and retrograde); different die to obv.

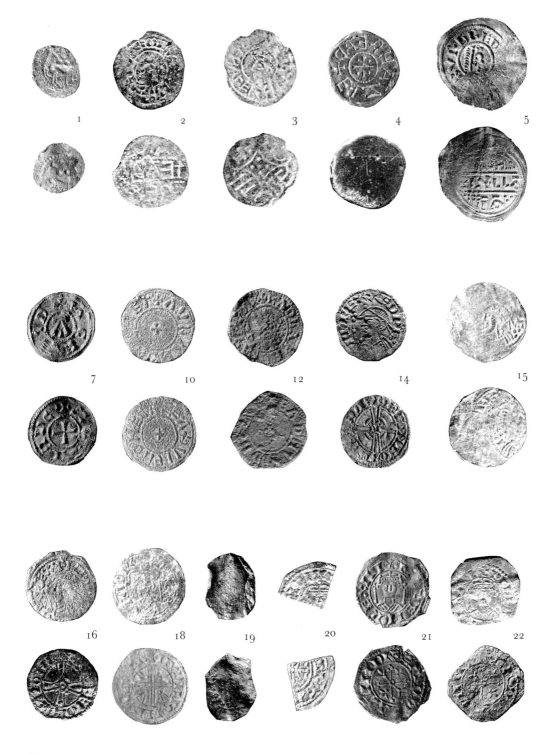

Fig. 4.10

1.33g; d. 15mm; 180°
North I, 121
Tilbury, Essex, 1986.
The reverse normally paired
with an obverse of this type is a
wolf whorl.

2. Coenwulf of Mercia, 796-821*
Portrait type, East Anglian mint
/ Eadwald of East Anglia, c.796-
8, Three Line type; double obv.
O: [+]COE[NVVLF REX] (incuse
and retrograde), same obv. as 3
R: AL[D] / +EADV / REX (incuse
and retrograde)
1.75g (chipped); d. 21mm; 90°
North I, 362/433
Canvey Island, Essex, 1988
Southend Museum

3. Coenwulf of Mercia, 796-821*
Portrait type, East Anglian mint
/ ?Eadwald of East Anglia,
c.796-98, Lozenge type, moneyer
Wihtred.
O: [+]COENVVLF / [REX] (incuse
and retrograde), same obv. as 2
R: [PI] / HT / RE / D[+] (incuse
and retrograge)
2.20g (chipped); d. 21mm; 315°
North 362/433; cf BLS Ea 3;
Canvey Island, Essex, 1987.
Southend Museum
This variety of the lozenge
reverse type is known for
Eadwald (cf BLS pl. VI, 3, a
different die of this variety) but
not for Coenwulf. Although it is
not possible to be certain
without matching this die on a
penny of Eadwald, it would
appear that this lead piece is a
mule between the same two
coins as the previous one: the
first of Coenwulf and the second
of the local king Eadwald whom
he overthrew to restore Mercian
power in East Anglia.

4. Athelstan I of East Anglia,
c.821/5 - c.840; uniface, obv.
only.*
O: AD +ELSAN RE (incuse and
retrograde)
13.62g; d. 21mm, w. 4mm; 0°
(as shown)
North I, 446 (var.)
Said to have been found at
Winchester, before 1950.

The present owner, Mr
J.Furner, acquired this piece
c.1950 in a miscellaneous group
of coins and jettons from a man
who told him that they had been
found by his late father, while
employed as a gardener by the
Bishop of Winchester, in the
latter's garden. It is no longer
possible to check this account.
This piece has the same reading
as the obv. of a penny in Leiden,
Netherlands, (Pagan, 1982,
p.61, no.VI), but although the
die is very similar it is not
identical. The author is grateful
to Dr Gay Van der Meer of the
Royal Coin Cabinet, Leiden,
who supplied photographs for
comparison. The reverse of the
Leiden coin is by the moneyer
Mon(ne); it has a plain cross
within the inner circle and
circumscription legend +MON
MON ET.

B Struck Type

5. Burgred of Mercia, 852-74
Lunette type a, not mint-signed
but probably London, moneyer,
Lulla.*
O: BVRGRED [REX]
R: MON / +LULLA / ETA, some
evidence of over-striking
3.78g; d. 26mm; 180°
North I, 423
Fitzwilliam Museum,
Cambridge, ex C.E.Blunt
collection.
Tilbury, Essex, 1986.
Part of the edge of the dies
(angled outline) is visible,
especially on the rev.

6. Alfred of Wessex, 871-99
BMC V, Cross and Lozenge, not
mint-signed but probably
London, moneyer, Ealdulf, c.875
or later; block of lead,
rectangular with rounded
corners, sides slightly concave.*
(See Fig 7.)
O: [+ÆLFRE] / D REX, outline of
die visible: rectangular
c.27 × 25mm with rounded
corners; defaced by two parallel
cuts across lower part of bust.

R: [+E] / AL / DV. / LF, outline
of die visible, rectangular
c.27 × 25mm with rounded
corners; gouging marks or just
corrosion?
163.1g; 37 × 34 × 14mm; 270°
Lyon 1968, pp.234; Stewart
1978, p.186.
Found in 1840 in St Paul's
churchyard, at the corner of
Canon Alley which formerly led
north from the churchyard into
Paternoster Row, London
(Gentleman's Magazine. 1841,
pp.244-5 and 498); presented to
the British Museum by C.Roach
Smith.
The weight of this piece is
close to half of that calculated
for the Roman pound (approx.
327g). For a discussion of Anglo-
Saxon weight systems see Lyon
1969, pp.204-22. Cf 13 and 17
for gouge marks on other heavy
pieces in the same catagory.

7. St Edmund Memorial Coinage
Post-Cuerdale type, East
Anglian mint, moneyer
uncertain, c.905-10.*
O: +SCEAID (S on its back;
slightly double-struck)
R: +A[ ]EEDC (ES retrograde)
2.2g; d. 19mm; 270°
North I, 483:1
Excavations at Ipswich, Suffolk,
1987.

8. Athelstan, 924-39
BMC IV, York, moneyer,
Adelbert, after 927; uniface, rev.
only.
O: AD(or Ð)EL[BERT], outline of
round die visible
3.10g; fragment,
c.20mm × 16mm; curved edge of
die visible
North I, 683; Pirie 1986, p.55,
No 48 (illustrated pl.VIa)
Excavations at Coppergate,
York, 1980.

9. Athelstan, 924-39
BMC V, York, moneyer, Regnald,
after 927; uniface, rev. only.
O: +REGNALD. MO EFORPI (L is
an inverted T), outline of round
die visible.

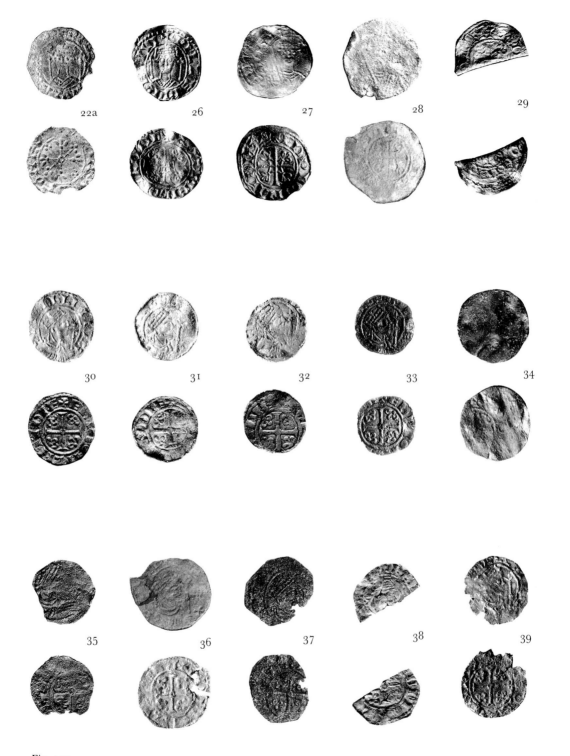

Fig. 4.11

6.20g; d. 30mm; three of the lay-out pellets beyond outer circle and a small arc of the edge of the round die visible
North I, 683; Pirie 1986, p.56, No 51 (illustrated pl.VIb)
Excavations at Coppergate, York, 1981.

10. Viking Kingdom of York
temp. Anlaf Sihtricsson, 941-4, moneyers Aura and Rathulf; double rev.*
O: +AVRA MO[NITR]E, same die as *SCBI* Glasgow 524 (of Regnald Guthfrithsson, *c*.941-3)
R: +RAÐVLF MOHETA, same die as *SCBI* Copenhagen 641 (of Anlaf Sihtricsson)
3.86g; d., 20mm; 135°
North I, 547/541; *SCBI* BM V, 1255
Find-spot unknown
presented to the British Museum by A.W.(later Sir Augustus) Franks in 1876.

11. Eadwi, 955-9
BMC Id (HR3), N.W. Mercian mint, probably Chester, moneyer, Frothric; lead strip rounded at one end, with a narrow neck at the other, broken off; bent double when found, obv. inside as illustrated in Pirie 1986, pl.VIII.
O: impressions of an obv. and a rev. die, both round-headed, one towards each end of the strip: i) +EADVVIG RE and ii) rosette / FROÐ / O + O / RIC M / rosette; outline of round die with lay-out pellets in margins outside the outer circle visible in each case
R: faint impression of i) above, not in register with ii), but towards the same end of the strip
71.95g; 153 × 44 × 1-2mm; Pirie 1986, pp.35-6 and p.57, No 59 (illustrated pl.VIII)
Excavations at Coppergate, York, 1981.

12. Edgar, 959-75
Reform type, London, moneyer, Eadmund, *c*.973-5.*

O: +E.A.GAR REX_ANGLOX
R: +EA.D.MVND M O LVN
1.89g (broken and mended); d. 21mm; 180°
North I, 752; BM E4299
Find-spot unknown
Purchased by the British Museum in 1838.

13. Ethelred II, 978-1016
Long Cross, Thetford, moneyer, Manna, *c*.997-1003, roughly rectangular block. (See Fig 7.)*
O: +ÆÐELRÆD REX AI, faint outline of die, rectangular with rounded corners
R: +MA [NA] MOÐ EOD, outline of die, rectangular with rounded corners
44.86g; max. diagonal, *c*.44mm, *c*.35 × 33 × 7mm with one rounded corner and the others ragged and unfinished; 180°.
North I, 744
Thetford, Norfolk, 1982; shown at the British Museum. Fitzwilliam Museum, Cambridge, ex Grierson collection, bought in the USA. There is gouging on both the obverse and the reverse which looks deliberate rather than accidental (*cf* 6 and 17), and the patination suggests that these marks are old.

14. Edward the Confessor, 1042-66
Expanding Cross (heavy issue, bust d), London, moneyer, Lifinc, *c*.1051-3.*
O: × EDPE: / RD REX
R: +C.IFINC ON L[V]NDI
1.46g; d. 20mm; 270°
North I, 823
Billingsgate spoil, 1983
Fitzwilliam Museum, Cambridge ex C.E.Blunt collection.

15. Edward the Confessor
Expanding Cross (heavy issue, bust d), *c*.1051-3; double obv.*
O: [+EADP]E / [RD REX]
R: Two imperfect off-centre impressions of the same die as the obv.
2.93g; d. 22mm; analysed

British Museum: lead
North I, 823
Excavations at Aldersgate St, London, 1984: ALG 84 [+] 2
Museum of London
This piece was first struck twice with the same die on one side (the reverse) and then, after the blank or sheet of lead has been turned over, was struck, still with the same die, on the other side (the obverse). There is no trace of any reverse die having been used. The piece has been cut out centring on the last (obverse) striking so that the reverse strikings are far off-centre.

16. Edward the Confessor
official Trefoil Quadrilateral obv. die with unofficial Expanding Cross rev. die, London, moneyer, Aelfwi, *c*.1050.*
O: +ED[PA] / .R REX.
O: [ ]LFI ON [ ]NDONI [ ] The N before D retrograde.
2.86g; d. 20mm; 270°
North I, 817 /820
Billingsgate spoil, 1984
The obverse appears to be a normal Trefoil Quadrilateral die rather than an Expanding Cross bust b variety which is confined to North Eastern mints; it is possible that the user knew that it would be a plausible obv. to use with a rev. die of the Expanding Cross type.

17. Edward the Confessor
Pointed Helmet, Winchester, moneyer, Aestan, *c*.1053-5.*
O: +EDPER. / D REX, same die as BMC 1412
R: +AESTAN ON PINCESTI, same die as BMC 1406
37.61g; d. 23mm; 5mm; 270°
North I, 825; Dolley 1953 pp. 175-8, pl. VI,3.
Excavations at Middle Brook Street, Winchester, 1953. Winchester City Museum.
The obverse is defaced by a small gouging mark *cf* 6 and 13.

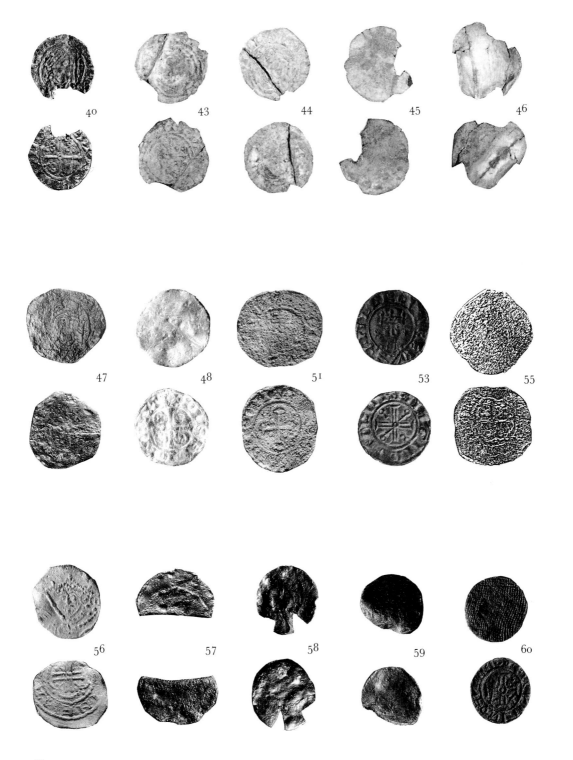

Fig. 4.12

18. Edward the Confessor
Pyramids, London, moneyer,
Dudinc, c.1063-66. The dies'
style is rough but is probably
official as some coins are
similar.*
O: +EADPARD REX
R: +IIVDNC ON LVNDII
1.52g; d. 20mm; 0°; analysed
British Museum: lead
North I, 831
Billingsgate spoil, 1985

19. Edward the Confessor
Pointed Helmet / Harold II,
1066, Pax, mint and moneyer
uncertain; double obv. Little is
visible on this crumpled piece
except the form of the two busts
whose identification is certain.*
0.89g; d. c.19mm; c.0°;
analysed British Museum: lead
North I, 825;
Excavations at Billingsgate,
1982 (in residual material): BIG
82 [4064] 2779
Museum of London

20. William I, 1066-87
cut quarter, BMC II, London,
moneyer, Ordgar, 1068-
c.1070.* (The dates for the
issues of William I and William
II here follow North, but there
is some reason to believe that
BMC VIII of William I may in
fact be the first type of William
II, with consequential
adjustments being required in
the dating of the types.)
O: [+PIL]LELM[VS REX]
R: [+O]RDGA[ ]
0.34g; 15mm; c.270°
North I, 843
Billingsgate spoil, 1985
The diameter of this piece
appears to be large, but this is
explained by some of the dies of
this type being a little wider
than normal, compounded by
the effects of corrosion. The
earliest known silver pennies of
Ordgar are of BMC type III;
this lead piece suggests that he
was already active in the
previous type.

21-2. William I
BMC IV, London, moneyer,
Eadwi, c.1072-4.
O: +PILLEM REX AI, same die as
26, a BMC IV/VI mule using a
rev.die of the moneyer Eadred
R: +EADPI [O]N LVNDI
North I, 844
Billingsgate spoil, 1983

No.21 2.51g; d. 22mm; 180°;
Mitchiner and Skinner 1985,
pl.41, 51 (this coin)*

No.22. 2.63g; rectangular
outline, 19 × 19mm; 225°. The
outline of this piece is
rectangular with the corners
cut off.*

22a. William I
BMC IV, York, moneyer
Hartholf, c.1072-4.*
O: +PIL[LEM RE]X A[NGL?]
R: +HARÐ[OL]F ON EO[ ]
1.27g (chipped); d. 19mm; 90°
North I, 844; same obv. die as
BMC 290 of same moneyer.
Find spot unknown
presented to the British
Museum by B.A.Seaby Ltd
in1931. See note on 49-50
below.

23. William I
BMC V, mint and moneyer
uncertain, c.1074-77. Coin not
examined by the writer;
included on basis of reference
below.
O: +[PILLE]M REX AN[?]
R: illegible; too little is visible
on the plate to see whether or
not it is from the same die as 24
1.38g; d. 19mm; die axis
uncertain
North I, 845; Mitchiner and
Skinner 1985, pl.41, 50.
Billingsgate spoil, before 1985.
A small wedge has been
deliberately cut out of the edge
cf 58.

24. William I
BMC V, London, moneyer,
Eadwi, c.1074-77. (See Fig 4.)*
Both visible sides struck from
the same die [+E]DPI ON
LIIN[DI]; the outline of the die,

rectangular with corners cut
off, is visible on both sides
7.76g; irregular outline,
c.33 × 29mm; analysed British
Museum: lead
North I, 845
Billingsgate spoil, 1983.
This piece is made up of four
layers of lead. There are traces
of at least three strikings by the
same die on one side, and two
on the other. It is possibly a
group of four double-sided lead
pieces squeezed together.

25. William I
BMC V, York, moneyer, Alief,
c.1074-77.
O: +PILLEM REX III
R: +ALE[I]F ON EF[RPNI]
1.37g (chipped and break
repaired); d. 20mm; 135°;
analysed University of
Bradford: lead
SCBI Yorkshire 759; same dies
as Lockett 945.
Clifford Street, York, acquired
by the Yorkshire Museum in
1894. See note on 49-50 below.

26. William I
BMC IV/VI, London, moneyer,
Eadred, c.1077-80.*
O: +PILLEM REX AI, same die as
21 and 22 above with a reverse
by the moneyer Eadwi
R: +EIIDRED ON LIIND
1.67g; diameter, 21mm; 90°;
analysed British Museum: lead
North I, 844/846;
Excavations at Billingsgate,
1982: BIG 82 [6978] 3617
Museum of London
Eadred is a rare moneyer,
hitherto known at London only
from a coin of the same type,
but from a different die, in the
Yorkshire Museum (SCBI
Yorkshire 1217). A moneyer of
this name appears at the Hythe
mint in BMC VIII.

27. William I
BMC VI, London, moneyer,
Edwi, c.1077-80.*
O: +PILLE[LM REX]
R: +EDPI ON LIINDII, double
struck, same die as BMC 417
1.79g; d. 21mm; 180°;

6   13   24

52

Fig. 4.13

analysed British Museum: lead
North I, 846;
Excavations at Billingsgate,
1982: BIG 82 [6978] 3392
Museum of London
This lead piece is a later
striking from the reverse die, as
a flaw has developed at the
right hand side of the lower
limb of the cross, less visible on
the silver penny. For × 2
illustrations see Fig 4.8.

28. William I
BMC VI, London, uncertain
moneyer (possibly Edwi on
spacing but dies different from
all others in the type),
c.1077-80.*
O: illegible
R: [ ]D[ ]ND[ ]
3.81g; d. 23mm; die axis
uncertain
North I, 846
Billingsgate spoil, 1985.

29. William I
BMC VI, London, moneyer,
Godwine, c.1077-80. Bent
almost double, obv. inside.*
O: illegible
R: + GODPINE ON LUN
1.59g; d. 21mm; die axis
uncertain; analysed British
Museum: lead
North I, 846;
Excavations at Billingsgate,
1982: BIG 82 [6978] 3618
Museum of London

30-5. William I
BMC VII, London, moneyer,
Edwi, c.1080-83; all from the
same pair of dies except obv. of
34 uncertain. All*
O: + PILLELM REX
R: + EDPI ON LVNDNE (N and E
ligatured)
North I, 847

30.   1.43g   19mm   0°
        Billingsgate spoil
        1984

31.   1.84g   19mm   180°
        Billingsgate spoil
        1985

32.   1.58g   18mm   180°

Billingsgate spoil
In or before 1986

33.   1.40g   17mm   180°
        Billingsgate spoil
        1984

34.   2.15g   20mm   uncertain
        Billingsgate spoil
        1984, obv. illeg. rev. very
        off-centre, but same die as
        others

35.   1.08g   18mm   90°
        Billingsgate spoil
        In or before 1987 (chipped)

36. William I
BMC VII, London, moneyer,
Edwi, c.1080-83.*
O: [+PI]LL[ELM RE]X, same die
as 37
R: +EDPI ON LVNDNE (N and E
ligatured), same die as 38
1.58g (broken but complete);
d. 20mm; 0°
North I, 847
Billingsgate spoil, 1985.
Numbers 36-38 may all be from
the same pair of dies but the
condition of the pieces makes it
impossible to be certain.

37. William I
BMC VII, London, moneyer
probably Edwi, c.1080-83.*
O: [+P]ILLELM [REX], same die
as 36
R: illegible
wt not recorded, chipped; flan
rectangular, 19 × 16mm, with
corners cut off; die axis
uncertain
North I, 847
Billingsgate spoil, 1984.

38. William I
BMC VII, London, moneyer,
Edwi, c.1080-83.*
O: + PILLELM [REX]
R: [+E]DPI ON L[VNDNE], same
die as 36
0.71g (broken fragment, about
half); d. 19mm; 180°
North I, 847
Billingsgate spoil
Presented to the British
Museum by Mr M.R.Allen in
1986.

39. William I
BMC VII, London, moneyer
probably Edwi, c.1080-83.*
O: [+P]ILLE[LM] REX
R: [+]E[ ] ON LIINDNE (N and
E ligatured)
1.45g (chipped); d. 19mm; 90°
North I, 847
Billingsgate, spoil, 1982;
Presented to the British
Museum by Mr T.G.Webb-
Ware in 1987.

40. William I
BMC VII, London, moneyer,
Edwi, c.1080-83*
O: [+PI]LLELM REX
R: [+E]DPI ON LIID[ ]
0.96g (chipped); a tiny
deliberate piercing at edge
above head; d. 18mm; 180°
North I, 847
Find-spot unknown, but
probably Billingsgate spoil;
shown at the British Museum,
1987.

41-2.William I
BMC VII, inscriptions illegible,
c.1080-83:

41. 1.67g   diameter and die axis
             unrecorded
             Billingsgate spoil
    1984

42. 1.03g   Billingsgate spoil
    1984

Shown at the Museum of
London; neither the lead pieces
nor photographs were
examined by the author.

43-6.Four lead pieces of William I
BMC VII, c.1080-83, chipped and
broken, found - crumpled
together - at Aveley, near
Greys, Essex, in a field a short
distance from the north bank of
the Thames; d. c.20mm.
It is possible that 43 could be of
Edwi, and therefore,
presumptively, of London but
as the pieces were in very poor
condition and only
photographs were examined, it
is not possible to be certain.
There is no evidence that any

spoil from Billingsgate was dumped at this site, and the findspot was reliably reported to Mr J.Bispham. All*

47. William I
BMC VIII/VII, uncertain mint and moneyer, c.1083-86.*
O: and R: inscriptions illegible.
3.51g; d. 22mm; die axis uncertain
North I, 848/847
Billingsgate spoil, in or before 1986.

48. William I
BMC VIII, Canterbury, moneyer, Winedi, c.1083-86.*
O: illegible
R: +PINEDI ON CNTI, same die as BMC 563
3.78g; d. 20mm; c.135°
North I, 848
Found in excavations at the Aula Nova site in 1977, just inside the main gate of the Priory of Christ Church, Canterbury, very close to the archbishop's palace, and a short distance from the north gate of the city, through which the road went to Fordwich, the port of Canterbury.
Winedi, who also worked at Romney where the archbishop held property, was probably an archiepiscopal moneyer. A full discussion by the author will appear in the forthcoming excavation report.

49-50. William I
Uncertain type(s), described as 'two leaden imitations of coins of William the Conqueror'.
Hall 1983 quoting Benson and Platnauer 1902.
Found during the under-pinning of Clifford's Tower, York, 1902.

The present whereabouts of these pieces is not known, but the William I of BMC type IV of York presented to the British Museum in 1931 (22a) whose findspot and date of discovery are unknown might possibly be one of them. A third lead piece

of William I, of BMC V, had previously been found in the same part of the city, in the area of Clifford's Tower, in 1894 (25).

51. William II, 1087-1100
BMC II, London, moneyer, Bate, c.1089-92.*
O: +PILLELM REX
R: +BIITE ON LIINDN
3.20g (corroded); d. 24mm; 270°
North I, 852
Find-spot unknown.
This piece was presented to the British Museum in the mid-nineteenth century by C. Roach Smith, most but not all of whose material came from London, so it is probable that it too was found there.

52. William II
BMC II, mint name illegible but moneyer Wulgar worked at several mints including London, c.1089-92; probably uniface; lead strip struck in centre with rev. die, one straight edge of which is visible; the thinner end (c.8mm wide) is hooked, which looks an original feature; the other (c.10mm wide) is broken off, but may have had a slot in it. The piece had been bent over double in the centre and then re-flattened. (See Fig 7)*
O: [+PV]LGAR ON [ ]
11.45g; 65 × 16 × c.1mm
North I, 852
Billingsgate spoil, early 1980s. acquired by the British Museum from Mr J.Hedges, 1988.

53. William II
BMC III, London, moneyer, Algar, c.1092-95.*
O: +PILLELM REI
R: +IILGIIR ON LIIN
3.03g; d. 20mm; 270°
North I, 853; same dies as British Museum coin 1925-2-1-1.
Find-spot unknown
Presented to the British Museum by L.A. Lawrence, 1924.

54. William II
BMC V, Thetford, moneyer, Godric, c.1098-1100.
O: +PILLELM RII
R: GODRC ON ÐTFR
4.51g; d. 21mm; die axis uncertain
North I, 856; Stewart 1978, pp.185-87, pl.36, E1.
Find spot unknown.

55. Stephen
BMC I, attributed in the standard works to Castle Rising, but see above discussion of the possibility that the mint is Richmond, Yorks., moneyer Bertold, 1135-c.1142. Enlarged photographs only examined on which details are clearer than on reduction on plate.*
O: +STIEFNE [:]
R: [+]BERTOLD ON [ ]
6.3g; outline c.21mm square with corners rounded off; 270°
North I, 873; same dies as British Museum coin 1921-5-19-170.
Bank of the river Swale below the castle at Richmond, Yorks., 1987.
The finder Mr G.D.Austin has kindly told me that in 1855 when the North York Rifles were laying out a parade ground inside the castle, they breached the walls and constructed a shute to dispose of the surplus soil onto the river bank below. Other coins and artifacts have been found in the same general area of this dump as the lead piece.

56. Stephen
BMC VII, mint and moneyer uncertain, c.1152-4*
O: illegible
R: [+]INEMA[ ]
2.51g; d. 21mm, angular outline, rev. off-centre; 180°
North I, 881
Billingsgate spoil, in or before 1986.

The obverse die cannot be matched, but the visible letters on the rev. suggest an expansion to 'Wineman'. The only recorded moneyer of this name is Winman of Salisbury, whose name is spelt differently and whose mint does not seem likely for a London find. Knowledge of type VII is very incomplete, and further as yet unrecorded moneyers at London and elsewhere are potential.

57-9. Three pieces with no visible designs, probably blank; all found in excavations at Billingsgate, 1982; analysed in British Museum, all lead; BIG 82 [6978] 3614-3616; Museum

of London:
All*

57. 1.72g d. 21m; about a third bent over double

58. 1.99g d. 18mm; pierced, two small wedges deliberately cut out of the edge cf 23

59. 1.48g d. 17mm; bent

60. Pseudo-coin type
R: loosely based on William I, BMC type VIII, London, moneyer, Godwine, prototype c.1083-6.*

O: impression of cloth, large chevron-barred A scratched into lead
R: + GODPINE ON LVNDI (retrograde)
1.29g; d. 17mm; 180°
North I, 848.
Billingsgate spoil, 1984.

The writer has examined only a photograph of this piece. Geoffrey Egan of the London Museum kindly examined the photograph and said that this object is not a bale seal.

Acknowledgements

I wish to acknowledge with gratitude the help of the following:

a) who have shown lead pieces at the British Museum and/or the Museum of London and have given permission for them to be included here; as the same pieces were often shown more than once by different people, they are not individually attributed:

M.R.Allen, G.D.Austin, J.Bispham, the late C.E.Blunt, G.Blunt, K.Bellringer, F.Bullard, M.Butcher, D.Elliot, B.Farrow, J.Furner, J.Gilbert, J.Hedges, D.Morgan, H.Norris, B.Parkinson, A.Pilson, Dr D.Rogers, A.Stewart, R.Varnham, T.G.Webb-Ware, J.Wood.

b) excavation directors and museum colleagues, other than those already mentioned above, who have given permission for unpublished lead pieces in their care to be included, or have helped in other ways:

Prof.T.V.Buttrey, Keeper of Coins and Medals, Fitzwilliam Museum, and M.A.S.Blackburn,

Cambridge (13; also 5 and 15 formerly in the collection of the late C.E.Blunt who had given permission for them to be included here); K.Crowe, Southend Museum (2 and 3); D.Dawson, Oxfordshire Museum Service, formerly of Canterbury Museum; Miss B.Green and Dr S.Margeson, Norwich Museum; Mrs E.Hartley, The Yorkshire Museum, for allowing 25 to be analysed; Dr M.Mays, The Yorkshire Museum, for drawing 52 to my attention; Miss E.J.E.Pirie, Leeds City Museum; Dr T.Tatton-Brown, former Director of the Canterbury Archaeological Trust and Mrs P. Garrard of the Canterbury Archaeological Trust (48); K.Wade and J.Newman, Suffolk Archaeological Trust (7).

c) who have discussed the problems of these pieces with me, in addition to those named above and throughout the text:

J.D.Brand; T.Dyson, Museum of London; Dr Marcus and Mrs S. Phillips; especially Dr J.P.C. Kent, Keeper of Coins and Medals, British Museum.

5.i EARLY MEDIEVAL PLANT USE AND ECOLOGY

Glynis Jones, Vanessa Straker and Anne Davis

This section brings together botanical evidence from early medieval deposits at a number of sites (Milk Street, Watling Court, Well Court, Peninsular House and Ironmonger Lane) in the City of London (see Fig 1.2). A range of feature types, including pits, occupation layers and hearths/ovens dating from the 9th or 10th to the 12th centuries, were sampled for plant remains. A total of 106 samples was taken of which 82 were from pits, and 12 each from occupation layers and hearths/ovens (Fig 5.1). Methodological problems are discussed in Appendix 5.1. Plant remains recovered from the samples are listed in Figs 5.4-5.15.

Plant Ecology and Human Activities

The exploitation of different plant species (wild, cultivated and imported) by the city dwellers of this period is discussed in Appendix 5.2. In conjunction with the ecology of some of these plants, it may be possible to throw light on some of the activities associated with the features from which they came (cf. Knörzer 1984).

Some wild plants exhibit fairly catholic habitat preferences and so provide little ecological information. Therefore, taxa which show a preference for more than three of the natural habitat groups listed in Appendix 5.2 were not considered further. Moreover, taxa which show a distinct preference for only one of the habitats listed were considered separately from those with broader preferences. The way in which taxa were classified is shown in Fig 5.16. Taxa were similarly classified according to their definite or potential uses (Fig 5.17).

Weed species are potentially the most useful group of plants for investigating local activities but they are probably also the most difficult to interpret, since many of them are tolerant of a particularly wide range of habitats, and detailed work on the ecology of weed species in Britain is badly needed (cf. Hall *et al* 1983). Nevertheless, weed species which do show a preference were further classified according to their preference for (or tolerance of) arable land (including species of the class *Secalinetea*), gardens (including species of the order *Polygono-Chenopodietalia*), very high nitrogen situations such as dung hills (including species of the order *Sisymbrietalia*) and heavily trodden ground such as paths and tracks (including species of the association *Lolio-Plantaginetum*) (Fig 5.18).

As most surviving literature and documentary evidence deals with large estates or church property, we know little about the use of garden or yard space in medieval towns and villages. In this area, therefore, archaeobotanical study can make a useful contribution to our knowledge of everyday life in early medieval London. Accordingly, cultivated plants and potential cultivars were further classified by their likely place of cultivation, ie. in fields, gardens or 'orchards' (Fig 5.18). Since many plants are grown for their edible leaves, stems or roots, which are not easily recognisable, most of the evidence for these plants comes from seed collected for propagation or plants accidentally allowed to 'go to seed'.

The sub-classifications of weeds and cultivars were based on a variety of sources, notably Braun-Blanquet (1936), Tüxen (1950), van Zeist (1974) but see also Jones (1958 and 1961), Bates (1935) and Bayliss (1963). Calculations were performed firstly using taxa which could be accurately identified to a single species or group of closely related species and secondly using less accurately identified taxa which, nevertheless, could be at least tentatively identified to a genus or closely related pair of genera. The former calculations were therefore based on a few accurately identified taxa and the latter on larger numbers of less accurately identified taxa. With few exceptions, the results of these two sets of calculations were broadly similar and further discussion is confined to these consistent results. Moreover, interpretations are based on associations of taxa rather than isolated occurrences of individual taxa.

Site	no. of samples:		
	from pits	from occupation layers	from hearths/ ovens
Milk Street	58 (24)	4	0
Watling Court	18 (6)	3	0
Peninsular House	4	3	3 (2)
Well Court	0	0	9 (2)
Ironmonger Lane	2	2	0

5.1 Distribution of samples according to feature type. In some cases several samples were taken from a single feature. The numbers in parentheses show the number of features sampled. In all other cases only one sample was taken per feature.

This investigation of human activities can probably best be achieved by considering the plant remains in relation to the types of feature from which they are derived. Each feature type will, therefore, be discussed in turn.

Pits

Pits make up the majority of features from which plant remains were recovered (see Fig 5.1) and they probably have the greatest range of possible functions of any feature type regularly encountered in urban excavations. They can be used as cess pits, for dumping household refuse and for temporary storage of commodities such as composting 'fertiliser' (Monk 1977). In addition, if they are left open, they also receive plant material through natural means.

Most of the pits considered here seem to have received plant remains from a variety of sources but it is possible, in some cases, to suggest a predominant function.

Some pits have a high proportion of plants from waste places, gardens or other disturbed ground, suggesting that they received most of their material from the surrounding area – an indication that they may have been uncovered. Potential garden cultivars (such as opium poppy, flax, dyer's rocket, celery, probable fennel and possible 'brassicas') were also found in these pits suggesting that there may have been cultivated areas nearby. Most of them also contained quantities of small fruit pips suggesting that they may have served partly as cess pits.

Other pits have a greater proportion of fruit pips suggesting that their primary function was

as cess pits. Some of these, and other pits, have quantities of sedge and/or rush seeds which may have come into town with flooring material which was later discarded in the pits. Large quantities of elder seeds were also found in some pits but it is impossible to say whether these were the remains of food, waste from tanning, or had simply got into the pits from nearby bushes. Weeds of waste places or gardens, in some pits, included 'dung-hill' weeds which may have grown around the edge of cess pits or may indicate the accumulation nearby of dung for use as fertiliser.

Three more pits provide the best examples of cess pits, containing many seeds which have been preserved by mineralisation presumably as a result of immersion in phosphate-rich faecal material. In two of the pits (one from Watling Court dating to the mid 12th century – Pit 59 cut 213; the other from Ironmonger Lane dating to the late 11th or 12th century – Pit 21 cut 177), arable weeds (such as *Agrostemma githago* and *Lithospermum arvense*) and other possible weeds of fields or gardens (eg. *Lapsana communis* and *Centaurea sp.*) predominate. These are accompanied, in the Watling Court pit, by a few cereal grains and numerous possible 'brassica' seeds, all in a mineralised condition. These two pits may give some indication of the basic diet of the time, which must have included cereals and probably vegetables. In contrast is another pit from Milk Street (pit 48), dating to the 12th century, in which, as well as the usual fruits, a large number of fig seeds and some grape pips were preserved. Both these species may have been imported (see above). Strawberry seeds were also more plentiful than usual. This may suggest greater access to luxury foods and imply a higher social status enjoyed by the individuals occupying this Milk Street property (cf. Green 1979a).

Caution is necessary though, as the difference could be simply seasonal if the two pairs of cess pits were in use at different times of year. Cereals (with their accompanying weeds) could well have been mostly locally grown and would have been stored for use throughout the year; so they would be a common component of cess deposits. Dried figs and raisins could, of course, also be stored but, if imported, it is likely that they would have come into the country when in season and, depending on the degree of their availability, they may have been consumed during part of the year only. They were not common, though, in the other, less obvious, cess pits in which plentiful remains of more local fruits were found. Were the more accessible local fruits stored (perhaps as preserves) in greater quantities than possibly imported ones or were they simply available to more people? Examination of other archaeological evidence is needed to complement the botanical study in answering this question. It should be noted that the apparent lack of cereal remains in the less obvious cess pits mentioned above may reflect nothing more than the different preservation conditions in these pits.

A 10th century pit (pit 45) from Milk Street is of particular interest. One context within this pit contained a large number of henbane seeds together with seeds of opium poppy. Henbane is a plant of waste places and its seeds are found in small quantities in a number of other pits. The quantity of seeds from this pit, however, and its association with opium poppy (which is also found in other pits), suggests that it was more than a casual weed on this occasion. Both species have medicinal properties and their seeds may have been kept for propagation. A single seed of probable cannabis/hemp (cf. *Cannabis sativa*) was found in another fill from the same pit. This suggests rather specialised activities in the vicinity. One could postulate the existence of a 'chemist's shop' in the area or, perhaps, a herb garden in which medicinal plants were grown. A range of other potential garden cultivars (flax, carrot, celery, dyer's rocket and possible 'brassicas') were also found in this pit.

Occupation Layers

Of the few occupation layers sampled, only six produced more than 50 seeds (1 from Milk Street, 1 from Watling Court, 2 from Peninsular House and 2 from Ironmonger Lane) and in two of these (one of the Peninsular House and one of the Ironmonger Lane samples) only the more robust taxa survived in a 'waterlogged' condition, though there were a few grains of carbonised wheat (mostly bread wheat) in the Ironmonger Lane sample. In fact, there was a tendency for robust seeds to be the most common category in the other occupation deposits. This is perhaps not surprising (see Appendix 1) as trampling of occupation surfaces may destroy many seeds, and waterlogging is less likely in occupation deposits than in many other features, such as pits, ditches and wells. The remaining Milk Street, Peninsular House and Ironmonger Lane samples also con-tained seeds of sedges and rushes, which would be expected if these were brought into town for use as flooring material. The Watling Court sample produced a number of potential food plants, including possible 'brassicas' as well as the more usual edible weeds and the Milk Street deposit included some seeds of henbane.

Hearths/ovens

Of the samples taken from within or near hearths or ovens, one group of related contexts from Well Court and one sample from Peninsular House produced large quantities of carbonised cereal grains. Carbonised remains are not unexpected from such contexts, exposure to fire being one of the prerequisites for this type of preservation. Their occurrence in substantial quantities in this context also makes it very unlikely that they are residual (see Appendix 5.1). Apart from their method of preservation, however, the plant remains from the two deposits are very different.

To take the Well Court contexts (context nos 1075-6) first, these samples date to the 10th or early 11th century and were part of an ash deposit thought to be rake-off from a nearby oven. The samples consist almost entirely of bread/club wheat (with some grains which could be of spelt or bread wheat) contaminated by occasional grains of oat, rye and barley. Weed contamination is low and the large seeds of corn cockle predominate.

Though the cereal species involved is bread wheat, this does not, in itself, suggest that the oven was used for baking. In fact, the discovery of whole grains rather suggests that it was used for grain drying at some stage prior to baking. The grain has evidently been cleaned free of chaff and weeds, as is commonly the case with wheat recovered from medieval urban deposits, indicat-ing perhaps that bread wheat was usually proces-sed before reaching town (Green 1979a). The crop seems to have been cleaned by sieving as well as winnowing, to judge from the large size of most of the weed seeds. It is probable that it was accidentally burnt while being dried prior to storage or, perhaps more likely in an urban con-text, while being hardened in preparation for grinding into flour (cf. Monk 1983). The oven could, of course, have been used for bread making also – we simply have no direct evidence for it, though the fact that the final stages of preparation of a grain suitable for bread making were carried

a. Oat (*Avena* sp.)

b. Rye (*Secale cereale*)

c. Hulled barley (*Hordeum cf. distichum*)

d. Bread wheat (*Triticum aestivum* s.l.)

5.2. Carbonised Cereal Grains from Peninsular House (context no. 1226)

out in this area may constitute indirect evidence. It has been suggested (Green 1979a) that, in early medieval towns, only middlemen and merchants stored quantities of unground grain, and this may be the case here.

The sample from a 10th century oven at Peninsular House (context no 1226) is quite different. Rather than being dominated by one species, it is composed of a number of different cereals. The most common cereal is oat, followed by rye and hulled barley and with some wheat (mostly bread/club wheat) (Fig 5.2). The oats could be wild or cultivated though the single lemma base found was of the cultivated species, *Avena sativa*, or possibly from an upper floret of a wild species, *A. ludoviciana*. Amongst the barley grains, none were obviously twisted (a characteristic of many six-row barley grains) though a large number of obviously straight grains were present suggesting the two-row species. The most striking thing about this sample, apart from the range of cereal species, is that it is heavily contaminated by carbonised weed seeds (Fig 5.3). Seeds of wild plants, many of them tiny, outnumber cereal grains by three to one though, when the larger size of the cereal grains is taken into consideration, these make up the bulk of the sample.

There are three possible interpretations for a sample of this type: (i) it represents a by-product or residue of grain cleaning, used perhaps to fuel the oven, (ii) it is the remains of a heavily contaminated crop (or crops) which has not been cleaned of weeds or (iii) it results from a mixture of waste used as fuel and cleaned crop from the drying chamber. In this case, the paucity of cereal culm nodes (indicating straw) and cereal rachis internodes (representing chaff) is inconsistent with residue from winnowing, the presence of large weed seeds and cereal grains argues against sieving residue and the predominance of well-formed cereal grains is suggestive of a crop product (cf. Hillman 1981a). A mixture of product and fuel is possible as weed seeds are often included with chaff and straw as tinder but the lack of evidence for chaff and straw suggests that the weed seeds arrived with the grain.

Many of the cereal grains (but none of bread wheat) had sprouted and loose sprouted embryos were common. This could mean that the grains were destroyed while being roasted as part of the malting process but by no means all the grains had sprouted and a more uniform germination is usually characteristic of this type of use (Hillman 1981b). Moreover, grain thought to have been

used in this way is not usually so heavily contaminated by weed seeds.

The cereals may have been destined for subsequent cleaning but perhaps a more likely explanation is that most of these cereals were intended as animal fodder where weed contamination (and possibly mixing of species) was considered unimportant. This suggestion receives some support from the fact that, although most of the more abundant wild species in the sample are common weeds of cultivation (eg. *Agrostemma githago*, corn cockle; *Anthemis cotula*, stinking mayweed; *Stellaria media*, chickweed; *Lapsana communis*, nipplewort; *Chenopodium album* type, fat hen; *Atriplex* spp., oraches and *Tripleurospermum maritimum*, scentless mayweed), some of the less well-represented species (eg. *Plantago lanceolata* type, ribwort; *Hypochoeris cf. radicata* cat's ear and numerous grasses including *Phleum* sp., timothy/cat's tail) are more characteristic of grassland, and timothy may be sown as hay grass. Other taxa (eg. *Bromus secalinus/mollis*, brome; *Vicia hirsuta/tetrasperma*, tare and *Rumex acetosella* agg., sheep's sorrel) could occur in arable fields or meadows. It has been noted by Greig (1984) that seeds of grassland plants tend to be under-represented compared with those of weeds and so the evidence from this sample may be sufficient to tentatively suggest the presence of hay, though no grass culm nodes were found. One possibility is that this sample represents a mixture predominantly of fodder 'crops' and, as such, might imply the stabling or stalling of animals in the City. Perhaps the sample results from spillage of material that was being dried to prevent further germination.

The weed seeds in the sample can also tell us something about the cultivation of the cereal crops. *Anthemis cotula* was by far the most numerous component of the weed flora and this species is particularly characteristic of heavy soils (Jones 1981). It is, of course, not possible to say whether all or only some of the cereals represented were grown on this type of soil. Indeed, if the oats are, after all, of the wild species *Avena ludoviciana*, this species too grows mostly on heavy soils in southern England (Clapham *et al* 1962) and so could simply indicate where some of the other cereals were grown. *Agrostemma githago* is an autumn-germinating species commonly associated with winter cereals, but some of the other well-represented species, such as *Stellaria media* and *Chenopodium album*, are more frequent amongst spring and summer crops and so it is likely that some of the cereals were sown in each

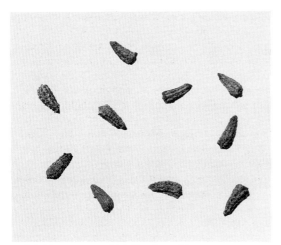

a. Stinking mayweed (*Anthemis cotula*)

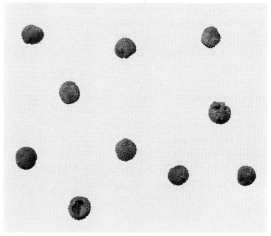

b. Chickweed (*Stellaria media*)

c. Nipplewort (*Lapsana communis*)

d. Ribwort (*Plantago lanceolata* type)

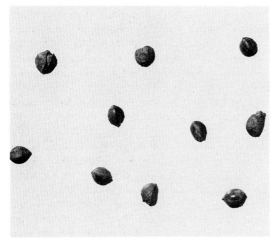

e. Sheep's sorrel (*Rumex acetosella* agg.)

5.3. Carbonised "Weed" Seeds from Peninsular House (context 1226)

season. This would not be surprising as rye, for example, is often autumn-sown and oat often spring-sown.

Conclusions

Recent redevelopment in other towns has also involved excavation of early medieval sites, and plant remains have been studied from a number of them. In general the taxa represented in London are similar to those from contemporary English centres such as York (Hall *et al* 1983), Durham (Donaldson 1979), Southampton (Green 1981), Winchester (Green 1981), Gloucester (Green 1979d) and Newbury (Green unpublished). None of the early medieval London sites studied so far has produced the remains of dyeing waste which have been found in deposits of a similar date in York (Tomlinson 1985). However, because of the vagaries of sampling and problems of differential preservation, interpretations cannot be based on the absence of certain categories of plant remains.

Some positive evidence for the use of sedges and rushes as flooring or roofing material is provided by occupation layers in London while small quantities of food and medicinal plants in these layers may represent spillage from food preparation and so on.

It is also clear that nearly all the pits in this study served, at least partly, as cess pits, though many of them received material from other sources too. Household rubbish, including flooring material, and locally growing plants contributed to their contents. Indeed, rubbish may have been deliberately added to act as a temporary seal. It has been suggested (Monk 1977) that such pits in Saxon Southampton were used for the deliberate composting of household refuse and dung for later use on arable fields outside the town. Certainly, this material would be suitable for such a use but, in early medieval London, there is no direct evidence (such as the thick sealing layer in some of the Southampton pits – Monk 1977) that it was conserved and later recovered. The material could equally well have been left *in situ* or used more locally as fertiliser on gardens, for the existence of which there is some direct evidence.

Potential garden cultivars and garden weeds, from some pits, suggest the existence of cultivated areas in the vicinity of the pits though caution is necessary when interpreting this kind of evidence (Hall *et al* 1983). Most of the evidence is for vegetable growing though one of the Milk Street pits, in particular, provides evidence for the cultivation or use of medicinal plants. There may have been a specialised building in the area of this pit or a garden area supporting a range of vegetable, fibre and medicinal plants. It has been suggested (Monk 1977) that the Saxons may have been the originators of the kitchen garden and late Roman deposits of 'dark earth' may indicate their existence even earlier (Macphail 1981). The samples from the City of London seem to support their presence by the early medieval period. Certainly, by the 14th century, garden produce was being sold in the City (Harvey 1981).

It is noticeable that exotic fruits such as figs and grapes are more common in some of the more important towns, notably Winchester, Southampton and London, and many of these major medieval towns were also ports handling a variety of imported goods. One of the cess pits from Milk Street provides evidence of greater access to luxury foods, such as fig, grape and possibly strawberry, which may be attributed to occupation of these areas by individuals of higher social status (cf. Green 1979a), though the seasonal use of fruits should not be overlooked.

It has also been possible to suggest whether charred grain samples from London represent food for human consumption or fodder for animals, by considering their state of preparation and the ecology of some of the species represented. Fully cleaned bread wheat may provide evidence for a merchant's or baker's establishment at Well Court and the mixture of oats, rye, barley (and perhaps hay) for the possible stabling or stalling of animals at Peninsular House.

Green (1979a and 1981) found oats and rye to be poorly represented in early medieval deposits from Wessex. He also notes (1979a) however, that both cereals were stored in a 12th century granary in Lydford, Devon, perhaps indicating that they were more common in south west England. The pollen evidence from Britain suggests that rye was common (Godwin 1975) and historical sources document its cultivation, but the pollen evidence has its drawbacks and the historical references to rye are sporadic (Green 1979a and 1981).

It has already been established (Green 1979a) that there are a number of reasons, including their use as fodder, why oats may be less well represented in archaeological deposits than documentary evidence might suggest. Green (1979a) also suggested that their cultivation as a cash crop may have contributed to their importance in later documents. The fact that rye as well as oats may have been found as a fodder crop in London could mean that the same arguments apply (cf. Green 1981). If fodder crops, unlike those used for human food or for brewing, were not normally processed in the vicinity of fires, then they would stand a much more slender chance of preservation by carbonisation. So, if rye were grown primarily for fodder, as has been suggested for oats (while wheat was used largely for baking and barley mostly for brewing – cf. Green 1979a), it would rarely enter the archaeological record.

A similar explanation may account for the occurrence of apparently two-row barley with the oats and rye. Most of the evidence from this period is for six-row barley (Green 1981, Jones 1981). It is at least possible that most of the six-row barley recovered to date was destined for human consumption while two-row barley was grown as fodder and is consequently under-represented. Clearly, more information is needed before this whole question of the use of cereal crops as food or fodder can be satisfactorily tackled. Finally, at least some of these crops appear, from the weed evidence, to have been grown on heavy soils, which may be contrasted with Green's (1979a) suggestion that in southern England their cultivation was restricted to poor (and, in that context, light) soils.

Appendix 5.1

Methodological Problems

Preservation and Contamination

The mechanisms by which plant remains are preserved in urban deposits have been discussed by Green (1979a and b, 1982) and some of the implications of his observations should be mentioned here. Plant remains from urban deposits can be preserved in three different ways; by waterlogging (ie. in anaerobic deposits), by mineralisation (ie. calcium phosphate replacement – Green 1979c) and by carbonisation (ie. by exposure to fire). Different types of deposit provide different preservation conditions (Green 1979a and b) and poor waterlogging can result in biased preservation of robust seeds (Monk 1977, Hall *et al* 1983).

Two major mechanisms of contamination are by redeposition and by biological activity. Residual material can become incorporated into later pit fills, for example, through the shovelling of earth from the ground surface to act as a sealing layer. This has been common practice with cess pits, and isolated mineralised and carbonised seeds, and even some robust waterlogged seeds (eg. *Sambucus*) may be included in this way. Similarly worms, insects and small mammals can carry seeds down into the soil and so contaminate early deposits with later, even modern, material (Keepax 1977) which is not usually distinguishable from earlier waterlogged remains. Such contamination is more likely to be a problem for periodically waterlogged deposits than for those that are permanently waterlogged. Carbonised or mineralised seeds would not normally be deliberately collected by animals but small seeds might be ingested by earthworms and occasional seeds fall into animal burrows and holes left by plant roots.

In London, usually only watefront sites or those with exceptionally deep stratigraphy produce truly waterlogged deposits. However, sites further from the river, such as those considered here, frequently expose damp deposits which are suitable for the preservation of plant remains by waterlogging. These deposits are particularly subject to biased preservation of waterlogged material and to problems of contamination by biological activity and, indeed, live earthworms were found in some deposits. However, fragile waterlogged remains and large concentrations of mineralised or carbonised seeds, which are unlikely to be residual, may be interpreted in relation to the context in which they were found.

Sampling and Processing

No unified sampling strategy was employed in the collection of samples from the sites discussed here and so the samples may not be representative of the full range of contexts encountered at each site. The way samples are distributed among feature types at the different sites is shown in Fig 5.1.

Often several samples come from the same pit or hearth and these were considered together unless there were marked differences between them.

Samples of approximately uniform size (about 10 litres) were taken at all sites and, for Milk Street, 1kg sub samples (or occasionally larger) were processed for plant remains. Orton (1983) conducted a statistical analysis on aspects of sampling policy which have a direct bearing on the analysis and he concluded that:

'The most serious obstacles to statistical analysis are the wide variation in sample size in terms of seeds per kg, and the practice of examining samples of different weights but expressing all on a 'per kg' basis. In theory, samples should all be the same size in terms of numbers of seeds, so that all could be expressed as 'per 100 seeds' or 'per 1,000 seeds' or whatever. There are of course severe practical problems: one could not, say, identify the first so many seeds found in a sample and expect this to be representative. One approach that might work would be to divide the sample into sub-samples, and examine them one at a time until the required number of seeds have been identified (sequential sampling). This approach would involve examining large quantities of samples in which seeds were scarce: perhaps this could be avoided by using a 'cut-off' criterion (similar to the 50 seeds per kg used here [in Orton's analyses]) so that these samples could be rejected before an enormous amount of sorting had taken place. A balance must be drawn between the need for statistically usable data and the amount of work needed to produce them.'

Orton (1983) p 24

In the light of Orton's comments on the Milk Street samples, a different subsampling policy was adopted for samples from the other sites discussed in this paper. As suggested by Orton, subsamples (of 250 g) were processed first and those which produced less than 12 seeds (equivalent to <50 per kg) were not processed further, though seeds from these subsamples were identified and recorded. A sequential sampling procedure was not followed, however, as the processing of large numbers of small samples is rather time consuming. Instead, for the more productive samples, the quantity of soil which must be processed to provide approximately 500 seeds was calculated from the subsamples. The figure of 500 seeds was based on calculations by van der Veen and Fieller (1982) which suggested that 384-541 seeds are sufficient to provide estimates of the relative proportions of taxa with an accuracy of 5% (in absolute terms) at a confidence level of 95-98%. This level of accuracy may be greater than required for some of the questions posed and so samples which produced at least 50 seeds (50 per kg for Milk Street) were also used in calculations.

It was often necessary to process large quantities of soil to achieve the required 500 seeds per sample and so the procedure used for processing soil samples was modified. The Milk Street samples and the 250 g subsamples from the other sites were processed by simple wet-sieving (cf.

Kenward *et al* 1980 – smallest mesh 250 microns) but many of the larger samples were processed by the wash-over technique of Kenward *et al* 1980 – smallest mesh 250 microns) with partial wet-sieving (smallest mesh 1mm). This technique is faster and equally effective for the recovery of all but the smaller mineralised seeds (Badham and Jones 1985) and so was used for samples containing no, few, or only large, mineralised seeds.

Interpretation

It is sometimes difficult, especially for water-logged remains, to distinguish plants which have been deliberately collected or grown for human use from those which have been deposited naturally or brought in inadvertently by man. This is less of a problem for carbonised remains since these must have been exposed to fire, implying some human involvement, though preservation by charring is biased in favour of plants that require processing in the vicinity of fires or that go into storage for long periods. Similarly, the most common cause of preservation by mineralisation in urban deposits is by immersion in phosphate-rich faecal deposits and so there is a greater chance of mineralised seeds providing evidence of human diet and indeed preservation by mineralisation is biased towards this kind of evidence. Even with these categories of material, however, it is possible that locally growing plants were accidentally charred or incorporated into faecal deposits. For a detailed discussion of these problems, see Green (1979a and b, 1982).

5.4. Plant remains from Milk Street, phase 1 pits (number of seeds per kg of soil).

Taxa	Context Numbers	pit 90 cut 2223		pit 42 cut 1397						pit 57 cut 1085		pit 93 cut 2116		
		[2208	2210]	[1118	1372	1373	1375	1376	1385]	[1041	1090]	[2140	2214	2215]
RANUNCULACEAE														
Ranunculus acris/repens/bulbosus	buttercups	—	—	0.5	0.2	6.3	1.6	—	—	0.7	—	—	—	—
Ranunculus sp.	—	1.6	—	—	—	—	—	—	—	—	—	—	—	—
PAPAVERACEAE														
Papaver cf. rhoeas	field coppy	—	—	—	—	—	0.3	—	—	—	—	—	—	—
Papaver somniferum L.	opium poppy	240.0	200.0	—	—	—	—	10.0	—	200.0	—	4.0	—	—
Papaver sp.	poppy	—	—	1.0	—	—	—	—	—	—	—	—	—	—
CRUCIFERAE														
Brassica/Sinapis spp.	—	4.8	—	—	—	—	0.2	—	—	—	—	—	—	—
Capsella bursa-pastoris (L.) Medic.	shepherd's purse	—	—	—	—	—	—	—	3.0	0.5	—	—	—	—
Camelina sativa (L.) Cranz	gold of pleasure	—	—	—	—	2.0	—	—	—	5.3	—	—	—	—
RESEDACEAE														
Reseda luteola L.	dyer's rocket	—	—	1.0	—	3.3	0.6	11.0	1.0	—	—	—	—	—
CARYOPHYLLACEAE														
Silene spp.	campions/catchflies	0.8	—	0.2	—	1.0	—	—	—	—	—	—	—	—
Lychnis flos-cuculi L.	ragged robin	—	—	—	—	0.7	—	—	3.3	—	—	—	—	—
Agrostemma githago L.	corn cockle	—	—	0.3	0.2	0.3	—	—	1.0	—	—	—	—	—
cf. Agrostemma githago	corn cockle	+	+	+	—	+	—	+	+	+	—	+	+	+
Stellaria media (L.) Vill.	chickweed	3.2	2.0	—	—	—	—	—	—	—	—	2.0	—	—
Stellaria graminea L.	lesser stitchwort	2.4	2.0	—	—	2.0	—	—	—	—	—	2.0	—	—
CHENOPODIACEAE														
Chenopodium album type	fat hen	—	—	8.0	3.0	—	37.2	500.0	5.0	35.0	—	2.0	1.0	33.0
Chenopodium murale		—	—	—	—	—	—	—	—	—	—	—	—	—
Chenopodium sp.	goosefoot etc.	18.4	16.0	—	—	10.0	2.0	13.0	2.0	—	—	17.0	—	—
Atriplex spp.	oraches	0.8	—	—	—	—	—	—	—	—	—	—	—	1.0
MALVACEAE														
Malva sylvestris L.	mallow	—	—	—	—	—	—	—	—	—	—	2.0	—	—
LINACEAE														
Linum usitatissimum L.	cultivated flax	—	—	—	—	—	—	—	—	0.7	—	—	—	—
VITACEAE														
Vitis vinifera L.	vine	—	—	—	—	—	0.7	4.8	—	—	—	—	—	—
LEGUMINOSAE														
cf. Lens culinaris	lentil	—	1.0	—	—	—	—	—	—	—	—	—	—	—
Vicia cf. tetrasperma	smooth tare	—	—	—	0.6	—	—	—	—	—	—	—	—	—
Vicia/Lathyrus spp.	vetch/tare/vetchling	—	—	—	—	—	0.2	—	—	—	—	—	—	—
ROSACEAE														
Rubus fruticosus/idaeus	blackberry/raspberry	160.0	9.0	0.9	0.4	70.0	100.0	100.0	0.5	166.7	—	—	—	—
Potentilla/Fragaria sp.	—	—	—	—	—	0.7	—	—	—	—	—	—	—	—
Fragaria vesca L.	wild strawberry	—	—	15.0	—	—	—	—	—	5.3	—	—	—	—
Rosa cf. canina	dogrose	—	—	—	—	—	4.8	—	—	—	—	—	—	—
Rosa sp.	rose	—	—	—	—	—	—	—	10.0	—	—	—	—	—
Prunus spinosa L.	sloe-blackthorn	—	—	—	—	—	3.4	—	—	—	—	—	—	—
Prunus cf. spinosa	sloe/blackthorn	4.0	—	—	—	—	—	—	—	—	—	—	—	—
Prunus domestica L.	plum/bullace	—	—	—	—	—	1.2	—	—	—	—	—	—	—
Prunus cf. cerasus	sour cherry	1.6	—	—	—	—	—	—	—	—	—	—	—	—
Prunus sp.	—	—	—	—	—	—	—	—	—	—	—	1.0	—	—
Crataegus monogyna Jacq.	hawthorn	—	—	—	—	—	3.0	—	—	—	—	—	—	—
Pyrus/Malus sp.	pear/apple	26.4	—	—	—	9.0	3.0	0.3	—	17.0	—	1.0	—	—
Rosaceae	NFI	—	—	—	—	—	—	0.3	—	—	—	—	—	—
UMBELLIFERAE														
Apium graveolens L.	celery	—	—	1.0	—	—	—	—	—	48.0	—	—	—	—
Apium sp.	—	—	—	—	—	—	0.2	—	—	—	—	—	—	—
Oenanthe cf. pimpinelloides	dropwort	—	—	—	2.0	0.7	1.2	—	—	—	—	—	—	—
Aethusa cynapium L.	fool's parsley	0.8	—	—	—	—	2.0	—	—	—	—	—	—	2.0
cf. Anethum graveolens	dill	—	—	—	—	—	—	1.7	—	—	—	—	—	—
Daucus carota L.	carrot	1.6	—	—	—	—	—	—	—	—	—	—	—	—
Umbelliferae	NFI	2.4	1.0	—	—	15.0	—	15.0	—	3.0	—	—	—	3.0
POLYGONACEAE														
Polygonum aviculare agg.	knotgrass	2.4	1.0	0.8	—	2.3	1.2	4.0	0.5	25.7	—	1.0	—	—
Polygonum persicaria L.	persicaria	0.8	—	—	—	—	—	—	—	—	—	—	—	—
Polygonum lapathifolium L.	pale persicaria	0.8	—	0.1	—	—	—	—	—	—	—	—	—	—
Polygonum convolvulus L.	black bindweed	4.8	—	—	—	0.7	0.2	0.3	—	—	—	—	—	—
Polygonum cf. convolvulus	black bindweed	—	—	—	—	—	—	—	+	—	—	—	—	—
Rumex spp.	docks	11.2	—	0.2	0.6	0.3	0.6	4.0	—	1.0	—	—	—	—
URTICACEAE														
Urtica urens L.	small nettle	—	—	6.0	2.0	2.0	0.9	90.0	5.8	21.3	—	—	—	1.0
Urtica dioica L.	stinging nettle	8.0	3.0	—	—	8.0	0.6	23.0	4.5	10.7	—	144.0	3.0	—
CORYLACEAE														
Corylus avellana L.	hazel	+	—	—	—	+	+	—	—	+	—	—	—	—

Taxa	Context Numbers	pit 90 cut 2223		pit 42 cut 1397						pit 57 cut 1085		pit 93 cut 2116		
		[2208	2210]	[1118	1372	1373	1375	1376	1385]	[1041	1090]	[2140	2214	2215]
MENYANTHACEAE														
Menyanthes trifoliata L.	bogbean	—	—	—	—	—	0.8	—	0.1	—	—	—	—	—
SOLANACEAE														
Hyoscyamus niger L.	henbane	—	—	—	—	—	—	—	—	—	—	16.0	—	—
Solanum nigrum L.	black nightshade	10.4	—	—	—	0.7	—	—	—	—	—	—	—	—
LABIATAE														
Lycopus europaeus L.	gipsy-wort	—	—	—	—	—	—	—	—	—	—	4.0	—	—
Prunella vulgaris L.	self-heal	—	—	—	—	—	—	—	5.0	—	—	—	—	—
Lamium cf. purpureum	red dead-nettle	—	—	—	—	—	—	—	—	6.0	—	—	—	—
Lamium sp.	dead-nettle	—	—	—	—	—	—	—	—	—	—	—	—	32.0
Galeopsis cf. tetrahit	common hemp-nettle	—	—	—	—	—	2.0	—	—	—	—	—	—	—
Labiatae	NFI	—	—	—	—	—	—	—	20.0	21.3	—	—	—	—
cf. Labiatae	NFI	8.0	—	—	—	—	0.9	16.0	—	—	—	—	—	—
CAPRIFOLIACEAE														
Sambucus nigra L.	elder	6.4	3.0	—	—	—	—	—	—	—	—	—	—	50.0
VALERIANACEAE														
Valerianella dentata (L.) Poll.	corn salad	—	—	—	3.0	3.0	—	—	—	—	—	—	—	—
COMPOSITAE														
Bidens tripartita L.	tripartite bur-marigold	—	—	—	—	—	0.2	—	—	—	—	—	—	—
Senecio cf. jacobea	ragwort	—	—	—	—	—	—	—	—	5.3	—	—	—	—
Anthemis cotula L.	stinking mayweed	0.8	2.0	5.0	9.0	0.7	18.4	600.0	12.5	141.0	—	—	—	—
Artemisia sp.	—	—	2.4	0.4	—	—	—	—	—	—	—	—	—	—
Cirsium sp.	thistle	—	—	—	—	—	—	—	—	9.0	—	—	—	—
Centaurea cf. nigra	lesser knapweed	—	—	0.1	—	—	—	—	—	—	—	—	—	—
Lapsana communis L.	nipplewort	0.8	—	0.4	—	—	3.6	46.0	—	7.7	—	—	—	—
Leontodon cf. autmnalis	autumnal hawkbit	—	—	—	—	—	3.6	—	—	—	—	—	—	—
Leontodon sp.	hawkbit	—	—	0.1	—	—	—	124.0	—	0.5	—	—	—	—
Sonchus cf. asper	spiny milk-/sow-thistle	—	—	—	—	1.3	—	—	—	—	—	—	—	—
Compositae	NFI	1.6	—	—	—	—	—	—	1.0	5.3	—	—	—	—
JUNCACEAE														
Juncus spp.	rushes	—	—	—	11.0	12.0	—	50.0	—	13.3	—	—	—	90.0
IRIDACEAE														
Iris pseudacorus L.	yellow flag	—	—	0.5	—	—	—	—	—	—	—	—	—	—
CYPERACEAE														
Eleocharis palustris type	spike-rush	0.8	—	8.0	4.0	25.0	4.5	22.0	3.6	30.0	—	—	—	—
Carex spp.	sedges	0.8	—	3.0	2.6	17.0	—	12.0	0.9	6.0	—	8.0	2.0	5.0
Cyperaceae	NFI	—	—	1.0	—	—	—	—	—	—	—	—	—	—
GRAMINEAE														
Avena sp.	oat	0.8	—	—	26.4	0.7	—	—	—	2.0	0.3	—	—	—
Hordeum sp.	barley	—	—	—	0.2	0.7	—	—	—	1.7	—	—	—	—
Triticum sp.	wheat	0.8	—	—	0.2	—	—	—	—	—	—	—	—	—
—	indeterminate cereal	—	—	—	0.8	3.7	—	—	—	3.0	—	—	—	—
Gramineae	NFI	5.6	—	—	—	1.7	1.0	23.0	1.0	18.7	—	—	—	—
Indeterminate		11.2	3.0	8.0	2.2	14.0	2.4	2.3	1.8	10.0	—	—	—	—
Total		547.2	243.0	61.5	68.4	215.4	206.6	1711.3	40.2	820.7	0.3	204.0	6.0	217.0

5.5. *Plant remains from Milk Street, phase 2 pits (number of seeds per kg of soil).*

Taxa	Context Numbers	pit 12 cut 36 48	pit 43 cut 1088 [1163]	1166]	[1213	1214	pit 45 cut 1344 1215	1310	1311]
RANUNCULACEAE									
Ranunculus acris/repens/bulbosus	buttercups	—	—	—	4.3	1.5	6.0	3.0	1.0
PAPAVERACEAE									
Papaver somniferum L.	opium poppy	20.0	—	—	92.0	209.0	36.0	15.0	0.7
FUMARIACEAE									
Fumaria officinalis L.	fumitory	—	—	—	—	0.5	—	—	—
CRUCIFERAE									
Brassica/Sinapis spp.	—	—	—	—	+	+	13.0	+	+
Capsella bursa-pastoris (L.) Medic.	shepherd's purse	—	—	—	—	—	—	—	2.0
Cruciferae	NFI	—	—	—	—	5.0	—	—	—
RESEDACEAE									
Reseda luteola L.	dyer's rocket	—	—	—	10.0	—	—	—	—
CARYOPHYLLACEAE									
Silene spp.	campions/catchflies	4.0	0.1	—	5.0	6.0	1.0	1.0	—
Agrostemma githago L.	corn cockle	—	—	—	—	—	4.0	—	1.0
cf. Agrostemma githago	corn cockle	+	—	+	+	+	+	—	+
Cerastium sp.	mouse-ear chickweed	—	—	—	—	—	—	10.0	—
Stellaria media (L.) Vill.	chickweed	—	—	—	2.0	—	3.0	5.0	—
Stellaria sp.	chickweed/stitchwort	—	—	1.0	—	2.0	—	—	—
Caryophyllaceae	NFI	—	—	1.0	—	—	—	—	1.0
CHENOPODIACEAE									
Chenopodium album type	fat hen	25.0	—	—	300.0	30.0	138.0	135.0	18.0
Chenopodium murale	—	—	—	—	30.0	91.0	24.0	—	1.4
Chenopodium cf. hybridum	maple-leaved goosefoot	—	—	—	0.2	—	—	—	0.1
Chenopodium sp.	goosefoot etc.	—	0.3	—	—	—	—	—	—
Atriplex spp.	oraches	—	—	—	11.0	2.0	90.0	4.0	1.0
Chenopodiaceae	NFI	—	—	—	2.0	3.0	—	—	—
MALVACEAE									
Malva sylvestris L.	mallow	—	—	—	—	—	—	1.0	1.4
LINACEAE									
Linum usitatissimum	cultivated flax	—	—	—	—	—	—	5.0	—
VITACEAE									
Vitis vinifera L.	vine	4.0	—	—	10.5	—	2.0	—	—
ROSACEAE									
Rubus fruticosus/idaeus	blackberry/raspberry	500.0	0.1	—	166.7	4.5	1000.0	600.0	13.7
Potentilla/Fragaria sp.	—	—	—	—	—	—	—	30.0	—
Prunus spinosa L.	sloe/blackthorn	95.0	—	—	2.3	—	17.0	—	—
Prunus cf. spinosa	sloe/blackthorn	—	—	—	—	—	—	9.0	—
Prunus domestica L.	plum/bullace	2.0	—	—	5.2	—	11.0	2.0	0.3
Prunus avium (L.) L.	cherry	—	—	—	—	—	—	1.0	—
Prunus cerasus L.	sour cherry	—	—	—	—	—	12.0	—	—
Prunus cf. cerasus	sour cherry	—	—	—	—	—	—	8.0	2.0
Prunus sp.	—	—	—	—	—	—	3.0	—	—
Crataegus monogyna Jacq.	hawthorn	28.0	—	—	1.8	—	49.0	—	—
Pyrus/Malus sp.	pear/apple	15.0	—	—	2.3	—	93.0	—	2.7
UMBELLIFERAE									
Apium graveolens L.	celery	—	—	—	3.0	3.0	10.0	6.0	—
Oenanthe cf. fistulosa	water dropwort	—	—	—	—	—	24.0	1.0	—
cf. Anethum graveolens	dill	—	—	—	0.3	—	—	—	—
Daucus carota L.	carrot	—	—	—	—	1.0	6.0	1.0	0.1
cf. Daucus carota	—	—	—	—	2.0	3.0	7.0	—	3.0
Umbelliferae	NFI	—	—	—	—	2.0	8.0	3.0	—
EUPHORBIACEAE									
Euphorbia helioscopia L.	sun spurge	—	—	—	0.3	0.5	—	1.0	0.1
POLYGONACEAE									
Polygonum aviculare agg.	knotgrass	—	—	—	63.0	15.0	36.0	25.0	4.6
Polygonum persicaria L.	persicaria	—	—	—	—	—	3.0	2.0	0.3
Polygonum lapathifolium L.	pale persicaria	—	—	—	—	—	15.0	8.0	0.9
Polygonum convolvulus L.	black bindweed	—	—	—	—	—	9.0	—	—
Polygonum cf. convolvulus	black bindweed	—	—	—	+	+	+	+	+
Rumex spp.	docks	4.0	—	—	1.0	9.0	7.0	14.0	1.4
URTICACEAE									
Urtica urens L.	small nettle	16.0	—	—	10.0	65.0	18.0	180.0	13.0
Urtica dioica L.	stinging nettle	—	—	—	36.0	91.0	—	240.0	113.0
CANNABIACEAE									
cf. Cannabis sativa	hemp	—	—	—	—	—	+	—	—
JUGLANDACEAE									
cf. Juglans regia L.	walnut	—	—	—	—	—	+	—	—
CORYLACEAE									

Taxa	Context Numbers	pit 12 cut 36 48	pit 43 cut 1088 [1163	1166]	[1213	1214	pit 45 cut 1344 1215	1310	1311]
Corylus avellana L.	hazel	—	—	—	+	+	+	—	—
SOLANACEAE									
Hyoscyamus niger L.	henbane	—	—	—	65.0	513.0	9.0	20.0	7.7
Solanum nigrum L.	black nightshade	8.0	—	—	—	41.0	—	—	—
SCROPHULARIACEAE									
Rhinanthus sp.	yellow rattle	—	—	—	—	0.5	—	—	0.3
LABIATAE									
cf. Mentha sp.	mint	—	—	—	—	1.0	—	—	—
Prunella vulgaris L.	self-heal	—	—	—	4.0	2.0	12.0	60.0	4.3
Lamium sp.	dead-nettle	—	—	—	—	7.5	—	1.0	—
Galeopsis sp.	hemp-nettle	—	—	—	—	—	1.0	—	—
cf. Labiatae	NFI	—	—	—	4.0	1.0	6.0	45.0	3.0
CAPRIFOLIACEAE									
Sambucus nigra L.	elder	—	—	0.3	1.0	3.0	1.0	—	0.3
COMPOSITAE									
Anthemis cotula L.	stinking mayweed	—	—	—	—	—	6.0	115.0	8.0
Cirsium sp.	thistle	—	—	—	0.3	2.0	—	—	0.7
Lapsana communis L.	nipplewort	—	—	—	6.5	8.0	54.0	48.0	7.0
Hypochoeris sp.	cat's ear	—	—	—	—	9.0	—	—	—
Leontodon sp.	hawkbit	—	—	—	8.0	2.0	3.0	35.0	5.0
Sonchus asper (L.) Hill	spiny milk-/sow-thistle	—	—	—	—	—	4.0	3.0	1.4
Taraxacum officinale Weber	dandelion	—	—	—	—	—	4.0	—	—
Compositae	NFI	—	—	—	—	2.0	5.0	—	3.0
JUNCACEAE									
Juncus spp.	rushes	10.0	—	—	12.0	108.0	96.0	120.0	1.4
CYPERACEAE									
Eleocharis palustris type	spike-rush	8.0	—	—	—	4.5	—	—	1.0
Carex spp.	sedges	4.0	0.3	0.5	5.3	15.0	4.0	6.0	2.0
Cyperaceae	NFI	—	—	—	11.0	2.0	—	—	0.1
GRAMINEAE									
cf. Avena sp.	oat	1.0	—	—	—	—	—	—	—
Triticum sp.	wheat	—	—	—	—	—	1.0	—	—
—	indeterminate cereal	—	—	—	—	3.5	—	—	—
Gramineae	NFI	—	—	—	4.0	7.0	90.0	100.0	0.9
Indeterminate		11.0	—	—	4.0	12.0	10.0	19.0	12.0
Total		755.0	0.8	2.8	886.2	1288.0	1951.0	1882.0	241.0

5.6. (Part 1) Plant remains from Milk Street, phase 4 pits (number of seeds per kg of soil).

Taxa	Context Numbers	pit 6 cut 34		pit 7 cut 47	pit 47 cut 141	pit 51 cut 1150					pit 53 cut 1122			pit 55 cut 1077
		[33	71]	76	1129	[1152	1138	1135	1131	1110]	[1107	1111	1109]	1064
PINACEAE														
Pinus sp.	pine	—	—	—	—	+	—	—	—	—	—	—	—	—
RANUNCULACEAE														
Ranunculus acris/repens/bulbosus	buttercups	—	—	—	0.2	0.8	—	0.4	0.8	1.0	1.0	—	—	2.0
Ranunculus sardous Crantz	hairy buttercup	—	—	—	—	—	—	—	—	—	—	—	—	0.3
Ranunculus cf. flammula	lesser spearwort	—	—	—	—	—	—	—	—	1.0	—	—	—	1.0
PAPAVERACEAE														
Papaver somniferum L.	opium poppy	—	—	—	0.2	3.2	—	—	3.2	3.0	—	—	—	1.0
FUMARIACEAE														
Fumaria officinalis L.	fumitory	—	—	1.0	0.5	—	0.6	0.2	—	—	—	—	—	—
CRUCIFERAE														
Brassica/Sinapis spp.	—	—	—	—	—	—	—	—	1.6	3.0	—	—	—	0.3
Thlaspi arvense L.	field penny-cress	—	—	—	—	—	—	—	0.4	—	—	—	—	—
Capsella bursa-pastoris (L.) Medic.	shepherd's purse	—	—	—	—	—	—	—	—	—	—	—	—	1.0
RESEDACEAE														
Reseda luteola L.	dyer's rocket	—	—	—	—	—	—	—	—	—	—	—	—	2.0
CARYOPHYLLACEAE														
Silene spp.	campions/catchflies	—	—	—	—	0.4	—	0.2	0.8	3.0	1.0	1.0	—	0.3
cf. Agrostemma githago	corn cockle	—	+	+	+	+	—	+	+	+	—	+	—	+
Stellaria graminea L.	lesser stitchwort	—	—	—	1.7	—	—	—	—	—	—	—	—	1.3
Caryophyllaceae	NFI	—	—	—	—	—	—	+	—	—	—	—	—	—
CHENOPODIACEAE														
Chenopodium album type	fat hen	—	—	—	2.8	—	—	—	—	—	—	2.0	12.0	13.7
Chenopodium murale		—	—	—	8.0	—	—	—	—	—	—	—	—	—
Chenopodium cf. hybridum	maple-leaved goosefoot	—	—	—	—	—	0.2	—	—	—	—	—	—	—
Chenopodium sp.	goosefoot etc.	6.0	—	—	—	11.6	—	3.0	27.2	18.0	13.0	—	—	4.0
Atriplex spp.	oraches	—	—	—	0.2	—	—	—	3.2	—	—	1.0	—	0.3
Chenopodiaceae	NFI	—	—	+	—	—	—	—	—	—	—	—	—	—
LEGUMINOSAE														
cf. Lens culinaris	lentil	—	—	1.0	—	—	—	—	—	—	—	—	—	—
ROSACEAE														
Rubus fruticosus/idaeus	blackberry/raspberry	—	—	26.0	0.3	20.0	1.0	0.6	11.2	22.0	1.0	7.0	—	94.7
Potentilla/Fragaria sp.	—	5.0	—	—	—	0.4	—	—	—	—	—	—	—	—
Fragaria vesca L.	wild strawberry	—	—	—	—	—	—	—	1.6	2.0	—	—	—	2.0
Prunus spinosa L.	sloe/blackthorn	—	—	—	—	138.0	—	—	—	—	—	—	—	—
Prunus cf. spinosa	sloe/blackthorn	—	—	—	—	—	—	—	—	—	—	—	—	1.0
Prunus domestica L.	plum/bullace	—	—	—	—	1.4	—	—	—	—	—	—	—	0.7
Prunus sp.	—	—	—	—	—	—	—	—	3.8	—	—	—	—	0.3
Pyrus/Malus sp.	pear/apple	—	—	+	—	21.6	—	—	—	2.0	1.0	—	1.0	55.0
UMBELLIFERAE														
Conium maculatum L.	hemlock	5.0	—	—	—	—	—	—	—	—	—	—	—	—
Apium graveolens L.	celery	—	1.0	—	—	—	—	—	—	—	—	—	—	—
Apium sp.	—	—	—	—	—	—	—	—	—	—	—	—	—	0.3
Daucus carota L.	carrot	—	—	—	—	—	—	—	—	1.0	—	—	—	0.7
Umbelliferae	NFI	3.0	1.0	—	—	—	—	—	—	1.0	—	—	—	—
EUPHORBIACEAE														
Euphorbia helioscopia L.	sun spurge	—	—	—	—	—	0.2	—	—	—	—	—	—	—
POLYGONACEAE														
Polygonum aviculare agg.	knotgrass	—	—	—	—	0.8	—	—	0.4	—	—	—	—	2.7
Polygonum lapathifolium L.	pale persicaria	—	—	—	—	1.0	—	—	0.4	—	—	—	1.0	—
Polygonum convolvulus L.	black bindweed	—	—	—	—	—	—	—	1.2	—	—	—	—	1.7
Rumex spp.	docks	—	—	—	1.8	0.8	—	0.4	2.0	5.0	—	1.0	1.0	2.0
URTICACEAE														
Urtica urens L.	small nettle	—	—	—	1.7	—	—	0.8	—	—	—	—	—	—
Urtica dioica L.	stinging nettle	85.0	—	—	61.7	0.8	0.8	—	—	—	—	—	—	5.0
CORYLACEAE														
Corylus avellana L.	hazel	—	—	—	—	+	—	—	—	—	—	—	—	+
SOLANACEAE														
Hyoscyamus niger L.	henbane	—	—	—	6.7	—	—	—	—	—	—	—	—	2.0
Solanum nigrum L.	black nightshade	—	—	—	—	—	—	—	—	—	—	—	—	1.0
LABIATAE														
Lamium sp.	dead-nettle	—	—	—	1.5	—	—	—	—	—	—	—	—	—
cf. Labiatae	NFI	—	—	1.0	22.0	0.8	—	—	—	—	1.0	—	—	—
CAPRIFOLIACEAE														
Sambucus nigra L.	elder	1.0	—	—	6.0	0.4	—	1.6	5.6	3.0	6.0	6.0	—	3.7
COMPOSITAE														
Anthemis cotula L.	stinking mayweed	—	—	4.0	—	4.8	—	—	—	—	—	—	—	11.0
Chrysanthemum segetum L.	corn marigold	—	—	—	—	—	—	—	—	—	—	—	—	1.0
Centaurea sp.	knapweed/thistle	—	—	—	—	—	—	—	—	—	—	—	—	3.7
Lapsana communis L.	nipplewort	—	—	—	—	—	—	—	—	—	—	—	—	1.0

Taxa	Context Numbers	pit 6 cut 34 [33	71]	pit 7 cut 47 76	pit 47 cut 141 1129	pit 51 cut 1150 [1152	1138	1135	1131	1110]	pit 53 cut 1122 [1107	1111	1109]	pit 55 cut 1077 1064
Leontodon cf. autumnalis	autumnal hawkbit	—	—	—	—	—	—	—	—	—	—	—	—	0.7
Sonchus asper (L.) Hill	spiny milk-/sow-thistle	—	—	—	—	—	—	—	—	—	—	—	—	0.7
Compositae	NFI	—	—	—	—	—	—	0.8	—	—	—	—	—	—
JUNCACEAE														
Juncus spp.	rushes	700.0	—	—	—	—	—	—	—	—	—	1.0	—	—
CYPERACEAE														
Eleocharis palustris type	spike-rush	3.0	—	—	—	2.2	—	—	2.4	—	—	—	—	1.0
Carex spp.	sedges	3.0	—	—	9.2	—	0.2	2.0	1.0	5.0	5.0	—	—	3.0
GRAMINEAE														
Avena sp.	oat	—	—	—	0.2	—	—	—	—	2.0	2.0	—	—	—
Hordeum sp.	barley	—	—	—	—	—	—	0.2	—	—	—	—	—	—
Triticum sp.	wheat	—	—	—	0.2	—	—	—	—	—	1.0	—	1.0	—
Secale cereale	rye	—	—	—	—	—	—	0.2	—	—	—	—	—	—
—	indeterminate cereal	—	—	—	0.7	—	—	—	—	—	—	—	—	—
Gramineae	NFI	—	—	1.0	—	—	—	—	4.8	—	—	1.0	—	—
Indeterminate		3.0	—	—	—	1.0	—	0.8	11.2	3.0	4.0	—	1.0	1.3
Total		814.0	2.0	34.0	125.4	210.0	3.0	11.2	82.8	76.0	35.0	20.0	17.0	223.3

5.6. (Part 2) Plant remains from Milk Street, phase 4 pits (number of seeds per kg of soil).

		pit 59 cut 1087	pit 60 cut 1086	pit 80 cut 1146		pit 88 cut 2042					pit 94 cut 2035		pit 96 cut 2463
Taxa	Context Numbers	1092	1091	[1144	1145]	[2041	2218	2224	2343	2444]	[2226	2227]	2456
RANUNCULACEAE													
Ranunculus acris/repens/bulbosus	buttercups	1.0	—	4.0	2.4	—	—	—	3.5	0.5	—	1.0	—
Ranunculus sp.	—	—	—	0.5	—	—	—	—	—	—	—	—	—
PAPAVERACEAE													
Papaver somniferum L.	opium poppy	7.2	—	0.5	4.0	—	—	—	—	—	6.7	—	—
CRUCIFERAE													
Brassica/Sinapis spp.	—	—	—	3.0	13.6	—	—	0.7	2.5	—	3.3	—	—
CARYOPHYLLACEAE													
Silene spp.	campions/catchflies	—	—	—	1.2	—	8.0	1.0	—	—	—	—	—
Lychnis flos-cuculi L.	ragged robin	—	—	—	—	—	—	—	5.0	—	—	0.3	—
Agrostemma githago L.	corn cockle	—	—	4.0	—	—	—	—	—	—	—	—	—
cf. Agrostemma githago	corn cockle	—	—	+	+	—	—	—	+	—	—	—	—
Stellaria media (L.) Vill.	chickweed	—	—	—	—	—	—	—	10.0	—	—	—	—
Stellaria holostea L.	greater stitchwort	—	—	—	—	—	—	3.3	—	—	—	—	—
Stellaria graminea L.	lesser stitchwort	—	—	5.0	—	—	—	—	—	—	—	—	—
cf. Stellaria alsine	bog stitchwort	—	—	—	—	—	—	—	—	—	—	0.7	—
Stellaria sp.	chickweed/stitchwort	—	—	—	—	—	—	—	—	—	—	6.7	—
Caryophyllaceae	NFI	—	—	1.0	1.6	—	—	—	1.0	—	1.0	—	—
CHENOPODIACEAE													
Chenopodium album type	fat hen	21.6	—	45.5	16.4	—	—	333.3	130.0	—	3.3	—	—
Chenopodium murale	—	0.8	—	—	—	—	—	—	—	—	—	—	—
Chenopodium cf. hybridum	maple-leaved goosefoot	—	—	—	—	9.0	—	—	—	—	—	—	—
Chenopodium sp.	goosefoot etc.	—	—	—	—	—	29.3	—	—	1.0	4.7	1.3	—
Atriplex spp.	oraches	1.6	—	—	0.8	—	—	—	24.0	—	—	—	—
Chenopodiaceae	NFI	—	—	14.5	—	—	—	—	—	—	—	—	—
LINACEAE													
Linum usitatissimum L.	cultivated flax	—	—	—	0.4	—	—	—	—	—	—	—	—
VITACEAE													
Vitis vinifera L.	vine	0.6	—	—	—	—	—	—	—	—	—	—	—
LEGUMINOSAE													
Leguminosae	NFI	—	—	—	—	—	—	—	—	—	—	0.3	—
ROSACEAE													
Rubus fruticosus/idaeus	blackberry/raspberry	540.0	1.0	—	400.0	—	—	0.3	10.0	1.5	—	0.3	3.0
Potentilla sp.	cinquefoil/tormentil	—	—	—	—	—	—	—	—	—	—	3.3	—
Potentilla/Fragaria sp.	—	—	—	—	—	—	—	—	—	—	—	0.7	—
Fragaria vesca L.	wild strawberry	—	—	—	—	—	—	—	—	—	10.0	—	—
Prunus spinosa L.	sloe/blackthorn	—	—	3.0	11.6	—	—	—	—	—	—	—	—
Prunus domestica L.	plum/bullace	1.0	—	—	6.0	—	—	—	—	—	—	—	—
Prunus cerasus L.	sour cherry	—	—	1.0	—	—	—	—	—	—	—	—	—
Prunus sp.	—	1.6	—	—	—	—	—	—	—	—	—	—	—
Pyrus/Malus sp.	pear/apple	—	—	1.0	120.0	—	—	—	—	1.0	—	—	—
Rosaceae	NFI	5.6	—	—	—	—	—	—	—	—	—	—	—
UMBELLIFERAE													
Chaerophyllum sp.	chervil	—	—	—	3.6	—	—	—	—	—	—	—	—
Conium maculatum L.	hemlock	—	—	—	—	—	—	—	—	—	—	0.3	—
Bupleurum cf. rotundifolium	hare's ear	—	—	6.5	—	—	—	—	—	—	—	—	—
Apium sp.	—	—	—	—	—	—	—	1.7	1.0	—	—	—	—
Oenanthe cf. fistulosa	water dropwort	—	—	0.5	—	—	—	—	—	—	—	—	—
Aethusa cynapium L.	fool's parsley	—	—	—	26.4	—	0.7	0.3	—	—	—	—	—
cf. Anethum graveolens	dill	—	—	0.5	—	—	—	—	—	—	—	—	—
cf. Daucus carota	—	—	—	0.5	—	—	—	—	—	—	—	—	—
Umbelliferae	NFI	—	—	—	—	—	—	0.3	1.0	—	—	—	—
CUCURBITACEAE													
Bryonia dioica Jacq.	bryony	—	—	—	—	—	—	—	16.5	—	—	—	—
EUPHORBIACEAE													
Euphorbia helioscopia L.	sun spurge	—	—	—	—	—	0.7	—	0.5	—	—	—	—
POLYGONACEAE													
Polygonum aviculare agg.	knotgrass	1.6	—	3.5	3.2	—	—	—	—	0.5	—	—	—
Polygonum cf. persicaria	persicaria	—	—	0.5	—	—	—	—	—	—	—	—	—
Polygonum lapathifolium L.	pale persicaria	—	—	0.5	—	—	—	—	3.5	—	—	—	—
Polygonum convolvulus L.	black bindweed	—	0.3	11.0	4.8	—	—	—	—	0.5	—	—	—
Rumex spp.	docks	—	—	13.5	6.8	—	—	—	7.0	—	0.3	—	—
URTICACEAE													
Urtica urens L.	small nettle	1.6	2.7	—	18.4	—	—	—	45.0	20.0	—	—	—
Urtica dioica L.	stinging nettle	19.4	1.3	—	12.0	—	—	—	—	—	—	10.3	—
MORACEAE													
Ficus carica L.	fig	—	—	—	—	—	—	—	—	—	—	0.3	—
SOLANACEAE													
Hyoscyamus niger L.	henbane	—	2.7	—	0.4	—	—	—	5.0	—	—	—	—
Solanum nigrum L.	black nightshade	—	—	—	—	—	—	25.0	—	—	—	—	—

Taxa	Context Numbers	pit 59 / cut 1087 / 1092	pit 60 / cut 1086 / 1091	pit 80 / cut 1146 / 1144	1145	pit 88 / cut 2042 / 2041	2218	2224	2343	2444	pit 94 / cut 2035 / 2226	2227	pit 96 / cut 2463 / 2456
SCROPHULARIACEAE													
Rhinanthus sp.	yellow rattle	—	—	—	—	—	—	—	5.5	—	—	—	—
LABIATAE													
Prunella vulgaris L.	self-heal	—	—	0.5	28.0	—	—	—	—	—	—	—	—
Lamium cf. purpureum	red dead-nettle	—	—	0.5	—	—	—	—	—	—	3.3	0.3	—
Lamium sp.	dead-nettle	—	—	—	14.8	1.0	11.7	40.0	—	—	0.3	1.0	—
Galeopsis cf. segetum	downy hemp-nettle	—	—	—	—	—	—	—	—	1.0	—	—	—
Galeopsis cf. tetrahit	common hemp-nettle	—	—	—	—	—	—	—	—	0.5	—	—	—
Galeopsis sp.	hemp-nettle	—	—	3.0	—	—	—	—	—	—	—	—	—
Labiatae	NFI	—	—	10.0	—	—	—	—	—	—	—	—	—
cf. Labiatae	NFI	0.2	—	20.5	20.4	—	—	—	—	—	—	—	—
CAPRIFOLIACEAE													
Sambucus nigra L.	elder	5.0	0.7	1.5	8.8	500.0	44.0	66.7	100.0	37.0	100.0	100.0	42.0
COMPOSITAE													
Anthemis cotula L.	stinking mayweed	—	—	15.0	36.8	—	—	—	50.0	—	—	—	—
Chrysanthemum segetum L.	corn marigold	—	—	15.5	10.4	—	—	—	—	—	—	—	—
Cirsium cf. arvense	creeping thistle	—	—	—	2.0	—	—	—	—	—	—	—	—
Centaurea cf. cyanus	cornflower	—	—	3.5	—	—	—	—	—	—	—	—	—
Centaurea cf. nigra	lesser knapweed	—	—	—	0.8	—	—	—	—	—	—	—	—
Lapsana communis L.	nipplewort	—	—	3.5	0.4	—	—	3.7	—	—	—	—	—
Hypochoeris sp.	cat's ear	—	8.0	—	—	—	—	—	—	—	—	—	—
Leontodon sp.	hawkbit	—	—	—	0.4	—	—	—	—	—	—	—	—
Picris echioides L.	bristly ox-tongue	—	—	3.0	—	—	—	—	—	—	—	—	—
Sonchus asper (L.) Hill	spiny milk-/sow-thistle	—	—	0.5	17.6	—	—	—	—	—	—	—	—
Taraxacum officinale Weber	dandelion	—	—	—	—	—	—	—	—	1.0	—	—	—
Compositae	NFI	—	—	3.0	0.8	—	—	—	—	—	—	—	—
ALISMATACEAE													
Alisma plantago-aquatica L.	water-plantain	—	—	—	—	—	—	—	—	—	3.3	0.3	—
LILIACEAE													
Convallaria/Ruscus sp.	lily-of-the-valley/ butcher's broom	—	—	—	—	—	—	—	—	5.0	—	—	—
JUNCACEAE													
Juncus spp.	rushes	—	2.7	5.0	—	—	—	6.7	40.0	50.0	133.3	11.3	—
CYPERACEAE													
Eleocharis palustris type	spike-rush	2.4	—	29.5	—	—	—	3.7	14.0	—	3.3	4.0	—
Carex spp.	sedges	0.4	5.0	57.5	3.2	—	—	7.3	11.0	—	7.3	4.3	4.0
Cyperaceae	NFI	—	—	—	—	—	—	—	—	—	2.3	—	—
GRAMINEAE													
Avena sp.	oat	—	—	—	0.8	—	0.3	—	—	—	—	—	—
Triticum sp.	wheat	—	—	—	0.4	—	0.3	—	—	—	—	—	—
—	indeterminate cereal	—	—	—	0.4	—	—	—	—	—	—	3.0	—
Gramineae	NFI	—	—	10.0	—	—	—	6.7	13.0	2.0	—	—	—
Indeterminate		1.6	1.7	12.5	4.0	4.0	—	6.0	15.0	—	4.3	1.3	—
Total		613.2	26.0	314.5	803.6	514.0	87.0	488.7	547.5	114.0	286.3	152.0	49.0

5.7. *Plant remains from Milk Street, phases 5-6 pits (number of seeds per kg of soil)*.

Taxa	Context Numbers	pit 37 cut 3205	pit 48 cut 1050			pit 54 cut 1083			pit 81 cut 1151				pit 91 cut 2007
		3084	1030	1031	1052	1025	1067	1015	1056	1062	1082	1128	2005
RANUNCULACEAE													
Ranunculus acris/repens/bulbosus	buttercups	—	3.4	5.0	2.0	9.0	1.3	—	22.0	12.0	28.0	1.0	2.0
Ranunculus cf. flammula	lesser spearwort	—	—	—	—	—	2.7	—	—	—	—	—	—
Ranunculus sceleratus L.	celery-leaved crowfoot	—	1.0	—	—	—	—	—	—	—	—	—	—
Ranunculus sp.	—	—	—	—	—	2.0	1.0	—	—	—	—	—	—
PAPAVERACEAE													
Papaver somniferum L.	opium poppy	—	2.0	—	7.5	13.0	6.7	2.0	—	—	—	—	—
FUMARIACEAE													
Fumaria officinalis L.	fumitory	—	0.2	—	—	—	—	—	—	—	—	—	—
CRUCIFERAE													
Brassica/Sinapsis spp.	—	—	2.2	3.2	3.0	6.0	1.3	—	17.0	8.0	4.0	—	1.0
Raphanus raphanistrum L.	wild radish/charlock	—	—	0.2	—	—	—	—	—	—	—	—	—
Capsella bursa-pastoris (L.) Medic	shepherd's purse	—	—	1.0	—	—	—	—	—	—	—	—	—
Camelina sativa (L.) Cranz	gold of pleasure	—	1.0	—	—	—	—	—	—	—	—	—	—
Cruciferae	NFI	—	—	—	5.0	—	—	—	—	—	—	—	—
CARYOPHYLLACEAE													
Silene spp.	campions/catchflies	—	0.4	0.4	—	—	0.5	—	2.0	—	2.0	—	—
Lychnis flos-cuculi L.	ragged robin	—	—	—	—	—	1.3	—	—	—	24.0	—	—
Agrostemma githago L.	corn cockle	—	—	—	—	—	—	—	2.0	2.0	1.0	—	—
cf. Agrostemma githago	corn cockle	—	+	+	+	+	+	+	+	+	+	+	—
Stellaria media (L.) Vill.	chickweed	—	—	—	—	—	—	—	—	—	4.0	—	—
Stellaria graminea L.	lesser stitchwort	—	—	—	—	—	—	—	—	—	2.0	—	—
Stellaria sp.	chickweed/stitchwort	—	—	—	—	—	—	—	—	—	—	2.0	—
CHENOPODIACEAE													
Chenopodium album type	fat hen	—	29.0	14.0	57.5	8.0	1.5	—	20.0	—	—	—	—
Chenopodium murale	—	—	1.0	—	7.5	—	1.3	—	—	—	—	—	—
Chenopodium cf. hybridum	maple-leaved goosefoot	—	—	1.0	—	—	—	—	—	—	—	—	—
Chenopodium sp.	goosefoot etc.	—	—	—	—	+	0.2	—	4.0	68.0	5.0	—	2.0
Atriplex spp.	oraches	—	3.4	3.2	2.8	8.0	9.2	—	9.0	—	—	—	—
Chenopodiaceae	NFI	—	—	—	3.0	3.0	0.5	—	6.0	—	—	—	—
LINACEAE													
Linum usitatissimum L.	cultivated flax	—	—	—	—	—	—	—	1.0	6.0	—	—	—
VITACEAE													
Vitis vinifera L.	vine	—	1.0	0.8	—	5.0	0.7	—	—	—	—	—	1.0
LEGUMINOSAE													
Pisum sativum L.	pea	—	—	0.8	—	—	—	—	—	—	—	—	—
cf. Lens culinaris	lentil	—	—	—	—	1.0	—	—	—	—	—	—	—
Vicia cf. tetrasperma	smooth tare	—	—	—	—	1.0	—	—	—	—	—	—	—
cf. Vicia faba	celtic bean/horsebean	—	—	0.4	—	—	—	—	—	—	—	—	—
Vicia/Lathyrus spp.	vetch/tare/vetchling	—	2.0	—	—	—	—	—	—	—	—	—	—
ROSACEAE													
Rubus fruticosus/idaeus	blackberry/raspberry	—	55.0	34.0	6.5	64.0	16.7	—	43.0	2.0	2.0	3.0	25.0
Potentilla sp.	cinquefoil/tormentil	—	—	—	—	—	33.3	—	—	—	—	—	—
Potentilla/Fragaria sp.	—	—	—	—	—	—	—	—	—	—	—	—	11.0
Fragaria vesca L.	wild strawberry	—	12.0	4.0	37.5	—	—	—	15.0	—	—	3.0	—
Rosa cf. canina	dogrose	—	—	—	—	1.0	—	—	—	—	—	—	—
Rosa sp.	rose	—	0.2	—	—	—	—	—	—	—	—	—	—
Prunus spinosa L.	sloe/blackthorn	—	—	—	—	1.0	1.3	—	—	—	—	—	—
Prunus cf. spinosa	sloe/blackthorn	—	2.2	2.0	1.0	—	—	—	—	—	—	—	—
Prunus domestica L.	plum/bullace	—	0.2	1.6	—	1.0	0.2	—	—	—	—	—	—
Prunus cerasus L.	sour cherry	—	—	—	—	—	—	—	—	—	33.0	—	—
Prunus cf. cerasus	sour cherry	—	0.2	—	—	1.0	—	—	—	—	—	—	—
Prunus sp.	—	—	—	+	—	—	—	—	3.0	—	—	—	—
Pyrus/Malus sp.	pear/apple	—	0.4	—	0.5	1.0	0.3	—	8.0	—	8.0	—	2.0
Rosaceae	NFI	—	—	—	—	—	—	—	4.0	—	—	—	—
UMBELLIFERAE													
Conium maculatum L.	hemlock	—	—	—	—	1.0	—	—	—	1.0	—	—	—
Bupleurum cf. rotundifolium	hare's ear	—	—	—	—	—	0.2	—	—	—	—	—	—
Bupleurum sp.	—	—	—	—	—	1.0	—	—	—	—	—	—	—
Apium graveolens L.	celery	—	—	0.8	—	—	—	—	—	—	—	—	—
Apium sp.	—	—	—	—	—	—	—	1.0	—	—	—	—	—
Aethusa cynapium L.	fool's parsley	—	—	—	—	—	0.8	—	—	—	—	—	—
cf. Daucus carota	—	—	—	—	—	8.0	2.2	—	—	—	—	—	—
Umbelliferae	NFI	—	—	—	2.8	—	0.3	—	—	1.0	—	—	—
EUPHORBIACEAE													
Euphorbia helioscopia L.	sun spurge	—	—	—	—	—	0.2	—	—	—	—	—	—
POLYGONACEAE													
Polygonum aviculare agg.	knotgrass	—	—	0.2	0.5	3.0	—	—	—	5.0	4.0	—	—
Polygonum persicaria L.	persicaria	—	—	0.2	—	1.0	—	—	1.0	1.0	—	—	—
Polygonum lapathifolium L.	pale persicaria	—	—	—	—	10.0	0.2	—	—	—	—	—	—

Taxa	Context Numbers	pit 37 cut 3205	pit 48 cut 1050			pit 54 cut 1083			pit 81 cut 1151				pit 91 cut 2007
		3084	[1030	1031	1052]	[1025	1067	1015]	[1056	1062	1082	1128]	2005
Polygonum convolvulus L.	black bindweed	—	—	—	0.3	—	0.3	—	—	1.0	—	—	—
Rumex spp.	docks	—	3.8	1.0	5.0	8.0	2.8	—	12.0	5.0	2.0	2.0	1.0
URTICACEAE													
Urtica urens L.	small nettle	—	—	—	10.0	—	—	—	—	—	—	—	—
Urtica dioica L.	stinging nettle	1.0	—	—	2.5	—	1.3	—	—	4.0	—	2.0	—
MORACEAE													
Ficus carica L.	fig	—	16.4	6.6	0.3	33.0	—	—	—	—	—	—	—
Morus nigra	mulberry	—	—	—	—	—	—	—	—	—	5.0	—	—
CORYLACEAE													
Corylus avellana L.	hazel	—	+	—	+	+	—	—	+	+	—	—	—
SOLANACEAE													
Hyoscyamus niger L.	henbane	1.0	19.0	10.0	12.5	—	0.2	—	—	—	—	—	—
Solanum nigrum L.	black nightshade	—	—	—	—	13.0	1.7	—	65.0	4.0	8.0	1.0	—
SCROPHULARIACEAE													
Scrophularia cf. nodosa	figwort	—	—	—	—	—	2.7	—	—	—	—	—	—
LABIATAE													
cf. Mentha sp.	mint	—	2.0	—	—	—	—	—	—	—	—	—	—
Lycopus europaeus L.	gipsy-wort	—	—	1.0	—	—	—	—	—	—	—	—	—
Stachys sp.	woundwort	—	0.2	—	—	—	—	—	—	—	—	—	—
Lamium cf. purpureum	red dead-nettle	—	—	—	—	—	—	—	—	—	—	3.0	—
Lamium sp.	dead-nettle	—	—	1.0	6.0	—	—	—	—	—	—	—	1.0
cf. labiatae	NFI	—	—	—	—	—	—	—	1.0	1.0	—	—	1.0
CAPRIFOLIACEAE													
Sambucus nigra L.	elder	9.0	1.4	1.4	5.8	—	3.2	—	5.0	—	—	1.0	4.0
COMPOSITAE													
Anthemis cotula L.	stinking mayweed	—	—	—	2.5	8.0	—	—	—	—	—	—	—
Chamaemelum nobile (L.) All.	chamomile	—	—	1.0	—	—	—	—	—	—	—	—	—
Chrysanthemum segetum L.	corn marigold	—	—	1.0	2.5	5.0	—	—	15.0	4.0	—	1.0	—
Cirsium cf. vulgare	spear thistle	—	—	—	—	—	—	—	6.0	—	—	—	—
Centaurea cf. cyanus	cornflower	—	—	—	—	—	—	—	—	—	1.0	—	—
Centaurea cf. nigra	lesser knapweed	—	0.2	—	—	—	—	—	—	—	—	—	—
Centaurea sp.	knapweed/thistle	—	—	—	—	—	—	—	3.0	—	—	—	—
Lapsana communis L.	nipplewort	—	—	3.0	2.5	1.0	—	—	6.0	5.0	—	1.0	—
Leontodon cf. autumnalis	autumnal hawkbit	—	—	—	—	—	—	—	5.0	—	—	—	—
Compositae	NFI	—	—	1.0	—	3.0	—	—	—	4.0	1.0	1.0	—
JUNCACEAE													
Juncus spp.	rushes	—	52.0	24.0	21.0	130.0	2.7	10.0	—	—	—	—	—
CYPERACEAE													
Eleocharis palustris type	spike-rush	—	4.2	—	11.0	42.0	4.0	—	36.0	8.0	14.0	9.0	1.0
Carex spp.	sedges	—	6.0	3.6	5.5	22.0	1.7	—	27.0	—	11.0	9.0	8.0
Cyperaceae	NFI	—	—	—	—	—	—	—	—	8.0	—	—	—
GRAMINEAE													
Avena sp.	oat	—	1.2	0.8	0.8	—	0.7	—	2.0	1.0	—	—	1.0
Hordeum sp.	barley	—	—	0.2	—	—	0.2	—	1.0	—	—	—	—
Triticum sp.	wheat	—	0.6	0.4	0.8	—	0.2	—	—	—	—	—	2.0
Secale cereale	rye	—	0.2	—	—	—	—	—	—	—	—	—	—
	indeterminate cereal	—	—	0.2	—	—	—	—	—	—	—	—	—
Gramineae	NFI	—	18.8	15.0	7.5	20.0	3.8	—	5.0	8.0	8.0	1.0	—
Indeterminate		—	9.0	11.0	5.0	2.0	4.2	—	6.0	1.0	6.0	5.0	5.0
Total		11.0	251.8	155.0	238.3	436.0	113.4	13.0	352.0	160.0	171.0	47.0	68.0

Taxa	Context Numbers	3152	Building 2 3161	3211
			3161	
RANUNCULACEAE				
Ranunculus acris/repens/bulbosus	buttercups	—	—	0.5
Ranunculus sp.	—	—	3.0	—
FUMARIACEAE				
Fumaria officinalis L.	fumitory	—	0.5	0.5
CRUCIFERAE				
Brassica/Sinapis spp.	—	0.5	1.0	—
RESEDACEAE				
Reseda luteola L.	dyer's rocket	1.5	—	—
CARYOPHYLLACEAE				
Silene spp.	campions/catchflies	—	—	0.5
Lychnis flos-cuculi L.	ragged robin	—	1.0	—
cf. Agrostemma githago	corn cockle	—	—	+
Stellaria media (L.) Vill.	chickweed	—	0.5	—
CHENOPODIACEAE				
Chenopodium album type	fat hen	—	—	0.5
Chenopodium sp.	goosefoot etc.	—	14.5	—
Chenopodium/Atriplex spp.	goosefoots/oraches	4.5	—	—
Chenopodiaceae	NFI	+	—	+
ROSACEAE				
Rubus fruticosus/idaeus	blackberry/raspberry	+	—	0.5
Potentilla erecta (L.) Rausch	tormentil	—	0.5	—
Fragaria vesca L.	wild strawberry	—	0.5	—
Pyrus/Malus sp.	pear/apple	—	—	+
UMBELLIFERAE				
Umbelliferae	NFI	—	—	0.5
POLYGONACEAE				
Polygonum aviculare agg.	knotgrass	1.0	2.0	—
Polygonum lapathifolium L.	pale persicaria	—	1.0	—
Polygonum convolvulus L.	black bindweed	—	—	0.5
Rumex acetosella agg.	sheep's sorrel	—	0.5	—
Rumex spp.	docks	—	1.5	0.5
Polygonaceae	NFI	—	—	1.0
URTICACEAE				
Urtica urens L.	small nettle	—	0.5	—
Urtica dioica L.	stinging nettle	3.0	14.5	1.0
SOLANACEAE				
Hyoscyamus niger L.	henbane	1.5	10.0	—
CAPRIFOLIACEAE				
Sambucus nigra L.	elder	1.0	1.0	—
COMPOSITAE				
Compositae	NFI	1.0	—	—
JUNCACEAE				
Juncus spp.	rushes	10.0	—	4.0
CYPERACEAE				
Eleocharis palustris type	spike-rush	—	—	6.5
Carex spp.	sedges	4.5	6.0	6.0
GRAMINEAE				
Triticum aestivum type	bread/club wheat	—	0.5	—
Triticum sp.	wheat	0.5	—	—
Secale cereale	rye	0.5	—	—
Indeterminate		—	1.5	0.5
Total		29.5	60.5	23.0

5.8. *Plant remains from Milk Street, phase 2 occupation surfaces (number of seeds per kg of soil).*

Taxa	Context Numbers	cut 139 94	cut 2121 2120
ROSACEAE			
Prunus sp.	—	—	4.0
cf. Prunus sp.	—	12.0	—
UMBELLIFERAE			
Apium sp.	—	—	4.0
CAPRIFOLIACEAE			
Sambucus nigra L.	elder	—	4.0
Indeterminate		4.0	—
Total		16.0	12.0

5.9. (above) Plant remains from Watling Court, phase 1 pits (number of seeds per kg of soil).

5.10. (below) Plant remains from Watling Court, phases 4-5 pits (number of seeds per kg of soil).

Taxa	Context Numbers	cut 705 [690	693]	cut 2587 [2543	2606]	[200	cut 213 202	203	204]	cut 711 [526	562	563	564	565	578]
RANUNCULACEAE															
Ranunculus acris/repens/bulbosus	buttercups	—	—	—	—	—	0.5	—	4.0	—	—	—	—	—	—
Ranunculus cf. sardous	hairy buttercup	—	—	—	—	—	0.3	—	4.0	—	—	—	—	—	—
Ranunculus cf. flammula	lesser spearwort	—	—	—	—	—	—	—	4.0	—	—	—	—	—	—
Ranunculus subgen. Batrachium (DC) A. Gray	crowfoots	0.5	—	—	—	—	—	—	—	—	—	—	—	—	—
Ranunculus cf. subgen. Batrachium	crowfoots	0.5	—	—	—	—	—	—	—	—	—	—	—	—	—
Ranunculus sp.	—	—	—	—	—	—	10.1	24.0	96.0	—	—	—	—	—	—
cf. Ranunculus sp.	—	—	—	—	—	—	0.8	—	—	—	—	—	—	—	—
PAPAVERACEAE															
Papaver cf. argemone	long prickly-headed poppy	—	—	—	—	—	—	—	20.0	—	—	—	—	—	—
Papaver somniferum L.	opium poppy	—	—	—	—	—	4.9	8.0	40.0	—	—	—	—	—	—
CRUCIFERAE															
Brassica/Sinapis spp.	—	5.4	—	—	4.0	8.0	14.8	72.0	264.0	—	—	—	—	—	8.0
Camelina sativa (L.) Cranz	gold of pleasure	—	—	—	—	—	0.3	—	—	—	—	—	—	—	—
CRUCIFERAE/LEGUMINOSAE															
Cruciferae/Leguminosae	NFI	—	—	—	—	—	0.3	—	—	—	—	—	—	—	—
RESEDACEAE															
cf. Reseda luteola	dyer's rocket	0.5	—	—	—	—	—	—	—	—	—	—	—	—	—
CARYOPHYLLACEAE															
Silene alba/noctiflora/vulgaris	campion	0.5	—	—	—	—	—	—	—	—	—	—	—	—	—
Silene vulgaris (Moench) Garcke	bladder campion	0.5	—	—	—	—	—	—	—	—	—	—	—	—	—
Silene cf. vulgaris	bladder campion	0.9	—	—	—	—	—	—	—	—	—	—	—	—	—
Silene cf. maritima	sea campion	0.5	—	—	—	—	—	—	—	—	—	—	—	—	—
Silene spp.	campions/catchflies	—	—	—	—	—	—	4.0	4.0	—	—	—	—	—	—
Agrostemma githago L.	corn cockle	—	—	—	—	—	1.3	4.0	32.0	—	—	—	—	—	—
cf. Agrostemma githago	corn cockle	—	—	—	—	—	0.3	—	—	—	—	—	—	—	—
Stellaria media (L.) Vill.	chickweed	0.9	—	—	—	—	0.8	—	—	—	—	—	—	4.0	—
Stellaria cf. graminea	lesser stitchwort	0.5	—	—	—	—	—	—	—	—	—	—	—	—	—
cf. Stellaria sp.	chickweed/stitchwort	—	—	—	—	—	1.0	—	—	—	—	—	—	—	—
CHENOPODIACEAE															
Chenopodium polyspermum	all-seed	0.5	—	—	—	—	—	—	—	—	—	—	—	—	—
Chenopodium album type	fat hen	21.4	12.0	—	—	—	—	—	—	—	—	—	—	—	—
Chenopodium cf. album type	fat hen	3.6	—	—	—	—	—	—	—	—	—	—	—	—	—
Chenopodium rubrum/glaucum	goosefoot	—	—	—	—	—	0.3	—	—	—	—	—	—	—	—
Chenopodium/Atriplex spp.	goosefoot/oraches	4.6	16.0	—	—	—	0.5	8.0	32.0	—	—	—	—	—	—
Atriplex spp.	oraches	10.4	12.0	—	—	—	—	—	—	—	—	—	—	—	—
cf. Atriplex sp.	orache	0.5	—	—	—	—	—	—	—	—	—	—	—	—	—
Chenopodiaceae	NFI	—	—	—	—	—	2.1	8.0	12.0	—	—	—	—	—	—
cf. Chenopodiaceae	NFI	—	—	—	—	—	—	—	8.0	—	—	—	—	—	—
MALVACEAE															
Malvaceae	NFI	—	—	—	—	—	0.3	—	—	—	—	—	—	—	—
LINACEAE															
cf. Linum sp.	flax	0.5	—	—	—	—	—	4.0	—	—	—	—	—	—	—
VITACEAE															
Vitis vinifera L.	vine	—	—	—	—	—	0.5	4.0	—	4.0	—	—	—	—	—
LEGUMINOSAE															
Vicia tetrasperma (L.) Schreb.	smooth tare	—	—	—	—	—	—	4.0	—	—	—	—	—	—	—
Vicia/Lathyrus spp.	vetch/tare/vetching	—	—	—	—	—	—	—	4.0	—	—	—	—	—	—

Taxa	Context Numbers	cut 705		cut 2587		cut 213				cut 711					
		[690	693]	[2543	2606]	[200	202	203	204]	[526	562	563	564	565	578]
Leguminosae	NFI	—	—	—	—	—	—	—	4.0	—	—	—	—	—	—
ROSACEAE															
Rubus cf. fruticosus agg.	blackberry	7.3	—	—	—	—	0.3	—	—	—	—	—	—	—	—
Rubus fruticosus/idaeus	blackberry/raspberry	2.3	—	—	—	—	—	4.0	16.0	—	—	—	—	—	—
Rubus fruticosus/idaeus/caesius	blackberry/raspberry/dewberry	3.2	—	—	—	—	0.3	—	—	—	—	—	—	—	—
cf. Potentilla/Fragaria sp.	—	—	—	—	—	—	—	—	4.0	—	—	—	—	—	—
Fragaria vesca L.	wild strawberry	0.9	—	—	—	—	2.3	—	72.0	—	—	—	—	—	—
Prunus spinosa L.	sloe/blackthorn	—	—	—	—	—	—	—	4.0	—	—	—	—	—	—
Prunus spinosa/avium/cerasus	sloe/cherry	—	—	—	—	—	0.3	—	—	—	—	—	—	4.0	—
Prunus sp.	—	—	—	—	—	—	0.3	—	—	—	—	—	—	—	—
Prunus spp.	—	3.6	—	—	—	—	2.6	4.0	52.0	—	—	—	—	8.0	—
cf. Prunus sp.	—	0.5	—	—	—	—	—	16.0	8.0	—	—	—	—	—	—
Pyrus/Malus sp.	pear/apple	0.5	—	—	—	—	0.3	8.0	8.0	—	4.0	—	4.0	—	—
cf. Pyrus/Malus sp.	pear/apple	—	—	—	—	—	0.5	4.0							
UMBELLIFERAE															
Chaerophyllum sp.	chervil	—	—	—	—	—	0.5								
Conium maculatum L.	hemlock	0.5	—	4.0	—	—	—								
cf. Conium maculatum	hemlock	—	—	—	—	—	0.8	4.0	4.0	—	—	—	—	—	—
cf. Bupleurum rotundifolium	hare's ear	—	—	—	—	—	—	—	12.0	—	—	—	—	—	—
Aethusa cynapium L.	fool's parsley	2.3	—	—											
Umbelliferae	NFI	—	—	—	—	—	1.0	—	4.0	—	—	—	—	—	—
cf. Umbelliferae	NFI	—	—	—	—	—	—	4.0	4.0	—	—	—	—	—	—
POLYGONACEAE															
Polygonum lapathifolium L.	pale persicaria	—	—	—	—	—	—	—	4.0	—	—	—	—	4.0	—
Polygonum cf. lapathifolium	pale persicaria	—	—	—	—	—	0.3	—							
Polygonum convolvulus L.	black bindweed	—	4.0	—	—	—	1.0	—	4.0	—	—	—	—	—	—
Polygonus cf. convolvulus	black bindweed	—	—	—	—	—	0.3	—							
cf. Polygonum convolvulus L.	black bindweed	—	—	—	—	—	—	—	28.0	—	—	—	—	—	—
Polygonum sp.	—	—	—	—	—	—	1.0	4.0	24.0	—	—	—	—	—	—
Rumex acetosella agg.	sheep's sorrel	0.9	—	—	—	4.0	0.3	4.0	8.0	—	—	—	—	—	—
cf. Rumex acetosella agg.	sheeps' sorrel	—	—	—	—	—	—	—	4.0	—	—	—	—	—	—
Rumex spp.	docks	0.5	4.0	—	—	—	1.0	12.0	20.0	—	—	—	8.0	8.0	—
Polygonaceae	NFI	—	—	—	—	—	—	—	4.0	—	—	—	—	—	—
POLYGONACEAE/CYPERACEAE															
Polygonaceae/Cyperaceae	NFI	1.4	—	—	—	—	4.4	8.0	40.0	—	—	—	—	—	—
cf. Polygonaceae/Cyperaceae	NFI	—	—	—	—	—	0.5								
URTICACEAE															
Urtica dioica L.	stinging nettle	—	—	—	4.0	4.0	—	—	4.0	—	—	—	—	—	—
Urtica sp.	nettle	—	—	—	—	—	0.5								
MORACEAE															
cf. Ficus carica	fig	—	—	—	—	—	0.3								
CORYLACEAE															
Corylus avellana L.	hazel	—	—	—	—	—	+	—	—	—	—	—	—	—	—
BORAGINACEAE															
Lithospermum arvense L.	corn gromwell	—	—	—	—	—	—	—	4.0	—	—	—	—	—	—
cf. SOLANACEAE															
cf. Solanaceae	NFI	—	—	—	—	—	0.3	—	4.0	—	—	—	—	—	—
LABIATAE															
Ballota nigra L.	black horehound	—	—	—	—	—	—	—	8.0	—	—	—	—	—	—
Lamium sp.	dead-nettle	—	—	—	—	—	0.3	—							
Marrubium vulgare L.	white horehound	—	—	—	—	—	—	—	4.0	—	—	—	—	—	—
cf. Labiatae	NFI	0.9	—	—	—	—	—	—	4.0	—	—	—	—	—	—
CAPRIFOLIACEAE															
Sambucus nigra L.	elder	5.0	—	—	4.0	4.0	0.5	—	—	—	12.0	—	—	4.0	4.0
RUBIACEAE															
Galium palustre L.	marsh bedstraw	—	—	—	—	—	—	4.0							
Galium aparine L.	cleavers	—	—	—	—	—	0.5								
Galium/Asperula sp.	bedstraw/woodruff	—	—	—	—	—	0.3								
cf. Galium/Asperula sp.	bedstraw/woodruff	—	—	—	—	—	0.3								
COMPOSITAE															
Anthemis cotula L.	stinking mayweed	3.2	—	—	—	—	1.0	—	32.0	—	—	—	—	—	—
cf. Anthemis cotula	stinking mayweed	—	—	—	—	—	—	—	4.0	—	—	—	—	—	—
Anthemis arvensis/cotula	mayweed/chamomile	—	—	—	—	—	0.3	—							
Anthemis sp.	mayweed/chamomile	—	—	—	—	—	3.6	—							
cf. Anthemis sp.	mayweed/chamomile	2.3	—	—	—	—	—	24.0	20.0	—	—	—	—	—	—
Chamaemelum nobile (L.) All.	chamomile	—	—	—	—	—	0.5	—	12.0	—	—	—	—	—	—
Centaurea cyanus L.	cornflower	—	—	—	—	—	—	—	4.0	—	—	—	—	—	—
Centaurea sp.	knapweed/thistle	1.8	—	—	—	4.0	15.8	24.0	276.0	—	—	—	—	—	—
cf. Centaurea sp.	knapweed/thistle	—	—	—	—	—	2.6	—	12.0	—	—	—	—	—	—
Lapsana communis L.	nipplewort	—	—	—	—	4.0	26.2	20.0	40.0	—	—	—	—	—	—

Taxa	Context Numbers	cut 705		cut 2587			cut 213			cut 711					
		[690	693]	[2543	2606]	[200	202	203	204]	[526	562	563	564	565	578]
cf. Sonchus sp.	milk-/sow-thistle	—	—	—	—	—	—	—	4.0	—	—	—	—	—	—
Compositae	NFI	—	—	—	—	—	4.4	—	4.0	—	—	—	—	—	—
cf. Compositae	NFI	—	—	—	—	4.0	0.5	—	—	—	—	—	—	—	—
ALISMATACEAE															
Alisma plantago-aquatica L.	water-plantain	—	—	—	—	—	0.3	—	—	—	—	—	—	—	—
CYPERACEAE															
Eleocharis palustris type	spike-rush	1.4	8.0	—	—	—	1.3	—	16.0	—	—	—	—	—	—
cf. Eleocharis palustris type	spike-rush	—	—	—	—	—	—	—	4.0	—	—	—	—	—	—
Scirpus spp.	club-rushes	0.5	—	—	—	—	—	—	—	—	—	—	—	—	—
Carex spp.	sedges	9.6	440.0	—	—	—	6.5	8.0	36.0	—	—	—	—	—	—
Cyperaceae	NFI	—	—	—	—	—	0.3	—	20.0	—	—	—	—	—	—
cf. Cyperaceae	NFI	—	—	—	—	—	2.9	4.0	24.0	—	—	—	—	—	—
GRAMINEAE															
Avena sp.	oat	—	—	—	—	—	3.4	28.0	48.0	—	—	—	—	—	—
cf. Avena sp.	oat	—	—	—	—	—	1.0	—	4.0	—	—	—	—	—	—
Hordeum sp.	barley	0.5	—	—	—	—	—	—	—	—	—	—	—	—	—
Triticum spelta/aestivum	spelt/bread wheat	0.5	—	—	—	—	—	—	—	—	—	—	—	—	—
Triticum aestivum type	bread/club wheat	0.5	—	—	—	—	0.5	—	16.0	—	—	—	—	—	—
Triticum sp.	wheat	—	—	—	—	—	0.3	—	—	—	—	—	—	—	—
cf. Secale cereale	rye	0.5	—	—	—	—	—	—	4.0	—	—	—	—	—	—
—	indeterminate cereal	—	—	—	—	—	3.4	—	32.0	—	—	—	—	—	—
Poa spp	poa	—	—	—	—	—	0.3	—	—	—	—	—	—	—	—
cf. Poa sp.	poa	—	—	—	—	—	—	—	24.0	—	—	—	—	—	—
Poa/Phleum sp.	poa/cat's tail	0.5	—	—	—	—	—	—	—	—	—	—	—	—	—
Bromus secalinus/mollis	rye-brome/lop-grass	—	—	—	—	—	1.0	4.0	—	—	—	—	—	—	—
Bromus cf. secalinus/mollis	rye-brome/lop-grass	—	—	—	—	—	—	—	8.0	—	—	—	—	—	—
Gramineae	NFI	2.3	—	—	—	—	4.4	8.0	112.0	—	—	—	—	4.0	—
cf. Gramineae	NFI	—	—	—	—	—	0.3	—	—	—	—	—	—	—	—
Indeterminate		6.8	16.0	—	—	4.0	16.4	48.0	188.0	4.0	4.0	—	—	8.0	—
Total		111.3	512.0	4.0	16.0	32.0	156.9	384.0	1824.0	8.0	4.0	16.0	8.0	48.0	12.0

5.11. *Plant remains from Watling Court, phase 4 occupation surfaces (number of seeds per kg of soil).*

Taxa	Context Numbers	776	Building 4 814	830
PAPAVERACEAE				
Papaver somniferum L.	opium poppy	0.2	—	—
CRUCIFERAE				
Brassica/Sinapsis spp.	—	21.3	—	—
CARYOPHYLLACEAE				
Silene cf. alba	white campion	0.2	—	—
Silene alba/noctiflora/vulgaris	campion	1.1	—	—
Silene vulgaris (Moench) Garcke	bladder campion	5.8	—	—
Silene cf. vulgaris	bladder campion	1.1	—	—
Silene vulgaris/maritima	bladder/sea campion	0.4	—	—
Silene cf. maritima	sea campion	0.4	—	—
cf. Silene sp.	campion/catchfly	0.2	—	—
Agrostemma githago L.	corn cockle	0.9	—	—
cf. Agrostemma githago	corn cockle	+	—	—
Myosoton/Stellaria sp.	chickweed/stitchwort	0.2	—	—
Stellaria media/graminea	chickweed/stitchwort	0.2	—	—
Stellaria cf. palustris	marsh stitchwort	0.4	—	—
Stellaria graminea L.	lesser stitchwort	2.2	—	—
Stellaria cf. graminea	lesser stitchwort	0.2	—	—
Stellaria sp.	chickweed/stitchwort	0.2	—	—
CHENOPODIACEAE				
Chenopodium polyspermum	all-seed	0.2	—	—
Chenopodium album type	fat hen	14.2	—	—
Chenopodium cf. ficifolium	fig-leaved goosefoot	0.4	—	—
cf. Chenopodium urbicum	upright goosefoot	0.2	—	—
Chenopodium sp.	goosefoot etc.	0.2	—	—
Chenopodium/Atriplex spp.	goosefoots/oraches	1.1	—	—
Atriplex spp.	oraches	16.9	—	—
Chenopodiaceae	NFI	0.2	—	—
MALVACEAE				
Malvaceae	NFI	0.2	—	—
LEGUMINOSAE				
cf. Vicia faba	celtic bean/horsebean	0.2	—	—
ROSACEAE				
Rubus fruticosus/idaeus	blackberry/raspberry	0.2	—	—
Potentilla/Fragaria sp.	—	0.2	—	—
Prunus domestica L.	plum/bullace	0.2	—	—
UMBELLIFERAE				
Chaerophyllum sp.	chervil	0.7	—	—
Torilis nodosa (L.) Gaertn.	knotted hedge-parsley	4.0	—	—
Bupleurum cf. rotundifolium	hare's ear	4.4	—	—
Oenanthe sp	dropwort	2.2	—	—
cf. Oenanthe sp.	dropwort	2.2	—	—
Daucus carota L.	carrot	0.2	—	—
POLYGONACEAE				
Polygonum aviculare agg.	knotgrass	0.4	—	—
Polygonum persicaria L.	persicaria	0.7	—	—
Polygonum convolvulus L.	black bindweed	1.6	—	—
Polygonum cf. convolvulus	black bindweed	0.2	—	—
Rumex acetosella agg.	sheep's sorrel	0.7	—	—
Rumex spp.	docks	67.3	—	—
Polygonaceae	NFI	4.9	—	—
POLYGONACEAE/CYPERACEAE				
Polygonaceae/Cyperaceae	NFI	2.2	—	—
URTICACEAE				
Urtica urens L.	small nettle	0.2	—	—
Urtica dioica L.	stinging nettle	47.6	—	—
Urtica sp.	nettle	0.4	—	—
PRIMULACEAE				
Anagallis arvensis L.	scarlet pimpernel	0.2	—	—
LABIATAE				
cf. Mentha sp.	mint	0.4	—	—
Labiatae	NFI	0.2	—	—
CAPRIFOLIACEAE				
Sambucus nigra L.	elder	1.3	8.0	4.0
RUBIACEAE				
Galium aparine L.	cleavers	0.2	—	—
COMPOSITAE				
Centaurea sp.	knapweed/thistle	0.2	—	—
Compositae	NFI	0.2	—	—

Taxa	Context Numbers	776	Building 4 814	830
CYPERACEAE				
Eleocharis palustris type	spike-rush	6.4	—	—
Eleocharis sp.	spike-rush	0.2	—	—
Carex spp.	sedges	8.4	—	—
GRAMINEAE				
Avena sp.	oat	0.4	—	—
cf. Avena sp.	oat	0.2	—	—
Hordeum sp.	barley	—	4.0	—
cf. Hordeum sp.	barley	—	—	4.0
Triticum aestivum type	bread/club wheat	0.2	—	—
Triticum sp.	wheat	0.2	—	—
—	indeterminate cereal	0.2	—	—
Indeterminate		10.2	—	4.0
Total		239.4	12.0	12.0

5.12. *Plant remains from Miles Lane pits (number of seeds per kg of soil).*

Taxa	Context Numbers	cut 118/119	cut 162/144	cut 159/154	cut 160/167	cut 172/173	cut 160/177	cut 205/195	cut 278 [200]	cut 278 [201]	cut 203/204	cut 251 [215]	cut 251 [227]
RANUNCULACEAE													
Ranunculus sceleratus L.	celery-leaved crowfoot	—	—	—	—	—	0.6	—	—	—	—	—	—
Ranunculus subgen. Batrachium (DC) A. Gray	crowfoots	—	—	—	—	—	—	0.3	—	—	—	—	—
PAPAVERACEAE													
Papaver rhoeas/dubium	field/long-headed poppy	—	—	—	—	—	—	—	—	—	—	—	0.3
Papaver argemone L.	long prickly-headed poppy	—	—	—	—	—	—	—	—	—	—	—	0.3
Papaver cf. argemone	long prickly-headed poppy	—	—	—	0.5	—	—	—	—	—	—	—	—
Papaver somniferum L.	opium poppy	—	—	—	0.5	—	—	—	—	—	—	—	—
CRUCIFERAE													
Brassica/Sinapsis spp.	—	—	—	—	0.5	—	—	—	0.6	—	—	—	—
RESEDACEAE													
Reseda luteola L.	dyer's rocket	—	—	—	—	—	—	—	0.1	—	4.0	—	—
CARYOPHYLLACEAE													
Silene alba/noctiflora	campion	—	—	—	0.3	—	—	—	—	—	—	—	—
Silene alba/dioica/noctiflora	campion	—	—	—	—	—	—	—	0.3	—	—	—	—
Silene alba/noctiflora/vulgaris	campion	—	—	—	—	—	0.3	—	0.3	—	—	—	—
Silene vulgaris (Moench) Garcke	bladder campion	—	—	—	—	—	—	—	—	—	—	—	0.3
Silene cf. vulgaris	bladder campion	—	—	—	1.9	—	—	—	0.6	—	—	—	—
Silene spp.	campions/catchflies	—	—	—	1.3	—	2.5	—	0.3	—	—	—	0.6
Lychnis flos-cuculi L.	ragged robin	—	—	—	—	—	0.3	—	—	—	—	—	—
Agrostemma githago L.	corn cockle	—	—	—	0.3	—	0.3	—	—	—	—	—	—
cf. Agrostemma githago	corn cockle	0.2	—	—	+	—	+	+	—	+	—	—	+
Stellaria media (L.) Vill.	chickweed	—	—	—	0.3	—	0.6	—	0.3	—	—	—	0.3
Stellaria graminea L.	lesser stitchwort	—	—	—	—	—	0.3	—	—	—	—	—	—
Stellaria sp.	chickweed/stitchwort	—	—	—	0.3	—	—	—	—	—	—	—	—
CHENOPODIACEAE													
Chenopodium album type	fat hen	0.2	—	—	4.8	—	9.8	17.3	20.0	60.3	24.0	6.0	7.3
Chenopodium hybridum L.	maple-leaved goosefoot	—	—	—	—	—	—	—	—	—	—	—	0.3
Chenopodium/Atriplex spp	goosefoots/oraches	—	—	4.0	0.5	—	1.3	—	—	1.4	—	—	—
Atriplex spp.	oraches	—	—	—	6.9	—	5.7	8.0	—	4.8	—	—	—
Chenopodiaceae	NFI	—	—	—	—	8.0	—	2.7	—	—	—	—	—
VITACEAE													
cf. Vitis vinifera	vine	—	—	—	—	—	—	—	0.1	—	—	—	—
LEGUMINOSAE													
Vicia/Lathyrus/Pisum sp.	vetch/tare/vetchling/pea	—	—	—	—	—	—	2.7	—	—	—	—	—
Leguminosae	NFI	—	—	—	—	—	—	1.3	—	—	—	—	—
ROSACEAE													
Rubus cf. fruticosus agg.	blackberry	—	—	—	1.1	—	4.4	—	—	3.5	225.0	—	0.6
Rubus fruticosus/idaeus	blackberry/raspberry	—	—	—	—	—	7.9	1.3	—	5.3	7.0	—	—
Rubus cf. idaeus	raspberry	—	—	—	—	—	0.3	—	—	—	—	—	—
Rubus fruticosus/caesius	blackberry/dewberry	—	—	—	—	—	—	—	—	0.1	—	—	—
Prunus spinosa L.	sloe/blackthorn	—	—	—	—	—	6.0	—	—	—	9.0	—	—
Prunus cf. spinosa	sloe/blackthorn	—	—	—	—	—	1.0	—	—	—	—	—	—
Prunus domestica L.	plum/bullace	—	—	—	—	—	1.3	—	—	—	18.0	—	—
Prunus cf. domestica	plum/bullace	—	—	4.0	—	—	0.6	—	—	—	25.0	—	—
Prunus sp.	—	—	—	—	—	—	1.9	—	—	—	—	—	—
Prunus spp.	—	—	—	—	—	—	—	—	—	—	13.0	—	—
Crataegus monogyna Jacq.	hawthorn	—	—	—	—	—	—	—	—	—	10.0	—	—
Pyrus/Malus sp.	pear/apple	—	—	—	—	—	0.6	—	—	—	12.0	—	—
UMBELLIFERAE													
Conium maculatum L.	hemlock	—	—	—	—	—	—	—	—	—	—	—	5.4
Apium sp.	—	—	—	—	14.1	—	1.3	6.7	—	—	—	—	—
Apium/Berula sp.	—	—	—	—	1.9	—	—	2.7	—	—	—	—	—
Oenanthe sp.	dropwort	—	—	—	—	—	—	—	0.1	—	—	—	0.6
Umbelliferae	NFI	—	—	—	1.3	—	1.3	—	—	—	4.0	—	—
POLYGONACEAE													
Polygonum aviculare	knotgrass	—	4.0	—	—	—	2.5	—	—	—	—	—	—
Polygonum persicaria L.	persicaria	—	—	—	—	—	0.3	—	—	—	—	—	—
Polygonum lapathifolium L.	pale persicaria	—	—	—	—	—	—	1.3	—	0.3	—	—	—
Polygonum convolvulus L.	black bindweed	—	—	—	0.5	—	—	2.7	—	1.6	—	—	—
Rumex spp.	docks	0.2	—	—	0.5	—	—	—	—	0.4	—	—	—
POLYGONACEAE/CYPERACEAE													
Polygonaceae/Cyperaceae	NFI	—	—	—	—	—	1.0	—	—	—	—	—	—
URTICACEAE													
Urtica urens L.	small nettle	—	—	—	0.3	—	1.0	—	—	—	—	—	2.2
Urtica dioica L.	stinging nettle	—	—	—	—	—	0.6	—	—	—	—	—	50.8
Urtica sp.	nettle	—	—	—	—	—	—	—	—	—	—	—	0.6
CORYLACEAE													
Corylus avellana L.	hazel	—	—	—	—	—	+	—	—	—	—	—	—
SOLANACEAE													

Taxa	Context Numbers	cut 118 / 119	cut 162 / 144	cut 159 / 154	cut 160 / 167	cut 172 / 173	cut 160 / 177	cut 205 / 195	cut 278 [200	201]	cut 203 / 204	cut 251 [215	227]
Hyoscyamus niger L.	henbane	—	—	—	—	—	0.3	—	—	—	—	—	0.6
Solanum nigrum L.	black nightshade	0.2	—	—	—	—	—	—	—	—	—	—	—
LABIATAE													
cf. Mentha sp.	mint	—	—	—	—	—	—	—	—	—	—	—	0.3
cf. Ballota nigra	black horehound	—	—	—	—	—	—	—	—	—	4.0	—	—
Lamium cf. purpureum	red dead-nettle	—	—	—	—	—	—	—	—	0.1	—	—	2.5
Lamium sp.	dead-nettle	—	—	—	—	—	—	—	—	0.1	—	—	0.6
Labiatae	NFI	—	—	—	—	—	—	—	—	0.1	—	1.0	0.6
CAPRIFOLIACEAE													
Sambucus nigra L.	elder	106.2	8.0	—	—	—	9.8	—	—	0.1	—	10.0	19.0
Sambucus nigra/ebulus	elder/danewort	3.9	—	—	—	—	—	—	—	—	—	—	0.6
RUBIACEAE													
cf. Galium palustre	marsh bedstraw	—	—	—	—	—	—	—	—	0.3	—	—	—
COMPOSITAE													
Anthemis cotula L.	stinking mayweed	0.2	—	—	0.3	—	1.0	—	—	—	—	—	0.3
Lapsana communis L.	nipplewort	—	—	—	0.5	—	—	—	—	—	—	—	—
Sonchus sp.	milk-/sow-thistle	—	—	—	—	—	1.3	—	—	—	—	—	—
Compositae	NFI	—	—	—	0.3	—	—	—	—	—	—	—	—
ALISMATACEAE													
Alisma plantago-aquatica L.	water-plantain	0.2	—	—	—	—	0.3	—	—	0.1	—	—	1.3
CYPERACEAE													
cf. Eriophorum sp.	cotton-grass	—	—	—	—	—	0.3	—	—	—	—	—	—
Eleocharis palustris type	spike-rush	0.9	—	—	0.5	—	1.3	1.3	—	2.7	—	—	13.3
Elocharis sp.	spike-rush	—	—	—	—	—	0.3	—	—	—	—	—	—
Scirpus spp.	club-rushes	—	—	—	—	—	1.9	—	—	—	—	—	—
Carex spp.	sedges	—	—	—	0.8	4.0	3.2	2.7	—	1.0	—	—	1.9
Cyperaceae	NFI	—	—	—	—	—	0.6	—	—	—	—	—	—
GRAMINEAE													
cf. Avena sp.	oat	—	—	—	0.3	—	—	—	—	—	—	—	—
Hordeum sp.	barley	0.5	—	—	—	—	1.6	4.0	—	0.6	—	—	0.6
Hordeum/Triticum/Secale sp.	barley/wheat/rye	0.2	—	—	—	—	—	—	—	—	—	—	—
Triticum spelta/aestivum	spelt/bread wheat	—	—	—	—	—	—	—	4.0	—	—	—	—
Triticum aestivum type	bread/club wheat	0.9	—	—	—	—	0.3	1.3	—	—	—	—	0.3
Triticum sp.	wheat	0.2	—	—	—	—	—	—	—	—	—	—	—
cf. Triticum sp.	wheat	—	—	—	0.3	—	—	—	—	—	—	—	—
Triticum/Secale sp.	wheat/rye	—	—	—	—	—	1.3	—	—	—	—	—	—
Secale cereale	rye	—	—	—	—	—	0.3	—	—	—	—	—	0.3
cf. Secale cereale	rye	0.2	—	—	—	—	0.3	—	—	—	—	—	—
—	indeterminate cereal	0.2	—	—	—	—	0.3	—	—	—	—	—	—
cf. Poa spp.	poa	0.2	—	—	—	—	0.3	—	—	—	—	—	—
Bromus secalinus/mollis	rye-brome/lop-grass	0.2	—	—	—	—	—	—	—	—	—	—	—
Gramineae	NFI	0.2	—	—	—	—	—	—	—	—	—	—	—
Indeterminate		1.1	8.0	—	1.6	—	9.8	8.0	—	2.6	—	4.0	7.0
Total		116.6	20.0	8.0	42.4	12.0	86.3	66.7	24.0	88.3	36.0	340.0	107.3

5.13. Plant remains from Peninsular House, phases 1-3 occupation surfaces, ovens and hearths; phases 2, 4 & 6 pits (number of seeds per kg of soil).

Taxa	Context Numbers	Building E6 [564	1226]	Building E14 1916	Building E19 [1211	1416	1431]	cut 257 296	cut 644 623	cut 184 627	cut 176 187
RANUNCULACEAE										
Ranunculus acris/repens/bulbosus	buttercups	—	—	—	—	—	0.3	—	—	—	—
Ranunculus sp.	—	—	—	—	—	—	0.3	—	—	—	—
PAPAVERACEAE										
Papaver cf. rhoeas	field poppy	—	5.0	—	—	—	—	—	—	—	—
Papaver rhoeas/dubium	field/long-headed poppy	—	10.0	—	—	—	—	—	—	—	—
Papaver somniferum l.	opium poppy	—	185.0	0.7	—	—	—	—	—	—	—
cf. Papaver somniferum	opium poppy	—	5.0	—	—	—	—	—	—	—	—
CRUCIFERAE										
Brassica/Sinapis spp.	—	—	75.0	1.3	—	—	—	—	—	—	—
cf. Brassica/Sinapis spp.	—	—	35.0	—	—	—	—	—	—	—	—
Raphanus raphanistrum L.	wild radish/charlock	—	—	1.3	—	—	—	—	—	—	—
Thlaspi arvense L.	field penny-cress	—	—	0.7	—	—	—	—	—	—	—
Cruciferae	NFI	—	100.0	—	—	—	—	—	—	—	—
cf. Cruciferae	NFI	—	—	—	—	—	0.3	—	—	—	—
CRUCIFERAE/LEGUMINOSAE										
Cruciferae/Leguminosae	NFI	—	120.0	—	—	—	—	—	—	—	—
RESEDACEAE										
Reseda luteola L.	dyer's rocket	—	—	0.7	—	—	0.3	—	—	—	—
VIOLACEAE										
Viola sp.	violet	—	—	11.0	—	—	—	—	—	—	—
CARYOPHYLLACEAE										
Silene alba/noctiflora	campion	—	—	0.7	—	—	—	—	—	—	—
Silene alba/noctiflora/vulgaris	campion	—	30.0	0.7	—	—	—	—	—	—	—
Silene vulgaris (Moench) Garcke	bladder campion	—	—	1.3	—	—	—	—	—	—	—
Silene cf. vulgaris	bladder campion	—	55.0	0.7	—	—	—	—	—	—	—
Silene cf. maritima	sea campion	—	5.0	—	—	—	—	—	—	—	—
Silene spp.	campions/catchflies	—	—	1.3	—	—	2.7	—	—	—	—
Agrostemma githago L.	corn cockle	—	220.0	—	—	—	—	—	—	—	—
cf. Agrostemma githago	corn cockle	—	10.0	+	—	—	+	—	—	—	—
Stellaria media (L.) Vill.	chickweed	—	655.0	0.7	—	—	—	—	—	—	—
Stellaria graminea L.	lesser stitchwort	—	20.0	0.7	—	—	—	—	—	—	—
Stellaria sp.	chickweed/stitchwort	—	180.0	—	—	—	—	—	—	—	—
Spergula arvensis L.	corn spurrey	—	—	0.7	—	—	—	—	—	—	—
CHENOPODIACEAE										
Chenopodium polyspermum	all-seed	—	—	0.7	—	—	—	—	—	—	—
Chenopodium album type	fat hen	10.0	120.0	251.0	—	—	27.5	—	—	—	—
Chenopodium cf. album type	fat hen	—	—	—	—	—	0.3	—	—	—	—
Chenopodium cf. ficifolium	fig-leaved goosefoot	—	—	0.7	—	—	—	—	—	—	—
cf. Chenopodium urbicum	upright goosefoot	—	—	6.4	—	—	—	—	—	—	—
Chenopodium/Atriplex spp.	goosefoots/oraches	10.0	865.0	7.7	—	4.0	6.6	—	—	—	—
Atriplex spp.	oraches	—	85.0	16.8	—	—	1.2	—	—	—	4.0
Chenopodiaceae	NFI	—	5.0	—	—	—	2.1	—	—	—	—
cf. Chenopodiaceae	NFI	—	5.0	—	—	—	—	—	—	—	—
LEGUMINOSAE										
Vicia hirsuta (L.) S. F. Gray	hairy tare	—	35.0	—	—	—	—	—	—	—	—
cf. Vicia hirsuta	hairy tare	—	170.0	—	—	—	—	—	—	—	—
Vicia/Lathyrus spp.	vetch/tare/vetchling	—	160.0	—	—	—	0.6	—	—	—	—
cf. Vicia/Lathyrus spp.	vetch/tare/vetchling	—	55.0	—	—	—	0.9	—	—	—	—
Vicia/Lathyrus/Pisum sp.	vetch/tare/vetchling/pea	—	—	—	—	—	0.3	—	—	—	—
Leguminosae	NFI	—	—	—	—	—	0.9	—	—	—	—
ROSACEAE										
Prunus sp.	—	—	—	—	—	—	0.3	—	—	—	—
Pyrus/Malus sp.	pear/apple	—	—	—	—	—	—	—	—	2.0	—
UMBELLIFERAE										
Chaerophyllum sp.	chervil	—	10.0	—	—	—	—	—	—	—	—
Conium/Petroselinum/Pimpinella sp.	hemlock/parsley/burnet saxifrage	—	30.0	—	—	—	—	—	—	—	—
Oenanthe sp.	dropwort	—	—	5.8	—	—	—	—	—	—	—
Umbelliferae	NFI	—	10.0	0.7	—	—	—	—	—	—	—
POLYGONACEAE										
Polygonum aviculare agg.	knotgrass	—	5.0	1.3	—	—	0.6	—	—	—	—
Polygonum persicaria L.	persicaria	—	—	0.7	—	—	0.3	—	—	—	—
Polygonum lapathifolium L.	pale persicaria	—	10.0	—	—	—	0.3	—	—	—	—
Polygonum convolvulus L.	black bindweed	—	5.0	6.4	—	—	—	—	—	—	—
Polygonum cf. convolvulus	black bindweed	—	10.0	—	—	—	—	—	—	—	—
cf. Polygonum sp.	—	—	5.0	—	—	—	—	—	—	—	—
Rumex acetosella agg.	sheep's sorrel	—	280.0	—	—	—	0.3	—	—	—	—
cf. Rumex acetosella agg.	sheep's sorrel	—	80.0	—	—	—	—	—	—	—	—
Rumex spp.	docks	—	70.0	1.3	—	—	—	—	—	—	—
Polygonaceae	NFI	—	5.0	—	—	—	—	—	—	—	—

Taxa	Context Numbers	Building E6 [564	1226]	Building E14 1916	Building E19 [1211	1416	1431]	cut 257 296	cut 644 623	cut 184 627	cut 176 187
cf. Polygonaceae	NFI	—	5.0	—	—	—	0.3	—	—	—	—
POLYGONACEAE/CYPERACEAE											
Polygonaceae/Cyperaceae	NFI	—	—	0.7	—	—	—	—	—	—	—
URTICACEAE											
Urtica urens L.	small nettle	—	—	2.6	—	—	0.3	—	—	—	—
Urtica dioica L.	stinging nettle	—	—	3.9	—	—	—	—	—	—	—
CORYLACEAE											
Corylus avellana L.	hazel	+	—	—	+	—	+	—	—	—	—
SOLANACEAE											
Hyoscyamus niger L.	henbane	—	—	—	—	—	0.3	—	—	—	—
LABIATAE											
cf. Mentha sp.	mint	—	—	0.7	—	—	—	—	—	—	—
cf. Ajuga sp.	bugle	—	—	—	—	—	0.3	—	—	—	—
PLANTAGINACEAE											
Plantago lanceolata type	ribwort	—	225.0	—	—	—	—	—	—	—	—
cf. Plantago lanceolata type	ribwort	—	15.0	—	—	—	—	—	—	—	—
CAPRIFOLIACEAE											
Sambucus nigra L.	elder	—	—	—	—	—	2.4	4.0	—	11.0	4.0
RUBIACEAE											
Galium aparine L.	cleavers	—	10.0	—	—	—	—	—	—	—	—
Galium aparine/tricornutum	cleavers/bedstraw	—	5.0	—	—	—	—	—	—	—	—
cf. Rubiaceae	NFI	—	—	0.7	—	—	—	—	—	—	—
VALERIANACEAE											
Valerianella cf. dentata	corn salad	—	—	—	—	—	0.6	—	—	—	—
COMPOSITAE											
Senecio sp.	ragwort	—	20.0	—	—	—	—	—	—	—	—
Anthemis cotula L.	stinking mayweed	25.0	9000.0	1.3	—	—	29.3	—	—	—	—
Anthemis sp.	mayweed/chamomile	—	15.0	—	—	—	—	—	—	—	—
Tripleurospermum maritimum (L.) Koch	scentless mayweed	—	100.0	—	—	—	—	—	—	—	—
Chrysanthemum segetum L.	corn marigold	—	—	—	—	—	0.9	—	—	—	—
Chrysanthemum cf. segetum	corn marigold	—	—	—	—	—	0.3	—	—	—	—
Lapsana communis L.	nipplewort	—	265.0	9.0	—	—	—	—	—	—	—
cf. Lapsana communis	nipplewort	—	20.0	—	—	—	—	—	—	—	—
Hypochoeris cf. radicata	cat's ear	—	40.0	—	—	—	—	—	—	—	—
Sonchus asper (L.) Hill	spiny milk-/sow-thistle	—	20.0	—	—	—	—	—	—	—	—
cf. Crepis capillaris	smooth hawk's-beard	—	60.0	—	—	—	—	—	—	—	—
Compositae	NFI	—	400.0	—	—	—	0.9	—	—	—	—
cf. Compositae	NFI	—	40.0	—	—	—	—	—	—	—	—
ALISMATACEAE											
Alisma plantago-aquatica L.	water-plantain	5.0	—	—	—	—	—	—	—	—	—
CYPERACEAE											
Eleocharis palustris type	spike-rush	—	—	5.8	—	—	17.0	—	—	—	—
Carex spp.	sedges	—	—	7.1	—	—	5.4	—	—	—	—
cf. Carex spp.	sedges	—	—	—	—	—	0.3	—	—	—	—
Cyperaceae	NFI	—	—	—	—	—	0.3	—	—	—	—
GRAMINEAE											
Avena fatua/ludoviciana	wild oat	—	5.0	—	—	—	—	—	—	—	—
Avena sp.	oat	20.0	2890.0	1.3	—	4.0	1.5	—	—	—	—
cf. Avena sp.	oat	5.0	215.0	—	—	4.0	—	—	—	—	—
Avena/Hordeum sp.	oat/barley	—	35.0	—	—	—	—	—	—	—	—
Avena/Secale sp.	oat/rye	—	10.0	—	—	—	—	—	—	—	—
Hordeum cf. distichum	two-row barley	—	585.0	—	—	—	—	—	—	—	—
Hordeum sp.	barley	5.0	—	—	—	—	0.3	—	—	—	—
cf. Hordeum sp.	barley	—	—	—	—	—	—	—	2.0	—	—
Triticum spelta type	spelt	—	20.0	—	—	—	—	—	—	—	—
Triticum spelta/aestivum	spelt/bread wheat	—	60.0	—	—	—	—	—	—	—	—
Triticum aestivum type	bread/club wheat	5.0	300.0	—	—	—	0.6	—	—	—	—
Triticum/Secale sp.	wheat/rye	—	40.0	—	—	—	—	—	—	—	—
Secale cereale	rye	20.0	945.0	—	—	—	—	—	—	—	—
cf. Secale cereale	rye	15.0	80.0	—	—	—	—	—	—	—	—
—	indeterminate cereal	5.0	240.0	—	—	—	—	—	—	—	4.0
cf. Festuca spp.	fescues	—	80.0	—	—	—	—	—	—	—	—
cf. Lolium perenne	rye-grass	—	25.0	—	—	—	—	—	—	—	—
cf. Vulpia sp.	fescue	—	15.0	—	—	—	—	—	—	—	—
cf. Poa annua	annual poa	—	—	—	—	—	0.6	—	—	—	—
cf. Poa sp.	poa	—	220.0	—	—	—	—	—	—	—	—
Bromus secalinus/mollis	rye-brome/lop-grass	10.0	540.0	—	—	—	—	—	—	—	—

Taxa	Context Numbers	Building E6		Building E14 1916	Building E19			cut 257 296	cut 644 623	cut 184 627	cut 176 187
		[564	1226]		[1211	1416	1431]				
cf. Agrostis sp.	bent-grass	—	240.0	—	—	—	0.3	—	—	—	—
Phleum sp.	cat's tail	—	65.0	—	—	—	0.3	—	—	—	—
cf. Phleum sp.	cat's tail	—	125.0	—	—	—	—	—	—	—	—
Milium sp.	millet	—	—	—	—	—	0.3	—	—	—	—
Gramineae	NFI	15.0	115.0	—	—	—	0.9	—	—	—	—
Indeterminate		10.0	955.0	7.7	—	—	2.7	—	—	—	—
Total		160.0	21775.0	362.0	0.0	12.0	112.0	4.0	2.0	13.0	12.0

5.14. (below) Plant remains from Well Court, phases 3-4 oven, hearth and related deposits (number of seeds per kg of soil).

Taxa	Context Numbers	Building 3 oven 1075	Building 4 ash from B3 oven					hearth 1200	Building 6 hearth	rake-off
			[1076	1132	1133	1134	1169]		[1020	1028]
RANUNCULACEAE										
Ranunculus acris/repens/bulbosus	buttercups	—	4.0	—	2.9	—	—	—	—	—
CARYOPHYLLACEAE										
Agrostemma githago L.	corn cockle	20.0	60.0	—	—	—	0.7	—	5.7	—
cf. Agrostemma githago	corn cockle	—	—	—	—	—	1.3	—	—	—
Stellaria sp.	chickweed/stitchwort	—	—	—	—	—	1.3	—	—	—
cf. Stellaria sp.	chickweed/stitchwort	—	—	—	—	—	1.3	—	—	—
CHENOPODIACEAE										
Chenopodium album type	fat hen	—	—	—	5.7	—	7.7	6.7	11.4	—
Chenopodium/Atriplex spp.	goosefoots/oraches	—	—	—	—	—	16.1	—	8.6	—
Atriplex spp.	oraches	—	—	—	—	—	0.7	—	—	—
cf. Atriplex sp.	orache	—	—	—	—	—	0.7	—	—	—
Chenopodiaceae	NFI	—	—	—	—	—	2.6	6.7	—	—
MALVACEAE										
Malva sp.	mallow	4.0	—	—	—	—	0.7	—	—	—
LEGUMINOSAE										
Medicago sp.	medick	—	—	—	—	—	—	—	2.9	—
Vicia/Lathyrus spp.	vetch/tare/vetching	—	—	—	—	—	5.8	—	—	—
Leguminosae	NFI	—	—	—	—	—	18.7	—	—	—
UMBELLIFERAE										
cf. Bupleurum sp.	—	—	—	—	—	—	0.7	—	—	—
POLYGONACEAE										
Polygonum sp.	—	—	—	—	—	—	1.3	—	—	—
Rumex acetosella agg.	sheep's sorrel	—	—	—	—	—	0.7	—	—	—
Rumex spp.	docks	—	—	—	—	—	1.3	—	—	—
Polygonaceae	NFI	—	—	—	—	—	0.7	—	—	—
POLYGONACEAE/CYPERACEAE										
Polygonaceae/Cyperaceae	NFI	—	—	—	—	—	—	13.3	—	—
URTICACEAE										
Urtica dioica L.	stinging nettle	—	—	—	—	—	1.9	—	—	—
CORYLACEAE										
Corylus avellana L.	hazel	—	—	—	—	—	+	—	+	—
PRIMULACEAE										
Anagallis sp.	pimpernel	—	—	—	—	—	3.2	—	—	—
LABIATAE										
Teucrium sp.	germander	—	—	—	—	—	0.7	—	—	—
cf. Labiatae	NFI	—	—	—	—	—	—	—	2.9	—
PLANTAGINACEAE										
Plantago lanceolata type	ribwort	—	—	—	—	—	0.7	—	—	—
CAPRIFOLIACEAE										
Sambucus nigra L.	elder	4.0	—	—	—	—	1.3	—	5.7	—
RUBIACEAE										
cf. Gallium aparine	cleavers	—	—	—	—	—	—	—	2.9	—
Galium/Asperula sp.	bedstraw/woodruff	—	—	—	—	—	1.3	—	—	—
COMPOSITAE										

Taxa	Context Numbers	Building 3 oven	Building 4 ash from B3 oven					Building 6 hearth	hearth	rake-off
		1075	[1076	1132	1133	1134	1169]	1200	[1020	1028]
Anthemis cotula L.	stinking mayweed	—	—	—	—	—	14.8	—	—	—
Compositae	NFI	—	—	—	—	—	3.2	—	—	—
SPARGANIACEAE										
cf. Sparganium sp.	bur-reed	—	4.0	—	—	—	—	—	—	—
CYPERACEAE										
Eleocharis palustris type	spike-rush	—	—	—	—	—	3.2	—	—	—
Carex spp.	sedges	—	—	—	—	—	2.6	—	—	—
GRAMINEAE										
Avena sp.	oat	8.0	24.0	—	—	—	1.9	—	—	—
cf. Avena sp.	oat	—	—	—	2.9	—	—	—	—	—
Hordeum vulgare	six-row barley	—	—	—	—	—	0.7	—	—	—
Hordeum sp.	barley	—	12.0	—	8.6	—	5.8	—	2.9	—
Hordeum/Triticum sp.	barley/wheat	—	4.0	—	—	—	—	—	—	—
Triticum spelta type	spelt	—	—	—	11.4	8.0	—	6.7	—	—
Triticum cf. spelta type	spelt	—	36.0	—	—	—	—	—	—	—
Triticum spelta/aestivum	spelt/bread wheat	400.0	512.0	40.0	25.7	20.0	1.3	40.0	5.7	—
Triticum aestivum type	bread/club wheat	600.0	2500.0	10.0	40.0	20.0	6.4	—	2.9	4.0
Triticum sp.	wheat	—	—	—	—	—	0.7	—	—	—
Triticum/Secale sp.	wheat/rye	12.0	44.0	—	—	—	—	—	2.9	—
Secale cereale	rye	—	20.0	—	—	—	—	—	—	—
cf. Secale cereale	rye	—	—	—	—	—	0.7	6.7	—	—
—	indeterminate cereal	—	320.0	5.0	5.7	—	—	—	11.4	4.0
cf. Festuca spp.	fescues	—	—	—	—	—	24.5	—	—	—
cf. Poa spp.	poa	—	—	—	2.9	—	4.5	—	—	—
Phleum sp.	cat's tail	—	—	—	—	—	1.3	—	—	—
Gramineae	NFI	—	—	—	—	—	11.6	—	—	—
cf. Gramineae	NFI	—	—	—	—	—	—	—	2.9	—
Indeterminate		—	4.0	—	—	—	32,9	6.7	—	—
Total		1048.0	3544.0	55.0	105.7	48.0	187.2	86.7	68.6	8.0

5.15. Plant remains from Ironmonger Lane, phase 2 occupation surfaces; phases 3-6 pits (number of seeds per kg of soil).

Taxa	Context Numbers	Building 1 298	2 279	cut 228 411	cut 177 172
RANUNCULACEAE					
Ranunculus acris/repens/bulbosus	buttercups	—	—	0.4	—
Ranunculus subgen. Batrachium (DC) A. Gray	crowfoots	1.0	—	—	—
cf. Ranunculus sp.	—	—	—	0.4	—
PAPAVERACEAE					
Papaver somniferum L.	opium poppy	0.3	—	—	—
CRUCIFERAE					
Brassica/Sinapsis spp.	—	0.5	—	0.4	0.7
RESEDACEAE					
Reseda luteola L.	dyer's rocket	0.3	—	—	—
CARYOPHYLLACEAE					
Silene alba/dioica/noctiflora	campion	—	—	—	0.4
Silena alba/noctiflora/vulgaris	campion	—	—	—	0.4
Silene cf. vulgaris	bladder campion	—	—	0.4	—
Silene spp.	campions/catchflies	0.3	—	—	—
Agrostemma githago L.	corn cockle	—	—	—	2.8
Stellaria media (L.) Vill.	chickweed	0.3	—	—	—
Spergula arvensis L.	corn spurrey	—	—	—	16.1
CHENOPODIACEAE					
Chenopodium polyspermum	all-seed	0.3	—	—	—
Chenopodium album type	fat hen	10.1	0.6	4.9	50.9
cf. Chenopodium urbicum	upright goosefoot	0.3	—	—	1.0
Chenopodium cf. rubrum/glaucum	red/glaucous goosefoot	0.3	—	—	—
Chenopodium/Atriplex spp.	goosefoots/oraches	1.6	—	0.4	3.9
Atriplex spp.	oraches	0.3	—	0.9	1.8
Chenopodiaceae	NFI	1.0	—	—	0.4
LEGUMINOSAE					
Vicia/Lathyrus spp.	vetch/tare/vetchling	0.3	—	—	—
ROSACEAE					
Potentilla sp.	cinquefoil/tormentil	0.5	—	—	—
Potentilla/Fragaria sp.	—	—	—	—	0.4
Fragaria vesca L.	wild strawberry	0.8	—	—	—
UMBELLIFERAE					
Conium maculatum L.	hemlock	1.3	—	—	0.4
Umbelliferae	NFI	0.3	—	—	—
POLYGONACEAE					
Polygonum persicaria L.	persicaria	0.3	—	—	—
Polygonum sp.	—	0.3	—	—	—
Rumex spp.	docks	—	—	—	0.4
POLYGONACEAE/CYPERACEAE					
Polygonaceae/Cyperaceae	NFI	0.3	—	—	—
URTICACEAE					
Urtica urens L.	small nettle	1.3	—	—	—
Urtica dioica L.	stinging nettle	1.3	—	—	—
MENYANTHACEAE					
Menyanthes trifoliata L.	bogbean	—	—	—	0.4
BORAGINACEAE					
Lithospermum arvense L.	corn gromwell	—	—	—	50.2
LABIATAE					
cf. Mentha sp.	mint	0.3	—	—	—
Lamium cf. purpureum	red dead-nettle	—	0.6	—	—
Lamium sp.	dead nettle	2.6	1.7	—	—
cf. Marrubium vulgare	white horehound	—	—	—	4.9
Labiatae	NFI	1.6	—	—	0.7
PLANTAGINACEAE					
Plantago lanceolata type	ribwort	—	—	—	0.4
CAPRIFOLIACEAE					
Sambucus nigra L.	elder	14.6	281.7	1.3	38.6
Sambucus nigra/ebulus	elder/danewort	1.3	7.4	—	—
RUBIACEAE					
Galium palustre L.	marsh bedstraw	—	—	0.9	0.4
COMPOSITAE					
cf. Athemis sp.	mayweed/chamomile	—	—	—	1.0
Centaurea sp.	knapweed/thistle	—	—	—	9.8
cf. Centaurea sp.	knapweed/thistle	—	—	2.7	—
Compositae	NFI	4.7	—	—	—
ALISMATACEAE					
Alisma plantago-aquatica L.	water-plantain	8.8	—	2.7	—
CYPERACEAE					
Eleocharis palustris type	spike-rush	2.1	0.6	13.3	24.9

Taxa	Context Numbers	Building		cut	cut
		1 298	2 279	228 411	177 172
cf. Eleocharis palustris type	spike-rush	—	—	—	1.4
cf. Eleocharis sp.	spike-rush	—	—	—	3.9
Carex spp.	sedges	6.5	0.6	4.4	9.1
GRAMINEAE					
Avena sp.	oat	—	0.6	—	—
Avena/Triticum sp.	oat/wheat	0.3	—	—	—
Hordeum sp.	barley	0.3	—	—	—
Triticum spelta/aestivum	spelt/bread wheat	—	1.1	—	—
Triticum aestivum type	bread/club wheat	0.3	6.3	—	—
Triticum sp.	wheat	0.3	1.7	—	—
cf. Secale cereale	rye	0.5	0.6	—	—
—	indeterminate cereal	—	1.7	—	—
Phleum sp.	cat's tail	0.5	—	—	—
Gramineae	NFI	0.5	—	—	0.4
Indeterminate		9.9	—	4.0	8.4
Total		77.7	305.1	37.3	233.7

Appendix 5.2

Habitats and Usage

As an aid to untangling the complex factors involved in the deposition of the plant remains discussed here, taxa were classified on the basis of their major habitat preferences (according to Clapham *et al* 1962) and some of their possible uses. There is much information available on the possible uses of plants; some is unreliable and has to be used with caution, and some is very helpful (eg. Grigson 1975 who quotes several early sources such as Cockayne 1866 and Gerard 1597). The categories used for classifying taxa are listed below:

A weeds of cultivated land
B weeds of waste places and disturbed ground
C plants of woods, scrub and hedgerows
D grassland plants
E plants of damp or marshy land
F edible wild plants
G medicinal plants
H wild plants with other economic uses
I cultivated plants

Many of the plants identified here fall into more than one of these categories and it would be misleading to assume that all wild plants which could have been eaten or functioned as raw materials for medicines, textiles, dyes etc were necessarily used in this way. Some evaluation of quantity, the assemblage as a whole, and a detailed consideration of its archaeological context is necessary before singling out a plant and suggesting that it had a specific use. A brief discussion follows of the plants identified in London, using the categories listed above to describe their habitats/uses.

A. Weeds of cultivated land

These are usually introduced into towns inadvertently with the cultivated plants (such as cereals) with which they were grown. Fragmented seeds of corn cockle (*Agrostemma githago*) were common in many pits and whole seeds preserved by mineralisation were occasionally found. This plant was a considerable pest of cornfields in the past and its seeds may have been incorporated into bread or broth with the cereals. They would therefore be an expected component of cess pit contents. It should be noted, however, that corn cockle seeds are actually poisonous to humans. Other species which were presumably brought into town as weeds of cereals include corn gromwell (*Lithospermum arvense*), charlock (*Raphanus raphanistrum*), fumitory (*Fumaria officinalis*), corn salad (*Valerianella dentata*) and fool's parsley (*Aethusa cynapium*), the first of which was also freqently found in a mineralised condition. Gold of pleasure (*Camelina sativa*) is a weed found in close association with flax, which also occurs in early medieval deposits. Many other plants in this group can also be found in other habitats.

B. Plants of waste places and disturbed ground

These plants are probably the most numerous on urban sites. Many reproduce very quickly and produce large quantites of seeds. They represent the 'background flora' on every urban site and some species such as goosefoots (*Chenopodium* spp.) and nettles (*Urtica* spp.) occur in large numbers and grow commonly on nutrient enriched soils associated with human activity. Plants in the daisy family (*Compositae*) such as thistles (*Cirsium* spp.) and dandelions (*Taraxacum officinale*) grow rapidly on waste ground and spoil heaps.

C. Plants of woods, scrub and hedgerows

This type of habitat is not well represented in the deposits, except by edible fruit and nut species. This is predictable for an urban situation where most of the inedible plants in this category, such as stitchworts and chickweeds (*Stellaria* spp.), could have been imported accidentally on the feet of animals or humans from locations outside the town. Many of the edible fruit and nut species probably did not grow locally but were introduced as food plants and are therefore discussed below (group F).

D. Grassland plants

These suggest grassy clearings or accidental importation into the town by incoming traffic, though many plants, such as thistles (*Cirsium* sp.) and nettles (*Urtica* spp.), are also associated with waste ground. Others, such as sedges (*Carex* spp.), were possibly gathered as flooring or thatching material from damp meadows, and grasses (Gramineae) may indicate hay collected as fodder. Buttercups (*Ranunculus* spp.) are found in a range of ecological conditions but are particularly common in meadows and could have been incidentally collected with sedges or hay.

E. Plants of damp or marshy land

Rushes (*Juncus* spp.), sedges and their close relatives (*Eleocharis*, *Scirpus* and most *Carex* spp.), hemlock (*Conium maculatum*) and water-dropworts (*Oenanthe* spp.) are conspicuous representatives of these conditions. They are commonly found growing on the banks of ditches or streams and, in early medieval London, they could have been gathered as flooring or thatching material (cf. Hall *et al* 1983), the rushes or sedges gathered deliberately and the others incidentally.

F. Edible wild plants

Seeds of blackberry or raspberry (*Rubus fruticosus/idaeus*) are common in these deposits and often occur in very large concentrations in pits. They are frequently among the contents of cess pits. Other woodland (group c) plants which are also edible are wild strawberry (*Fragaria vesca*) and sloe (*Prunus spinosa*). Hazelnuts (*Corylus avellana*), although not found in large quantities, are present in several pits. Apples (*Malus* sp.) were probably collected from woods and hedgerows and brought into town as well as deliberately grown, along with pears (*Pyrus* sp.), as an orchard plant. Elder (*Sambucus nigra*) is found in a wide range of habitats and could easily have been growing on waste ground within the urban area. It was probably collected for making into wine, preserves etc. A great many wild plants are edible. Goosefoot (*Chenopodium*), for instance, is a member of the spinach family and is itself edible as well as being a common weed.

G. Medicinal Plants

Practically every wild plant is reputed in the herbals to have some medicinal value. It is, however, unclear whether their use was widespread. Opium poppy (*Papaver somniferum*) contains strong alkaloids and henbane (*Hyoscyamus niger*) is known for its use as a hypnotic and brain sedative (Grigson 1975). Both plants were found in quantity in some deposits and are discussed below. Very probably a wide range of common plants was utilised, in infusions and poultices, for minor afflictions and injuries.

H. Wild plants with other economic uses

Elderberries (*Sambucus nigra*) have properties which could be used in the tanning process (Buckland *et al* 1974). Large numbers of elder seeds were found in some deposits and smaller accumulations in others. There is, however, little other evidence to support their use in tanning (Hall *et al* 1983). Seeds of weld (*Reseda luteola*) were found in several deposits. This plant produces a yellow dye but is also a common weed and in view of the low numbers found it may not have been utilised here.

I. Cultivated plants

A few seeds of cultivated pulses including pea (*Pisum sativum*), Celtic bean (*Vicia faba*) and possible lentil (cf. *Lens culinaris*) were found, usually in a mineralised condition. Carbonised cereal grains were more abundant and securely dated finds include bread/club wheat (*Triticum aestivum s.l.*), hulled barley (probably including two-row barley – *Hordeum cf. distichum*), rye (*Secale cereale*) and oat (*Avena* sp.).

Orchard species are also common in many deposits and include plum/bullace (*Prunus domestica*), cherry (*P. avium*) and sour cherry (*P. cerasus*), some of which could also have grown wild, and a single find of mulberry (*Morus nigra*). Mulberry was probably introduced to Britain in the Roman period but may have died out completely in the Dark Ages (Harvey 1981). Grape (*Vitis vinifera*) and fig (*Ficus carica*) pips were frequent in some contexts and may be from imported fruits though both can be grown in southern Britain.

A number of potential 'garden' cultivars were encounted in some deposits. Occasional seeds of flax/linseed (*Linum usitatissimum*) must presumably have arrived with plants cultivated for their fibres or oil though no direct evidence for their use (such as retting facilities) is provided by the present study. Taxa which could have been cultivated as vegetables include celery (*Apium graveolens*), carrot (*Daucus carota*), probable fennel (cf. *Foeniculum vulgare*) and possible 'brassicas' (*Brassica/Sinapis* spp.). Opium poppy has already been mentioned and can be grown as a flavouring, for its oil or for medicinal use. The only culinary herb identified with certainty is Alexanders (*Smyrnium olusatrum*), from Milk Street pit 42, which is known to have been used as a pot herb from Roman times. This was unfortunately identified too late to be included in the tables or calculations.

	A	B	C	D	E	I
Ranunculus sardous	X	X		X		
,, flammula				X		
,, sceleratus				X		
,, subgen. Batrachium				X		
Papaver rhoeas	X	X				
,, rhoeas/dubium	X	X				
,, argemone	X					
,, somniferum			X			X
,, sp.	X	X				X
Fumaria officinalis	X					
Brassica/Sinapis spp.	X	X				X
Raphanus raphanistrum	X					
Thlaspi arvense	X	X				
Capsella bursa-pastoris	X	X				
Camelina sativa	X					X
Reseda luteola	X	X				X
Hypericum sp.			X	X	X	
Silene alba	X	X	X			
,, alba/noctiflora	X	X	X			
,, alba/dioica/noctiflora	X	X	X			
,, vulgaris	X	X		X		
Lychnis flos-cuculi			X	X	X	
Agrostemma githago	X					
Cerastium sp.	X	X	X			
Stellaria media	X	X				
,, holostea			X			
,, palustris				X		
,, graminea			X	X		
,, alsine				X		
Spergula arvensis	X					
Chenopodium polyspermum	X	X				
,, album	X	X				
,, ficifolium	X	X				
,, urbicum	X	X				
,, hybridum	X	X				
,, rubrum/glaucum	X	X				
,, sp.	X	X				
Atriplex spp.	X	X				
Malva sylvestris	X					
,, sp.	X	X	X			
Linum usitatissimum						X
,, sp.			X			X
Vitis vinifera						X
Medicago sp.			X	X		
Pisum sativum						X
Lens culinaris						X
Vicia hirsuta	X		X			
,, tetrasperma			X			
,, faba						X
Rubus fruticosus		X				
,, idaeus		X				
,, fruticosus/idaeus/caesius		X	X			
Potentilla erecta		X	X	X		

	A	B	C	D	E	I
Fragaria vesca			X	X		
Rosa canina			X			
,, sp.			X			X
Prunus spinosa			X			
,, domestica			X			X
,, avium			X			X
,, cerasus			X			X
,, sp.			X			X
Crataegus monogyna			X			
Pyrus/Malus sp.			X			X
Chaerophyllum sp.			X	X		
Torilis nodosa	X			X		
Conium maculatum			X			
Conium/Petroselinum/Pimpinella			X	X	X	X
Bupleurum rotundifolium	X					
Apium graveolens				X	X	
,, sp.				X	X	
Apium/Berula sp.				X	X	
Oenanthe fistulosa				X		
,, pimpinelloides				X	X	
,, sp.				X	X	
Aethusa cynapium	X					
Foeniculum vulgare		X				X
Anethum graveolens		X				X
Daucus carota				X		X
Bryonia dioica		X				
Euphorbia helioscopia	X	X				
Polygonum aviculare agg.	X	X				
,, persicaria	X	X		X		
,, lapathifolium	X	X		X		
,, convolvulus	X	X				
Rumex acetosella	X			X		
Urtica urens	X	X				
Cannabis sativa		X				X
Ficus carica						X
Morus nigra						X
Anagallis arvensis	X					
,, sp.	X			X	X	
Corylus avellana		X				
Menyanthes trifoliata				X		
Lithospermum arvense	X					
Hyoscyamus niger		X				
Solanum nigrum		X				
Scrophularia nodosa				X	X	
Rhinanthus sp.	X	X		X		
Lycopus europaeus					X	
Prunella vulgaris			X	X	X	
Stachys sp.	X			X		X
Ballota nigra				X		
Lamium purpureum	X	X				
,, sp.	X	X				
Galeopsis segetum	X					
,, tetrahit	X	X				
,, sp,	X	X				
Marrubium vulgare		X				
Teucrium sp.				X	X	X

	A	B	C	D	E	I
Plantago lanceolata type				x		
Sambucus nigra		x	x			
,, nigra/ebulus		x	x			
Galium palustre					x	
,, aparine		x	x			
,, aparine/tricornutum	x	x	x			
Valerianella dentata	x					
Bidens tripartita					x	
Senecio jacobea		x				
Anthemis cotula	x	x				
,, sp.	x	x				
Chamaemelum nobile		x		x		
Tripleurospermum maritimum	x	x				
Chrysanthemum segetum	x					
Artemisia sp.		x	x			
Cirsium vulgare	x	x				
,, arvense	x	x				
Centaurea cyanus	x	x				
,, nigra		x		x		
,, sp.	x	x		x		
Lapsana communis		x	x			
Hypochoeris radicata				x		
Leontondon autumnalis		x		x		
,, sp.		x		x		
Picris echioides		x	x			
Sonchus oleraceus	x	x				
,, asper	x	x				
,, sp.	x	x			x	
Crepis capillaris		x		x		
Taraxacum officinale		x		x		
Alisma plantago-aquatica					x	
Naja sp.					x	
Convallaria/Ruscus			x			
Juncus spp.		x		x	x	
Iris pseudacorus					x	
Sparganium sp.					x	
Typha sp.					x	
Eriophorum sp.					x	
Eleocharis palustris type					x	
,, sp.					x	
Scirpus spp.					x	
Carex spp.			x	x	x	
Avena fatua/ludoviciana	x					
,, sp.	x					x
Hordeum distichum						x
,, vulgare						x
Triticum spelta						x
,, aestivum						x
,, sp.						x
Secale cereale						x
indet. cereal						x
Festuca spp.			x	x		
Lolium perenne		x				
Vulpia sp.		x		x		
Bromus secalinus/mollis	x	x		x		
Phleum sp.				x	x	

	A	B	C	D	E	I
Milium sp.			x	x	x	

A = weeds of cultivated land
B = weeds of waste places and disturbed ground
C = plants of woods, scrub and hedgerows
D = grassland plants
E = plants of damp or marshy land
I = cultivated plants

5.17 Classification of Taxa According to Potential Uses

	F	G	H
Ranunculus acris/bulbosus		x	
,, flammula		x	
,, sp.		x	
Papaver rhoeas		x	x
,, rhoeas/dubium		x	x
,, somniferum		x	x
,, sp.		x	x
Brassica/Sinapis spp.		x	x
Camelina sativa			x
Reseda luteola			x
Viola sp.		x	
Hypericum sp.		x	
Silene vulgaris	x		
,, sp.	x		
Myosoton/Stellaria sp.		x	
Stellaria holostea		x	
,, sp.		x	
Spergula arvensis	x		
Chenopodium album	x		x
,, sp.	x		x
Atriplex spp.	x	x	x
Malva sylvestris	x		
,, sp.	x		
Linum usitatissimum	x		x
,, sp.	x		x
Vitis vinifera	x		
Pisum sativum	x		
Lens culinaris	x		
Vicia faba	x		
Vicia/Lathyrus sp.	x		
Rubus fruticosus	x	x	x
,, idaeus	x		
,, fruticosus/idaeus/caesius	x	x	x
Potentilla erecta		x	x
,, sp.		x	x
Fragaria vesca	x	x	x
Rosa canina		x	
,, sp.		x	

	F	G	H
Prunus spinosa		x	
,, domestica	x	x	
,, avium	x	x	
,, cerasus	x	x	
,, sp.	x	x	
Pyrus/Malus sp.	x		
Conium maculatum		x	
Conium/Petroselinum/Pimpinella	x	x	
Apium graveolens	x		
,, sp.	x		
Apium/Berula sp.	x		
Foeniculum vulgare	x	x	
Anethum graveolens	x		
Daucus carota	x	x	
Bryonia dioica		x	
Euphorbia helioscopia		x	
Polygonum aviculare agg.		x	
,, persicaria			x
,, convolvulus	x		
,, sp.	x	x	
Rumex sp.	x	x	
Cannabis sativa			x
Ficus carica	x		
Morus nigra	x		
Anagallis arvensis		x	
,, sp.		x	
Corylus avellana	x		
Menyanthes trifoliata	x	x	
Hyoscyamus niger		x	
Solanum nigrum	x		
Scrophularia nodosa		x	
Rhinanthus sp.		x	x
Lycopus europaeus			x
Prunella vulgaris		x	
Stachys sp.		x	
Ballota nigra		x	
Lamium sp.		x	
Galeopsis tetrahit			x
,, sp,			x
Marrubium vulgare		x	
Teucrium sp.		x	
Ajuga sp.		x	
Sambucus nigra	x		
,, nigra/ebulus	x	x	x
Galium aparine		x	
,, aparine/tricornutum		x	
Asperula/Galium		x	
Senecio jacobea		x	
,, sp.		x	
Anthemis cotula		x	x
,, arvensis/cotula		x	x
,, sp.		x	x
Chamaemelum nobile	x	x	
Chrysanthemum segetum			x
Artemisia sp.		x	x
Cirsium sp.	x	x	

	F	G	H
Centaurea cyanus		x	x
,, nigra		x	
,, sp.		x	x
Lapsana communis	x		
Leontondon sp.	x		
Picris echioides		x	x
Taraxacum officinale	x	x	
Alisma plantago-aquatica		x	
Convallaria/Ruscus		x	x
Juncus spp.			x
Iris pseudacorus		x	x
Scirpus spp.			x
Carex spp.			x
Avena sp.	x		
Hordeum distichum	x		
,, vulgare	x		
Triticum spelta	x		
,, aestivum	x		
,, sp.	x		
Secale cereale	x		
indet. cereal	x		

F = food plants
G = medicinal plants
H = plants with other economic uses

5.18 Classification of Potential Weeds According to Preferences/Tolerances

preference for arable land

Papaver argemone
Fumaria officinalis
Raphanus raphanistrum
Agrostemma githago
Spergula arvensis
Vicia hirsuta
Torilis nodosa
Bupleurum rotundifolium
Aethusa cynapium
Lithospermum arvense
Galeopsis segetum
,, tetrahit
Valerianella dentata
Chrysanthemum segetum

preference for gardens

Euphorbia helioscopia
Polygonum persicaria
,, lapathifolium
Anagallis arvensis
Lamium purpureum

Sonchus oleraceus
   ,,   asper

preference for very high nitrogen situations

Chenopodium ficifolium
        ,,   rubrum/glaucum
Urtica urens

tolerance of trodden ground

Polygonum aviculare agg.

5.19 Classification of Potential Cultivars According to Likely Type of Cultivation

usually grown in gardens

Papaver somniferum
Brassica/Sinapis spp.
Camelina sativa
Reseda luteola
Linum usitatissimum
   ,,   sp.
Pyrus/Malus sp.
Conium/Petroselinum/Pimpinella
Apium graveolens
   ,,   sp.
Apium/Berula sp.
Foeniculum vulgare
Anethum graveolens
Daucus carota
Cannabis sativa

often grown in fields

Pisum sativum
Lens culinaris
Vicia faba
Avena sp.
Hordeum distichum
   ,,   vulgare
Triticum spelta
   ,,   aestivum
   ,,   sp.
Secale cereale
indet. cereal

fruit trees

Vitis vinifera
Prunus domestica
   ,,   avium
   ,,   cerasus
   ,,   sp.
Ficus carica
Morus nigra

Acknowledgements

Thanks are due to Patrick Allen, Alan Vince and the Finds Section at the DUA who provided useful information. We are grateful to Francis Green, Mick Monk and Clive Orton for permission to cite their unpublished work and we are particularly indebted to Paul Tyers who wrote the computer programmes for inputting and analysing the data and to Keith Badham for his assistance with the laboratory work.

5.ii PARASITE REMAINS

Clare de Rouffignac

Introduction

In recent years, the recovery of parasite remains from archaeological deposits has become more common as awareness of the technique has increased (Jones 1982, de Rouffignac 1987). It is now a well-established fact that parasitic worm infestations were endemic in historical populations (Grieg 1982, 51) as the eggs of various species can survive for a considerable time under certain conditions in cess-pits, drains and occupation layers.

The most common eggs recovered are from *Ascaris* sp (round-worm or maw-worm) and *Trichuris* sp (whip-worm). Neither species have an intermediate host, but the fertilised eggs are passed on in contaminated food and drink or via soiled hands (Horne 1985, 301-2). Widespread incidence of parasitic worms therefore occurs when standards of hygiene are low and sanitary practices are minimal. Light infestations cause little discomfort, but large numbers of worms can give rise to a variety of symptoms without being fatal. Egg production is in the thousands per worm per day, with considerable variation, but the proportions of *Trichuris* sp to *Ascaris* sp eggs are approximately 3:1 in well-preserved archaeological samples (Pike 1975).

The identification of eggs is via the shape and size of the species involved. Worms of various trichurid species affect many mammals, but the eggs of *Trichuris trichiura*, which parasitises man, are of a size range different to other species (Beer 1976). Measurement of the eggs can therefore be used to enable identification of species. If the size range encountered suggests that *Trichuris trichiura* is present, it can be assumed that the accompanying ascarid eggs are of *Ascaris lumbricoides*, the human parasite, rather than *Ascaris suum*, the similar sized round-worm which parasitises pigs.

The retrieval of parasite remains is useful for studying patterns of sewage disposal in the past, especially with regard to identifying pit function according to the presence or absence of eggs. Attempts at quantification have proved useful, with Jones (1985) listing various levels for faecal input into archaeological features from parasite egg concentrations. For this study, samples with over 1000 ova per gram (opg) are considered as containing a substantial amount of faecal material, whilst 100 opg or less are 'background' levels.

A note of caution must be added, however, as preservational problems have been encountered with samples which have been allowed to dry out. Various writers, including Pike and Biddle (1966) and Pike (op cit.) have noted the potential effects of drying out soil samples, including the fact that *Ascaris lumbricoides* eggs are far more resistant to decay (Hyman 1951) than eggs of *Trichuris sp* Thus in dry samples, ascarid eggs may outnumber trichurid eggs, and in well-preserved samples a high proportion of *Ascaris lumbricoides* eggs may indicate drying and re-wetting in antiquity. These comments must therefore be borne in mind when the results from this study are considered in interpretation.

Methodology

The condition of each sample was noted (very dry to very wet) before a 0.5g sub-sample was disaggregated in a solution of sodium triphosphate. Droplets were then examined at x100 for the presence or absence of parasite eggs. If eggs were present, quantification was carried out after Jones (1985). 2g of sample was soaked in 28ml of sodium triphosphate solution, then passed through a 250 μm sieve. Aliquots of 0.15ml from the filtrate were examined and all the eggs present were counted and their condition noted. Calculations were then performed to give ova per gram of soil.

If sufficient numbers of trichurid eggs were present, 100 complete specimens were measured and the mean and standard deviation calculated to confirm that the eggs present were from *Trichuris trichiura*.

Results

Approximately 150 samples were examined from Saxon features on the following sites: Peninsula House (PEN 79), Pudding Lane (PDN 81), Ironmonger Lane (IRO 80), Well Court (WEL 79), Milk Street (MLK 76) and Watling Court (WAT 78). The majority of these samples were taken from what were interpreted during excavation as being primary rubbish fills of pits. Some samples were taken from occupation deposits, mainly in the hope of finding industrial residues.

Samples from pits of all dates from CP1 to CP5 were represented and parasite eggs were found in samples of all dates. In several cases the proportion of ascarid to trichurid eggs suggests that the sample had partially dried, either in antiquity or since collection. The quantities of eggs in these samples is no guide to the original composition of the deposit. In others, however, the quantity of eggs suggests that the deposit originally consisted predominantly of human cess. Where more than 100 trichurid eggs were present in a sub-sample their dimensions were measured and proved to be *Trichuris trichiura*.

Conclusions

It can be seen from the results obtained that parasite eggs, whilst not ubiquitous, are fairly common in samples from Saxon sites examined for this study. This confirms once more the widespread occurrence of parasitic worm infestations in historical populations. However, preservational changes in the condition of some of the samples has created a somewhat distorted view of the distribution of parasite remains.

This is especially true for some of the samples from pits and occupation layers, which gave proportions of *Ascaris* sp to *Trichuris* sp eggs not normally expected from archaeological deposits, or contained no eggs at all.

From the evidence gained from the pits it can be seen that most of them were used at some time for the disposal of cess. This tended to be either as a primary function merely for sewage dumping, or as a general rubbish pit with some faecal input as well as domestic refuse. However, the interpretations made for pits from which only single con-

Fig 5: results by site, sorted by ceramic phase and pit number. Key: X negative, ? positive but subjected to drying, L positive but low, H high

Pudding Lane CP1: P47 - L, P48 - H, CP3: B1 use - X, B3 - X.

Milk Street CP1: (all pit samples discarded after completion of botanical remains study) B1 - B and X (very dry), CP2: Third and fourth phases of use of B1 - X, First phase of disuse of B4, disuse of third phase of B4 - X, Use of B5 - X.

Watling Court Undated: P5 - L, P6 backfill - L, P39 - L, P92 - H, CP1: P9 - H, P12 primary use - H, P12 backfill - X, P15 - cess and rubbish fill, P18 - L, P23 L, P38 - X, CP3: P76 - L. CP4: B3 - L, First use of B4 - X (3 samples) and L, Second phase of use of B4 - X and L (one sample, noted as 'cessy' during excavation), Disuse of B4 - X, P40 - X, P43 disuse - H, P46 - L, P47 - X, P52 backfill - H, P61 primary fill - L, P61 backfill - X, P62 - H, P63 - L, P65 backfill - L. CP5: P48 - L, P60 backfill - L, P95 - L, P99 - L, P121 disuse - X, P122 - X.

Peninsula House CP1: External levels contemporary with B10, CP2: P62 - L.

Ironmonger Lane CP1: Building 2 - L, CP2: Disuse of B1 and B2 - L, CP3: P23 - H. CP5: P27 - L.

Well Court CP1-3: P89 - L, CP4: P18 - X.

texts were examined must be viewed tentatively, multiple samples from a series of contexts provide a far more reliable guide to pit function. As only a small number of samples had sufficient trichurid eggs to enable confirmation of the species as *Trichuris trichiura*, it can only be assumed that most of the faecal material dumped in the pits was human in origin.

The backfilling of features with faecal material mixed with organic refuse was determined from a number of the samples, but, as previously mentioned, the primary fills were not examined from those pits where this occurred and therefore the interpretation of pit usage can only be very partial.

The very variable results for samples of occupation deposits from within buildings indicate some small amounts of faeces, other site layers also appeared to indicate some faecal input. Whilst it was not expected to retrieve large numbers of eggs from such contexts, these samples tended to be far less well preserved than those from pits and this certainly affected the results obtained. Unfortunately there is little published data on parasite eggs obtained from occupation deposits, but Jones (1985 *op cit*) suggests likely sources as casual defecation by children, 'treading in' of faeces from outside sources, and use of abandoned buildings as latrines.

The widespread occurrence of parasite eggs from both pits and occupation deposits point to standards of health and hygiene which though considerably lower than those of today cannot be quantified, since no information about the actual levels of infestation exists due to factors such as preservational changes and variable egg production by worms, and the actual numbers of worms in the gut. The recovery of parasite remains has proved useful, however, in the interpretation of a number of Saxon features, in the interpretation of botanical remains from the same contexts, and cannot be overlooked as a technique for regular future use.

6. METALLURGY

Justine Bayley, Ian Freestone, Anne Jenner and Alan Vince

Introduction

Fragments of slag, hearth lining, crucibles, 'motif' pieces, a hoard of lead ingots and an ingot mould recovered from late Saxon and Norman contexts in London suggest that metalworking was widespread throughout the city, but no site has produced evidence for the existence of a permanent professional metalworking 'factory'. While this may be due to the vagaries of excavation, other late Saxon towns have produced such evidence. This study, part of a wider one of metalworking in the Roman and later City, is based on a combination of the excavated evidence and material from the Museum of London collections.

Slag from several excavations was examined by Kevin Brown (then of the Oxford Institute of Archaeology) and divided into classes. The weight of slag in each class was measured but the low quantities involved suggested that none of the slag need be contemporary with the deposits in which it was found and therefore no further analysis was undertaken. Fragments of hearth lining were similarly scarce and never found in sufficient profusion to show that an industrial hearth had existed nearby. Examination by X-ray fluorescence (XRF) spectrometry showed most to have a fuel-ash glazed surface. The ceramic fabric of the fragments contains inclusions typical of local deposits but, given the heterogeneous nature of the drift geology of London, no attempt was made to define fabric groups or suggest precise sources. Scraps of metal, which in most cases might either be production waste or fragmentary artefacts, were only superficially examined. None could be shown to be unfinished artefacts or waste that had been prepared for use as raw materials. A group of lead ingots, recovered from a pit at Watling Court dated to the mid 12th century (CP5), are sufficiently unusual to warrant special study, which is in progress, and are therefore not included in this report. An ingot mould, Fig 3.50,

No 175, cut into a re-used Roman tile, was examined using XRF to see if the metal cast in it could be identified; no firm conclusion could be reached.

As these studies have all proved either inconclusive or are still in progress, the main information on Saxon and Norman metalworking in London is that obtained from the analysis of crucibles, which often have the advantage of being datable from their form and fabric even when not recovered from Saxon or Norman contexts. In total over 500 fragments of crucible have been recovered from the City of London and of these 132 are of Saxo-Norman types. They are from three main sources: the Museum of London reserve collection, which contains mainly complete examples and has therefore been used to illustrate the range of forms found (Nos 1, 3-4, 9, 11-22, 25-6, and 31-2); the pre-DUA excavations carried out by the Guildhall Museum (Nos 10 and 27); and the DUA collection (Nos 2, 5-8, 23-4, and 28-30). The fraction of the collection that was recovered from Saxon and Norman contexts was divided into fabric groups and a sample of sherds from apparently unused crucibles from each fabric group was examined to determine the raw materials used for their manufacture and their qualities as refractories. The inner surfaces of the used crucibles were analysed to identify, where possible, the alloys which had been melted in them and an attempt made to relate use to fabric and properties.

Analytical methods and samples analysed

For the investigation of crucible fabrics and their properties, a selection of twenty sherds was taken from the DUA collection. These sherds were chosen, as far as possible, on the basis of the apparent absence of evidence of use, such as glazing, distortion, bloating or surface contamination.

Thus they were most likely to allow the characterisation of the fabrics and their properties without interference due to contamination by fuel-ash and metal oxide fluxes, or modification of the mineralogy by extreme temperatures. In addition to 10 sherds from Saxo-Norman crucibles the sample also included a range of Roman and later medieval crucibles for comparative purposes. These are not discussed in detail here, but their compositions are reported by Freestone and Tite (1986).

Polished thin sections were prepared and the fabrics examined in the petrological microscope. A computer-assisted image analyser was used to measure the volume proportion and grain size distribution of the quartz sand fraction in selected sherds (size greater than 0.0625mm; number frequency analysis, cf. Middleton *et al* 1985). The microstructures of the sherds were examined using the scanning electron microscope (SEM) and the chemical composition of the bulk samples, the fine-grained matrixes and selected inclusions were determined using the energy dispersive X-ray analyser (EDXA) in the SEM. In addition selected samples were re-fired in a furnace at temperatures of 1100° and/or 1200°C in a reducing atmosphere, mounted in epoxy resin, polished and their microstructure examined in the SEM to determine any changes that had occurred.

Following an examination of all the crucibles and sherds under low magnification (x10–x30), all those with visible traces of vitreous deposits or metals were analysed semi-quantitatively by XRF. Some of the remaining sherds were also analysed but as these all produced non-diagnostic results (see below) it was not considered worth analysing the remainder of the pieces, which are marked n/a in Figs 6.14–6.17. These sherds however had almost certainly been used as crucibles.

Fabrics and forms of crucibles

Petrographic and elemental analysis revealed a range of ceramic fabrics. As the predominant inclusion in every case was quartz, the criteria used to differentiate the fabrics were predominantly textural and the elemental data (Fig 6.13) were used to support these subdivisions.

The analytical results essentially confirm and embellish the classification based on the examination of the sherds in hand specimen. The crucibles fall into three main groups:

Stamford ware

This has finer and less abundant quartz and silt (Fig 6.1). It differs from the other groups in terms of its low potash, K_2O, content and typically has lower iron oxide, FeO (Fig 6.2). In two of the four sections argillaceous inclusions are present with sharp to merging boundaries which seem to be the result of failure to blend the clay completely during preparation (cf Whitbread 1986). In three of the samples the quartz is poorly sorted while

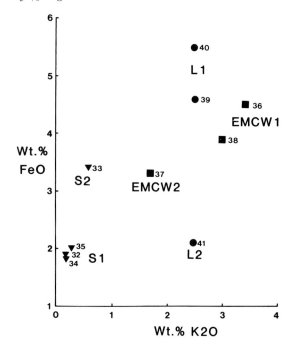

6.1. SEM *image of Stamford ware crucible.*

6.2. *Comparison of* FeO *and* K_2O *in analysed crucible fabrics by % weight.*

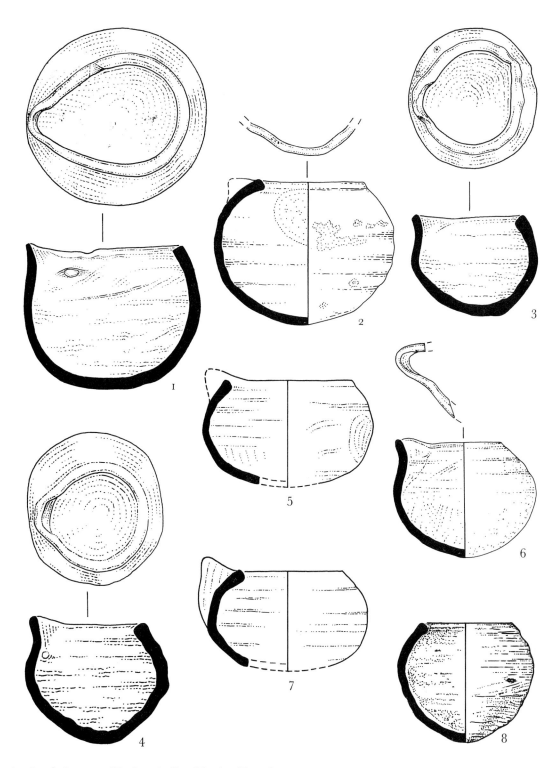

6.3. Stamford ware crucibles from the City of London. Nos 1–8.

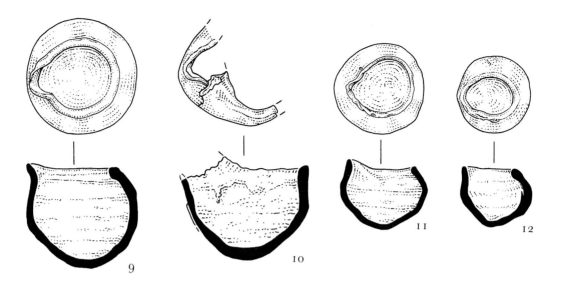

6.4. Stamford ware crucibles from the City of London. Nos 9–12.

in the fourth it is well sorted; the sherds with poorly-sorted quartz grouped closely in chemical composition and so were designated a sub-fabric s1, while the fourth was designated s2 (Fig 6.1). Comparison with thin sections of domestic Stamford ware from the DUA collection revealed closely similar fabrics. All of the crucibles have a similar form, thrown on a wheel with the base later formed by hand (Nos 1-2) but they varied considerably in size. This is shown both by their profiles and from their capacities (measured to the nearest 10ml using dry rice). The crucibles have thin walls, often only a few millimetres thick.

Early Medieval Coarse Whiteware (EMCW)

This forms a distinctive group, the fabric of which has not been closely paralleled in any domestic pottery. It is typically a white-firing clay tempered with 20-30% of a medium grade quartz and flint/chert sand. Tentatively two sub-fabrics have been identified within this group. EMCW1 consists of two grey-white sherds containing predominantly monocrystalline quartz with mean diameter 0.34mm (Fig 6.5) and EMCW2 consists of one red-brown sherd in which flint/chert and polycrystalline quartz are much more common and with a lower mean diameter of 0.24mm

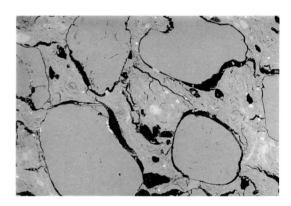

6.5. SEM *image of Early Medieval Coarse Whiteware crucible (*EMCW1*).*

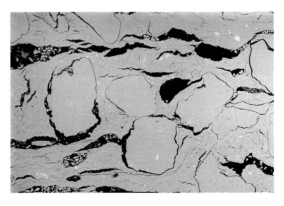

6.6. SEM *image of Early Medieval Coarse Whiteware crucible (*EMCW2*).*

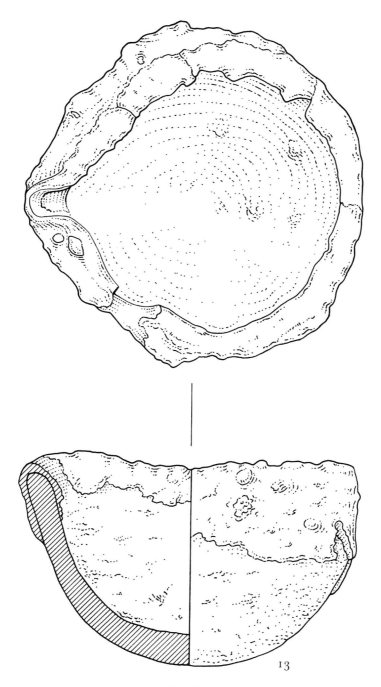

6.7. Early Medieval Coarse Whiteware crucibles from the City of London. No 13.

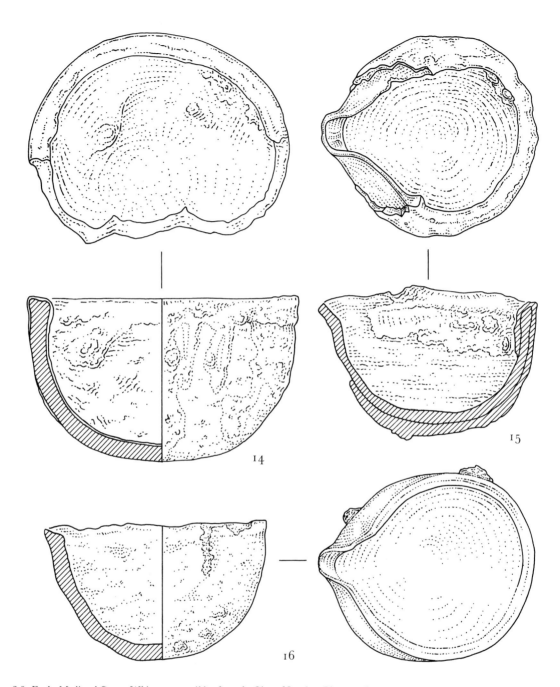

6.8. Early Medieval Coarse Whiteware crucibles from the City of London. Nos 14–16.

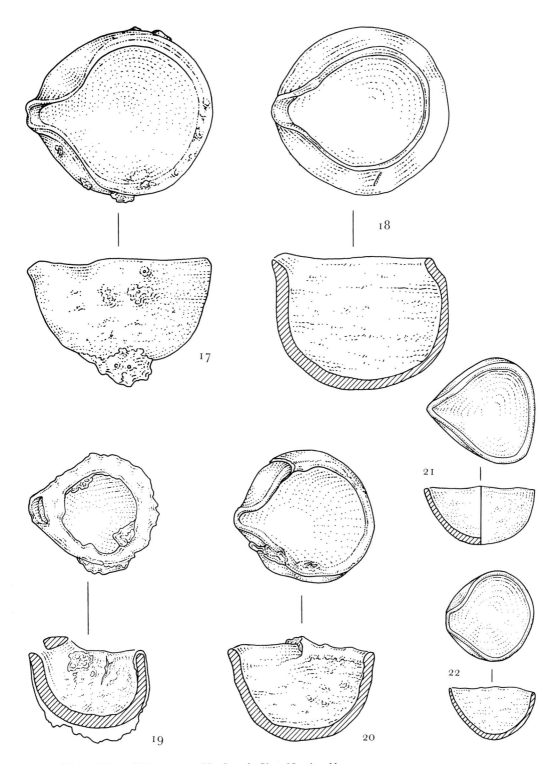

6.9. *Early Medieval Coarse Whiteware crucibles from the City of London. Nos 17–22.*

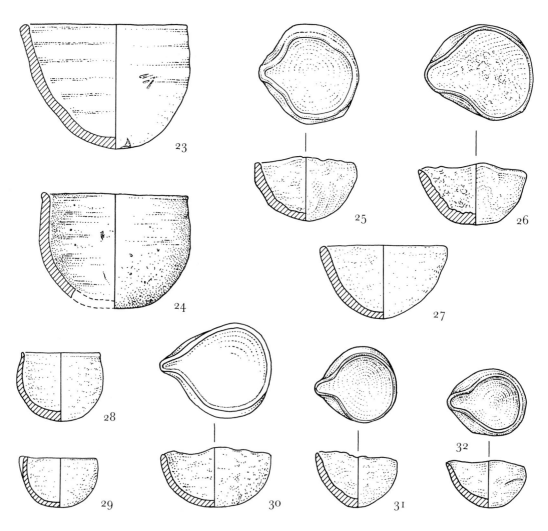

6.10. London-type ware crucibles from the City of London. Nos 23–32.

(Fig 6.6). There is some evidence for a chemical separation between EMCW1 and EMCW2 (Fig 6.1). There is considerable variation in form and size amongst these crucibles, all of which seem to have been formed by hand (Nos 13-22). A few appear to copy the globular form of the Stamford ware vessels but most are simple hemispheres. Few vessels were sufficiently complete to allow measurement of their capacities.

London-type ware

Two of the remaining three sherds contain 12-13% fine quartz sand, grading down into coarse silt (Fig 6.11). They also contain occasional rounded red-brown 'glauconitic' pellets and in this sense, and in terms of their important coarse silt/very fine sand component, appear closely related to London-type ware pottery fabrics. A precise match was not found, as the crucibles are at the upper end of the range of quartz contents in London-type ware, but texturally London-type ware is very variable. The quartz in the third sherd is again fine-grained, but it lacks the silty component of the others and its relation to London-type ware is more doubtful. Chemically the sherd (L2, Fig 6.1) is distinct from the others (L1, Fig 6.1). These vessels are much rarer than those of Stamford ware or EMCW and were invariably small, hemispherical forms (Nos 23-32). There are no complete examples known.

6.11. SEM *image of London-type ware crucible.*

Identification of Metal Alloys

The results of the XRF analysis of the inner surfaces of the crucibles were initially recorded as the height of the major peak produced by each element of interest, ie copper (CU), tin (SN), zinc (ZN), lead (PB), silver (AG) and gold (AU). Antimony (SB) was also detected on a few sherds and mercury (HG) on one complete pot, though this latter case was probably post-excavation contamination. The height of the iron peak was also recorded as this element is present mainly in the clay of the crucible fabric and can be considered as an internal standard. It is almost impossible to compare directly the absolute peak heights as the numbers recorded depend not only on the duration of the analysis, but also on the size of

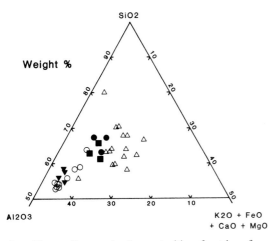

6.12. *Ternary diagram showing composition of matrices of analysed crucibles.*

the sherd, the proportion of its surface covered by metal-rich deposit and the varying sensitivities of the individual elements to XRF analysis.

To allow easy comparison of the results the data has been processed and the presence of an element is shown in Figs 6.14–6.17 by one of a series of symbols. By comparing the heights of the other peaks to that of the iron peak it was possible to say whether the elements they represented were present in significant amounts. Where the peaks were very weak an asterisk was entered in the 'metal melted' column which indicates that the crucible has been used to melt non-ferrous metal of some sort but that its nature cannot now be determined. Crucibles which showed no evidence of surface contamination under low magnification, and which therefore were unlikely to yield evidence of alloy use, were not analysed and are marked n/a in the figures.

Interpreting the results to provide information on the nature of the metals being melted is at least partly a subjective judgement as a number of different, almost unquantifiable, factors have to be taken into account. The information sought is the composition of the metal but what has been recorded is that average composition of the crucible slag and any corroded metal droplets trapped in it. Extrapolating from one to the other is not an exact science and it is this uncertainty that introduces the subjectivity to the interpretation.

One element that is notable for its almost universal presence is zinc. Because of its chemical nature zinc both diffuses into the crucible fabric and becomes chemically bound in the slag layer. As a result of its volatility it is often detected at apparently significant levels even where it only formed a very minor component of the alloy being melted. For this reason crucibles where major or minor amounts of zinc were detected but no other elements were present at significant levels have also been marked with an asterisk in the figures.

Figs 6.14–6.17 present the analytical results for the crucibles made of Stamford ware, London-type ware and EMCW. The results are summarised in Fig 6.8 which shows all types were used to melt both silver and copper alloys but in different proportions. (The results for the crucibles from Milk Street are presented separately as no data is available as to their fabric. Judging by the analytical results they are most likely to be Stamford ware or London-type ware.)

Fig 6.17 suggests that Stamford ware was preferentially selected for melting silver, London-type ware was used for both silver and copper

sample	BMRL no	sample	SiO$_2$	TiO$_2$	Al$_2$O$_3$	FeO	MgO	CaO	Na$_2$O	K$_2$O	P$_2$O$_5$	SO$_2$
Stamford												
PDN81 [2370] <700>	25832	Bulk	60.2	2.1	32.8	2.0	0.5	1.3	–	0.2.	0.3	–
PDN81 [2370] <700>	25832	Matrix	54.7	2.2	38.7	1.9	0.5	1.1	–	0.2	–	–
NFW74 [84] <536>	25833	Bulk	60.0	1.8	32.1	3.4	0.4	1.1	–	0.4	–	–
NFW74 [84] <536>	25833	Matrix	60.0	1.8	32.1	3.4	0.4	1.1	–	0.4	–	–
MLK76 [2001] <21>	25834	Bulk	61.6	1.9	32.7	1.8	0.5	1.0	–	0.1	–	–
MLK76 [2001] <21>	25834	Matrix	57.1	2.3	36.6	1.8	0.3	1.1	–	0.2	–	–
PDN81 [1502] <1741>	25835	Bulk	63.7	1.9	30.3	2.1	0.3	0.9	–	0.2	–	–
PDN81 [1502] <1741>	25835	Matrix	55.8	2.0	37.6	2.0	0.5	1.0	–	0.3	–	–
EMCW												
OPT81 [58] <1486>	25836	Bulk	74.5	0.5	16.1	3.1	1.0					
OPT81 [58] <1486>	25836	Matrix	59.6	0.8	26.4	4.5	1.2	1.3	–	2.0	0.7	0.4
PDN81 [592] <184>	25837	Bulk	72.5	0.7	17.5	2.3	0.5	2.3	–	3.4	0.8	0.3
PDN81 [592] <184>	25837	Matrix	61.2	1.0	28.4	3.3	0.6	1.3	0.7	1.0	0.4	–
ER1210 <2>	25838	Bulk	72.9	0.8	17.7	3.8	0.9	2.0	0.8	1.7	0.9	–
ER1210 <2>	25838	Matrix	64.9	1.1	24.8	3.9	1.1	0.6	0.7	2.2	–	–
								0.6	–	3.0	–	–
London-type												
BIS82 [967] <435>	25389	Bulk	74.4	0.8	15.3	3.6	1.0	1.2	–	2.2	–	–
BIS82 [967] <435>	25389	Matrix	66.0	0.7	22.2	4.6	1.4	1.2	–	2.5	–	–
WAT78 [3894] <1046>	25840	Bulk	77.6	0.7	13.6	3.5	0.7	1.0	–	1.5	0.6	0.3
WAT78 [3894] <1046>	25840	Matrix	61.7	0.7	25.2	5.5	1.2	1.4	–	2.5	0.6	0.4
OPT81 [54] <1330>	25841	Bulk	77.5	0.7	15.8	1.7	0.7	0.8	–	1.8	–	–
OPT81 [54] <1330>	25841	Matrix	66.7	0.8	25.3	2.1	0.9	1.3	–	2.5	–	–

6.13. Composition of crucibles from the City of London.

alloys, while the EMCW crucibles were used mainly for copper alloys. To confirm this conclusion, a statistical chi-squared test was carried out on the data in Fig 6.18. Alloys were grouped as copper based or silver, the single example of lead was neglected. The chi-squared statistic thus evaluates the significance of the association between the three main crucible types and two basic alloy groups, for a total of 38 crucibles with identifiable alloy residues (ie 10 silver, 28 copper-based). A chi-squared value of 16 with 2 degrees of freedom was obtained indicating a better than 99% probablity that the distribution was not obtained by chance. The highest individual contribution to the chi-squared statistic was contributed by the silver/Stamford ware cell in the table and it may be concluded that a high degree of significance can be attached to the association between Stamford ware crucibles and the melting of silver.

Key to Figs 6.14–6.17

+ + + major quantity detected by XRF
+ + minor quantity detected by XRF
+ trace quantity detected by XRF
? possible trace detected by XRF
* no reliable interpretation possible
n/a not analysed

site	context	acc no	extra outer layer	Cu	Zn	Au	Pb	Ag	Sn	metal melted	fig no
BIG 82	3073	5663			+++					*	
BIS 82	547	432	yes	++	++		+	+++		silver	
BIS 82	662	429	yes	+	++		+			*	
GPO 75	420	3701		?	++					*	
GM 136	ER 751	1		+	+++		+			*	
PDN 81	638	250		++	+++		+	+++		silver	
PDN 81	682	254			+++					*	
SWA 81	2119	3712	yes	++	++		+	+++		silver	
WAT 78	0	34	yes	++	+++		+++		+++	leaded gunmetal	
WAT 78	2549	1068		+++	+++		+++		+++	leaded gunmetal	
WAT 78	3559	217		+	+++					*	
Watling House		20235								not analysable	4
Probably Stamford ware											
GM 131	ER 1151	2		+	++		+	+++		silver	
BIG 82	3801	5672		+			+++		?	*	
GPO 75	1148	3760		++	+++		?	+++		silver	
GPO 75	1195	4146			++					*	
SM75	222	458		++	++			+++		silver	

6.14. Analytical results for Stamford ware crucibles.

Properties of Crucibles

Fragments of selected crucibles were refired at 1100° and/or 1200°C for an hour to determine their ability to withstand high temperatures. By 1100°C all crucibles had undergone changes in microstructure and these become more marked by 1200°C but none had undergone coarse bloating or distortion and it appears that all of the crucibles could have withstood temperatures of this order for realistic melting periods. The Stamford ware s1 fabric was substantially more refractory than the other crucibles which, allowing for a little postburial contamination of the EMCW sherds by phosphate (Fig 6.13), all showed similar behaviour. Even this latter somewhat less refractory group of crucibles was comparable to the most refractory earthenware pottery (Roman whiteware) studied to date in the British Museum Research Laboratory by Dr Michael Tite and others.

Chemical compositions of the crucibles (Fig 6.13) bear out these conclusions. Fig 6.12 compares the clay matrix analyses of the crucibles (neglecting the coarse quartz inclusions which remain essentially inert during use) with 20th-century clay building bricks (Worrall 1975) and modern fireclay refractories (Highley 1982). The components K_2O, FeO, MgO, and CaO are fluxes which degrade the refractory properties of the ceramic, while high Al_2O_3 relative to SiO_2 should improve its ability to withstand high temperatures. It can be seen that all of the crucibles may be expected to be refractory relative to typical brick clay as they have lower flux contents while Stamford ware clays in particular compare closely in composition with modern fireclay bricks, due to their low flux and high Al_2O_3 contents.

Other desirable properties of crucibles include great strength (they will have held considerable weights of metal and have been handled with tongs at high temperatures), resistance to thermal stresses due to variations in temperature within the vessel, as well as resistance to thermal shock due to sudden change in temperature and also resistance to corrosion by oxidised metal and by fuel-ash (Percy 1861, Searle 1940). Comparison of the SEM photomicrographs (Figs 6.1, 6.5, 6.6 & 6.11), all at the same magnification, reveals some of these properties. The voids in the fabrics, which

site	context	acc no	extra outer layer	Cu	Zn	Au	Pb	Ag	Sn	metal melted	fig no
GM 41	ER 425	1		+++	+++		+		?	brass	
BIG 82	3516	5669								n/a	
BIG 82	3558	4447								n/a	
BIG 82	3738	4479								n/a	
BIG 82	3831	5674	yes	+	+		+	+++		silver	
BIG 82	3884	5675								n/a	
BIG 82	4285	4448		+	+++					brass ?	
BIG 82	5400	5687		+++	+		+++			leaded copper	
BIS 82	401	421		+++	+		+++		?	leaded copper/ bronze	
BIS 82	600	385								n/a	
BIS 82	630	430		+++			++			copper	
BIS 82	724	424								n/a	
BIS 82	805	386		+	+					*	
BIS 82	925	428								n/a	
GM 131	ER 1167	7		+++	+		+		?	copper/? brass	
CLE 81	166	109								n/a	
CLE 81	395	407								n/a	
GM 29	ER 1205	1		+++	?		++			copper	
GPO 75	585	1144		+	+++					*	
GPO 75	585	4584								n/a	
GM 4	ER 1069C	16								n/a	
HOP 83	22	37								n/a	
HOP 83	222	34								n/a	
HOP 83	226	30								n/a	
IME 83	160	88		+++	+		+			leaded brass	
IRO 30	119	11		+	+		+			leaded brass	
LH 74	102	591		+++			+		+++	bronze	
MLK 76	3087	979			+					*	
OPT 81	58	1489		+	+		?			*	
OPT 81	69	1319		+	+++			?		*	
OPT 81	74	1463	yes	+	+	+				*	
PDN 81	1143	1222								n/a	
PDN 81	1173	1220		+	+++					*	
PDN 81	1191	1224								n/a	
PDN 81	1252	1221		+	+		+			*	
PDN 81	1943	1226	yes							n/a	
PDN 81	1947	1225								n/a	
PDN 81	2371	1953		+	+++					*	
PDN 81	32	172								n/a	
PDN 81	579	181								n/a	
PDN 81	58	173								n/a	
PDN 81	618	286		+	+		+			*	
PDN 81	635	285		+	+					*	
PDN 81	643	255								n/a	
PDN 81	644	257		+	+++					*	

site	context	accn no	extra outer layer	Cu	Zn	Au	Pb	Ag	Sn	metal melted	fig no.
PDN 81	645	358								n/a	
PDN 81	673	360		+	+					*	
PDN 81	684	311								n/a	
PDN 81	698	361								n/a	
PDN 81	84	169		?	+++					*	
PDN 81	91	256								n/a	
PDN 81	1995	1223								n/a	
POM 79	1272	315		?	+					*	
RAG 82	97	658		+	+					brass?	
SLO 82	335	76								n/a	
SSL 84	7	58								n/a	
SWA 81	2277	3716								n/a	
SWA 81	2279	3718								n/a	
TR 84	201	562								n/a	
WAT 78	2091	1014								n/a	
WAT 78	3891	749								n/a	
WAT 78	3901	1048								n/a	
HOP 83	223	47		+	+		+			*	
POM 79	668	141		+	+					*	
POM 79	1318	312								n/a	
SH 74	451	703								n/a	
PDN 81	569	178								n/a	
Bishopsgate		26423		+++	?		+++		?	leaded copper (+ Sb)	
Bank of England		14708		+++	?		+			copper (?Sb)	14
Bank of England		14712		+++	+		+++		+	leaded bronze (+ Sb)	
In Thames		13173		+++	+		+		+	bronze	16
Lombard St	1865	6192		+			+			copper	18
St Thomas' Hosp		13177		+++	+		+		+	gunmetal	17
''		13175		+++	+++		+		+	brass?	
''		13178	yes	+++	+		+			brass	19
Probably early medieval coarsewhite ware											
GM 131	ER 1180	2		+	+++		+		+++	gunmetal?	
GM 131	ER 1142	2								n/a	
GM 4	ER 1238	4		+	?					copper?	
PDN 81	579	183								n/a	
PDN 81	602	252								n/a	
WAT 78	2086	363		+	+++					*	
WAT 78	2215	774								n/a	
WAT 78	2548	1066								n/a	

6.15. Analytical results for Early Medieval Coarse Whiteware crucibles.

site	context	accn no	extra outer layer	Cu	Zn	Au	Pb	Ag	Sn	metal melted	fig no
BIG 82	4330	4278								*	
GM4	ER 1076B	18	yes	+++	+++		+		+++	gunmetal	10
OPT 81	54	1329		+	+		+++	+++		silver	
WAT 78	2195	1013		+	+		?	+++		silver	
POM 79	2275	510								not used	30
Miscellaneous London ware											
ACW 74	2	276		+++	+		+++			leaded copper	
ACW 74	2	277		+++	?		+++			leaded copper	
EST 83	126	109		?	+					*	
GM 76	ER 460	3								not used	27
Bank of England		14711		+	+		+			leaded copper	
Bank of England		14713		+			+++			leaded copper?	
Poultry		22010								not used	21
Blomfield St		13183		?	?					not used	32
London Wall		13182		?						not used	31
Gresham House		A24618		+	+		+	+++	+++	silver ? (+Hg)	26
Salters Hall		24392					+			lead?	25

6.16. Analytical results for London-type ware crucibles.

appear black, are of two major types: firstly, elongate voids which are parallel to the surfaces of the vessels, with their direction controlled by the original orientation of the clay minerals, and, secondly, voids which have opened up around the surfaces of the quartz grains. The formation of both types of voids is related to a marked increase in the volume of quartz which occurs when it is heated through 573°C. When a crucible is fired the elongate cracks open up to accommodate this expansion of the quartz grains. When the crucible cools the quartz shrinks back to the low temperature form, leaving the elongate voids and opening up a space around each quartz grain. As might be expected, these voids become greater in size and more abundant the coarser and more abundant the quartz grains (Figs 6.1, 6.5, 6.6 & 6.11). We can expect a ceramic fabric to be weaker the larger and more abundant the voids within it are and on this basis the Stamford ware (Fig 6.1) is a stronger ceramic than the other crucibles. This has allowed the production of much finer, thinner-walled vessels. Further, the coarser-grained more porous crucible fabrics are more likely to corrode and be penetrated by slag or metal with subsequent loss of material.

Several authors have argued that quartz temper was detrimental to thermal stress and shock resistance in archaeological ceramics during use because of its high coefficient of thermal expansion, in particular that associated with the volume change at 573°C. Woods (1986) however has observed that many cooking wares were made in quartz-tempered fabrics. The presence of abundant quartz in the fabrics of widely used types of crucible, which would have been subjected to extreme thermal stresses, supports Woods' view that the effects of quartz are not critically deleterious. The SEM study reveals that the quartz expanded to some extent in the initial firing.

Therefore, the fabric was opened up when initially fired so that during use expansion of the quartz grains filled up the voids, and did not impose stresses on the matrix.

To sum up, the crucibles were made from relatively refractory clays which were therefore quite well suited to the purpose. They could withstand temperatures of at least 1200°C which, given the melting points of silver and many copper alloys in the range 900°-1000°C, would allow 200°C or so superheat so that the metal remained fluid while pouring and casting. Even so, at least the Stamford ware and probably the London-type ware crucibles appear to have been made from

site	context	accn no	extra outer layer	Cu	Zn	Au	Pb	Ag	Sn	Metal melted	fig no
MLK 76	224	89		?	+++					*	
MLK 76	1056	287	yes	+	+					*	
MLK 76	3067	365		+	+++		+	+		silver	
MLK 76	262	531		?	+++		+			*	5
MLK 76	3084	860		+	+					*	
MLK 76	3143	867		+	+		+	+		silver	
MLK 76	224	963		?	+		+			*	7
MLK 76	3104	1563		+	+++					*	
MLK 76	33	1651		+	+					*	
MLK 76	1080	1655		+	+		+			*	
		1657								not used	
		1653								not used	
		874								not used	
		859								not used	
		520								not used	
		215								not used	

6.17. Analytical results for crucibles from Milk Street, London (probably all Stamford ware).

the same or similar raw materials to those used for domestic pottery. While the quartz in the EMCW is coarse relative to domestic pottery, the clay composition is close to that of the London-type ware crucibles (Figs 6.12, 6.13). These observations are consistent with the specification of Theophilus that the clay to be used should be that 'from which earthenware pots are made' (Hawthorne and Smith 1963). Theophilus also suggests that white or grey-firing clays are to be preferred, these of course are low in the oxides of Iron, potent fluxes which would have reduced the ability of the crucible to withstand high temperatures, and that it was desirable to avoid when selecting a refractory clay.

Of the crucibles studied, the Stamford ware appears to offer superior qualities in terms of ability to withstand high temperatures, and probably strength and corrosion resistance. Resistance to thermal stress and shock is a complex phenomenon and not easy to predict; however, the potentially deleterious effects of the quartz inclusions were reduced by its opening effect on the ceramic microstructure in all fabrics. Stamford ware contains less abundant and finer quartz and on this basis it is to be expected that Stamford ware might have been the preferred crucible type for the more valuable alloys as is indicated by its strong association with the melting of silver.

Discussion

Stamford ware crucibles were widely used in both Lincoln and York at this period but they were long-distance imports to London and so are unlikely to have been used unless they were in some way superior to the locally-produced fabrics. Their almost exclusive use for silver, a more valuable metal than copper alloys, reinforces this suggestion of higher quality, which is in turn borne out by the investigation of the properties of the fabrics themselves. However, as all fabrics appear to have been used quite frequently as metallurgical crucibles it is evident that all were sufficiently refractory to withstand the temperatures to which they were exposed and, as the melting points of silver and copper alloys are very close, there are unlikely to have been any significant differences in the operating temperatures used for melting most of the alloys noted here. The exception is a single sherd from a vessel used to melt lead, which has a substantially lower melting point.

It is probable that the properties of Stamford ware made it a much more reliable crucible to use, less prone to failure due to accidental rough handling, temperature overshoot or sudden shock. Furthermore, the thin-walled Stamford ware vessels were probably easier to handle and pour and their relatively smooth surface finishes did not so readily trap metal particles or act as sites for corrosion by slag. These features probably combined to offer sufficient saving of wasted metal, either in perception or in reality, to encourage the craftsmen to use Stamford ware crucibles which, as imports, are likely to have been more expensive.

In order to improve performance, some crucibles appear to have been modified before use. In some cases an added outer layer of less refractory clay which is usually deeply vitrified and vesicular has been added (Nos 13, 15 & 19). This is a common feature on wheel-thrown crucibles of Roman and early medieval date. The reason for this extra layer is unknown, but it would have protected the vessel from thermal shock as it was removed from the fire and would have increased its thermal capacity, keeping the metal molten for a little longer, allowing more time to pour it into a mould. In a few cases the added clay has been extended up over the rim of the crucible to make a bar across the top of the vessel, just behind the pouring lip (eg No 19). This bar would have kept back any crucible slag floating on the molten metal when pouring it into a mould thus helping to produce cleaner castings.

One factor which is difficult to judge from small sherds is the overall size of the vessel. In general larger crucibles would not have been used for melting precious metals which were expensive and hence tended to be used in smaller quantities. Stamford ware crucibles are often quite small with diameters typically in the range 30–70mm though larger examples are known (Bayley 1982). The one complete vessel from Watling House had a maximum diameter of 90mm.

The more complete London ware and miscellaneous London ware crucibles fell into the same size range with the exception of two vessels from the Bank of England (MOL Acc Nos 14711 and 14713) which had diameters of 140-160mm and had been used to melt leaded copper. The two sherds with similar metal deposits were both from thick-walled vessels which must have been of similar diameters. This suggests that two distinct sizes of crucibles were made from London ware, the first with diameters of 40–80mm which were, like Stamford ware crucibles, mainly used to melt silver, and the second, with diameters of around 150mm which were used mainly to melt copper alloys (but note MOL 1013 from Watling House which is of the larger size but was used for silver). The larger vessels can be seen as a development towards the very large-volume, thick-walled vessels that are common in the later medieval period.

The EMCW crucibles show a considerable range of sizes, from 70mm up to over 150mm diameter with no particular favoured sizes. The sherds which are too small to suggest vessel diameters have very variable thicknesses (3 to 10mm) and thus also indicate a considerable range of crucible sizes. There is some correlation between sherd thickness and the composition of the alloy melted in the vessel; leaded alloys were melted in medium or large vessels while unleaded alloys were found on small or medium sized crucibles. This makes sense as leaded alloys were used for relatively massive castings where the lack of strength of the metal was not important. Wrought metalwork and smaller castings tend to be made of unleaded alloys as they have the necessary physical properties. The vessels where XRF suggested unalloyed copper was melted are all of different sizes which can be interpreted as showing that copper was used in both large and small quantities, or that the XRF results are misleading and that these crucibles originally contained both leaded and unleaded copper alloys. The larger vessels are comparable in size with the larger London ware crucibles but even the smaller EMCW crucibles are larger than most of the Stamford ware and smaller London ware ones. One EMCW crucible from St Thomas's Hospital (MOL 13177) had an external diameter of 90mm and contained 120ml up to the slag 'tidemark' inside. This is equivalent to about 1kg of metal.

Conclusions

Metals worked in Saxon and Norman London included a range of copper alloys including bronze, brass and gunmetal. These alloys were melted in crucibles made in at least three fabrics. Two of these are likely to have been made in the London region and the third, Stamford ware, is

alloy	Stamford	London	EMCW	Milk St
silver	6	3	1	2
copper	0	0	6	0
brass	0	0	5	0
gunmetal	0	1	2	0
bronze	0	0	2	0
leaded bronze	0	0	1	0
leaded gunmetal	2	0	0	0
leaded brass	0	0	0	2
leaded copper	0	4	3	0
lead	0	1	0	0
alloy identifiable	8	9	22	2
alloy unknown	8	2	18	8
not analysed	1	0	43	0
not used	0	5	0	6
total analysed	17	16	83	16

6.18. Summary of analytical results.

imported. Stamford ware offered significant advantages in its physical properties and was favoured for the melting of silver. The small sample of metallurgical debris which has been retrieved sets a limitation to any inferences that can be drawn as to any distribution of metalworking activity in London during this period. This is compounded by the high proportion of crucible sherds which yield no information on alloy use. Of 132 crucibles or crucible sherds examined in the present study, it was possible to assign an alloy type to only 41 with any confidence. It thus appears that any further advances in this area must await the accumulation of a substantially larger sample or the discovery of evidence for permanent workshops.

Acknowledgements

We thank Dr Morven Leese for advice on the interpretation of the chi-squared test.

Appendix 6.1:

CONCORDANCE OF SITE AND
CONTEXT OR MUSEUM OF LONDON
ACCESSION NUMBER FOR
CRUCIBLES ILLUSTRATED IN FIGS
6.3–6.4, 6.7–6.10

Stamford-type ware

1 MOL ACC NO 30.38/13
2 PDN [2370]
3 MOL ACC NO 30.38/10
4 MOL ACC NO 20235
5 MLK [262]
6 MLK [2001]
7 MLK [224]
8 MLK [3080]
9 MOL ACC NO P11
10 GM4 ER1076B
11 MOL ACC NO 15970
12 MOL ACC NO 59.94/46

Early Medieval Coarse White ware

13 MOL ACC NO 11862
14 MOL ACC NO 14708
15 MOL ACC NO A27779
16 MOL ACC NO 13173
17 MOL ACC NO 13177
18 MOL ACC NO 6192
19 MOL ACC NO A27575
20 MOL ACC NO 13178
21 MOL ACC NO 22010
22 MOL ACC NO 13180

London-type ware

23 GPO [263]
24 BIS [967]
25 MOL ACC NO 24392
26 MOL ACC NO A24618
27 GM76 ER460
28 GPO [364]
29 GPO[1]
30 POM [2275]
31 MOL ACC NO 13182
32 MOL ACC NO 13183

7.i DENDROCHRONOLOGY

TREE-RING ANALYSIS OF OAK TIMBERS FROM MILK STREET

Jennifer Hillam and Cathy Groves, University of Sheffield Dendrochronology Laboratory

Introduction

Samples from eleven oak (*quercus spp.*) timbers from Milk Street were examined at the Sheffield Dendrochronology Laboratory during 1985. The samples were from contexts dated to the 10th, late 11th to early 12th and late 12th to early 13th centuries. Of these, five samples contained rings which were, in places, too close together to be distinguished reliably. The remaining six samples consist of five timbers from a single pit (Pit 45, group 1 - 10th century) and one timber from another pit (pit 81, group 3 - late 12th to 13th century).

The samples were prepared and measured using methods outlined elsewhere (Hillam 1985). The resulting tree-ring curves were compared with each other both visually and on the microcomputer using the method of Baillie and Pilcher (1973), which gives a value of Student's *t* for each position of overlap. Generally, a *t* value of 3.5 or over is significant as long as it is accompanied by an acceptable visual match. Where acceptable matches were found the data were averaged to produce a site master curve. This process produced three independent curves: MLK1 which was produced from three curves, MLK2 which was produced from two curves and a single sample, MLK3.

A full report of this work has been deposited in the Museum of London, Department of Urban Archaeology Archive (Hillam and Groves 1985). This includes the data from the six measured samples and a list of the reference chronologies used in the study.

Pit 45

MLK1. This curve, formed by timbers 871, 1679 and 1680 could not be dated conclusively. This is probably due to the shortness of the ring patterns (44, 50 and 48 measured rings respectively).

Samples with more than 50 rings are preferred as these can be dated more readily. However, as all three samples are probably contemporary their relative felling date is after year 61 (arbitrary).

MLK2. The curve is composed of samples 1673 and 1674. When compared with various reference curves from Britain and Europe acceptable matches were found when the MLK2 curve covered the period AD785-904 (Fig 7.1).

Chronology	Student's *t*	Reference
City medieval	5.4	SDL unpub.
Coppergate New 10th	3.9	SDL unpub.
Exeter	3.5	Hillam 1980
Exeter Goldsmith	4.5	Morgan 1984
Germany Trier area	4.0	Hollstein 1980

7.1 : Correlation of MLK2 *with reference chronologies.*

There is no sapwood present on either timber and therefore only *termini post quos* for the felling of the timbers can be given. Taking 10 years as the minimum number of sapwood rings, these are AD906 and AD914, but the actual felling dates could be much later.

Pit 81

MLK3. Several tentative dates were obtained for sample 412 but the sequence, comprising 98 measured rings, could not be dated. There are many problems associated with the dating of single timbers and it is often preferable to have a large number of short ring sequences rather than one long one (Hillam *et al* 1987). If the other two samples from this phase (1677 and 1681) had been measurable they might have replicated this

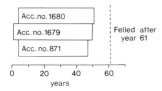

7.2 : MLK I *relative chronology.*

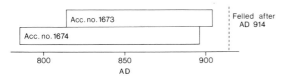

7.3 : MLK3 *absolute chronology.*

sequence and provided a conclusive date for the timber, which had 21 rings of sapwood.

Acknowledgements
The work was financed by the Historical Buildings and Monuments Commission for England.

7.ii ARCHAEOMAGNETIC DATING

A. J. Clark, Ancient Monuments Laboratory, HBMC(E)

Archaeomagnetic dates were obtained from two late Saxon structures from the City of London. The technical data will be published elsewhere but the dates themselves are published here together with an archaeological evaluation (supplied by Alan Vince).

AML-854792 Botolph Lane Building PEN12. Samples obtained from a clay oven floor (Vol 1 pp.98–9, Fig 95). The date, at the 68% confidence level, is probably 9th century. The magnetic stability of the material is not very good and the date is therefore not highly reliable.

The oven was in one of the latest surviving floor levels in its sequence and pottery found in earlier contexts would indicate a construction date in the later 10th century at the earliest.

AML-854791 Well Court, Building WEL3. Samples obtained from a clay oven floor (Vol 1 pp.61–2, Figs 50, 92). The date, at the 68% confidence level is *c*.950-1000. The result was, however, somewhat off the reference curve to the east, possibly due to compass error. The date given is from the nearest part of the curve.

Very little pottery was found in levels associated with Building WEL3 or from earlier contexts. What there was could date from the late 9th to the early 11th century. Building WEL3 was succeeded by another timber building and a sherd of Early Surrey Coarseware was found in the construction levels of this building. This would suggest a mid 11th century construction date and presumably only a slightly earlier date for the abandonment of Building WEL3 and its oven. The archaeological evidence and the archaeomagnetic date appear to be in broad agreement.

8. THE DEVELOPMENT OF SAXON LONDON

by Alan Vince

Summary

Although there was apparently a decline in the intensity of occupation of London in the late 4th century it has the latest dated town defences in Britain. Nevertheless, it is probable that by the middle of the 5th century, when the first evidence of Saxon activity in this part of the Thames Valley is found, the intra-mural area had largely been given over to agriculture or scrub, apart from areas occupied by ruined and deserted buildings. It is possible that it continued to act as a refuge for the surrounding region but such a function leaves little if any archaeological trace.

From the late 6th or early 7th century onwards there is evidence, both from excavation and the distribution of artefacts, for the existence of a large settlement outside the walls, along the present-day Strand; while a few finds suggest that small religious and lay estates may have existed within the walls. The Strand settlement declined during the 9th century and it is to this period, or even later, that the extensive post-Roman re-occupation of the intra-mural City can be dated.

Excavations within the City walls have shown that much of the street system is primary to the re-occupation and that some of these streets were occupied by buildings from their foundation onwards. The majority of the evidence for late Saxon London, however, comes from analysis of the contents of rubbish pits. From these, there is evidence for an increase in overseas trade and in the working of copper alloys and precious metals at the end of the 10th or early in the 11th century. Conversely, there is no evidence for any major change in trade or economy in the middle of the 11th century, corresponding to the Norman Conquest.

Late Roman London (Fig 8.1)

To understand the fate of London in the 5th century it is necessary to consider the situation in the last years of Roman rule. The features of late Roman London which might affect its post-Roman history are the size of the occupied area, the range of activities taking place in London and the physical limitations which Roman land-use may have placed in the way of later occupants. Knowledge of London in this period is limited, owing to the truncation of late Roman and later stratigraphy over much of the intra-mural City, and to the difficulties in interpreting the surviving evidence. There are therefore significant divisions of opinion as to the state of the Roman settlement at the end of the 4th century.

Defences

Londinium was provided with a defensive land wall at the end of the 2nd century. Similarity of construction, dating evidence and the quality of the work (which contained mainly new materials) all suggest that this wall was not built to counter an immediate threat. Parts, probably all, of the river frontage of the settlement were protected in the mid-3rd century by a wall of similar construction but during the 4th century the riverside was completely enclosed by the hurried construction of walls containing reused sculpted stone (Sheldon and Tyers 1983, 359-61; Hill *et al* 1980). Reused stonework was also incorporated into the foundations of bastions, added at regular intervals around the eastern landward circuit in the mid-4th century or later. Parts of this defensive system were being rebuilt at the very end of the 4th century, to judge from the discoveries at the Tower of London (Parnell 1977, 98), but, surprisingly, in a less hurried style than the mid-4th-century work.

Intra-mural occupation

Given the clear evidence for the continuing importance of London's defences throughout the late Roman period, it is surprising, perhaps, to find that on most intra-mural excavations there was a radical change in the nature of the occupation at about the time of their construction. Shops, workshops, bathhouses and a complex interpreted as the Governor's palace were all apparently demolished and in several cases replaced by a layer of dark earth (Horsman *et al* 1988, 23, 26, 28 and 30). This deposit typically contains abraded Roman pottery, of 3rd- to 4th-century date, and has produced a substantial collection of Roman coins, predominantly of the late 3rd century but including issues down to the mid-4th century. In some areas, foundations of late Roman buildings have been recorded cutting through this dark earth, showing that later Roman stratigraphy had been truncated. There

8.1 London in the late 4th century. Late Roman inhumation burials are shown as crosses while coin finds are shown as black dots.

is certainly little evidence that dark earth was accumulating in the late 4th century, and none at all for its growth in the 5th to 9th centuries. Nowhere, however, has a soil profile been seen to have developed in the dark earth. Therefore, either the deposit was disturbed (by horticulture, agriculture or human occupation) inhibiting soil formation, or a soil did develop but was removed at or before the late Saxon occupation, taking with it evidence for 5th- to 9th-century activity.

The coins found in DUA excavations and before suggest that commercial activity in London was in relative decline (compared with that in unwalled 'towns' or 'villages' for example) in the 4th century, and the total number of coins found in London which could have been current at the end of the 4th century is remarkably small (cf. Reece 1980, 88-9). There are, for example, more coins of the house of Theodosius from a single small excavation at the roadside settlement of Old Ford, to the north-east of London, than from the whole of the intra-mural area. Coins of late 4th-century date come mainly from the south-east fringe of the City, from sites just north of the

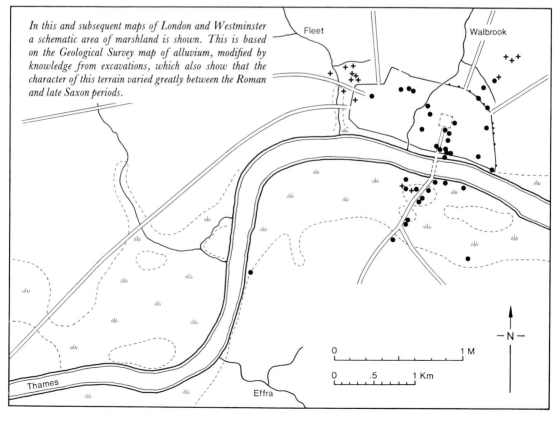

Thames and east of the site of the Roman bridge. Excavations in this area reveal patchy evidence for continued urban life; for example, a bath building at Pudding Lane was altered in or after the third quarter of the 4th century, but there is little evidence from the site for occupation after that date (Milne 1985, 33). A short distance to the east was the Billingsgate bathhouse. This was still in use, but not kept clean, after c.380 and when its tile roof collapsed it was left where it fell.

Cemeteries

Even if the walled area was not occupied intensively it was still regarded as part of the City, since no late Roman burials have been found within the walls. Outside the main gates, and across the bridge in Southwark, extensive cemeteries have been found. Those to the north-west and east of the city have revealed evidence for intensive burial during the later Roman period, although the absence of grave goods in the later 4th-century burials makes the end of use of these cemeteries difficult to determine. A chip-carved buckle from Smithfield, now in the British Museum, was probably from a grave of c.400 or later.

Function of settlement

There is as little evidence for the function of London at the end of the 4th century as there is of its extent and character. The most obvious characteristic, and one which is known to have survived into the medieval period, is the defensive circuit. In front of the riverside wall, however, there were no timber quays constructed after the mid-3rd century, and little evidence that the 3rd-century quay continued in use into the later Roman period. Fragments of Eastern Mediterranean micaceous ribbed amphorae and North African cylindrical amphorae are, however, quite frequent in late Roman assemblages in London but are not found on the sites of contemporary rural settlements in the Thames valley (for example none is known from the huge collections of 4th-century material from various sites in Essex catalogued by the Chelmsford Archaeological Trust, pers comm C Going). These amphorae must have been imported direct to London, although the port itself could conceivably have been moved outside the walled area. Documentary evidence and an ingot of silver, found at Tower Hill in 1777, reflect London's role as a treasury for Britain (Merrifield 1983, 241-4).

Until the introduction of Christianity, London was a major religious centre, although most of the pagan temples were probably demolished to provide materials for the 4th-century defences (Merrifield 1983, 246). London was the seat of a bishop in the late 4th century, although the location of his church is unknown.

To summarise, therefore, it seems that London had lost its commercial and manufacturing sectors during the 3rd century and had acquired a role as a fortified area containing administrative buildings, temples, bathhouses and, presumably, some domestic residences. The settlement seems to have had less of an economic role in the 4th than in the 2nd century and, unless the administration was taken over by British authorities in the early 5th century (as it is suggested took place at Wroxeter), the City may well have been an empty shell by the time the first Saxon settlers arrived in the mid-5th century.

The 5th and 6th centuries

In the area within the walls in which Theodosian coins are found there have been only three controlled excavations. At Pudding Lane the only strata dating to the late 4th or early 5th century record the silting of a drain and the consequent formation of a pond or marsh (Milne 1985, 35; Horsman et al 1988, 16-17, Fig 8). At Billingsgate bathhouse a deposit on the floor of one room produced Theodosian coins, and was therefore accumulating during the period 380-400, to be sealed immediately by the collapsed roof of the building (Marsden 1980, 180). This debris was still exposed in the mid-5th century or later when a button brooch of that date was lost between the tiles (Welch 1975, 91). There is no evidence for the date of abandonment of the south-east corner of the City, now occupied by the Tower of London, but only because here too the vital archaeological evidence has been removed (Parnell 1977, 98-9). It is still possible that evidence for early 5th-century occupation will be found but already there is sufficient evidence to show that London contrasts with Verulamium and Wroxeter, where such occupation can be demonstrated, even if its duration at those places is uncertain.

This lack of evidence for continued sub-Roman occupation contrasts with positive evidence for continuity of occupation at local villas, both in the Chilterns and in Essex (Branigan 1973; Drury and Rodwell 1980, 71-5); the survival of the whole rural landscape in parts of Essex (Drury and Rodwell 1980, Figs 22 and 23); and for the continuation of the town of Verulamium, probably as an urban settlement, well into the 5th century. On the other hand, recent excavations in Canterbury suggest that it shared the fate of London (Tatton-Brown 1982, 81-2). If London itself was unoccupied before the beginning of Germanic settlement within 20 miles of the City (at sites such as Mucking and Croydon, Hawkes 1982, 67) then it is perhaps surprising that no early settlements have been found on the fertile brickearth terraces surrounding London. If a sub-Roman political authority still existed where was it based? The answer may lie in the outskirts of London, or it may be that political control over the London area had moved to Verulamium.

Mid Saxon London (Figs 8.2-8.5)

Although the *Anglo-Saxon Chronicle* records that London was the refuge for the British of Kent after the battle of Crayford (*Crecganford*) in 456, the first reliable reference to London in post-Roman historical sources is in the early 7th century, when it was chosen by Pope Gregory to be the seat of an archbishop. What this implies for the status of London at this time is difficult to determine. Gaulish and Mediterranean bishoprics of this period were urban and it was evidently Gregory's intention to create an urban archbishopric for the new ecclesiastical province in England. The political realities which his bishop, Augustine, encountered in England evidently forced changes in the original plan and London in 604 became the seat of the bishop of the East Saxons, under an archbishop at Canterbury. Abandoned Roman forts and towns were given by Saxon kings to religious communities during the 7th century for their monasteries (Rigold 1977, 70-1) and bishoprics were established at Dorchester-on-Thames and Winchester in 634 and 662 respectively. However in these last two cases it is possible

8.2 London in the late 6th or 7th centuries. The black dots represent a variety of types of find but exclude sherds of chaff-tempered pottery (plotted on Fig 8.3) since these could be of later date.

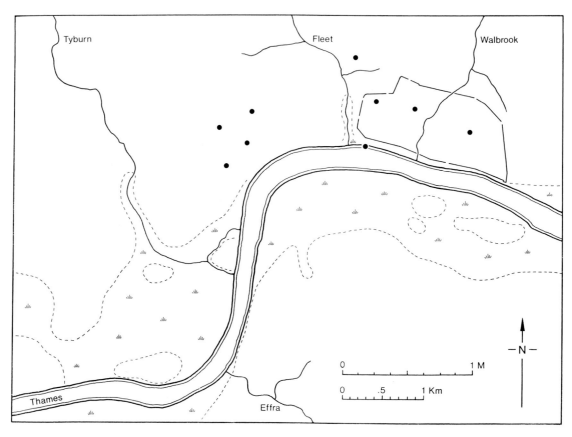

that the Roman towns were already administrative centres, even if they housed a very small permanent population. London's Roman past was obviously in the minds of contemporaries, as when in the early 9th century Bishop Helmstan of Winchester described his recent consecration 'in the illustrious place, built by the skill of the ancient Romans, called throughout the world the great city of London' (Stenton 1971, 56). No physical remains of the 7th-century cathedral have yet been found. The earliest Saxon artefacts in the area of the present cathedral are a late 9th-century lead weight from St Paul's churchyard, to the north-east of the cathedral, and the mid-11th-century Scandinavian-style grave slab found to the south-east of the cathedral. From the beginning of the 7th century onwards, London had a varied political history. It was probably the centre for local administration of a division of the East Saxon kingdom. At times two kings of Essex ruled concurrently and, although there is no conclusive evidence that they ruled separate areas, it is quite likely that London lay at the centre of one sub-kingdom.

The northern boundary of the territory looking to London may be that taken by the medieval diocesan boundary, since these territories have been shown elsewhere to preserve very early administrative divisions, corresponding to 7th-century kingdoms or sub-kingdoms (Sawyer 1978, 146 and Fig 8). Whereas the local administrative network is likely to have remained stable or to have developed gradually from the 7th to the 11th centuries, the overlordship of the area can be shown to have been complex and subject to rapid change and upheaval. In the early 7th century, London was under the hegemony of the kings of Kent but upon the death of Aethelbert this control collapsed, at least temporarily. Bishop Cedd was a Mercian appointee and his successor, Wine, obtained his seat from Wulfhere of Mercia in 666. Mercian control of London seems to have been almost continuous from the late 7th to the late 9th century, although the laws of Hlothere and Eadric of Kent refer both to the hall of the kings

8.3 London in the late 7th to early 9th centuries. The majority of the finds plotted here are sherds of Ipswich or chaff-tempered wares or coin finds.

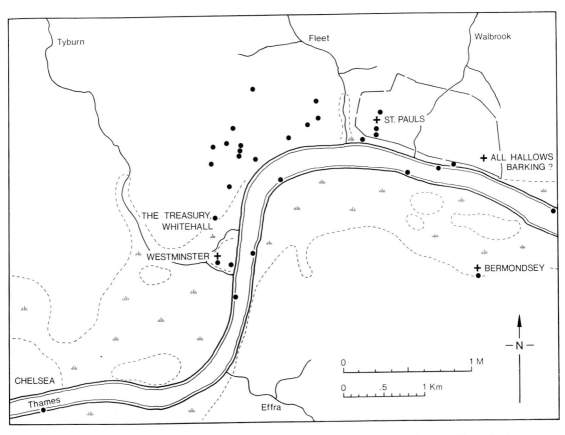

of Kent and to their reeve in London. This may indicate a brief re-assertion of Kentish power in the late 7th century, within the period 673 to 686. By 732, however, London was securely under the control of Aethelbald of Mercia since between that date and 748 he issued a series of charters granting relief from toll from ships landing at London to various religious houses. Some of these grants were confirmed by early 9th-century Mercian kings but by that time the kingdom of Wessex was rising in power and influence and the capture of London by Egbert of Wessex in the early 9th century was apparently commemorated by the issue of coinage bearing the legend 'LUNDONIA CIVIT' (Dolley, 1970, Pl19). Nevertheless, the City does not seem to have remained in West Saxon hands for more than a year. From this evidence it is clear that the control of London was often disputed and that its capture was regarded in the early 9th century as a matter of importance. It is likely, therefore, that it would always have had a royal hall and king's reeve, as recorded by the Kentish kings. In the mid-9th century this hall may have been 'by the west gates', since that was the location of the reeve Ceolmund's haga (Whitelock 1968, No 92, 487-8). Nevertheless, councils in the London area did not always meet in London itself. Chelsea, for example, was a more popular venue in the late 8th and 9th centuries and was the location of a meeting at which the restoration of London was discussed in 898/9 (Dyson 1978, 201).

The reeve would have commanded a garrison and it has been suggested that two of the rich Kentish 7th-century cemeteries (Sarre and Buckland) belonged to such garrisons controlling the port of Dover and the route from mainland Kent to Thanet (Chadwick-Hawkes, 1969, 191-2). Their characteristic features are a high proportion of male burials with weapons, including swords, and an unusually high quantity of imported Frankish goods. No such cemetery has yet been found in the London area (Mucking cemetery I is both too early and too distant to be considered) but there are a few finds from within the walls which may

8.4 The position of London on the boundaries of several Saxon kingdoms. The marked sites are either mid-Saxon wics or cathedrals.

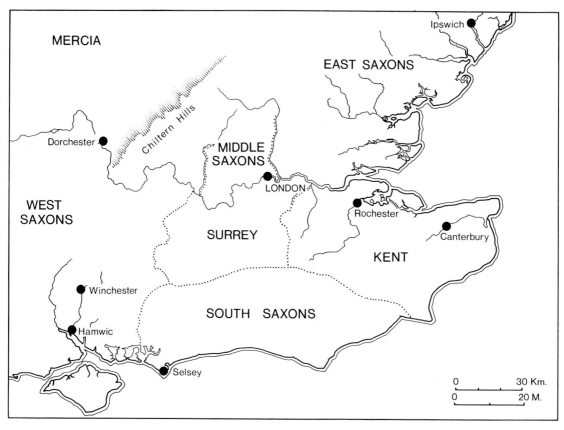

be relevant. There are three recorded finds of Frankish pottery, all early finds and only two with precise provenances (see page 00, Nos 301-3). One of these pots is a roller-stamped greyware jar from Gresham Street while the other is an undecorated dish from Christ's Hospital, Greyfriars. The third pot is a further roller-stamped greyware jar (Evison 1979, Fig 14f, Plᵥɪᴀ & xc). All three pottery vessels are complete and more likely to have come from burials than occupation sites. However, until similar discoveries are made in controlled archaeological excavations there is always the possibility that the vessels are recent imports, given London provenances to aid their sale.

The growth of trade through London can be demonstrated by numismatics. London was almost certainly one of the first substantial mints in England, producing, from the 630s onwards, a gold coinage which included the name of the mint (Sutherland 1948; Stewart 1978). The only provenanced find of these early coins is at Crondall, on the border between Hampshire and Surrey, although a related coin was found in the Pas-de-Calais. In the late 7th century this gold coinage was replaced first by a debased gold, then by silver and finally debased silver coinage, known today as the denarial or sceatta coinage. A few of these sceattas have a blundered London mint-mark and stylistic comparison enables others to be placed in the same class (Rigold 1977, series L). Initial work on the distribution of find-spots has also led to the putative attribution of other types to London, or at least to Essex (Metcalf 1984). However, much work remains to be done on the provenance of the denarial coinage. Nevertheless, analysis of the distribution of these putative London coins, and comparison of those with other suggested mints, shows that London may have been second only to Kent in production. Coins minted in London are also more widely dispersed than most others. East Anglian runic sceattas, for example, are hardly ever found outside the boundaries of the kingdom where they were produced.

The importance of London to the Saxons may well have been not only for international trade but because it lay on the boundary between several kingdoms, acting as a port of trade between Kent, Essex, Wessex (the kings of which certainly controlled Surrey briefly in the late 7th century) and Frisia. It has been suggested that many Roman *vici* were similarly situated on the boundaries between *civitates* (Phythian-Adams 1977, 78). When Bede described London as a 'mart of many nations' it is possible that this was the concept he had in mind. Excavations within the walls have made it clear that no large mid-Saxon settlement existed there, although the cathedral may have been the focus for a small non-religious settlement close to the precinct, and there is sparse evidence for rich burials or settlement to the north of the cathedral (see above). Similar 'negative evidence' comes from Southwark, shown by extensive excavation to have been a gravel-capped island surrounded by marsh until late in the medieval period. Considerable erosion took place there between the late Roman period and the 11th or 12th century. This erosion suggests that Southwark was completely abandoned at some stage during which time the archaeological deposits were subjected to natural weathering. By contrast, the majority of early to mid-Saxon finds from the London area are either from an area to the west of the walls, along the north bank of the Thames between Whitehall and the Fleet valley, or from the river itself. These finds can be considered in three categories. Firstly, there are those which either definitely or potentially come from burials. Secondly, those, mainly loom-weights and potsherds, which are most likely the evidence for occupation sites together with the results of controlled excavations, a source of information almost completely lacking until 1985. Thirdly there are finds, such as coins and metal-work, which indicate activity in the area but of an indeterminate nature.

The evidence for Saxon cemeteries in the London area is tantalising but in general sparse. Outside the walls, the St Martins-in-the-Fields area is a potential location for a rich burial since in the 13th century the bishop of London had to condemn Londoners who were desecrating consecrated land in their search for buried treasure there (Thomas and Thornley 1938, *sub anno* 1298). A burial accompanied by two glass bowls of late 6th or early 7th-century date was discovered in the early 18th century underneath the new portico of the church (Harden 1956, 142) while a gold finger-ring from Garrick Street (now in the British Museum) might also have come from a burial. No early to mid-Saxon swords are known from sites within the walls but a high quality sword pommel was found at Fetter Lane. This is dated to the end of the 8th century by its ornamentation (Wilson 1964, 148-9, No 41) and is therefore less likely to have come from a burial than to be an accidental loss. To this short list can now be added a burial from Jubilee Hall, to the south of Covent Garden in the Strand area, excavated in 1985 (Whytehead 1985), which may date to the 6th or 7th century; another single burial from a site at Bedfordbury excavated in 1987 (Cowie and Whytehead 1989) and a 6th-century short long cross brooch from 'Tower Street'. The latter find is in the British Museum and no further indication of its provenance is known (the two possibilities are (Great) Tower Street in the south-east of the walled City or Tower Street off Shaftesbury Avenue in the Strand area).

The evidence from within the City walls is much less impressive. At least one spearhead has been found in the intra-mural City, at Poultry, but, being broken in half, need not have come from a burial (Wheeler 1935, 168-9, Fig 39, No 7). Another was found in a medieval water-front dump at New Fresh Wharf (pers comm J Clark), presumably the result of disturbance somewhere within the walls during the medieval period.

8.5 Greater London in the mid-Saxon period. Within the area of the London boroughs (shown by the dotted line) the search for mid-Saxon evidence has been thorough.

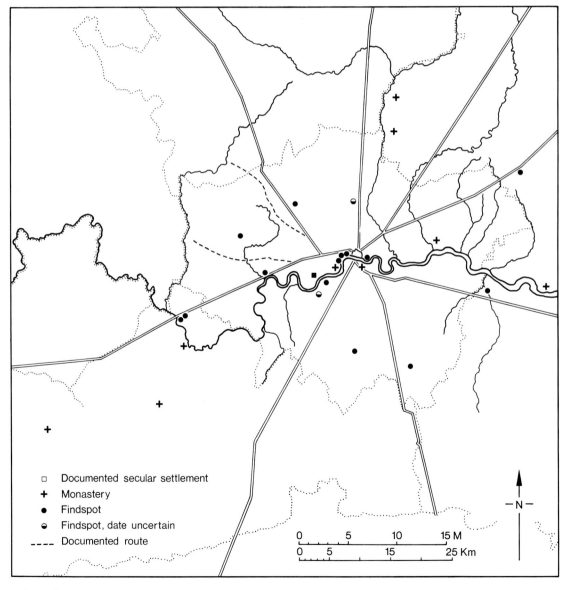

Documented secular settlement
+ Monastery
• Findspot
⊖ Findspot, date uncertain
---- Documented route

0   5   10   15 M
0 5   15   25 Km

- N -

0   5   10   15 M
0 5   15   25 Km

- N -

- N -

- N -

- N -

Few of these Saxon burials have been recorded satisfactorily and in most cases both the date and nature of the discovery are disputable. Nevertheless, taken as a whole, the concentration of evidence to the north of the Strand between Charing Cross and Kingsway might suggest that burials took place in a zone set back from the river frontage. If so, the Tower Street brooch would take its origin back to the 6th century, while the finds from Drury Lane and St Martins-in-the-Fields would show that it was in existence in the 7th century. Finds of Ipswich-type ware and mid-Saxon rubbish pits in the same area and further to the north show that this area was eventually used for domestic occupation.

Later, definitely Christian, Saxon burials in the Strand area have been found at St Brides church, pre-dating an 11th-century or later pit (Grimes 1968, 184, Fig 42 and Pls 81-3). These graves were lined with stones, a trait noted in several late Saxon to early Norman cemeteries within the walls (Schofield in White 1988, 22-5), and are probably therefore of 12th-century or earlier date. There were undoubtedly graveyards at the monasteries of Westminster and Bermondsey from at least the late 8th century as at St Paul's from the beginning of the 7th century (although there is as yet no archaeological evidence for any of them before the 11th century). However, the first two were closed communities unlikely to have had burial rights over the surrounding population. Whether St Paul's cathedral had extensive graveyards, sufficient to account for the whole population of London inside and outside the walls in the mid-Saxon period remains to be proved and is certainly unlikely. Mid Saxon Christian burials might, for example, be expected at St Andrew Holborn, a church described as 'old' in a charter of the mid-10th century granting the area of the Strand settlement to Westminster (Gelling 1954). Excavations at Saxon Southampton have shown that the mid Saxon settlement was probably served by a number of small churches, as well as the minster church of St Mary (Brisbane 1988).

Evidence of settlement can be graded from the undeniable, actual structural evidence with associated dating and artefactual evidence, to the possible, where one or more unassociated finds of a type likely to be derived from a settlement have been discovered. Traces of buildings have been found at the Treasury, Whitehall (Huggins forthcoming), and at Jubilee Hall. The former probably dates to the late 8th or 9th centuries while occupation at the latter site may start earlier but finish at about the same time (Whytehead forthcoming). Mid Saxon occupation is also likely at Arundel House and the site of Savoy Palace, both just to the south of the Strand, but here the evidence consisted solely of unstratified pottery and loom-weights (Wheeler 1935, 139-141; Hammerson 1975, 209-10; Haslam 1975, 221-2). The pottery from these sites suggests a 7th-century or earlier date for the start of occupation at the Savoy and an 8th-or 9th-century date for the occupation at Arundel House. An assemblage from Tottenham Court, consisting solely of chaff-tempered sherds, including one stamped sherd, may therefore be earlier than those noted above and at present stands apart from the main concentration of finds (Whytehead and Blackmore 1983, 82-4). Further finds of pottery and loom-weights consist of single finds, mostly from the Strand area; from the Adelphi (to the south of the Strand); Kingsway and Fetter Lane (Blackmore 1983, 84). These finds probably represent only a fraction of those discovered before 1985. For example, the British Museum accession register records that the Adelphi loom-weight was one of 'hundreds' recovered. Since 1985 excavations and recording by the Department of Greater London Archaeology of the Museum of London have increased the number of actual and potential occupation sites considerably.

Three sites within the walls have produced small collections of chaff-tempered pottery. All are immediately south of St Paul's. One, at 29-31 Knightrider Street, is actually close to the south boundary of the precinct of St Paul's cathedral while the other two are close to the river. Only one other chaff-tempered sherd is known from the intra-mural City, found in an 11th-century context at New Fresh Wharf, where it is presumed to be residual. A collection of annular loom-weights from the site of a City bastion, now in the Passmore Edwards Museum, is not precisely provenanced but, from the recorded date of discovery could be from one of two bastions, both of late Roman date, which were located on either side of Aldgate (pers comm P Marsden). A pit containing a comb fragment of probably mid-Saxon date excavated at Plough Court, Lombard Street, is further tantalising evidence for occupation within the City walls in the mid-Saxon or early late Saxon period (Pritchard, Part 3 p.194).

Stray finds, which need not indicate occupation or burial on the site, consist mainly of metalwork recovered from the Thames. In most cases either the precise findspot is unrecorded or the finds themselves are not closely datable. Those which can be given both a date and a provenance are shown in Fig 8.3, and this does convey the size of the collection, much of which is held by the British Museum and the Museum of London. This concentration of metalwork, even though only loosely provenanced, is another indication of the importance of London in the mid-Saxon period. Coins and other non-ferrous metal finds are presently being recovered in increasing numbers through the activities of metal detectors users, but here too the majority of finds appear to come from the Thames foreshore and therefore may well not be close to the original place of loss, since the Saxon foreshore either lies buried underneath medieval deposits or was eroded by the river during the Saxon period. Vast stretches of the present foreshore only came into existence in the 15th century or later and any Saxon finds found within it must have been dumped there during the late or post-medieval periods.

Four numismatic finds are well-provenanced, although unstratified and unassociated. Two are stray coin finds of 9th-century date, one from Northumberland Avenue (Burgred, c.865-74) and Fleet Street (Coenwulf, 798-c.802). The others are hoards. The Middle Temple hoard, deposited c.840, was found during rebuilding at Hare Court, just south of Fleet Street, and presumably close to the mid-Saxon waterfront. The other, the Waterloo Bridge hoard, was found in the Thames silt during rebuilding of the bridge in the 1880s. This hoard, dated c.870, could either have been thrown into the river or be from a 9th-century wreck. Its position, at the base of the third pier from the south on the east side of the bridge, demonstrates that the hoard could not have been flung into the water from the shore, unless it was attached to something buoyant. Dolley has emphasised that the deposition dates of these hoards correspond with recorded Viking sackings of London, but the significance of their location outside of the walled area has only recently been noted.

The earliest coin hoard found inside the walls is from Bucklersbury and, although poorly recorded, appears to be dated early within the period c.880-899 (Blackburn forthcoming). This too was a period of Viking activity in the Thames valley. Firstly, there must have a siege of London between 880 and 883 (which had taken place by 883 according to the *Anglo-Saxon Chronicle* (Garmonsway 1953, *sub anno* 883) and then there

was a period of unrest in the 890s, leading to the construction of fortresses by King Alfred on either side of the Lea to protect the area against a group of Vikings encamped 20 miles to the north (Stott Part 4 p.288; Garmonsway 1953, *sub anno* 896). Also found within the walls was a lead weight bearing the impression of coin dies of Alfred (BMC type V, dated by Mark Blackburn to c.875-80). This weight, found at St Paul's churchyard in 1841-3, at the same time as the discovery of a late Saxon or early medieval graveyard, was probably intended to be half a pound. It could have been used by a moneyer, or a trader, or it may have been an official standard weight (Archibald Part 4 p.335). The first reference to the existence of such standards in London is of 10th-century date (Stenton 1970, 30). In this regard, it is noteworthy that St Paul's churchyard is the traditional location of the folkmoot of London and a place where both minting and the regulation of trading might be expected at an early date. Whatever date is ascribed to the manufacture or function of the weight there is no means of demonstrating that it was lost in the City within the period of currency of the coins whose dies it bears, although this is the natural interpretation.

There is no other archaeological evidence relevant to the precise date of the large-scale reoccupation of the walled area and the demise of the Strand settlement, but the general absence of overlap between the ceramic types used in the latest Strand settlement and those used in the earliest intra-mural occupation suggests that both settlements were never extensively occupied at the same time and that changes in the nature of the trade through London took place during the same period. On the one hand, a change in the terms used in documents to describe London, from -wic (or *vicus*) to -bury, took place in the 850s, giving force to the suggestion that the shift in settlement took place a third of a century earlier than the documented 'restoration' of London in 886 (Tatton-Brown 1986). On the other hand, a recent study of the coinage of Alfred by Blackburn suggests that the number of moneyers operating in London declined sharply, from about ten to two (Ludig and Beagstan) during the later part of Alfred's reign (Blackburn forthcoming). This decline probably dates to the mid 890s and suggests that there was a delcine in the flow of bullion into London which lasted into the reign of Edward the Elder. It is possible that one reason for the dcline in bullion was the abandonment of the Strand settlement and the commercial failure of the new, walled, town. This interpretation would suggest that the Strand settlement continued to function beyond the 'restoration' of 886 but that initial occupation of the walled city was on too small a scale for archaeological excavation to have revealed it.

The explanation for the demise of the extramural settlement must take account of the similar changes noted at York, Southampton, Quentovic and Dorestad, although not every extramural trading settlement shifted in the late 9th century. At Ipswich, for example, the medieval town directly overlies the mid- and late Saxon settlements. Three factors relevant to most of these cases were the increasing danger to sea-going trade brought about by the Vikings during the 9th century; changes in the nature of the estuaries in which the settlements were located; and the possibility of a general economic crisis.

In the case of London, and probably elsewhere as well, the Viking threat had been present for a century during which time no attempt to either defend the Strand settlement, nor move it to a more easily defended place, can be detected. It is nevertheless likely that the walled area acted as a refuge during this period, perhaps explaining some of the finds of mid-Saxon metalwork found within the walls. Neither the Whitehall nor Jubilee Hall sites has produced physical evidence for Viking attack, such as burnt horizons or pits filled with fire debris.

Another explanation often put forward for the shift in these settlements is the silting-up of the rivers where they lay. Some major change can certainly be seen in the action of the Thames during this period. It has been noted above that the Roman riverside wall was originally constructed above high water level but by the medieval period had been subjected to considerable river erosion. Similarly, whereas the river constantly built up deposits along the northern Thames foreshore during the 1st to 3rd centuries, and again from the 11th century onwards, there is no evidence of any substantial build-up in the intervening period. This suggests either that the build-up of foreshore deposits was caused in some way by the human activity along the waterfront (such as the impedance of the river flow by jetties or groynes) or that the river was more erosive between the late Roman and the 10th centuries.

Other changes are to be noted further up-river. The confluence of the Tyburn and the Thames, and presumably that of other streams as well, became clogged with mud late in the Saxon period so that, for example, mud flats built up around the gravel eyot of Thorney. The reason for this change appears to be that the convergence of fresh and salt water causes particles held in suspension in the fresh water to precipitate and form mud, a process known as flocculation. By the mid-10th century the areas around the mouths of the Tyburn and Fleet were known as 'fens', *bulunga fen* at the mouth of the Tyburn and *lunden fen* at the mouth of the Fleet, whereas *c*.800 or later, when the Westminster Palace sword was deposited almost immediately below the present site of the Victoria Tower, the foreshore consisted of gravel. Small variations in Mean Sea Level and the movement of the tidal head of the Thames were probably responsible for these changes, but their precise effect upon the ability of ships to navigate the river and to be landed and unloaded are difficult to calculate. It is most unlikely that such changes were sufficiently rapid to bring about a change in settlement in the middle of the 9th century but the possibility of environmental change being a factor in the development of the settlements must be taken seriously. It is most likely that the actual explanations for these shifts in settlements are intricately linked.

London, Southampton, Dorestad and Quentovic appear to have depended for their existence to an overwhelming degree upon international trade and would therefore have been even more sensitive to fluctuations in the volume of trade than medieval towns, which had a broader base, serving social and political functions as well as economic ones. A study of the pottery in London shows that there is virtually no imported pottery in use in the 10th century compared with substantial quantities in the 9th and 11th centuries. Taking this evidence at its face value we can suggest that there was a decline in overseas trade. We can certainly demonstrate that occupation within the walls was underway long before the first archaeological signs of activity along the waterfront (see p.24). The London data would suggest that there was a recession in international trade in the late 9th century, (Hodges 1982, 151-61), even though trade was being encouraged in London at the highest level (Dyson 1978, 211-12). Two themes therefore run through the development of London in the late 9th century: firstly, the decline of London as an international trading settlement, a role which it did not fully recover until late in the 10th century; and, secondly, the foundation of a defended fortress and market town by Alfred as part of the burghal system.

The Development of Saxon London   419

Late Saxon London

There is a scatter of 9th-century material from one end of the Strand settlement to the other. Such an extensive area of settlement implies that there was a substantial population to be accommodated within the walls, unless the decline in the international trading functions of the town, suggested above, brought about a decline in the overall population of London before its relocation.

One of the tasks of archaeology is therefore to identify the areas of the City occupied in the late 9th to early 10th centuries. At present, however, this aim is frustrated by our inability to define an archaeological horizon of this date. It is suggested that the City pottery sequence starts at this time, but there is no proof that it did not start, say, in the mid-10th century. Late 9th to early 10th century occupation can therefore only be examined through the excavation of deeply stratified sites, such as those at Botolph Lane and Pudding Lane

described by Horsman *et al* (1988, 12-21). On these sites a long succession of buildings and other activity has been excavated. An upper date bracket for the sequence can be fixed using pottery and coins, and the duration of the sequence can then be estimated.

Even on these sites there is no proof that the occupation sequences did not begin, say, in the late 10th century, although any shorter sequence is unlikely. Stray coin finds confirm a sudden upsurge in activity in the late 10th century although late 9th century coin finds are known from the City (Stott, Part 4, p.288) while the decorative metalwork and bonework includes little which is stylistically earlier than the Win-

8.6 London in the later 9th to mid 10th centuries. Pottery finds are excluded from this map, because they cannot be dated with enough accuracy, and the findspots are all coins. The street grid shown is that which can be inferred to have existed by the 890s from the Queenhythe charters. The estate of the Bishop of Worcester is shown hatched.

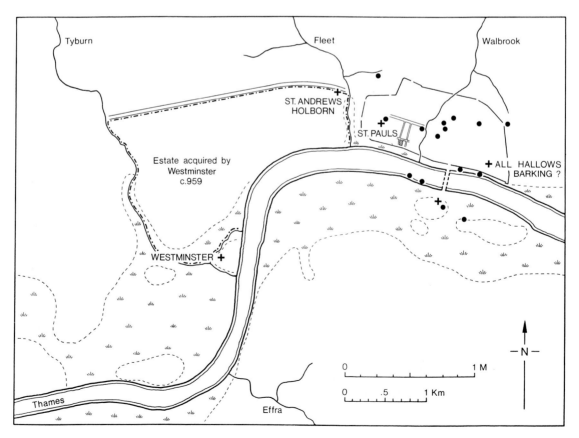

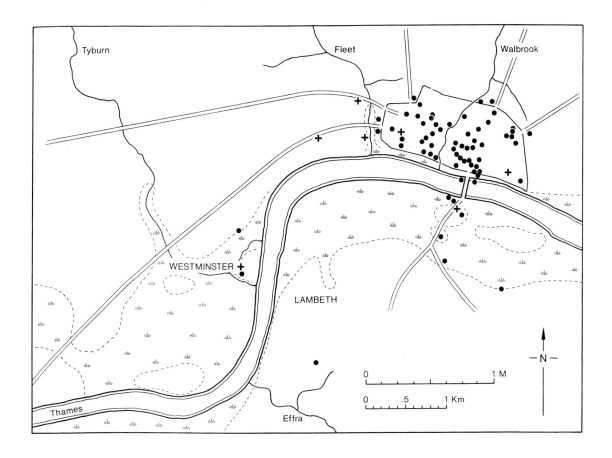

8.7 *London in the later 10th and early 11th centuries. The findspots shown are pottery and coins. Crosses mark the position of churches.*

chester and Ringerike styles of the late 10th and early 11th centuries (Pritchard, Part 3). Even decorated artefacts, however, are often too broadly dated to contribute to this debate.

Although we cannot yet use archaeology to demonstrate the extent of the first late Saxon settlement inside the walls of the City, and may suspect that this is because it was comparatively small, there is both historical and archaeological evidence to suggest that the late 9th to early 10th century town was planned, in the sense of having a formal rectilinear grid of streets unrelated to the earlier Roman pattern. Dyson has shown through a study of two charters of the late 9th century that part of this grid, at Queenhithe, was apparently laid out at the instigation of Alfred the Great and was certainly in existence at the end of his reign (Dyson 1978, 200-15). At Well Court, Bow Lane (one of the streets involved in this grid) was shown

to be of 10th-century or earlier date, and may well be a 9th-century construction as inferred from the documentary sources (Milne in Horsman *et al* 1988, 29). In the eastern half of the City, the origin and date of similar streets is less clear. At Botolph Lane a layer of make-up underlying both the lane and buildings constructed on its west side contained several potsherds which are certainly of late 9th-century or later date (LSS, see Part 2) (Milne in Horsman *et al* 1988, 16). This gives a relative date for the construction of the eastern street grid and the introduction of LSS pottery but still leaves the absolute date undetermined, since it is quite possible that the street grid running north from Queenhithe predates that laid out east of the Walbrook. The alternation of straight and crooked north-south streets leading off East Cheap has suggested to Milne that the former streets may be 'primary' and the latter 'secondary', or at least of differing function and importance (Milne in Horsman *et al* 1988, 19-21). Unfortunately, it was not possible to excavate underneath Pudding Lane and so it is possible

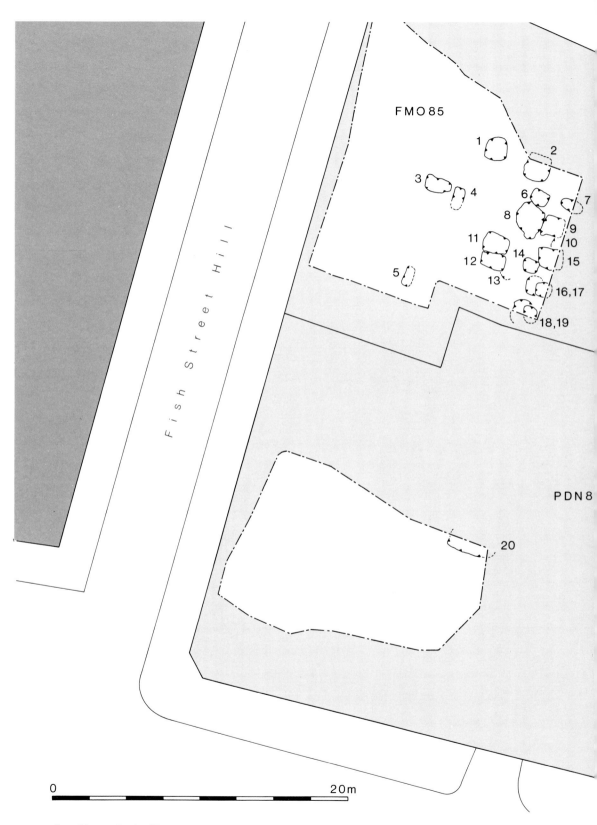

FMO85

1
2
3
4
6
7
8
9
10
11
12
14
15
13
5
16,17
18,19

PDN8

20

0   20m

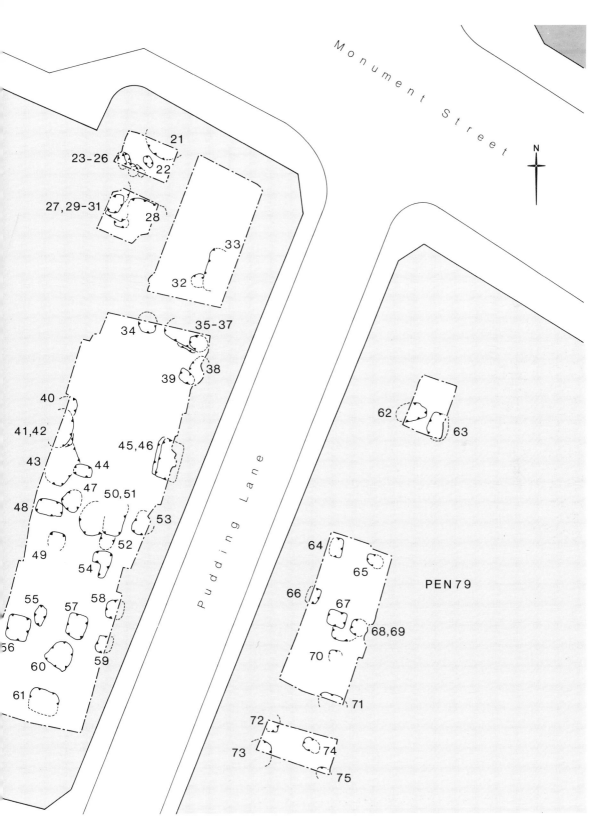

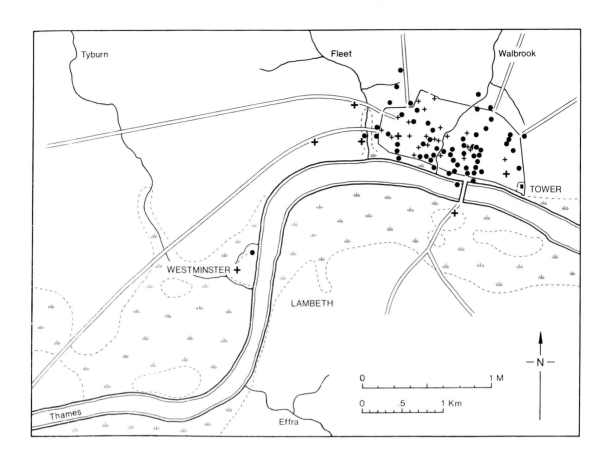

8.9 London in the late 11th to early 12th centuries. The findspots are pottery only. The absence of finds along the Strand reflects the lack of excavation on frontage sites whilst the apparent desertion of Southwark is due to the lack of data at the time of compilation (1987).

that it existed as a back lane as early as Fish Street Hill and Botolph Lane. The difference in its layout might then be due to the lack of 'official' interest in its construction.

A major change in the street pattern took place along the waterfront following the demolition of the Roman riverside wall. No documentary record of this demolition is known but it is likely that it took place after the Norman Conquest (Dyson 1980, 7-10), although whether for strategic reasons or to make access to the waterfront

8.8 Previous page: Rubbish pits to the northeast of London Bridge. The overall distribution of 10th- to 12th-century pits on the Fish Street Hill (FMO85) Pudding Lane (PDN81) and Botolph Lane (PEN79) sites. The dating evidence and finds assemblages from these pits is catalogued in Appendix M1.

easier cannot be determined. The first references to Thames Street, which lies immediately over the demolished riverside wall at the south-west corner of the City, date to the middle of the 12th century. A late 11th- to mid-12th-century date for the lowest metallings of Thames Street and St Peters Hill was given by pottery and a coin of William I from the 1981 Peter's Hill excavation (PET81). Streets and lanes which originally ran down to the wall, perhaps passing through gates onto the foreshore in some cases, were extended to the south of Thames Street both at the same time as the construction of that street and subsequently while minor lanes leading south from Thames Street were constructed as the reclamation of the waterfront extended (Dyson 1988). Despite the uncertainty as to the rate of growth of the 10th-century town, the distribution of pits and other contexts producing pottery of Ceramic Phase (CP) I shows that by the beginning of the 11th century, at the latest, most of the major street frontages were occupied (Fig 8.7). Features dating to the following phases, dating probably to the early to

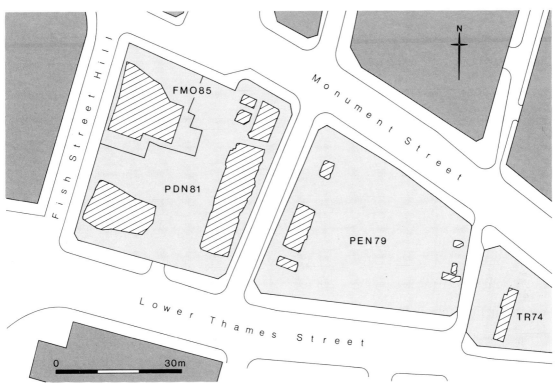

8.10 Location of excavated areas. Undated pits are shown in outline on Figs 8.11-13. Pits with a broad date range are shown on each relevant plan in outline.

8.11 Pits and buildings dating to the 10th or early 11th centuries (CP1 & CP2).

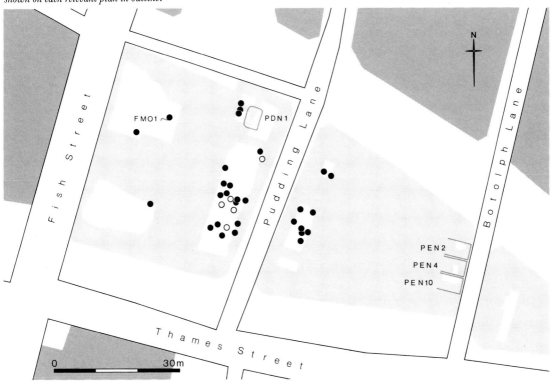

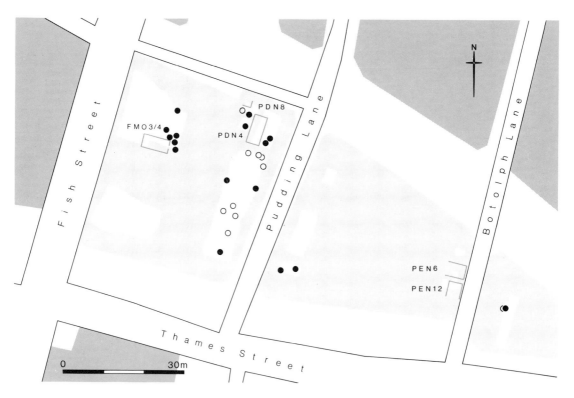

8.12 Pits and buildings dating to the early to mid 11th century (CP3 & CP4).

8.13 Pits and buildings dating to the late 11th to mid 12th centuries (CP5).

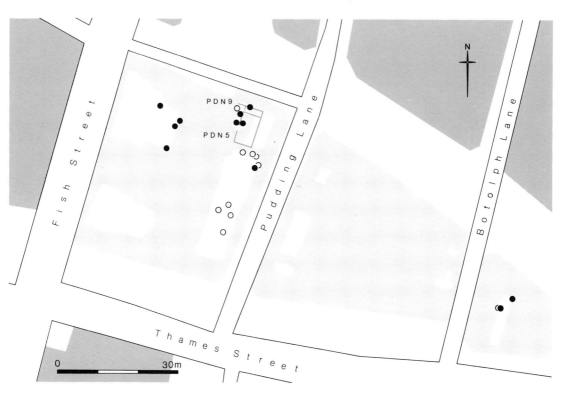

mid-11th century (CP2 and CP3) appear to be rarer, although this may be partly an artificial effect arising from the less distinctive nature of the pottery or the shorter duration of the phases. A comparable distribution map cannot be constructed because dating depends purely on the composition of associated groups of vessels. Nevertheless, a similar area of occupation is suggested. Even in the mid-11th to early 12th centuries (CP4 and CP5) there are few significant differences in pottery distribution, and by inference in occupation (Fig 8.9). By this date, however, occupation outside the walls at Aldersgate and Aldgate can be demonstrated, together with the infilling of the area to the west of St Paul's and just inside the City wall (as demonstrated by excavations at the Central Criminal Court (Marsden 1967, 189-221) and a re-examination of the finds from the pits found there). The finding of a lead flan stamped with the coin dies of Edward the Confessor from Aldersgate demonstrates both that this ribbon development outside the gates probably started before the Norman Conquest and, if Archibald's interpretation of these pieces is correct, that toll was probably collected just outside the gate (Archibald, Part 4, p.340).

Excavation of the area to the north of London Bridge has shown that, even if the area under occupation had not increased between the 10th and the 11th centuries, there was an intensification of occupation. This is shown most clearly by the Pudding Lane excavations, which indicate that occupation close to Pudding Lane can be dated to the late 10th century (Horsman et al 1988), and that this can be best explained as infilling at the backs of properties fronting onto Fish Street Hill. This process of infilling of the original grid chequers must have continued well into the post-Conquest period, as at Peter's Hill (see above). A reconstruction of the topography of some parts of the City is possible, based on the area excavations at Pudding Lane and Botolph Lane to the east of the Walbrook (Milne in Horsman et al 1988) and Milk Street and Watling Court to the west (Schofield and Allen forthcoming). Alignment of cess and rubbish pits shows the continuity of property boundaries at Milk Street from the 10th to the 13th centuries, which can be traced in documentary sources thereafter. In the east there may have been more change in the topography, following the demolition of the Roman riverside wall and the construction of Lower Thames Street, the reclamation of

land to the south of this street, followed by the rebuilding of London Bridge in the late 12th century and the reclamation and development of the waterfront.

The churches of London can supply further evidence for the nature of the topography of the late Saxon City. Several have been excavated and their full publication is in preparation (Schofield et al). Although post-excavation analysis is not yet complete several aspects of their development are clear. Firstly, there is no archaeological evidence that any of these churches had a pre-urban origin. The only church for which a 7th to 9th century date can be proved is St Paul's cathedral. There may have been other churches or chapels in the cathedral complex, such as that of St Gregory, to the south of the medieval church (although the surviving illustrations of this church show that the medieval structure was built in the 12th century). It has been suggested that other intra-mural churches, such as St Alban Wood Street originated as chapels on intra-mural but non-urban estates, but the siting of many of these churches at street corners (as at St Albans Wood Street) suggests that most were built to serve an urban population living in the surrounding streets. Excavations at St Alban Wood Street revealed an undated early stone building which could as easily be of 10th to 11th century date as earlier, especially considering that it seems to have been planned from the start as a two-cell building (Grimes 1968, 205-6). Another church for which an early origin has been postulated is All Hallows Barking. From the late 11th century this church belonged to Barking Abbey and it has been suggested that the church and other property in the City was granted to the abbey in the 7th century. A blocked arch composed of tile was exposed in the church after the blitz (Taylor and Taylor 1965, 399-400). The corbelled effect used in the arch, the re-use of Roman building materials and a possible historical context for the connection with Barking (the foundation of the abbey by

8.14 The street pattern in London. This series of maps is based on the survey of London's streets made after the Great Fire of 1666. It therefore excludes the northeast part of the city, which was not affected by the fire and therefore not planned. The top map shows the eastern and western grids, both in existence in the 10th century. The middle map shows additions to the grid, such as Pudding Lane, which were in existence by the 11th century, while the bottom map shows the streets laid out over the demolished riverside wall which would have been established in the late 11th or early 12th centuries and extended with the waterfront up to the mid 15th century.

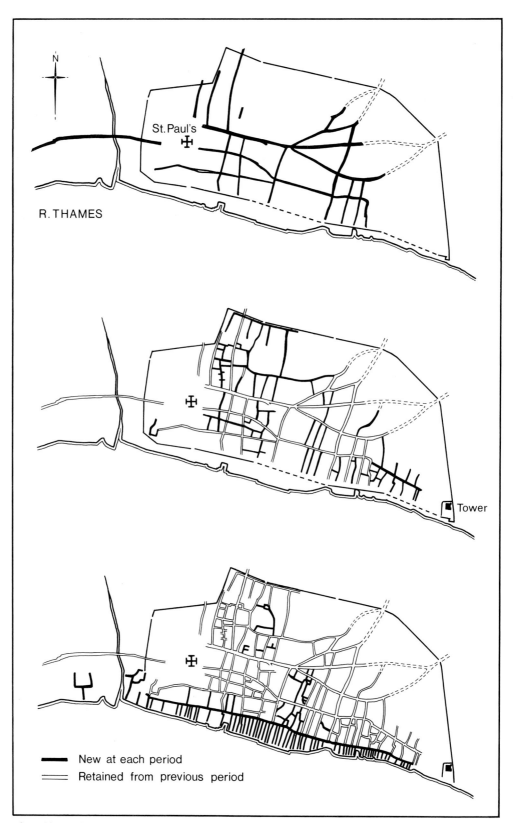

N

St. Paul's

R. THAMES

Tower

New at each period
Retained from previous period

Eorcenwald, bishop of London, in the late 7th century) have all led to the attribution of an early date to its construction. Furthermore, the fragments of walling recognised as the same build as the arch show that the Saxon church cannot have been a simple two-cell structure but must have either had a *porticus* or an aisle (Taylor and Taylor 1965, Fig 182). It is certainly not inconceivable that the nuns of Barking had a refuge in London, such as the monks of Lympne were granted within the walls of Canterbury in the 9th century.

Whatever the date of All Hallows Barking, a solid case can be made for placing the origin of many of the medieval churches in the City in the late Saxon period, although few (if any) are as early as the late 9th century. Firstly, there is the evidence of archaeology. Excavations at St Nicholas Acon, St Mildred Bread Street and St Nicholas Shambles suggest an origin in the mid- or late-11th century while St Peter Paul's Wharf can probably be dated to the late 11th to mid-12th century. A study of the dedications of London's churches by Brooke and Keir (1975, 122-147) shows that many can be dated to the mid-11th century or later, although it is always possible that this is due to earlier churches being given new dedications. Finally, documentary evidence demonstrates that some churches are of pre-Conquest 11th-century origin, for example All Hallows Gracechurch Street which was granted to Christ Church Canterbury in a mid-11th-century charter (Brooke and Keir 1975, 135). Since dedications, documents and archaeology all lead to the same conclusion, it is likely that in most cases we can take the evidence at face value. The conclusions from this study are that about 20 churches can be dated to the later 11th or 12th centuries, but that no church except St Paul's itself can be yet be demonstrated - archaeologically or through documents - to have been in existence in the late 9th to mid-10th century.

It seems therefore that the small urban churches of London appeared late in the late Saxon history of the City, and that they cannot be used to determine the areas occupied in the late 9th to mid-10th centuries. What they do show, by the size and shape of their parishes, is the location of the highest population density in, at the latest, the 12th century. Brooke and Keir make the point that the central parishes were established after the City was built up, since their boundaries are more tortuous than those of the peripheral and extra-mural parishes.

The churches outside the gates of London (three dedicated to St Botolph, and one each to St Sepulchre and St Giles) all bear dedications which are most likely to have arisen in the early 12th century or later (Brooke and Keir 1975, 143-7). None of these churches has yet been examined archaeologically but excavation has shown that the earliest post-Roman occupation immediately outside the gates dates to the mid-11th to early 12th centuries. This suggests that outside the walls, as in general inside, the churches were not a primary settlement feature.

The ward boundaries of the City appear to have been established in the late 10th to early 11th centuries (Brooke and Keir, 1975, 168) and therefore tell us nothing of the initial Alfredian occupation of the City. Like the churches, they reflect the distribution of population in the late 10th or early 11th century and confirm the inferences drawn from pottery that all the main streets of the City were occupied by c.1000. The smaller size of some of the wards in the eastern half of the City might suggest that the densest settlement was by this time to be found fronting onto the Bishopsgate to London Bridge route and the major streets leading off it.

Archaeological and other evidence combines to show that before the Norman Conquest the majority of the intra-mural City was built up, at least along the major streets, and soon after this there is evidence for a spread outside the walls, to the east at Aldgate, to the north at Bishopsgate, Cripplegate and Aldersgate and to the south in Southwark. Only to the west of the City is the late Saxon topography still unclear. Although there was a substantial settlement there in the mid-Saxon period very few archaeological finds can be dated to the later 9th, 10th or 11th centuries. In contrast, the church of St Andrew Holborn, referred to as an old wooden church in the mid-10th century, probably survived from the mid-Saxon period, and a similar case could be made for St Bride's, which was certainly the site of a late Saxon cemetery. There was probably a church at St Clement Danes in the mid-11th century, while the late 6th- or 7th- century burial under St Martin-in-the-Fields also raises the possibility of a continuous religious use from the mid-Saxon period to the first documentary record of the church in the 13th century (even if the Saxon burial was pagan). Activity in the 10th or early 11th centuries at Whitehall is suggested by a few potsherds residual in medieval pits on the Treasury site (LSS, Huggins forthcoming), although the first definite evidence of medieval

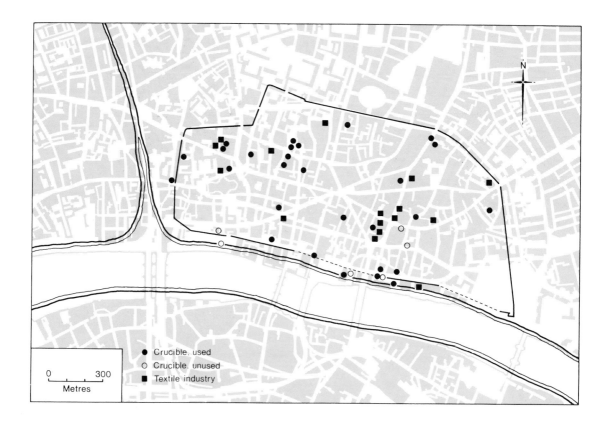

occupation there is of late 11th- to mid-12th-century date (CP5). By and large, the evidence still suggests that there was no continuity between the mid-Saxon and medieval occupation in this area, bearing in mind that no excavation has yet taken place in a centrally-placed site fronting onto the Strand or Fleet Street.

The archaeological evidence sheds relatively little light on the lifestyle of late Saxon Londoners. Artefacts are few and mostly of a mundane nature. This, however, tends to be a feature of late Saxon finds from all classes of settlement and probably results from the fact that the more prestigious belongings were either made from organic materials (such as wood, horn, leather and textiles) which have survived only in small quantities or from precious metals which when broken were recycled. The presence of silk amongst the textile fragments from Milk Street and the quality of some of the woollen cloth found there contrast sharply with the pottery and other artefacts from the same site. A similar contrast can be seen between the late Saxon decorated metal and ivory finds with a London provenance (Wilson 1964) and those from current excavations. The total

8.15 Industrial waste from late Saxon sites within the city. Comparison with Fig 8.7 shows that most excavated sites produced evidence for either textile manufacture or metalworking.

absence of lead or lead alloy brooches and copper alloy hooked tags from recent sites must be misleading when one considers the number of such finds reported as a result of the use of metal detectors on spoil from City excavations. Only perhaps with the antler combs do we have a class of artefact which was both highly prized to its users and has survived well (Pritchard, Part 3, p.196).

Excavations in the City have revealed numerous traces of trades and industries of late Saxon date. The evidence for clothworking has been summarised by Pritchard (1984, 63-7). It consists of groups of clay loom-weights, spindle-whorls of various materials, and bone pin-beaters, (further examples are described by Pritchard, Part 3, pp.165, 205). There is not a sufficient concentration of finds in any one area to suggest that the industry was localised, nor even that it was operating on more than a domestic scale. Sherds of 11th- to 12th-century cooking pots have been

SCEATTA FINDS ●

REMISSION OF TOLLS ■

CROSS-CHANNEL PORTS ▼

RHENISH QUERNS ○

POTTERY ◇

0   300 miles

0   500 km

found with a pink staining on the interior, due to madder (Taylor, Part 3, p.168). These, we suggest, were most likely to have been used to dye wool. However, the distribution of these sherds across the City and the absence of local concentrations (they are associated with typical domestic refuse) suggests that this operation too took place on a very small scale, dispersed throughout London. Four glass linen-smoothers have been found in 11th- to early 12th-century contexts in the City (Pritchard, Part 3, p.173). They were used to give a glaze to linen and by the 16th century were used commercially in the finishing process before the cloth was sold, although they were also used in the home. There is no evidence for

8.16 Trade into and out of London in the mid-Saxon period. The sceattas plotted are those thought to have been minted in London. Sites with charters giving remission of tolls in the port of London are shown as squares. Quentovic and Dorestad are the documented destinations of ships setting out from London. The white diamonds mark the supposed sources of pottery found in the Strand settlement.

a concentration or for an association with other clothworking debris.

Ironworking is represented at most excavated sites, mainly by smithing slag, although there is great difficulty in distinguishing contemporary debris from residual Roman material. There is no concentration of slag, furnaces or unfinished goods to suggest a blacksmiths' quarter although a pair of tongs from the floor of a late 10th-century building at Pudding Lane (PDN1) may show the location of one smithy (Pritchard, Part 3, No 21; Horsman *et al* 1988, 37-8). Workers in lead and copper alloys and in precious metals are represented by crucibles and two hoards - the Cheapside hoard of pewter jewellery and the St Mary-at-Hill hoard of late 11th-century coins and a gold brooch set with sapphires and pearls contained within a crucible. At site after site crucible fragments occur as part of otherwise typical domestic assemblages. They show scant evidence for localisation, not even within certain pits on a site, nor for production on a large scale (Fig 8.16). It is notable, however, that they are absent from definite 10th-century contexts and are most common in late 11th-century and later deposits (Bayley *et al*, Part 6, Figs 6.14-17). Moulds, of clay or stone, and iron tools of various sorts must have been used with these crucibles (for example to produce brooches of the Cheapside Hoard type) but only one possible ingot mould has so far been recognised (Pritchard, Part 3, p.116). The most

interesting of these metalworking artefacts are undoubtedly the bone motif pieces, possibly used to try out designs or for practice. London has produced 13 examples, one stratified in a late 10th-century context, one in a late 11th- to early 12th-century context and one in a late 12th-century waterfront dump (although probably a much earlier piece, see Pritchard, Part 3, No 206). Taken with the crucible evidence these finds show that from the end of the 10th century onwards an extensive decorative metalworking industry existed in London but the paucity of earlier evidence is quite striking.

Two roughed-out Rhenish lava quernstones were found used in the footings of an 11th-century building (PDN3) at Pudding Lane (Horsman *et al* 1988, 39 & Fig 26; Pritchard, Part 3, p.162). These may have been destined for trans-shipment in

8.17 Trade into and out of London in the 11th and 12th centuries. The black dots mark the origin of merchants mentioned in contemporary documents and the open circles the sources of pottery found in 11th- and early 12th-century deposits in the city.

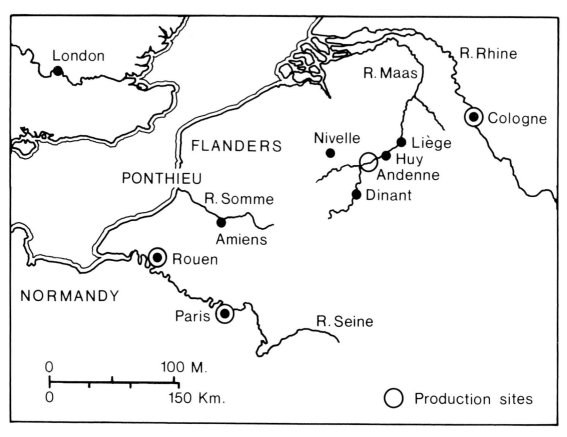

their rough state or it may have been standard practice to shape Rhenish quernstones in London. Occasional offcuts of bone and antler have been found but nothing yet to suggest that comb, casket or handle-making ever formed a substantial activity in the City (Pritchard, Part 3, p.175). Leather offcuts have been found, but most of the leather is from discarded worn shoes or other artefacts rather than from the manufacture of new ones (Pritchard, Part 3, p.211). Likewise, no pit has yet been demonstrated as having been used for tanning or flax-retting.

Archaeological evidence for industry after industry therefore points to the same conclusion. Unlike many Saxon towns, which seem to have contained such concentrations of artisans that they must have been producing goods for the market, the evidence for industries that archaeology can demonstrate in London is found in such small quantities, and is dispersed in such a way, as to suggest that the City was, at most, self-sufficient in their products (Fig 8.16). The one craft which has the strongest archaeological claims to have been operating on more than a domestic level, non-ferrous metalworking, is the only one for which we can demonstrate a late flowering, a century after the reoccupation of the City. Furthermore London is the only major late Saxon town not to have had its own pottery industry (Vince 1983, and Part 2, p.39). Perhaps from the very beginning of the settlement these noxious industries had been banished to the suburbs, or to the surrounding villages but maybe, even at this date, the population of London, which archaeological evidence suggests was low until the later 10th century, earned their living either by providing services for the ecclesiastical community or through various aspects of trade.

Some of the earliest documentary evidence for Saxon London is concerned with trade and it is perhaps in the demonstration of contacts between London and its trading partners that archaeology can contribute most (Figs 8.17 & 8.18). As noted above when discussing the Pudding Lane quernstones, many of the items passing through London, even those which could leave an archaeological trace, are likely to have gone straight through the City without leaving a record of their presence. Thus, minor and incidental imports and exports, such as pottery, probably stand for a much larger invisible trade.

The pottery from the mid-Saxon settlement, although still known from too small a sample, is sufficient to show that the majority of sherds in the 8th to 9th centuries were produced at Ipswich. They probably entered London as an incidental cargo on board boats engaged in coastal shipping (Vince 1984, Fig 11). A substantial minority of the collection is of continental origin, including types paralleled in the vast collection from Saxon Southampton (Hodges 1982; Timby 1988). There is little concrete evidence for the precise sources of these wares, although sherds with parallels in Belgium and northern France, and the Rhineland, have been noted (Blackmore and Redknap 1988).

The character of the pottery found in the earliest ceramic phase in the late Saxon City is completely different. Virtually no imported wares are known, nor are there any examples of 10th-century Ipswich-Thetford wares (despite the presence of wares from this source in both the mid-Saxon settlement and in later 11th- and 12th-century contexts). Instead, the overwhelming majority of sherds found came from a source to the west of the Chilterns, the precise location of which is not known. The link between the London and Oxford regions at this date is interesting in view of the fact that in the early 10th century London and Oxford were linked politically, being the central places of regions transferred from Mercia to Wessex (Garmonsway 1953, *sub anno* 913). The absence of continental imports in London is remarkable. It is inconceivable that London could have supported a thriving merchant class, in contact with much of western Europe and the north sea coast, without the occasional imported pot being brought into the City. This suggests that the assumption that the documentary evidence of the late 10th century and after throws light on the earlier 10th century may be mistaken. The importance of trade in the late 9th- or early 10th-century City is certainly debatable. The only solid piece of evidence seems to be Athelstan's Grately Ordinance which allotted London more moneyers than either Canterbury or Winchester. The study of the coins themselves shows that these moneyers existed but it is only an assumption that the size of the London mint reflects the volume of trade passing through the City. Given the absence of archaeological evidence for trade or industry it is more likely that the mid-10th-century mint was placed in London for political reasons, or even as a gesture recalling London's traditional position as one of the principal mints of England. It may be that the need to stimulate a sluggish economy was amongst the reasons why Alfred granted the

Queenhithe charters in the late 9th century and they are certainly no evidence that trade was flourishing within the refounded town.

By contrast, from the later 10th century onwards evidence from documentary, numismatic, archaeological and ceramic sources points in the same direction; namely to the rapid growth of London both in population and as a trading centre. Undoubtedly the most important evidence for this growth is that included in Ethelred II's fourth law code, traditionally dated $c.1000$. The towns and regions whose merchants were given privileges by Ethelred (Fig 8.18) were the same as those which supplied pottery to the mid-11th century and later citizens (undoubtedly as an incidental consequence of the presence of a traffic between these places and London). The English pottery too is quite different in character and source from that of the late 9th to 10th centuries. A wide range of sources are represented and we can demonstrate that the City was being supplied by a network of potteries within a circle of 30 kilometres radius around the City. By this time the numbers of actual coins and named moneyers confirm London's place as one of the major mints in England (although not represented amongst Scandinavian collections by as many coins as Winchester, which may have been the main collection point for the Danegeld (Brooke and Keir, 1975, 379)). Similarly, activity along the Thames waterfront, either in the form of landing stages or hards on the foreshore or of the heightening of the waterfront by the construction of a bank of clay laced with timber, can now be seen to date from the later 10th and 11th centuries rather than the earliest late Saxon City. Part of the reason for this seems to be that the waterfront was protected by the Roman riverside wall. It is likely that the wall survived to a considerable height along the whole of its circuit and it certainly stood 3 metres or more in the extreme south-west corner of the City in an exposed position where it had poor foundations. East of the Walbrook it was protected from erosion by the earlier timber waterfronts some metres to the south. While trading undoubtedly took place on the foreshore in front of the wall access inland must have been difficult. This, as well as the probable desire of the king and the citizens of London to restrict the landing of goods for the purpose of gathering custom, would probably have led to the concentration of activity at a few localities, either where Roman gates still stood or where new gates had been inserted (Dyson, 1988). Finally it has

been noted that the distinctive timber cellars found in excavations in London appear to date to exactly this period, although the earliest (FMO1) significantly situated in a property fronting onto Fish Street Hill, was constructed in CP1 (Horsman et al 1988, 49-51). The only other sunken-featured buildings dating to the late 9th or 10th centuries (MLK1 and IRO1), would not be out of place in an early or mid-Saxon rural settlement and cannot really be seen as the ancestors of these much larger cellars (Horsman et al 1988, 52-5, 64-5). Whether used for the storage of goods in transit or the storage of goods for sale (for example casks of wine, Schofield and Allen forthcoming) these cellars imply flourishing trade and a healthy surplus (Horsman et al 1988, 109).

The effect of the Norman Conquest on the material culture of everyday Londoners was slight. This is shown most clearly by the pottery, since it is impossible to distinguish groups of mid- and late 11th century pottery (see Jenner and Vince, Part 2), and by the continuity of building techniques, and property boundaries into the post-Conquest period. The major breaks in the pottery sequence took place both earlier (between $c.1040$ and $c.1055$ according to the Billingsgate evidence) and later, with the introduction of locally-produced glazed jugs in the late 11th century, and wheelthrown cooking pots in the late 12th century. There are similar complex developments in other artefacts (Pritchard, Part 3, p.121). There is too little ironwork to provide any pattern and this is also true of bonework. Antler combs, however, do show a change between those in CP1-3 deposits and those from CP4 and later assemblages. Leather footwear underwent several changes during the 11th century and some of these do appear to have taken place in the later part of the century. There are some differences between late-11th-century and earlier artefacts and some changes may well have taken place at the time of the Norman conquest. However, any contribution made by craftsmen, fashions or artefacts from Normandy can only have been small. There is probably more evidence for the influence of Scandinavian culture on England following Cnut's conquest than there is for the Normans. One can be fairly sure, therefore, that the artisans supplying London in the late 11th and early 12th centuries were working in industries which originated in England before the conquest and were working predominantly for an Anglo-Saxon, or, more accurately, an Anglo-Scandinavian, market. Topographically, by contrast the construction of the Norman White Tower, Baynards Castle and Montfichet Tower must have had an effect on the layout and fortunes of the City, and the White Tower would undoubtedly have dominated the eastern skyline. Nevertheless, by and large, archaeology reveals the middle years of the 11th century as a time of continuity in the life of the City.

BIBLIOGRAPHY

Aartsbisschoppelijk Museum Utrecht, 1972 *From Willibrord to World Council. Some aspects of the spiritual life in Utrecht through the Middle Ages*, Utrecht

Adams, J H, 1967 A new type of cresset stone?, *Cornish Archaeol*, **6**, 47-57

Adams Gilmour, L *et al*, 1988 *Early medieval pottery from Flaxengate*, (The archaeology of Lincoln, **17/2**)

Addyman, P V & Hill, D H, 1968 Saxon Southampton: a review of the evidence, part 1, *Proc Hampshire Field Club & Archaeol Soc*, **25**, 61-93

—— & Hill, D H, 1969 Saxon Southampton: a review of the evidence, part 2 *Proc Hampshire Field Club & Archaeol Soc*, **26**, 61-96

——, 1969 Late Saxon settlements in the St Neots area: II. The Little Paxton settlement and enclosures, *Proc Cambridge Antiq Soc*, **67**, 59-93

——, Hopkins, B G & Norton, G T, 1972 A Saxo-Norman Pottery-kiln producing stamped wares at Michelmersh, Hants, *Medieval Archaeol*, **16**, 127-30

Alexander, J & Binski, P (eds), 1987 *Age of Chivalry Art in Plantagenet England 1200-1400*, Royal Academy of Arts

Alexander, J & Kaufmann, M, 1984 Manuscripts in *English Romanesque Art 1066-1200* (Zarnecki, G, Holt, J & Holland, J eds) Catalogue of the exhibition held at the Hayward Gallery, London, 5th April – 8th July, 1984, Arts Council of Great Britain, 81-133

Allan, J P, 1984 *Medieval and Post-Medieval Finds from Exeter, 1971-1980* Exeter Archaeol Rep, **3**, Exeter City Council and the University of Exeter

Allen, P, 1985 A plan for the City, *Popular Archaeol*, **6** (12), 24-7

Ambrosiani, K, 1981 *Viking Age combs, comb making and comb makers in the light of finds from Birka and Ribe*, Stockholm Studies in Archaeology, **2**

Arbman, H, 1943 *Birka I: Die Gräber*, Stockholm/Uppsala

Archer, I, Barron, C & Hardy, V, 1988 *Hugh Alley's Caveat. The Markets of London in 1598* London Topographical Society Publication No **137**, London 1988

Archibald, M M & Oddy, 1979 The technique of some forged silver pennies in Oddy, W A (ed) *Scientific Studies in Numismatics*, British Museum Occasional Paper No **18**, 81-90, London

——, 1974 English medieval coins as dating evidence in Casey, J & Reece, R (eds) *Coins and the Archaeologist*, British Archaeol Rep, **4**, 234-71

Armitage, K H, Pearce, J E & Vince, A G, 1981 Early medieval roof tiles from London, *Antiq J*, **61**, 359-62

Armstrong, E C R, 1922 Irish bronze pins of the Christian period, *Archaeologia*, **72**, 71-86

ASMH Blackburn, M (ed) *Anglo-Saxon Monetary History*

Atkin, M W, 1978 Saxon bronze brooch from Threxton, Little Cressingham, *Norfolk Archaeol*, **37**, 134

Ayers, B, 1988 *Digging Deeper. Recent Archaeology in Norwich*

BLS Blunt, C E, Lyon, C S S & Stewart, B H I H, 1963 The coinage of southern England, 796-840, *BNJ*, **32**, 1-74 [The numbers quoted refer to the numbers in the corpus in the paper cited and not to page numbers]

BMC *A catalogue of English coins in the British Museum: Anglo-Saxon series*, vol I, London 1887, and *vol II*, London, 1893, and *The Norman Kings*, 2 vols, London [The numbers quoted refer to the numbers in the appropriate catalogue and not to page numbers] see also Grueber & Keary 1887-93; Brooke 1916

BNJ *British Numismatic Journal*, London

Backhouse, J, Turner, D H & Webster, L E (eds), 1984 *The Golden Age of Anglo-Saxon Art, 966-1066*

Badham, K & Jones, G, 1985 An experiment in manual processing of soil samples for plant remains, *Circaea*, **3** (1), 15-26

Baillie, M G L & Pilcher, J R, 1973 A simple crossdating program for tree-ring research, *Tree-Ring Bulletin*, **33**, 7-14

Baines, P, 1977 *Spinning Wheels, Spinners and Spinning*, New York

Ballard, A, 1913 *British Borough Charters*, Cambridge

Barlow, F, 1983 *William Rufus*

Bascombe, K, 1987 Two charters of King Suabred of Essex in Neale, K (ed) *An Essex Tribute to S F Emerson*, 85-96

Bates, G H, 1935 The vegetation of footpaths, sidewalks, cart-tracks and gateways, *J Ecology*, **13**, 470-87

Batiscombe, C F (ed), 1956 *The Relics of St Cuthbert*

Bayley, J, 1979 The glassworking residues in Heighway, C M, Garrod, A P & Vince, A G, Excavations at 1 Westgate Street, Gloucester, 1975, *Medieval Archaeol*, **23**, 201-2

——, 1982 Non-ferrous metal and glass-working in Anglo-Scandinavian England: an interim statement, *J European Study Group on Physical, Chemical and Mathematical Techniques Applied to Archaeology*, PACT, **7** (2), 487-96

——, 1985 *Note on an enamelled disc from Billingsgate*, Ancient Monuments Lab Rep

Bayliss, B, 1963 Botanical field work in a school garden, *The London Naturalist*, **42**, 19-20

Beaurepaire, C de, 1873 Les méreaux de la vicomité de l'Eau et des chanoines de Nôtre-Dame de Rouen, *Bulletin de la comm et antiq de Seine inferieur 1873*, at 399-400

Beckwith, J, 1969 *Early Medieval Art, Carolingian, Ottonian, Romanesque*, revised edn

——, 1972 *Ivory Carving in Early Medieval England*

Beer, R J S, 1976 The relationship between *Trichuris trichiura* (Linnaeus 1758) of man and *Trichuris suis* (Schrank 1788) of the pig, *J Research in Veterinary Science*, **20**, 47-54

Benson, A & Platnauer, H M, 1902 Notes on Clifford's Tower, *Annual Report of the Yorkshire Philosophical Society*, 68-74

Bersu, G & Wilson, D M, 1966 *Three Viking Graves on the Isle of Man*, Soc Medieval Archaeol Monogr Ser, **1**

Besborodov, M A, 1957 A chemical and technological study of ancient Russian glasses and refractories, *J Soc Glass Technol*, **41**, 168-84

Biddle, M *et al* 1976 *Winchester Studies I. Winchester in the early middle ages*, Oxford

—— & Collis, J, 1978 A new type of 9th and 10th-century pottery from Winchester *Medieval Archaeol* **22**, 133-5

—— & Quirk, R, 1962 Excavations near Winchester Cathedral 1961, *Archaeol J*, **119**, 150-94

——, 1976 Towns in Wilson, D M (ed) *Archaeology of Anglo-Saxon England*, 99-150

——, 1984 London on the Strand, *Popular Archaeol*, **6** (1), 23-7

——, (ed) 1990 *Objects and Economy in Medieval Winchester*, Winchester Studies **7/2**

Black, G, 1977 The redevelopment of 20 Dean's Yard Westminster Abbey, 1975-77, *Trans London Middlesex Archaeol Soc*, **28**, 190-210

Blackburn, M & Bonser, M, 1984 Single-finds of Anglo-Saxon and Norman coins, part 1, *BNJ* **54**, 63-73

—— & Bonser, M, 1985 Single-finds of Anglo-Saxon and Norman coins, part 2, *BNJ* **55**, 55-78

—— & Lyon, S, 1986 Regional die-production in Cnut's Quatrefoil issue in Blackburn, M (ed) *Anglo-Saxon Monetary History*, 185-200

—— & Pagan, H, 1986 A revised check-list of coin hoards from the British Isles *c* 500-1100 in Blackburn, M (ed) *Anglo-Saxon Monetary History*, 291-314

——, 1984 A chronology for the sceattas in Hill, D & Metcalf, M *Sceattas in England and on the Continent*, British Archaeol Rep, **128**, 165-74

——, Colyer, C & Dolley, R H M, 1983 *Early Medieval Coins from Lincoln and its shire c 770-1100* (*The Archaeology of Lincoln*, **6/1**)

Blackmore, L & Redknap, M, 1988 Saxon and Early Medieval Imports to the London area and the Rhenish Connection in Gaimster, D R M, Redknap, M & Wegner, H-H (eds) *Zur keramik des Mittelalters und der beginnenden Neuzeit in Rheinland – Medieval and later pottery from the Rhineland and its markets* BAR Int Ser **440**, 223-239

——, 1983 The Anglo-Saxon and medieval pottery, in Whytehead, R & Blackmore, L, Excavations at Tottenham Court, 250 Euston Road NW1, *Trans London Middlesex Archaeol Soc*, **34**, 81-91

Blomqvist, R & Mårtensson, A W, 1963 *Thulegrävningen 1961*, *Archaeologica Lundensia*, **2**, Lund

——, 1938 Medeltida svärd, Dolkar och slidor funna i Lund, *Kulturen*, 134-69

Blunt, C & Dolley, R H M, 1977 Coins from the Win-chester excavations 1961-73, *BNJ*, **47**, 135-8

——, 1955-7 The coinage of Ecgbeorht, king of Wessex, 802-39, *BNJ*, **28**, 467-76

——, 1961 The Coinage of Offa, in Dolley, R H M (ed) *Anglo-Saxon Coins*, 39-62

——, 1962 Tenth-century halfpennies and C Roach Smith's plate of coins found in London, *BNJ*, **31**, 44-8

——, 1974 The Coinage of Aethelstan 924-39: a Survey, *BNJ*, **42**, 35-158

——, 1974a A new coin of Baldred, King of Kent, *BNJ*, **44**, 75-6

——, Lyon, S & Stewart, I, 1963 The Coinage of Southern England 796-840, *BNJ*, **32**, 1-74

Brade, C, 1978 Knöcherne Kernspaltflöten aus Haithabu in Schietzel, K (ed) *Das Archäologische Fundmaterial III der Ausgrabung Haithabu. Berichte über die Ausgrabungen in Haithabu* **12**, 24-35, Neumünster

Branigan, K, 1973 *Town and Country: The Archaeology of Verulamium and the Roman Chilterns*

Braun-Blanquet, J, 1936 *Prodrome des Groupements Vegetaux, Classe des Rudereto-Secalinetales*, **3**, Montpellier

Britnell, R H, 1978, English markets and royal administration before 1200, *Economic History Review*, 2nd Series, **31**, 183-96

Brøgger, A W & Shetelig, H, 1928 *Osebergfundet II*, Oslo

Brooke, C assisted by Keir G, 1975 *London 800-1216: the Shaping of a City*, London

Brooke, G, 1916 *Catalogue of English Coins in the British Museum*, Norman Kings, 2 vols

Brooks, N & Graham-Campbell, J, 1986 Reflections on the Viking-Age silver hoard from Croydon, Surrey in Blackburn, M (ed) *Anglo-Saxon Monetary History*, 91-110

Brown, P D C, 1973 Linen heckles in Brodribb, A C C, Hands, A R & Walker, D R (eds) *Excavations at Shakenoak Farm, near Wilcote, Oxfordshire, Part IV*, 134-6

Buckland, P C, Greig, J R A & Kenward, H K, 1974 York: an early medieval site, *Antiquity*, **48**, 25-33

Buckton, D, 1986 Late tenth and eleventh-century cloisonné enamel brooches, *Medieval Archaeol*, **30**, 8-18

Butler, V & Dolley, R H M, 1958-9 New light on the nineteenth-century find of pence of Aethelred II from St Martin's-le-Grand, *BNJ*, **29**, 265-74

Capelle, T 1976 *Die frühgeschichtlichen Metallfunde von Domburg auf Walcheren* vol 2, *Nederlandse Oudheden* **5**, Amersfoort

Carrington, P, 1977 Chester: Castle Esplanade Hoard Pot (CHE/CEH) in Davey, P J (ed) *Medieval Pottery from Excavations in the Northwest*, 12-13

Chapman, H, Metal objects in Miller, L, Schofield, J & Rhodes, M *The Roman Quay at St Magnus House, London*, London Middlesex Archaeol Soc Special Paper, **8**, 235-9

Charleston, R J, 1984 *English Glass and the Glass used in England, circa 400-1940*

Charleston, R J, Davies, W & Grew, F O, forthcoming

Seventeeth-century glassworking at Aldgate, City of London

Cherry, J, 1975 A bronze buckle and buckle plate in Steane, J M & Bryant, G F Excavations at the deserted medieval settlement at Lyveden 4th Report, *J Northampton Museums and Art Gallery*, **12**, 106-7

Clapham, A R, Tutin, T G & Warburg, E F, 1962 *Flora of the British Isles*

Clark, J, 1973 Early medieval pottery from pit P4 in Chapman, H & Johnson, J, Excavations at Aldgate and Bush Lane House in the City of London, 1972, *Trans London & Middlesex Archaeol Soc*, **24**, 1-73

——, 1980a *Saxon and Norman London*, Museum of London

——, 1980b A Saxon knife and a shield mount from the Thames foreshore, *Antiq J*, **60**, 348-49

——, forthcoming *Medieval Finds from Excavations in London: Horses and Horse Harness*

Clarke, R R & Dolley, R H M, 1958 The Morley St Peter Hoard: the significance of the find *Antiquity*, **32**, 102-3

Clarke, H & Carter, A, 1977 *Excavations in King's Lynn 1963-1970*, Soc Medieval Archaeol Monogr Ser, **7**

Clason, A T, 1980 Worked bone and antler objects from Dorestad, Hoogstraat I in Van Es, W A & Verwers, W J H *Excavations at Dorestad I The Harbour: Hoogstraat I, Nederlandse Oudheden* **9**, Amersfoort, 238-47

Cockayne, T O, 1866 *Leechdoms, Wortcunning and Starcraft of Early England*

Collis, J & Kjølbye-Biddle B, 1979 Early medieval bone spoons from Winchester, *Antiq J*, **59**, 375-91

Colyer, C & Jones, M J, 1979 Excavations at Lincoln, second interim report; excavations in the lower walled town 1972-8, *Antiq J*, **59**, 375-91

Cottrill, F, 1935 Bone trial-piece found in Southwark, *Antiq J*, **15**, 69-71

Cowgill, J, de Neergaard, M & Griffiths, N, 1987 *Medieval Finds from Excavations in London: I Knives and Scabbards*

Cowie, R, 1987 Lundenwic: Unravelling the Strand, *Archaeology Today*, **8** (5), 30-4

Crosby, D D B & Mitchell, J G, 1987 A survey of British metamorphic hone stones of the 9th to 15th centuries AD in the light of Potassium-Argon and natural remanent magnetization studies, *J Archaeol Science*, **14**, 483-506

Crowfoot, E G, 1983 The Textiles in Evans, A C (ed) *The Sutton Hoo Ship Burial vol 3, I,* 409-62

Cunliffe, B W, 1964 *Winchester Excavations, 1949-1960,* vol **1**

——, 1976 *Excavations at Porchester Castle, vol II: Saxon,* Rep Res Comm Soc Antiq London, **33**

Davidan, O I, 1970 Contacts between Staraja Ladoga and Scandinavia, *Varangian Problems* Scando-Slavica supplement I, Copenhagen, 70-91

Davies, B & Richardson, F E, forthcoming *A Dated Type Series of Roman Pottery from London. Part 1 : c.AD50-160* CBA Res Rep

Densem, R & Seeley, D, 1982 Excavations at Rectory

Grove, Clapham 1980-81, *London Archaeol*, **4** (7), 177-84

Dodwell, C R, 1982 *Anglo-Saxon Art. A New Perspective*

Dolley, R H M & Blunt, C, 1961 The chronology of the Coins of Alfred the Great 871-99 in Dolley, M (ed) *Anglo-Saxon Coins*, 77-95

—— & Grover, B, 1983 The 1981 Chelsea Reach (London) find of Second Hand pennies of Aethelred II, *Numismatika Meddelanden*, **33**, 85-99

—— & Metcalf, M, 1961 The Reform of the English Coinage under Eadgar in Dolley, M (ed) *Anglo-Saxon Coins*, 136-68

—— & Morrison, K, 1963 Finds of Carolingian Coins from Great Britain and Ireland, *BNJ*, **32**, 127-39

—— & Skaare, K, 1961 The Coinage of Aethelwulf, King of the West Saxons 839-58 in Dolley, M (ed) *Anglo-Saxon Coins*, 63-76

—— & Talvio, T, 1977 The twelfth of the Agnus Dei pennies of Aethelred, *BNJ*, **47**, 131-3

——, 1952-4 Two unpublished Hoards of Late Saxon Pence in the Guildhall Museum, *BNJ*, **27**, 212-3

——, 1953, A piedfort lead trial-piece of Edward the Confessor, *BNJ*, **27**, 175-8

——, 1960 Coin Hoards from the London area, *Trans London Middlesex Archaeol Soc*, **20**, 37-50

——, 1970 *Anglo-Saxon Pennies*, British Musem

Donaldson, A, 1979 Plant life and plant use in Carver, M O H, Three Saxo-Norman Tenements in Durham City, *Medieval Archaeol*, **23**, 55-60

Drury, P & Rodwell, W, 1980 Settlement in the late Iron Age and Roman periods in Buckley, D G (ed) *Archaeology in Essex to AD 1500*, CBA Res Rep, **34**, 59-75

Du Cange, Domino (Henschel, G A L, ed), 1840 *Glossarium mediae et infirmae Latinitatis cum supplementis integris D P Carpenterii*, Paris

Dumas, F, 1979 Les monnaies normandes (Xe-XIIe siècles) avec un répertoire des trouvailles, *Revue Numismatique*, **21**, 84-140

Duncan, S & Ganiaris, H, 1987 Some sulphide corrosion products on copper alloys and lead alloys from London waterfront sites in Black, J (ed) *Recent Advances in the Conservations and Analysis of Artifacts*, 109-18

Dunning, G C, 1932 Medieval finds in London, *Antiq J*, **12**, 177-8

——, 1958 A Norman pit at Pevensey Castle and its contents, *Antiq J*, **38**, 205-17

——, 1959 Anglo-Saxon Pottery – A Symposium, *Medieval Archaeol*, **3**, 31-78

——, 1977 Mortars in Clarke, H & Carter, A, *Excavations in King's Lynn 1963-1970*, Soc Medieval Archaeol Monogr Ser, **7**, 320-47

——, Hurst, J G, Myres, J N L & Tischler, F, 1959 Anglo-Saxon Pottery – A Symposium, *Medieval Archaeol*, **3**, 1-78

Durham, B, 1977 Archaeological Investigations in St Aldates, Oxford, *Oxoniensia*, **42**, 83-203

Dyson, A & Schofield, J, 1981 Excavations in the City of London Second Interim Rep, 1974-78, *Trans*

London Middlesex Archaeol Soc, **32**, 24-81

——, 1975 St Mildred, Bread Street: Documentary Survey in Marsden, P, Dyson, A & Rhodes, M, Excavations of the Site of St Mildred's Church, Bread Street, London, 1973-1974, *Trans London Middlesex Archaeol Soc*, **26**, 181-208

——, 1978, Two Saxon land grants for Queenhithe in Bird, J, Chapman, H & Clark, J (eds) *Collectanea Londiniensia: Studies in London Archaeology and History presented to Ralph Merrifield*, London Middlesex Archaeol Soc Special Paper, **2**, 200-15

——, 1980 London and Southwark in the Seventh Century and Later, *Trans London Middlesex Archaeol Soc*, **31**, 83-95

——, 1984 Saxon London in Haslam, J (ed) *Anglo-Saxon Towns*, 285-314

——, 1985 Early harbour Regulations in London in Herteig, A (ed) *Conference on Waterfront Archaeology in Northern European Towns, No 2*, Bergen

——, Schofield, J & Steedman, K, in preparation *The Saxon and Medieval Waterfront of London*

EHD I Whitelock, D (ed) 1979, *English Historical Documents* **1** c 500-1042, 2nd edn

East, K, 1983 The shoes in Evans, A C (ed) *The Sutton Hoo Ship Burial vol 3*, II, 788-810

Egan, G & Pritchard, F A, forthcoming *Medieval Finds from Excavations in London: Dress Accessories*

——, 1985-6 Finds Recovery on Riverside Sites in the City of London, *Popular Archaeol*, **6** (14), 42-50

English Romanesque Art 1066-1200 (Zarnecki, G, Holt, J & Holland, J eds) Catalogue of the exhibition held at the Hayward Gallery, London, 5th April – 8th July, 1984, Arts Council of Great Britain

Evans, A C (ed) 1983 *The Sutton Hoo Ship Burial vol 3*

Evison, V I, 1955 Anglo-Saxon Finds near Rainham, Essex, with a study of glass drinking horns, *Archaeologia*, **96**, 159-95

——, 1964 A decorated seax from the Thames at Keen Edge Ferry, *Berkshire Archaeol*, **61**, 28-36

Evison, V I, 1966 A caterpillar-brooch from Old Erringham Farm, Shoreham-by-sea, Sussex, *Medieval Archaeol*, **10**, 149-51

——, 1970 The Anglo-saxon cemetery in Eagles, B N & Evison, V I Excavations at Harrold, Bedfordshire 1951-53, *Bedfordshire Archaeol*, **5**, 38-55

——, 1979 *A Corpus of Wheel-thrown pottery in Anglo-Saxon Graves*, Royal Archaeol Institute Monograph

von Feilitzen, O, 1937 *The pre-Conquest personal names of Domesday Book*, *Nomina Germanica*, **3**, Uppsala

Fillon, B 1850, *Les monnaies de France*, Fontenay-Vendée

Finucane, R, 1977 *Miracles and Pilgrims*

FitzStephen, W, (H E Butler trans), 1934 *A Description of London* in Stenton, F M *Norman London. An Essay*, 25-32

Forgeais, A, 1886, *Collection de plombs historiés trouvés dans la Seine*, 5th series, Paris

Fox, C, 1920-21 Anglo-Saxon Monumental sculpture in the Cambridge district, *Proc Cambridge Antiq Soc*, **23**, 15-45

Freestone, I C & Tite, M S, 1986 Refractories in the ancient and pre-industrial word, *High Technology Ceramics, Past, Present and Future, Ceramics and Civilisation*, **3**, 35-63

Fuglesang, S H, 1978 Stylistic groups in Late Viking art, in Lang, J (ed) *Anglo-Saxon and Viking Age Sculpture and its Context: papers from the Collingwood Symposium on Insular Sculpture from 800 to 1066*, British Archaeol Rep, **49**, 205-23

——, 1980 *Some Aspects of the Ringerike Style*, Odense

GMC 1908 Library Committee of the Corporation of the City of London, *Catalogue of the Collection of London Antiquities in the Guildhall Museum*

Galloway, P, 1976 A note on descriptions of bone and antler combs, *Medieval Archaeol*, **20**, 154-6

Garmonsway, G N (Trans), 1972 *The Anglo-Saxon Chronicle*

Gedai, I, 1985-6, in *Numizmatikai Közlöny* **84-85**, Budapest, 55 and pl XII

Gentleman's Magazine, September 1836

Gerard, J, 1597 *The Herbal or Generall Historie of Plants*

Gettens, R J & Stout, G L, 1966 *Painting Materials, a Short Encyclopaedia*, Dover edn, New York

Godwin, H, 1975 *History of the British Flora*, 2nd edn

Goodall, A R, 1981 The medieval bronzesmith and his products in Crossley, D W (ed) *Medieval Industry*, CBA Res Rep, **40**, 63-71

Goodall, I H, 1984 Non ferrous metal objects in Rogerson, A & Dallas, C *Excavations in Thetford 1948-59 and 1973-80*, East Anglian Archaeol Rep, **22**, 68-75

——, I H, 1979 The Iron Objects in McCarthy, M & Williams, J H (eds) *St Peter's Street Northampton Excavations 1973-76*, 268-73

——, I H, 1980 The objects of copper alloy in *North Elmham vol II*, East Anglian Archaeol Rep, **9**, 499-505

——, I H, 1981 The medieval blacksmith and his products in Crossley, D W (ed) *Medieval Industry*, CBA Res Rep, **40**, 51-62

——, I H, 1984 Iron objects in Rogerson, A & Dallas, C *Excavations in Thetford 1948-59 and 1973-80*, East Anglia Archaeol Rep, **22**, 77-106

Gosling, K, forthcoming Two recent finds from London, in Bammesberger, A (ed) *Old English Runes and their Continental background*, Eichstätt

Gover, J E B, Mawer, A & Stenton, F M, 1942 *The Place-names of Middlesex*, English Place-name Society, **18**

Graham-Campbell, J, 1978 An Anglo-Scandinavian ornamented knife from Canterbury, Kent, *Medieval Archaeol*, **22**, 130-33

——, 1980 *Viking Artefacts, A Select Catalogue*

——, 1982 Some new and neglected finds of 9th-century Anglo-Saxon ornamental metalwork, *Medieval Archaeol*, **26**, 144-51

Gras, N S B, 1918, *The early English customs system*, Cambridge

Green, F J, 1979a *Methods and results of archaeobotanical analysis from excavations in southern England with especial reference to Winchester and urban settlements of the 10th-15th centuries*, unpublished M Phil thesis, Southampton University

Green, F J, 1979b Collection and interpretation of botanical information from medieval urban excavations in southern England in Körber-Grohne, U (ed) *Festschrift Maria Hopf, Archaeo-Physika*, **8**, 39-55

——, 1979c Phosphatic mineralisation of seeds from archaeological sites, *J Archaeol Science*, **6**, 279-84

——, 1979d The plant remains in Heighway, C M, Garrod, A P & Vince, A G, Excavations at 1 Westgate Street Gloucester, *Medieval Archaeol*, **23**, 186-90

——, 1981 Iron age, Roman and Saxon crops: the archaeological evidence from Wessex in Jones, M & Dimbleby, G (eds) *Environment of Man: the Iron Age to the Anglo-Saxon Period*, British Archaeol Rep, **87**, 129-53

——, 1982 Problems of interpreting differentially preserved plant remains from excavations of medieval urban sites in Hall, A R & Kenward, H K (eds) *Environmental Archaeology in the Urban Context*, CBA Res Rep, **43**, 40-6

——, unpublished The plant remains from Newbury

Greig, J, 1984 The palaeoecology of some British hay meadow types in van Zeist, W & Casparie, W A (eds) *Plants and Ancient Man: Studies in Palaeoethnobotany*, Rotterdam

Grew, F & de Neergaard, M, 1988 *Medieval Finds from Excavations in London: Shoes and Pattens*

Grieg, J R A, 1976 Garderobes, sewers, cess-pits and latrines, *Current Archaeol*, **85**, 49-52

Grierson, P & Blackburn, M, 1986 *Medieval European Coinage*, **1** The Early Middle Ages (5th-10th centuries)

——, 1982, *Byzantine coins*, London

Grierson, S, 1986 *The Colour Cauldron*

Grigson, G, 1975 *The Englishman's Flora*

Groenman-van Waateringe, W, 1984 *Die Lederfunde von Haithabu (Berichte über die Ausgrabungen in Haithabu, 21)* (ed K Schietzel), Neumünster

Grove, L R A, 1940 A Viking bone trial-piece from York Castle, *Antiq J*, **20**, 285-7

Grueber, H & Keary, C, 1887/93 *A Catalogue of English Coins in the British Museum*, Anglo-Saxon Series, 2 vols

Guildhall Catalogue, see GMC

Hald, M, 1972 *Primitive Shoes*, Publications of the National Museum Archaeological Historical Series **1/13**, Copenhagen

Hald, M, 1980 *Ancient Danish Textiles from Bogs and Burials*, Copenhagen

Hall, A R, Kenward, H K, Williams, D & Greig J R A, 1983 *Environment and living conditions at two Anglo-Scandinavian sites* (The Archaeology of York, **14/4**) CBA London

——, Tomlinson, P R, Taylor G W & Walton, P, 1984 Dyeplants from Viking York, *Antiquity*, **58**, 58-60

Hall, R A, 1983, Lead trial pieces of William I from York castle *Seaby's Coin and Medal Bulletin* November 1983, 284-5

——, 1984 *The Excavations at York. The Viking Dig*

Hamerow, H, 1987 *The pottery and spatial development of the Anglo-Saxon settlement at Mucking, Essex* D.Phil Thesis submitted to the University of Oxford

Hammerson, M, 1975 Excavations on the site of Arundel House in the Strand, WC2, in 1972, *Trans London Middlesex Archaeol Soc*, **26**, 209-51

Harden, D B, 1956 Glass vessels in Britain and Ireland, AD 400-1000 in Harden, B D (ed) *Dark Age Britain. Studies presented to E T Leeds*, 132-67

——, 1970 *Glass in London*

——, 1976 The glass in Cunliffe, B W, *Excavations at Porchester Castle, vol II: Saxon*, Rep Res Comm Soc Antiq London, **33**, 232-4

——, 1984 The glass in Rogerson, A & Dallas, C, *Excavations in Thetford 1948-59 and 1973-80*, East Anglian Archaeol Rep, **9**, 116

Harding, P & Gibbard, P, 1983 Excavations at Northwold Road, Stoke Newington, North-east London, 1981, *Trans London Middlesex Archaeol Soc*, **34**, 1-18

Harris, J, 1987 Thieves, harlots and stinking goats: fashionable dress and aesthetic attitudes in Romanesque Art, *Costume*, **21**, 4-15

Harvey, J, 1981 *Medieval Gardens*

Haslam, J, 1975 Excavations on the site of Arundel House in the Strand, WC2, in 1972, *Trans London Middlesex Archaeol Soc*, **26**, 221-42

Hawthorne, J G & Smith, C S (eds), 1979 *On Divers Arts. The Treatise of Theophilus*, Dover edn, New York

Hedges, J W, 1978 The loom-weights in Collis, J, *Winchester Excavations Vol II: 1949-1960*, 33-9

Heighway, C M, 1979 Miscellaneous small finds in Heighway, C M, Garrod, A P & Vince, A G, Excavations at 1 Westgate Street, Gloucester 1975, *Medieval Archaeol*, **23**, 201

Henderson, J, 1986 Beads and rings in Tweddle, D, *Finds from Parliament Street and Other Sites in the City Centre* (The Archaeology of York, **17/4**), 210-26

Hendriks, A, 1964 Karolingisch schoeisel uit Middelburg in Trimpe Burger, J A, Een oudheidkundig onderzoek in de Abdij te Middelburg in 1961, *Berichten van de rijksdienst voor het oudheid-kundig bodemonderzoek*, **14**, 112-16

Hendy, M F, 1985, *Studies in the Byzantine Monetary economy c 300-1453*, Cambridge

Highley, D E, 1982 *Fireclay*

Hill, C, Millett, M & Blagg, T, 1980 *The Roman Riverside Wall and Monumental Arch in London: Excavations at Baynard's Castle, Upper Thames Street, London 1974-76*, London Middlesex Archaeol Soc Special Paper, **3**

Hill, D & Metcalf, M (eds) 1984 *Sceattas in England and on the Continent*, British Archaeol Rep, **128**

Hillam, J & Groves, C, 1985 Tree-ring analysis of oak timbers from Milk Street, London, Archive Report, Museum of London

——, 1985 Theoretical and applied dendrochronology: how to make a date with a tree in Phillips, P (ed) *The Archaeologist and the Laboratory*, CBA Res Rep, **58**, 17-23

——, 1987 BIG 82 Dendrochronological Analysis Archive Report

——, forthcoming Dendrochronological Analysis in Dyson, A, Schofield, J & Steedman, K, in preparation *The Saxon and Medieval Waterfront of London*

_____, Morgan, R A & Tyers I, 1987 Sapwood estimates and the dating of short ring sequences in Ward, R G W (ed) *Applications of Tree-ring Studies. Current Research in Dendrochronology and Related Areas* British Archaeol Rep, **S-333**, 165-85

Hillman, G C, 1981a Reconstructing crop husbandry practices from charred remains of crops in Mercer, R J (ed) *Farming Practice in British Prehistory*, 123-162

_____, 1981b Spelt kilning at Roman Catsgore in Somerset in Leech, R H (ed) *Excavations at Catsgore, Somerset 1970-3* (CRAAGS Excavation Monogr Ser **2**)

Hinton, D A & Welch, M, 1976 Objects of iron and bronze in Cunliffe, B W, *Excavations at Porchester Castle, vol II: Saxon*, Rep Res Comm Soc Antiq London, **33**, 195-219

_____, 1974 *A Catalogue of the Anglo-Saxon Ornamental Metalwork 700-110 in the Department of Antiquities, Ashmolean Museum*

_____, 1986 Coins and commercial centres in Anglo-Saxon England in Blackburn, M (ed) *Anglo-Saxon Monetary History*, 11-26

Hodges, R A, 1981 *The Hamwih pottery: the local and imported wares from 30 years' excavations at Middle Saxon Southampton and their European context* Southampton Archaeol Res Comm Rep, **2**, CBA Res Rep, **37**

Hoffman, M, 1964 *The Warp-weighted Loom*, Oslo

Holwerda, J H, 1930 Opgravingen an Dorestad, *Oudheidkundige Mededeelingen*, **11**, 32-93

Hooson, A, forthcoming A Dated Type-series of London medieval pottery: South Hertfordshire greyware, *Trans London Middlesex Archaeol Soc*

Horne, P D, 1985 A review of the evidence of human endoparasitism in the pre-Columbian New World through the study of coprolites, *J Archaeol Science*, **12**, 299-310

Horsman, V, 1983 Saxon buildings near Billingsgate, *Popular Archaeology*, **5** (4), 28-32

_____, Milne, C & Milne, G, 1988 *Aspects of Saxo-Norman London* **I**, London Middlesex Archaeol Soc Special Paper, **11**

Hrubý, V, 1957 Slovanské kostěné, predměty a jejich výroba na moravé, *Památky Archeologicke*, **48**, 118-217

Hubener, W, 1972 Gleicharmige bugelfibeln der Merowingerzeit in Westeuropa, *Madrider Mitteilungen*, **13**, 211-69

Huggins, P J, 1978 Excavations of Belgic and Romano-British Farm with Middle Saxon Cemetery and Churches at Nazeingbury, Essex, 1975-6, *Essex Archaeology and History*, **10**, 29-117

Huggins, R, forthcoming Excavations at 11 Downing Street, Westminster, *Trans London Middlesex Archaeol Soc*

Hughes, H & Lewis, P, 1988 Paint palettes in T B, James & A M, Robinson, *Clarendon Palace: the History and Archaeology of a Medieval Palace and Hunting Lodge*, Rep Res Comm Soc Antiq London, **45**

Hundt, H J, 1981 *Die Textil and Schnurreste aus der frühgeschichtlichen Wurt Elisenhof*, Studien zur Küstenarchäologie Schleswig-Holsteins, Series A

Elisenhof Band 4, Frankfurt am Main

Hunter, J, 1980 The glass in Holdsworth, P (ed) *Excavations at Melbourne Street, Southampton 1971-6*, CBA Res Rep, **33**, 59-72

_____, 1990 The glass in Biddle, M (ed) *Objects and Economy in Medieval Winchester*, Winchester Studies, **7** (2)

Hunter, R, 1979 Appendix: St Neots' type ware, in McCarthy, M & Williams, J H (eds) *St Peter's Street Northampton Excavations 1973-76*, 230-40

Hurst, J G, 1955 Saxo-Norman pottery in East Anglia: part I General discussion and St Neots' ware, *Proc Cambridge Antiq Soc*, **49**, 43-70

_____, 1956 Saxo-Norman pottery in East Anglia: part II Thetford ware, *Proc Cambridge Antiq Soc*, **I**, 42-60

_____, 1957 Saxo-Norman pottery in East Anglia: part III Stamford ware, *Proc Cambridge Antiq Soc*, **51**, 37-65

_____, 1961, The kitchen area of Northolt Manor, Middlesex, *Medieval Archaeol*, **5**, 211-99

_____, 1976a Anglo-Saxon and medieval in *The Archaeology of the London area: Current knowledge and problems*, London Middlesex Archaeol Soc Special Paper, **I**, 60-7

_____, 1976b The pottery in Wilson, D M (ed) *The Archaeology of Anglo-Saxon England*, 283-348

Hyman, L H, 1951 *The Invertebrates: Acanthocephela, Aschelminthes and Entoprocta*, New York

JBAA *Journal of the British Archaeological Association*

Jankuhn, K, 1943 *Die Ausgrabungen in Haithabu (1937-39)*, Berlin/Dahlem

Jensen, J S, 1983, Et prøvestykke fra Svend Estridsens Lundemønt, *Nordisk Numismatisk Unions Medlemsblad*, Feb 1983, 2-4

Johnson, C (Trans), 1950, *The Course of the Exchequer by Richard son of Nigel*, London

Jones A W, 1958 The flora of the City of London bombed sites, *The London Naturalist*, **37**, 189-210

_____, 1961 The vegetation of the South Norwood or Elmers End sewage works *The London Naturalist*, **40**, 102-14

_____, 1982 *Human Parasite Remains: Prospects for a Quantitative Approach*

_____, 1985 *Trinchurid ova* in archaeological deposits: their value as indicators of ancient faeces in Fieller, N R J, Gilbertson, D D & Ralph, N G A (eds) *Paleobiological Investigations. Research Design, Methods and Analysis*, British Archaeol Rep **S- 266**, 105-99

Jones, D M (ed), 1980 *Excavations at Billingsgate Buildings 'Triangle', Lower Thames Street, 1974*, London Middlesex Archaeol Soc Special Paper, **4**

Jones, M U, 1980 Mucking and early Saxon rural settlement in Essex in Buckley, D G (ed) *Archaeology in Essex to AD 1500*, CBA Res Rep, **34**, 82-6

Jones, M, 1981 The development of crop husbandry in Jones, M & Dimbleby, G (eds) *The Environment of Man: the Iron Age to the Anglo-Saxon Period* British Archaeol Rep, **87**, 95-127

Jones, P & Moorhouse, S, 1981 The Saxon and medieval pottery in Robertson-Mackay, R, Blackmore, L, Hurst, J G, Jones, P, Moorhouse, S & Webster,

L, A group of Saxon and medieval finds from the site of the neolithic causewayed enclosure of Staines, Surrey, with a note on the topography of the area, *Trans London Middlesex Archaeol Soc*, **32**, 107-31

——, 1982 Saxon and early medieval Staines, *Trans London Middlesex Archaeol Soc*, **33**, 186-213

——, forthcoming Late Saxon and Medieval Pottery from Reigate

Jones, W T, 1980 Early Saxon cemeteries in Essex in Buckley, D G (ed) *Archaeology in Essex to AD 1500*, CBA Res Rep, **34**, 87-95

Jope, E M & Threlfall, R J, 1959 The twelfth-century castle at Ascot Doilly, Oxfordshire: its history and excavation, *Antiq J*, **39**, 219-73

——, 1964 The Saxon building-stone industry in Southern and Midland England, *Medieval Archaeol*, **8**, 91-118

Keene, D, 1985 *Cheapside before the Great Fire*, Economic and Social Research Council

Keepax, C, 1977 Contamination of Archaeological deposits by seeds of modern origin with particular reference to the use of flotation machines, *J Archaeol Science*, **4**, 221-9

Kendrick, T D & Raleigh Radford, C A, 1943 Recent discoveries at All Hallows, Barking, *Antiq J*, **23**, 14-8

——, 1938 An Anglo-Saxon Cruet, *Antiq J*, **18**, 377-81

Kenward, H K, Hall, A R & Jones, A K G, 1980 A tested set of techniques for the extraction of plant and animal macrofossils from waterlogged archaeological deposits, *Science & Archaeology*, **22**, 3-15

Kilmurry, K, 1977 The production of red-painted pottery at Stamford, Lincs. *Medieval Archaeol*, **21**, 180-6

——, 1980 *The Pottery Industry of Stamford, Lincs c AD 850-1250*, British Archaeol Rep, **84**

Knörzer, K-H, 1984 Veranderungen der Unkrautvegetation auf rheinischen Bauernhöfen seit der Romerzeit *Bonner Jarhrbücher*, **184**, 479-503

Knight, J, 1972 A 12th-century stone lamp from Llangwm Uchaf, Monmouthshire, *Medieval Archaeol*, **16**, 130-33

Lambraki, A, 1980 Le cipolin de la Karystie. Contribution à l'étude des marbres de la Grèce exploités aux époques romaine et paléochrétienne, *Revue Archeologique*, 31-62

Larsen, A J, 1970 *Skomaterialet fra Utgravningene i Borgund på Sunnmøre 1954-62*, Årbok for Universitetet Bergen : Humanistisk Serie No 1, Bergen-Oslo

——, forthcoming *Skotöyet fra Gullsko-området, Bryggen Bergen*, Bryggen Papers

Lasko, P, 1984 Ivory carvings in *English Romanesque Art 1066-1200* (Zarnecki, G, Holt, J & Holland, J eds), Arts Council of Great Britain, 210-31

Levison, W, 1946 *England and the Continent in the Eighth Century*

Lindstrom, M, 1976 Nålar av ben, horn och brons in Mårtensson, A W, Uppgrävt förflutet för P K-banken i Lund, *Archaeologica Lundensia*, **7**, 275-8

Ling Roth, H, 1909 *Hand Woolcombing*, Bankfield Museum Notes, Ser 1, **6**

Lockett number refers to lot number in Lockett Sale,

English Part I, Glendining, London, 6.vi.1955

Loyn, H R, 1961 Boroughs and Mints AD 900-1066 in Dolley, R H M (ed) Anglo-Saxon Coins, 122-35

——, 1962, *Anglo-Saxon England and the Norman Conquest*, Harlow

——, 1977 *The Vikings in Britain*

——, 1986 Progress in Anglo-Saxon Monetary History in Blackburn, M *Anglo-Saxon Monetary History*, 1-10

Ludtke, H, 1985 *Die mittelalterliche Keramik von Schleswig Ausgrabung Schild 1971-1975* (Ausgrabungen in Schleswig Berichte und Studien, **4**), Neumünster

——, 1989 *The Bryggen Pottery 1: Introduction and Pingsdorf Ware* The Bryggen Papers Supplementary Series **4**

Luneau, V, 1906 Quelque deniers normandes inédits du XIe siècle, *Revue Numismatique*, **10**, 306-16

Lynn, C J, 1984 Some fragments of exotic porphyry found in Ireland, *J Irish Archaeol*, **2**, 19-32

Lyon, C S S, 1968, Address by Stewart Lyon, President of the British Numismatic Society, *BNJ* **37**, 216-38

——, 1969, Address by Stewart Lyon, President of the British Numismatic Society, *BNJ* **38**, 204-22

Lyon, C S S & Stewart, I, 1961 The Northumbrian Viking coins in the Cuerdale hoard in Dolley, R H M (ed) *Anglo-Saxon Coins*, 96-121

——, 1966-70 Historical Problems of Anglo-Saxon coinage (Presidential addresses to the British Numismatic Society), *BNJ*, **35-39**

MacGregor, A, 1976 Bone skates; a review of the evidence, *Archaeol J*, **133**, 57-74

——, 1978 Industry and commerce in Anglo-Scandinavian York in Hall, R A (ed) *Viking Age York and the North*, CBA Res Rep, **27**, 37-57

——, 1982 *Anglo-Scandinavian Finds from Lloyds Bank, Pavement and Other Sites*, (The Archaeology of York, **17/3**)

——, 1985a *Bone, Antler, Horn and Ivory. The Technology of Skeletal Materials*

——, 1985b Note on the ivory comb in Blair, J & Mckay, B, Investigations at Tackley Church, Oxfordshire, 1981-4: the Anglo-Saxon and Romanesque phases, *Oxoniensia*, **50**, 38-40

Mack, R, 1966 Stephen and the Anarchy 1135-41, *BNJ*, **35**, 38-112

Macphail, R, 1981 Soil and botanical studies of the 'dark earth' in Jones, M & Dimbleby, G (eds) *The Environment of Man: The Iron Age to the Anglo-Saxon Period Brit Archaeol Rep*, **87**, 309-331

Mann, J E, 1982 *Early Medieval Finds from Flaxengate 1: Objects of antler, bone, stone, horn ivory, amber and jet*, (The Archaeology of Lincoln, **14/1**)

Mann, J G, 1931 *Catalogue of Sculpture*

Manning, W H, 1976 Blacksmithing in Strong, D & Brown, D (eds) *Roman Crafts*, 143-53

Margeson, S & V, Williams, 1985 The Artefacts in Ayers, B, *Excavations within the North-East Bailey of Norwich Castle 1979*, East Anglia Archaeol Rep, **28**, 27-33

——, 1982 Worked bone in Coad, J G & Streeten, A D F, Excavations at Castle Acre Castle, Norfolk

1972-77: country house and castle of the Norman Earls of Surrey, *Archaeol J*, **139**, 241-55

Marsden, P, 1967 Archaeological finds in the City of London, 1963-4, *Trans London Middlesex Archaeol Soc*, **21**, 189-223

———, 1968 Some Discoveries in the City of London: 1954-9, *Trans London Middlesex Archaeol Soc*, **22**, part 1, 32-42

———, 1980 *Roman London*

Mason, D J P, 1985 Excavations at Chester, 26-42 Lower Bridge Street 1974-6: the Dark Age and Saxon periods. *Grosvenor Museum Archaeological Excavation and Survey Reports* **3**

Meaney, A, 1964 *A Gazetteer of Early Anglo-Saxon Burial Sites*

Mechanic's Magazine, 1827-8

Megaw, J V S, 1960 Penny Whistles and Prehistory, *Antiquity*, **34**, 6-13

Mellor, M, 1980 Late Saxon pottery from Oxfordshire: Evidence and speculation!, *Medieval Ceramics*, **4**, 17-27

Menghin, W, 1983 Völkerwanderungszeit und Frühes Mittelalter, in *Die Vor-und Frühgeschichtliche Sammlung Germaniches Nationalmuseum Nürnberg*, Stuttgart, 162-201

Merrifield, R, 1983 *London City of the Romans*

Metcalf, M & Walker, D, 1967, The Wolf Sceattas, *BNJ*, **26**, 11-28

———, 1977 Geographical Patterns of Minting in Medieval England, *Seaby's Coin and Medal Bulletin*, 314-7, 353-7 & 390-1

———, 1980 Continuity and change in English monetary history c 973-1086, part 1, *BNJ*, **50**, 20-49

———, 1981 Continuity and change in English monetary history c 973-1086, part 2, *BNJ*, **51**, 52-90

———, 1984 Monetary circulation in southern England in the first half of the eighth century in Hill, D & Metcalf, M (eds) *Sceattas in England and on the Continent*, British Archaeol Rep, **128**, 27-70

———, 1986 The monetary history of England in the tenth century viewed in the perspective of the eleventh century, in Blackburn, M (ed) *Anglo-Saxon Monetary History*, 133-58

Meyer, O, Wyss, M, Coxall, D J & Meyer, N, 1985 *Bilan des Fouilles. Saint-Denis. Recherches Urbaines 1983-1985*, Saint-Denis

Middleton, A P, Freestone, I C & Leese, M N, 1985 Textural analysis of ceramic thin sections: evaluation of grain sampling procedures, *Archaeometry*, **27**, 64-74

Milne, G, 1985 *The Port of Roman London*

Mitchiner, M & Skinner, A, 1983, English tokens, c 1200-1425, *BNJ*, **53**, 29-77

———, 1985 Contemporary forgeries of English silver coins and their chemical compositions: Henry III to William III, *NC*, **145**, 209-36

———, 1984 Rome: Imperial portrait tesserae from the city of Roman and Imperial tax tokens from the province of Egypt, *NC*, **144**, 95-114

Moltke, E, 1985 *Runes and Their Origin. Denmark and Elsewhere* (trans P G Foote), Copenhagen

Monk, M A, 1977 *The plant economy and agriculture of the Anglo-Saxons in southern Britain: with particular reference to the mart settlements at Southampton and Winchester*, unpublished M Phil thesis, Southampton University

———, 1983 Post-Roman drying kilns and the problems of function: a preliminary statement in Corrain, D O (ed) *Irish Antiquity. (Essays and Studies presented to Professor M J O'Kelly)*, Cork

Moore, D T & Ellis, S E, 1984 Hones in Rogerson, A & Dallas, C, *Excavations in Thetford 1948-59 and 1973-80*, East Anglia Archaeol Rep, **22**, 107-11

Morris, C, 1982 Aspects of Anglo-Saxon and Anglo-Scandinavia lathe-turning in McGrail, S (ed) *Woodworking Techniques before AD 1500*, BAR International Ser, **129**, 245-61

Morrisson, C, 1981, Monnaies en plomb byzantines de la fin du VIe et du début du VIIe siècles, *Rivista Italiana di Numismatica* **83**, 119-32

Müller-Wille, M, 1976 *Das Bootkammergrab von Haithabu (Berichte über die Ausgrabungen in Haithabu*, **8**) (Schietzel, K ed), Neumünster

Munsell, 1969 *Munsell Book of Color*, Baltimore, Maryland

Musty, J, Wade, K & Rogerson, A, 1973 A Viking pin and an inlaid knife from Wicken Bonhunt, Essex, *Antiq J*, **53**, 287

Myres, J N L, 1937 Three styles of decoration on Anglo-Saxon Pottery, *Antiq J*, **17**, 424-37

———, 1977 *A Corpus of Anglo-Saxon Pottery of the Pagan Period* 2 Vols

NC *Numismatic Chronicle*, London

Napier, A S & Stevenson, W H (eds), 1895 *Anecdota Oxoniensia. The Crawford collection of early charters and documents*, Oxford

National Museum of Ireland, 1973 *Viking and Medieval Dublin*, Dublin

Nordman, C A, 1931 Nordisk ornamentiki Finlands Jarnlder, *Nordisk Kultur*, **27**, 180-201

North I & North, J J, 1980 *English Hammered Coinage, I*, 2nd edn, London

Noss, A, 1976 *Før Strykejernet, Slikejake og Mangletre*, Oslo

O'Meadhra, U, 1979 *Early Christian, Viking and Romanesque Art: Motif Pieces from Ireland*, Theses and Papers in North-European Archaeology **7**, Stockholm

Ó'Ríordáin, B, 1971 Excavations at High Street and Winetavern Street, Dublin, *Medieval Archaeol*, **15**, 73-85

Oakley G E & Hunter, J, 1979 The glass in McCarthy, M & Williams, J H (ed) *St Peter's Street Northampton Excavations 1973-76*, 296-302

———, 1979 The worked bone in McCarthy, M & Williams, J H (ed) *St Peter's Street Northampton Excavations 1973-76*, 308-18

Oikonomedes, N, 1986, *A collection of dated Byzantine lead seals*, Washington DC

Okasha, E, 1967 An Anglo-Saxon inscription from All Hallows, Barking-by-the-Tower, London, *Medieval Archaeol*, **11**, 249-51

———, 1971 *Hand-list of Anglo-Saxon Non-Runic Inscriptions*

———, 1981 Three inscribed objects from Christ Church Place, Dublin in Bekker-Nielsen, H, Foote, P & Olsen, O (eds) *Proceedings of the Eighth Viking Congress*, Odense, 45-51

Orton, C, 1983 *Statistical analysis of seed samples from the Milk Street Pit Project*, Archive Report, Museum of London

Owen-Crocker, G R, 1986 *Dress in Anglo-Saxon England*

Pagan, H E, 1965 Coinage in the Age of Burgred, *BNJ*, **34**, 11-27

———, 1982, The coinage of the East Anglian kingdom from 825 to 870, *BNJ* **38**, 41-83

———, 1986 Coinage in southern England 796-874, in Blackburn, M (ed) *Anglo-Saxon Monetary History*, 45-66

Parnell, G, 1977 Excavations at the Tower of London, 1976-7, *London Archaeol*, **3** (4), 97-9

Parsloe, G, 1928 Notes on the site of the Roman bridge at London, *An Inventory of the Historical Monuments in London*, 192-4

Pearce, J E, Vince, A G & White, R, 1982 *A Dated Type-Series of medieval pottery in London, Part 1 : Mill Green ware*, London and Middlesex Archaeol Soc **33**, 266-298

———, Jenner, M A, 1985 *A Dated Type-series of London Medieval Pottery : Part 2, London-type Ware*, London Middlesex Archaeol Soc Special Paper, **6**

———, 1988 *A Dated Type-series of London Medieval Pottery : Part 4, Surrey Whitewares*, London Middlesex Archaeol Soc Special Paper, **10**

Peers, C & Raleigh Radford C A, 1943 The Saxon Monastery of Whitby, *Archaeologia*, **89**, 27-88

Percy, J, 1961 *Metallurgy, Vol 1 Part 1 : Fuel ; Fireclays*

Persson, J, 1976 Kammar in Martensson, A W, Uppgrävt förflutet för PK-banken i Lund, *Archaeologica Lundensia* **7**, 317-32

Phythian-Adams, C, 1977 Rutland reconsidered, in Dornier, A (ed) *Mercian Studies*, 63-84

Pike, A W & M Biddle, 1966 Parasite eggs in Medieval Winchester, *Antiquity*, **40**, 293-6

———, 1975 Parasite eggs, in Platt, C & Coleman-Smith, R, *Excavations in Medieval Southampton 1953-69, Vol 1*

Pinder-Wilson, R, 1976 Glass, in *The Arts of Islam* The Arts Council of Great Britain

Pirie, E J E, 1986 *Post-Roman coins from York excavations 1971-81*, (The Archaeology of York, **18/1**)

Platt, C, & Coleman-Smith, R, 1975 *Excavations in medieval Southampton, 1953-69*

Pritchard, F A, 1982 *Swan Lane Medieval Building Material*, Archive Report, Museum of London

———, ———, 1984 Late Saxon Textiles from the City of London, *Medieval Archaeol*, **28**, 46-76

———, 1986 Ornamental stonework from Roman London, *Britannia*, **17**, 169-89

———, forthcoming Leatherwork in Hurst, H R, *11-17 Southgate Street, Gloucester*

Prou, M, 1886, Tiers de sou d'or Mérovingiens de Tidiriciacum, *RN*, **40** 3rd Series **4**, 203-17

Prou, M, 1890, Inventaire sommaire des monnaies Mérovingiennes de la collection Amécourt acquis par la Bibliothèque Nationale, *RN*, **44** 3rd Series **8**, 271-357

RN *Revue Numismatique*, Paris

Rahtz, P A, 1974 *Pottery in Somerset AD400-1100* in Evison, V I, Hodges H and Hurst, J G (eds) *Medieval Pottery from Excavations, studies presented to G. C. Dunning*, London

Rahtz, P A, 1979 *The Saxon and Medieval Palaces of Cheddar*, British Archaeol Rep **65**

Read, C H, 1887 Appendix : On an iron sword of Scandinavian type found in London, now in the British Museum ; and a bronze stirrup of the same period found near Romsey, in Hampshire, in the possession of Philip B Davis Cook, Esq *Archaeologia*, **50**, part II, 530-33

Reece, R, 1980 Town and Country : the end of Roman Britain, *World Archaeol*, **12** (1), 77-92

Rhodes, M, 1975 Saxon and medieval pottery in Marsden, P, Dyson, A & Rhodes, M, Excavations on the Site of St Mildred's Church, Bread Street, London, 1973-1974, *Trans London Middlesex Archaeol Soc*, **26**, 181-208

———, 1980a Saxon pottery in Jones, D M (ed) *Excavations at Billingsgate Buildings 'Triangle', Lower Thames Street, 1974*, London Middlesex Archaeol Soc Special Paper, **4**, 139-41

———, 1980b Wood and woody tissue, in Jones, D M (ed) *Excavations at Billingsgate Buildings 'Triangle' Lower Thames Street, 1974*, London Middlesex Archaeol Soc Special Paper, **4**, 144

———, 1980c The Saxon Pottery in Hill, C, Millett, M & Blagg, T, *The Roman Riverside Wall and Monumental Arch in London*, London Middlesex Archaeol Soc Special Paper, **3**, 97-8

———, 1980d Other finds from the Riverside Wall excavation in Hill, C, Millett, M & Blagg, T, *The Roman Riverside Wall and Monumental Arch in London*, London Middlesex Archaeol Soc Special Paper, **3**, 110-12

———, 1986 Stone objects in Miller, L, Schofield, J & Rhodes, M, *The Roman Quay at St Magnus House, London*, London Middlesex Archaeol Soc Special Paper, **8**, 240-5

Richardson, F E, 1986 Roman Pottery in Miller, L, Schofield, J & Rhodes, M, *The Roman Quay at St Magnus House, London*, London Middlesex Archaeol Soc Special Paper, **8**, 96-138

Richardson, K M, 1959 Excavations in Hungate, York, *Archaeol J*, **116**, 51-114

Riddler, I D, forthcoming *Organic Materials*, Southampton Finds, Vol 3

———, forthcoming, Eine Stielkamm aus Haithabu, in Schietzel, K (ed) *Das archäologische Fundmaterial der Ausgrabung Haithabu (Berichte über die Ausgrabungen in Haithabu)*, Neumünster

Rigold, S & Metcalf, M, 1984 A revised check-list of English finds of sceattas in Hill, D & Metcalf, M (eds) *Sceattas in England and on the Continent*, British Archaeol Rep, **128**, 245-68

Rigold, S E, 1968 The double minsters of Kent and

their analogues, *JBAA*, **31**, 27-37

―――, 1977 The Principal Series of English Sceattas, *BNJ*, **47**, 21-30

Roach Smith, C, 1854 *Catalogue of the Museum of London Antiquities*

―――, 1859 *Illustrations of Roman London*

Robinson, P, 1981 A pin of the later Saxon period from Marlborough and some related pins, *Wilts Archaeol Magazine*, **74/75**, 56-60

Roesdahl, E, Graham-Campbell, J, Conner, P & Pearson, K (eds), 1981 *The Vikings in England and in their Danish Homeland*, The Anglo-Danish Viking Project

Rogerson, A & Dallas, C, 1984 *Excavations in Thetford 1948-59 and 1973-80*, East Anglia Archaeol Rep, **22**

Rosenberg, M, 1922 *Zellenschmelz, III: Geschichte der Goldschmiedekunst auf technischer Grundlage* Frankfurt-am-Main

―――, de Rouffignac, C, 1987 Mediaeval biology: Mediaeval man and his worms, *Biologist*, **34** (4), 187-90

Rouyer, J, 1864, Notes concernant des méreaux et d'autres pieces du même genre. Méreaux fiscaux etc, *RN*, **30** New Series **9**, 444-59

Ruding, R, 1817 *Annals of the Coinage of Britain*

Rüger, C B, 1970 Römische Ziegelbruchstüke aus Haithabu in Schietzel, K (ed) *Das archäologische Fundmaterial I der Ausgrabung 1963-64*, (Berichte über die Ausgrabungen in Haithabu, **4**), Neumünster, 74-6

SCBI 1, Grierson, P, 1958 *Sylloge of Coins of the British Isles*, The Fitzwilliam Museum, Cambridge, part 1 Ancient British and Anglo-Saxon coins

SCBI 2, Robertson, A S, 1961 *Sylloge of coins of the British Isles*, The Hunterian Museum, Glasgow. Part I. The Anglo-Saxon coins in the Hunterian and Coats collections

SCBI 4, Galster, G, 1964 *Sylloge of coins of the British Isles*, The Royal Danish Collection, Copenhagen. Part I. Ancient British and Anglo-Saxon Coins before Aethelred II

SCBI 7, Galster, G, 1966 *Sylloge of Coins of the British Isles*, The Royal Danish Collection, Copenhagen, part 2 Anglo-Saxon coins, Aethelred II

SCBI 8, Dolley, R H M, 1966 *Sylloge of Coins of the British Isles*, Hiberno-Norse coins in the British Museum

SCBI 11, Blunt, C & Dolley, R H M, 1969 *Sylloge of Coins of the British Isles*, Reading University, Anglo-Saxon coins

SCBI 13, Galster, G, 1970 *Sylloge of Coins of the British Isles*, The Royal Danish Collection, Copenhagen, part 3a, Cnut

SCBI 14, Galster, G, 1970 *Sylloge of Coins of the British Isles*, The Royal Danish Collection, Copenhagen, part 3b, Cnut

SCBI 15, Galster, G, 1970 *Sylloge of Coins of the British Isles*, The Royal Danish Collection, Copenhagen, part 3c, Cnut

SCBI 17, Gunstone, A, 1971 *Sylloge of Coins of the British Isles*, Midland Museums, Ancient British, Anglo-Saxon and Norman coins

SCBI 20, Mack, R P, 1973 *Sylloge of Coins of the British Isles*, R P Mack Collection Ancient British, Anglo-Saxon and Norman coins

SCBI 21, Pirie, E J E, 1975 *Sylloge of coins of the British Isles*, Yorkshire Collections

SCBI 28, Smart, V J, 1980 *Sylloge of coins of the British Isles*, Cumulative index of Volumes 1-20

SCBI 30, Brady, J D, 1982 *Sylloge of Coins of the British Isles*, American Collections

SCBI 34, Archibald, M M & Blunt, C E, 1986 *Sylloge of coins of the British Isles* British Museum V, Athelstan to the reform of Edgar

SCBI BM V see SCBI 34

SCBI Copenhagen see SCBI 4

SCBI Glasgow see SCBI 2

SCBI Yorkshire see SCBI 21

Sachsen und Angelsachsen, 1978 Helms-Museum, Hamburg

Saville, A, Haddon-Reece, D & Clark, A, 1985 Salvage recording of Romano-British, Saxon, medieval and post-medieval remains at North Street, Winchcombe, Gloucestershire *Trans Bristol Glos Archaeol Soc* **103**, 113-23

Sawyer, P, 1986 Anglo-Scandinavian trade in the Viking age and after in Blackburn, M (ed) *Anglo-Saxon Monetary History*, 185-200

Schietzel, K, 1970 Hölzerne Kleinfunde aus Haithabu Ausgrabung in *Das archäologische Fundmaterial I der 1963-64 (Berichte über die Ausgrabungen in Haithabu*, **4**), Neumünster, 77-91

Schofield, J, in preparation *The Early Church in London*

Searle, A B, 1940 *Refractory Materials*

Sheldon, H & Tyers, I G, 1983 Recent dendro-chronological work in Southwark and its implications, *London Archaeol*, **4** (13), 355-61

Shetelig, H, (ed), 1940 Viking Antiquities in Great Britain and Ireland, Part II, Oslo

Spufford, P, 1963 Continental Coins in Late Medieval England, *BNJ*, **32**, 127-39

Stenton, F M, 1934 *Norman London An Essay* Historical Association Leaflets Nos 93 & 94

―――, 1970 Norman London in Stenton, D M (ed) *Preparatory to Anglo-Saxon England: Being the collected papers of Frank Merry Stenton*, 23-47

―――, 1971 *Anglo-Saxon England*

Stewart, I, 1967 *The Scottish Coinage* (revised edn)

―――, 1978 Anglo-Saxon gold coins, in Carson, R & Kraay, C (eds) *Scripta Nummaria Romana*, 143-72

―――, 1978, A lead striking of William II's last coin-type, *NC*, **138**, 185-7

―――, 1984 The early English denarial coinage *c* 680-*c* 750 in Hill, D & Metcalf, M (eds) *Sceattas in England and on the Continent*, British Archaeol Rep, **128**, 5-26

―――, 1986 The London mint and the coinage of Offa in Blackburn, M (ed) *Anglo-Saxon Monetary History*, 27-44

Stott, P, 1984 Recent finds of sceattas from the River Thames in London in Hill, D & Metcalf, M (eds) *Sceattas in England and on the Continent*, British Archaeol Rep, **128**, 241-4

Sutherland, C, 1948 *Anglo-Saxon Gold Coinage in the Light*

of the Crondall Hoard

Swallow, A W, 1975 Interpretation of wear marks seen in footwear *Transactions of the Museum Assistants' Group for 1973*, **12**, 28-32

Szabó, M, Grenander-Nyberg, G & Myrdal, J, 1985 *Die Holzfunde aus der frühgeschichtlichen Wurt Elisenhof*, Studien zur Kustenarchäologie Schleswig-Holsteins, Series A Elisenhof, Band **5**, Frankfurt-am-Main

Tatton-Brown, T, 1986 The Topography of Anglo-Saxon London, *Antiquity*, **60**, No 228, 21-8

Tempel, W-D, 1969 *Die Dreilagenkämme aus Haithabu. Studien zu den Kämmen der Wikingerzeit in Nordseeküstengebiet und Skandinavien*, Dissertation, Göttingen

———, 1972 Unterscheide Zwischen den Formen der Dreilagenkämme in Skandinavien und auf den Friesischen Wurten vom 8 bis 10 Jahrhurdert, *Archaeologisches Korrespondenzblatt*, **2**, 57-9

———, 1979 *Die Kamme aus der frühgeschichtlichen Wurt Elisenhof, Studien zur Küstenarchäologie Schleswig-Holsteins*, Series A Elisenhof Band **3**, Frankfurt am Main, 151-74

Temple, E, 1976 *Anglo-Saxon Manuscripts 900-1066. A Survey of Manuscripts Illuminated in the British Isles, Vol 2*

Thomas, A H & Thorley, I D, 1938 *The Great Chronicle of London*, (reprinted Gloucester)

Thompson, D V, 1956 *The Materials and Techniques of Medieval Painting*, New York

Thompson, J, 1986 A return to tradition, *Hali*, **30**, 14-21

Thompson, J D A, 1956 *Inventory of British Coin Hoards AD 600-1500*

Thompson, M W, 1967 *Novgorod the Great*

Thornton, J H & Goodfellow A V, 1958 Leather shoes in Stead, I M, Excavations at the south corner tower of the Roman fortress at York, 1956, *Yorkshire Archaeol J*, **39**, 525-30

———, 1969 Leather in Addyman, P V, Late Saxon settlements in the St Neots area : II. The Little Paxton settlement and enclosures, *Proc Cambridge Antiq Soc*, **67**, 91

———, 1975 A glossary of shoe terms, *Transactions of the Museum Assistants' Group for 1973*, **12**, 44-8

———, 1977 Leatherwork in Durham, B, Archaeological Investigations in St Aldates, Oxford, *Oxoniensia*, **42**, 155-60

———, 1979 Leather artifacts and manufacture in Carver, M O H, Three Saxo-Norman tenements in Durham City, *Medieval Archaeol*, **23**, 26-36

Timby, J R, 1988 Middle Saxon pottery in Andrews, P (ed) *The Coins and Pottery from Hamwic*, Southampton Finds, Vol 1, 73-124

Tomlinson, P, 1985 Use of vegetative remains in the identification of dyeplants from waterlogged 9th-10th century deposits at York, *J Archaeol Science*, **12**, 269-83

Tristram, E W, 1944 *English Medieval Wall-Paintings, I. The Twelfth Century*

Turner, D H, 1984 Illuminated manuscripts in Backhouse, J, Turner, D H & Webster, L (eds) *The Golden Age of Anglo-Saxon Art 966-1066*, 46-87

Tuxen, R, 1950, Grundriss einer Systematik der nitrophilen Unkraut-gesellschaften in der Eurosibirischen Region Europas, *Mitteilungen der Floristisch-soziologischen Arbeitsgemeinschaft N F*, **2**, 94-175

Tweddle, D, 1980 Putting on the style *Interim, Bulletin of the York Archaeological Trust*, **7** (2), 22-28

———, 1982 Scabbard and miscellaneous leatherwork in MacGregor, A, *Anglo-Scandinavian finds from Lloyds Bank, Pavement and Other Sites* (The Archaeology of York, **17/4**), 142-3

———, 1986 *Finds from Parliament Street and Other Sites in the City Centre* (The Archaeology of York, **17/4**)

Tylecote, R F & Gilmour B J J, 1986 *The Metallography of Early Ferrous Edge Tools and Edged Weapons*, British Archaeol Rep, **155**

Tylecote, R F, 1981 The medieval smith and his methods in Crossley, D W (ed) *Medieval Industry*, CBA Res Rep, **40**, *42-50*

Ulbricht, I, 1978 Die Geweihverarbeitung in Haithabu *Die Ausgrabungen in Haithabu*, **7**, Neumünster

———, 1984 *Die Verarbeitung von Knochen, Geweih und Horn im mittelalterlichen Schleswig (Ausgrabungen in Schleswig*, **3**) (ed V Vogel), Neumünster

Van Es, W A & Verwers, W S, 1980 *Excavations at Dorestad I The Harbour: Hoogstraat I*, Nederlandse Oudheden, **9**, Amersfoort

VCH 1909 *Victoria History of the Counties of England*, London

Ivan der Veen, M & Fieller, N, 1982 Sampling seeds, *J Archaeol Science*, **9**, 287-98

Vierck, H, 1984 *Archäologische und naturwissenschaftliche Untersuchungen an Siedlungen im deutschen Kustengebiet II* (eds H Jankuhn, K Schietzel & H Reichstein), Acta Humaniora, Weinheim

Vigeon, E, 1977 Clogs and wooden shoes, *Costume*, **11**, 1-27

Vince, A G & Bayley, J, 1983 A Late Saxon glass finger ring from the City of London, *Trans London Middlesex Archaeol Soc*, **34**, 93-4

Vince, A G, 1977 Some Aspects of Pottery Quantification *Medieval Ceramics* **1**, 63-74

———, 1979 Appendix 1 in C M Heighway, A P Garrod and A G Vince Excavations at 1 Westgate Street, Gloucester *Med Arch* **23**, 170-181

———, 1983a *The Medieval Ceramic Industry of the Severn Valley* Ph.D. Thesis, University of Southampton

———, 1983b In search of Saxon London: the view from the pot shed, *Popular Archaeol*, **5** (4), 33-7

———, 1984 The Aldwych: Saxon London discovered, *Current Archaeol*, **93**, 310-2

———, 1985a Comment: the limestone spindlewhorls from Berrington Street in *Hereford City Excavations Vol 3: The Finds*, CBA Res Rep, **56**, 14

———, 1985b The processing and analysis of the medieval pottery from Billingsgate Lorry Park 1982 in Herteig, A E (ed) *Conference on waterfront archaeology in north European towns No 2 Bergen 1983*, 157-168

_____, 1985c Part 2: the ceramic finds in Shoesmith, R (ed) *Hereford City Excavations Volume 3: The Finds CBA Research Rep* **56**, 34-82

_____, 1985d The Saxon and Medieval Pottery of London: A Review *Medieval Archaeology* **29**, 25-93

_____, 1990 *Saxon London: an archaeological investigation* B A Seaby

_____, forthcoming Saxon and Medieval Pottery in Hurst, H R, *11-17 Southgate Street, Gloucester*

Volkers, H H, 1965, *Karolingische Münzfunde der Früzeit*, Göttingen

Waateringe, 1984 see Groenman-van Waateringe, W, 1984

Waddington, 1927 Viking sheath of leather, *Antiq J*, **7**, 526-7

Wade, K, 1980 A Settlement of Bonhunt Farm, Wicken Bonhunt, Essex in Buckley, D G (ed) *Archaeology in Essex to AD 1500*, CBA Res Rep **34**, 96-102

Wade, K & Blinkhorn, P, forthcoming Anglo-Saxon Pottery from Ipswich

Wallace, P F, 1987 The economy and commerce of Viking Age Dublin, in Düwel, K, Jankuhn, H, Siems, H & Timpe, D (eds) *Untersuchungen zu Handel und Verkehr de vor-und frühgeschichtlichen Zeit in Mittel – und Nordeuropa, IV. Der Handel del Karolinger– und Wikingerzeit*, Abhandlungen der Akademie der Wissenschaften, Göttingen Philologisch-Historische Klasse, **156**, 200-45, Göttingen

van de Walle, A, 1961 Excavations in the ancient centre of Antwerp, *Medieval Archaeol*, **5**, 123-36

Walton, P, 1989 *Textiles, Cordage and Raw Fibre from 16-22 Coppergate* (The Archaeology of York, **17/5**)

Ward Perkins, J B, 1940 *Medieval Catalogue*, London Museum Catalogue, **7**

Waterman, D M, 1948 Viking antiquities from Sawdon, N R Yorks *Antiq J*, **28**, 180-3

_____, 1959 Late Saxon, Viking and early Medieval finds from York, *Archaeologia*, **97**, 59-105

Watkins, M J, 1983 Finds from minor sites in Heighway, C M, *The East and North Gates of Gloucester and associated sites, Excavations 1974-81*, Western Archaeol Trust Excavations Monograph, **4**, 210-2

Watson, J, 1986 *The identification of the handles of two reversible knives from Billingsgate 1982*, London, Ancient Monuments Lab Rep **29/86**

Webster, G, Dolley, R H M & Dunning, G C 1953 A Saxon treasure hoard found at Chester, *Antiq J*, **33**, 22-32

Welch, M G, 1975 Mitcham grave 205 and the chronology of applied brooches with floriate cross decoration, *Antiq J*, **55**, 86-95

West, B, 1982 A note on bone skates from London, *Trans London Middlesex Archaeol Soc*, **33**, 303

West, S E, 1963 Excavations at Cox Lane (1958) and at the Town Defences, Shire Hall Yard, Ipswich (1959), *Proc Suffolk Institute of Archaeology*, **29**, 232-303

Westell, W P, 1935 Bronze objects found in Hertfordshire, *Antiq J*, **15**, 350-1

Wheeler, A, 1980 Fish remains in Jones, D M (ed) *Excavations at Billingsgate Buildings Triangle, Lower Thames Street, 1974*, London Middlesex Archaeol Soc Special Paper, **4**, 161-2

Wheeler, R E M, 1927 *London and the Vikings*, London Museum Catalogue **1**

Wheeler, R E M, 1935 *London and the Saxons*, London Museum Catalogue **6**

Whitbread, I K, 1986 The characterisation of argillaceous inclusions in ceramic thin sections, *Archaeometry*, **28**, 79-88

White, W J, 1988 *Skeletal remains from the cemetery of St Nicholas Shambles, City of London*, London Middlesex Archaeol Soc Special Paper, **9**

Whytehead, R & Blackmore, L, 1983 Excavations at Tottenham Court, 250 Euston Road, NW1, *Trans London Middlesex Archaeol Soc*, **34**, 73-92

Whytehead, R, 1984 Site watching at Gardiner's Corner, *Trans London Middlesex Archaeol Soc*, **35**, 37-58

_____, 1985 The Jubilee Hall site reveals new evidence of Saxon London, *Rescue News*, **37**

Wild, J P, 1970 *Textile Manufacture in the Northern Roman Provinces*

Wilde, K A, 1953 Die Bedeutung der Grabung Wollin 1934, *Beiheft zum Atlas der Urgeschichte*, 2 edn, Hamburg

Willcox, G H, 1977 Exotic plants from Roman waterlogged sites in London, *J Archaeol Science*, **4**, 269-82

Wilson, D M, 1960 An Anglo-Saxon ivory comb, *The British Museum Quarterly*, **23** (1), 17-18

_____, 1964 *Anglo-Saxon Ornamental Metalwork 700-1100 in the British Museum*

_____, 1969 A late Anglo-Saxon strap-end in Biddle, M, Excavations at Winchester, 1968, *Antiq J*, **49**, 326-8

_____, 1975 Tenth-century metalwork in Parsons, D (ed) *Tenth-century Studies*, 200-48

_____, 1976 Craft and industry in Wilson, D M (ed) *The Archaeology of Anglo-Saxon England*, 253-81

_____, (ed), 1976 *The Archaeology of Anglo-Saxon England*

_____, 1983 A bone pin from Sconsburgh, Dunrossness in O'Connor, A & Clarke, D V (eds) *From the Stone Age to the 'Forty-Five'*, 343-9

Wilthew, P, 1987 Metallographic examination of medieval knives and shears in Cowgill, J, de Neergaard, M & Griffiths, N, *Medieval Finds from Excavations in London: I. Knives and Scabbards*, 62-74

Woods, A, 1986 Form, Fabric and Function: Some observations on the cooking pot in Antiquity, *Ceramics and Civilisation*, **2**, 157-72

Wormald, F, 1973 *The Winchester Psalter*

Worrall, W E, 1975 *Clays and Ceramics Raw Materials*

van Zeist, W, 1974 Palaeobotanical studies of the settlement sites in the coastal area of the Netherlands, *Palaeohistoria*, **16**, 226-371

ACKNOWLEDGEMENTS

Many people have been involved in the production of these papers and it is only possible to mention here those whose work behind scenes has made the production of the report possible.

Tony Dyson, the general editor for all DUA publications, has himself made several important contributions to the study of Saxon London and has consequently taken an even closer interest in the progress of this work than normal. As always, his advice and criticism is gratefully acknowledged. Steve Roskams, Val de Hoog, Clive Orton and Jo Groves have all made substantial contributions to the study of the Milk Street pits. Mike Rhodes coordinated the post-excavation analysis of many of the New Fresh Wharf/St Magnus House finds. Paul Tyers, when DUA Computer Supervisor, made many contributions, especially by developing new systems to cope with the problems of simultaneous analysis of the finds from over a dozen excavations.

Especial thanks are due to Mick Griffiths for many of the figures contained in this volume. Figs 8.8 and 8.10-11 are the work of Majella Egan.

Funding to carry out the post-excavation analysis was provided first by the Department of the Environment and subsequently by English Heritage (HBMC).

Those whose contributions has been predominantly in a particular field have been acknowledged at the end of the part concerned.

SUMMARIES IN FRENCH AND GERMAN

Resumé

Au 9ème siècle, le centre de l'agglomération de Londres fut transporté, presque surement à la demande royale, du Wic non-fortifié placé le long du Strand jusqu' à l'intérieur des murs de la cité romaine, qui jusque là ne comprenait guère plus que la cathédrale St Paul et la communauté qui la servait. Après un début lent, Londres grandit au 10ème et 11ème siècle d'une façon spectaculaire et vers le milieu du 11ème siècle la ville était devenue un port animé ayant des liens avec la Scandinavie, la région du Rhin et le nord de la France.

Dans ce volume, on a présenté les diverses études entreprises sur les artefacts et les indices du paléo-environnement provenant de sites situés à l'intérieur des murs de la cité dont les dates s'étagent de la fin du 9ème siècle au milieu du 12ème. On y trouvera huit parties de tailles inégales dont la première est une discussion sur la nature des gisements d'où proviennent les indices. Ils consistent pour la plus grande part de couches de base des fosses-dépotoirs. Les couches d'habitation associées à ces fosses ont été enlevées il y a bien longtemps, en particulier au moment où l'on a creusé des caves.

La deuxième partie comprend un groupe de céramique saxonne de la Cité de Londres et également le raisonnement que l'on a fait pour justifier le choix du cadre chronologique qui se retrouve dans presque tous les autres articles. De plus, on y verra comment il a été possible de retrouver la source, ou la région de la source, de la majorité de la céramique de la Cité en utilisant ensemble l'analyse pétrologique et l'étude de la céramique provenant des sites contemporains de la campagne environnante.

Les artefacts étaient faits de bois de cerf, d'os, d'alliage de cuivre, d'argile cuite, de verre, de fer, d'ivoire, de plomb, de cuir, de pierre et de bois; ils ont présentés dans la troisième partie du volume. Tous les artefacts retrouvés dans les couches du 10ème et 11ème siècle sont inclus sauf ceux provenant de sites dont les informations stratigraphiques n'ont pu être obtenues. Les objets en cuir sont d'un intérêt car ils ont en nombre suffisant pour permettre de faire remonter la séquence des styles et techniques jusqu'au 10ème siècle alors qu'elle n'allait jusqu'à maintenant que du 12ème au 15ème siècles.

On a retrouvé relativement peu de pièces de monnaie des époques saxonne et normande dans les fouilles récentes. Cependant, l'étude de pièces retrouvées antérieurement et la comparaison des pièces de monnaie de la Cité avec celles de la région environnante est très importante pour interpréter la céramique et les autres artefacts. On a donc inclus dans la quatrième partie de ce volume un catalogue illustré de ces pièces. Dans un article sur les objets en plomb, on propose l'idée que ceux - ci étaient des sortes de reçus pour péage.

Les problèmes de résidualité et de contamination qui touchent les études de la céramique et autres artefacts touchent aussi les macrorestes botaniques; ils sont exposés dans la 5ème partie. Mais, malgré ces problèmes, les résultats de l'analyse des restes botaniques se sont avérés utiles. L'absence de certains éléments de la balle des céréales, les rachis par example, montrent que les grains apportés à Londres avaient été vanés et criblés au préalable; en particulier, un ensemble composé uniquement de grains de froment provenant de Well Court. Dans la partie 5.2, une étude de la présence d'œufs de parasites a montré qu'il n'est pas possible de différencier entre les couches qui sont uniquement composées d'excréments humains, celles qui contiennent une grande proportion de ces déchets et celles qui n'en contiennent que quelques éléments.

Dans la sixième partie, on trouvera les résultats préliminaires de l'étude des creusets de l'époque saxonne récente. Il y est démontré que l'on préférait les creusets en céramique de Stamford à ceux d'une autre origine surtout pour la fonte de l'argent. La distribution des fragments de creusets laissent à penser que le travail du métal se pratiquait à une petite échelle dans toute la ville habitée, et par ailleurs leur distribution stratigraphique montre qu'il n'y a eu que peu ou pas de travail de métal non-ferreux avant le début du 11ème siècle.

La 7ème partie comprend deux rapports sur la datation scientique des gisements saxons récents utilisant respectivement la dendrochronologie et l'archéomagnétisme.

Finalement, le développement topographique et fonctionnel de Londres depuis l'époque romaine tardive jusqu'a la conquête normande est résumé dans la 8ème partie; les données contenues dans les volumes Un et Deux de cette série y sont utilisées. Le but principal de ce chapître est de donner un cadre archéologique aux artefacts saxons trouvés à l'intérieur des murs de la Cité, bien que ce faisant il soit nécessaire de se tourner vers les agglomérations situées à l'extèrieur des murs le long du Strand et à Southwark dont le développement est intimement lié à celui de la ville intra-muros.

On a donné une bibliographie unique pour l'ensemble du volume car les divers rapports citent en général les mêmes publications. A la suite du texte imprimé, l'on trouvera des microfiches comprenant les rapports site par site qui permettront au lecteur de voir les liens entre la stratigraphie, la céramique, les autres artefacts et les indices du paléo-environnement d'un même endroit. De plus amples informations peuvent être obtenues sur demande à la section des archives du Musée de Londres.

Zusammenfassung

Im späten 9. Jahrhundert wurde das Zentrum der Londoner Besiedlung vom unbefestigten *wic* am Strand hinter die römischen Stadtmauern verlegt. Hier hatten bis dahin wenig mehr als die Kathedrale und einige Gemeindehäuser gestanden. Dieser Wechsel geschah mit ziehmlicher Sicherheit auf Befehl des Königs. Nach einem zögernden Anfang entwickelte sich London im 10. und 11. Jahrhundert zu erstaunlichen Ausmaßen. Mitte des 11. Jahrhunderts hatte die Stadt einen blühenden Hafen und Handel mit Skandinavien, dem Rheinland und Nord Frankreich.

Dieser Band umfaßt mehrere Studien über Funde und Umweltfragen der Stadt hinter den Mauern zwischen dem 9. und 12. Jahrhundert. Das erste von acht unterschiedlich langen Kapiteln ist eine kurze Einführung und beschreibt die Art der Lagen aus denen die Funde kamen, und zwar meist die unteren Schichten von Abfallgruben, deren Oberflächen schon in alter Zeit durch Kelleranlagen verloren gegangen sind.

Das zweite Kapitel behandelt eine Gruppe sächsischer Töpferwaren aus der umfriedeten Stadt und erörtert den chronologischen Ablauf, auf dem auch die meisten anderen Kapitel aufgebaut sind. Durch eine Materialanalyse unter Einbeziehung von Tonwaren zeitgleicher Fundorte aus der Umgebung wurde es außerdem möglich, den Ursprung oder doch die Herkunftsgegend der Ware aus der City zu bestimmen.

Das dritte Kapitel befaßt sich mit kleinen Funden, wie Geweih- und andere Knochen, Elfenbein, Leder, gebranntem Ton, Glas, Stein, Bronze, Eisen, Blei und Holz. Alle Funde, die stratigraphisch sicher dem 10. und 11. Jahrhundert zugeschrieben werden können, sind hier behandelt, die unsicheren sind ausgelassen. Besonders interessant ist das Lederwerk. Da reichlich vorhanden, konnten Sequenzen von Stilformen und Techniken, die früher dem 12. bis 15. Jahrhunderts zugeordnet waren, jetzt bis ins 10. Jahrhundert zurückbelegt werden.

Das vierte Kapitel beschreibt Münzen und enthält auch einen illustrierten Katalog. Jüngste Ausgrabungen brachten relativ wenig sächsische und normannische Münzen zu Tage. Deshalb sind die Untersuchungen früherer Funde und der Vergleich von Münzen innerhalb der Mauer mit denen der umliegenden Orte sehr wichtig für das Verständnis der Töpferwaren und anderer Funde. Außerdem werden hier noch Bleistücke erwähnt, die wahrscheinlich als Hafenzollbestätigungen gedient haben.

Das fünfte Kapitel beschäftigt sich mit dem Problem der offensichtlich "zu alten" und "zu jungen" Funde in Lagen. Dieses betrifft sowohl Scherben, Kleinfunde als auch botanische Überreste. Trotz dieser Schwierigkeit hat die Untersuchung der pflanzlichen Reste einen Wert: des Fehlen von Spreu läßt auf den Import von geworfeltem Korn, die Reinheit des Weizens in Wellcourt auf vorangegangenes Sieben schließen. Teil 5.11 untersucht die Häufigkeit von Parasiteneiern in Kompostlagen und zeigt, daß man unterscheiden kann zwischen Lagen die vollkommen, und solchen die nur zum Teil aus verrottetem menschlichen Kot bestehen, sowie anderen mit lauter zufälligen Bestandteilen.

Im sechsten Kapitel werden die vorläufigen Resultate einer Untersuchung über spätsächsische Schmelztiegel dargestellt. Es zeigt sich, daß Stamford Tiegeln für die Silberschmelze bevorzugt wurden. Während die Verteilung der Schmelztiegel auf kleine Werkstätten überall in der City hinweisen, zeigt der stratigraphische Zusammenhang mit andern Funden, daß vor dem frühen 11. Jahrhundert kaum etwas anderes als Eisen verarbeitet wurde.

Im siebenten Kapitel sind zwei kurze Berichte über wissenschaftliches Datieren spätsächsischer Lagen veröffentlicht, hauptsächlich mit Hilfe von Dendrochronologie und Archeaomagnetismus.

Das achte Kapitel behandelt schliesslich die topographische und funktionelle Entwicklung Londons von der spätrömischer Zeit bis zur normannischen Besetzung. Dabei wird Material der beiden früheren Bände dieser Serie benutzt. Das Hauptanliegen dieser Studie ist, den archaologischen Zusammenhang der sächsischen Funde innerhalb der Stadtmauer herzustellen. Um dies zu ermöglichen, musste aber auch die Umgegend mit einbezogen werden, denn die Entwicklung im Strand und in Southwark ist eng mit der City verbunden.

Da viele dieser Artikel sich auf dieselben Veröffentlichungen beziehen, wurde eine gemeinsame Bibliographie zusammengestellt. Im Anhang befinden sich Microfilme mit den individuellen Ausgrabungsberichten. Sie ermöglichen dem Leser im einzelnen Stratigraphy, Scherben, Kleinfunde und Umweltdaten bis in ihre Lage zurückzuverfolgen. Weitere Einzelheiten sind von der Datenabteilung des Museum of London auf Anfrage erhältlich.

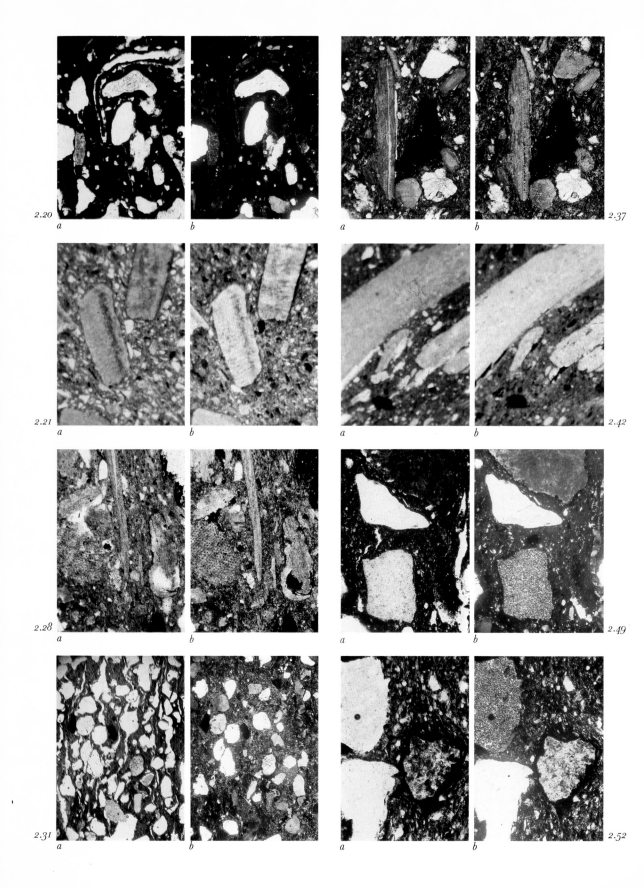

2.20   a   b

2.37   a   b

2.21   a   b

2.42   a   b

2.28   a   b

2.49   a   b

2.31   a   b

2.52   a   b

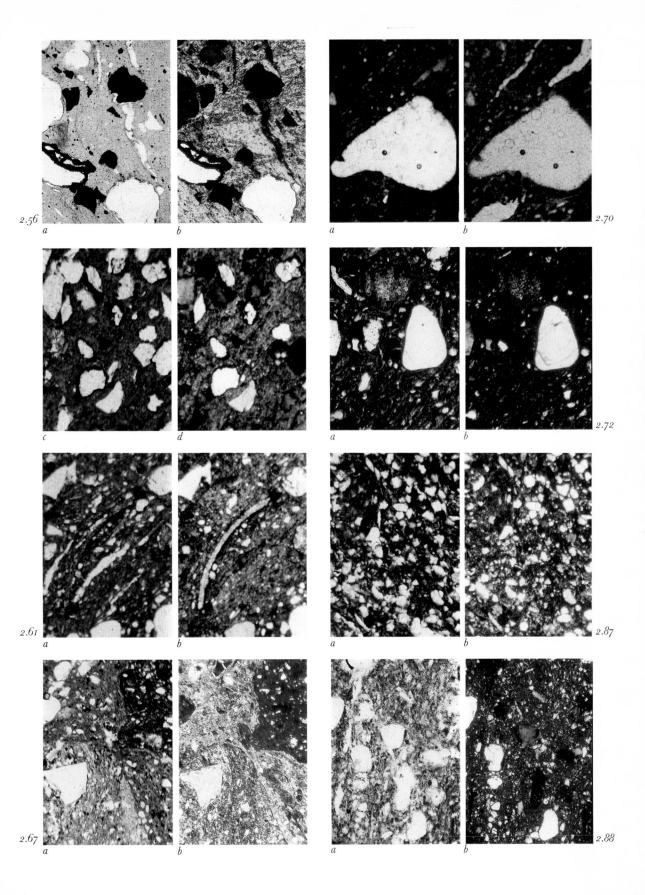

2.56 a b

2.70 a b

c d

2.72 a b

2.61 a b

2.87 a b

2.67 a b

2.88 a b

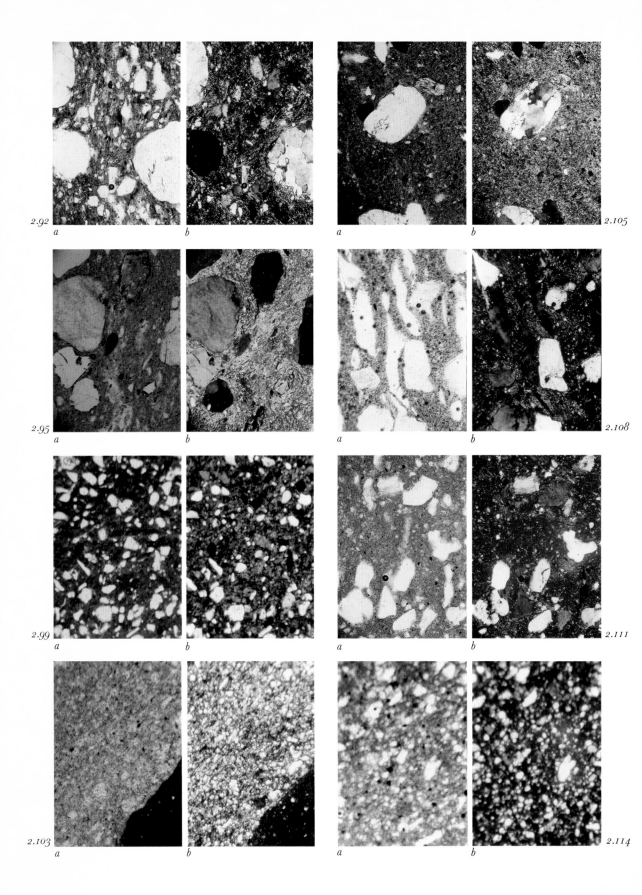

2.92 a b

2.95 a b

2.99 a b

2.103 a b

2.105 a b

2.108 a b

2.111 a b

2.114 a b

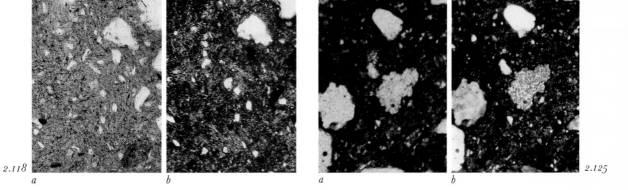

2.118   a   b   a   b   2.125